Oracle BPM Suite 11g Developer's Cookbook

Over 80 advanced recipes to develop rich, interactive business processes using the Oracle Business Process Management Suite

Vivek Acharya

[PACKT] PUBLISHING enterprise
professional expertise distilled

BIRMINGHAM - MUMBAI

Oracle BPM Suite 11g Developer's Cookbook

First published: April 2012

Production Reference: 1180412

Published by Packt Publishing Ltd.
Livery Place
35 Livery Street
Birmingham B3 2PB, UK.

ISBN 978-1-84968-422-4

www.packtpub.com

Cover Image by Artie Ng (artherng@yahoo.com.au)

Credits

Author
Vivek Acharya

Reviewers
Ramakrishna Kandula
Arun Pareek

Acquisition Editor
Rukshana Khambatta

Lead Technical Editor
Hyacintha D'Souza

Technical Editors
Apoorva Bolar
Priyanka S
Naheed Shaikh

Copy Editors
Brandt D'Mello
Leonard D'Silva

Project Coordinator
Vishal Bodwani

Proofreader
Lesley Harrison

Indexer
Rekha Nair

Graphics
Manu Joseph

Production Coordinator
Nilesh R. Mohite

Cover Work
Nilesh R. Mohite

About the Author

Vivek Acharya is an Oracle Consultant currently working as a professional freelancer. He has been in the design, development, consulting, and the Architect world for approximately seven years while working in Oracle Practice at GE, IBM, and HP. He is an Oracle Certified Expert as an Oracle Fusion-SOA 11g Implementation specialist and an Oracle-BPM 11g Implementation Specialist.

He has experience and expertise in Oracle Fusion - SOA, BPM, Webcenter, Spaces, BAM, Mediator, B2B, BI, AIA, WebLogic, Workflow, Rules, Webcenter, ECM, IDM, Oracle Fusion Applicaitons, SaaS, OnDemand, and so on. He loves everything to do with Oracle Fusion Applications, Oracle SOA, Oracle BPM, Social BPM, Cloud Computing, Salesforce, SaaS, and BSM

He has been author of a couple of books on Distributed Systems, has an interest in playing synthesizer, and loves travelling.

You can add him at `http://www.linkedin.com/pub/vivek-acharya/15/377/26awrite`, read about him at `http://acharyavivek.wordpress.com/`, and can write to him at `vivek.oraclesoa@gmail.com`.

Acknowledgement

No one walks alone, and when one is walking the journey of life, just where do you begin to thank those that joined you, walked beside you, and helped you along the way? So, perhaps this book and its pages will be seen as "thanks" to all of you who have helped make my life what is today.

Much of what I have learned over the years came as the result of being a son to my caring father and mother, and brother to Alankar. They have their own ways of inspiring me, and have subconsciously contributed a tremendous amount to the content of this book.

I would like to thank Richa, without whom nothing is possible.

I also have to thank Prashant, Ankur, RamaKrishna, Vijay, and Nitin with whom I have worked on several projects on SOA and BPM.

I also have to thank Rukshana and Jovita from the Packt Publication team for their belief in me and for giving their time to polish the manuscript.

Last, but not the least, I would like to thank the Almighty.

About the Reviewers

Ramakrishna Kandula has more than seven years of rich experience in IT. He has been involved in Full Life Cycle Implementations, where he has worked as a technical lead in various capacities from gathering requirements to production support and maintenance across various implementations in Oracle Applications, SOA, and BPM Suite technologies.

He has completed his Bachelor's in Technology in Computer Science from JNTU, Hyderabad, India and has done many thesis presentations on different technology projects during his graduation course.

He has also worked as a Technology trainer and mentor for fresh graduates and experienced correspondents in various organizations throughout his career.

Arun Pareek is an SOA Practitioner working on SOA-based Implementation projects in the capacity of a Consultant and Architect for over five years now. He is also an IASA-certified Software Architect and is currently co-authoring a book on Oracle SOA Suite Administration for Packt Publishing. He has been actively working on the SOA Suite of products for both BEA and Oracle, including technologies such as Service Bus, AIA, BPEL, BAM, BPA, and BPMN. He has a knack for designing systems that are scalable, performant, and fault tolerant and is an enthusiast of automated continuous integration techniques. He is also an active blogger on these technologies and runs a popular blog at `http://beatechnologies.wordpress.com`.

I would like to appreciate the encouragement I had from my parents for helping me to achieve many things in my life. A special note of thanks to my wonderful wife Karuna for her constant support, cooperation, and patience, without which it would have been impossible for me to manage my work and life together.

www.PacktPub.com

Support files, eBooks, discount offers and more

You might want to visit www.PacktPub.com for support files and downloads related to your book.

Did you know that Packt offers eBook versions of every book published, with PDF and ePub files available? You can upgrade to the eBook version at www.PacktPub.com and as a print book customer, you are entitled to a discount on the eBook copy. Get in touch with us at service@packtpub.com for more details.

At www.PacktPub.com, you can also read a collection of free technical articles, sign up for a range of free newsletters and receive exclusive discounts and offers on Packt books and eBooks.

PACKTLIB®

http://PacktLib.PacktPub.com

Do you need instant solutions to your IT questions? PacktLib is Packt's online digital book library. Here, you can access, read and search across Packt's entire library of books.

Why Subscribe?

- Fully searchable across every book published by Packt
- Copy and paste, print and bookmark content
- On demand and accessible via web browser

Free Access for Packt account holders

If you have an account with Packt at www.PacktPub.com, you can use this to access PacktLib today and view nine entirely free books. Simply use your login credentials for immediate access.

Instant Updates on New Packt Books

Get notified! Find out when new books are published by following @PacktEnterprise on Twitter, or the *Packt Enterprise* Facebook page.

Table of Contents

Preface

Organizations find that it's the business process that constitutes the heart of an enterprise and is a differentiating factor. They've found that it's the processes that make or break an enterprise. Operational efficiency is a differentiating factor, and research shows that it's the processes that provide operational efficiency, business visibility, and agility to an enterprise. They've concluded that, for business process and business process management, Oracle BPM guarantees better decision making and faster Enterprise response by giving enterprises high visibility into business processes.

Oracle BPM, with its continuous improvement methodology, offers process automation, agility, process improvement, adaptability, and strong collaboration of business and IT, and increases predictability, incorporate measure, and provision traceability. It lowers IT costs, enables inclusion of changes faster, and empowers business and at the same time dramatically increases customer satisfaction.

Oracle BPM is meant for all types of processes. It's based on a unified process foundation, user-centric design, and social BPM interactions. Unified process foundation, powered by a unified process engine, will streamline process development, and deployment and monitoring, and will synchronize design and runtime environments. User-centric design will empower participants with the right set of tools.

Social BPM enables social collaboration with Enterprise 2.0 and Web 2.0, which are offered by Spaces and offer collaboration and communication. Enterprise 2.0 also offers publishing with wikis, blogs, and Mashups. Social BPM offers enterprise-wide collaboration.

Oracle BPM unifies with Oracle SOA suite and offers agility. Oracle ADF offers rich process interactions. Oracle Business Activity Monitoring offers analytics, monitoring, and end-to-end visibility. Oracle Business Rules offers decision logics, Oracle UCM offers document workflows, and AMX offers approval flow management. Oracle BPM also unifies with Business Intelligence, Complex Event Processing, and Oracle security. BPM offerings, such as application extensions and workflow consolidation drive SOA expansion.

Oracle BPM sits on top of Oracle SOA and it's the first BPMS product to execute BPMN 2.0. This empowers organizations, as what they are modeling is what they would automate and execute.

This book encompasses vision, modeling, simulation, implementation, measurement, execution, collaboration, monitoring, management, and administration of Business Processes through Oracle BPM 11g, and covers BPM unification with SOA, ADF, AMX, Workflows, Rules, WCM, and UCM through BPM 11g; and includes implementing social collaboration by Enterprise 2.0, and Web 2.0 through Spaces.

What this book covers

Chapter 1, Process Modeling, starts with laying the foundation of, and demonstrating how to implement the modeling of business processes for a Use Case of a fictitious organization that needs Oracle BPM to be implemented on its site. You will learn to model business process with BPM and will uncover the BPM application development lifecycle. The main emphasis is on modeling a fictitious organization, creating business process flow, and creating and defining projects, roles, organization units, swimlanes, and data objects. It covers gateways in detail while focusing on business catalog. It includes working with MDS and publication of BPM projects to MDS. It also covers communication with external process and services.

Chapter 2, Process Implementation, emphasizes how developers implement the process. This chapter answers the question *How do you move from a model to a running process that automatically routes tasks, brings right forms, applies rules, stores data, and so on?* You will switch gears, and as a Process Developer, implement a running process. In this chapter we will discuss how to define interactive tasks, common interactive tasks, and to generate task forms. It also demonstrates how to create data associations, assign the outcome of tasks to data objects, and create data associations for conditional flows. The assignment of Human Tasks to different interactive tasks and implementation of service tasks are also covered.

Chapter 3, Process Deployment and Testing, looks at building, deploying, testing, analyzing, and debugging Oracle BPM processes.

Chapter 4, Business Rules in BPM process, covers applying advance routing rules in Oracle BPM processes, application of business objects, conflict resolution, gateways, and Human Tasks. Emphasizing on rules, it will explore rule containers such as dictionaries, Bucketsets, decision tables, and if-else decision components in rules and testing of rules.

Chapter 5, Human Workflow in BPM process, focuses on advanced concepts in human workflow, architecture, human workflow management in Oracle BPM, task patterns, routing, defining parallel and serial stages, skipping rules, runtime ad-hoc task assignments, approval groups, functions, task assignments, participant types, rule-based task assignments, deadline, escalation policies, and much more.

Chapter 6, Process Simulation, looks at process simulations, defining simulation definitions and models, and examines reengineering of BPM process to improve performance and analyze results.

Chapter 7, Developing a UI using Oracle ADF for BPM Process, covers ADF frameworks and describes how to build user interfaces for end-user interaction. It puts emphasis on ADF-BC components, entity and view objects, Web Service data control, and a different approach to create task display forms. You will also learn how Oracle BPM 11g sits on top of SOA and leverages Oracle ADF.

Chapter 8, Exception Management, explains the strategies of how exceptions are handled in Oracle BPM 11g, with detailed coverage of the fault management framework. It examines handling of exceptions in tasks, subprocess, and processes while covering different categories of faults.

Chapter 9, BPM & SOA in Concert, explores how Oracle SOA and Oracle BPM, in tandem, can help in enabling the success of Enterprise-wide BPM. You will witness how, together, they provide an Enterprise computing an end-to-end Enterprise BPM offering. It covers Oracle BPM and JMS interaction and defines communicating with other BPMN processes and services. Uncover Oracle BPM services and learn different ways to interact with BPM processes.

Chapter 10, End User Interaction, gives you a chance to experience the power of Social BPM and witness an Oracle offering on Social BPM. Examine social collaboration by Enterprise 2.0 and Web 2.0, which are offered by Spaces. Explore spaces—workspace and process space—and build a social network to collaborate, communicate, announce, blog, post, and poll.

Chapter 11, Manage, Monitor, and Administer BPM Process, provides a blueprint of how Oracle BPM and BAM work in tandem and offer process analytics. In this chapter, we examine Oracle BPM and BAM integration, provisioning of monitoring using dashboards, and the course of incorporating analytics and monitoring in BPM using BAM, uncovering business indicators, marks, counters, custom dashboards, and so on. We will see how Oracle EM is used for administering and monitoring of Oracle SOA infrastructure, and Oracle BPM.

Appendix - A, Oracle BPM - Application Development Lifecycle, covers how the Oracle BPM application development lifecycle helps in achieving process automation, agility, continuous process improvement, and adaptability, offers strong collaboration of business and IT, and increases predictability, incorporating measure and provision traceability.

Appendix - B, Approval Management, helps you to master approval management through the Oracle BPM Approval Management extension (AMX). We will examine the extension of human workflow services with complex approval patterns through Approval Management extension (AMX).

What you need for this book

To explore modeling, implementation, deployment, testing, Social BPM, and AMX using the Oracle BPM Suite through recipes in this book, you will need the following software installed on your machine/site:

- Oracle Database
- Oracle RCU
- Oracle WebLogic Server
- Oracle SOA Suite (includes Oracle BPM Suite)
- Oracle WebCenter
- Oracle JDeveloper

Demos and examples used throughout this chapter and book are created on Database 11g, RCU 11.1.1.5, Oracle WebLogic server 10.3.5, SOA Suite 11.1.1.5.0, Oracle WebCenter 11.1.1.5, and JDeveloper 11.1.1.5.0, on a Windows 7 64-bit machine. BPM Suite gets installed when you install Oracle SOA Suite. Update JDeveloper for SOA and BPM.

Who this book is for

If you are a BPM,Oracle SOA, or Oracle Fusion Applications - developer, designer, architect, or end-user looking to develop BPM solutions without impediments, then this is the best guide for you.The book assumes that you have fundamental knowledge of BPM.

Conventions

In this book, you will find a number of styles of text that distinguish between different kinds of information. Here are some examples of these styles, and an explanation of their meaning.

Code words in text are shown as follows: "Enter name as `SalesToContractSM`."

A block of code is set as follows:

```
CREATE OR REPLACE PRODECURE CHECKOPPORTUNITY (
OPPID IN VARCHAR2,
OPPTYPE OUT VARCHAR2,
OPPREV OUT VARCHAR2) AS
BEGIN
SELECT OPPORTUNITYTYPE, OPPORTUNITYREVISION INTO OPPTYPE, OPPREV
FROM VALIDATEOPPORTUNITY
WHERE OPPORTUNITYID = OPPID;
END;
```

New terms and **important words** are shown in bold. Words that you see on the screen, in menus or dialog boxes for example, appear in the text like this: "Open the Resource Palette, by selecting the menu **View | Resource Palette**"

[Warnings or important notes appear in a box like this.]

[Tips and tricks appear like this.]

Reader feedback

Feedback from our readers is always welcome. Let us know what you think about this book—what you liked or may have disliked. Reader feedback is important for us to develop titles that you really get the most out of.

To send us general feedback, simply send an e-mail to `feedback@packtpub.com`, and mention the book title through the subject of your message.

If there is a topic that you have expertise in and you are interested in either writing or contributing to a book, see our author guide on `www.packtpub.com/authors`.

Customer support

Now that you are the proud owner of a Packt book, we have a number of things to help you to get the most from your purchase.

Errata

Although we have taken every care to ensure the accuracy of our content, mistakes do happen. If you find a mistake in one of our books—maybe a mistake in the text or the code—we would be grateful if you would report this to us. By doing so, you can save other readers from frustration and help us improve subsequent versions of this book. If you find any errata, please report them by visiting `http://www.packtpub.com/support`, selecting your book, clicking on the **errata submission form** link, and entering the details of your errata. Once your errata are verified, your submission will be accepted and the errata will be uploaded to our website, or added to any list of existing errata, under the Errata section of that title.

Piracy

Piracy of copyright material on the Internet is an ongoing problem across all media. At Packt, we take the protection of our copyright and licenses very seriously. If you come across any illegal copies of our works, in any form, on the Internet, please provide us with the location address or website name immediately so that we can pursue a remedy.

Please contact us at `copyright@packtpub.com` with a link to the suspected pirated material.

We appreciate your help in protecting our authors, and our ability to bring you valuable content.

Questions

You can contact us at `questions@packtpub.com` if you are having a problem with any aspect of the book, and we will do our best to address it.

1
Process Modeling

In the first chapter, you will start with laying the foundation for, and demonstrating how to implement the modeling of, business processes for a Use Case of a fictitious organization that needs Oracle BPM to be implemented at their site. Recipes will demonstrate how to create and model business processes using **Business Process Management Notation and Modeling** (**BPMN**) within the Oracle Business Process Management Suite and how to create an organizational model that mimics your real-world organization.

In this chapter you will learn the following:

- Modeling business processes with BPM
- Simulating the BPM Application development lifecycle
- Modeling a fictitious organization
- Creating Business Process Flow
- Creating and defining Projects
- Defining Role and Organization Units
- Organizing processes using swimlanes
- Adding user interaction to Process Flow
- Controlling Process Flow—Defining exclusive gateways
- Controlling Process Flow—implementing exclusive gateways
- Controlling Process Flow—Parallel gateways
- Controlling Process Flow—Sequence flows
- Communicating with external processes and services
- Changing the value of Data objects in your process
- Creating Business objects in Business Catalog
- Adding documentation to the Flow Element
- Creating MDS for BPM
- Publishing a BPM Project in BPM Studio to MDS

Introduction

Business Process Management (**BPM**) is for process transparency, process intelligence, business empowerment, and business alignment. This chapter explores recipes to carry out a model business process, using Oracle BPM Suite 11g. **Business Architecture** lays the blueprint for operating and transforming the Enterprise. Business Architecture includes various models that define business goals, objectives, initiatives, and metrics. Business Architecture models business functions, both internal and external. They also encompass organizational models to depict roles, responsibilities, and collaborations to define how, and by whom, defined functions will be provided and used. Along with this, Business Architecture defines the business rules and policies to infuse governance, so that stakeholders can adhere and enforce policies. Steps to achieve business transformation objectives are also defined.

However, one Business Architecture element that is of interest for us in this book is, **Business Process Models**. Business Process Models define the activities, steps, and information flow between processes, to carry out business functions.

As BPM is a part and element of Enterprise architecture, they need to be designed so that the Enterprise can fully reap the rewards of Oracle BPM. While designing business processes, we are not just automating and managing processes; it's more about how an enterprise adapts to a comprehensive view of business processes, where one has to take the overall Enterprise architecture into account and not just automating and managing business processes. Hence, you can look at BPM adoption in an Enterprise as an element of Enterprise architecture.

With BPM, an enterprise can achieve the goal of automation. It can now model a business process, make associations with human workflow and IT applications, and infuse **Business Rules Management Systems** (**BRMS**). In combination with SOA and BRMS, enterprises can achieve extremes of agility. Oracle BPM will offer business agility whose process impact is directly proportional to process complexity. BPM is used for continuous process improvement as well.

Oracle BPM methodology is an agile strategy and an iterative approach to Business Process Management. It is well-suited to this era of ever-changing business processes, where there is a demand for continuous incremental improvement. Traditional methodologies were code-centric, rarely Model Driven; they always overlook the KPI, lacked continuous improvement, and had no vision beyond the current single project. For BPM, a methodology was required that could address these inadequacies; that could bridge the gap between IT and Business.

Oracle BPM methodology as a foundation for Business Process Implementation, as an Enterprise element, offers many benefits, such as the following:

- Business-driven: You will witness, in the BPM lifecycle, that business leadership and the Enterprise Architect work closely. This leads to process improvements with continuous alignment with business needs.
- Evaluation: Evaluation of IT assets enables effective planning. Gaps in the IT landscape can be identified and accessed, and required enhancements can be specified.
- Predictability: With simulation and analysis of processes, BPM incorporates predictability, so that results and costs can be determined in advance and with a high degree of accuracy and confidence.
- Bridging the Business-IT gap: Business stakeholders are involved at every step of process design and development. Information is exchanged at every engineering step. A Process or Business Analyst always works with Process Architects. Business Process Analysts, with their process, business and modeling skills, capture and model processes, drive process optimization, recommend changes, incorporate change requests from business, direct UAT, identify rules, define KPI's, and work with Process Architects for technical coordination.
- Traceability: With Process Analysis, you can capture the key decisions and associated motivation artifacts to support impact analysis and enable traceability throughout the business process lifecycle.
- Measurablity: With Process Analysis you can monitor your business processes, which enables a feedback loop, enabling continuous improvement.
- Adaptability: BPM methods and activities can be integrated with existing methods and new methods, with ease.
- Role Definition: Clear definition of duties.

The prerequisites to explore modeling, implementation, and deployments, using Oracle BPM Suite through recipes in this book, are that the following software be installed at your machine/site:

- Oracle Weblogic Server
- Oracle SOA Suite (includes Oracle BPM Suite)—BPM Suite gets installed when you install Oracle SOA Suite.
- Oracle Database
- Oracle Jdeveloper (with updates for SOA and BPM configured)

> Demos and examples used throughout this chapter and book are created on WebLogic server 10.3.5, SOA Suite 11.1.1.5.0, and JDeveloper 11.1.1.5.0 on a Windows 7, 64-bit machine.

BPM Application development lifecycle

Just as SOA enables IT Agility, BPM enables Business Agility. Process Impact is directly proportional to Process Complexity. BPM allows for continuous process improvement.

It is argued that BPM enables organizations to be more efficient, more effective, and more capable of change than a functionally focused, traditional, hierarchical management approach. It's the BPM that provides Process Management to serve business agility and manage complex business processes. An Oracle BPM Application's development lifecycle has many phases, such as:

- Vision
- Model
- Implementation
- Deployment
- Runtime

This application development lifecycle is equally applicable to any type of BPMN Process, be it a Standard process, Orchestration process, or Choreographic process. Most process modelers, and even you, after reading this book and creating a model, must be more familiar with defining the flow of activities. This is called a Standard process or an Orchestration process. In Choreography processes, the focus is not on orchestrations of work performed by the participants but rather on the exchange of messages/information between participants.

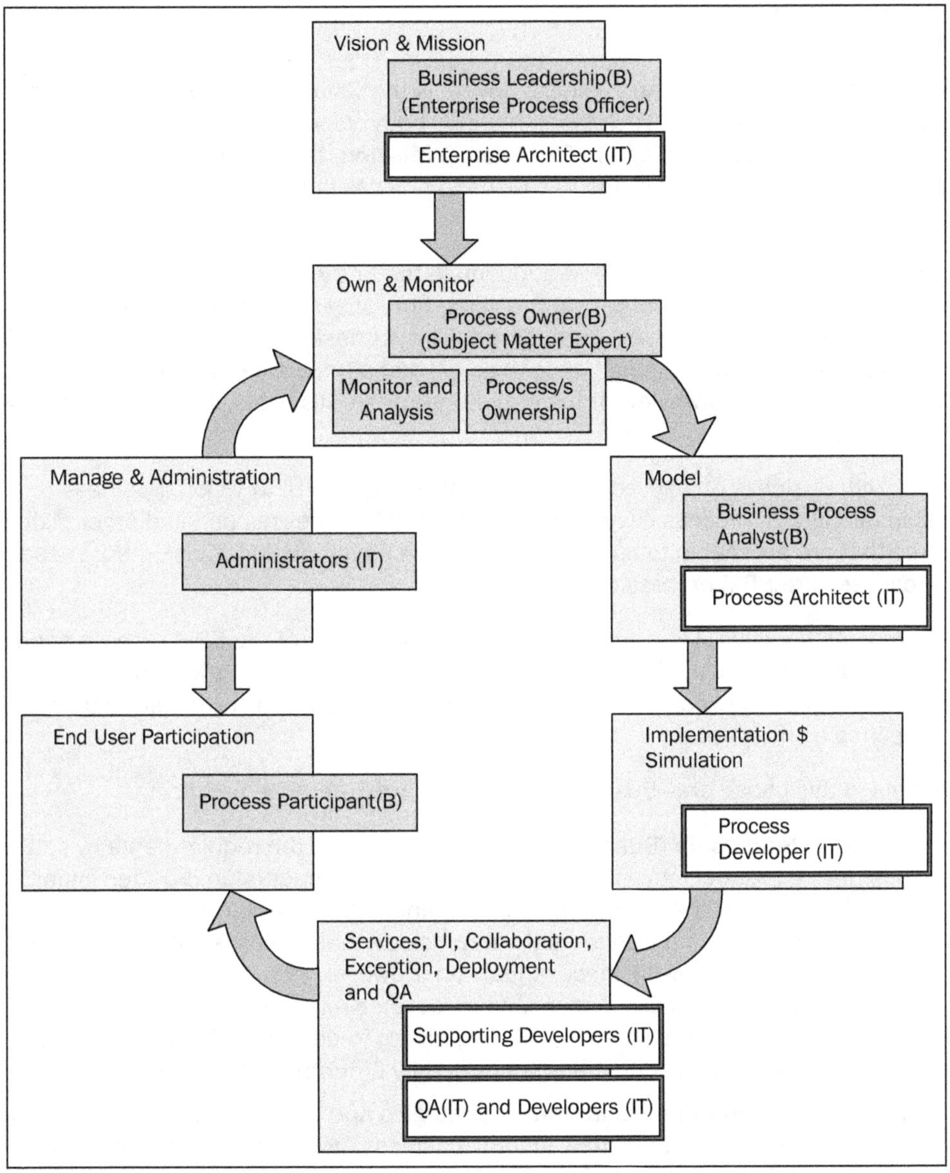

User personas

There are user personas for every phase of the Application Development lifecycle, as different phases require interaction from different types of users.

Vision

Making BPM adoption Enterprise business-driven, is the vision laid by the leadership and coordinated by Enterprise-wide Architects. It brings both business and process agility. As you can see in the preceding diagram for **Vision & Mission**, the business leadership and Enterprise Architect work closely, and this leads to process improvements with continuous alignment with business needs.

This phase lays the foundation for BPM adoption in the Enterprise with automation and continuous improvement guaranteed, at the same time staying aligned with business needs. You can term it as planning, strategy, analysis, or design. Planning is must for a BPM initiative to succeed. BPM planning needs to go beyond a departmental level and must incorporate a comprehensive view of the entire enterprise—it's goals, operations, processes, and IT Systems.

Alignment with business objectives must be the strategy for a BPM vision. Business leadership, along with process owners, must analyze the processes and find other high-value processes that are amenable to automation and have a high benefit-to-risk ratio. These high-value processes are BPM process candidates.

An Enterprise Architect will then analyze the technical aspects of the BPM process candidates and create a BPM road map. This road map will describe the current state and future vision, and identify the gaps between the two. A road map to get from the current state to the desired state is defined as the mission.

Participants in this phase are—Business leadership and Enterprise Architects.

- **Business leadership** (Business Participant) will drive the requirements by setting business goals, objectives, and priorities. Business leadership provides initial inputs, such as high-level vision definition and mission statements. They fund the BPM initiative. Business leadership may include many roles, such as Executive Management, Line-of-Business, and so on. However, let's define them as Enterprise Process Officers, who are responsible for developing a process-centric culture, system, and behaviors. They use BPM Analytics to determine business process changes. Business leadership is supported by Enterprise Architects.
- **Enterprise Architects** ensure that IT strategies and standards are applied. Along with Business Leadership, they identify business architecture inputs to BPM and help determining the needs for major business process changes.

Model

During this stage, a Process Analyst creates process models based on real-world business processes and problems. Oracle BPM provides three distinct tools for modeling business processes. Each tool has a different role within the Oracle BPM Suite. The tool you use depends on your business requirements, the stage of the application development cycle, and your user persona.

- Oracle BPM Studio
- Oracle Business Process Composer
- Oracle Business Process Analysis Suite (BPA)

Models are simply a way for Process Analysts to document processes in a structured way. Process Analysts model the flow of a business process and document its steps. They are assisted by Process Architects with their technical skills. Process Analyst and Process Architect are the critical roles in the automation of business process. One has a greater business focus and the other has a technical orientation.

This bridges the business-IT gap. Business Process Analysts, with their process, business, and modeling skills, capture and model processes, drive process optimization, recommend changes, incorporate change requests from business, direct UAT, identify rules, define KPI, and work with the Process Architect for technical coordination.

The participants in modeling are as follows:

- Process Analysts: They are also termed as Business Process Analysts. They are involved in Process Modeling and have the relevant skills. They are responsible for:
    - Capturing and managing the graphical business process models
    - Driving process optimization
    - Recommending changes
    - Handling process change requests from the business
    - Incorporating incremental process improvements
    - Identifying and coding business rules
    - Working in User Acceptance Testing.

  They work closely with the Process Architect for technical coordination.

- Process Architects: They coordinate with the Process Analysts in Process Modeling. It's a role that we also identify as Solution Architect. However, they have modeling skills and process implementation skills, too.

  They are responsible for:

  - Analysis and design of technical aspects for the process
  - Defining technical integration strategies
  - Technical specification for new IT capabilities
  - Directing system and integration testing

Implementation

After Process Analysts model business processes, Process Developers are responsible for creating business applications based on these models. Using Oracle BPM Studio, Process Developers implement reusable services and integrate other business systems. Implementation may include the following types of tasks, generally performed by Process Developers:

- Refining the process model
- Making technical configurations

They implement defined rules. They can create a user interface and can incorporate Exception management. However, they have secondary developers to perform specialist technical tasks, for example, an Oracle ADF expert can create dynamic ADF pages to be used as Task Forms. Some other developer with Exception Handling expertise can perform that on the process. An integration expert can incorporate SOA stuff into the process, and so on.

After a Process Developer finishes the implementation, the application is compiled and deployed like other SOA composite applications. It can be compiled and deployed using Oracle BPM Studio.

Process Developers: Also termed as Process Designers, they implement the process model to make it executable by configuring data mappings, defining data, and transforming activity input and output. They may not be knowledgeable about business processes, but rely on Process Models for implementations. They have the following responsibilities:

- Rapidly create business processes using tools. Tools Required: BPM Studio
- Creating implementation Artifacts.
- Populating business catalog with rich implementation artifacts.

Deployment

This phase includes testing and deployment. Process Developers or a supporting deployment team can perform process deployment.

For testing, either a developer or a **QA** can be involved. Different phases involve participation from different people. Generally, developers will perform the Unit testing. System and Integration testing will be performed by the QA and directed by Process Architects. **User Acceptance Testing** (**UAT**) will witness involvement of Process Analysts and QAs. Once UAT is completed, the process is deployed to runtime.

Deployment is the process of transferring an Oracle BPM project from the development environment to the runtime environment. This can be either a testing or production runtime environment. After finishing the integration of business processes with backend systems and reusable services, Process Developers create and compile a working, process-based application. This application is then deployed to Oracle BPM Runtime. Oracle BPM Suite contains the following typical scenarios for deploying to Oracle BPM Run Time:

- Deployment directly from Oracle BPM Studio
- Deployment directly from Business Process Composer
- Deployment using an exported SAR file
- Deployment using the **WebLogic Scripting Tool** (**WLST**)

Once the process is deployed to runtime, it's available to end users.

Runtime

After an application is deployed, the runtime environment makes the Oracle BPM application available to process participants, based on the roles assigned in the organization where the business processes were deployed. This stage is divided into the following distinct functions:

End user interaction

Process participants and process owners are responsible for interacting with the running application using process workspace. Process Analysts and owners can also monitor the process and revise **Oracle Business Rules** at runtime.

End user participants: Process participants are the end users or process performers in a business process who perform the human aspects of the business process task and perform interactive activities. They provide task execution details to the Process Analyst and are involved in Acceptance Testing. They should be contacted and interviewed at the time of Process Automation, as it's a must for process design to know what they actually do. They have many roles, such as supervisor, sales manager, sales representative, business analyst, agents, clerks, and so on.

Oracle BPM flow will automatically route these tasks to a participant, based on his/her role, and they have to log in (either to Oracle BPM workspace or Process Spaces) and perform their activity. End user interaction to running process is performed by logging on to either Oracle BPM Workspace or Process Spaces.

Administrators are responsible for maintaining running business applications and the overall runtime infrastructure, using Oracle Enterprise Manager and the Oracle Weblogic Server administration console.

Administrators or Operation Managers are responsible for the following:

- Configuring and Monitoring SOA Infrastructure
- Configuring BPMN Process Service Engine
- Integrating Oracle BPM with External Monitoring, such as Oracle Business Activity Monitoring, and many more.

Process management and monitoring

Process owners are responsible for monitoring and maintaining running processes using process workspace. Process Analysts and owners use Oracle Business Process Analysis to monitor the real-time performance of business processes. The participant is process owner in this phase.

Process owners are the subject matter experts for the business process (es). They own a process or processes. They are responsible for:

- Assisting the Business Process Analyst (B) throughout the modeling
- Assisting the Business Process Administrators (IT) throughout runtime—they require considerable business knowledge
- Managing Process flow
- Assigning tasks
- Defining rules and objectives
- Analyzing end-to-end Business Process Performance
- Making process-specific decisions to resolve conflicts like the gap between departmental silos of business process activities where ownership is undetermined and knowledge is sparse. Process owners resolve such issues, as they are the process experts responsible for the end-to-end flow of key business processes.
- Advocating recommendation for Enterprise-wide process improvements.
- They are also responsible for the monitoring business process(es) that they own.

Modeling business processes with BPM

Modeling is the first phase of the BPM Application development lifecycle, as the preceding diagram shows, and is carried out by Process Analysts. It lays the foundation for Process Development, by creating a model of the process to be implemented. Oracle BPM Suite 11g provides a rich set of applications to perform modeling.

How to do it...

During the phase of modeling you will learn the following:

1. Simulating a BPM Application development lifecycle
2. Modeling a fictitious organization
3. Creating Business Process Flow
4. Defining process participants, Roles, and Organization Units
5. Defining the start and end of your process
6. Adding user interaction to your Process Flow
7. Controlling your Process Flow using gateways and sequence flows
8. Communicating with external processes and services (optional)
9. Creating Process Data objects
10. Adding documentation to Flow Elements and processes
11. Handling information in your process design
12. Configuring activity instance attributes
13. Developing arguments, scope, and access
14. Creating data associations
15. Developing transformations
16. Creating MDS for BPM

How it works...

The Oracle BPM Suite provides two primary applications for modeling and implementing business processes:

- **Oracle BPM Studio** supports Business Process Management Notation (BPMN) 2.0. It is a component of the Oracle BPM Suite that provides a user-friendly environment.
- **Business Process Composer** provides a user friendly environment for editing processes and process templates created in Oracle BPM Studio.

You will simulate, model, define, interact, control, and document, using Oracle BPM Studio. As this is the chapter in which you will model the Business Process, you will act as a Process Analyst and you will use Oracle BPM Suite 11g BPM Studio to model the Business Process.

Simulating the BPM Application development lifecycle

By simulating BPM Application development lifecycle, you will define the strategy, paradigm, and Use Cases. As a Process Analyst, you will use BPM Studio to create BPM Process Models. Based on these models, Process Developers will implement the BPM applications and deploy it to BPM runtime.

Using BPM Studio, a Process Analyst can do the following:

- Model business processes
- Define business rules and performance indicators
- Simulate processes
- Determine the optimal resource requirements to achieve specified SLAs

How to do it...

The steps to define strategy, paradigm, and Use Case are:

1. Chose between BPA and BPM Suite.

   If your answer is 'YES' to following requirements, then you need BPM as a tool:

   - If you are concentrating only on a process and not enterprise-wide modeling
   - If you have human-centric Use Cases that require flexibility and collaboration
   - If you have to focus on the project at hand and not on your total enterprise
   - If you have the tactical/implementation of the processes, BPM Suite works best

   If your answer is 'YES' to following requirements, then you need BPA as a tool:

   - If you have a strategic/pre-implementation work, such as as-is, to-be, gaps, requirements definition, and so on, BPA works best
   - If you need to focus on higher-level, enterprise-wide modeling that might be done using rigorous methodologies, use Oracle BPA
   - If you need the ability to model other things that relate to processes, such as systems, data, people, organizations, and services that represent the Enterprise, use BPA
   - If you need models that relate not only to processes but to other parts of the enterprise, as well, use BPA

2. Define modeling approach:

   If it is bottom-up, then:

   - Create projects in BPM Studio
   - Populate projects with reusable artifacts, such as data services, and so on
   - Publish to MDS—Projects or Templates can be published to MDS
   - From Process Composer, check out published BPM projects
   - Customize and use these projects to create new processes

   Else if it is top-down ,then:

   - Create high-level abstract Process Flows (blueprints) from scratch using BPM Composer
   - Publish them to MDS
   - Check into BPM Studio and refine them
   - Deploy

3. Define the Use Case:

   - Determine the business requirements
   - Model the required business processes using Oracle BPM Studio
   - Create simulation models for "as-is" and "to-be" processes or models. Implement the processes by integrating each element of the process with backend systems and reusable services
   - Compile the Oracle BPM project as a composite application
   - Deploy the application to the runtime environment
   - Interact with the deployed processes as part of a running business application
   - Maintain and monitor the running process-based applications

How it works...

You can start modeling in either BPA Suite or BPM Suite. However, as a Process Analyst, you will choose BPM Suite to model, because you have answered 'YES' to all questions asked when choosing between BPA and BPM, in favor of BPM. Along with it, BPM Suite offers predictability, traceability, adaptability, is measurable, and bridges the gap between Business and IT. As a Process Analyst, you have some knowledge of the business process and can collaborate with business users to enrich the modeling outcomes.

As a Process Analyst, in this chapter, you will probably follow the bottom-up modeling paradigm as your modeling strategy. **Metadata Store** (**MDS**) enables modeling paradigms. The MDS repository is used for creating a shared, collaborative work environment across multiple BPM Studios and process composers.

There's more...

In addition to the modeling methods described in the preceding text, there are different ways by which a Process Analyst can model business processes, such as the following:

- Implementing a modeling Use Case with Business Process Composer, by creating Process blueprints. These blueprints will be used by developers to create project templates and store them into Oracle MDS. After this, Process Analyst will use these project templates again to create projects, and finally, to deploy them.
- You can even use Oracle BPA suite to model the processes by designing the business architectures, analyzing the processes that will be candidates for BPM projects, and then creating process models and importing them into Studio to finally make them available at runtime.

Modeling a fictitious organization

Our fictitious organization "FusionNX", located at `http://www.fusionnx.net/`, has a number of business processes. Let's take into consideration FusionNX's Sales Quote business process to implement the modeling phase.

How to do it...

1. Define the Business Process and the tasks inside it:
    - Define SalesToContract as a process that you will model for the Sales Quote process of FusionNX
    - Create SalesToContract as the main process
    - Define Enter Quote, Business Analysis, Approvals, and Contract Finalization as different tasks inside it.
2. Define who the participants are and what role they will play in process development and at runtime:
    - Define users who will participate in different tasks/work in the process, such as Sales Representatives, Approvers, and so on, in the SalesToContract process, which you will model for the Sales Quote process of FusionNX.

3. Define what data will be associated with the process:
    - Define quote data, as per `Quote.xsd`, for the SalesToContract process, which you will model for the Sales Quote process of FusionNX.
4. Define the outcome of the process as a whole and outcomes of the different tasks:
    - Enlist outcomes of all the tasks that you have rejected or approved as possible outcomes of the Approvals task; also enlist all other tasks for the SalesToContract process which you will model for Sales Quote Process of FusionNX.

How it works...

As per the Use Case listed in the preceding text, the Process Analyst will determine the business requirement and will come up with with the Process Flow, user persona, data meant for the process, and outcome of the process. The resulting conclusion is an understanding of the business requirement specific to FusionNX's Sales Quote business process.

The following information is required by Process Analyst to design the Business Process Model:

- Process Flow
- Process participants: Users ,Groups, and organizational roles
- Data: Business data, and input and output of each process step, and process as a whole
- Outcomes: Possible Outputs from human workflow, process steps, and the process as a whole.

Creating Business Process Flow

Using the Business Process Flow, you will model the process the `sales quote` for FusionNX and in the `SalesToContract` business process meant for the creation of `Sales Quote`. The `SalesToContract` business process implements a solution for sales representatives to submit the sales quotes and manage all the approvals within a particular sales organization. The sales quote travels through many phases and gets finalized. Once finalized, it's saved in FusionNX's Enterprise database.

How to do it...

The SalesToContract process has many tasks. Let us define the major tasks of the SalesToContract business process:

1. Defining the task—Enter sales quote
    - Task: Entering a sales quote is a Sales Representative's solution process to:
    - Submit the sales quote:
        i. Manage approvals
        ii. Role: Sales Representative
    - Data: Input and output business data is `Quote`.
    - Outcomes: The Sales Representative, as a process participant, is responsible for the creation of a sales quote. He will create the sales quote initially, and after rejections from Approvers, edit it as well.

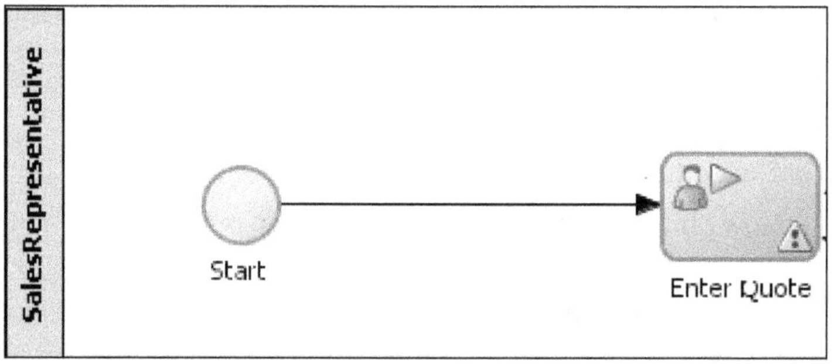

2. Defining the task—Business Analyst review
    - Task: Sales quote review
    - Role: Business Analyst
    - Data: Input and Output business data is "Quote" (`Quote.xsd`)
    - Outcome: The Business Analyst as process participant can either approve or reject the quote.

If approved: The process continues forward.

Else: On rejection, the flow token reaches the Sales Representative again, to refine and resubmit the quote.

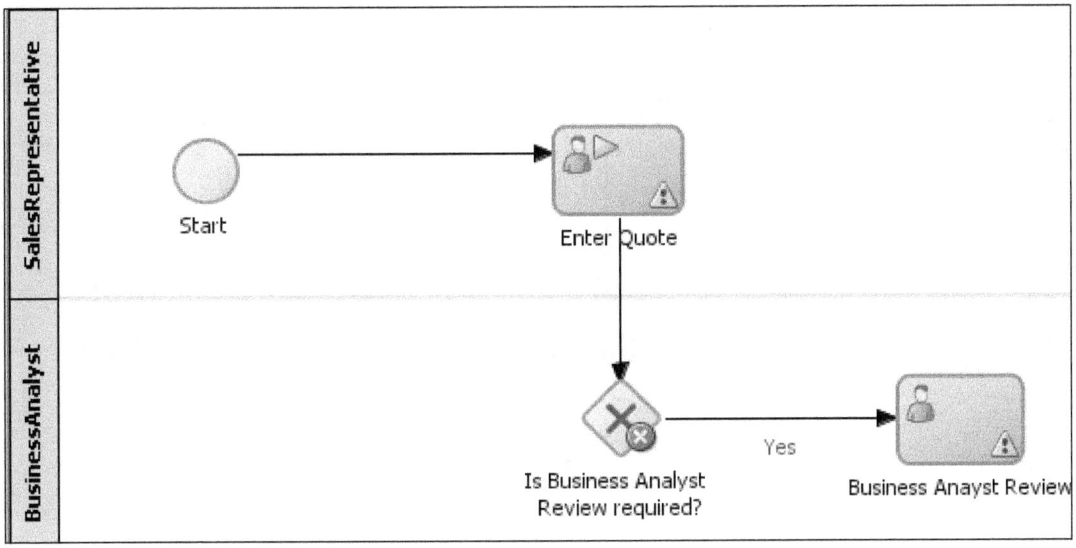

3. Defining the task—Quote Approval
    - Task: Quote Approval has two parallel tasks
        i. Deal Step Approval
        ii. Term Step Approval
    - Roles: Approvers
    - Data: Input and Output business Data is "Quote" (`Quote.xsd`)
    - Outcomes: Approver as Process Participant can either APPROVE or REJECT the quote

If Approved: The Process continues forward.

Else: On rejection, the process reaches the Sales Representative again, to refine and resubmit the quote.

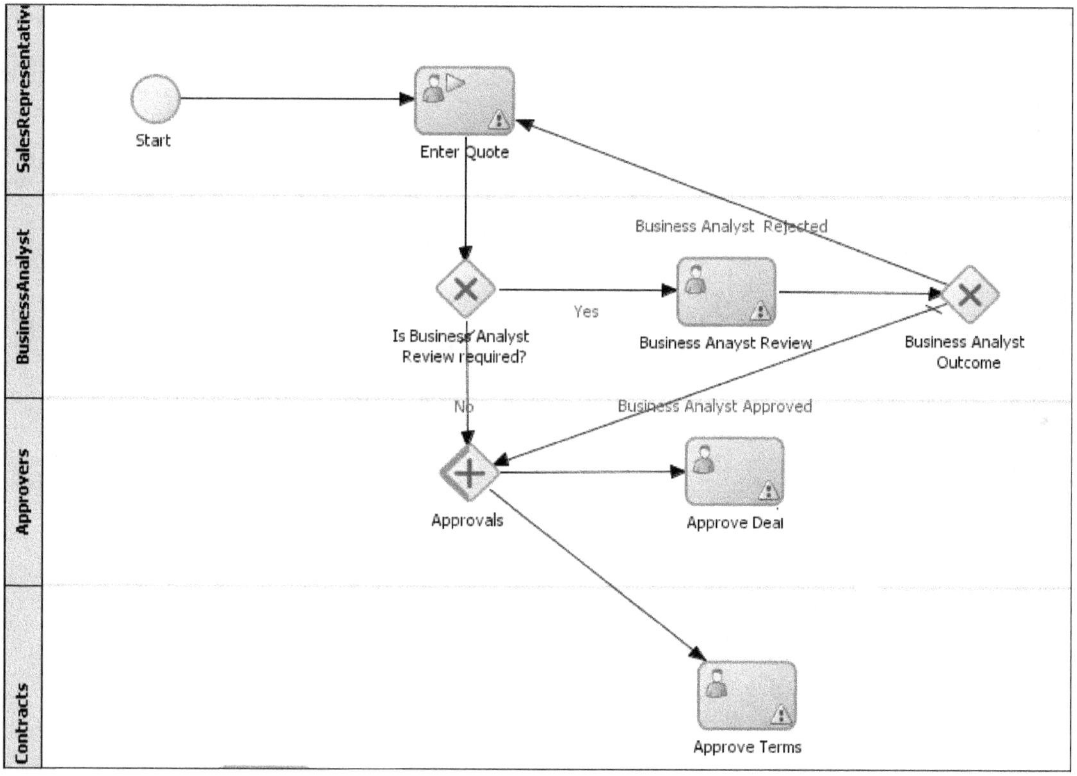

4. Defining the task—Finalize Contract
    - Task: Contract Finalization
    - Role: Contracts
    - Data: Input and Output Business Data is "Quote" (`Quote.xsd`)

- Outcome: The quote is saved in the Enterprise database by external service call

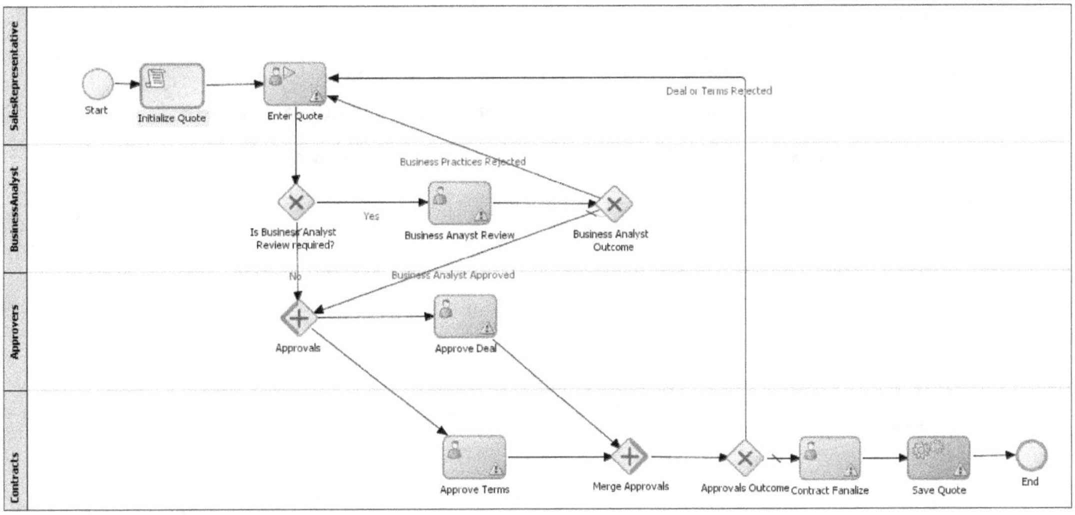

How it works...

Task definition is the primary objective of Process Flow definition. The Process Analyst has to define roles and responsibilities, which depend on the task definitions. The Process Analyst can choose any tools to carry out the task definition. However, he must try and understand the process to the best of his ability.

Approve Deal is used for approving the deal structure of the quote, and the **Approve Terms** step is used for approving the terms of the quote.

Creating and defining projects

You will need a container for the resources that are used to create and support business applications created using Oracle BPM. Oracle BPM projects are based on SOA projects, but they include the additional functionality of the Oracle BPM Suite, including BPMN processes.

How to do it...

You will use JDeveloper as the IDE to work with BPM Studio. The version of JDeveloper used is 11.1.1.5.0. This is done as follows:

1. Start the JDeveloper Studio (11.1.1.5.0). Choose the default role, to enable all the technologies. You can also choose the **BPM Process Analyst** role.
2. Click on **File | New | All Items**, and choose **BPM Application**:

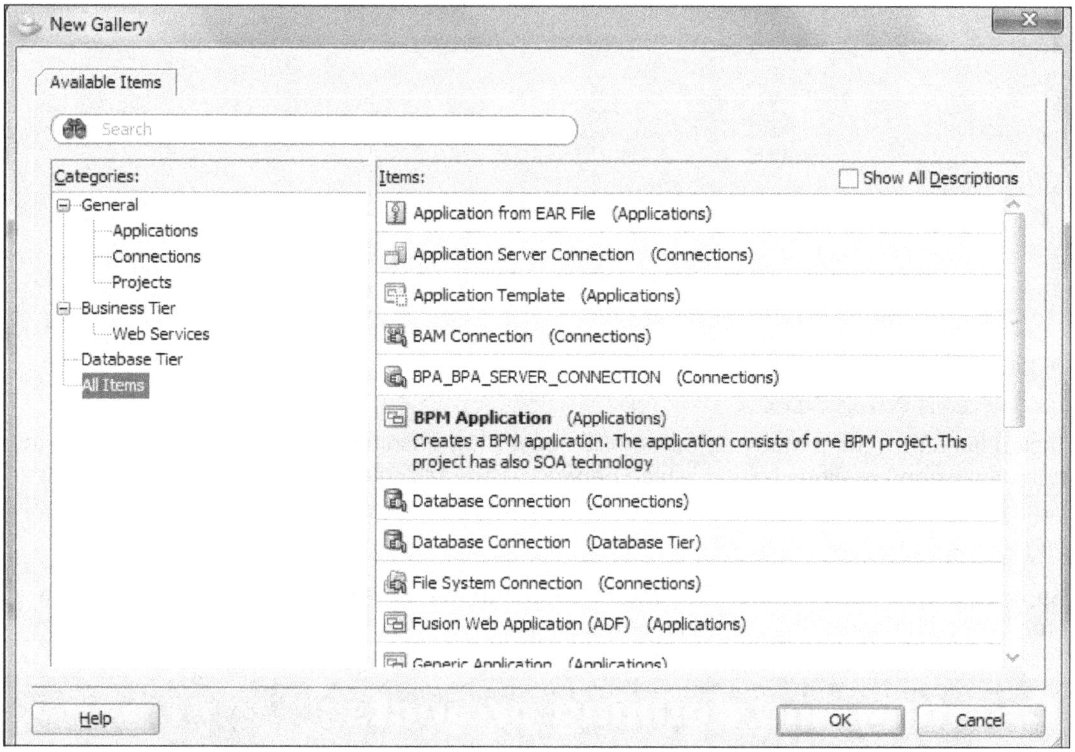

3. Give a name to the application, say **FusionNX_Application**.
4. We will create an application as we are starting the demo. In subsequent chapters and demos, we will use the same chapter.

5. Click on the **Application** menu, to the right of the application name in JDeveloper and click **New Project...**.

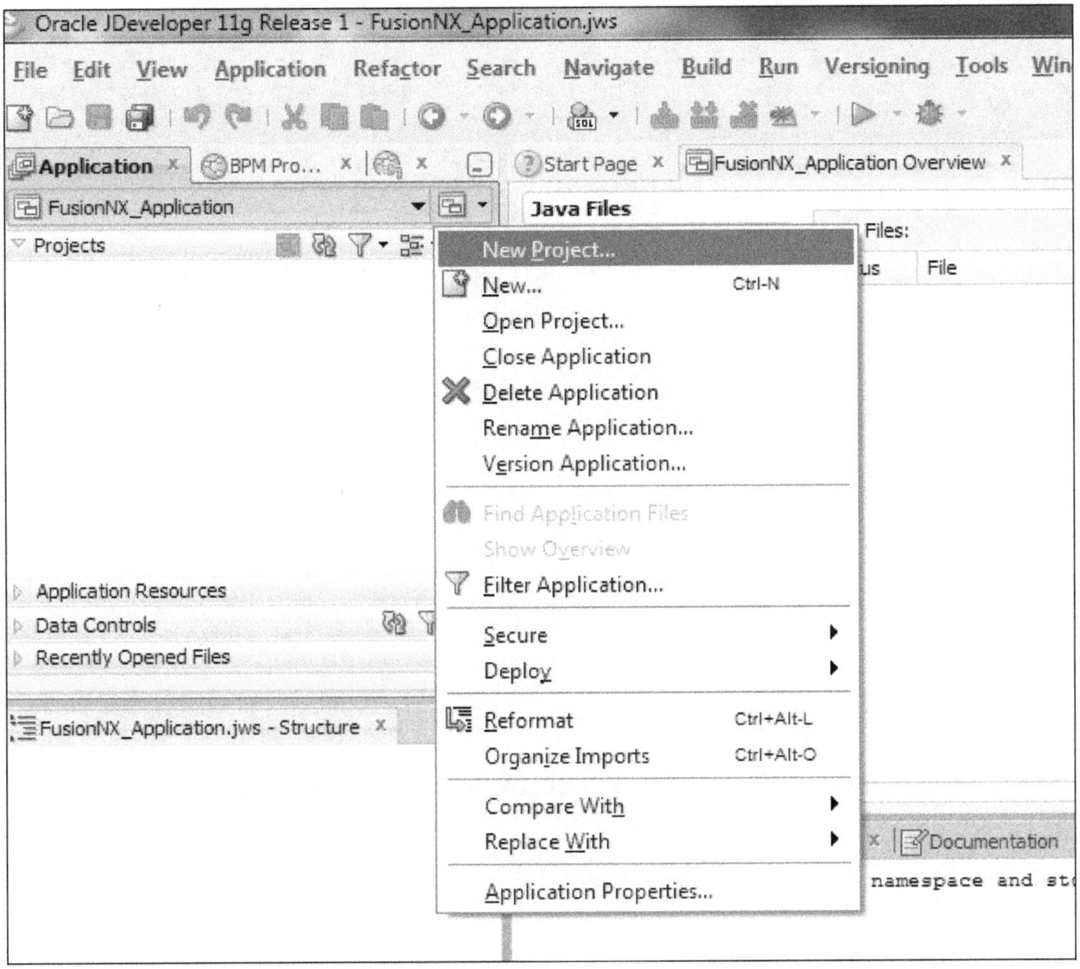

6. Choose **BPM Tier** in the project gallery, and select **BPM Project**:

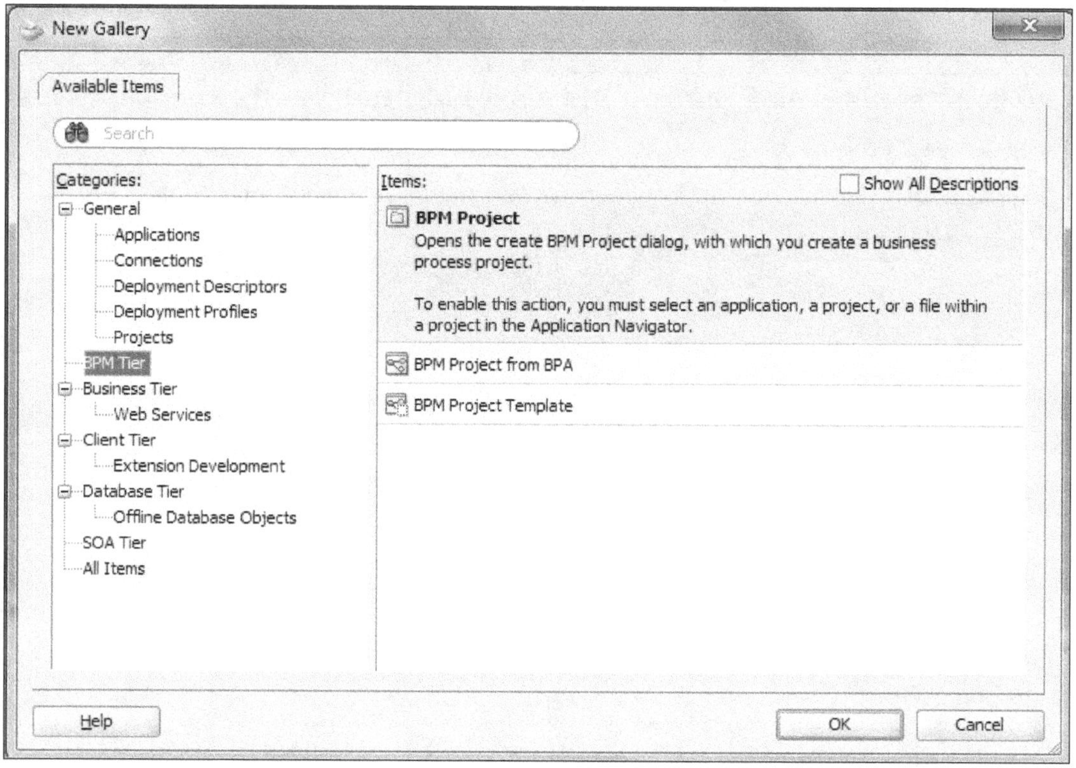

7. Enter the Project details such as **Project Name** (`SalesQuoteToContractDemo`) and specify the **Directory** where it will get saved.
8. Make sure that both **BPM** and **SOA** are selected.

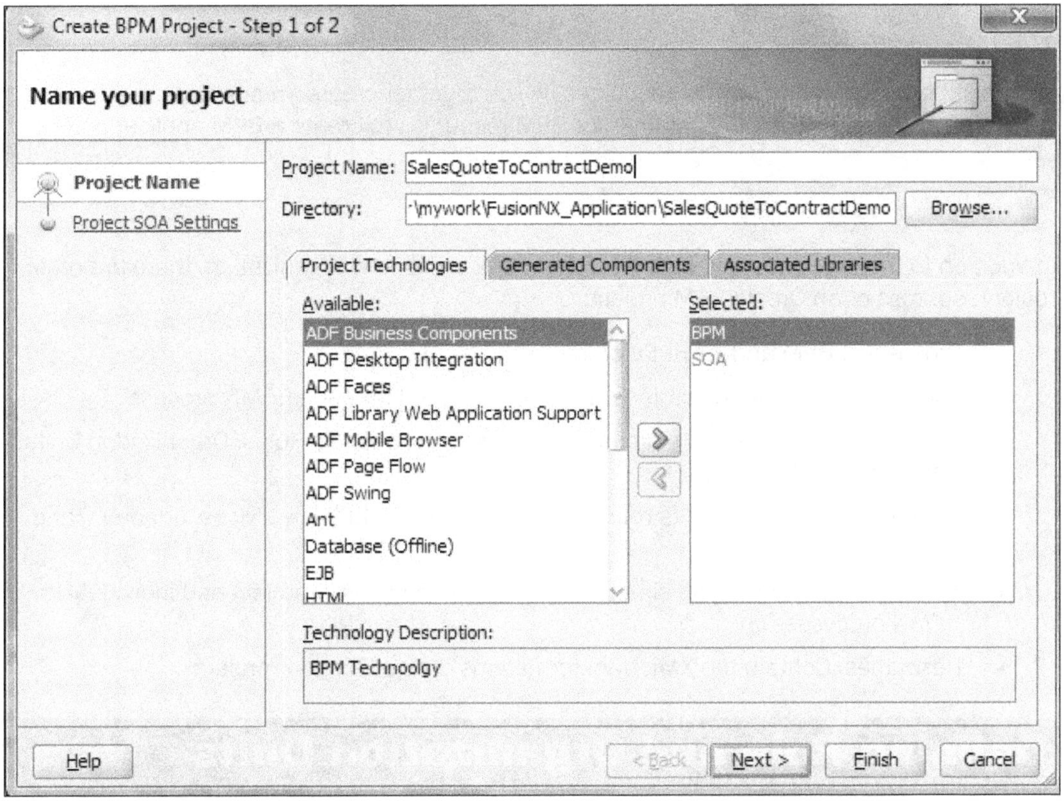

9. A new Project will get created and will appear in the Project navigator, with a structure of resources, as shown:

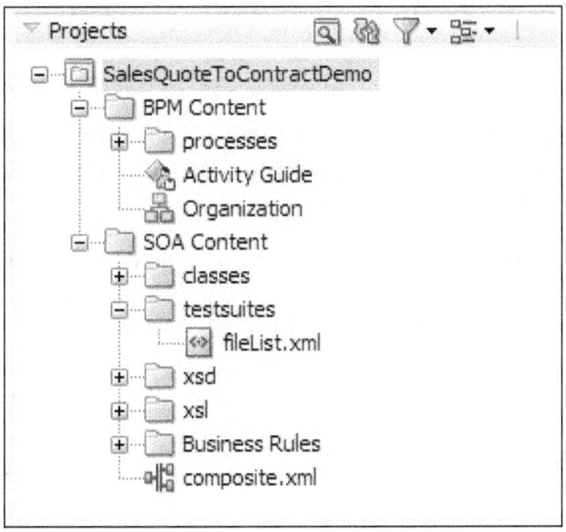

How it works...

You must be aware that to handle resources, which together create an application, you need a container. And **Projects** is the container for BPM resources to create a BPM application.

There's more...

In addition to the two resources of BPM project, Processes and Organization, there are other major resources of an Oracle BPM project:

- Processes: BPM and/or BPEL processes
- Activity Guide: Includes project milestones defined for each BPMN process
- Organization: Includes the organization elements, such as Roles, Organization Units, Calendars, and Holiday rules
- Business Catalog: Includes reusable components including services, adapters, and human tasks
- Simulations: Includes the simulation models defined for a project and individual BPMN processes
- Resources: Contain the XML transformations defined for your project

Defining Role and Organization Units

Once finished with defining a process model, you, as Process Analyst, will define the roles (who will perform which responsibility/task) and Organization Units (Organization association, Calendar rules, and Holiday rules). You will define Application Roles in the BPM Studio, and those Application Roles are mapped to organizational users.

Getting ready

Roles authorize the people with a set of responsibilities (tasks) to perform. Later, you divide the tasks based on these roles by creating **swimlanes** in the process. Each horizontal swimlane is associated with a role.

The roles we will create in **Project | Organization** are logical roles. **LDAP** defines the actual users, and during deployment of BPM projects, logical roles are mapped to LDAP roles. Use BPM Studio to map roles to specific users using LDAP.

How to do it...

Now, you have created Application and Project. You already know the Process Flow. Let's create the processes. However, we still don't know "who will perform what", that is, the roles yet need to be defined. Let's organize our Processes, based on roles and Organization Units. Every process has some task/work to be performed. It's the Roles that help decide who has the responsibility to perform the task/work.

Creating a Role

You will create application roles, and later, these roles will be mapped to organizational users. This is done as follows:

1. Double-click **Organization** in the **Project navigator**. Project Editor will open the **Organization** window.
2. Select the **Roles** tab.
3. Click the "add" (**+**) icon to add roles.
4. The role name dialog appears. Enter **Name** of the role, say `Sales Representative`. Repeat this step to create other roles listed.

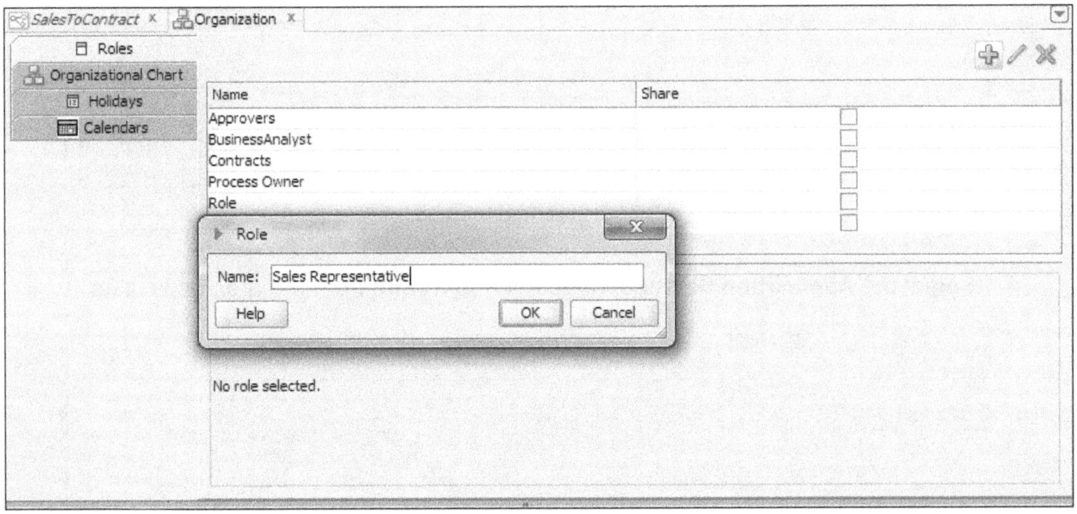

Associating Roles with members

Here, you will map Application Roles to organizational users. This is done as follows:

1. Click the **Roles** tab in **Organizations**.
2. In the **Roles | Members** section, choose **User** as the **Type**.

3. Click on **Browse** (Identity lookup browse).

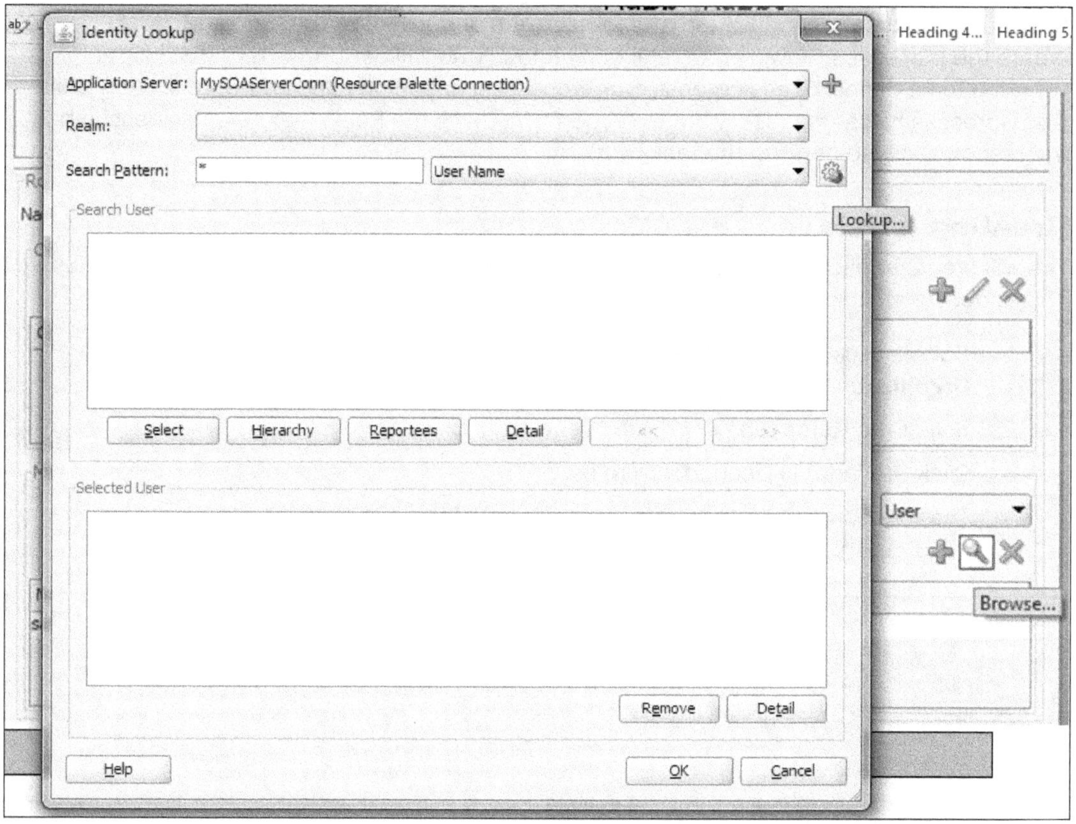

4. Select the **Application Server** connection and **Realm** from the drop-down lists.

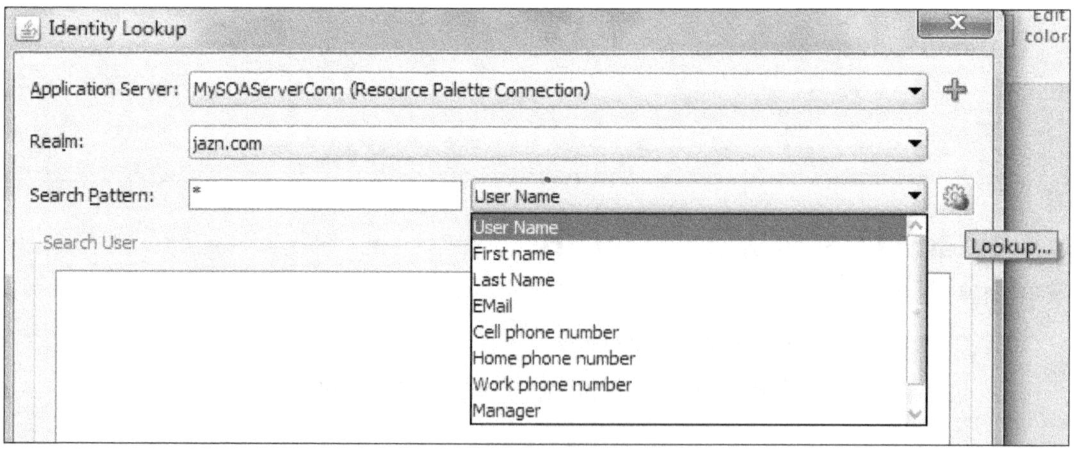

5. In **Search Pattern**, specify *(search all) and select **User Name** from the drop-down list as the search string. This will list all the users in the **Realm**.
6. Select the **User**. As you are associating members to the Sales Representative role, choose a user (member) meant to perform the Sales Representative role.

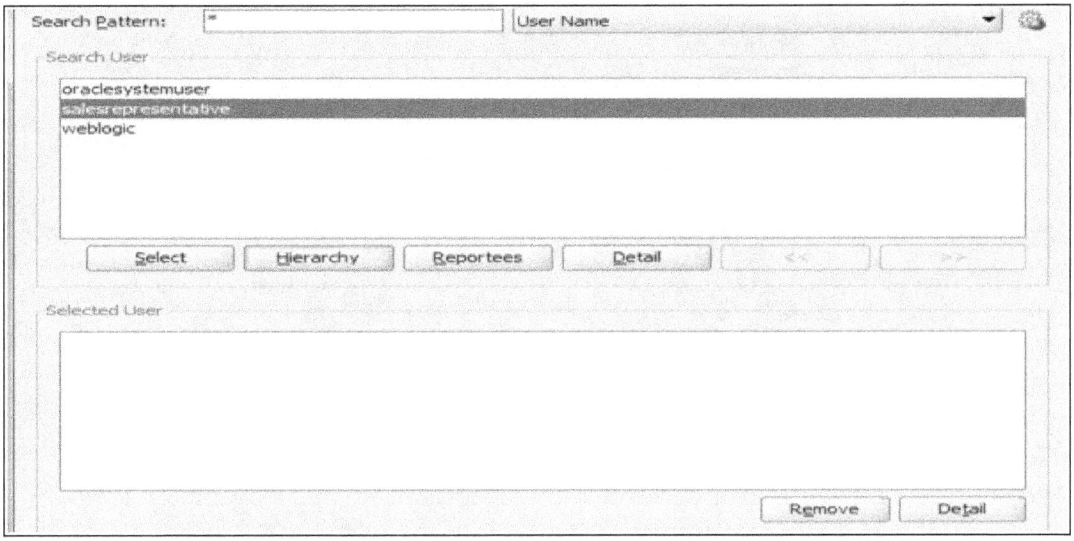

7. Repeat the preceding steps for all the users and associate them with members.

> However, in actual scenarios, Process Analysts need not know which user in the organization is mapped to application roles. This assignment is typically done by Process Admins through the Worklist Application or EM.

Creating Organization Units

Organization units represent a division in an organization, and once defined, process participants might be assigned to one of the organizational units. This is done as follows:

1. Click **Organization**, in the Project navigator, and select the **Organizational Chart** tab.

2. Click **+** to add an organization unit root node, which will contain organization units based on geography; say **FusionNXorganizationUnit**:

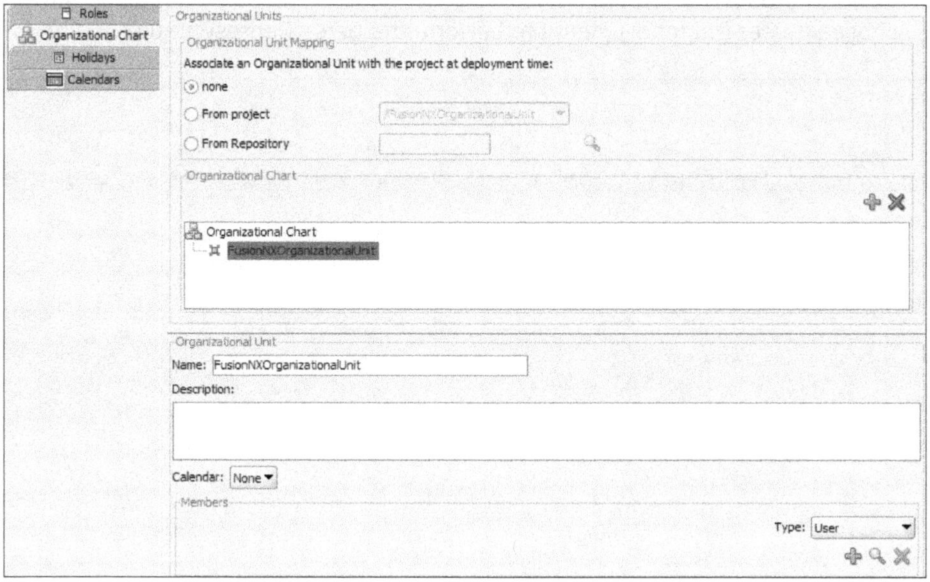

3. Let's say your Sales Representative is from **APJ | India**. However, for his/her sales quote he/she needs approvals from the APJ head.

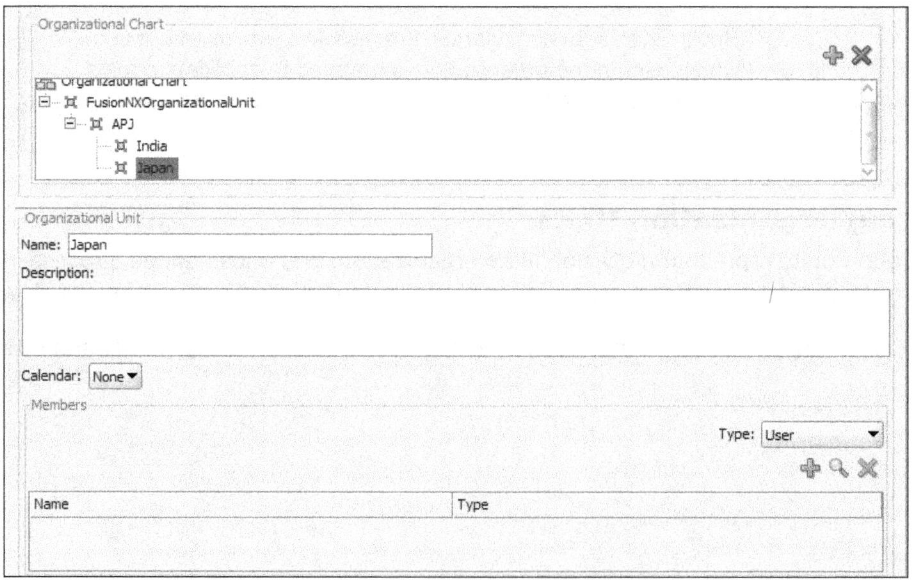

4. When you have finished the preceding steps, click **Save.**

Associating members to Organization Units

The Organization Units and Roles defined in BPM Studio are abstract. They need to be mapped to your real-world organization FusionNX. During deployment of your project, the components of the modeled organization and roles are mapped to your real-world organization:

1. In **Organization**, select the **Organization Unit** tab.
2. Scroll to **Members Section**. Select **User** as the **Type** and click **Browse**, to browse **Identity Lookup**.
3. Select **Application Server** and **Realm.**
4. In **Search Pattern**, search for all (*), with **User Name** as search string.
5. When users are listed, choose the appropriate user to associate with the Organization Unit. Say, for **APJ | India**, associate Sales Representative user and APJ with Approvers.

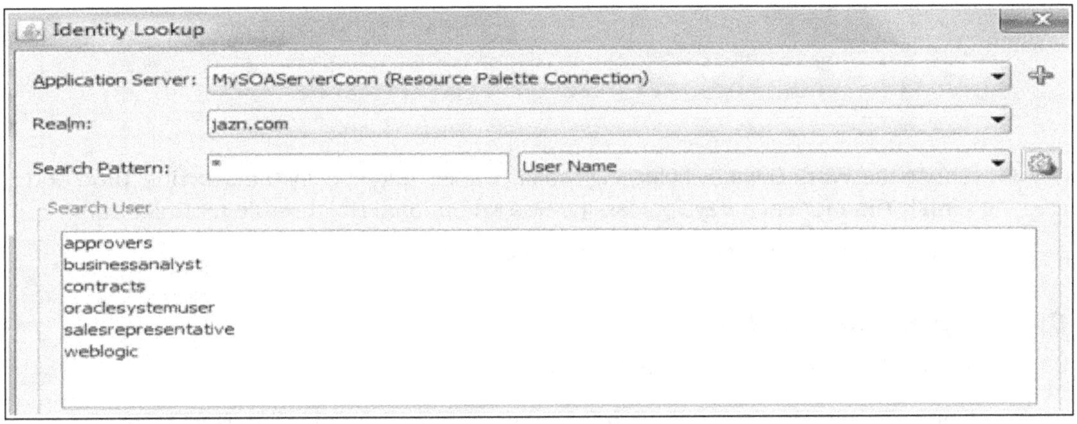

6. When you are finished, click **Save.**

Creating Calendar Rules for Organization Units

In this section, you will define the working hours of an individual, as follows:

1. In the **Organization Unit** editor window, select the **Calendar** tab.
2. Click the "add" (+) icon to create a calendar, say `FusionNXCal`.

3. Click the created **Calendar** rule to define **Time Zone** and **Work Days** with hours:

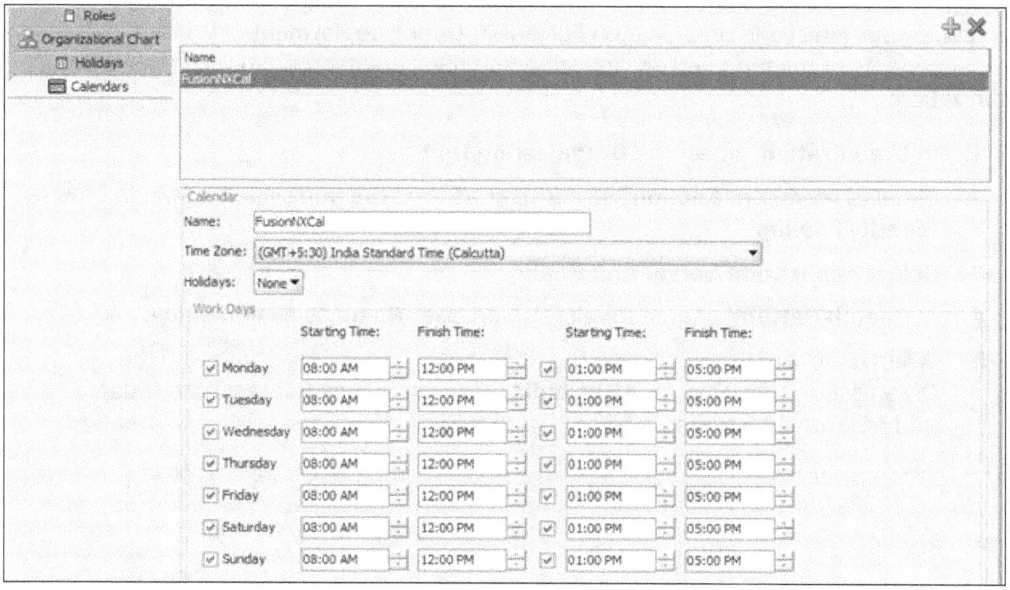

4. Chose the **Work Days** by selecting the checkbox, and specify the **Starting Time** and **Finish Time** for each day.You can include an optional Holiday rule for Calendars.
5. When you have finished the preceding steps, click **Save**.

Creating Holiday rules

Use the following steps to create a Holiday rule:

1. Open JDeveloper in the default role and go to **View | Application Navigator**.
2. Select **FusionNX_Application**, which you have just created, and select the **SalesQuoteToContractDemo** project, which you have already created. This is the Project navigator.
3. In the Project navigator go to **Open Organization**.
4. In the **Organization Unit** editor window, select the **Holiday** tab
5. Click the "add" (**+**) icon to create a Calendar, say **FusionNXHolidayRule**.
6. Select **Holiday Rule** and click the "add" (**+**) icon.
7. Provide the following details for the Holiday rule, and then click **OK**.
    - **Description**: Fill in a description of the Holiday rule
    - **Type**: **Common** (**Common/Fixed**)
    - **Date**: This refers to the dates for this Holiday rule. To specify a range, you must create a new entry for each day

8. When you have finished the preceding steps, click **Save**.

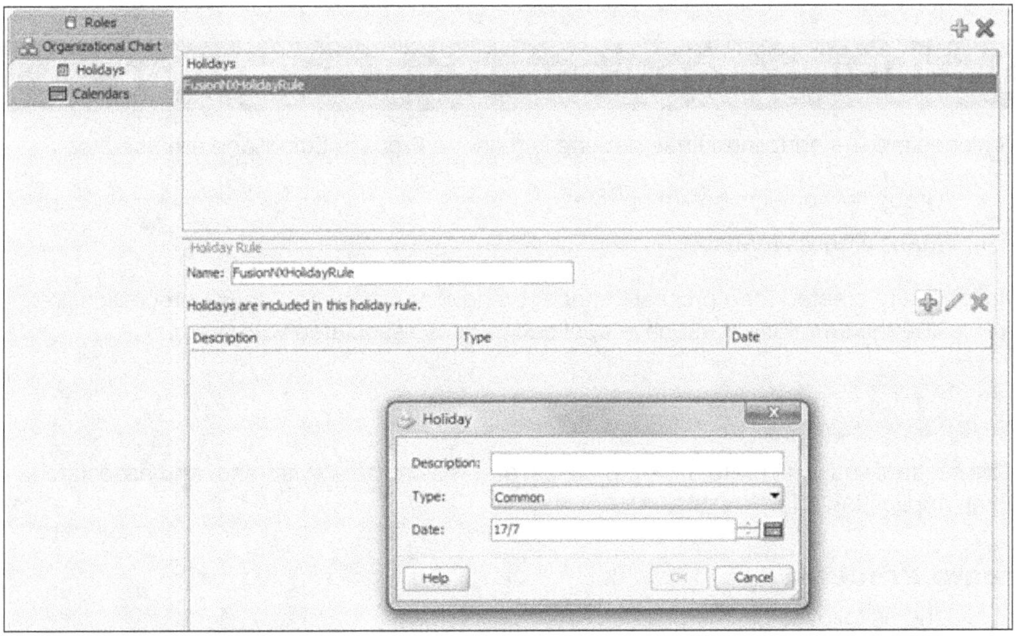

How it works...

Creating roles works only when Process Analyst has the Process Flows defined. This has resulted in the following list of Roles:

- Sales Representative
- Business Analyst
- Approvers
- Contracts

Roles are defined in Organization Resources inside the BPM Project. Check the preceding screenshot of the Project navigator; you can identify **Organizational Chart** in it. **Organizational Chart** is used to define Roles, Organization Units, Calendar Rules, and Holiday rules.

Associating roles to members allows you to define what members of your real-world organization are responsible for performing the activities and tasks within your process.

FusionNX operates in multiple geographical locations and has sales units that are divided based on geography, say America, EMEA, APJ, and so on. Hence, organization units were categorized by geography. You know that the Sales Representative is from APJ in the India Organization Unit and that the Approver is from APJ.

To define when resources are working in an Organization, create Calendar rule, and to define when resources are not working, define **Holiday rules** in an organization.

Organizing processes using swimlanes

Swimlanes are the horizontal lines running across the Process Editor and are used to:

- Group flow objects based on roles
- Make process readable.

Swimlanes are created for a process, hence you have to create and define processes first. Tasks inside the swimlane must have application roles associated with them.

How to do it...

In this section, you will create a BPM process, and will create a swimlane, and associate it with an application role.

Create Process

This is done as follows:

1. Go to the Project navigator and right-click **processes** (this will open the new gallery).
2. From **Categories**, choose **BPM Tier**.
3. Select **Process** to create a process.
4. Click **OK**.

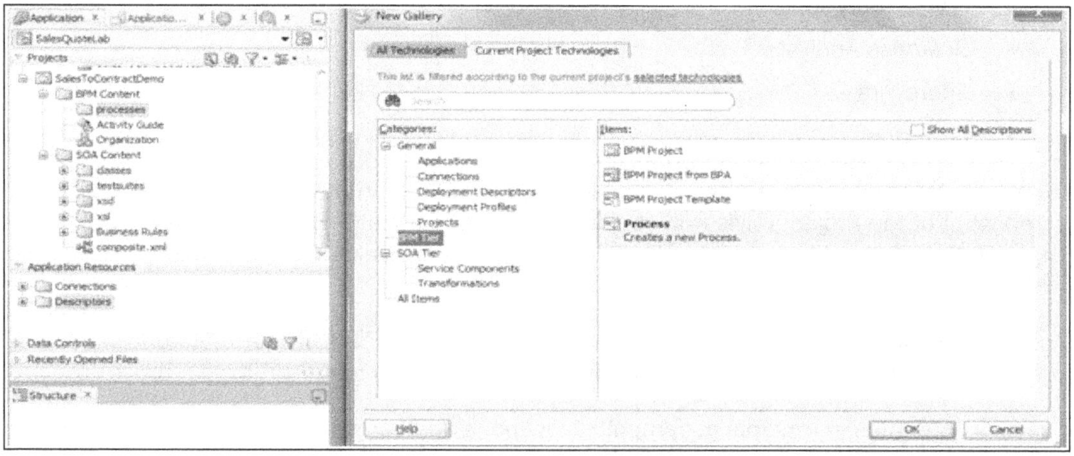

5. The **BPMN Process** definition dialog opens up.
6. Enter process name and choose **Type**:
   - Process name: `SalesToContract` process:
   - Process Type: **Manual Process** (no **Start** and **End** event)
   - Process Instance initialization: A **None** start event followed by a user task defined with the initiator pattern will result in Process Instance initialization.
7. Click **Next**.
8. In the **Advance** tab, go to **Select | Inherit Project Default**.
9. Click **Finish** and **Save**.

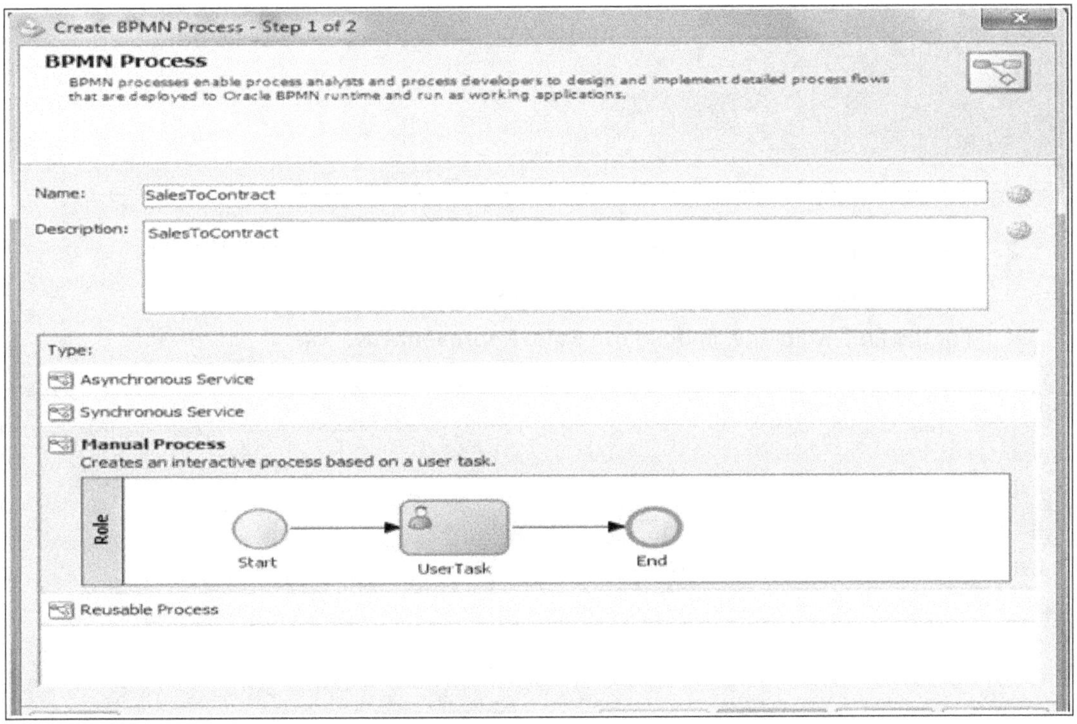

Adding swimlanes

Follow the ensuing steps to create swimlanes:

1. Click **Add Role** in the Project Editor, as shown:

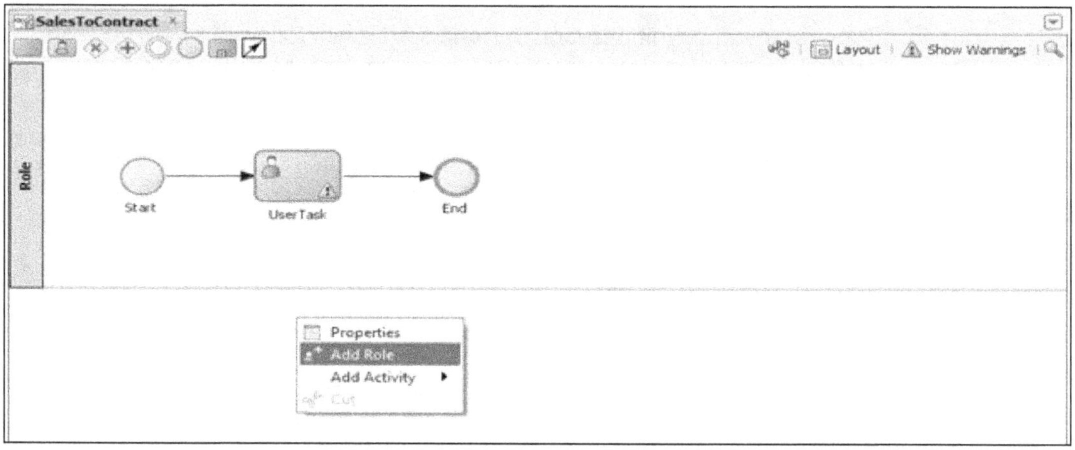

2. It will open a **Role** properties dialog box.
3. From the **Role** properties, choose the **Role**.
4. For the first swimlane, choose the **SalesRepresentative** role:

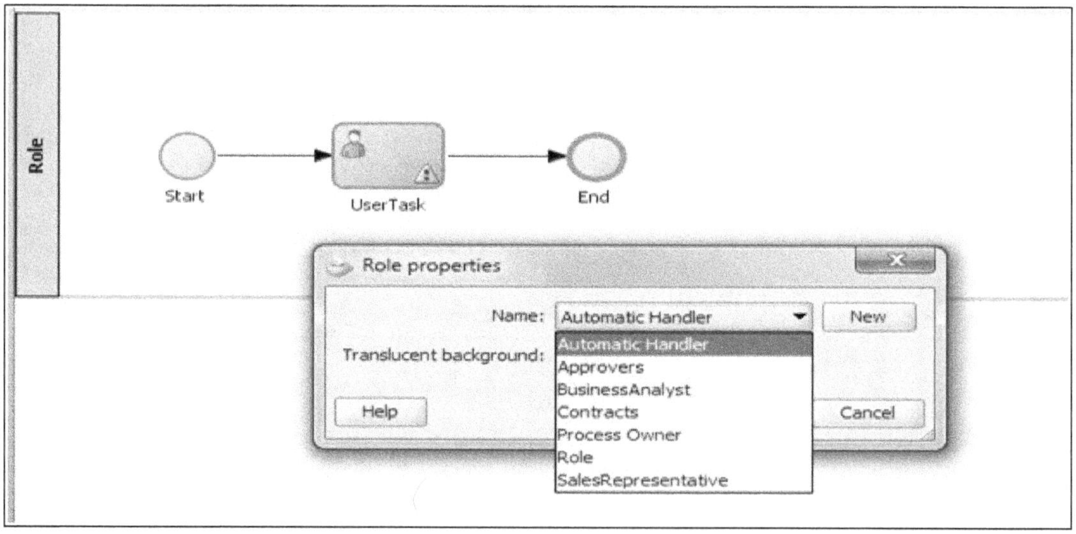

5. Repeat the preceding steps to create swimlanes for **BusinessAnalyst**, **Approvers** and **Contracts** roles too.

6. For **SalesRepresentative**, **BusinessAnalyst**, **Approvers** and **Contracts** roles, the swimlanes will look like the following:

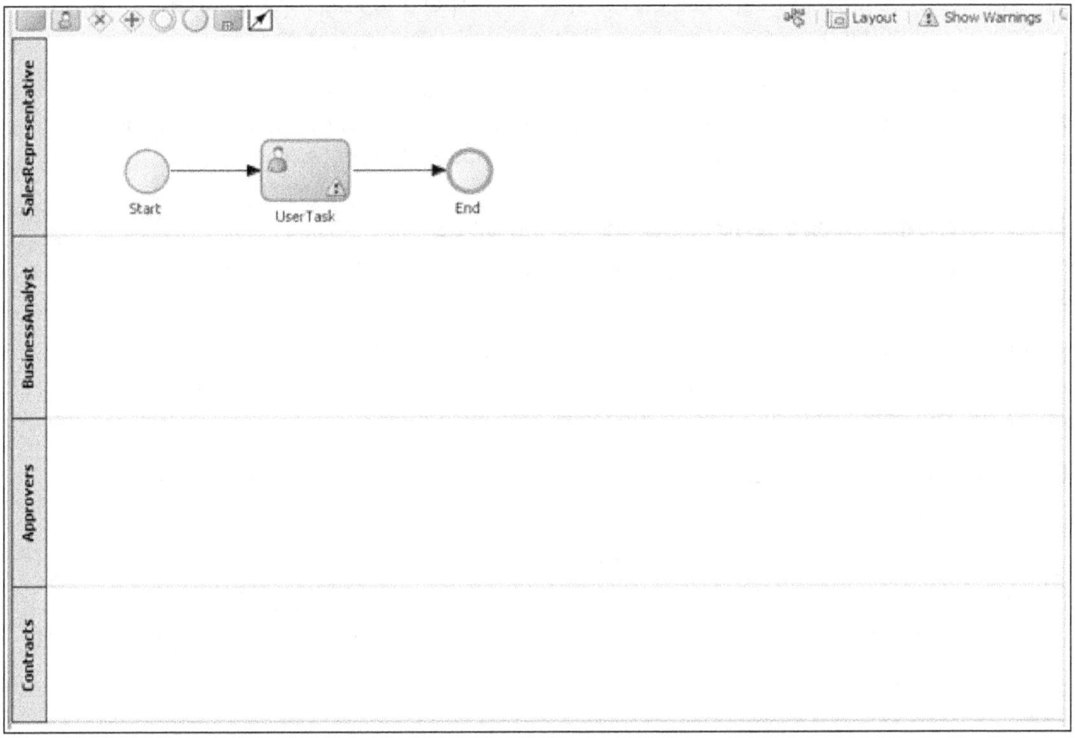

7. When you have finished the preceding steps, click **Save**.

How it works...

The **None** start event will not trigger the Process Instance. However, it is required while triggering a process instance using the following flow objects:

- `Receive task` must have a `Create Instance` property set to `true`

  OR

- `User task` must be implemented with the initiator pattern

In the SalesToContract process, since the process contains a User task implemented with the initiator pattern, the **None** start event triggers a process instance.

By default, a default role and a single horizontal swimlane get created in the Project Editor. You can make it work by either renaming the first default swimlane or following the preceding steps.

There's more...

Process Instance creation depends on the type of start event. FusionNX's **SalesToContract** process is a manual process, as we have chosen while creating the process.

Triggering of a Process Instance: For SalesToContract, we have a User task following the **None** start event, which has an initiator pattern defined. This will result in initialization of a Process Instance. **None** start event will not accept input arguments.

Defining the Start and End of a Process

Start events: A Start defines the starting point of a process. Start means initialization of the Process Instance.

End Events: An End event defines the end of a process. When the token reaches the end event, it gets consumed and the instance gets completed. The SalesToContract process will end when the contract is finalized in the **Contracts** swimlane.

Since the SalesToContract process will end once the contract is finalized, follow the ensuing steps:

1. Drag the **End** event to the **Contracts** swimlane.
2. Delete the sequence flow from **User Task** in the **SalesRepresentative** swimlane to **End** event by right-clicking the sequence flow, as shown in the following screenshot:

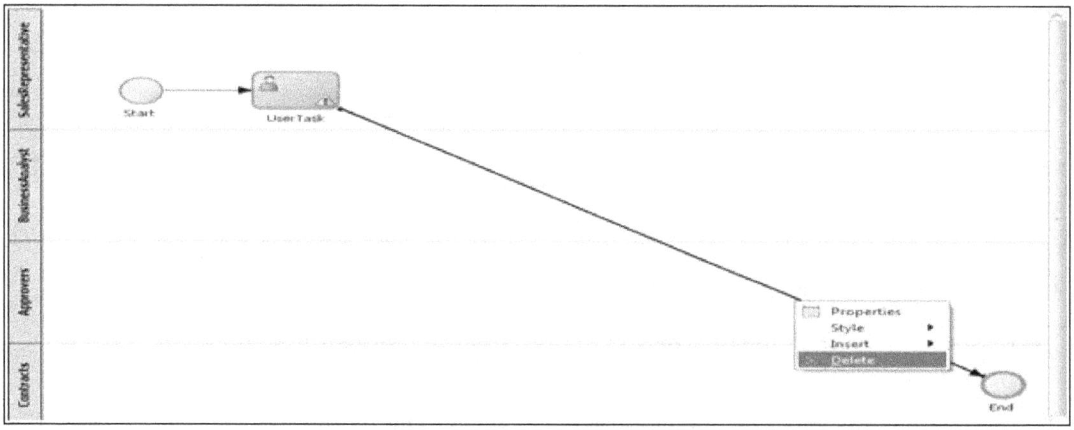

3. Delete the created **User Task**, `Default`, as we will create a User task with initiator pattern to initiate the Process Flow.
4. When you have finished the preceding steps, click **Save**.

Adding user interaction to Process Flow

The Process participant's interaction is enabled in the SalesToContract process by Human Tasks. You will create a User task in the process, where a process participant is required to perform tasks.

How to do it...

In the SalesToContract process, inside the **SalesRepresentative** swimlane, the user with the Sales Representative role has the task of entering quote information.

Create a User task, which will prompt the **Sales Representative**, to enter quote information, as follows:

1. Click on the process name (**SalesToContract**) in the Project navigator. This will open the Process Editor.
2. Click on **Component Palette | BPM Components** and select **Activities**, in the list.
3. Click on **Interactive | Initiator**. You will create a human task of the **Initiator** type:

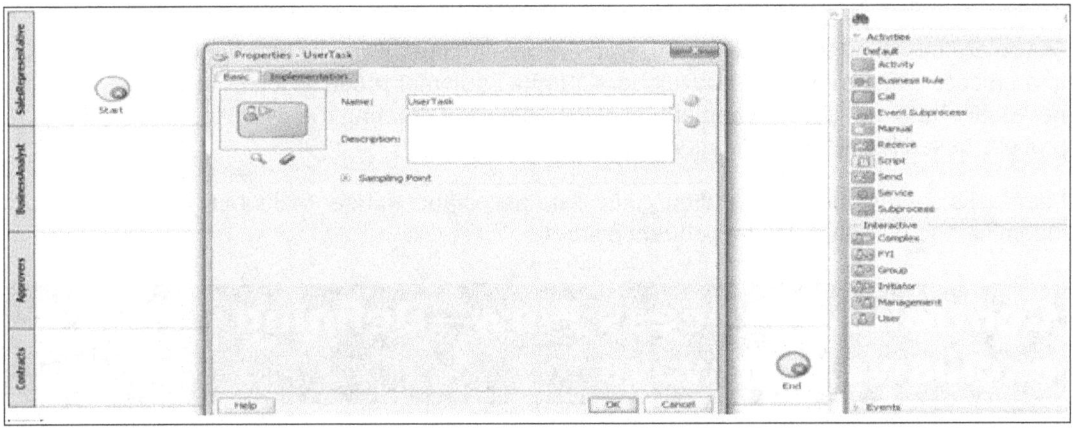

4. Enter name of the User task as **Enter Quote**.
5. Click on the sequence flow icon, at the top middle of the Process Editor.
6. Create an outgoing sequence flow from **Start Event | Enter Quote**.
7. Create the sequence flow as "unconditional".

8. Click on **Sequence flow**, and open the **Sequence Flow Properties** dialog box, wherein you can create Conditional sequence flows as well.

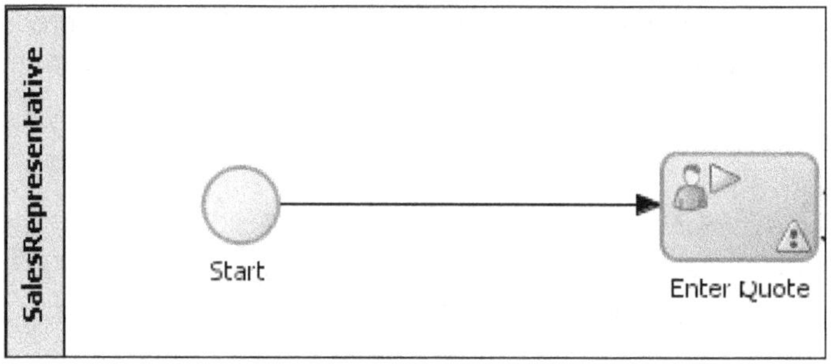

9. When you have finished the preceding steps, click **Save**.

How it works...

The Process participant interacts with BPM Workspace in BPM Suite. This can be a simple interaction, such as entering a form, or part of a more complicated workflow that requires input from multiple process participants.

As you are modeling the process, you, as a Process Analyst, will only add the user task to a process diagram. Process Developers, during implementation, will create the necessary human tasks and implement them as part of creating the overall process-based business application.

User tasks contain incoming and outgoing data associations. User tasks may also contain incoming and default outgoing sequence flows.

Controlling Process Flow—Defining exclusive gateways

You will be modeling Task # 2 (Business Analyst Review), which is performed by the Business Analyst role, in the Business Analyst swimlane.

Getting ready

The Business Analyst will review the Sales quote and he/she can either APPROVE or REJECT the Quote.

If Approved: The process continues forward.

Else: On Rejection, the process reaches the Sales Representative again, to refine and resubmit the quote.

How to do it...

Create User Task

Perform the following steps to create a User task:

1. Select **Project navigator**, click **Process | Project Editor**.
2. In the Project Editor, at the the **BusinessAnalyst** swimlane, create a User task, which is performed by the Business Analyst to review the quotation.
3. Select **Component Palette | BPM | Activities** and select **User task**.
4. Drag **User task** from **Interactive Activities** and position it in the swimlane.
5. Name the User task `Business Analyst Review`.
6. When you have finished the preceding steps, click **Save.**

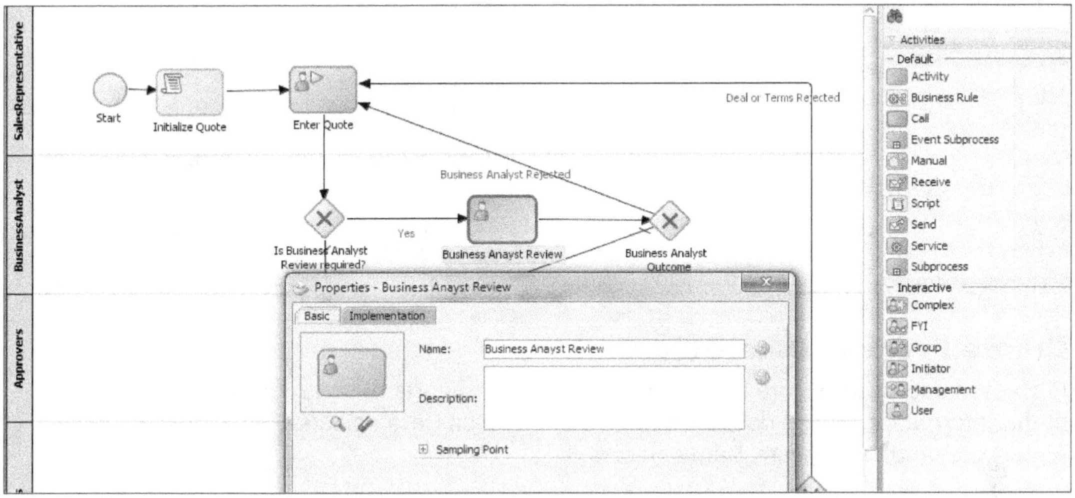

Create a Condition Switch

Before the Business Analyst performs the review on the sales quote and either rejects or approves the quote, you will check if a Business Analyst Review is required or not.

If required: Proceed to the Business Analyst Review User task.

Else: Proceed to Approvers review.

1. Select **Component Palette | BPM | Gateways**.
2. Select **Exclusive Gateway**, click on the **Business Analyst** swimlane, and position it where you want to create the Condition switches.

3. It will open a **Properties** dialog box. Enter basic information:

   Name: **Is Business Analyst Review required**? This will get displayed on the Process editor on the Exclusive Gateway.

4. Create an unconditional sequence flow from **Enter Quote** (Initiator User task) to the **Is Business Analyst Review required?** Exclusive Gateway.
5. When finished, click **Save**.

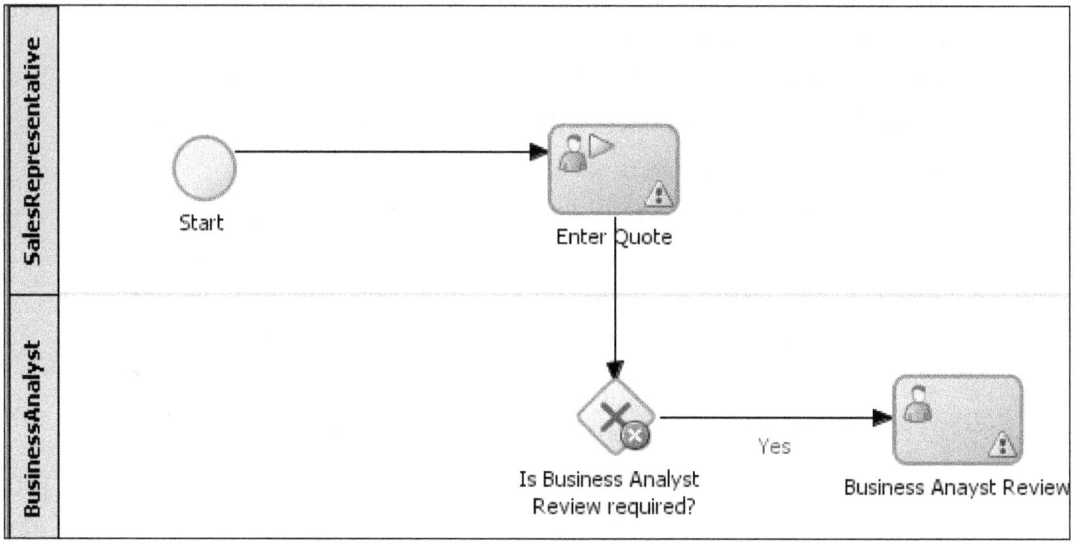

Create Process Data Object

Processes access and store information, and BPM supports data structures to keep track of this information. These data structures are—Process Data objects, Project Data objects, Arguments, and Subprocess Data objects.

Process Data objects—They store information related to each process instance you create. The value of these data objects is different for every instance in the process. However, the structure of the data object is the same for all process instances. When you define a process, you must define the data object to store information. You must also define in which part of the process you assign a value to these data objects. The value of data objects may come from user input, from external systems, or might be calculated based on other process data objects. When you create an instance, the Process Engine assigns `Null` as the default value for all the process data objects defined for that process. Later on, the activities in the process assign values to these variables.

Project Data objects—The processes in a BPM project often have a set of data they share. The value of this data is different for every instance in each of those processes; they only share the necessity to keep track of that data. Project data objects allow you to ensure that all the processes in a certain project keep track of a set of data. Then each process has to assign and update the value of this data.

You can create project data objects as follows:

1. In the Project navigator, click on the process name, **SalesToContract**.
2. You can see a **Structure** panel open at the lower-left corner of the JDeveloper screen.
3. Right-click **Process Data Objects**. Click **New** to create a Data object.
4. Enter the following details for the Process data object:
    - **Data Object name:** `BusinessAnalystReviewRequire`
    - **Type:** `Boolean (Bool)`

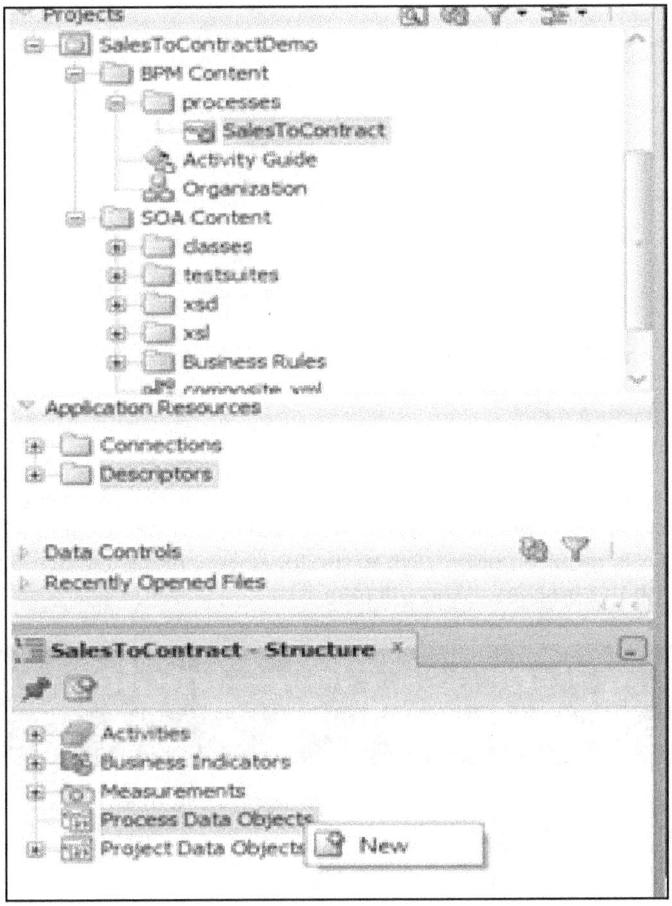

5. Create a conditional sequence flow from **Exclusive Gateway** to **Business Analyst Review** User task.
6. This will open sequence a **Flow properties** dialog.
7. In the **Description** tab, enter **Name of the Sequence flow** as `Yes`.
8. In the **Properties** tab, click on **Expression Builder** and set the value of the Process Data object as **BusinessAnalystReviewRequire == true**.

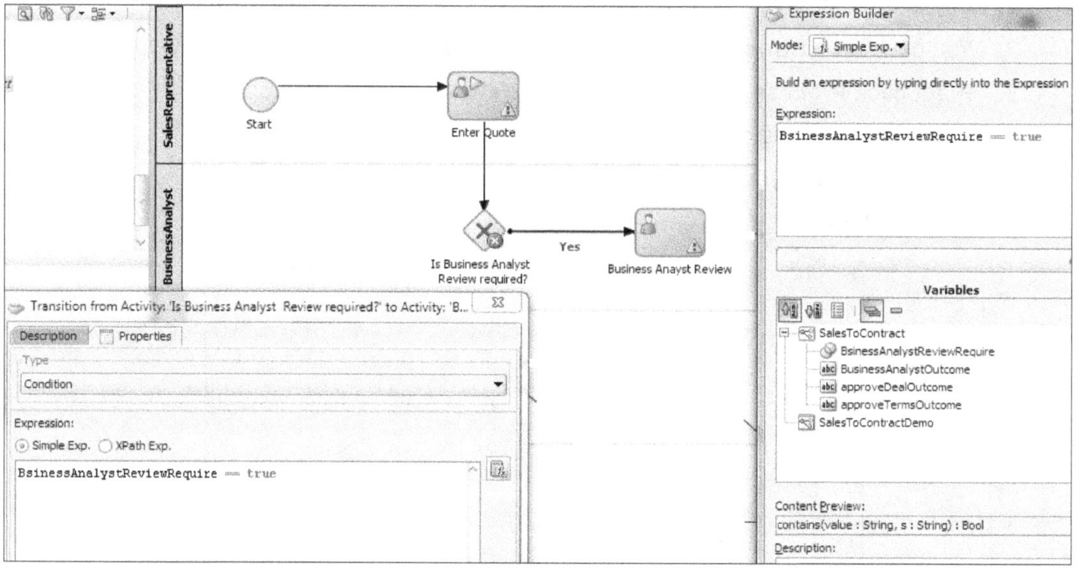

9. When you have finished the preceding steps, click **Save**.

How it works...

This User task, Business Analyst Review, will be performed by the Business Analyst to review the quotation. However, even before a review is carried out by the Business Analyst, you will check if a review is required or not. When the token reaches Exclusive Gateways, it will determine what path the process token will take.

Controlling Process Flow—Implementing Exclusive Gateways

The Business Analyst will either reject the quote or approve it, to switch the token flow, based on Business Analyst Review User task.

How to do it...

Perform the following steps to implement Exclusive gateways:

1. Create an Exclusive Gateway for the condition switch.
2. Create an Exclusive Gateway to check on the Business Analyst Approval Outcome.
3. Select **Component Palette | BPM | Gateways** and select **Exclusive Gateway**.
4. Next, click on the **BusinessAnalyst** swimlane and position it where you want to create the condition switches. In this case, place it after the **Review** task (User task).
5. It will open a Properties dialog box. Enter basic information, such as:
   - **Name**: `Business Analyst Outcome`

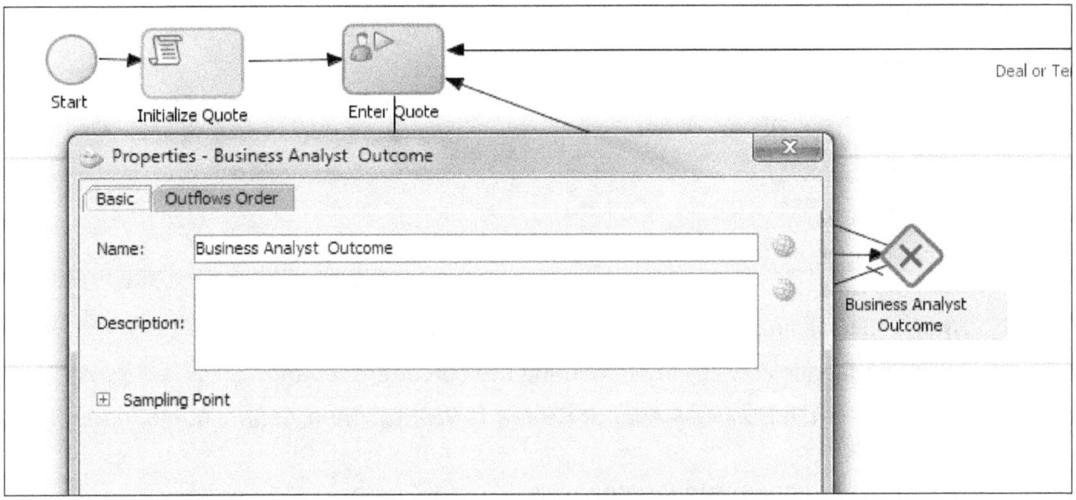

6. When you have finished the preceding steps, click **Save**.

Create a Process Data object to hold outcome of the `Business Analyst Review` User task as follows:

1. Click the process name **SalesToContract** in the Project navigator.
2. You can see that a **Structure** panel opens at the lower left corner of the JDeveloper screen.
3. In the **Structure** panel, on the lower-left side, right-click **Process Data Objects** and click **New**, to create a new Data object.

4. Enter the following details for the Process Data object:
   - Data object name: `BusinessAnalystOutcome`
   - **Type: String**
   - Enable **Auto Initialise**.

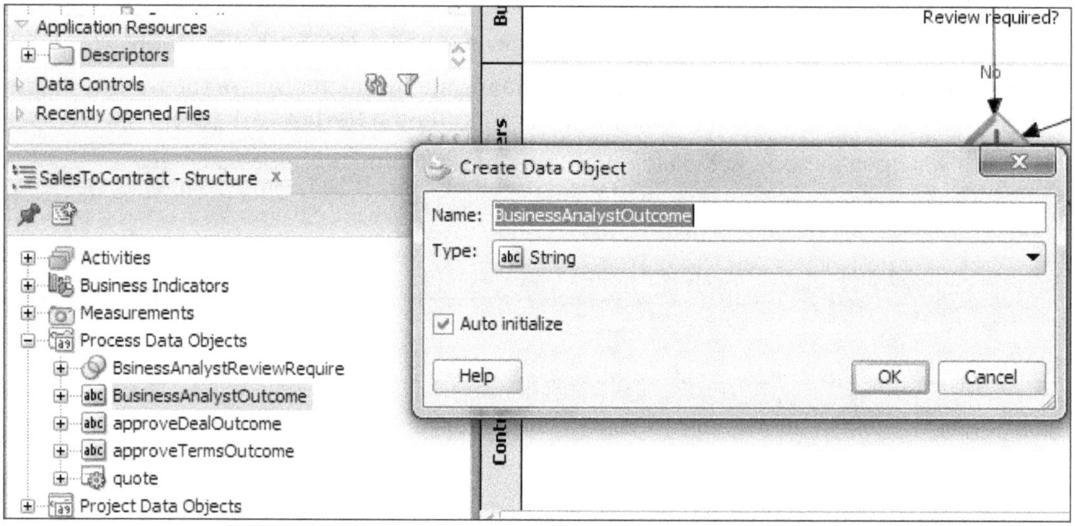

5. When you have finished the preceding steps, click **Save**.
6. Create Sequence flows by implementing the outcome scenario:

   If outcome of the Business Analyst Review is REJECT: Then, send a quote to the Sales Representative.

   Else: Send it to Approvers for approvals.
7. Case: REJECT
   - Create a Conditional Sequence flow from Business Analyst Outcome Gateway to User Task (Enter Quote)
   - Click on sequence flow to open the **Properties** dialog
   - Enter basic information as follows:
   - In the **Description** tab ,enter **Name: Business Analyst Rejected**
   - In the **Properties** tab:
   - Select **Type** as **Condition** (to implement conditional sequence flow)
   - In the **Expression** section, click **Expression Builder**

- In **Expression Builder**, select **Mode** as **Simple expression**
- From the **Variables** section, chose the Data object **BusinessAnalystOutcome** and set value as: **BusinessAnalystOutcome=="REJECT"**

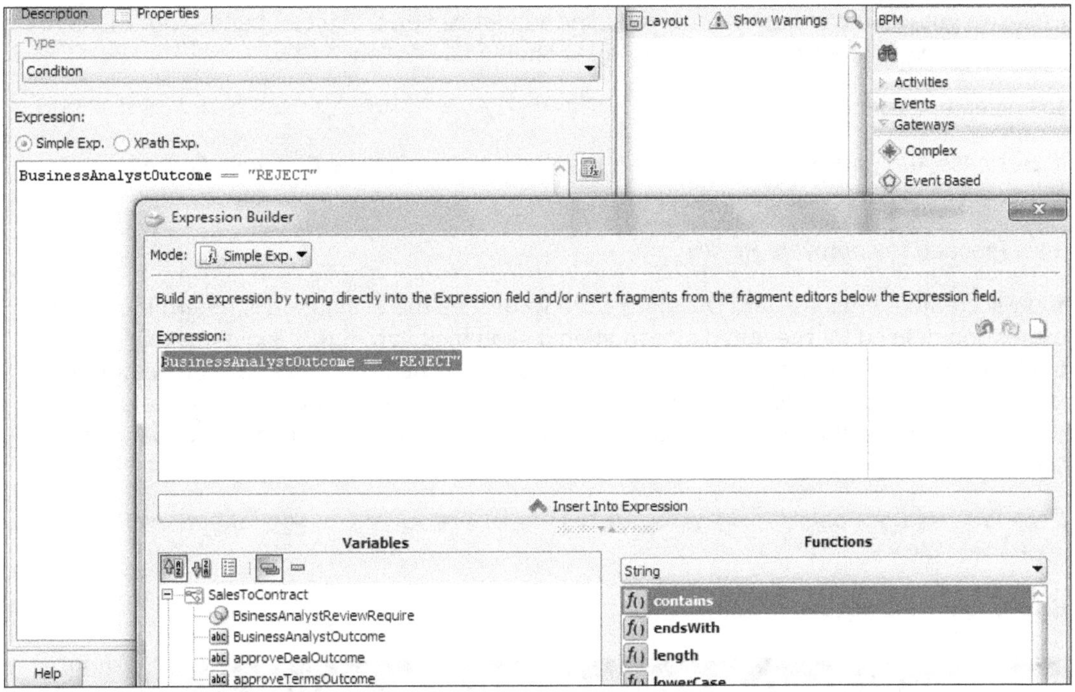

- Click **OK**
- When you have finished the preceding steps, click **Save.**

8. Case: APPROVE
   - Create an unconditional sequence flow from Gateway (Business Analyst Outcome)to Approvals(Parallel gateway), in the **Approvers** swimlane
   - Enter basic information such as:
   - In the **Description** tab, enter **Name:** `Business Analyst Approved`
   - In the **Properties** tab, select **Unconditiona**l as **Type**(to implement unconditional sequence flow)
   - When you have finished the preceding steps, click **Save**.

How it works...

Exclusive gateways used for the conditional switch discussed in the preceding text are flow objects that define the flow of process. Gateways define what path the process token will take. Exclusive gateways have conditional outgoing sequence flows. You can build expressions to determine if your process continues down a conditional sequence flow.

To implement Conditional Switch:

If: Business Analyst Review is required = Yes, then proceed to the Business Analyst Review User task.

Else: Proceed to Approvers Review.

You will create a Process Data Object to store values, as the evaluation is determined by the expression defined for the outgoing conditional sequence flow. If this evaluates to true, then the Process Flow proceeds down the `Yes` path (towards the Business Analyst Review User task). If it evaluates to false, then the Process Flow proceeds down the path of the default outgoing sequence flow. The condition in the sequence flow will be based on values of Process Data object `BusinessAnalystReviewRequired`.

If the Process Data object `BusinessAnalystReviewRequired = True`*, then choose the sequence flow* `Yes`

Else: Choose the sequence flow `No`

Controlling Process Flow—Parallel gateways

Task # 3, Quote Approval has 2 parallel tasks:

- Deal Step Approval
- Term Step Approval

They need to be performed in parallel by the Approvers and Contracts roles.

How to do it...

I. Create a Parallel gateway

1. Move to **Component Palette | BPM | Activities**.
2. Click **Gateways**, and select **Parallel Gateway**.
3. Drag it to the Project Editor, in the **Approvers** swimlane.

4. Enter basic information into the properties dialog of the gateway, such as:
    - **Name: Approvals**
5. When you have finished the preceding steps, click **Save**.

II. Create a User task

> You need to create two User tasks in the Process Model, which will perform the Approval deal and Approval terms tasks, by the Approvers and Contracts roles, respectively.

1. Go to **Component Palette | BPM | Activities**.
2. Click **User task** in interactive activities.
3. Click in the **Approvers** swimlane, where you want to position this User task.
4. Enter the following details in the **Properties** dialog of the User task:
    - In the **Base** tab, enter **Name** as `Approve Deal`
    - In the **Implementation** tab, leave the default, as we will implement it in the implementation phase of the development cycle
5. When you have finished the preceding steps, click **Save**.
6. Go to **Component Palette | BPM | Activities**.
7. Click **User task** in interactive activities.
8. Click on the **Approvers** swimlane, at the point where you want to position this User task.
9. Enter the following details in the **Properties** dialog of the User task:
    - In the **Base** tab, enter **Name** as **Approve Terms**
    - In the **Implementation** tab, leave the default, as we will implement it in the implementation phase of the development cycle.
10. When you have finished, click **Save**.

III. Create sequence flows

Create unconditional sequence flows from the **Approvals** Parallel gateway to **Approve Deal** and **Approve Terms** User tasks.

1. Click on the sequence flow on top of the Process Editor.
2. Create a Sequence flow (Unconditional) from the **Approvals** Parallel gateway in the **Approvers** swimlane to the Approve Deal User task.
3. Similarly, create a Sequence flow (Unconditional) from the **Approvals** Parallel gateway in the **Approvers** swimlane to the **Approve Terms** User task.
4. When you have finished the preceding steps, click **Save.**

IV. Create Process Data objects

Create Process Data objects to store the outcome of the Approve Deal and Approve Terms User tasks.

1. Click the process name **SalesToContract** in the Project navigator.
2. You can check the open **Structure** panel at the lower-left corner of the JDeveloper screen.
3. In the **Structure** panel, on the lower-left side, right-click the Process Data object, and click **New**, to create a new Data object.
4. Enter the following details for the Process data object:
    - Data object name: `approveDealOutcome`
    - **Type**: **String**
    - Enable **Auto Initialize**
5. Enter Following Details for the Process data object :
    - Data Object name : `approveTermsOutcome`
    - **Type**: **String**
    - Enable **Auto Initialize**
6. When you have finished the preceding steps, click **Save**.

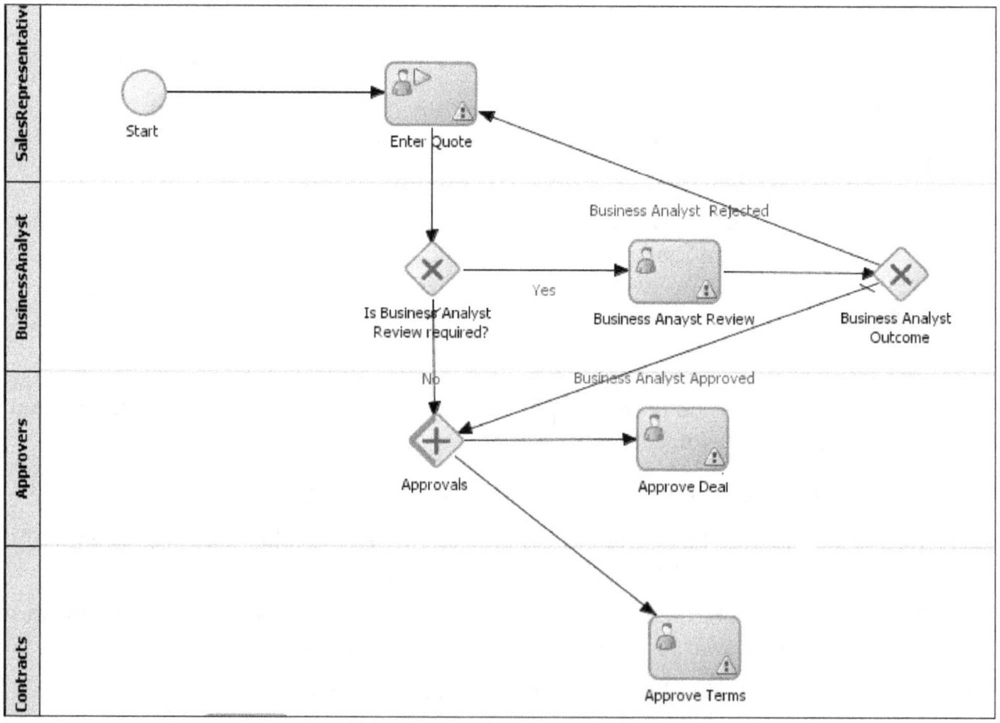

How it works...

The Parallel Gateway guides the process token to perform two or more tasks simultaneously.

The Parallel Gateway:

- Splits your process into two or more paths when you want your Process Flow to follow all paths simultaneously
- When a token reaches a parallel gateway, the parallel gateway creates a token for each outgoing sequence flow

Controlling Process Flow—Sequence Flows

Task # 4 is performed at the Contracts swimlane by the Contracts role. You will merge the outcome of the `Approval Deal` and `Approval Terms` User tasks. Data objects that have already been created (`approveDealOutcome` and `approveTermsOutcome`) will contain the values of outcome from the Approve Deal and Approve Terms User tasks, respectively.

How to do it...

1. Merge Outcome: Merge the outcome of `Approve Deal` and `Approve Term` User tasks:
   - Go to **Component Palette | BPM | Gateways**
   - Click on **Parallel Gateway**
   - Click on the **Contract**s swimlane, where you want to place the Parallel Gateway
   - Name the Parallel Gateway `Merge Approvals`
   - Create an unconditional, unnamed sequence flow from the `Approve Deal` and `Approve Terms` User tasks to the gateway `Merge Approvals`.
   - When you have finished the preceding steps, click **Save**
2. Create a Finalize User task:
   - Go to **Component Palette | BPM | Activities**
   - Select a User task from the interactive section
   - Click on the **Contracts** swimlane and position User task before the**End** event
   - In the User task **Properties** window, enter the following:
   - In the **Basic** tab, enter **Name** = **Contract Finalize**
   - Leave the implementation tab as default
   - When you have finished the preceding steps, click **Save**

- Create an unconditional sequence flow from the gateway `Approvals Outcome` to the `Contract Finalize` User task.
- Name the sequence flow as **Approved**
- When you have finished the preceding steps, click **Save**

3. Switch on `Approve Deal` and `Approve Terms` outcome:

   Post merger, you have to switch on the outcome of Approve Deal and Approve Terms User tasks. Create Exclusive Gateway to implement conditional switch on outcomes.

   - Go to **Component Pallet | BPM | Gateway** and select Exclusive Gateway
   - Click on the Contracts swimlane, where you want to place the Exclusive Gateway
   - Name the gateway `Approvals Outcome`
   - When you have finished the preceding steps, click **Save**

4. Create sequence flows:

   To implement the outcome scenario

   If the outcome of Approve Deal OR Approve Terms User tasks is REJECT, then send the quote back to the Sales Representative

   Else: Send it to Finalize Contract User task

5. When REJECT:

   - Click on the sequence flow icon on top of the process editor to create a sequence flow
   - Create a conditional sequence flow from the gateway **Approvals Outcome** to the **Enter Quote** User task.
   - Enter the following information in the properties of the sequence flow:
   - In the **Description** tab, enter **Name** = `Deal` or `Terms Rejected`
   - In the Properties tab, Type = Condition
   - In the **Expression** section, choose **Simple Expression**
   - Select **Expression Builder**
   - You can find the `approveDealOutcome` and `approveTermsOutcome` process Data objects. They hold the outcome values from User tasks:
   - **approveDealOutcome == REJECT** or **approveTermsOutcome == REJECT**
   - When you have finished, click **Save**

6. When APPROVE:
    - Create an unconditional sequence flow from the Gateway `Approvals Outcome` to the `Contract Finalize` User task.
    - Name the sequence flow `Approved`
    - When you have finished the preceding steps, click **Save**

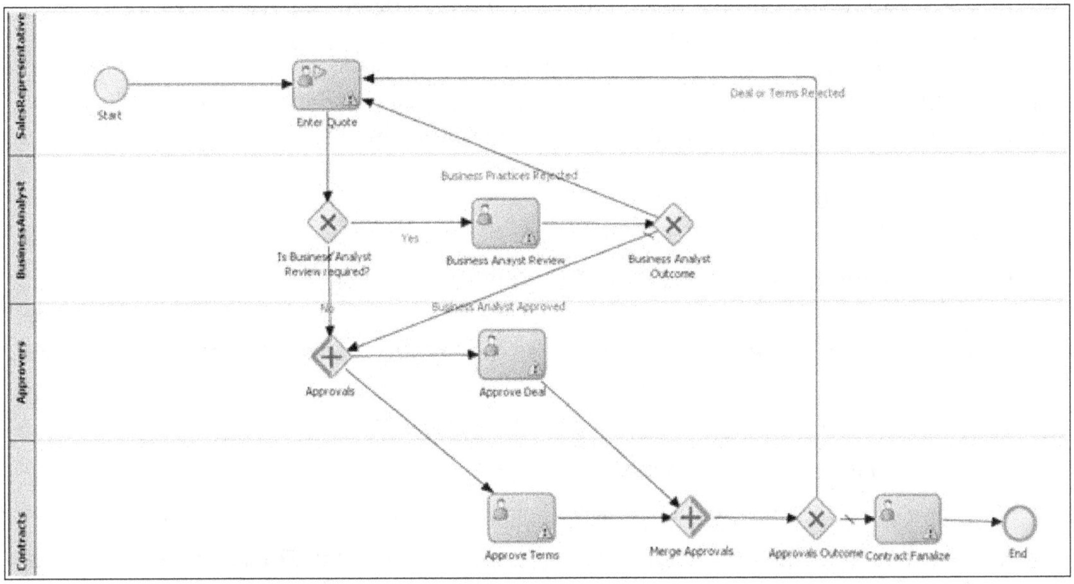

How it works...

As per Process Flow:

If: the outcomes for the `Approve Deal` *or the* `Approve Terms` *User tasks' is* `REJECT`, *then the Sales Representative will reenter the quote information.*

Else: The contract will be finalized.

You can also use the parallel gateway to merge process paths split by the parallel gateway. The merge of the parallel gateway waits for a token to arrive from each of the incoming sequence flows. After all tokens arrive, only one token is passed to the outgoing sequence flow.

In addition, you should design your process so that a token arrives for each incoming sequence flow, for the merging parallel gateway. If you do not, your process can freeze if the merger is expecting tokens that do not arrive.

Communicating with external processes and services

Till this point, you have finalized the contract. Let's save the contract information in the database. We can achieve it by communicating with either an external service, which performs the service of interacting with the desired database and performs an insert operation into it. This external service could be a BPEL Service, Mediator service, Adapter Service, or another BPM Process itself. Let's take the case of invoking an Adapter Service (Database Adapter) to perform the insert operation. As a Process Analyst, you will model the service call in the process. However you will implement it in Implementation phase.

How to do it...

1. Go to **Component Palette | BPM | Default Activities** and select the **Service Task** activity.
2. Click on the **Contract** swimlane between the **Finalize Contracts** User task and **End** event.
3. This will open the **Properties** dialog for the **Service Task** activity.
4. In the **Basic** tab, enter **Name** as `Save Quote`.
5. Leave other tabs as default. We will implement it at the implementation phase.
6. Create an unconditional sequence flow from the **Contracts Finalize** User task to the **Save Quote** service and from the **Save Quote** service to the **End** event.
7. When you have finished the preceding steps, click **Save**.

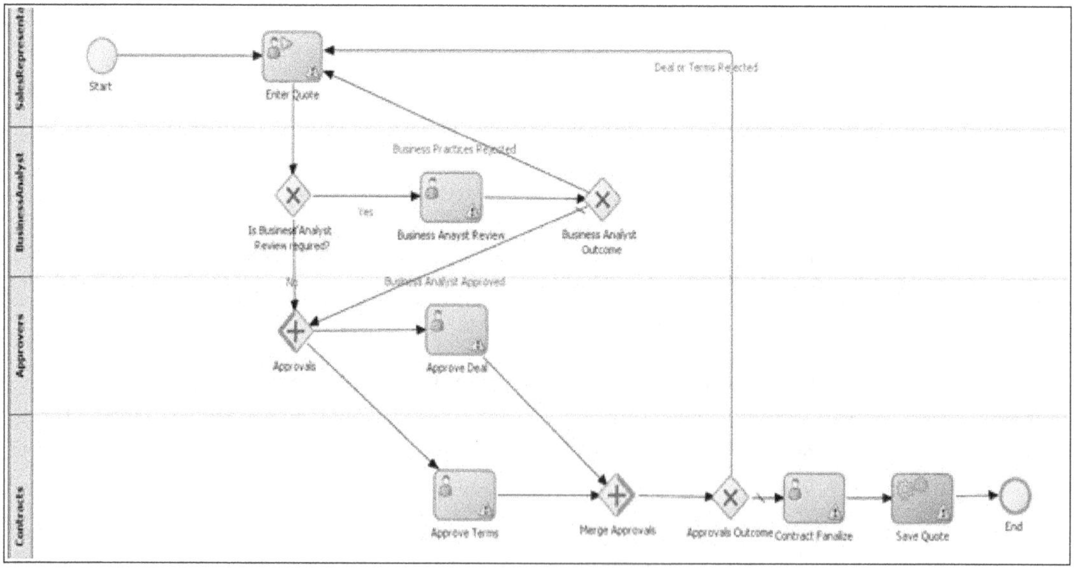

How it works...

Process Analysts can add the service task when they know that a process must invoke an external service or process to communicate with other processes and services, such as BPMN process, BPEL process, SOA service, Adapter Services and mediator services.

Service task invokes processes and service, synchronously. When the service task invokes a process or service, the token waits at the service task until a response is returned. After the response is received, the token continues to the next sequence flow in the process.

There's more...

Service Adapter (Database Adapter) will be configured in `Composite.xml`.

In the Service Activity **Save Quote** properties, on the **Implementation** tab, you can browse the service that you will carry out in the Implementation phase to implement it.

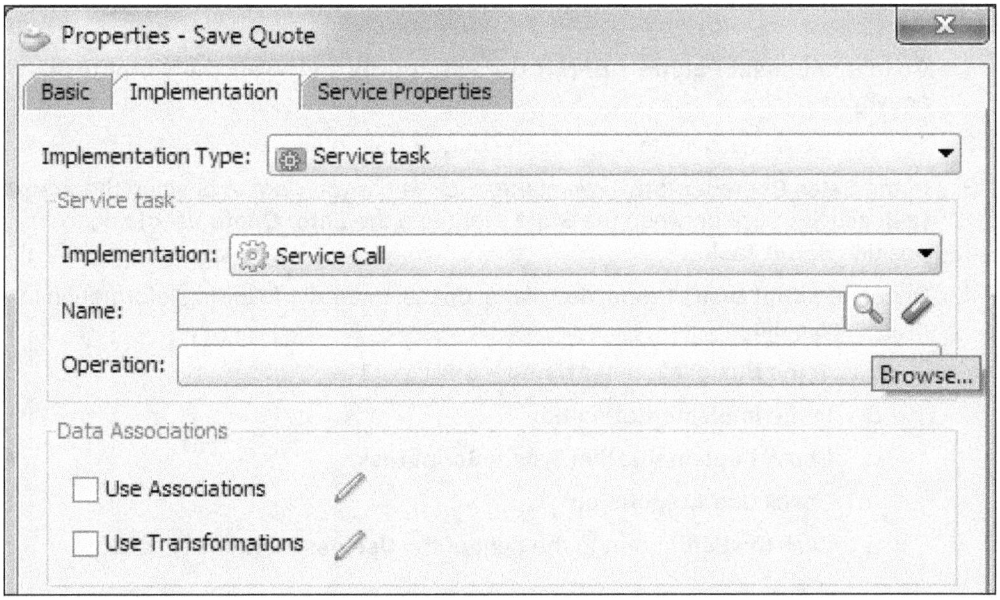

Changing the value of Data objects in your process

You have created a couple of Process Data Objects while modeling the **SalesToContract** process. However, you have never initialized those Data objects.

The following Data objects were created during modeling:

- `BusinessAnalystOutcome` (to hold the outcome of the Business Analyst Review User task)
- `approveDealOutcome` (to hold the outcome of the Approve Deal User task)
- `approveTermsOutcome` (To hold the outcome of the Approve Terms User task)

Let's try to change Process Data object values and initialize them in the process.

How to do it...

1. Go to **Component Palette | BPM | Default Activity** and select the **Script task** activity.
2. You will use this activity to initialize the `Quote` Data objects.
3. In the **Sales Representative** swimlane, click where you want to position the **Script task** activity. Click between the **Start** event and the **Enter Quote** User task, to position **Script Task**.
4. Once the **Script task | Properties** dialog opens, enter the following information in the properties dialog:
    - In the **Basic** tab, enter **Name** = `Initialize Quote`
    - In the **Implementation** tab
    - Chose **Implementation Type** = **Script task**
    - Check **Use Association**
    - Click the **Edit** button to the right of the **Use Associations** checkbox

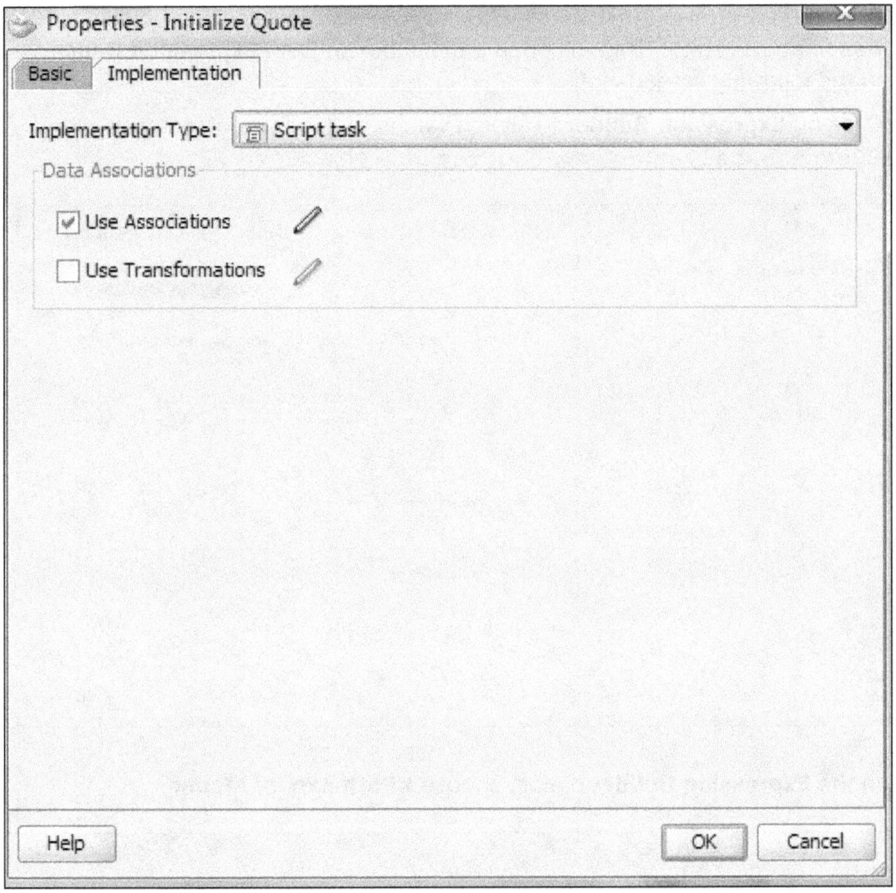

5. The **Data Associations** editing dialog will open.
6. On the right side of the dialog box, list the Data objects created so far in the process.

7. Drag the `BusinessAnalystReviewRequired` process Data objects to the **Data Associations** editor. This will open a blank box with an **Expression Builder**, as shown in the following screenshot.
8. Click on **Expression Builder** to assign values to this Data object, say `BusinessAnalystReviewRequired` Data object:

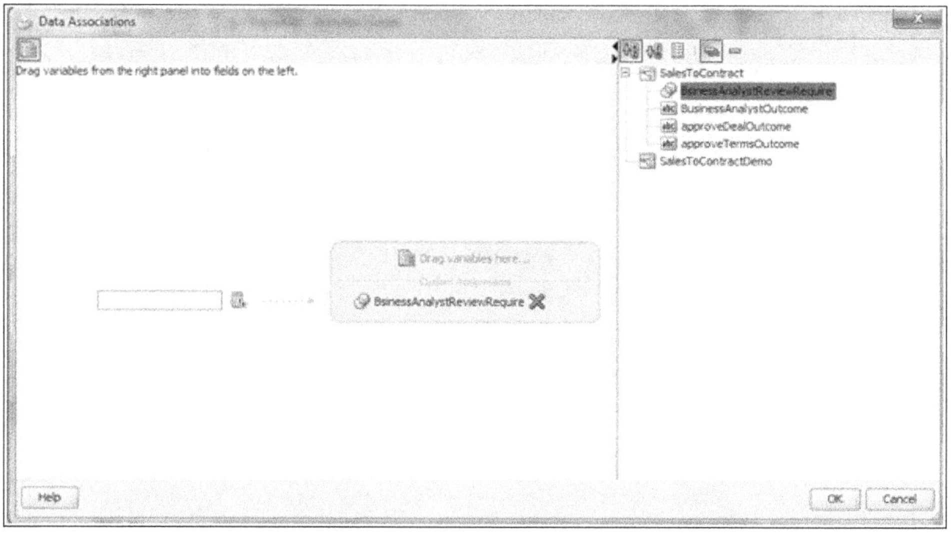

9. In the **Expression Builder** dialog, choose **XPath Exp** for **Mode:**

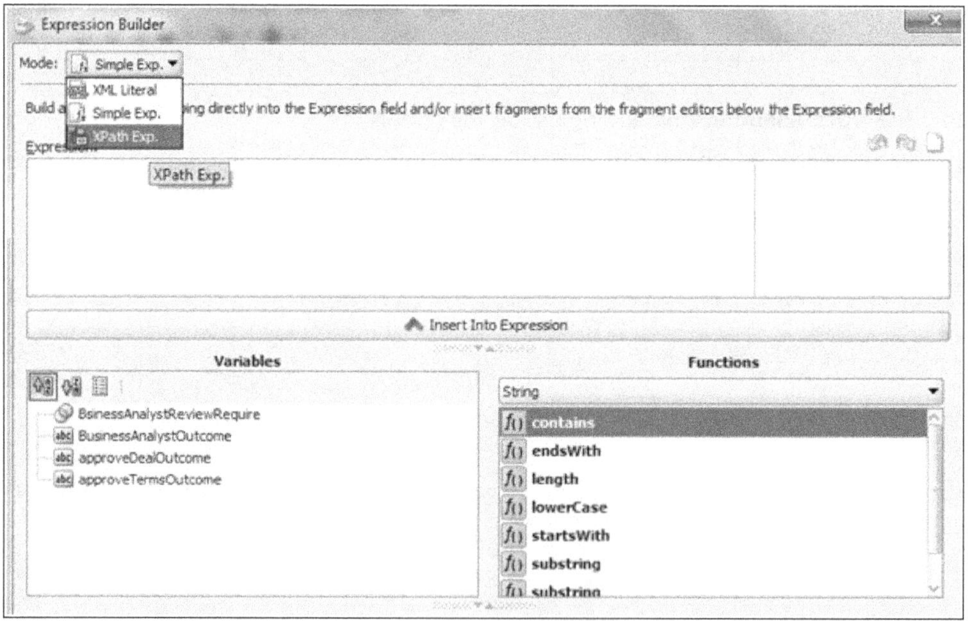

10. In the **Expression** editor, enter `false()` to assign `false()` as initial value to the **BusinessAnalystReviewRequire** Data object.
11. Click **OK**, and when you have finished the preceding steps, click **Save**.

How it works...

Script Tasks are used to change Process Data objects values. So when the process token reaches the script task, it will initialize those Data objects.

The script task is used to:

- Change values of Data objects within your process
- Change the values of Data objects outside of another flow object
- Set initial values of Data objects at the beginning of a process

Project Data objects are Data objects that you define in a project. As with other flow objects that accept data associations, you can use expressions to change the values of Data objects.

Creating Business objects in a Business Catalog

The main elements of a business process are tasks and information related to those tasks. The information of a process may change as you run the process. This information defines the state of a process at a given time. According to the value of this information, the instance may take one path or another. This information defines the state of a process at a given time.

You may store this information in an external system also.

The Sales Quote example process uses the following information:

- Approval flow
- Approval terms outcome
- Quote

BPM data objects have two characteristics: Data Object Name and Data Object Data Type. The business catalog is a repository that stores the reusable components you use to implement some flow objects in BPMN processes. The business catalog stores the following types of components:

- Errors
- Events
- Human Tasks
- Business Rules

- Service Adapters
- Synthesized Types
- BPEL Processes and Mediators
- Business Objects
- Business Exceptions

The Business Catalog holds the different types of Services (System, BPEL processes, Task Services, Rule Services) as well as Business objects (Data). There are different folders for holding different types of BPM artifacts. Some folders have a lock to indicate that the artifacts inside them cannot be deleted. Business objects allow you to model and develop the business entities that are part of your process using the Object Oriented paradigm. Using Business objects simplifies the management of the data in your process by encapsulating the data and business behavior associated with the business entity it represents. A **Business object** is composed of a set of attributes and a set of methods.

- Attributes store the data related to the entity you are modeling.
- Methods manipulate the value of these attributes, or perform calculations based on their values.

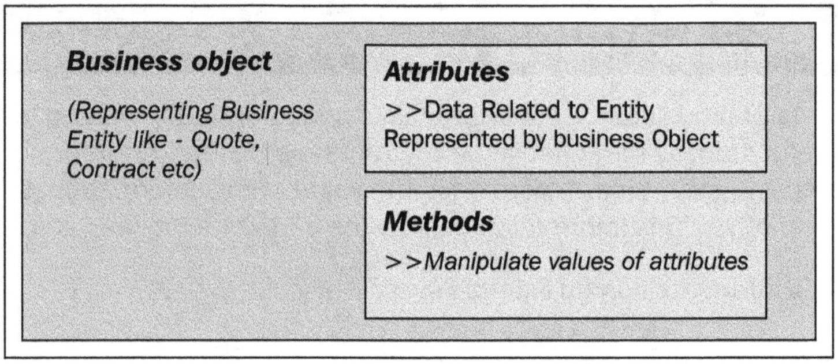

In a Sales Quote example, you can identify the business entities **Quote**, **Contract**, and so on.

You can create Business objects either manually, or based on an XML schema element or complex type, or by customizing a synthetic type in the types.

How to do it...

You will use BPM Studio to create the `Quote` Business object represented by XML Schema. These Business objects will be stored under **Business Catalog**.

1. In the BPM Project navigator, right-click on **Business Catalog**, select **New**, and then select **Business Object**.

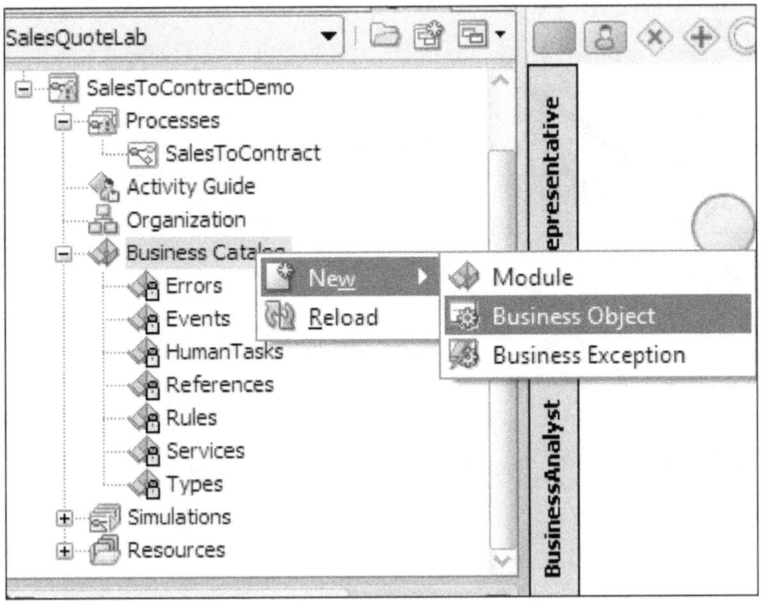

This will bring up the **Business Object** dialog, as follows:

2. Type `Quote` in the **Name** field.

3. Click on the magnifying glass icon next to the **Destination** module. This will bring up the **Module List** dialog. Click on the **New** symbol to add a module with the name `Data` under **Business Catalog**.

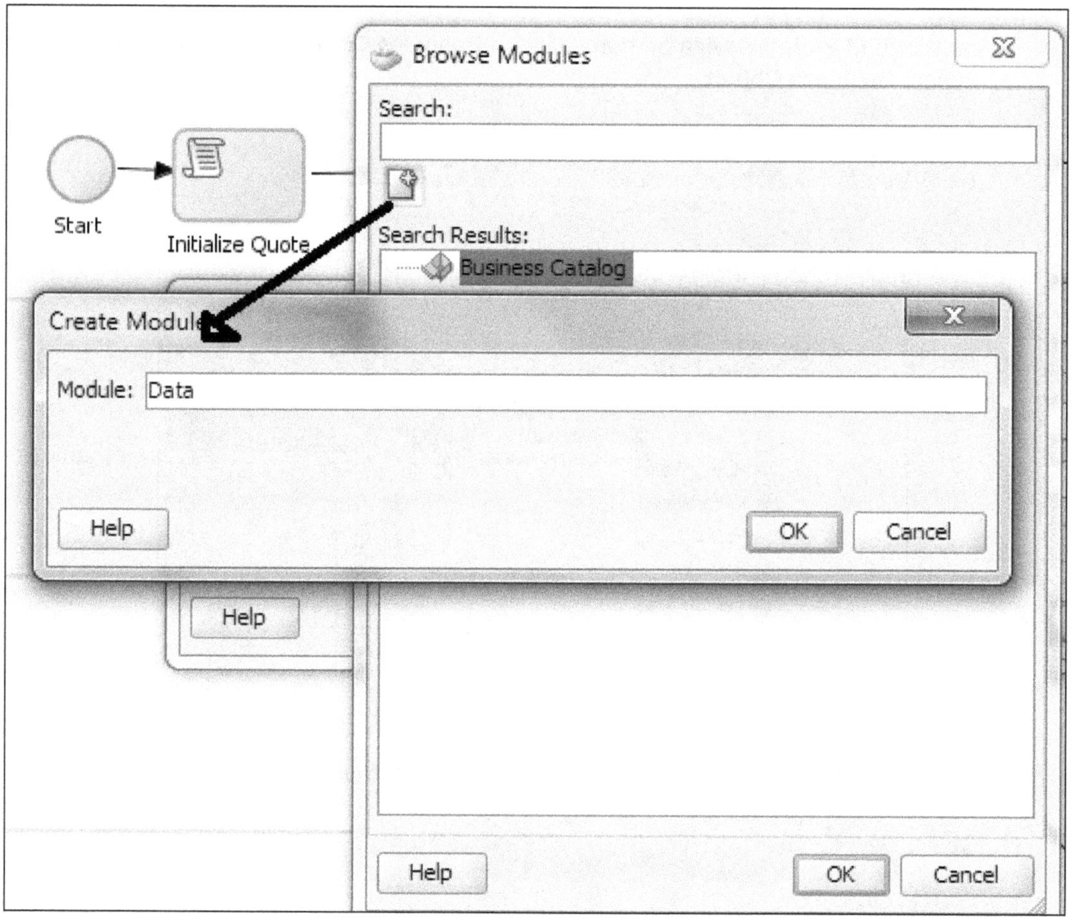

4. Click **OK**.
5. Select the **Based on External Schema** option and click the magnifying glass icon. This brings up the **Type Chooser** dialog. Click on the **Import Schema Files** icon on the top-right corner to import an XSD file into your BPM Project.

6. Select the **Copy to Project** option in the **Import Schema File** dialog and select the magnifying glass icon.

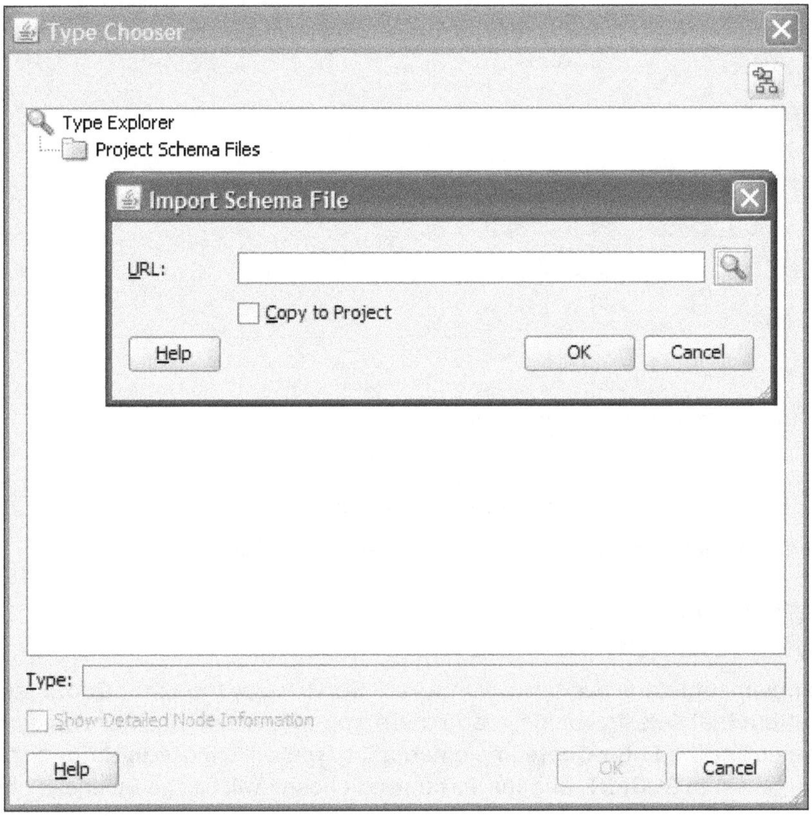

7. This brings up the **SOA Resource** browser window. Locate and select the `Quote.xsd` file.
8. Click **OK** to close the **SOA Resource** browser and click **OK** again on the **Localize Files** dialog.
9. Expand the **Project Schema Files** folder in **Type Chooser**, and select the **Quote Request** element. Click **OK** and then **OK**, again.

10. The Quote Business Object opens. You can add description and documentation details here, as desired. When finished, close the **Quote** window.

11. You have now created the Business object **quote**.
12. When you have finished the preceding steps, click **Save**.

How it works...

When you implement Interactive tasks with a Task Service, say the **Enter Quote** task, you choose a pattern that sets its outcome, and there, you will choose Business object as the task parameter. For the **Enter Quote** Implementation, you will choose **Initiator** as the **Pattern**, outcome will be set to **SUBMIT**, and the **Parameter** chosen will be the Business object **quote**.

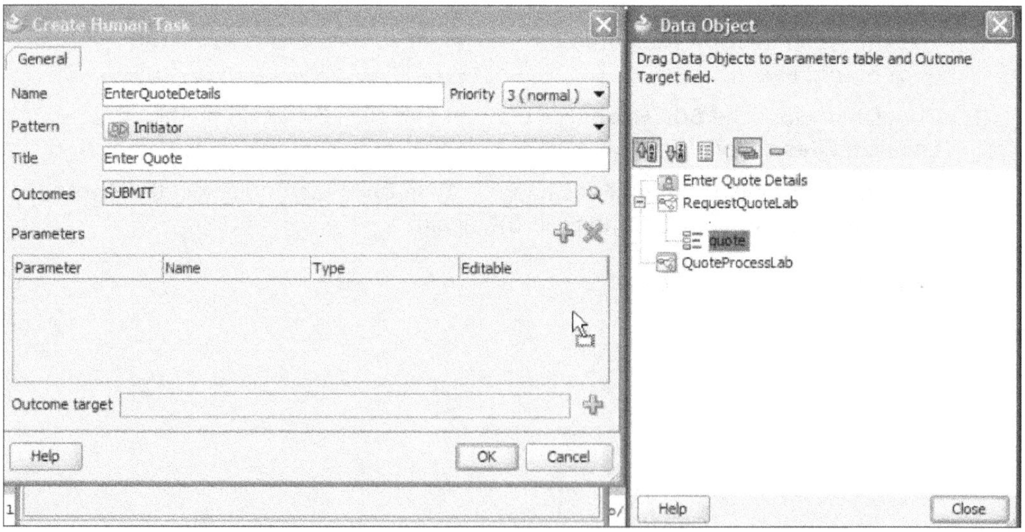

Adding documentation to the Flow Element

The Oracle BPM Suite 's BPM Studio provides process documentation features too. Within the documentation Windows allows you add documentation for the entire process or for each flow object within your process. You can create end user and Use Case documentation for your processes.

- End User Documentation: This is the documentation the process participants see using the Oracle BPM Workspace application.
- Use Case documentation: This is the documentation that Process Analysts and Process Developers see when updating a business process.

How to do it...

Adding documentation to the Flow Element in a process is done as follows:

1. Open the process **SaleToContract**.
2. From the **View** menu select **Documentation**.
3. Select the flow object within your process that you want to document.
4. You can even add documentation for the whole process or any of its individual elements.
5. From the drop-down list, select the type of documentation you want to add.
6. You can choose either **Documentation** or **Use Case Documentation**, based on your requirements.
7. Enter your documentation.
8. When you have finished, click **Save**.

How it works...

Have a look at the **Documentation** tab in the following screenshot. On the upper-left side, you can find the process name given (SalesToContract), as you are documenting the entire process. However, you can choose any Flow Element and its name will appear there, and then you can document for that particular Flow Element too.

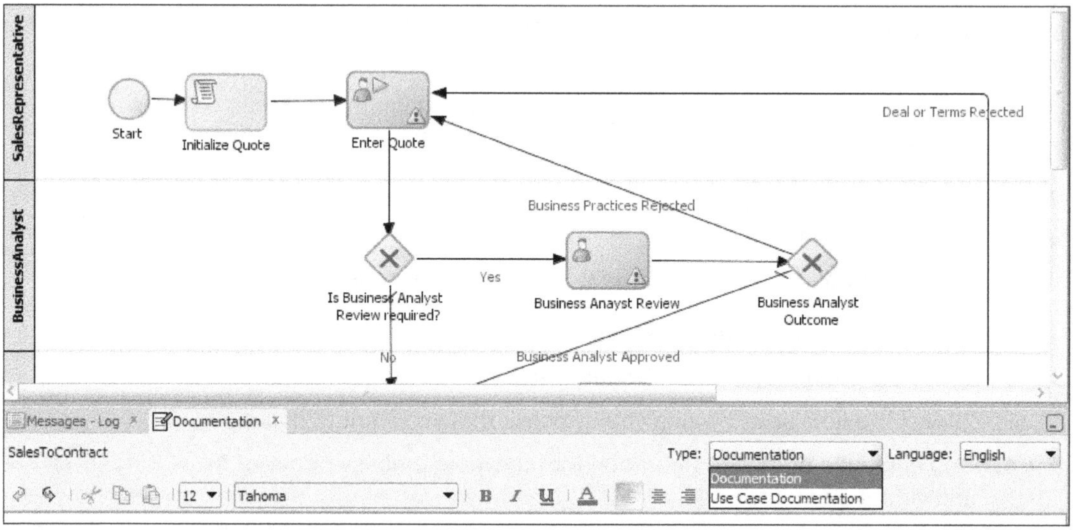

Creating MDS for BPM

Oracle **Metadata Service** (**MDS**) repository is an Oracle Fusion Middleware component that stores metadata for certain types of deployed applications. Oracle BPM uses this repository when deploying applications to runtime. In addition to using Oracle MDS to store information about deployed applications, Oracle BPM also creates a partition in the MDS repository to store projects and project templates.

When an MDS connection is created, BPM partitions are created. These partitions are used by both Oracle BPM Studio and Business Process Composer to share projects and project templates.

The Oracle BPM MDS repository contains the following default folders:

- `Public`: Contains all shared Oracle BPM projects.
- `Templates`: Contains all project templates.

You can create additional subfolders within these folders, to organize your projects and project templates. The Oracle BPM Metadata Services repository is installed as part of the Oracle BPM runtime installation. After this installation is complete, you must configure your Oracle BPM Studio installation to connect to the repository.

How to do it...

Here you will create an MDS for BPM:

1. Open JDeveloper in the default role.
2. Open **Resource Palette**, by selecting **View** | **Resource Palette**.

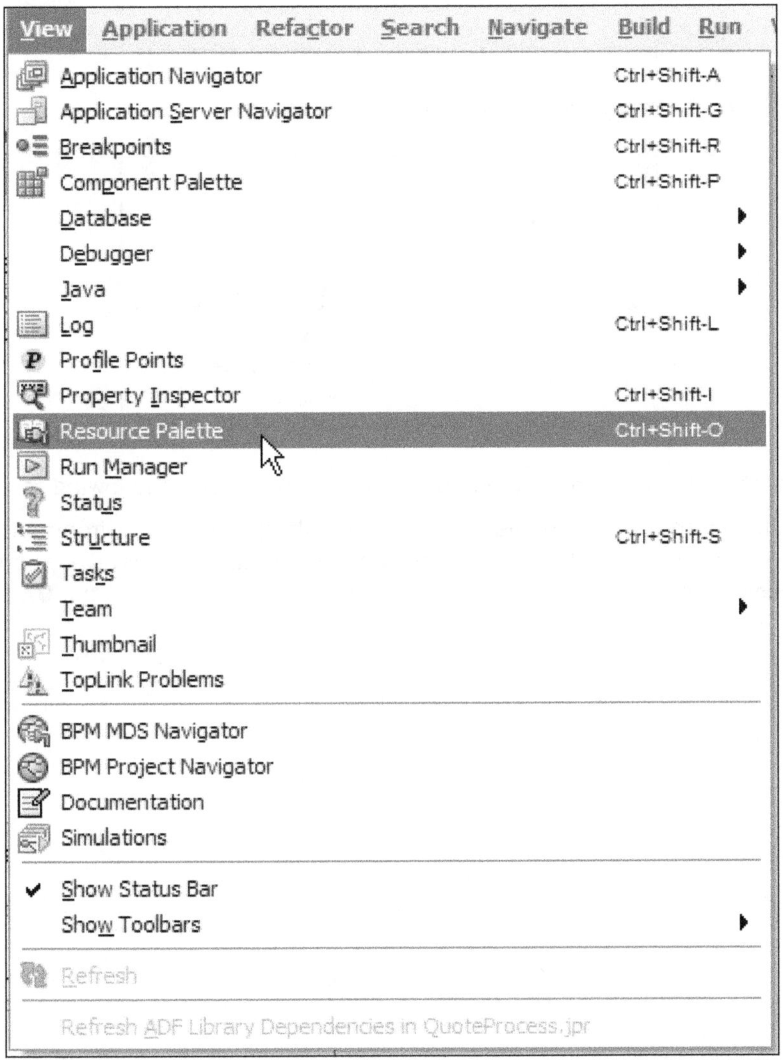

3. Go to **IDE Connections**. Click on the folder with the **+** sign.

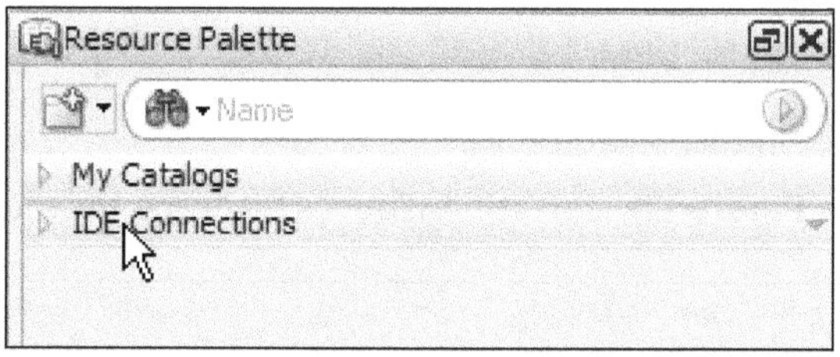

4. Right-click on **New Connection** and then **Database**.

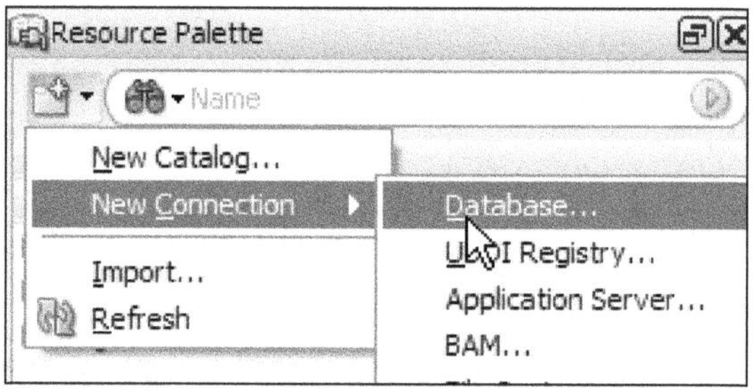

5. Create a database connection to the MDS, as shown in the following screenshot.
6. Get the database TNS details and fill the details as per your environment. Once you're done, you can check the connection by pressing the **Test Connection** button; a **Success!** message appears, if the parameters are correct. Click the **OK** button.

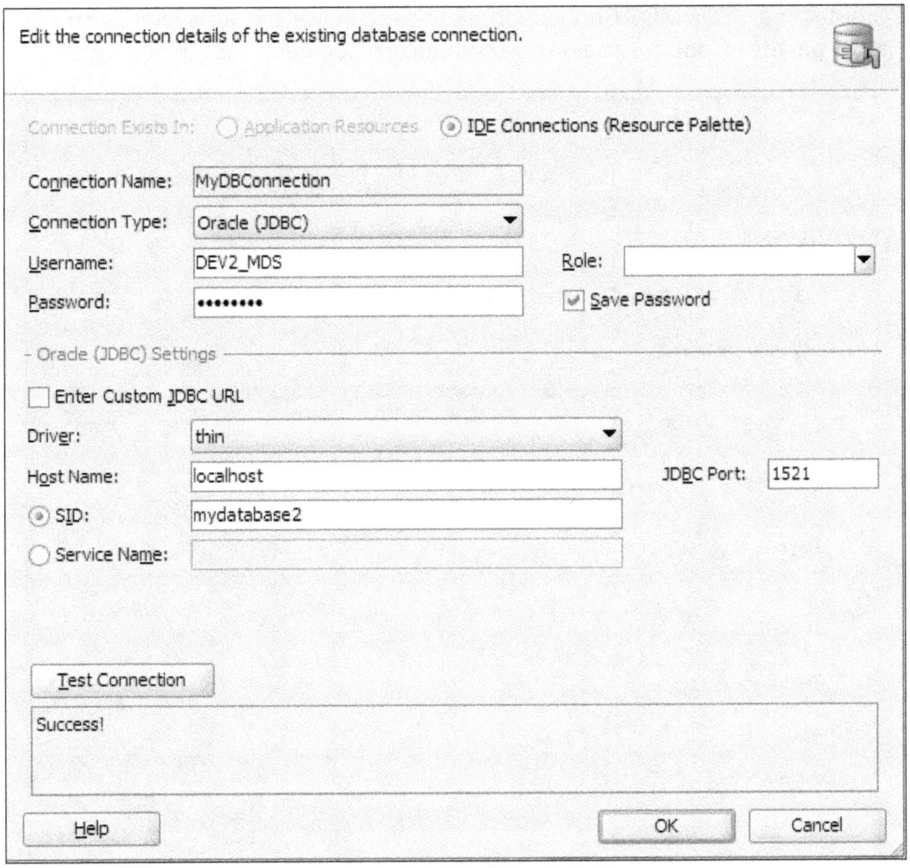

7. Right-click on **New Connection** and select **New Connection** and select **SOA-MDS**.

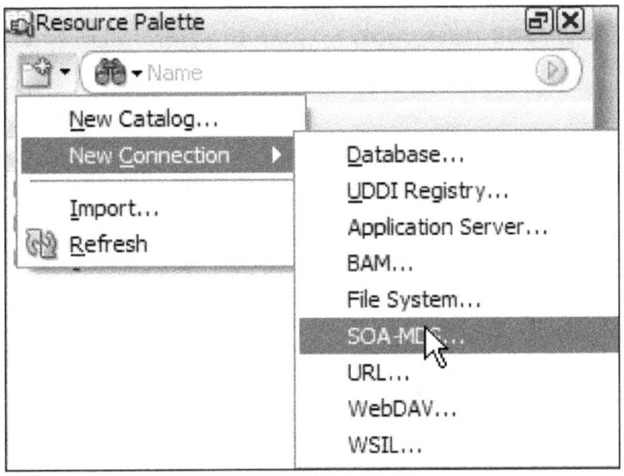

8. Create a new SOA MDS Connection, as started in the previous step. In the **Select MDS partition**, **obpm** should be automatically selected. Test the connection.

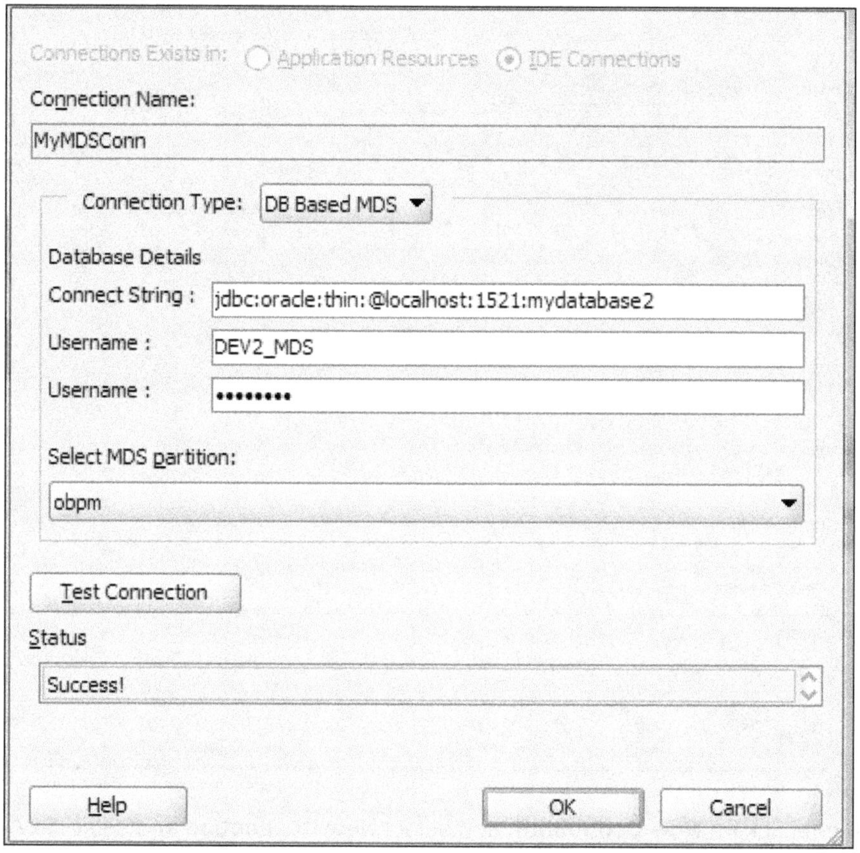

9. Go to **View | BPM MDS Navigator**, to open the BPM MDS Navigator.

10. Open **Configure Connection** and choose the SOA MDS Connection that you just defined.

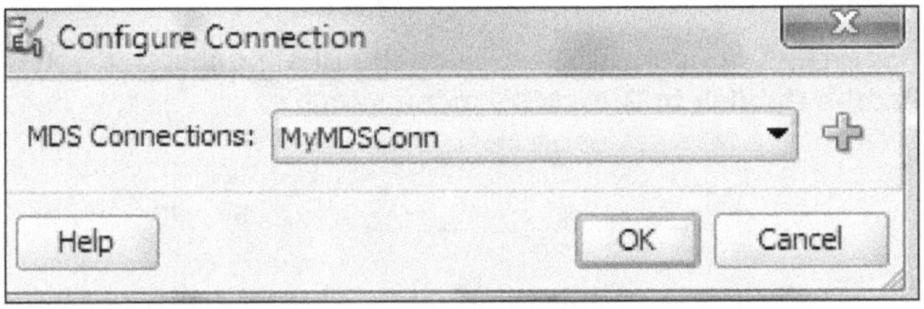

11. Check that root folders **Public** and **Templates** are shown in **BPM MDS Navigator**.
12. When you have finished the preceding steps, click **Save**.

How it works...

The Oracle BPM Metadata Service browser enables you to view the contents of the Oracle BPM MDS repository and perform related tasks. You can perform the following tasks using this browser:

- Publish projects and project templates.
- Create and configure Oracle BPM MDS connections.
- Check out and lock projects and project templates

Publishing a BPM Project in BPM Studio to MDS

Getting ready

Publishing a project to the Oracle BPM MDS repository enables you to share projects and project templates with other Process Analysts and Process Developers. Once a project or project template is published to the repository, it can be accessed by other Process Analysts and developers using either Oracle BPM Studio or Business Process Composer.

How to do it...

Follow the steps of this section to publish a BPM project in BPM studio to MDS:

1. Go to BPM Project navigator, right-click on the BPM project that you want to publish, and select the **Publish to BPM MDS** menu item.

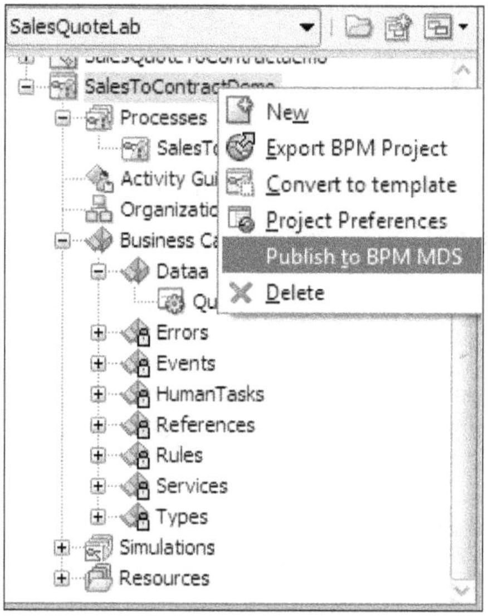

2. The **Publish to BPM MDS** dialog pops up. Keep the default name of QuoteProcessLab, Check the **Override** box, and click **OK**.

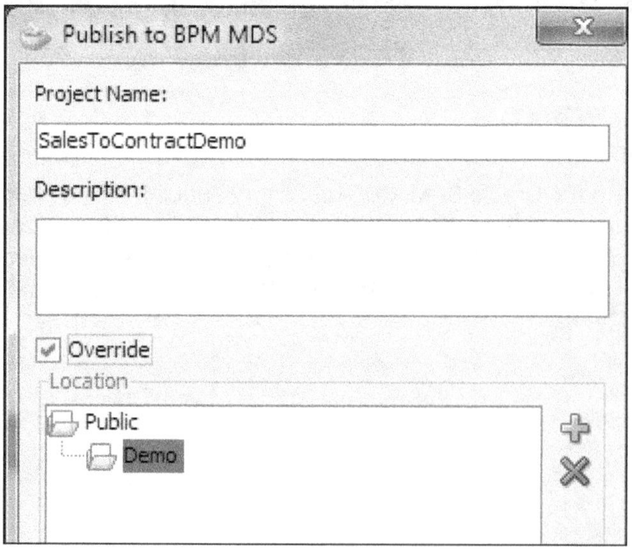

3. To see the project just published, go to the BPM MDS navigator and expand the **Public** folder; the project should be listed in the correct location folder.

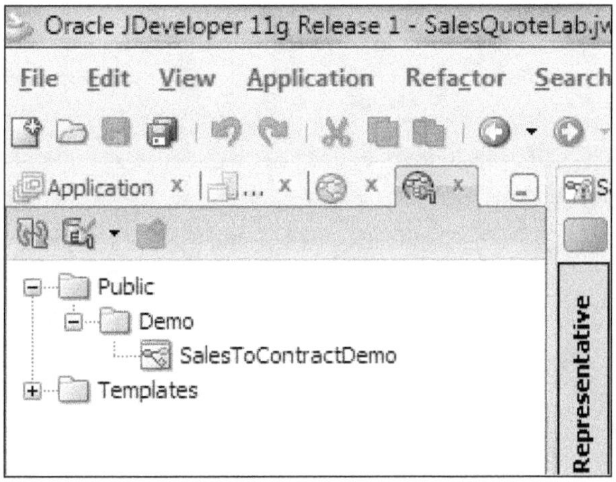

4. If you published a BPM Template Project, then you would find it in the **Templates** root folder.
5. When you have finished the preceding steps, click **Save**.

How it works...

After publishing projects to the Oracle BPM MDS repository, business users can use them to create new deployable BPM projects. You can use them in BPM Composer too.

2
Process Implementation

In this chapter, we will look at how developers implement the process. This chapter answers the question "How do you move from a model to a running process?", which automatically routes tasks, brings the right forms, applies rules, stores data, and so on.

The main tool to be used is BPM Studio, which you have used in *Chapter 1, Process Modeling*, while developing the model as a Process Analyst. You will focus on implementing the model. However, the same model that was developed as a Process Analyst will be used. You can switch gears as you are now a Process Developer and are going to implement a running process.

This chapter will focus on the implementation tasks and cover the following topics:

- Defining an Interactive task
- Generating a Task Form for an Interactive task
- Defining an Interactive task for the Finalize activity
- Creating a common Interactive task
- Generating a common Task Form
- Assigning the same Human Task to different Interactive tasks
- Creating Data associations
- Implementing service tasks
- Assigning the outcome of Interactive tasks to Data objects
- Configuring Data association for conditional flows

Introduction

BPM is a strategy for managing and improving the performance of a business through continuous optimization of the business processes in a closed loop cycle of modeling, implementation, simulation, execution, and measurement. The typical life cycle for BPM is shown as follows:

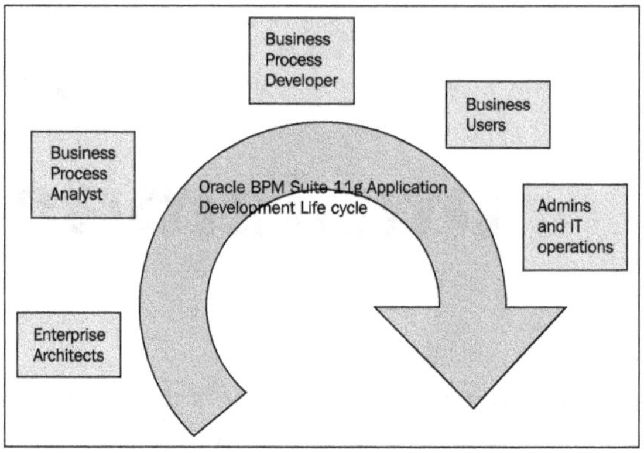

The process model created in *Chapter 1, Process Modeling*, has to be implemented before it can be executed on the BPM runtime engine. The Process Developer/IT Developer role is responsible for the implementation. Implementation of the process model involves the creation of implementation artifacts, creation of data types and data mapping, handling of exception conditions, transactional conditions, and compensation logic.

For human interactions managed by the BPM engine, the Human Task implementation artifacts and their associated user interfaces have to be implemented. In addition, the roles have to be mapped to an LDAP user or group before deployment. Similarly, the business rules also have to be implemented. Furthermore, these business rules can be dynamically changed by the business user at runtime to meet the changing needs of the business. Finally, implementation of the process model involves creation of complex data types, variables, and transformation logic to convert data from one format to another.

After the Process Analyst models the process, developers need to implement the process. In this step, developers perform the following actions:

- Refine the model
- Bring technical configuration into the model
- Assign values to measurements and KPIs
- Make a deployable application.

For example, developers define technical components such as sending notifications to perform tasks, forms for participation, and integration of processes with backend systems and other systems.

We will go from a process model to a running process, which automatically routes tasks to assigned participants, brings the right forms, applies business rules that a developer defines, calls the services, stores data, and so on.

BPMN elements include activities (Task and subprocesses), events, and Gateways. BPMN has many types of tasks such as the following:

- User tasks: These are for human steps managed by the workflow component of BPMN runtime engine.
- Manual tasks: These are for human steps not managed by the workflow component of the BPMN runtime engine.
- Service tasks: These are for synchronous system interaction.
- Send and Receive tasks: These are for asynchronous interaction.
- Script tasks: These are for scripting needs
- Call tasks: These are for calling other BPMN processes.

Developers perform implementation tasks for each activity such as defining tasks, rules or services, binding components to their activities, or mapping data (input and output). For each Gateway, they include conditional transitions, define expressions that determine branching, and finally deploy and test.

Defining an Interactive task

An **Interactive task** adds human interaction in the BPMN process. This recipe will delve into defining an Interactive task.

Getting ready

User tasks are tasks that need user interactions. Check the model that you have created. Rectangle green boxes represent the User tasks. They are also called Interactive tasks.

How to do it...

To implement a User task, you need to define a service component called Human Task, associate it with the activity, and then map data into and out of the activity. As we mentioned earlier, you must have already defined the Business and Data objects. As a developer, you will perform the following activities for implementing a User/Interactive task:

- Defining a Human Task
- Binding it to an activity
- Mapping data input and output to the activity

There are two approaches to working with Human Tasks in Oracle BPM:

- Creating the Human Task using the SOA Human Task editor
- Creating the Human Task using the simplified interface that Oracle BPM provides

You will be using the second option of creating a Human Task using the simplified interface that Oracle BPM provides. BPM Studio offers a number of Human Task patterns such as simple patterns for individual users/groups and initiator patterns for those who initiate the process (in this case, it's the sales representative). Swimlane roles are used to determine assignments.

In *Chapter 1, Process Modeling*, you defined the outline of the process and specified only the name and description for the activities. Now, in order to execute the process, you need to implement the process activities. Every Interactive task has to be bound to a **Task Service**. You can either browse for existing Task Services or create one on the fly. Multiple Interactive tasks can share the same Task Service.

Let's create a new Task Service for the `Enter Quote` activity.

1. Launch BPM Studio.
2. Select **Default Roles** when asked for the developer type.

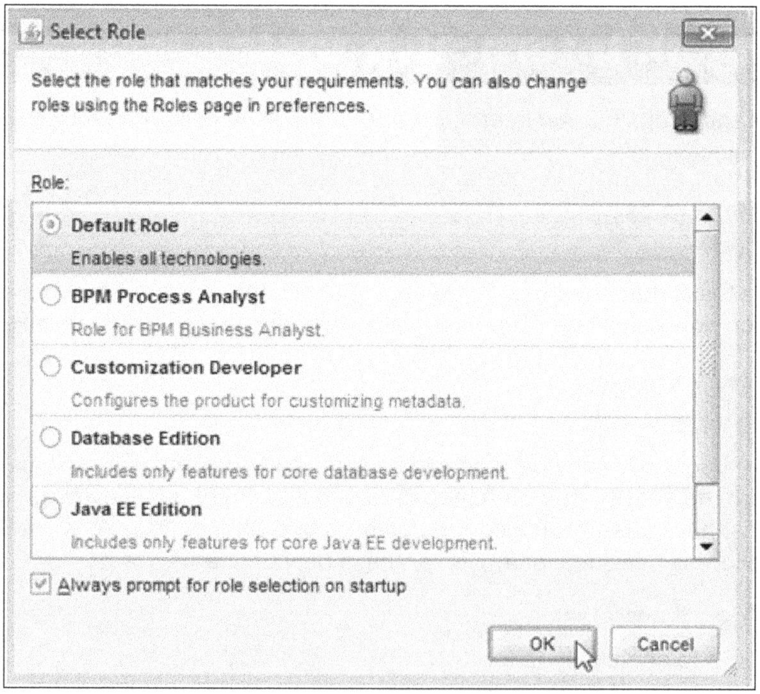

3. Click on the Project name in the project navigator, as shown in the following screenshot. This will open the modeled project in the designer.

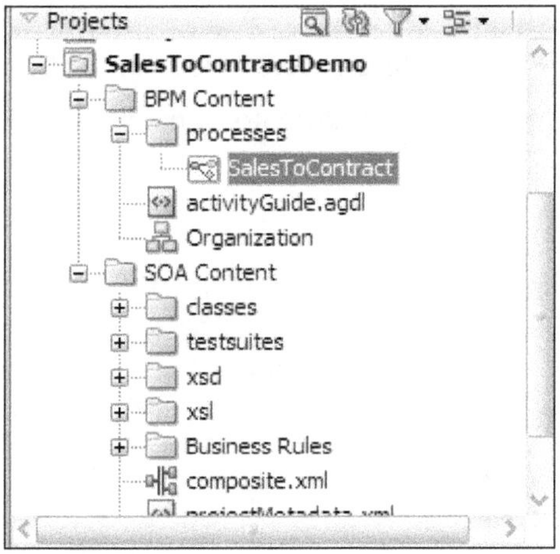

4. Right-click on the **Enter Quote Details** User activity and select **Properties**.

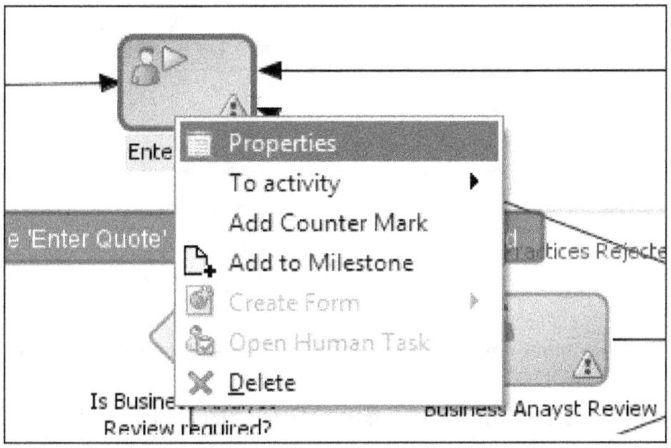

5. In the **Properties** dialog, click the **Implementation** tab.
6. Click the **+** sign next to **Human Task** to add a Human Task.

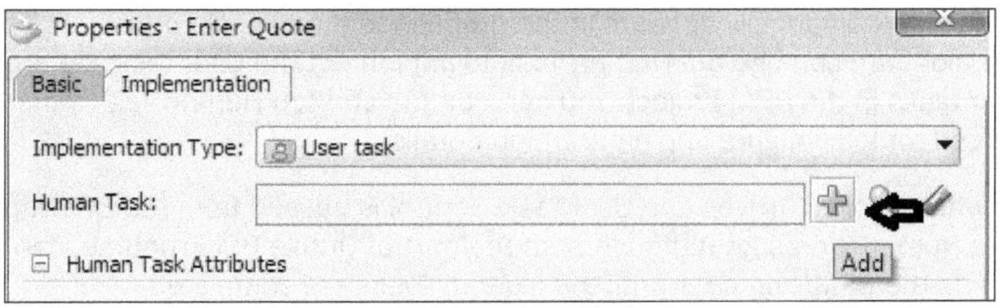

7. In the **Create Human Task** dialog, enter the name `EnterQuoteDetails`.
8. Select **Initiator** as **Pattern**. This will automatically set the outcome to **SUBMIT**.
9. Type in `Enter Quote` as the title.
10. Click on the green **+** next to **Parameters** to launch the Data object dialog.
11. Drag **quote** from the Data object navigator window to the **Parameters** section.
12. Set the **Parameter** to **Editable**.
13. Click **OK** twice.

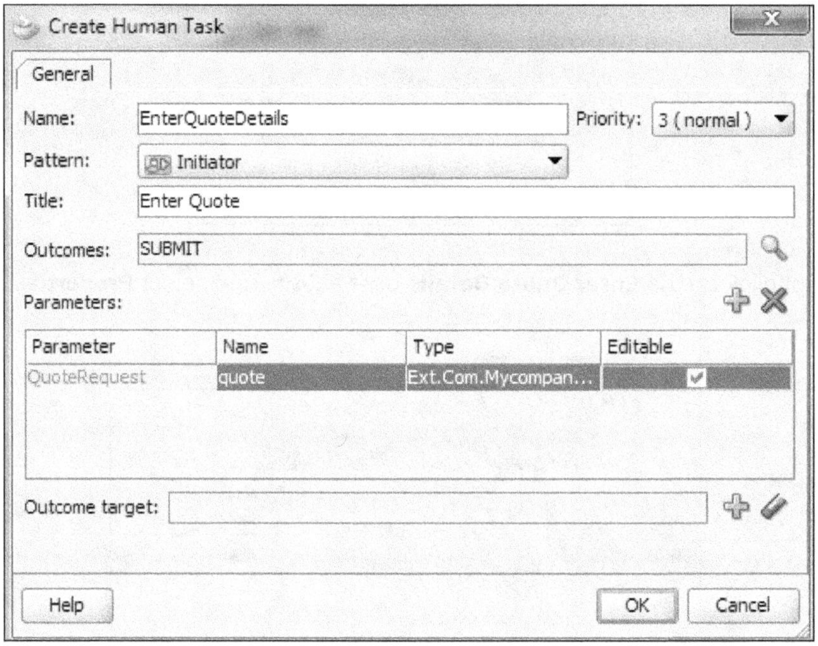

14. You have just finished creating the **EnterQuoteDetails** Task Service.
15. When you have finished following the preceding steps, click **Save**.

How it works...

The Human Task automatically appears in the predefined module, *Human Tasks*, in the business catalog. You can use the Human Task to implement the User task you are editing or other user tasks in the BPM project. You can edit the created Human Task using the SOA Human Task editor to configure implementation details.

At runtime, when a token arrives at a User task, control is passed from the BPMN process to the Oracle Human Workflow. Although both are part of Oracle BPM runtime, control is not passed back to the BPMN process until the Human Tasks are completed.

After the workflow is complete, control is passed back to the BPMN process. Any required Data objects are passed back to the user task, and the token moves to the next sequence flow of the process.

However, Human Tasks are independent from BPMN processes. If you terminate a BPMN process while it runs a User task, the associated Human Task keeps running independently. When you define a Human Task in BPM, the callback is implicitly defined.

Generating a Task Form for an Interactive task

Now we have a Human Task created for the User task and they are connected as well. However, when this task is assigned to someone who performs an action on it, he/she must have a user interface to interact with. We will now develop a user interface like an ADF Form for interaction.

How to do it...

In this section, you will learn how to create a Task Form for an Interactive task:

1. Launch BPM Studio.
2. Navigate to BPM Project Navigator.

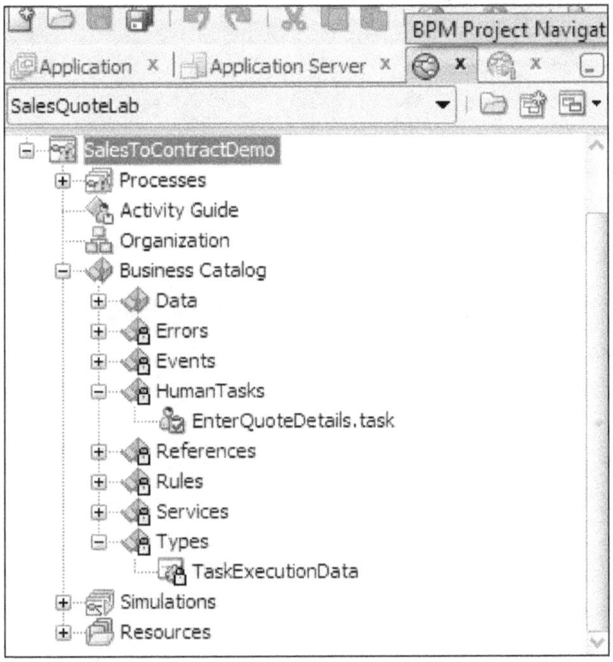

3. Expand the **SalesToContractDemo | Business Catalog | Human Tasks** folder to examine the newly created Task Service. You can click on the **Types** folder to see the associated types.
4. Double-click the **EnterQuoteDetails.task** file to open the Task editor with the Task Service definition.

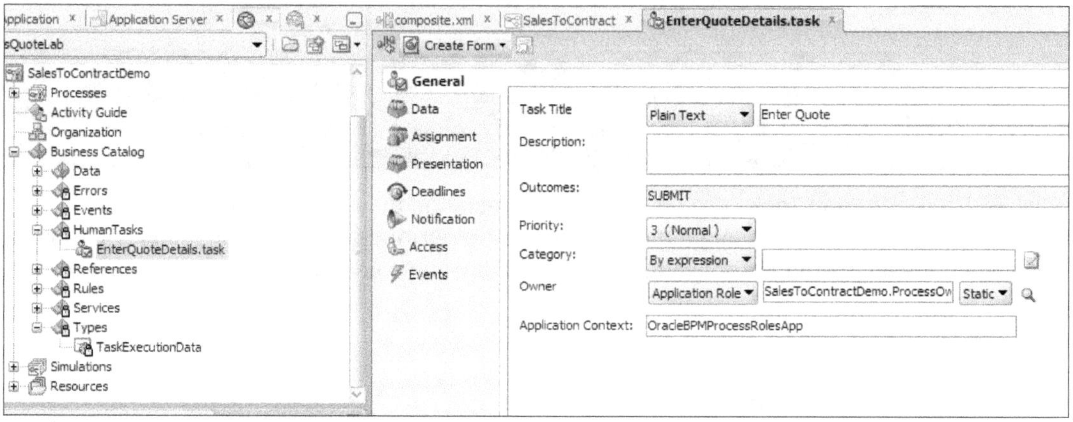

5. Click on **Auto Generate Task Form** from the **Create Form** pop-up, found at the top of the Task Form.

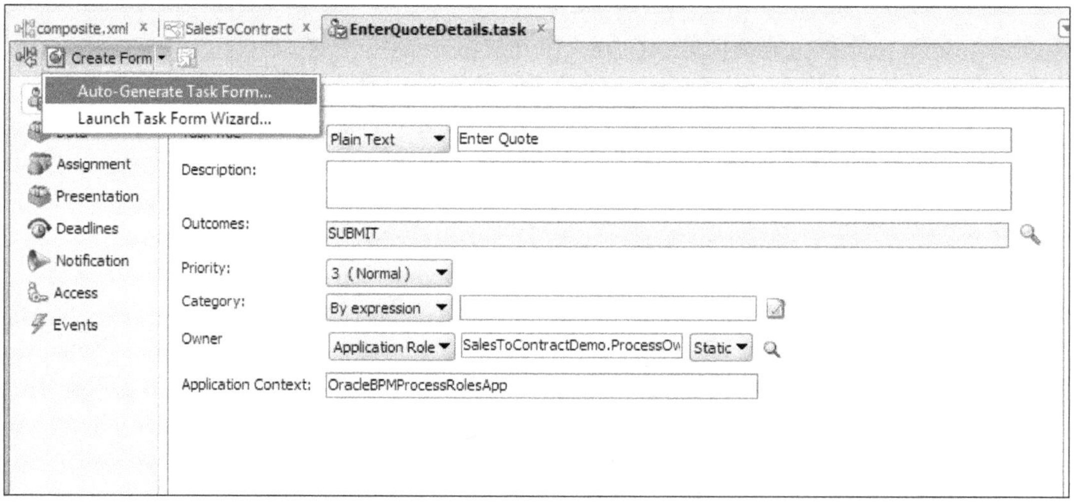

6. Task Forms are kept in a separate project, as they have different dependencies and deployment requirements. Hence it will open a **Create Project** form to create a separate project for the user interface. You need to provide a name for the project, say `EnterQuoteUI`.

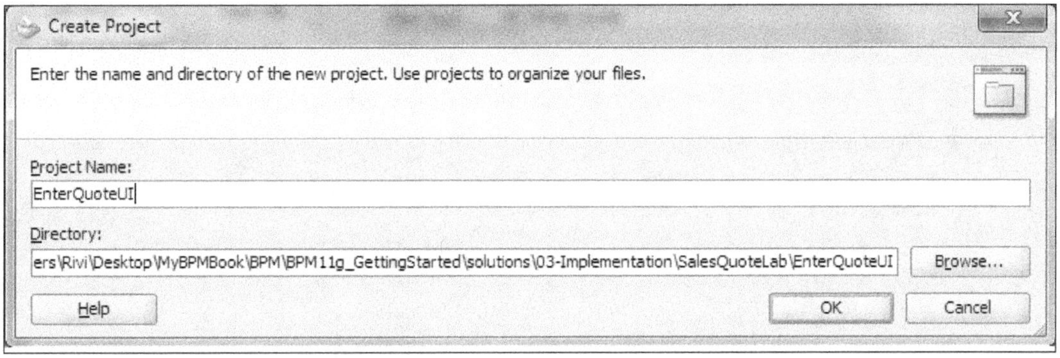

7. Click **OK**.

   When you click **OK**, several actions will take place such as creating a new project, creating necessary files, and so on. This will take few minutes and you need to wait until it's done. The user interface for the Task Service is generated automatically. Many dialogs will open to give you an opportunity to do some customization. For the time being, you can click **OK** on them too.

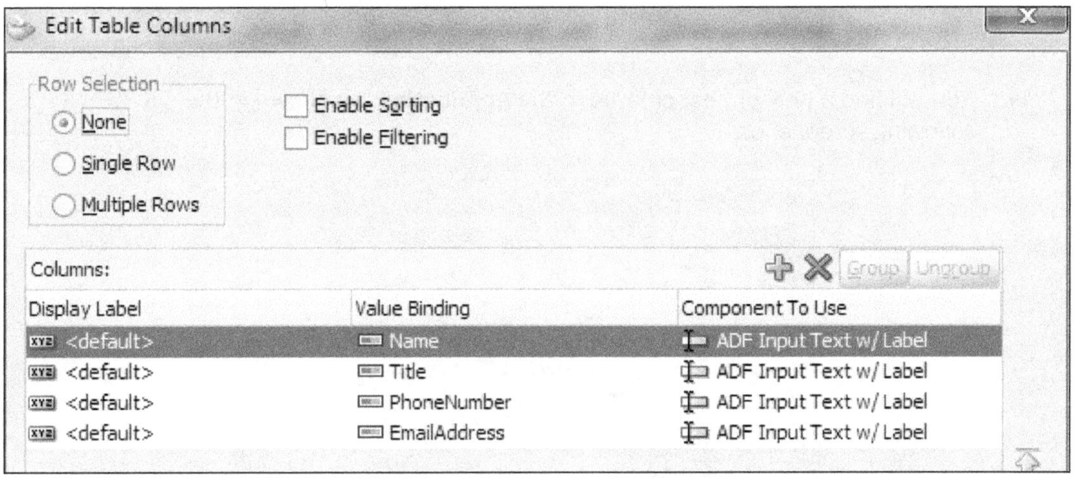

8. The designer will get initiated in the course of action. Hence you are advised to wait for some time.

9. When you have finished following the above steps, click **Save**. You should see a screen as follows:

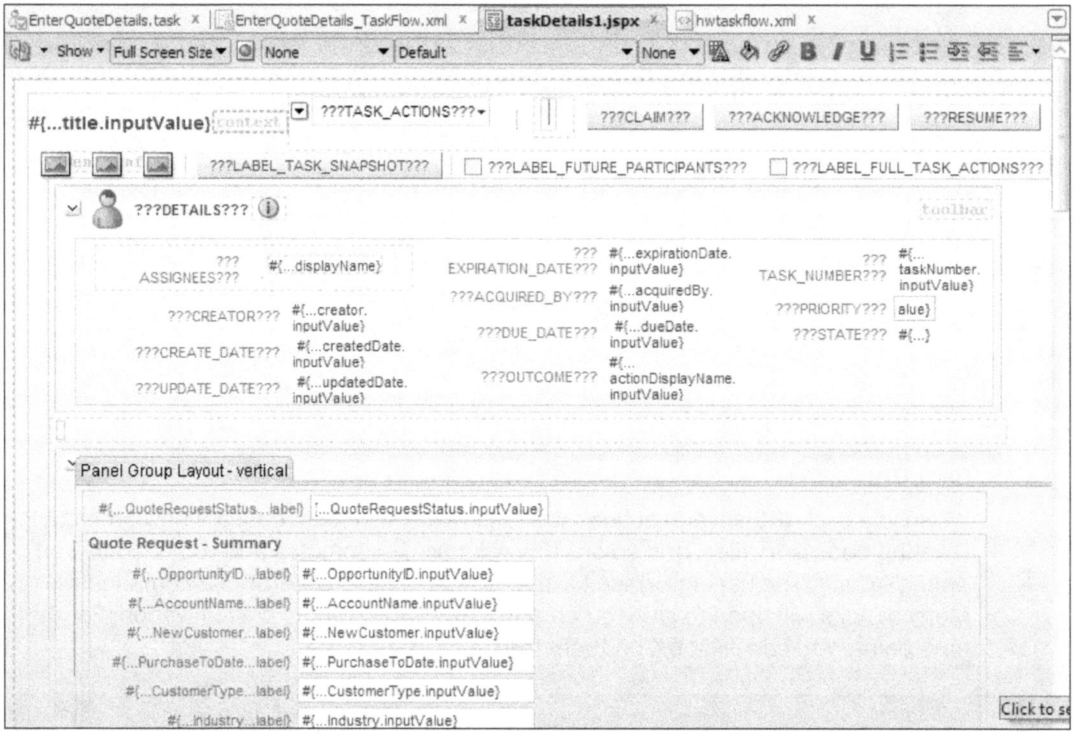

10. You will find a new project created in the **Application**, as shown in the following screenshot:

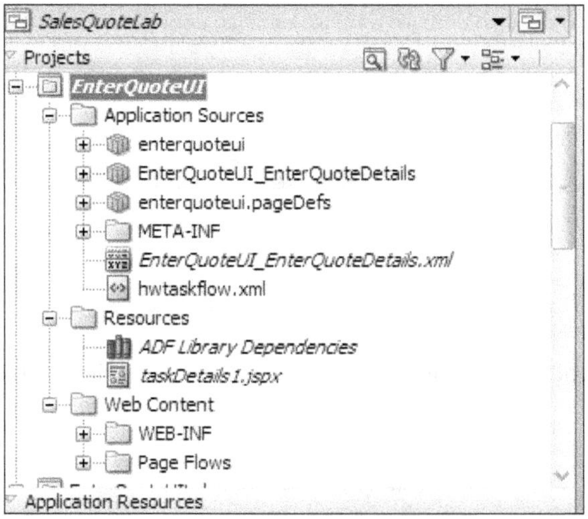

How it works...

As your SOA Composite includes a Human Task, you need a way for users to interact with the task. The integrated development environment of Oracle SOA Suite includes **Oracle Application Development Framework** (**Oracle ADF**) for this purpose. With Oracle ADF, you can design a Task Form that depicts the Human Task in the SOA composite.

If you check in the Project navigator into the newly created project, `EnterQuoteUI`, you will find:

- The Task Form generated is a Java Server Page XML (`.jspx`) file.
- The `hwtaskflow.xml` file is created to capture the details on connecting with the service engine. By default, it uses remote EJB to connect to the workflow server. Oracle SOA server URL and port are automatically determined by using the WebLogic server runtime MBeans. However, you can override these by explicitly specifying the URL and port information here.

There's more...

You can create a Task Form by using either the **Auto-Generate Task Form** option or the **Launch Task Form Wizard**.

Generating a Task Form using Launch Task Form

Here you will learn how to initiate a Task Form generation using wizards, as follows:

1. Expand the **SalesToContractDemo | Business Catalog | Human Tasks** folder to examine the newly created Task Service. You can click on the **Types** folder to see the associated types.
2. Double-click the `.task` file to open the Task Editor with the Task Service definition.
3. Click on **Launch Task Form Wizard** from the pop-up **Create Form**, found at the top of the Task Form.

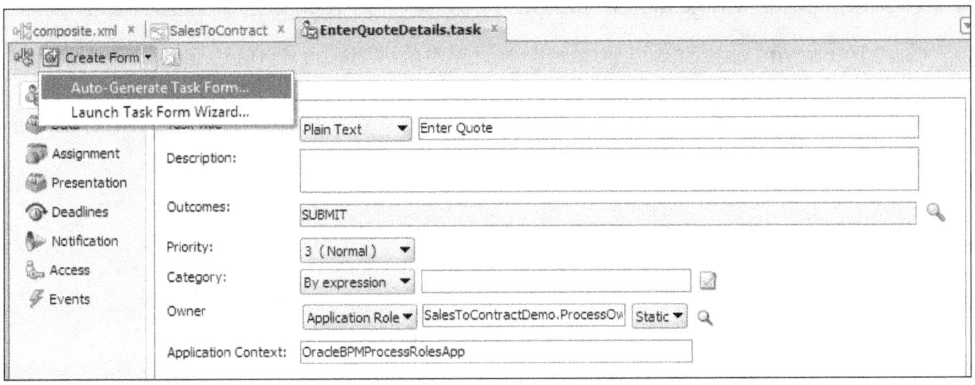

4. Provide a Project name, a directory path, and click **OK**.
5. Once you complete the wizard, a form is generated. (Refer to the section *Generating Task Form using Wizard in Chapter 3, Process Deployment and Testing*).
6. When you have finished following the preceding steps, click **Save**.
7. Defining an Interactive task for the Finalize Activity

The last User task in the process is to finalize the contract with the Contracts role. Input and Output Business Data is saved in "Quote" (`Quote.xsd`), and finally the quote is saved in the Enterprise database by an external service call.

How to do it...

In this section, you will create an Interactive task:

1. Right-click the **Finalize Contract** User task in the designer.

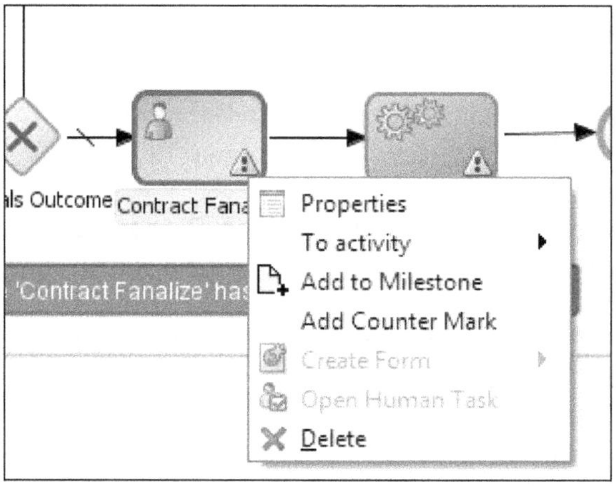

2. Go to the **Properties** and **Implementation** tab.
3. Click the green **+** plus sign to create a new Human Task.
4. Give the **Name** as `FinalizeContracts` and **Title** as `Finalize Contracts`.

5. Click on the browsing icon to the right of **Outcomes** to change the outcome from **APPROVE** or **REJECT** to **OK**.

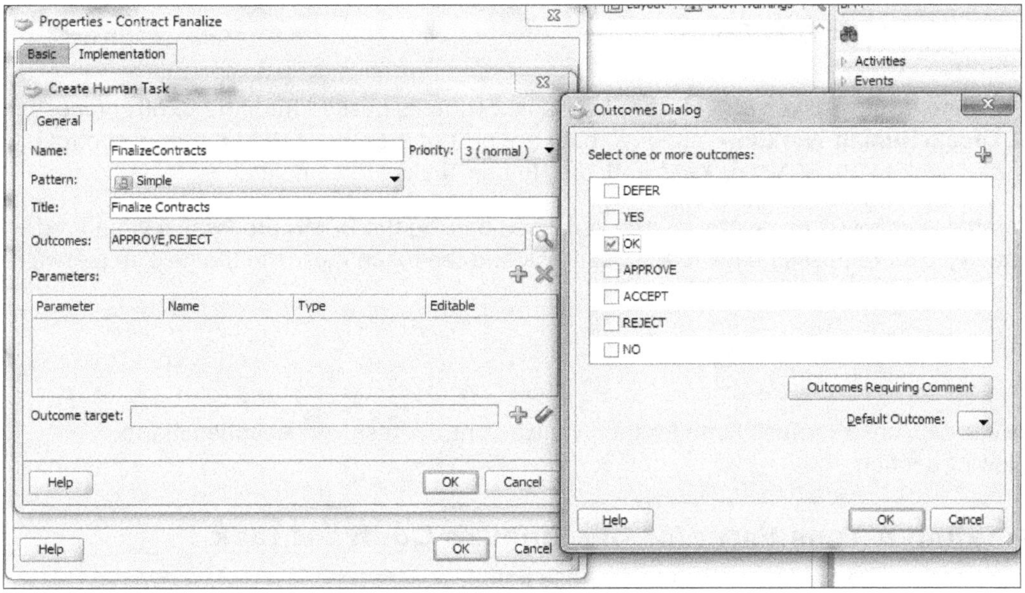

6. In the **Human Task** dialog, click the green plus(**+**) icon next to **Parameters**, drag in the `quote` Data object, select **Editable**, and click **OK**.

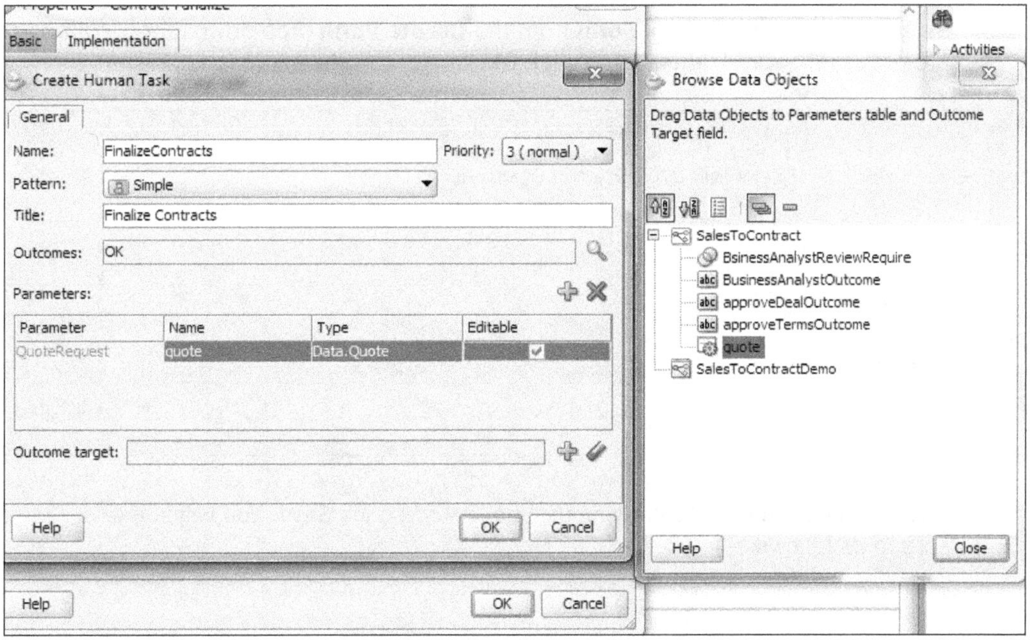

7. Click **OK**.
8. When you have finished following the preceding steps, click **Save**.

How it works...

At runtime, when a token arrives at a User task, control is passed from the BPMN process to the **Oracle Human Workflow**. Although both are part of the Oracle BPM runtime, control is not passed back to the BPMN process until the Human Tasks are completed.

After the workflow is complete, control is passed back to the BPMN process; any required Data objects are passed back to the User task and the token moves to the next sequence flow of the process.

There's more...

We can also create a Task Form for the Finalize Contract task, as described in the following section.

Creating a Task Form for the Finalize Contract task

In this section, you will learn to create a Task Form:

1. Go to **BPM Project navigator**.
2. Double-click the `FinalizeContracts.task` file under **Business Catalog | Human Tasks**.
3. Select **Auto-Generate Task Form** from the **Create Form** drop-down menu. Name the project **FinalizeContractsUI** and click **OK**.

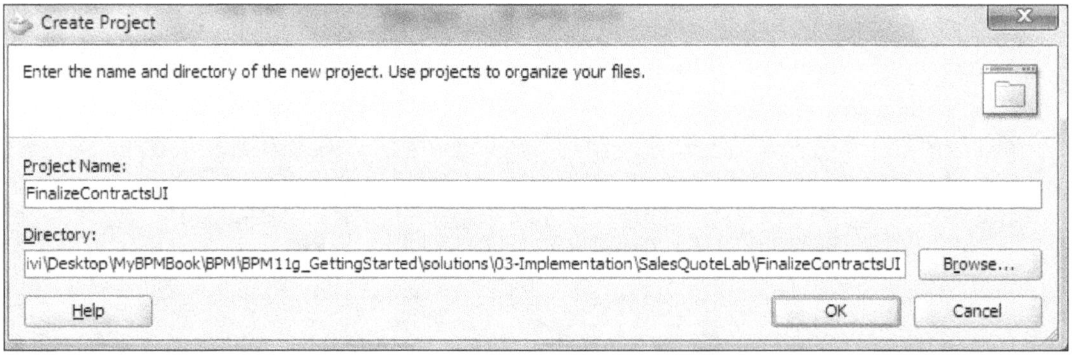

4. When you have finished following the above steps, click **Save**. You will see a screen as follows:

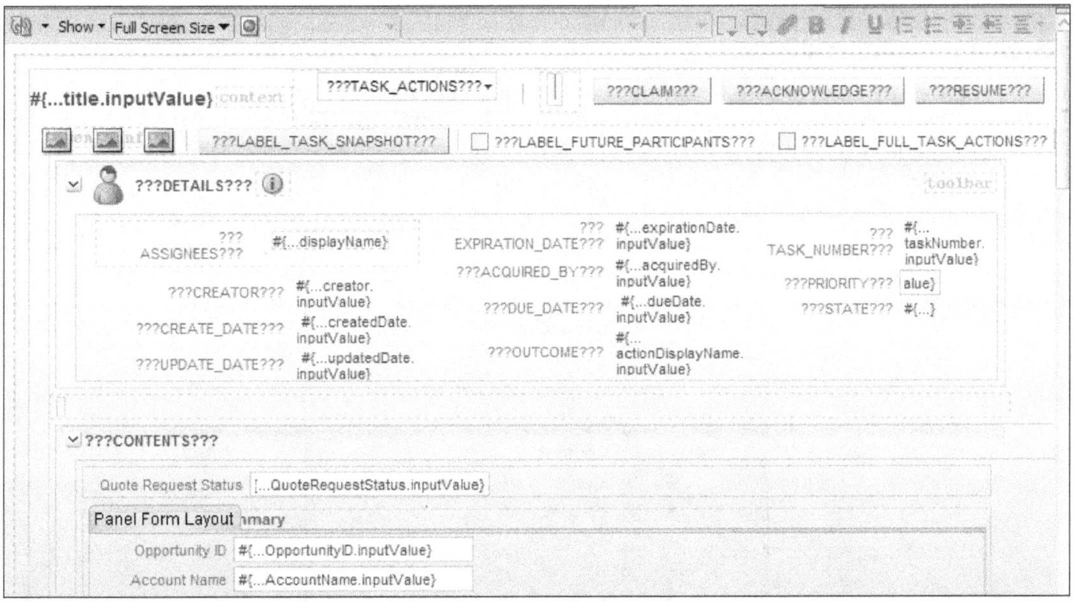

Creating a common Interactive task

The following screenshot shows the final modeling process:

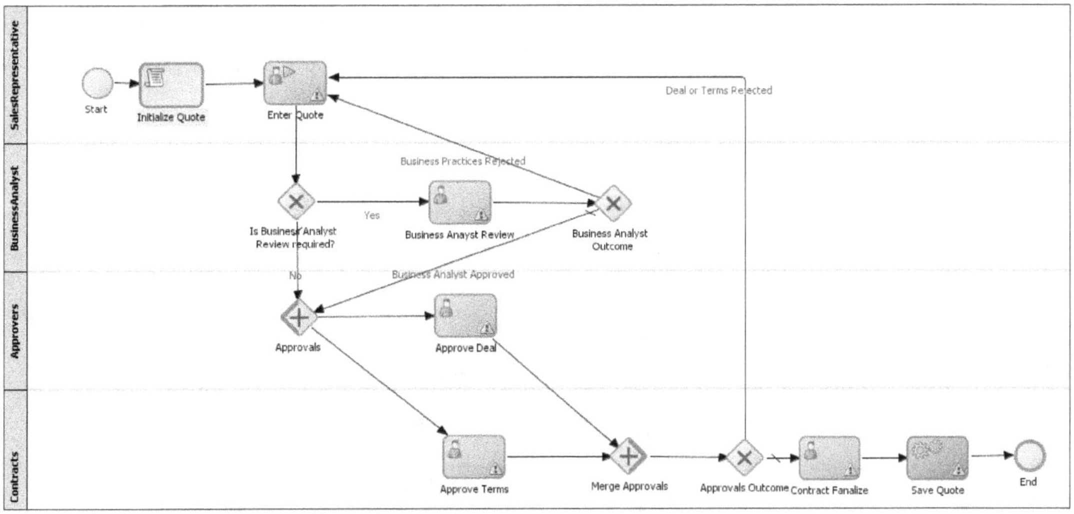

Interactive tasks such as **Business Analyst Review**, **Approve Deal**, and **Approve Terms** share common outcome and payloads. So you can create one Task Form and one Task for them and reuse it.

How to do it...

In this section, you can create a common Interactive task as follows:

1. Click on the project name in the project navigator, as show in the following screenshot. This will open the modeled project in the designer.

2. Right-click the **Business Analyst Review** activity and select the **Properties** window and then the **Implementation** tab:

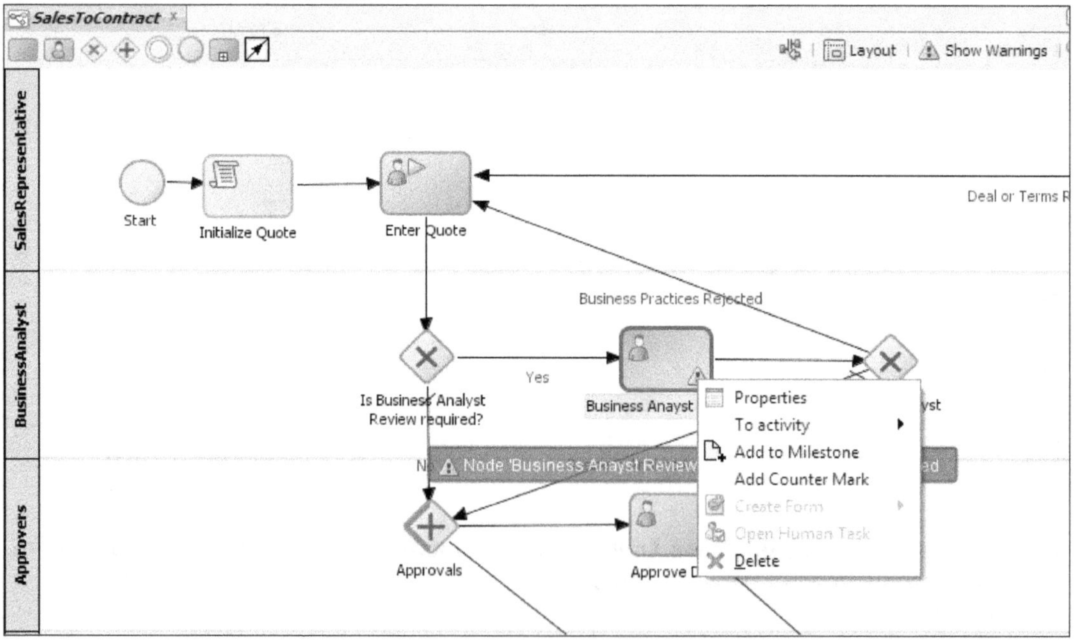

3. Click the **+** symbol to create the Task Service.
4. Enter the name as **ApproveQuote**.
5. Select the **Pattern** as **Simple**.
6. Enter the title as `Approve Quote` and add the parameter **quote** with the **Editable** checkbox checked.
7. Let **Outcomes** be default—**APPROVE, REJECT**.
8. The **Approve Quote** properties dialog looks like the following screenshot:

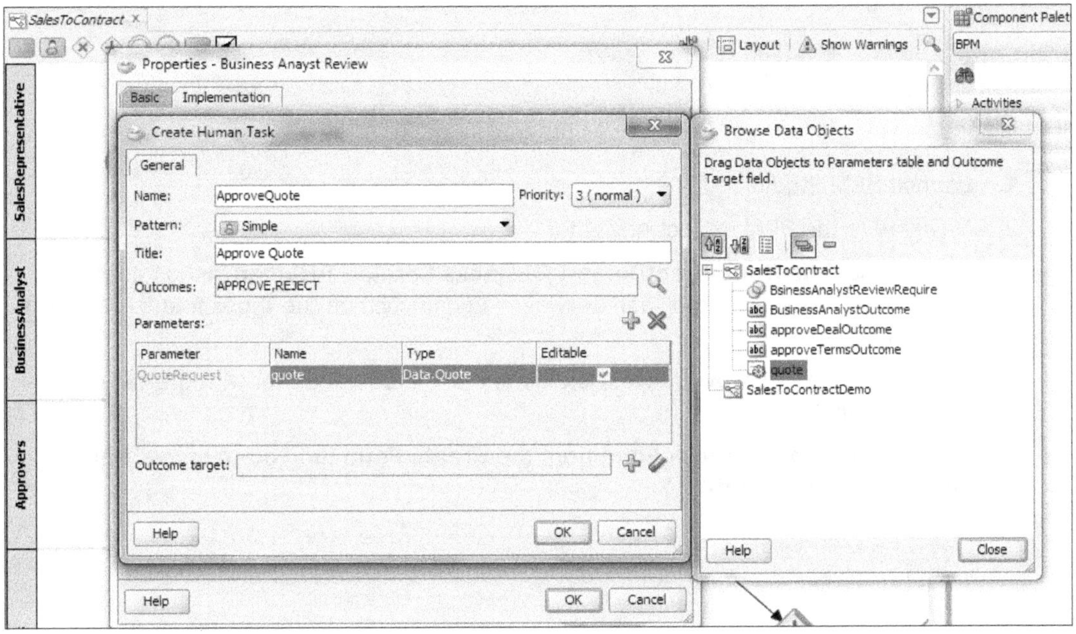

9. Click **OK**.
10. When you have finished these steps, click **Save**.

How it works...

At runtime, when a token arrives at a User task, control is passed from the BPMN process to the Oracle Human Workflow. Although both are part of the Oracle BPM runtime, control is not passed back to the BPMN process until Human Tasks are completed.

After the workflow is complete, control is passed back to the BPMN process. Any required Data objects are passed back to the User task and the token moves to the next sequence flow of the process.

However, Human Tasks are independent from BPMN processes. If you terminate a BPMN process while it runs a User task, the associated Human Tasks keep running independently.

Generating a common Task Form

Now, we have a Human Task created for the User task, and they are connected as well. However, when this task is assigned to someone who performs an action on it, he/she must have a User Interface to interact with. You will develop a User Interface like an ADF Form for interaction. The three tasks will use the same Task Form for interaction.

How to do it...

In this section, you will learn to generate a common Task Form:

1. Launch BPM Studio.
2. Navigate to the BPM Project navigator.
3. Expand the **SalesToContractDemo | Business Catalog | HumanTasks** folder to examine the newly created Task Service. You can click on the **Types** folder to see the associated types.
4. Double-click the **ApproveQuote.task** file to open the Task Editor with the Task Service definition.
5. Select **Auto-Generate Task Form** from the **Create Form** drop-down menu. Name the project **ApproveQuoteUI**.

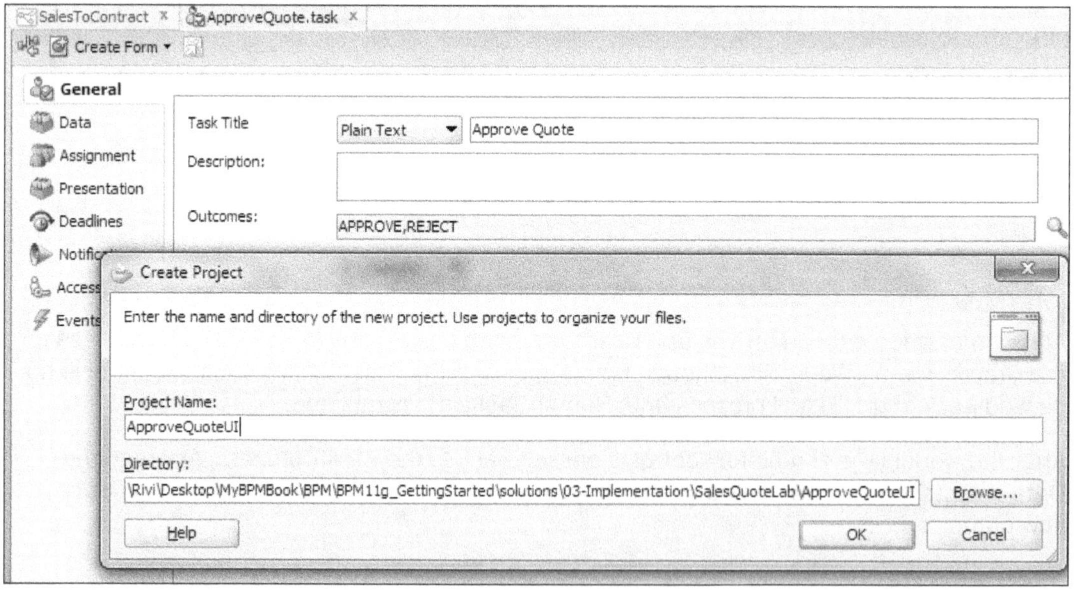

6. Click **OK**. When you click **OK**, several actions will take place such as creating a new project, creating the necessary files, and so on. This will take a few minutes and you need to wait until it's done. The user interface for the Task Service is generated automatically. Many dialogs will open to give you an opportunity to perform some customization. For the time being, you can click **OK** on them too.
7. When you have finished following the preceding steps, click **Save**. You will find a screen for `taskdetails1.jspx`.

How it works...

You can find a project, `ApproveQuoteUI`, created in the Project navigator. If will contain a Task Form.

(Java Server Page XML `(.jspx)`) and an `hwtaskflow.xml` file is also created to capture the details on connecting with the service engine. By default, it uses remote EJB to connect to the workflow server. The Oracle SOA server URL and port are automatically determined by using the WebLogic server runtime MBeans. However, you can override these by explicitly specifying the URL and port information here.

Assigning the same Human Task to different Interactive tasks

Interactive tasks, including `Business Analyst Review`, `Approve Deal`, and `Approve Terms`, share common outcomes and payloads. So you will create one Task Form and one task for them and reuse it. You have already created a Human Task, `Approve Quote`. As `Approve Deal` and `Approve Terms` share a common payload, `Business Analyst Review`, you will use the same Human Task as their Interactive task too.

How to do it...

You can assign one task to different Interactive tasks as follows:

1. Click on **Process** in the Project navigator.
2. Right-click on the **Approve Deal** User task and select **Properties**.

3. From the **Implementation** tab, select the magnifying glass icon. Select **Approve Quote** from the list and click **OK** to return to the dialog.

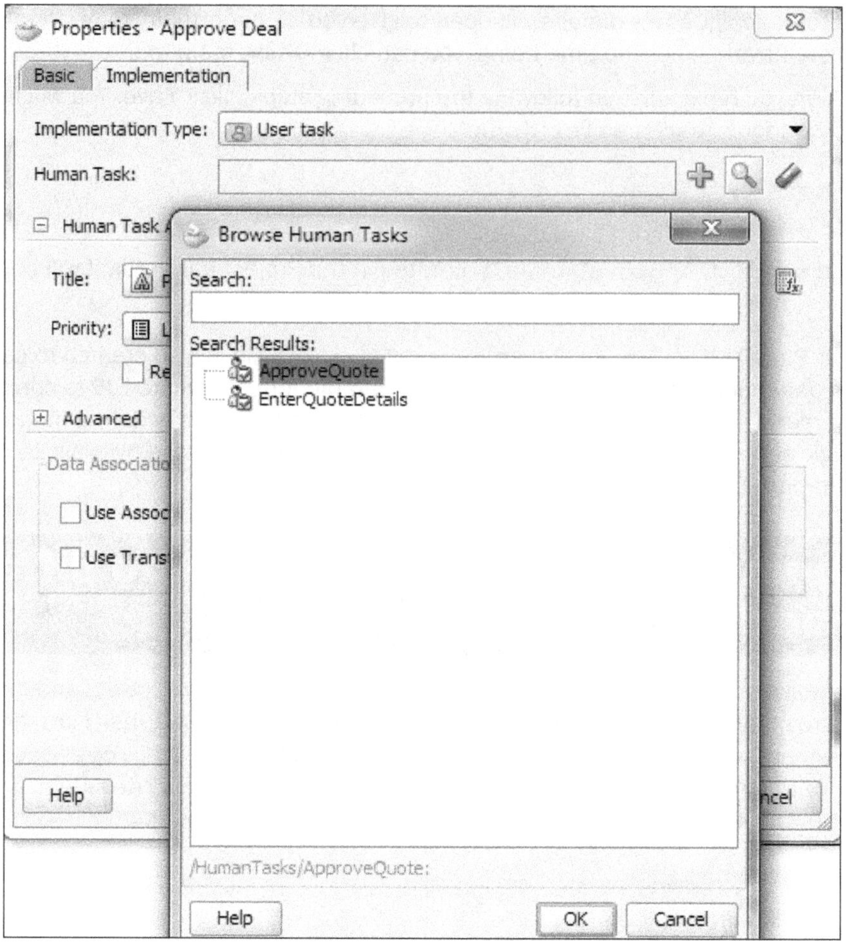

4. Give a new title to the **Human Task**:

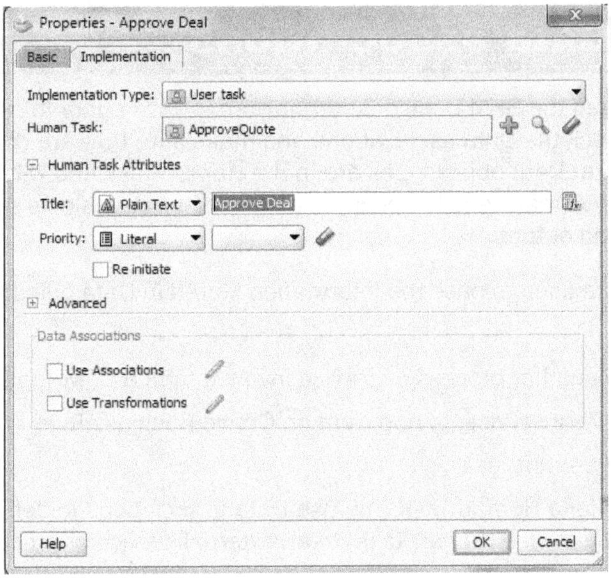

5. Click **OK**.
6. When you have finished following these steps, click **Save.**
7. Repeat the preceding steps for the **Approve Terms** Interactive task. Back in the **Approve Terms** dialog, we'll override the **Title** to be `Approve Terms`. Click **OK**.

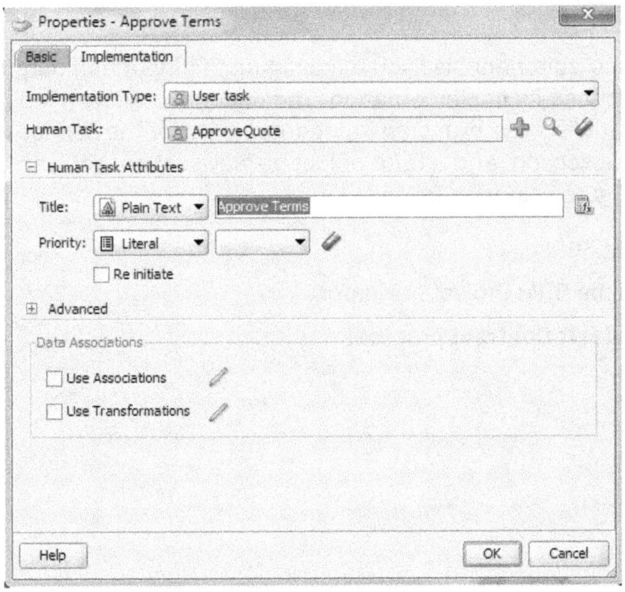

8. When you have finished following the preceding steps, click **Save**.

Creating Data associations

Whether you have used the BPM Design Editor or Human Task editor to define the Human Task, you need to check the Data associations and make sure they are correct. The application knows what Data object types are in the Human Task and will list them for you in the center area, but you may need to specify exactly which Data objects should be mapped to each type as input and output.

Data associations are used to pass the information stored in Data objects in the following contexts:

- To and from another process or service invoked from a BPMN process
- In a Human Task service, to and from an Oracle Business Rule
- To and from a script task

You are doing it here for a Human Task. You use Data associations to define the input and output from a flow object (like Human Task) to an external service or process.

> It is important to note that although the inputs and outputs are defined in the Data associations for a flow object, the defined values are passed to the implemented systems and services.

How to do it...

The Data associations' editor enables you to configure the input and output values passed between a flow object and its implementation. The editor contains an input section, flow object interface (it lists the expected input arguments for the service or process implemented), output section, and a Data object display section. You can create Data associations to configure values as follows:

1. Launch BPM Studio.
2. Navigate to the BPM Project navigator.
3. Click the **SalesToContract** process.

4. Right-click the **Enter Quote** task and click **Properties**.

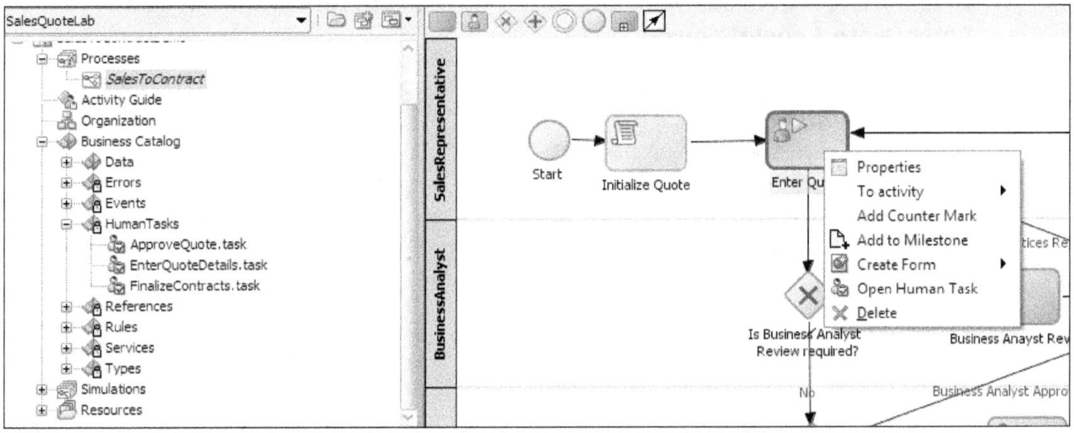

5. Go to the **Implementation** tab and then the **Data Association** section.
6. Check **Use Association** and click on the pencil icon to its right.

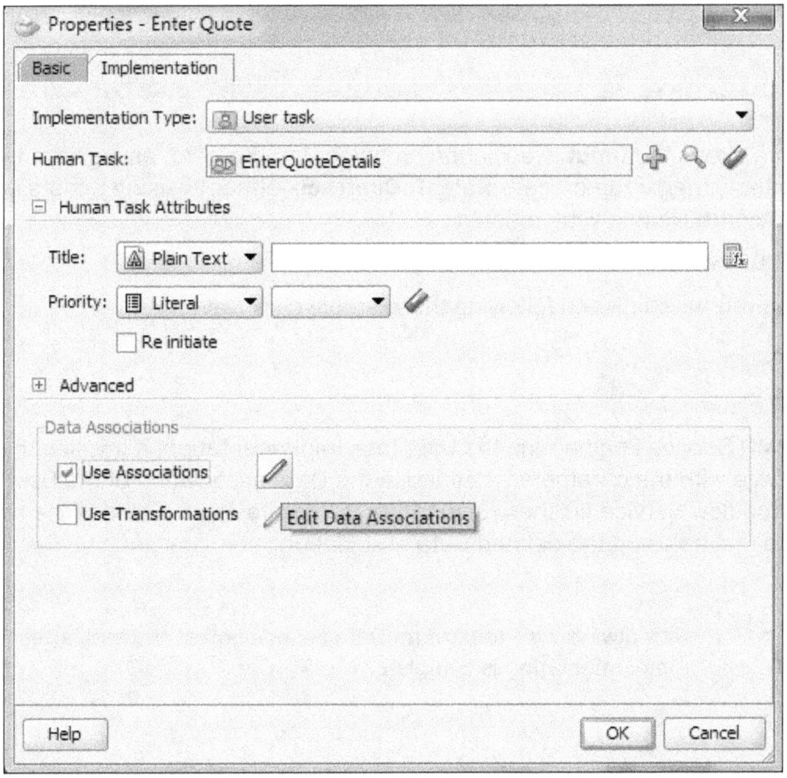

7. You will reach the **Data Associations** editor.
8. Drag the **quote** from the Data objects section to the **Output** box to the right of **Enter Quote | quoteRequest**.

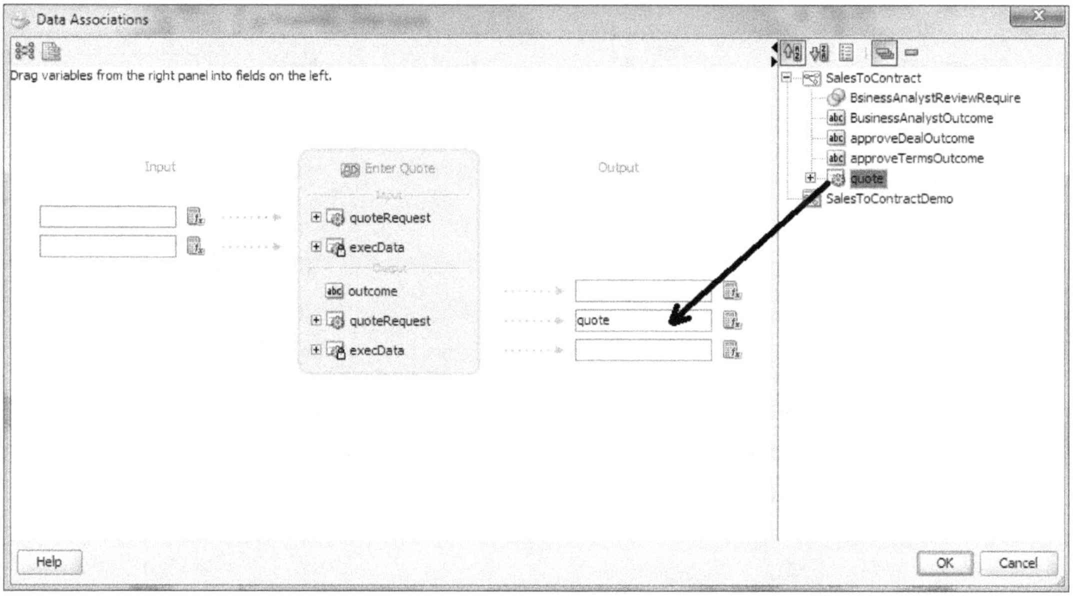

9. You can keep the **Input** association empty for the moment; as we have two options to initiate/trigger the process **SalesToContract**—either by using Scripts or the y Sales Representative role with Initiate task.
10. Click **OK** twice.
11. When you have finished following these steps, click **Save.**

How it works...

When the BPMN Service Engine runs the User task implementation, it invokes the Human Workflow Service with the parameters defined in the Data association of the User task. When the Human Workflow Service finishes running the Human Tasks, it provides the results to the BPMN Service Engine using the defined Data association.

> It's always wise to perform Data association at the end, after implementation is complete.

There's more...

While creating Human Tasks directly from our Interactive tasks, the Data associations are completed automatically for `Business Analyst Review` and `Finalize Contract` tasks. Our other Interactive tasks (`Approve Deal` and `Approve Terms`) were associated with the existing `Approve Quote` task, so we'll have to create the Data associations for these manually.

Checking Existing Data associations

Follow the ensuing steps to check Data associations:

1. Right-click **Business Analyst Review** or **Finalize Contract** task.
2. Choose the **Properties | Implementation** tab.
3. Go to the **Data Association** section.
4. You can find that **Data Association** is already created for both the tasks.
5. Click on the pencil icon used for editing to the right of **Data Association** to check the association for the respective tasks.

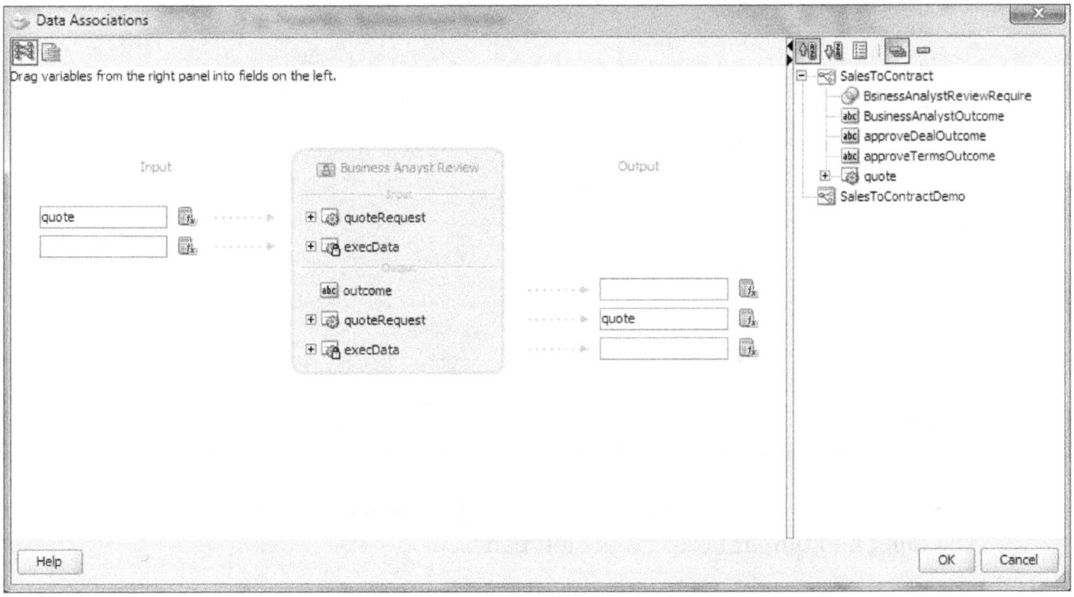

6. When you have finished following the preceding steps, click **Save**.

Creating Data mappings for Approve Deal and Approve Terms activities

The Interactive (**Approve Deal** and **Approve Terms**) activities were associated with the existing **ApproveQuote** task, so we'll have to create the data associations for these manually.

1. Right-click on the **Approve Deal** activity, choose **Properties**, and go to the **Implementation** tab.
2. Check **Use Associations** and click the pencil icon.

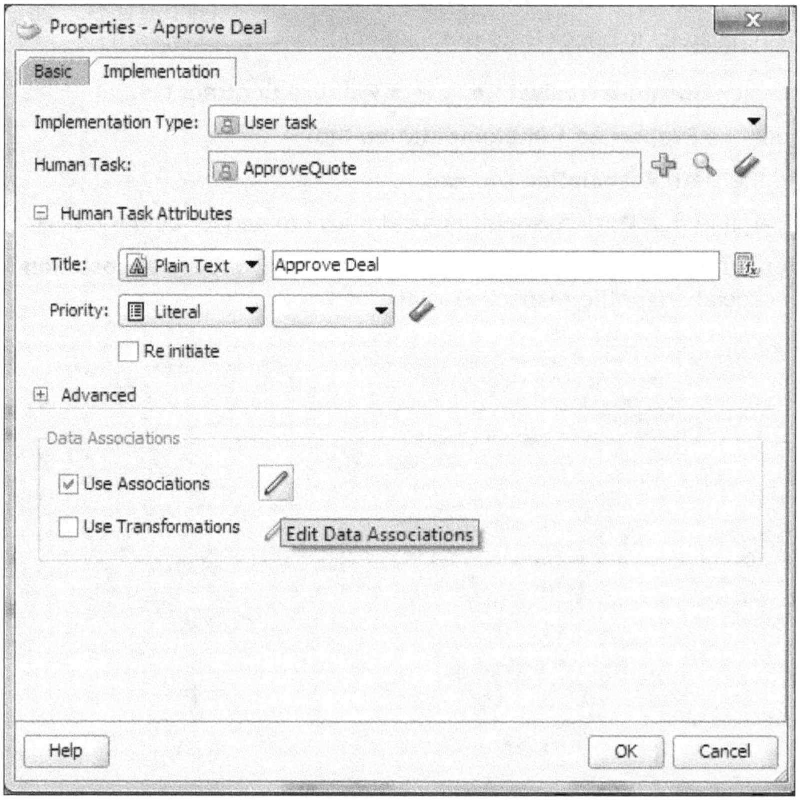

3. Drag the Data object **quote** from the Data object display panel on the right to both the **Input** and **Output** boxes on the left panel.

> Make sure you drag the Data object to the correct boxes, as shown in the following screenshot (`quote` matches to `QuoteRequest` on both Input and Output).

4. Click **OK**.

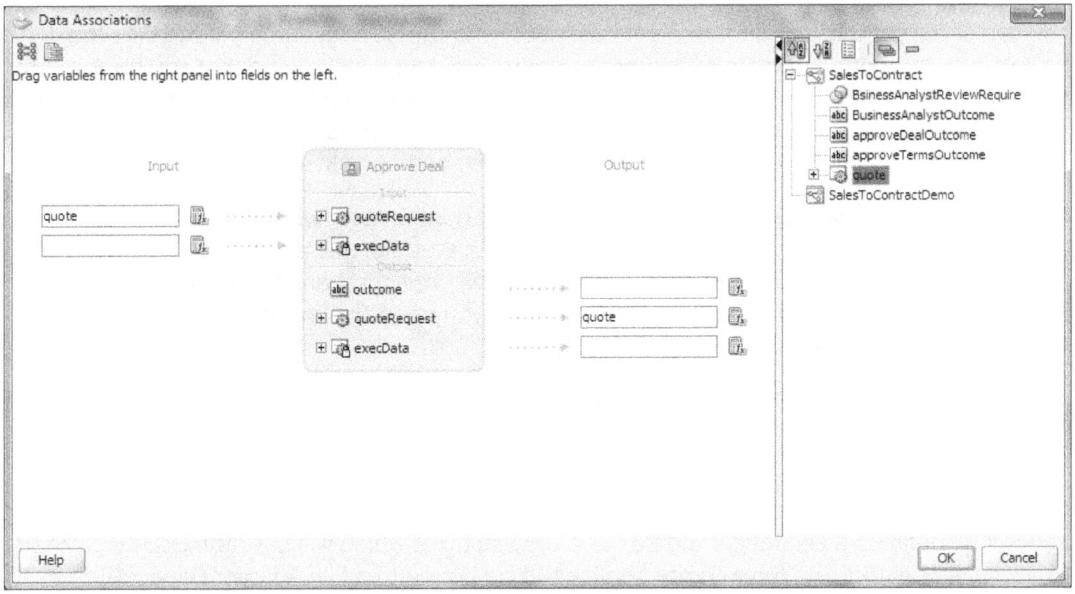

5. Repeat the same steps for **Approve Terms**.
6. When you have finished following the preceding steps, click **Save**.

Implementing service tasks

If you need to communicate to other processes and services, you can use service tasks. You have added a service task (`Save Quote`) while modeling as a Process Analyst, as you were aware at that point of time that your process will need to invoke a service. Now, as a Process Developer, you can implement the necessary services. You can use the service task to invoke other BPMN processes, BPEL processes, SOA service adapters, and Mediators that are exposed as services.

In our example, the `SaveQuote` activity is a service task. It represents an automated (or system) invocation step.

The service task has similar behavior to the Send and Receive task pair and the Message throw and Catch event pair. The primary difference is that the service task is used to invoke processes and services synchronously.

How to do it...

You can use a composite editor to create services, and the SOA resource palette lists the type of service components and adapters you can configure. You will find that you have many options in the component palette. For example, you could define a BPEL Process Service if you want to call a BPEL Process, a Database Adapter service if you want to write to a database, or even a File Adapter service if you want to write to a file on the disk.

You can even find a Web Service Adapter, which is generic—it's for web services that are not already listed. You can use a wizard to configure a Web Service adapter from scratch. You need to define a service and bind it to the activity. Configuration of the service varies according to which kind of service is selected. Then you need to map data input and output. Hence the steps can be summed up as follows:

- Define a service (configure the operation)
- Bind it to the activity
- Map data input and output

You will be defining a service for the `Save Quote` activity, which will save the `quote` payload to a local filesystem. The **Save Quote** service task is bound to a File Adapter Service

1. Go to **Application Navigator | SalesToContract | SOA Content** and click **composite.xml**, as shown in the following screenshot:

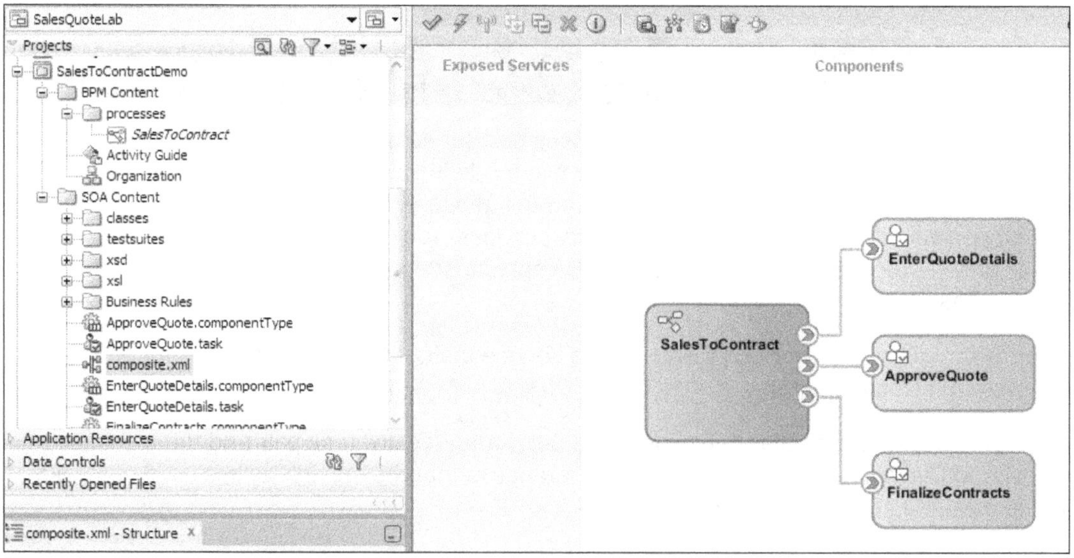

2. Go to the **Component Palette** on right-hand side of the **Composite Editor** and drag-and-drop **File Adapter** from **Component Palette** into the composite editor's **External Reference** panel:

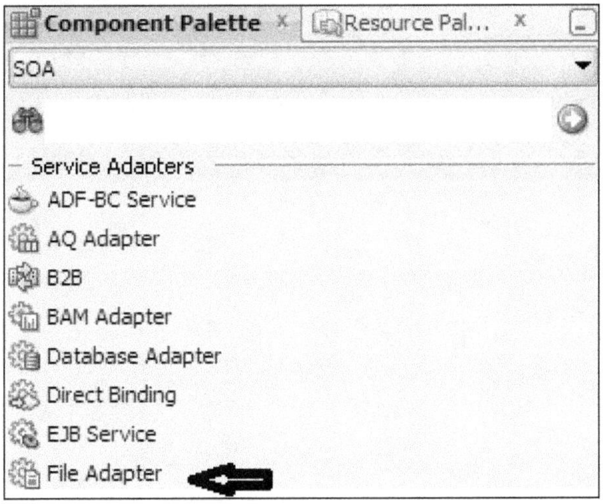

   This will open the **FILE Adapter** Configuration Wizard.

3. Complete the Configuration Wizard to create a **Save Quote** service to write to a file location. Click **Next** on the **Welcome** page of the wizard.
4. Enter Service Name: **SaveQuote**.
5. On the **Define Interface** dialog, click the radio **Define From Operation and schema**.

   WSDL is used to define the adapter interface. This WSDL is generated by the operation and schema, which we will choose later in this wizard. By choosing this option, you are directing WSDL to define an adapter interface that will be generated later.
6. Click **Next**.

7. Chose the **Operation** type—**Write File**, and click **Next**.

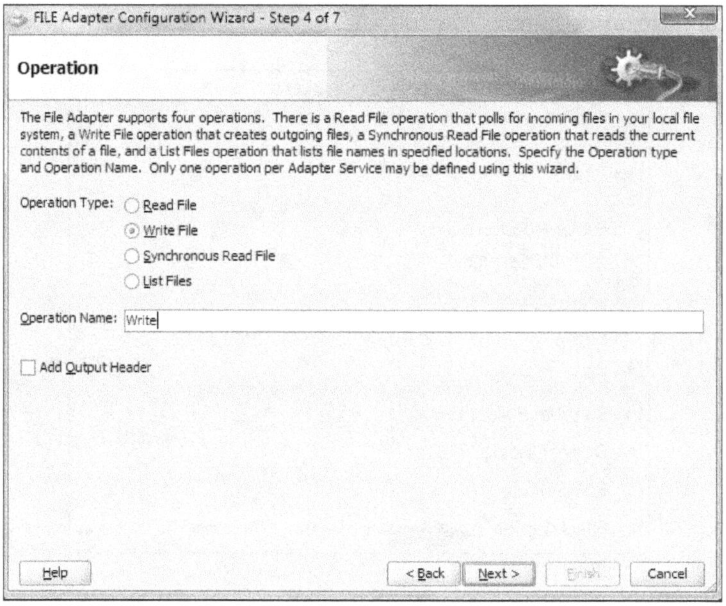

8. While configuring the file, you can choose the logical name of the directory where the file will be kept. Say `QuoteOutputFileLoc` and give a **File Naming Convention:** `Quote_%SEQ%.xml`.

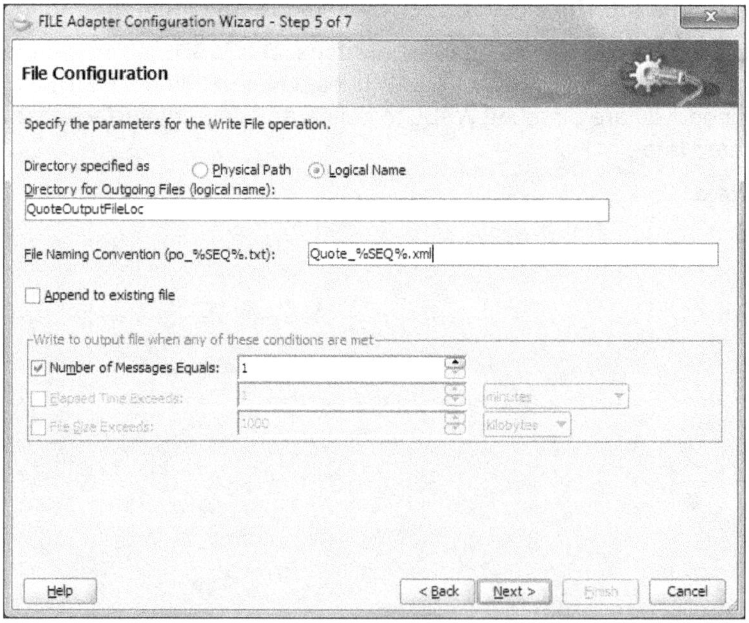

9. While defining the message schema, click on **Browse Schema** in front of the URL in the **Message Schema** section. This will open the **Type Chooser**. Expand **Project Schema Files**.

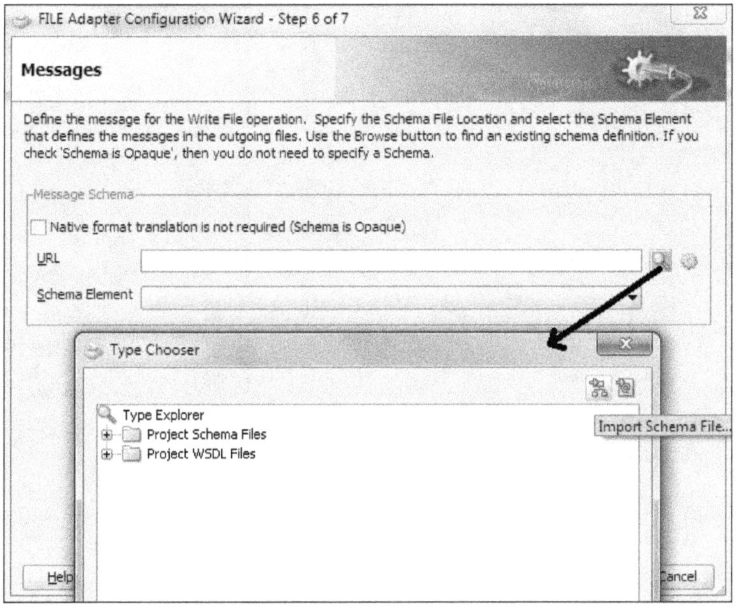

10. Choose **QuoteRequest** in **Quote.xsd** and click **OK**.

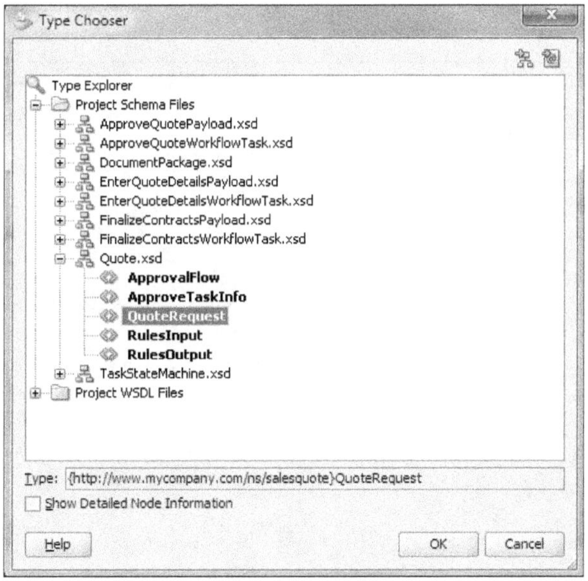

11. Click **Next**, and then **Finish** in the last dialog box of the file configuration wizard.
12. When you have finished following the preceding steps, click **Save**.

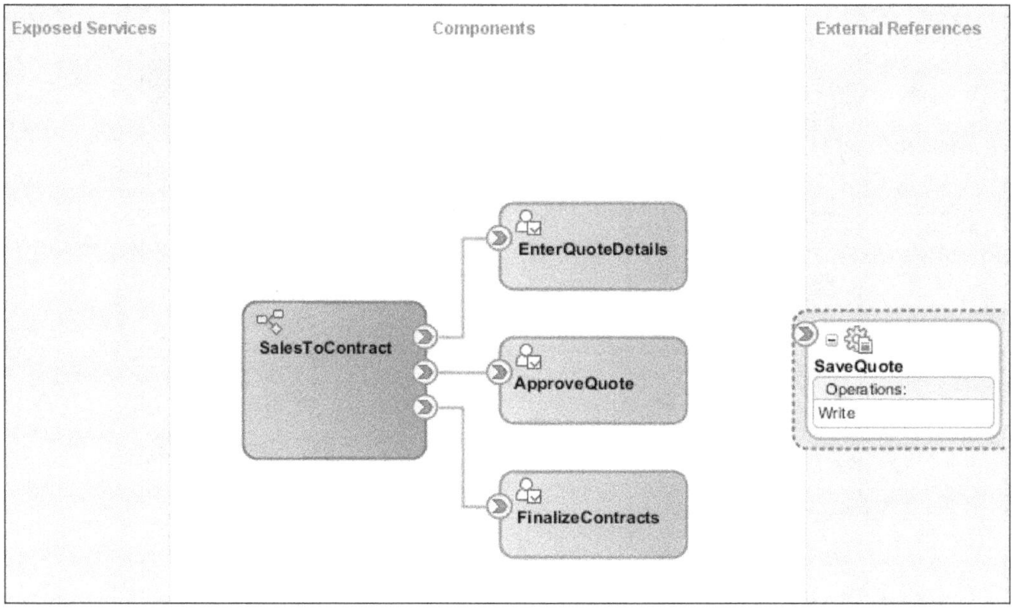

13. Go to **BPM Project Navigator | SalesToContractDemo(Project) | Business Catalog | Services | Externals**.

    You can find the **SaveQuote** External service to verify its creation.

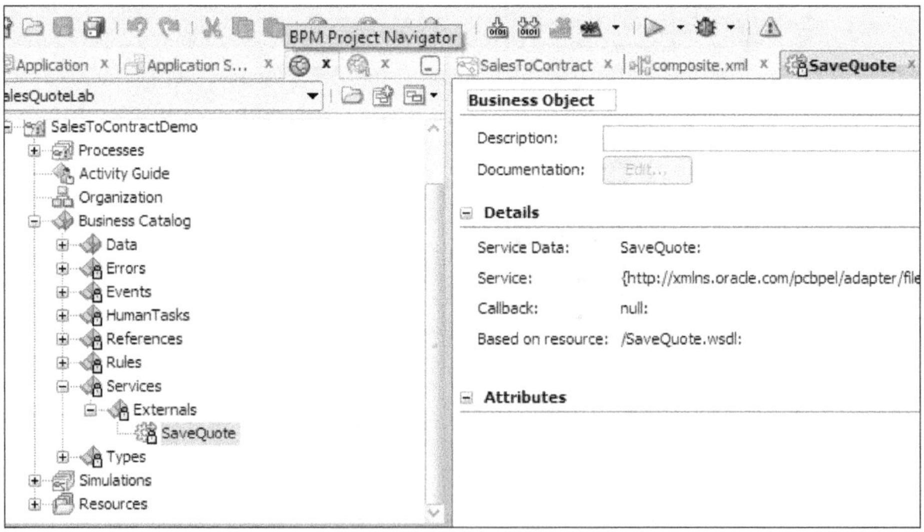

14. In the BPM Project navigator, open the process **SalesToContract**, right-click the **Save Quote** activity, and select **Properties.**
15. Click on the **Implementation** tab in the **Properties** dialog.
16. In the **Service task** section, choose **Service Call** as the **Implementation**.

    Click on the browsing icon to the right to search for the service:

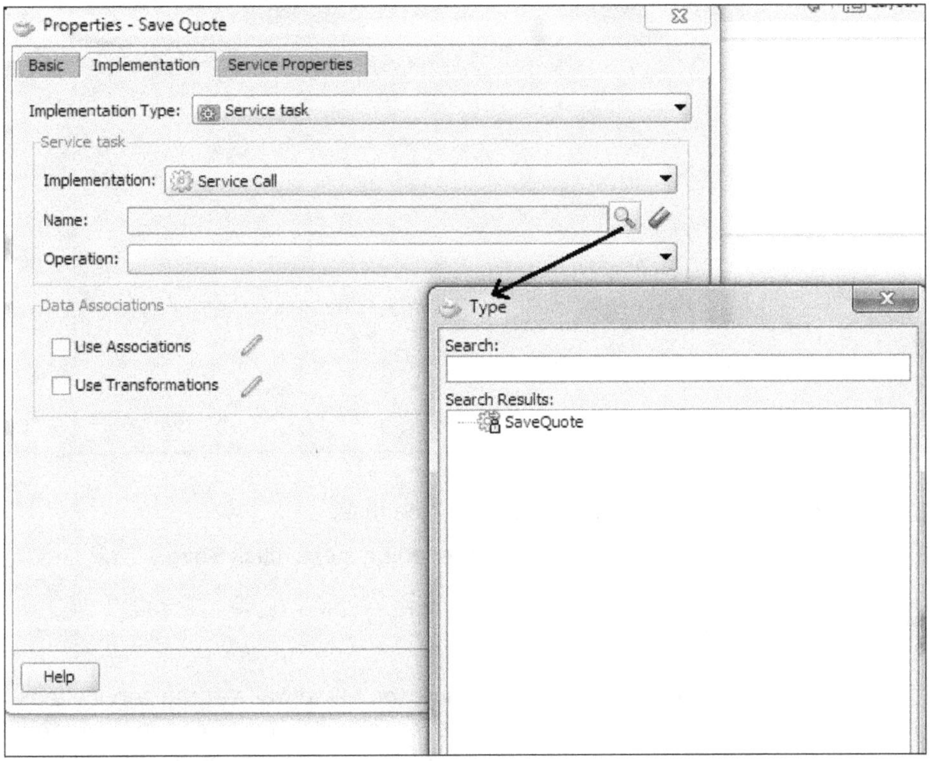

17. From the search result of the **Service**, choose the service you have created to write to a file—**SaveQuote.** This will bind the activity with the service.
18. In **Operation**, choose **Write**. (However, as the service has only one operation, it will get automatically populated).

    Go to the **Data Associations** section. You can check the **Use Associations** to perform input-output mappings.
19. Click the pencil icon to the right of **Use Associations** to edit it. This will open the **Data Association** dialog.

20. Drag-and-drop the `quote` Data object from the right-hand panel to the Inputs area and click **OK**.

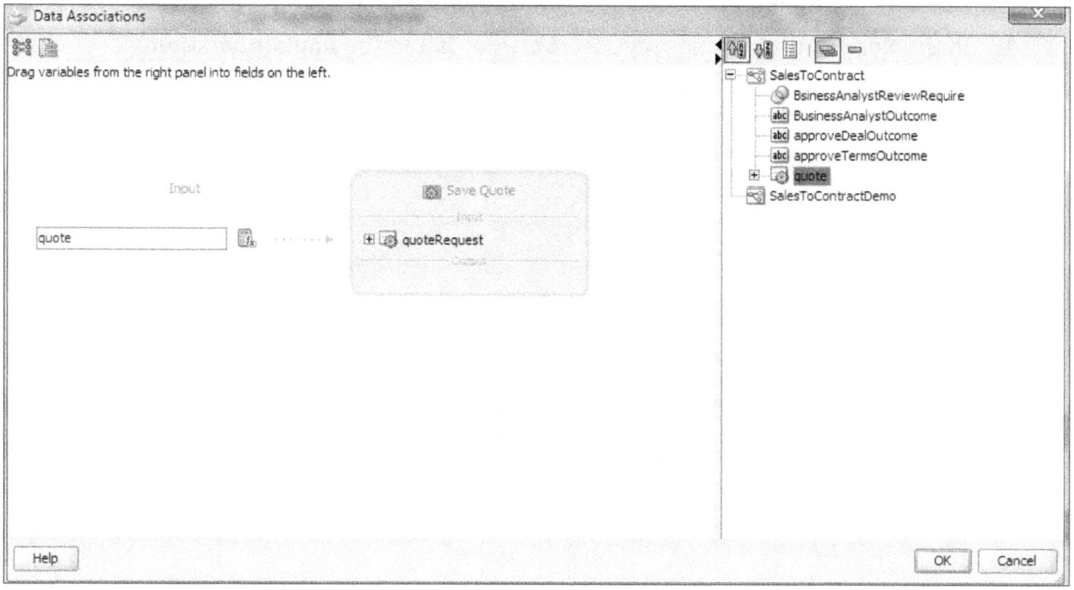

21. Click **OK** to complete the **Save Quote** service task.
22. When you have finished following the preceding steps, click **Save**.

How it works...

When the service task invokes a process or service, the token waits at the service task until a response is returned. After the response is received, the token continues to the next sequence flow in the process. You use service tasks to invoke synchronous operations in services and BPMN processes. By **synchronous**, we mean that when the BPMN service engine runs a service task, it invokes the operation specified in the service task and waits for a response. In this case, data for `quote` is provided to the `SaveQuote` file service, which writes it to a file location.

> Services are not reserved for service tasks; they can also be used to implement message events as well as the Send and Receive tasks.

Assigning the outcome of an Interactive task to Data objects Interactive tasks come with outcomes. You have defined these outcomes when you configured the Human Task Implementation artifact. Like you have set **Submit** as the outcome for **Enter Quote Human Task**, you have to assign these outcome values to Data objects to be used in the process, as shown in the following screenshot:

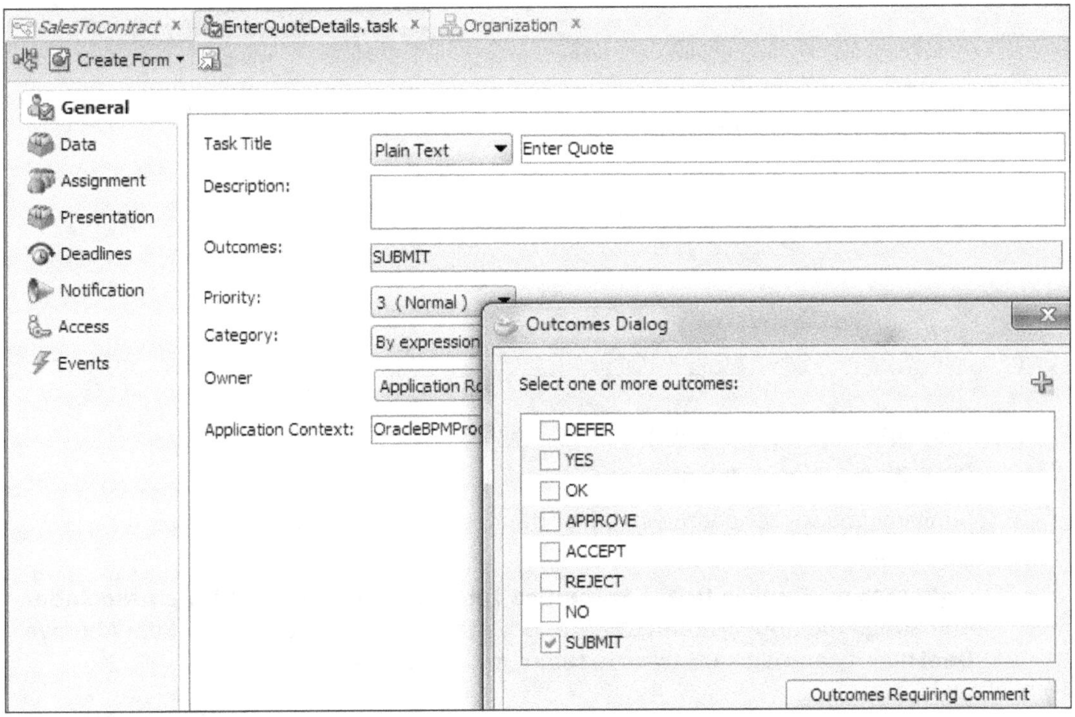

How to do it...

You can remember that you have already created `BusinessAnalystOutcome`, `approveDealOutcome`, and `approveTermsOutcome` as a Data object in *Chapter 1, Process Modeling*, to hold values while you modeled the process. You will assign the outcome of the `Business Analyst Review` activity to the `BusinessAnalystOutcome` Data object, and similarly you will assign the outcomes of the `Approve Deal` and `Approve Terms` activities to the `approveDealOutcome` and `approveTermsOutcome` Data objects, respectively.

1. Go to the **Application Navigator | Project | SalesToContract Process | Business Analyst Review** activity.
2. Right-click the **Business Analyst Review** activity, select **Properties**, open the **Implementation** tab, and then click the pencil icon next to **Use Associations** to bring up the **Data Associations** window.

3. Drag-and-drop the **BusinessAnalystOutcome** Data object from the right-hand panel to the box indicated on the **Output** panel.

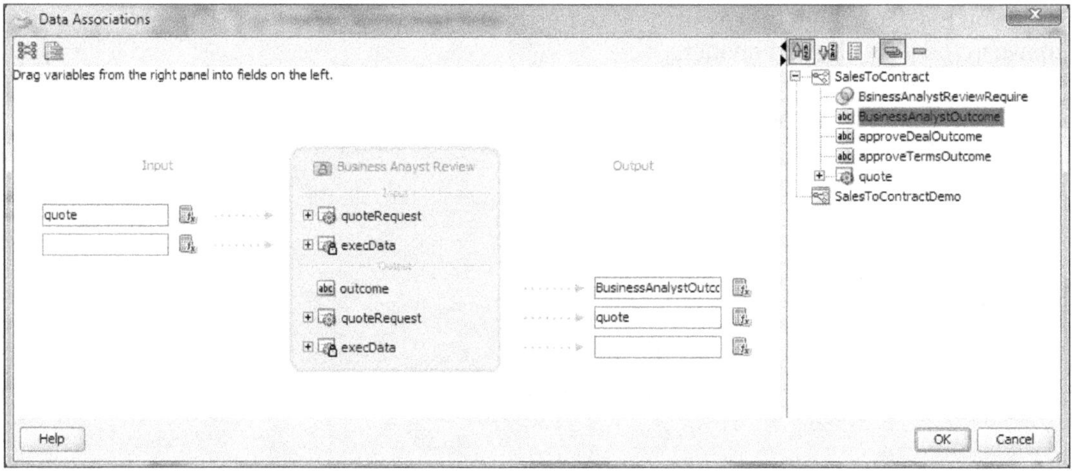

4. Click **OK** to return to the **Properties** dialog.
5. Click **OK** to return to the designer.
6. Similarly, you will repeat the steps for the `Approve Deal` and `Approve Terms` activities too.
7. Right-click on **Approve Deal | Properties | Implementation Tab | Data Association** and assign the `approveDealOutcome` Data object to the outcome of the **Approve Deal** activity and click **OK** twice to return to the designer:

8. Right-click on **Approve Terms | Properties | Implementation Tab | Data Association**, assign the `approveTermsOutcome` Data object to the outcome of the **Approve Terms** activity, and click **OK** twice to return to the designer.

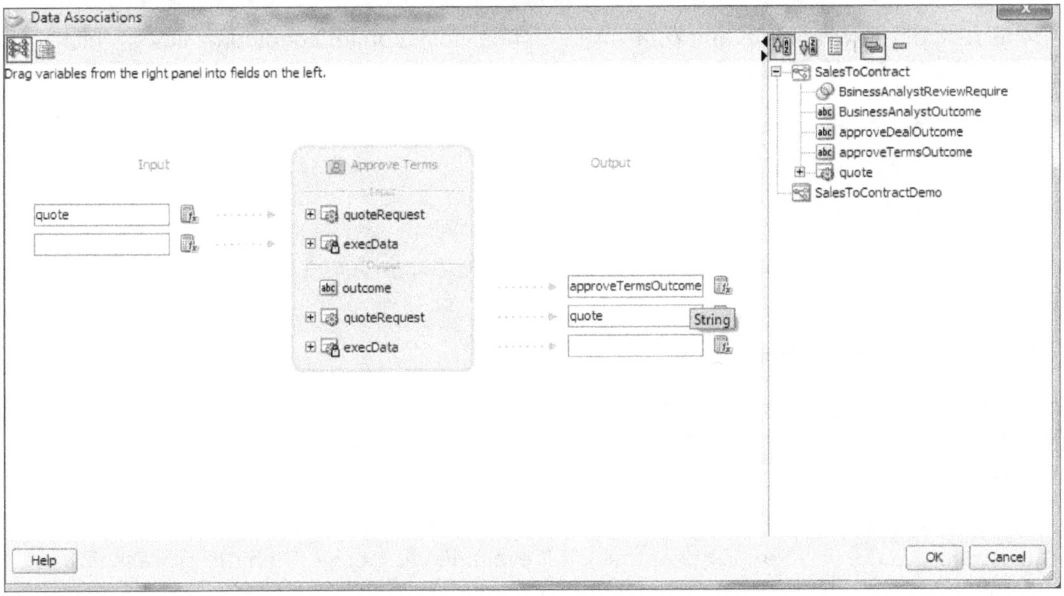

9. When you have finished following the preceding steps, click **Save**.

How it works...

When the token returns back to the process from the Human Task, it brings the outcome with it. These outcomes will be assigned to the Data objects, based on the Data association defined in the properties of the activities.

> You created a script task in *Chapter 1, Process Modeling*, to initialize values. You have created a process Data object, `BusinessAnalystReviewRequired`, and assigned the values of `false ()` in the section *Changing the Value of Data Objects in Your Process* in *Chapter 1, Process Modeling*. These values will be required while conditionally branching from the Gateways.

Configuring a Data association for conditional flow

In this recipe, you will create and configure a Data association for conditional flows, which defines the flow the BPMN process token will take.

Getting ready

To implement the Conditional switch:

If: `Business Analyst Review Required` *= Yes, then proceed to Business Analyst Review User Task*

Else: Proceed to Approvers Review

You have created a process Data object, `BusinessAnalystReviewRequired,` to store values, as the evaluation is determined by the expression defined for the outgoing conditional sequence flow.

If this evaluates to `true`, then the process flow proceeds down the `Yes` path (Towards the `Business Analyst Review` User task). If it evaluates to `false`, then the process flow proceeds down the path of the default outgoing sequence flow.

The condition in the sequence flow will be based on values of the process Data object `BusinessAnalystReviewRequired`

If: `BusinessAnalystReviewRequired` *= True, then choose the sequence flow 'Yes'*

Else: Choose the Sequence Flow 'No'

Similarly, you have to specify the Data object-based conditional expression for the **Business Analyst Rejected** and **Deal** or **Terms Rejected** paths. You will do this for the three paths, numbered as follows:

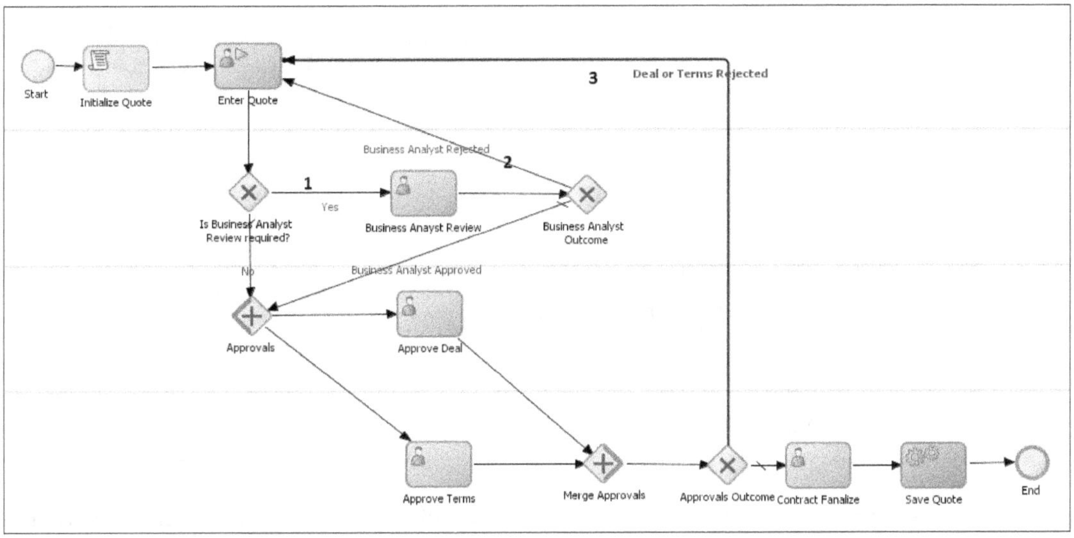

How to do it...

You will configure data association for flow conditions in this section, as follows:

1. Go to **Project | SalesToContract Process** and right-click on the conditional path (the first sequence path in the preceding figure), that is, the outcome from **Is Business Analyst Review Required?** Gateway.
2. Click on **Properties** and go to the **Properties** tab in the **Properties** dialog.
3. Chose **Type = Condition and Expression = Simple**.
4. Enter the expression `BsinessAnalystReviewRequire == true`.

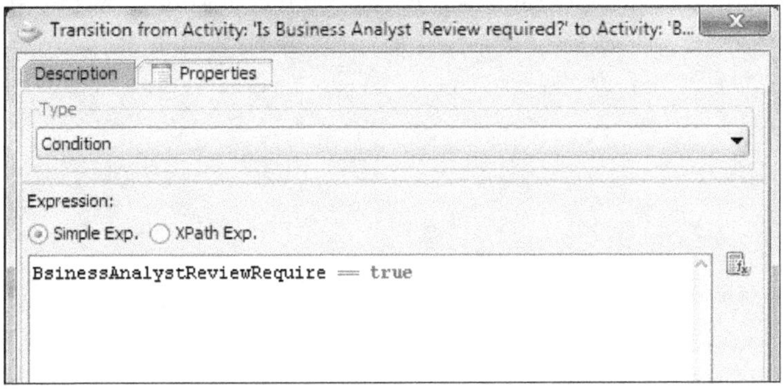

5. Click **OK** twice to return back to the designer.
6. Repeat the same steps for the **Business Analyst Rejected** conditional flow and enter the following expression: `BusinessAnalystOutcome == "REJECT"`.

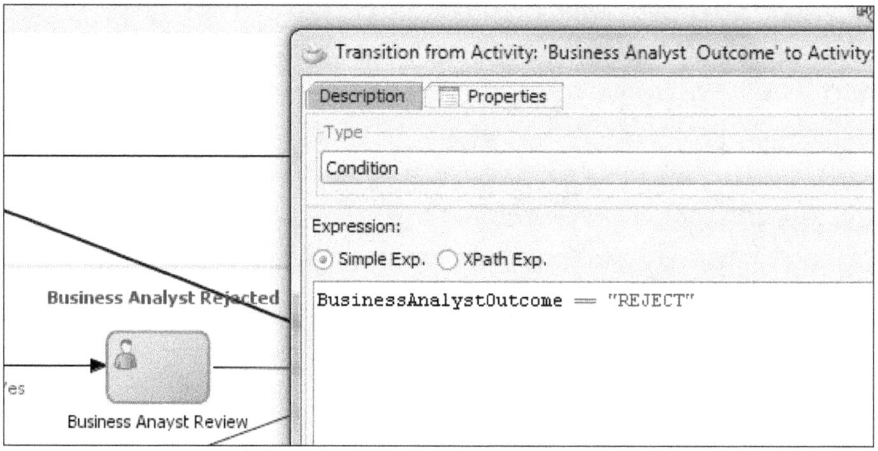

7. Repeat the steps for the **Deal** or **Terms Rejected** conditional flow as well, and enter the following in the Expression Builder: `approveDealOutcome == "REJECT"` or `approveTermsOutcome == "REJECT"`.
8. When you have finished following the preceding steps, click **Save**.

How it works...

This outcome that you set in the Human Tasks is available as an action on the Task Forms. Consider then that you log in to BPM Workspace with the user `sales representative`. You can find **Enter Quote** as a task assigned to the user. When you click the **Enter Quote** task, it will open an **Enter Quote** Task Form with the outcome as **Submit**. You click on **Submit** to initiate the process. The Business Practices Review, Approve Deal, and Approve Terms steps have two possible outcomes—**APPROVE** and **REJECT**. These Human Task outcomes can be evaluated to perform conditional branching and split the sequential flow of the process into conditional flows.

3

Process Deployment and Testing

In this chapter, we will look at how developers build, deploy, test, analyze, and debug the process. Once you have completed the implementation tasks, you would want to deploy and test the project before you roll it out into the test/production environment. You can deploy your project as an SOA Composite application from BPM Studio, EM Console, or Business Process Composer.

This chapter will focus on deployment tasks such as:

- Connecting to Application Server running SOA Suite
- Making/Compiling a BPM Project
- Deploying the Project
- Testing Process: Triggering the Process
- Analyzing Process Instance
- Debugging the Process

Introduction

BPM Deployment is the process of transferring an Oracle BPM project from the development environment to the runtime environment. This can be either a testing or production runtime environment. After finishing the integration of business processes with backend systems and reusable services, process developers create and compile a working process-based application. The application is then deployed to Oracle BPM runtime.

Oracle BPM Suite contains the following typical scenarios for deploying to Oracle BPM runtime:

- **SAR File**: Deployment using an exported SAR Archive file—Oracle BPM Studio and Business Process Composer enable you to export applications using a SAR file. The SAR file can be deployed to runtime by business administrators using Oracle Enterprise Manager. In a production environment, this is generally how applications are deployed.

  Such deployments are carried out through the **Enterprise Manager** console. **EM** provides capabilities to deploy, un-deploy, re-deploy, as well as start and stop BPM composites. This option requires the SAR or corresponding file to be created.
- **JDeveloper**: BPM Projects can be deployed using JDeveloper. You will use JDeveloper to perform deployment of a BPM Project in this chapter.
- **WLST**: Deployment using the **WebLogic Scripting Tool** (WLST)—Oracle BPM provides customized WLST commands for managing and deploying Oracle BPM projects.
- **Ant**: Deployment can be scripted using `ant` scripts. Oracle BPM Suite has these scripts created out of the box for use.

Connecting to the Application Server running SOA Suite

This section will demonstrate how connections to the Application server are created.

Getting ready

You need to deploy the project to the application server that is running Oracle SOA Suite / BPM Suite. Hence you will first establish a connection with the WebLogic Application Server, which is running Oracle SOA Suite (BPM Suite).

How to do it...

You will be creating a Standalone Server connection:

1. Start Oracle J Developer, and select **Default Role**, and click **OK**.
2. Go to **View | Application Server navigator**.

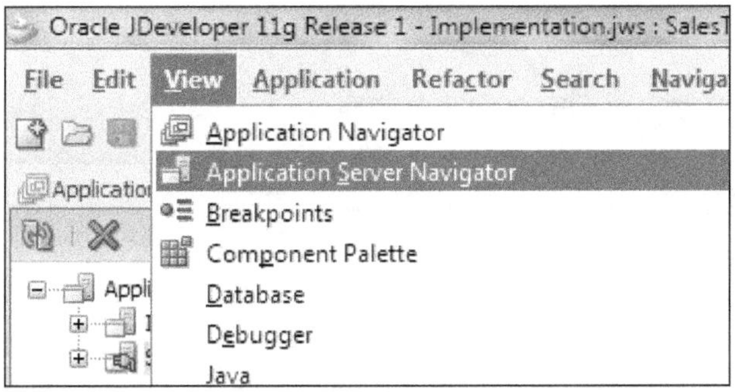

3. Right-click **Application Servers** and choose **New Application Server**. This will open a **Create Application Server** Connection Wizard.
4. Choose the usage of **Application Server** as **Standalone Server**.
5. In the **Name** and **Type** tab, enter the name of the connection, say `SOA_AS_Conn`. You can choose any connection name. You have to select **Connection Type** as `Weblogic 10.3` because we have SOA Suite installed on the Weblogic Server.
6. Click **Next**.
7. In the Authentication tab, enter the WebLogic Server admin **Username** (`weblogic`) and **Password** (`Welcome1`) or whatever you have for your WebLogic Server.

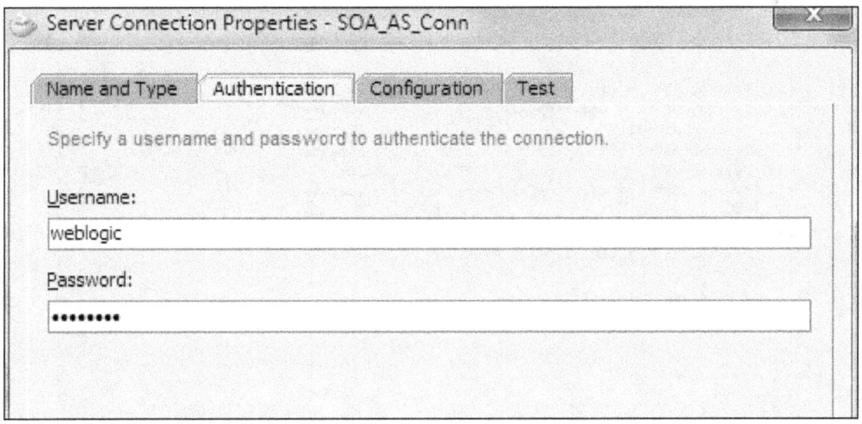

8. Click **Next**.

9. In the **Configuration** tab, enter **Weblogic Hostname** (in my case, it was `localhost`) and the Admin port for SSL and Non-SSL (`7001`), and then enter the **Weblogic Domain**. Like, in my case, it's `soa_domain`.

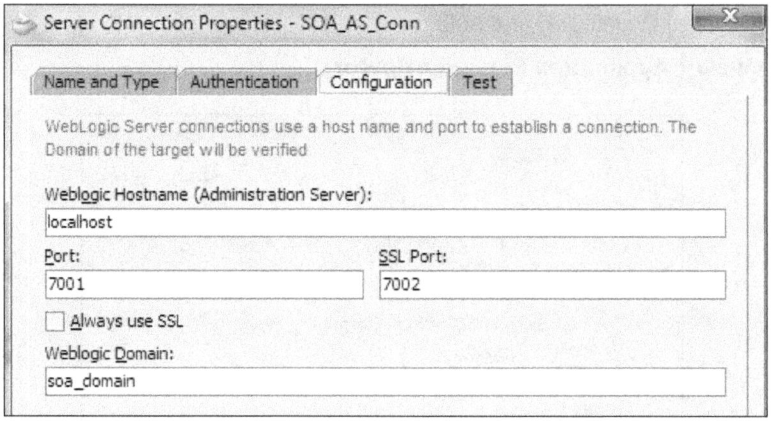

10. Click **Next**.
11. Now you can test the connection. Click on the **Test Connection** button to test the connection. All the nine tests should result in **success**. Once done, click **OK**. Make sure you configure your JDeveloper proxy settings if you are trying to connect to the SOA domain across a proxy or a firewall.

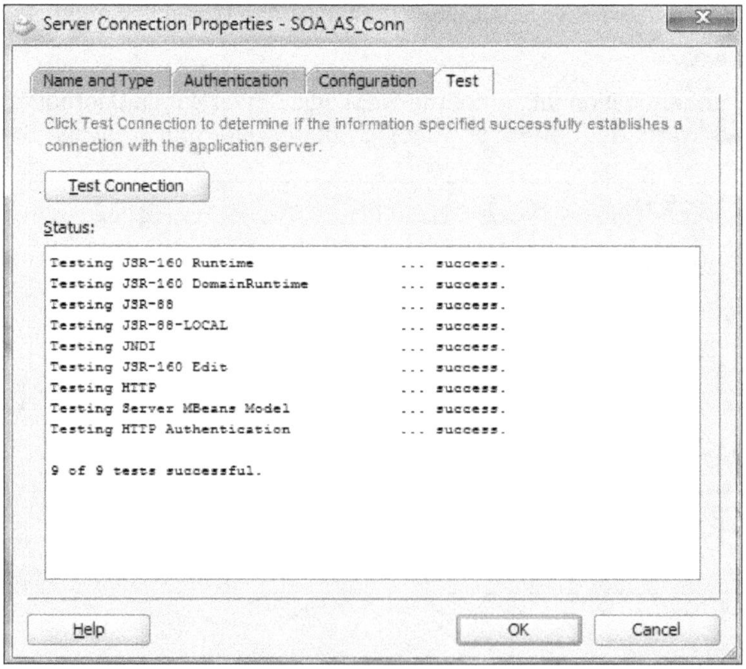

How it works...

Connection to the server is established with the credentials given like login and password. However, due importance must be given while entering the domain name, Server port, and other details.

Building and Compiling a BPM Project

In this section, you will learn to make (build) and compile your BPM project before deployment.

Getting ready

Before starting the deployment process to a BPMN Service Engine, you must build your BPM project. After you build the BPM project, the Compiler Log window displays the results. If the build is successful, then you can deploy to the BPMN Service Engine. If there are any errors, you can select the **Compiler** tab and click the errors to open the corresponding editor and correct them.

How to do it...

1. Go to J Developer and click on the **Application** navigator.
2. Choose the project and right-click on it.
3. Select **Make SalesToContractDemo.jpr**, which is the `ProjectName.jpr`.

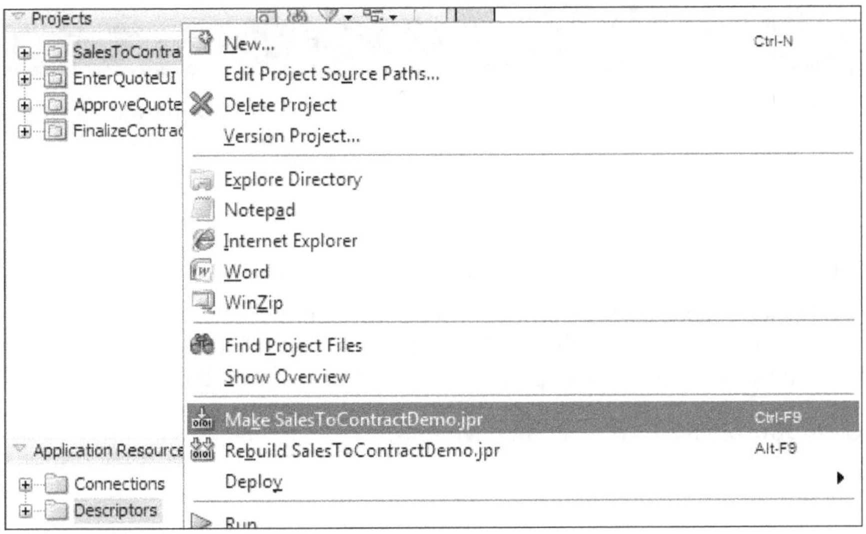

How it works...

Oracle JDeveloper compiles the BPM Project. The Compiler Log window displays the results of the compilation. If there are errors, you can correct them too.

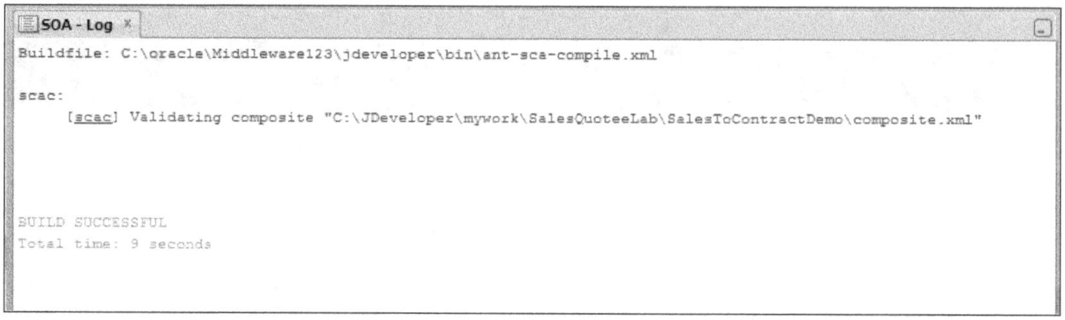

After you successfully build a BPM Project, you can deploy it to a BPMN Service Engine.

> As the logical roles are often mapped to LDAP Group(s) or User(s) at deployment time, you have to assign Users to Logical Roles. Before deploying the application, you connect to the internal LDAP realm within the WebLogic server and map those roles to the LDAP users. However, you have already done the assignment of LDAP users to logical roles in *Chapter 1, Process Modeling*.

Deploying the Project

You will now deploy the BPM project that you have just compiled. During wizard-based deployment from JDeveloper as well, the project is first compiled and a SAR file is created for the project in the deploy folder of the project's filesystem.

How to do it...

Deployment is the process of transferring an Oracle BPM project from the development environment to the runtime environment. In this section, you will deploy the Project using JDeveloper. Later you will perform deployment with other methods too:

1. Go to **JDeveloper | Application navigator**.

2. Choose and right-click on the BPM Project **SalesToContractDemo**.

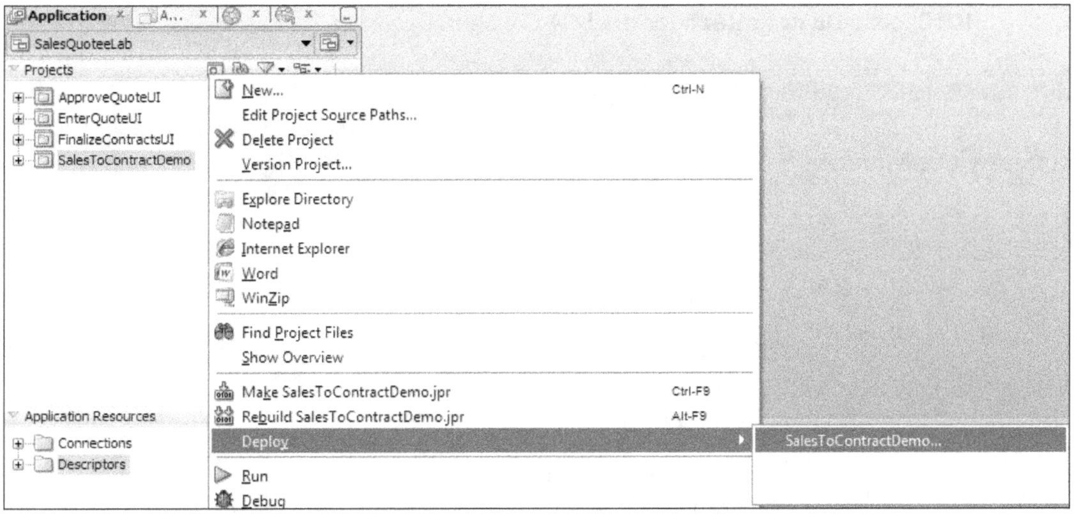

3. The **Deployment Action** Configuration Wizard will start up. As you are deploying to an application server , choose **Deploy To Application Server** in the deployment action list and click **Next**.

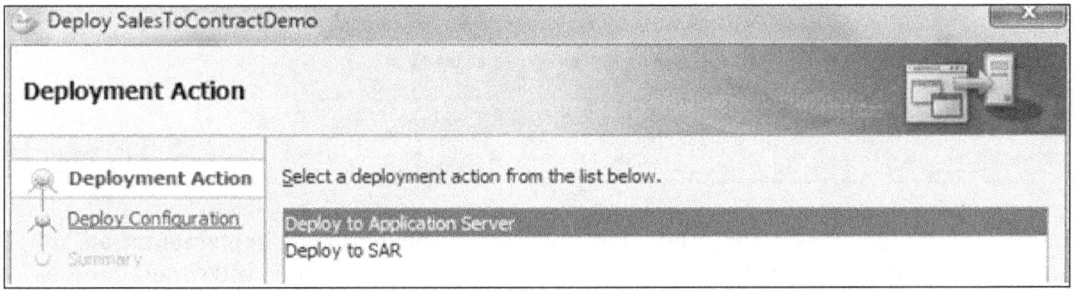

4. Enter `1.0` as **Revision** in the **Deploy Configuration** step. Select the **Mark composite revision as default** and **Overwrite any existing composites with the same Revision ID**. Choose **Do not attach** for the SOA Configuration Plan.

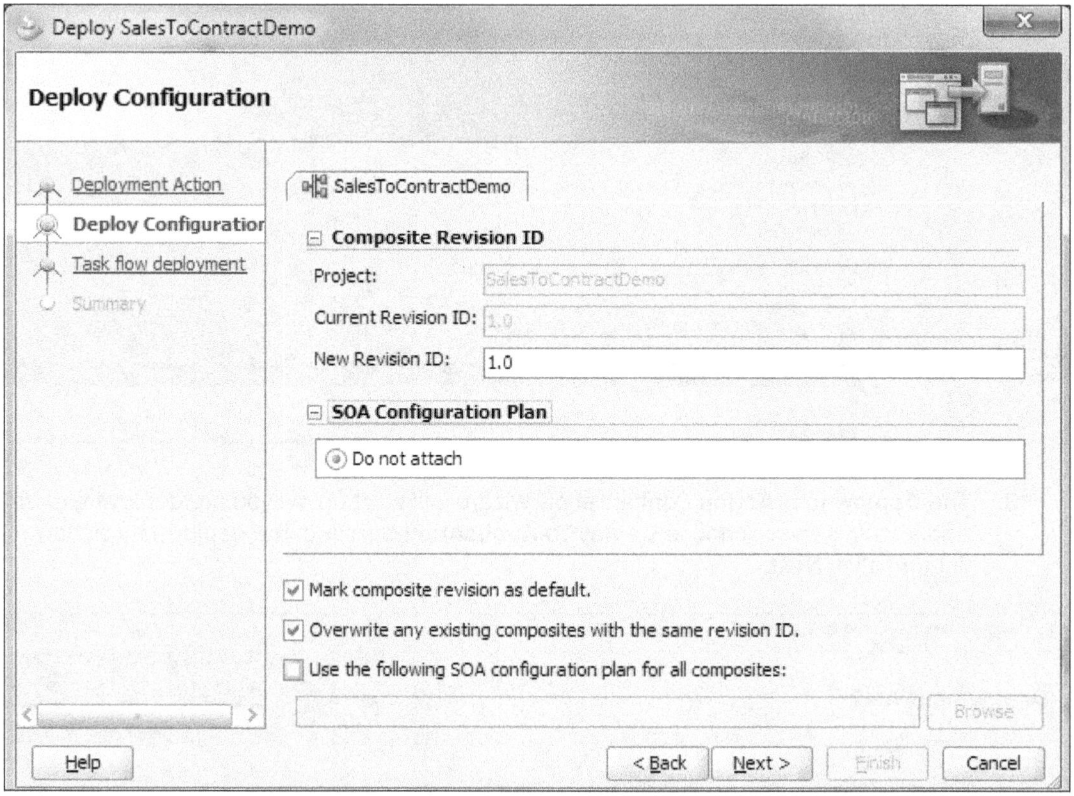

5. In the **Task flow deployment** step, choose the **Application** as **Implementation**. You will find that the **User Interface** projects that you created when you generated Task Forms for the Human Tasks are listed. Choose/select all of them and click **Next**.

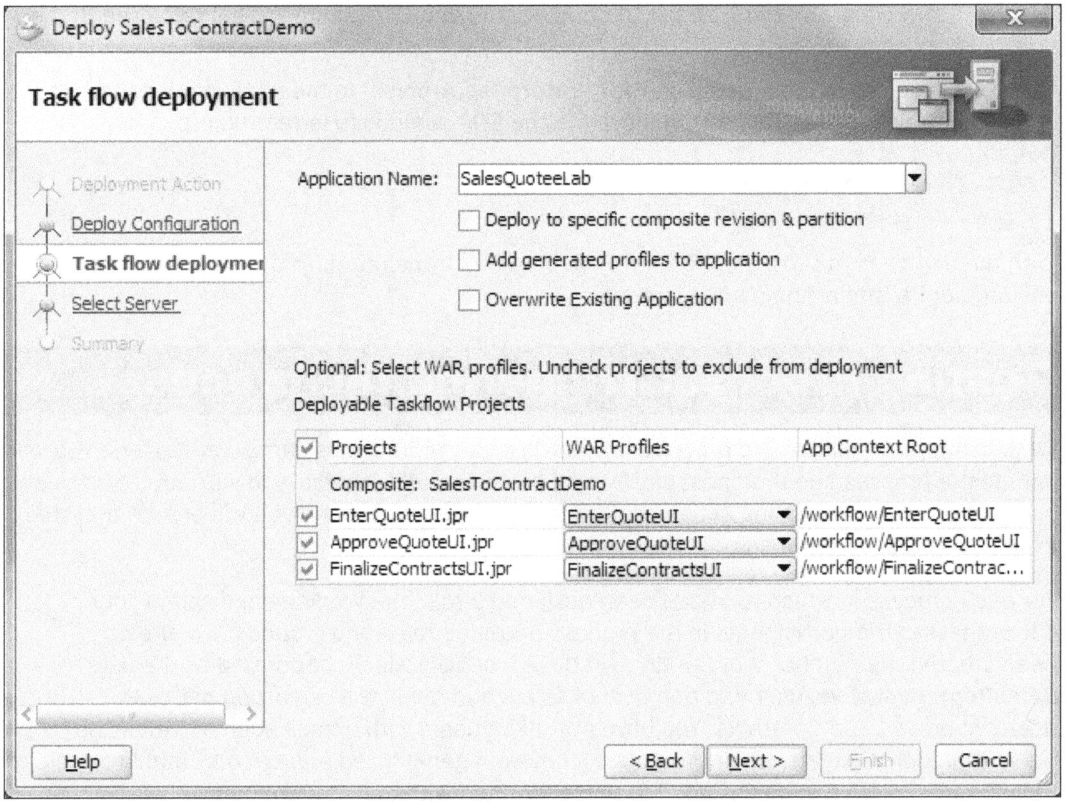

6. Select the application server connection (`SOA_AS_Conn`) that you have created in the preceding text.
7. Click **Finish**. It will take time to compile and deploy the project.
8. When completed, you can check the status of deployment in **Deployment - Log**.

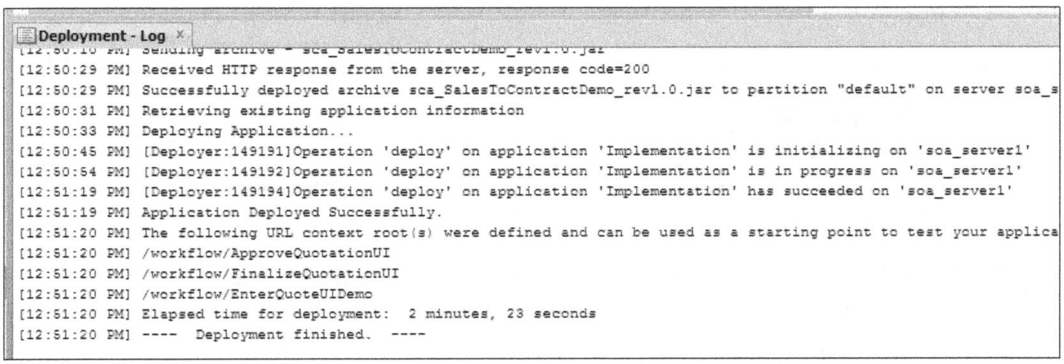

9. If there are no errors, all the UI Components and Composite will get deployed to the application server.
10. UI project is deployed as an **EAR** (**Enterprise Archive**) to the application server. The composite application is deployed to the SOA composite infrastructure.

How it works...

With the deployment process, the BPM Project will be transferred from the development environment to the runtime environment.

Testing Process: Triggering the process

While testing, we will run the process as you will log in with various sample end users. You will initiate the process and then advance it to all possible paths, that is, you will test it across all possible flows by performing actions on the task in the work list and you will ensure that the expected paths are followed.

For each process in which you have been assigned a role, the Workspace displays your current tasks. The participants in the process and their roles and groups have already been created. Remember that the `Enter Quote` activity will be performed by the user **SalesRepresentative**, user and approval of terms and deals will be carried out by the users, Approver, and Contracts. You have not taken users with names such as 'Adam' as SalesRepresentative and so on. You have followed a generalized approach by making a role of SalesRepresentative to be assigned to a user created with the same name.

Role	User	Task
SalesRepresentative	salesrepresentative	Enter Quote Activity
BusinessAnalyst	businessanalyst	Business Review Activity
Approvers	approver	Approve Deal Activity
Contracts	contracts	Approve terms and Finalize Contacts activities

How to do it...

As a user, you can log in to **Workspace** . It's the common place where end users log in to participate in the process.

1. Go to the following URL to log in the Business Process Workspace: `http://localhost:8001/bpm/workspace/`.
2. Log in with the credentials: `salesrepresentative/Welcome1`.

3. Go to the **Applications** in **Workspace** and click on the Process name **SalesToContract v1.0** that you have deployed.
4. You have logged in as `salesrepresentative`. This is the user that has the role `SalesRepresentative`, which has an Initiator Task. When you click on the application, it will generate a task which will be available in the Inbox of the user, `SalesRepresentative`.

5. You can find that **Worklist Views** has an **Inbox**. Click on **Inbox**, and the task assigned to you (when logged in as `SalesRepresentative`) is listed on the right-hand side of the screen, that is, the **Enter Quote** task.

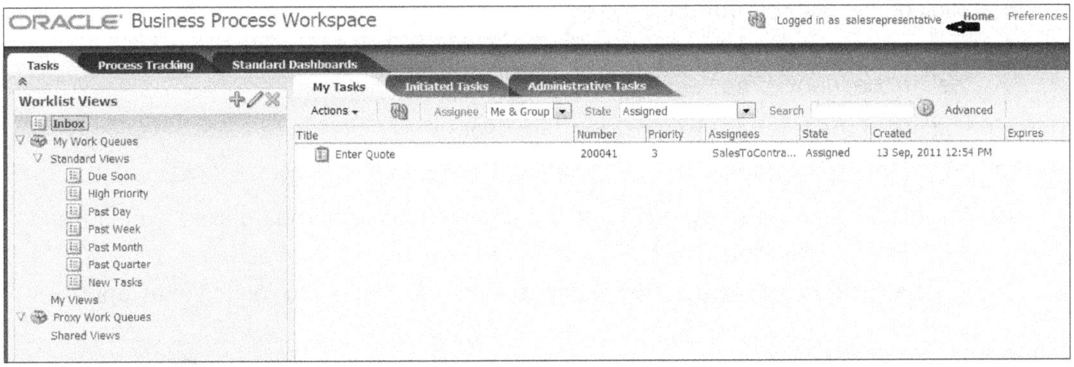

6. Double-click on the **Enter Quote** task to open it in a new window.

7. In the **Enter Quote** window modify quote **Details**. As you have used a script task to initialize the values of `Quote`, they are available here. You can change them too, but keep them as it is for now.

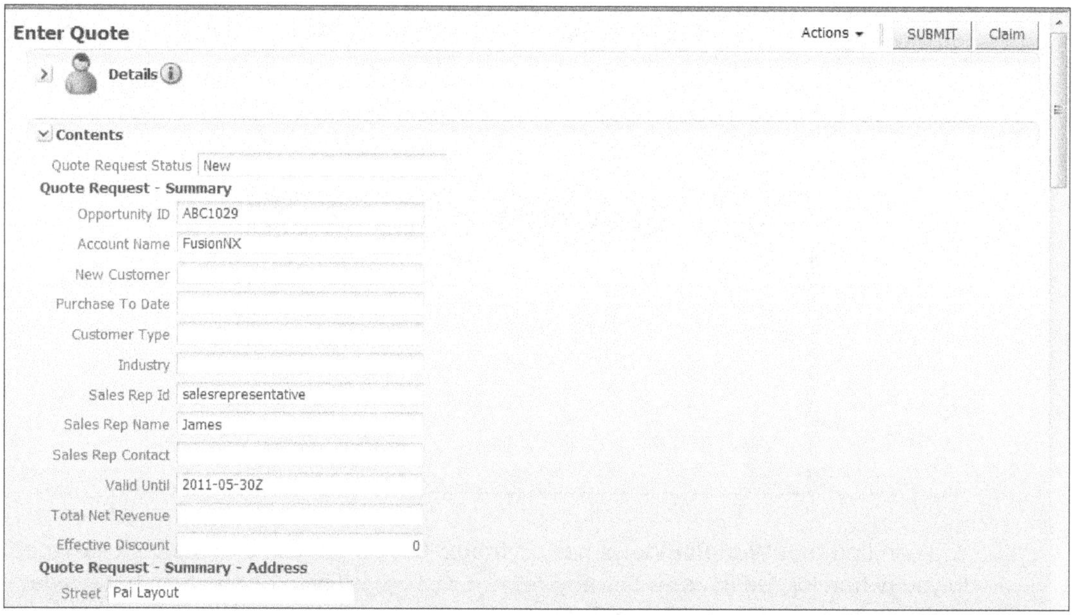

8. Click on the **Submit** button.
9. The task has now moved ahead and you will find that it has moved from the enlisted task in the Inbox of `salesrepresentative`.
10. Log out of the `salesRepresentative` user.
11. Log in with the Approver role with the user credentials: `approver/Welcome1`.
12. The process now has now moved to the Approver role and the Contracts role for the Approve Deal and Approve Terms tasks respectively.
13. Double-click on the **Approve Deal** task assigned to you when you log in as **approver**.

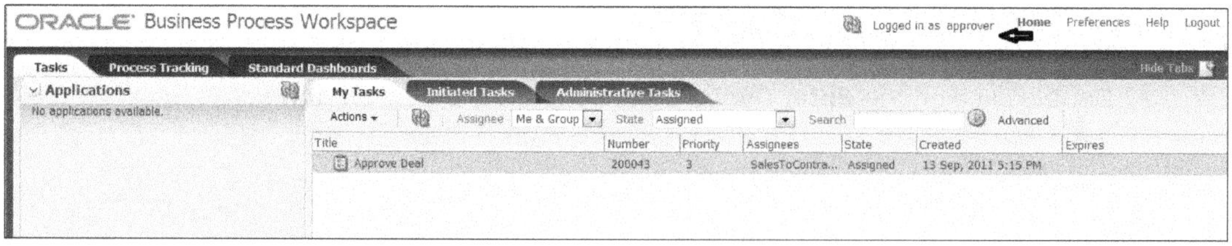

14. Click on **Approve** to approve the **Approve Deal** task.

15. The task will move from the task list of the Approver user.
16. Log out of **approver**.
17. Log in again with the credentials `contracts/Welcome1` to perform the **Approve Terms** and **Finalize Contract** tasks.
18. Double-click on the **Approve Terms** task assigned to the `contracts` user.

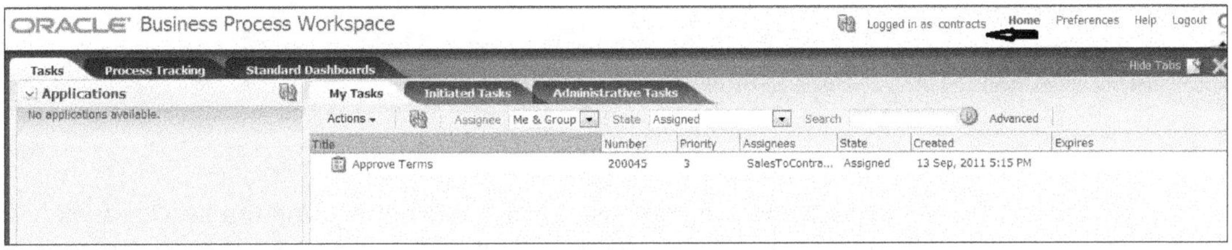

19. Click on the **Approve** button to approve the **Approve Terms** task.

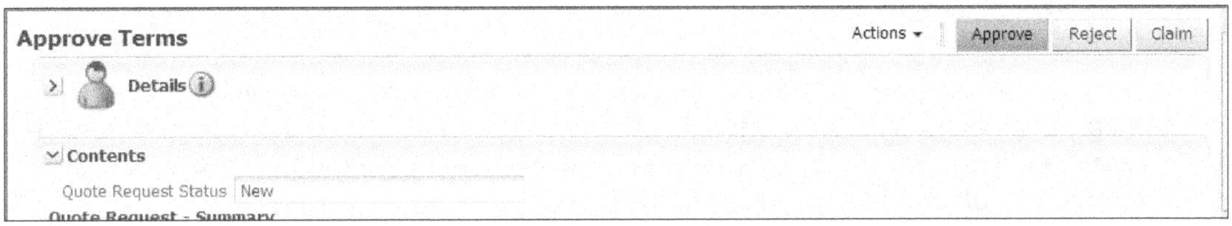

20. Double-click the **Finalize Contracts** task assigned to the `contracts` user.

21. You will find that as soon as you approve, the task moves out of the list. However, as the same user is also going to finalize the contract, as the **Finalize Contracts** task is assigned to the user Contracts:

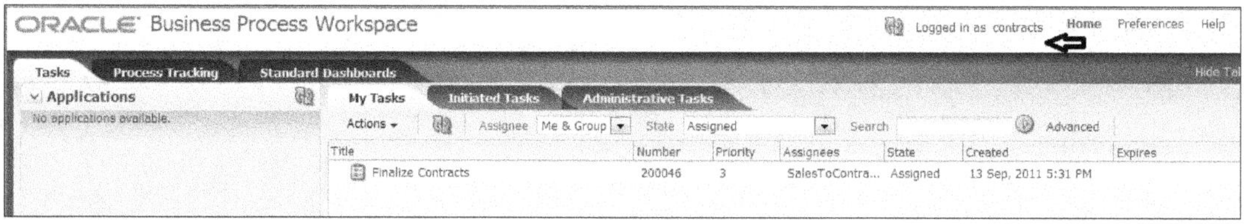

22. Click **OK** to finalize the contract.

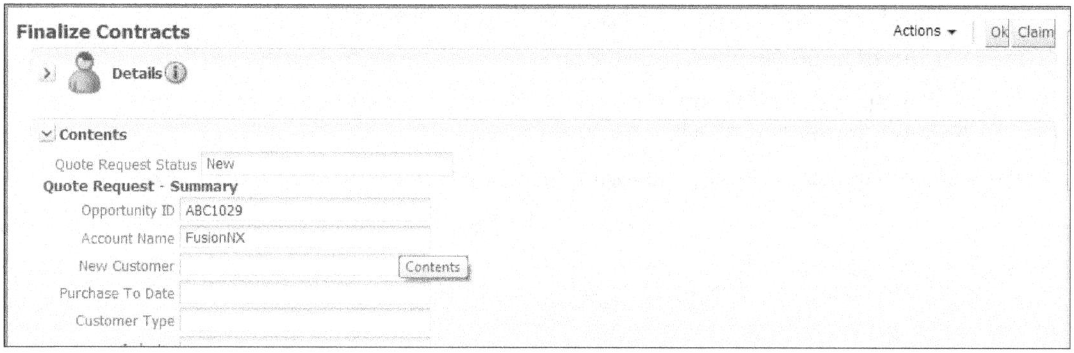

23. Go to the Output directory which you have given while configuring the service task `SaveQuote`, which is a file adapter. In my case, it's `TEMP/QuoteOutput`. You can find a quotation file created there.

How it works...

When you log in as the user `salesrepresentative` (the Initiator of the process) and click on the application name **SalesToContractv1.0**, the process gets triggered. The **Enter Quote** task is assigned to `salesrepresentative`. Once you submit the **Enter Quote** task, the token moves to another task.

As you have already set the **BusinessAnalystReviewRequired** Data object to `false()` in the Script Task `Initialize Quote`, so when the token **Is business Analyst Review Required?** is switched on, it will not move to the **Yes** path but take the **No** Path, as shown in the following screenshot:

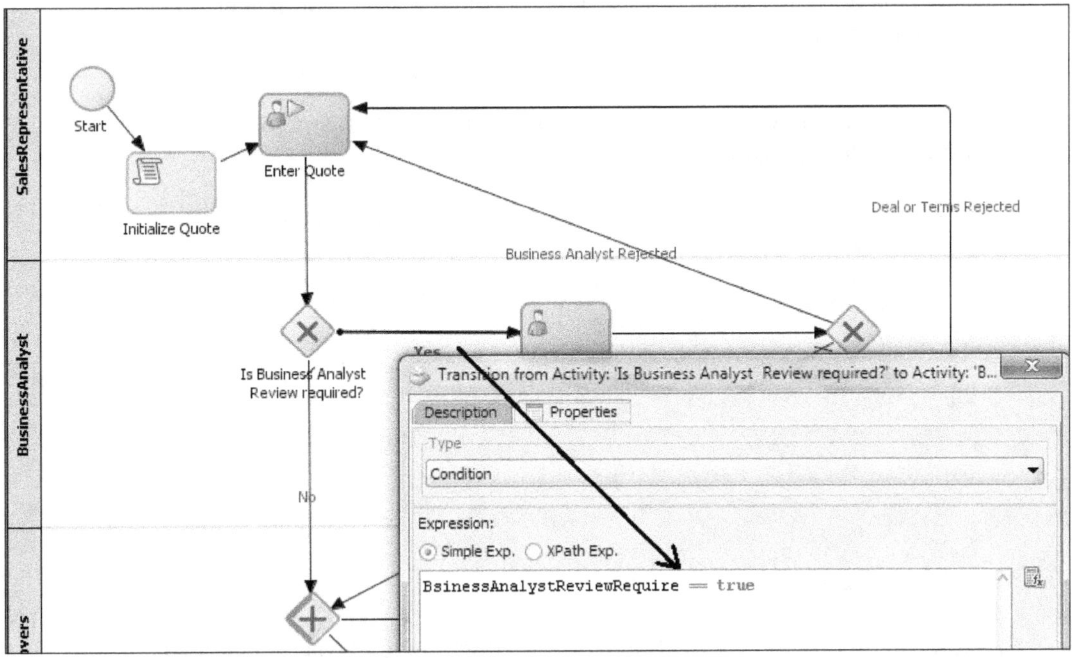

Hence the token will reach the Approve Deal and Approve Quote simultaneously, as you have used a parallel Gateway. Once both are approved, the `contracts` role user will finalize the contract and the SaveQuote service will save the quote in a file location.

There's more...

Files can be attached to tasks and also you can add notes in the comments section.

Attaching files and adding notes

In this section, you will learn to add files and notes to tasks as follows:

1. Go to BPM Workspace and log in with the `salesrepresentative` credentials.
2. Open the assigned task from the task list is in the Inbox , double-click on it. It will open the `Enter Quote` task.
3. Scroll down to the **Comments** and **Attachment** section at the end.
4. In the **Attachment** section, click on the green plus (**+**) sign to open the **Add attachment** file browser.

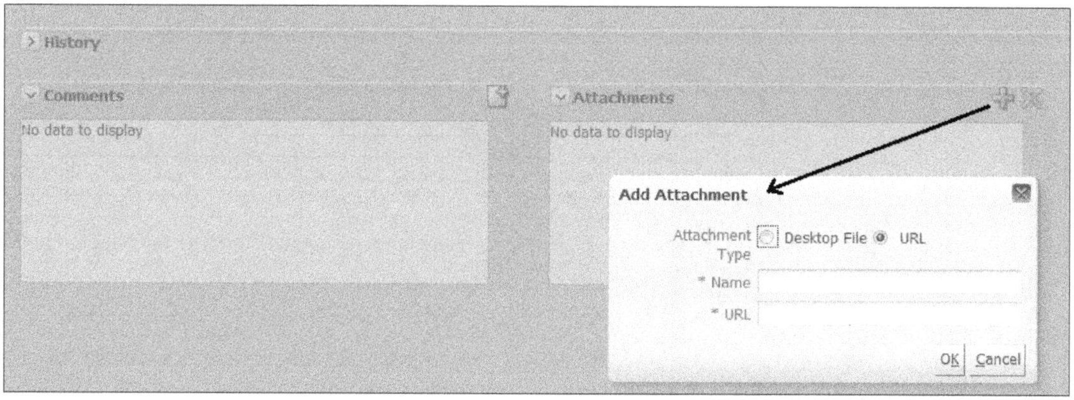

5. You can browse the file to attach the file attachment . It will appear as a link for other participants.
6. You can also add a note in the **Comments** section.

> For any user to add a note, the task item status should not be processed or completed. Also, while configuring the task UI, we had checked the **Is Editable** to be `true`. Hence any approver can also make changes in the form values submitted by the sales representative.

Analyzing process instances

You may now be interested in knowing the path your process has taken and if it has met the expected path. You can analyze, view an audit trail, and monitor your process instance through process tracking in Oracle BPM Workspaces.

How to do it...

1. Log in to Oracle BPM Workspace with the credentials `salesrepresentative/Welcome1`.
2. Click on the **Process Tracking** tab.
3. On the right-hand side, click on **Advanced** to search for the Process Instance.
4. Enter the eligibility criteria for the search as follows:

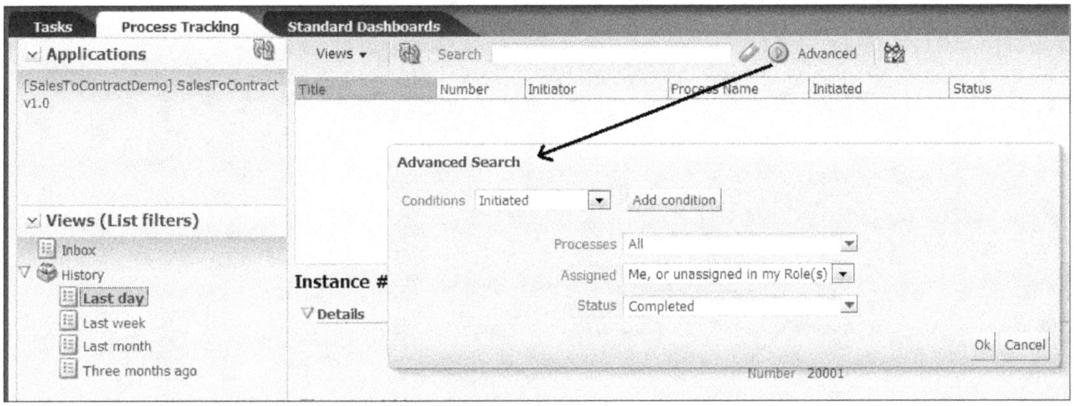

5. You can find the instance listed. Click on the instance row and you can find instance **Details** on the lower side of the window.

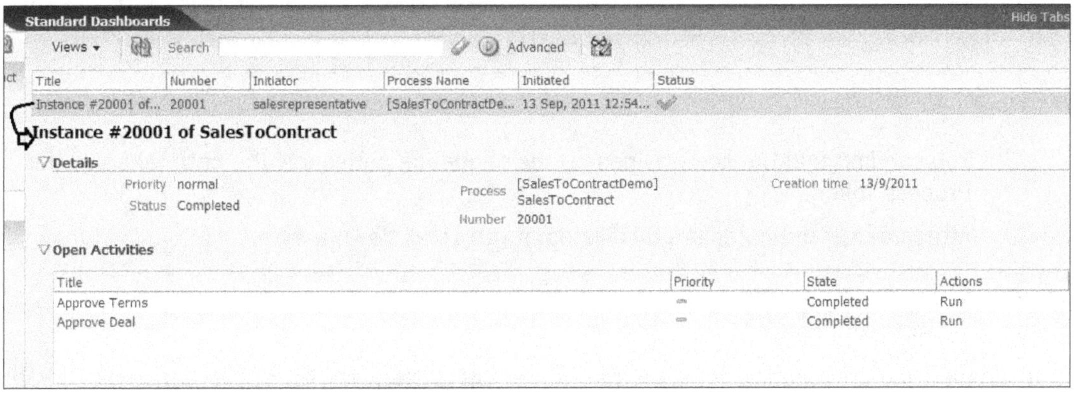

6. Scroll down to the **Audit Trail** section and expand it.

7. Choose the Graphical Radio to view the audit in graphical form.

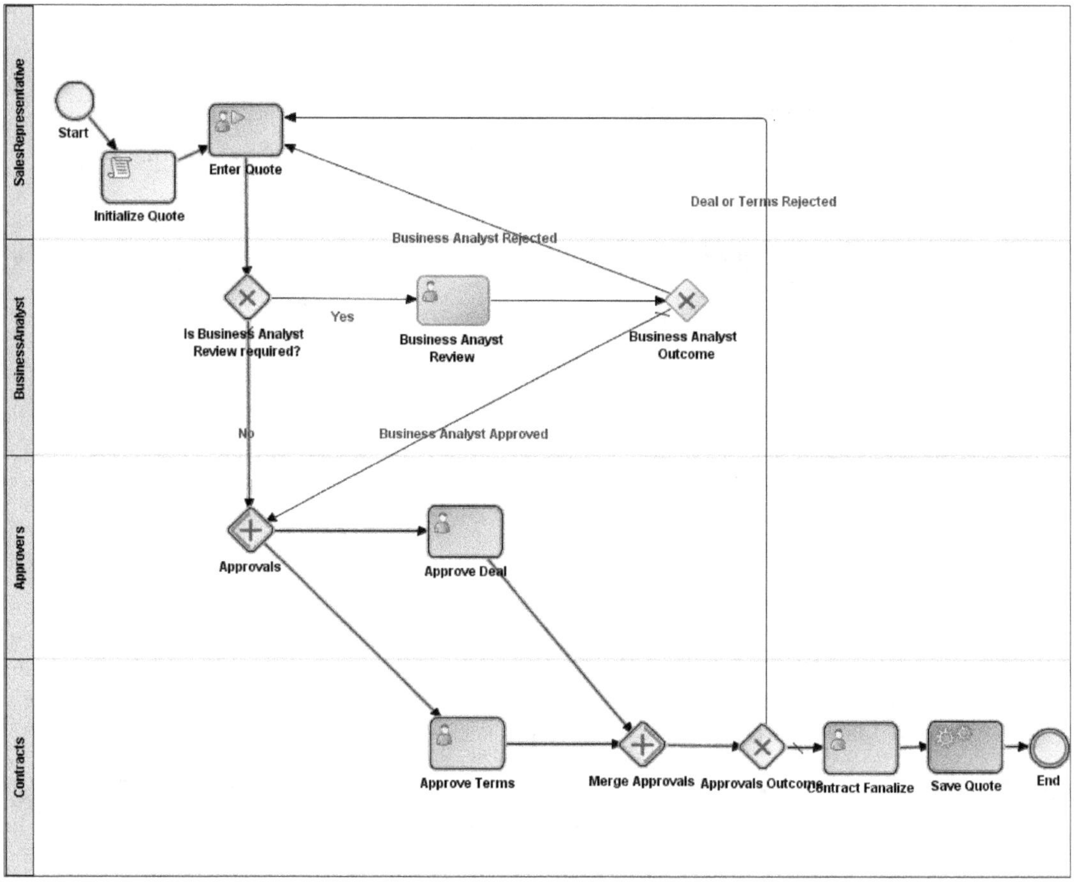

8. You can find that the screen lines on the sequence path show the path taken by the Process Token.
9. Attachments and notes are also listed, if you scroll down a little.

There's more...

You can also find an instance being created in the **EM** (**Enterprise Manager**) console and you can use it to view the Audit Trail of the process.

Instance tracking from EM Console

1. Log in to the WebLogic EM Console with credentials `weblogic/Welcome1`.
2. Go to **SOA-INFRA | Default | SalesToContractDemo**, where the partition is **Default** and **SalesToContractDemo** is the project you have deployed.

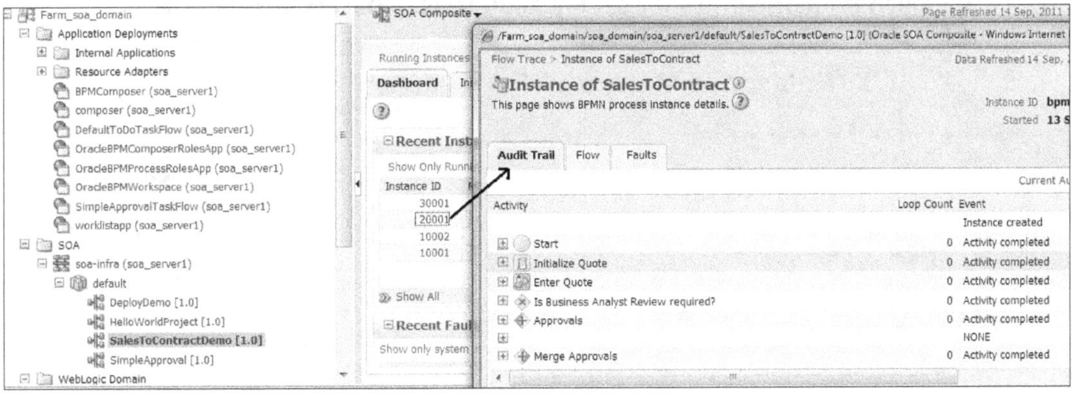

3. Click on the **Instance ID 20001**. It's the same Instance ID that you have found in BPM Workspace too.
4. The Instance window opens and you can check the flow, can find the fault details, if any, and trace the audit trail too.

Debugging the process

While you are testing the process and things are not working as expected, for example, a process instance takes the wrong branch or the approval flow is not what you were expecting, you can debug the process by setting the Audit Level to `Development`. Setting the Audit Level is done in the Enterprise Manager.

First you will set the Audit level to Development mode and then you will initiate a new process instance in the Business Process Workspace to witness the effects of this change in debugging.

How to do it...

This section will cover how to debug a process instance. It is done as follows:

1. Go to the **Enterprise Manager** console **| SOA-Infra | SOA Administration** and click **Common Properties**. This will set the **Audit level** to **Development** mode.

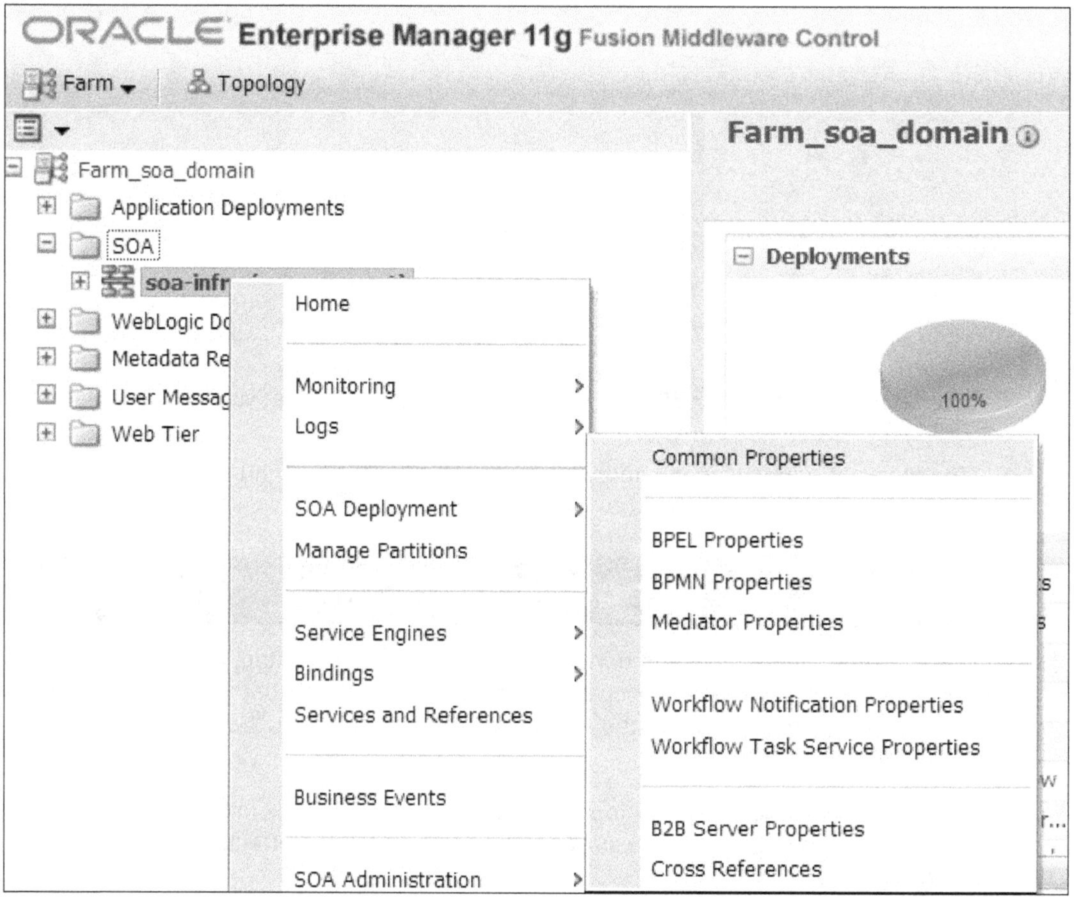

2. Also tick the **Capture Composite Instance State** check box.

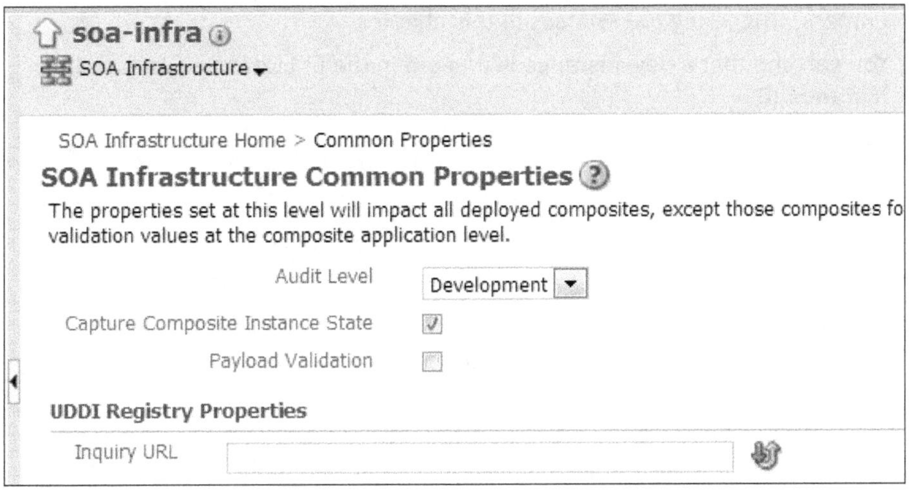

3. In the EM Console, click on the old instance that you have created while following the steps in the section *Testing Process : Triggering the Process*, in this chapter.
4. The Instance number is `20001` and you can find that no data values are displayed at each activity. It just shows that an instance is created for the activity, after which the instance left the activity.

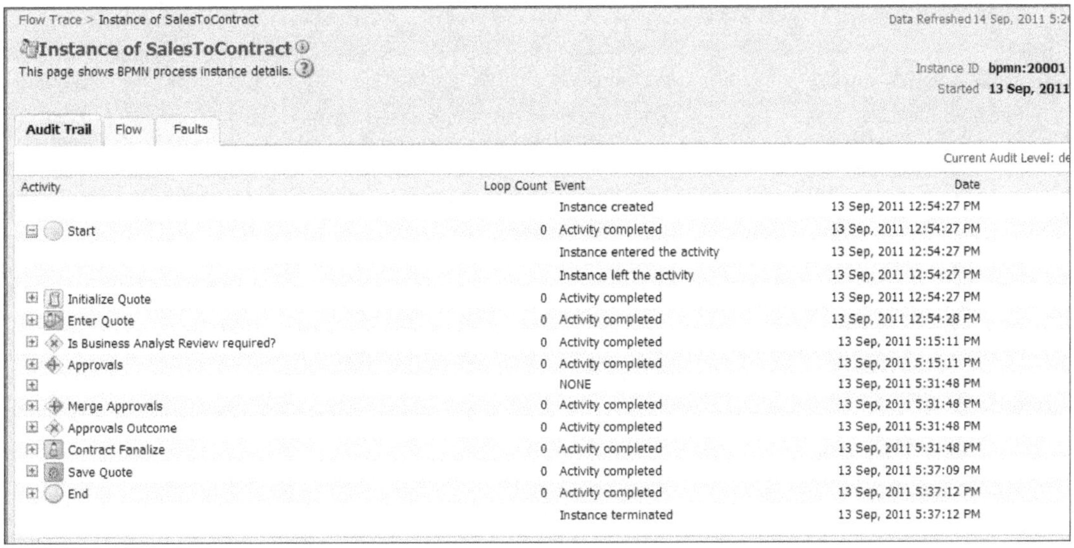

5. Log in to Oracle BPM Workspace with the `salesrepresentative` credentials and reinitiate the process instance with the following the steps in the section *Testing Process : Triggering the Process* in this chapter.

6. You can find that a new instance is created in the EM Console. Click on the **Instance ID**.

7. In the trace section, click on the process name **SalesToContract**.

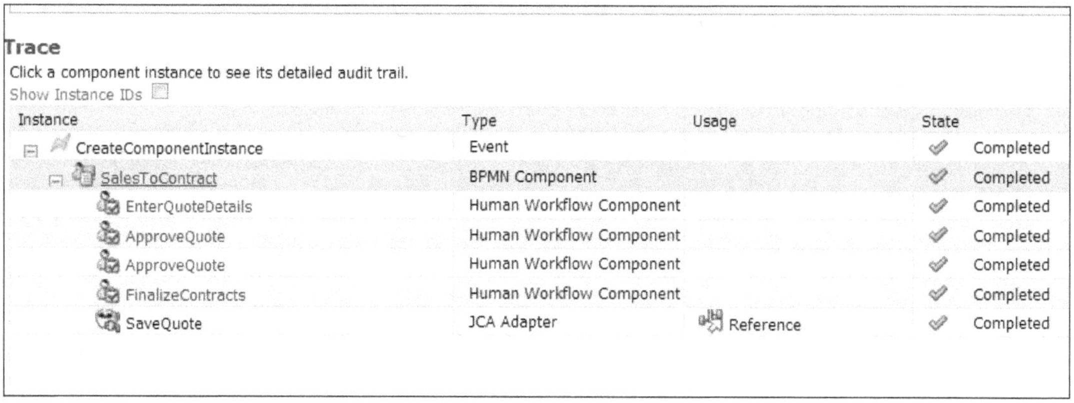

8. In the **Audit Trail** tab, you can find that blue links are clickable and display data values at that particular point in the process.

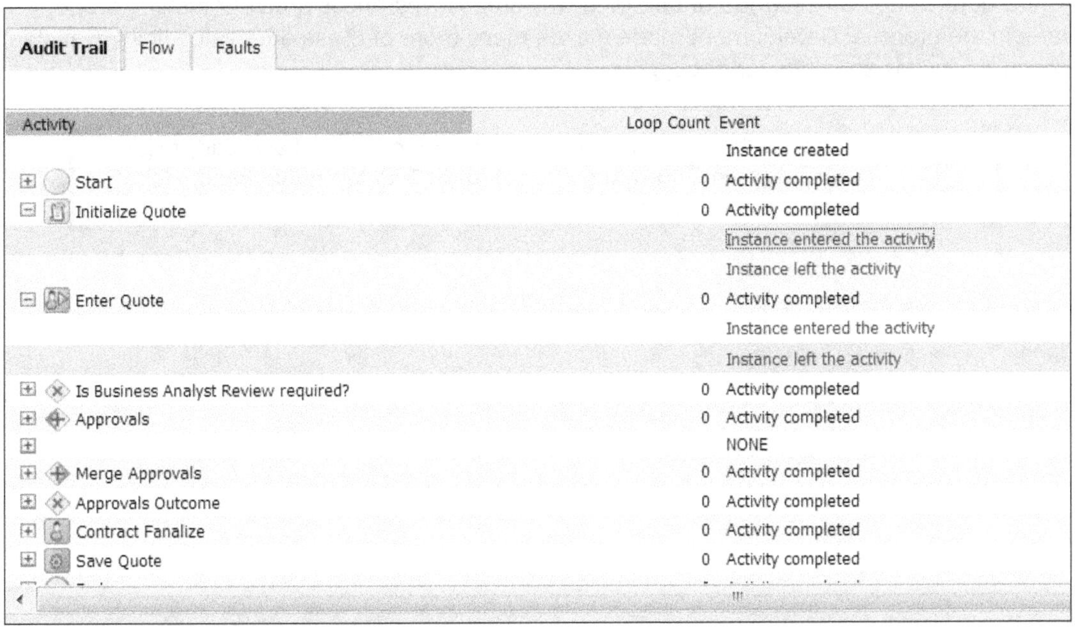

9. Click on **Instance Entered the activity** for the **Enter Quote** task and you can find the data associated with the activity.

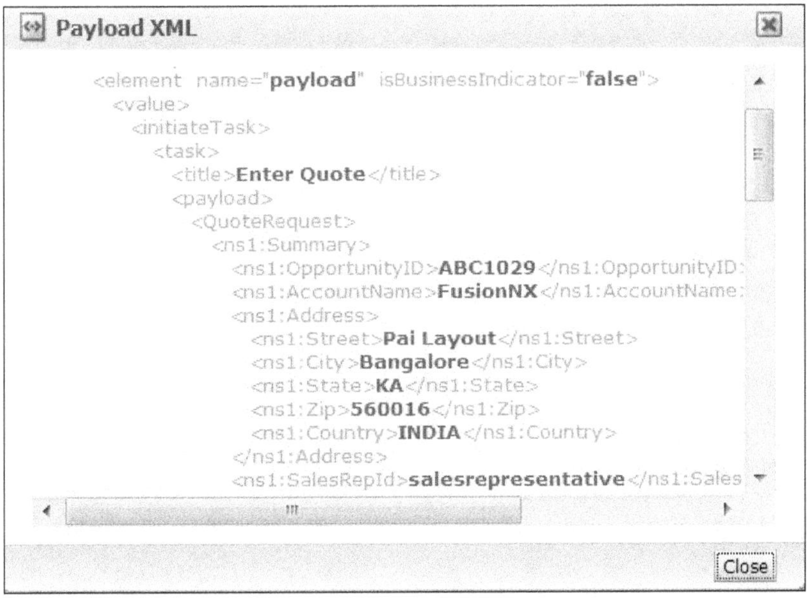

How it works...

These data values will help you understand why process instances aren't branching properly later in the process. Development mode makes many more of these data value links available, which is why it is so useful for debugging.

> When you have finished debugging your process and are ready to go into production, don't forget to set **Audit Trail** to **Production** mode to minimize the impact on performance.

4

Business Rules in the BPM Process

In this chapter you will see how developers use advance routing rules in Human Workflow. You will learn to use facts, functions, IF/THEN, Decision Tables, Bucketsets, rulesets, decision components, and other features of Oracle Business rules. You will learn to implement business rules using BPM Studio and will customize rules at runtime using BPM Composer.

This chapter will focus on implementation tasks such as the following:

- Extending Human Tasks
- Adding a Business object
- Creating a Dictionary
- Defining Global and Bucketsets
- Defining the rule: Decision Table
- Adding gateways and Human Tasks
- Defining the rule: IF/THEN
- Testing the rules

Introduction

Business rules focus on decision making and policies. Business rules can be included in cases where you need dynamic processing, Human Task routing, data validations, and so on. A Decision component, also called a Business rule service component, supports the use of Oracle Business rules in an SOA composite application.

Business rules are statements that describe business policies or key business decisions. For example, computations such as discounts or premiums, or say a business rule for a car rental company might specify that if the driver's age is less than twenty-one, the application must be denied. Business rules can perform calculations, such as calculating a credit score, and they can result in changes to the flow by setting values that determine how the process branches.

Rules follow either an **IF/THEN** structure or can be expressed in a spreadsheet-like format called Decision Tables. You write rules and Decision Tables in terms of fact types and properties. Fact types are often imported from the Java classes, XML schema, Oracle ADF Business Component view objects, or may be created in the Rule designer. Fact properties have a name, value, data type, and an optional Bucketset. A **Bucketset** splits the value space of the data type into buckets that can be used in Decision Tables, choice lists, and for design time validation.

A decision function provides a contract for invoking rules from Java or SOA (from an SOA composite application or from a BPEL process). The contract includes input fact types, rulesets to run, and output fact types. A ruleset is a group of rules and Decision Tables. A dictionary is a group of rulesets, facts, and Bucketsets. It is an XML file that stores the application's rulesets and the data model.

Business rules can be used as a Decision component or as a library in a Java application. A **Decision component** is a mechanism for publishing rules and rulesets as a reusable service that can be invoked from multiple business processes. A Decision component can be used within a SOA composite and wired to a BPEL component. It can be used within a SOA composite and used directly to run business rules, or be used with the dynamic routing capability of Mediator, or be used with the advanced routing rules in Human Workflow.

Some facts about Business rules are as follows:

- They use the Rete algorithm as the foundation of Oracle Business rules.
- This rule-based system consists of:
    - A **rule base** which contains the appropriate business policies or other knowledge encoded into IF/THEN rules and Decision Tables
    - **Working memory**, which contains the information that has been added to the system.
    - The **Inference Engine** Rules engine, which processes the rules and performs pattern-matching to determine which rules match the facts for a given run through the set of facts. Oracle Business Rule Engine is an inference-based engine. You just have to load the facts into Rule Memory and it will evaluate the outcome based on implicit inference.
- This rule-based system is a data-driven, forward-chaining system.
- Rules fire sequentially, not in parallel. Note that rule actions often change the set of rule activations, and thus, change the next rule to fire.

- They follow an inference cycle, that is, facts cause rules to fire and firing rules can create more facts, which in turn can fire more rules.

BPM Studio and Business Process Composer, both have Rule designers which you can use during development.

As you are moving ahead and implementing the process as a Process Developer, you will use BPM Studio. However, the Business Analyst and Process Analyst use Business Process Composer. Whatever the tool you use, business rules are deployed to the business rules MDS, which is a data store that interacts with the business Rules engine at runtime.

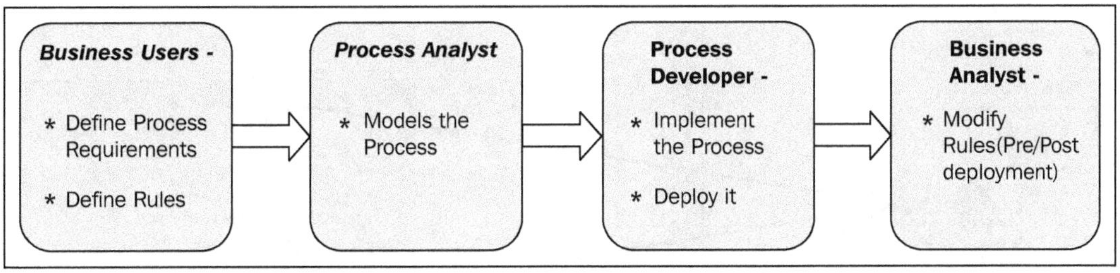

You modeled the process, as a Process Analyst, in *Chapter 1, Process Modeling*, and as Process Developer, you implemented the process in *Chapter 2, Process Implementation* and deployed the process in *Chapter 3, Process Deployment and Testing*. There are cases when you need to implement rules in the process. Let's say you want to check if a customer is a new customer or an old customer, and if he/she is a new customer you want management approval. Or consider a new customer who has bought a quantity greater than 100, and you can approve a 10% discount to the customer. Such rules can be implemented in processes. However, as you use rules, they become dynamic and one can change those rules at any time without bringing changes in the process (application code) itself. Separating the business rules from application code allows business analysts to change business policies quickly, with graphical tools. The Rules engine evaluates the business rules and returns decisions or facts that are then used in the business process.

You can use Business rules in BPM in the following areas:

- As a component in the BPMN process
- In the BPM Workspace for user-defined task management and vacation rules
- In Human Workflow to identify the proper recipient for a task assignment
- For dynamic service binding in the composite

Once the process is deployed and running, through Business Process Composer, users can read and make changes to Business rules. When they commit those changes, they take effect immediately, without taking the process offline.

Extending Human Tasks

Remember, you have created one Human Task, **ApproveQuote.task**, and have used it for three user activities: **Business Analyst Review**, **Approve Deal**, and **Approve Terms**.

As you are going to bring many changes to the Human Task, and create new tasks and rules in this chapter and next the chapter too, you will create separate Human Tasks and their forms for **Business Analyst Review** and **Approve terms**. **Approve Deal** will continue to use the same **ApproveQuote.task** form.

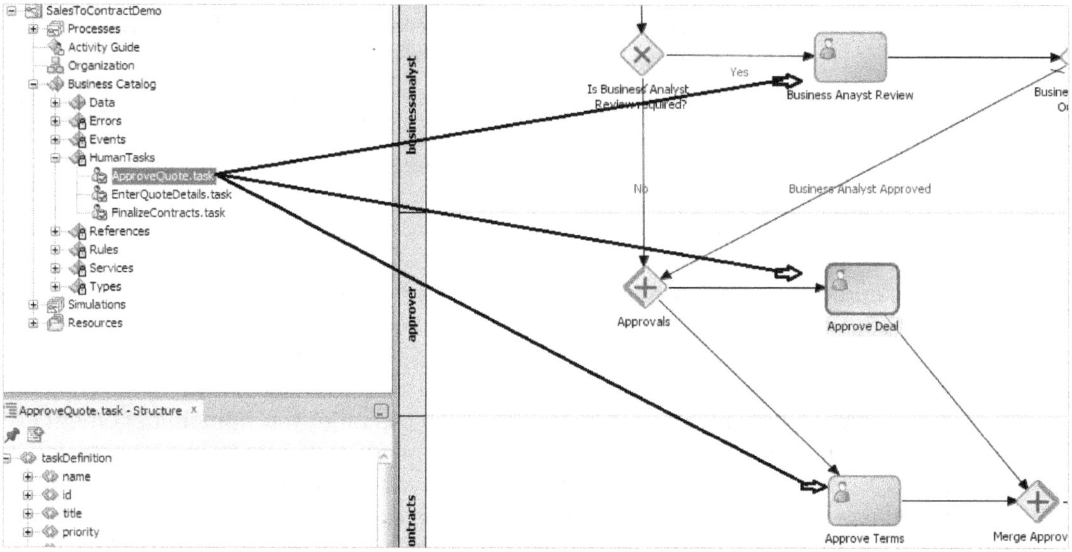

How to do it...

In this section, you will generate a user interface for the Human Tasks, as follows:

1. Start Oracle JDeveloper, select **Default Role**, and click **OK**.
2. In the BPM navigator, click on the process **SalesToContract**. This will open the process flow in the design area.
3. Right-click the task **Business Analyst Review** and select **Properties**.
4. In the **Properties** dialog, go to the **Implementation** tab.
5. Click on the green plus (**+**) icon to the right of Human Task, to **Create Human Task**.
6. Enter Human Task details, as shown in the following screenshot. Add **quote** as a parameter to the task.

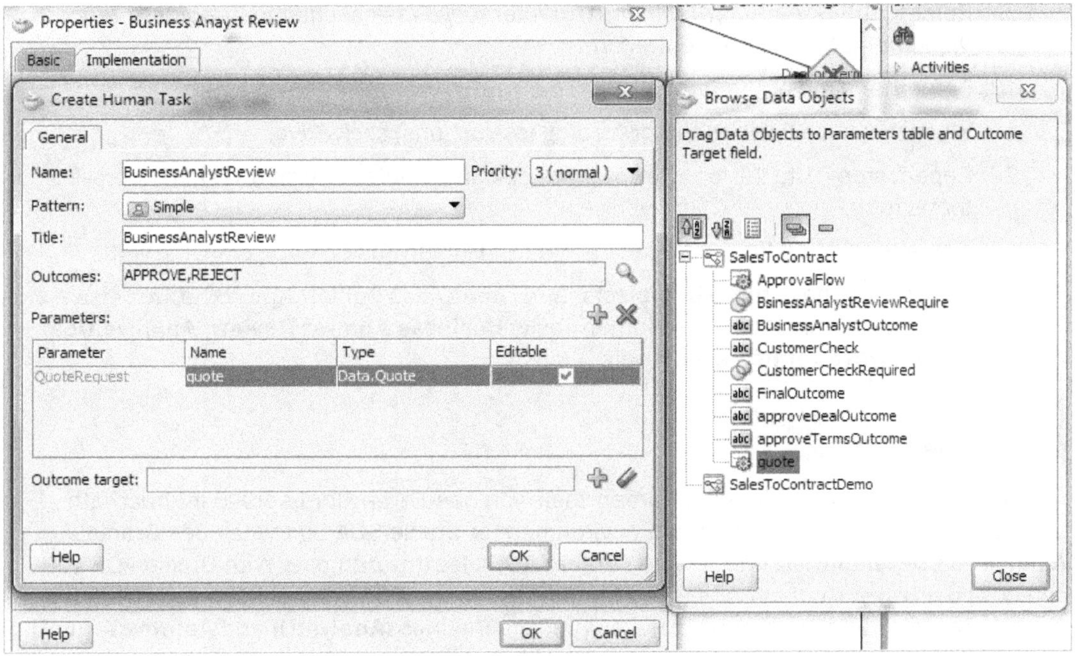

7. This will create a task **BusinessAnalystReview**, which you can verify from **BPM Project navigator | Business Catalog | Human Task**.
8. Click on the `.task` file and click **Create Form | Auto generate Task Form**, to generate ADF UI for the Human Task.

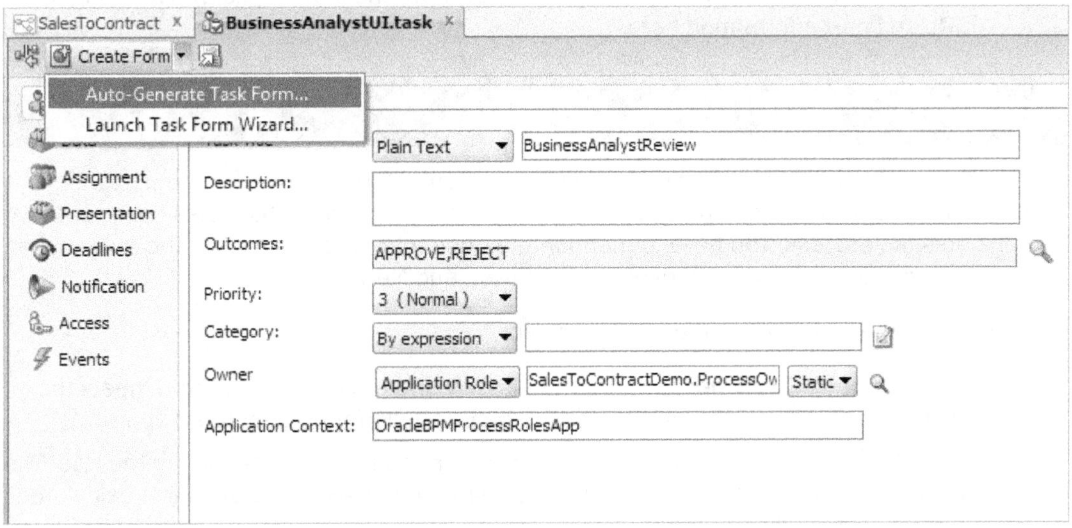

9. Refer to the *Generating Task form for Interactive task* section in *Chapter 2, Process Implementation*, to create the form.
10. Enter the name of the form as `BusinessAnalystUI`.
11. When you have finished the preceding instructions, click **Save**.
12. Repeat steps 1 to 11 for `Approve Terms` and create a Human Task to approve terms for it.
13. Name the ADF UI for the `Approve Terms` Human Task as `ApproveTermsUI`.
14. You will now have three UI projects: `BusinessAnalystUI`, `ApproveQuoteUI`, `ApproveTermsUI`, for the Human Tasks **Business Analyst Review**, **Approve Deal** and **Approve Terms**, respectively.

How it works...

As your SOA Composite includes a Human Task, you need a way for users to interact with the task. The integrated development environment of Oracle SOA Suite includes **Oracle Application Development Framework** (**Oracle ADF**), for this purpose. With Oracle ADF, you can design a task form that depicts the human task in the SOA composite. If you check the project navigator, under the newly created projects **BusinessAnalystUI** and **ApproveTermsUI**, you can find the following:

- The task form generated is a Java Server Page XML (`.jspx`) file.
- A `hwtaskflow.xml` file is created to capture the details on connecting with the service engine. By default, it uses remote EJB to connect to the workflow server.The Oracle SOA server URL and port are automatically determined by using the WebLogic runtime server MBeans. However, you can override these by explicitly specifying the URL and port information here.

Adding a Business object

Let's understand how rules are defined. You have implemented the `SalesToContract` process for quote fulfillment. You have quote data to be entered while the sales representative user initiates the process. You have to mention the Customer Type while filling the quote data. Customers are categorized as—Premium, Gold, Silver, and New.

Business Users have defined some rules, such as:

- **Rule 1, Check Customer**: If a customer is new and the quantity entered meets the defined range of values, the process will move ahead for management approval.

  Level 1 and Level 2 approval in the management chain is also defined in the rule. The level of management approval is defined by the rule itself. The discount is calculated in the rule, based on quantity.

- **Rule 2, Check Discount**: If the discount offered to a customer is greater than the specified threshold value, and if it's a Premium customer, then Business Analyst Review is not required.
- However, if it's not a Premium customer, then a `Business Analyst Review` is required.

Have a look at Rule 1, Check Customer. You need to have a Business object to hold values of Level 1 and Level 2 flags, level details, modified discount, and so on.

Look at `Quote.xsd`, which you have used for the implementation of the process. You can find the **ApprovalFlow** element of the complex type **ApprovalFlowType**, as shown in the following screenshot:

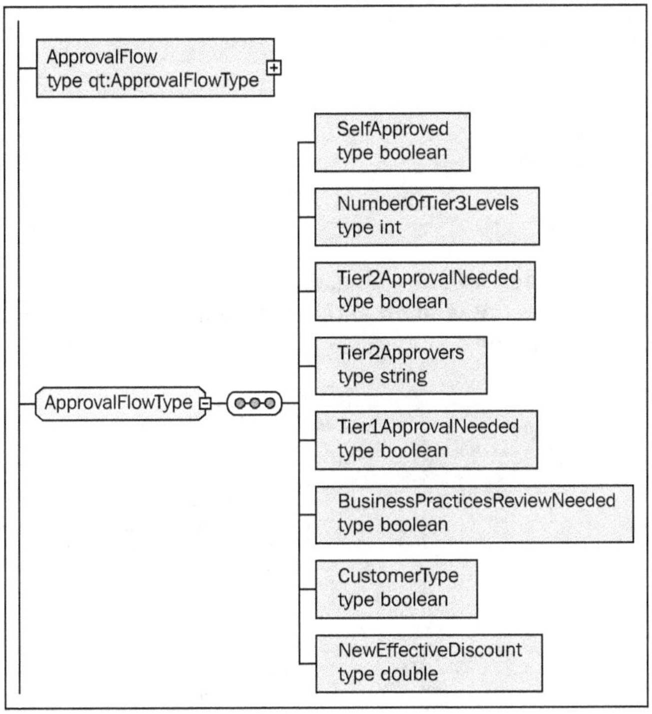

You will add this Business object to the process.

How to do it...

In this section, you will deal with the creation of Business objects:

1. Start Oracle JDeveloper, select **Default Role**, and click **OK**.
2. Go to **BPM Project navigator | Project | Business Catalog**.

3. Right-click **Data Module | New** and select **Business Object**.

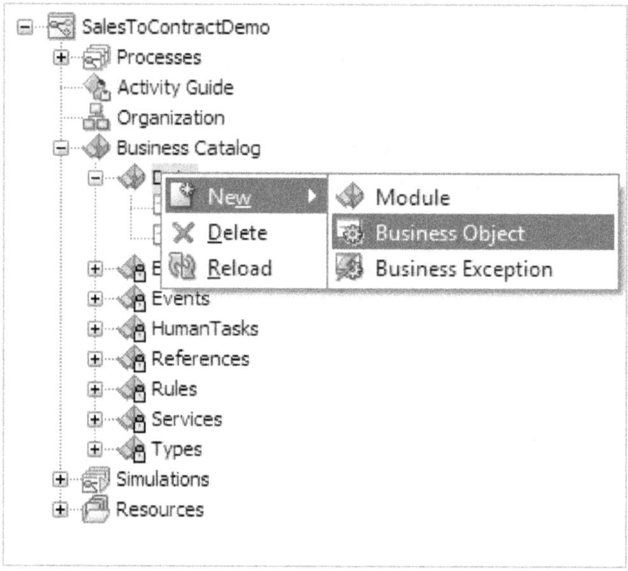

4. In the **Create Business Object** dialog, enter the Business object name as `ApprovalFlow`, check **Based on external schema**, and select **ApprovalFlow** from **Quote.xsd** schema:

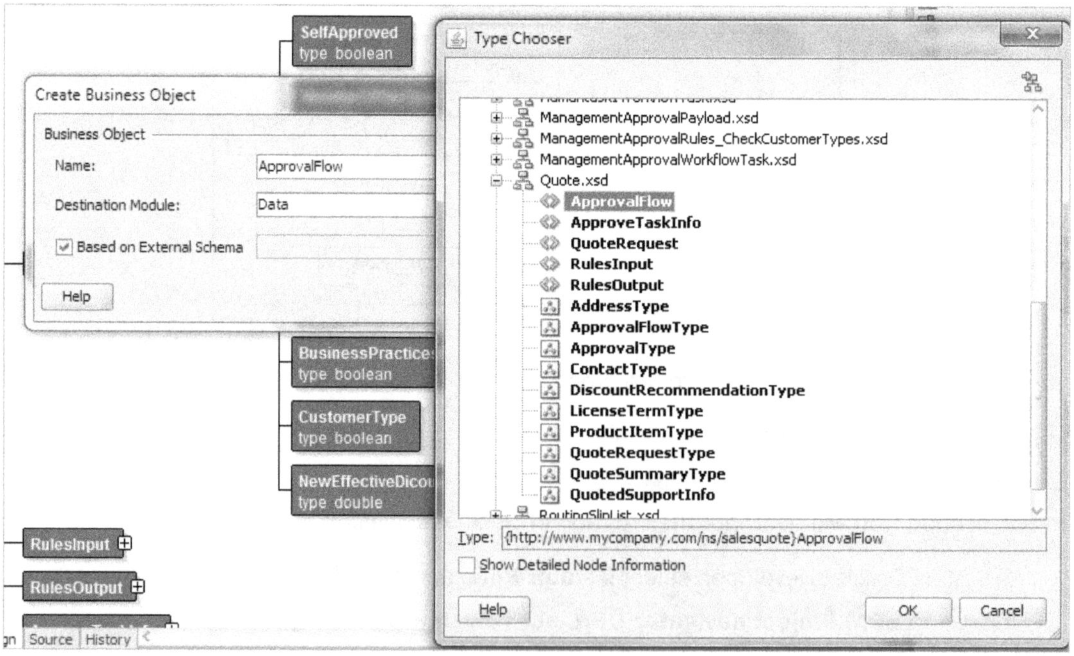

5. Click on the process name in the Application navigator. You can find a structure window in the lower-left corner of JDeveloper. You have a Business object created. Let's create a Process Data object based on this Business object.
6. In the **Structure** window, right-click **Process Data object** and select **New**.
7. In the **Create Data Object** dialog, enter name of process Data object as `ApprovalFlow`, select **Type** as **Component**, and select **ApprovalFlow** as the component.

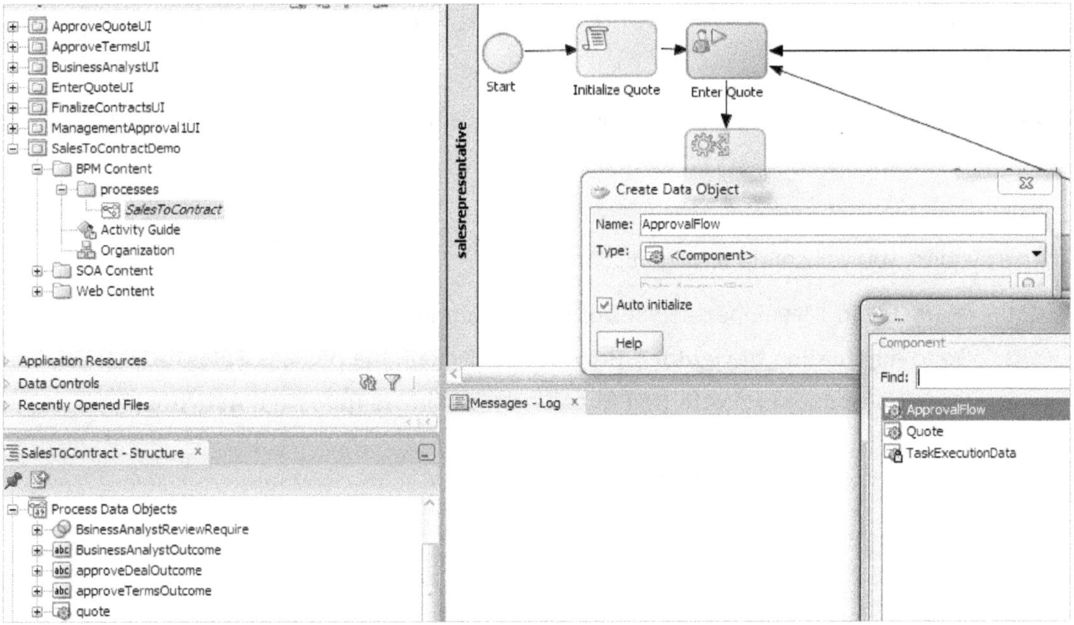

8. When finished, **Save**.

How it works...

When you implement business rules, such as **Check Customer** and **Discount Check**, you will use the Business and Process objects as output facts. In the Rule designer, you make Business objects and their methods known to Oracle Business rules, using fact types that are part of a data model. You can create fact types and Bucketsets before you create rules. The fact that you have created just now is an XML fact, as it's imported from existing sources by specifying XML Schema (`Quote.xsd`).

In Oracle Business rules, facts that you can run against the rules are Data objects that have been asserted. Each object instance corresponds to a single fact. Elements and types defined in XML Schema can be imported into the data model so that instances of types can be created, asserted, modified, and retracted by rules.

Creating a dictionary

A **dictionary** is an Oracle Business rules container for facts, functions, globals, Bucketsets, links, decision functions, and rulesets. A dictionary is an XML file that stores the application's rulesets and the Data model. Dictionaries can link to other dictionaries. Oracle JDeveloper creates an Oracle Business rules dictionary in a "rules" file.

> You can create as many dictionaries as you need. A dictionary may contain any number of rulesets.

Rules dictionaries are use to hold rule facts, functions, tables, and other components.

How to do it...

In this section, you will create a rules dictionary:

1. Start Oracle JDeveloper, select **Default Role**, and click **OK**.
2. Go to **Application Navigator | Project** and click on the process **SalesToContract**.
3. Go to **Component Palette | BPM** and click **Business Rule** from **Activities**.

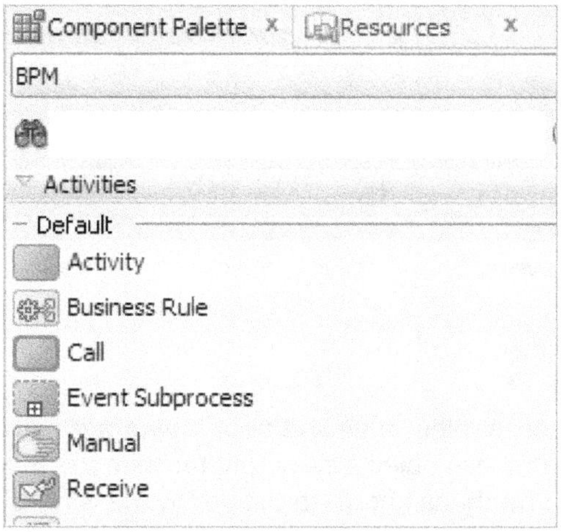

4. Click on the **salesrepresentative** swimlane, between **Enter Quote** user task and **Is Business Analyst Review Required?** gateway.

5. You will find the **BusinessRuleTask | Properties** dialog:

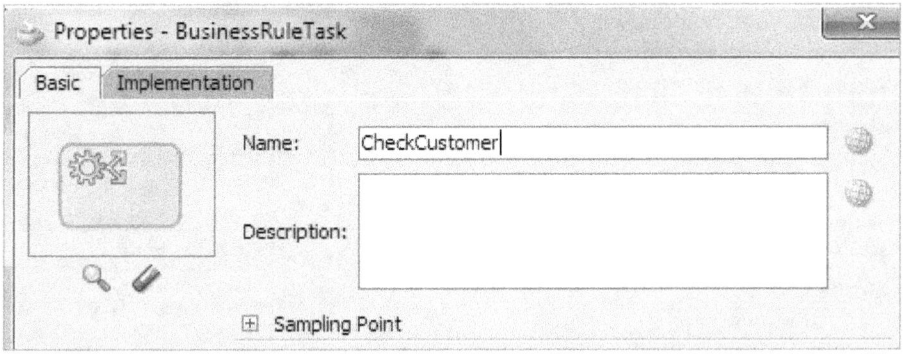

6. Enter the Business Rule Task name as `CheckCustomer`.
7. Click on the **Implementation** tab and click the green plus (**+**) icon to add a Business Rule.
8. You will find that a **Create business Rule** dialog opens up.
9. Go to the **General** tab of the dialog and enter rule **Name** `CheckCustomer`.
10. In the input and output section, click on the green plus (**+**) icon to add input and output Data objects:

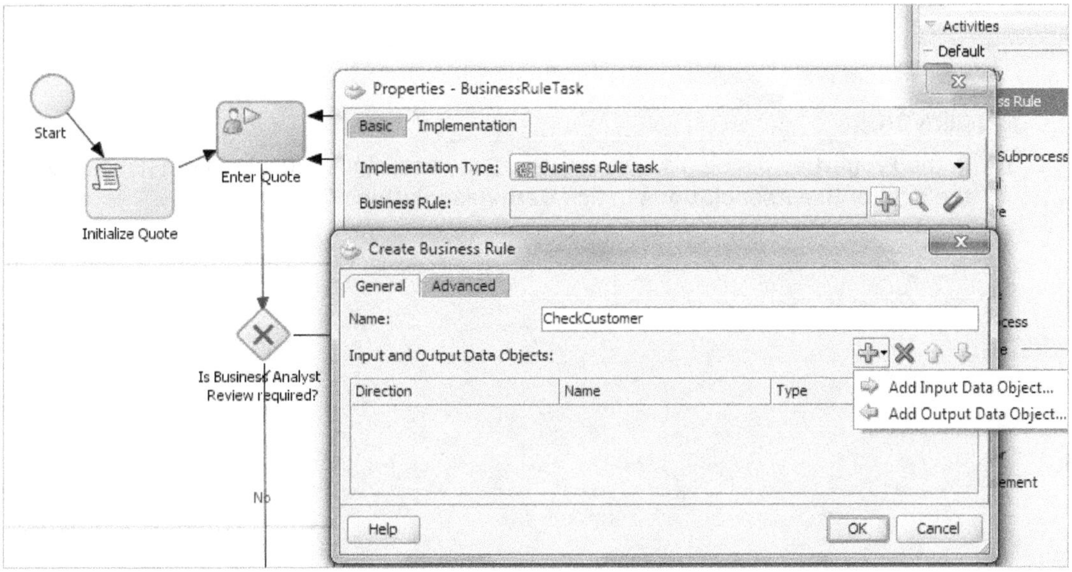

11. Click **Input Data Object** and browse for the object **quote**, and click **Output Data Object** and browse for the object **ApprovalFlow**, as the input and output of the Business rule, respectively:

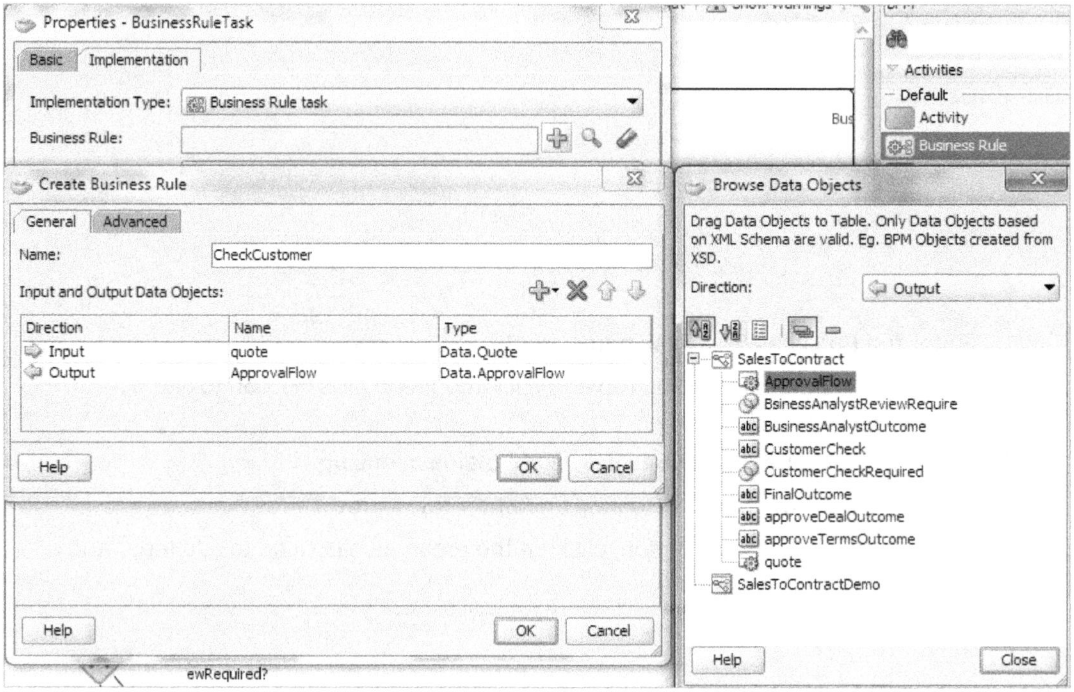

12. Click **OK**.
13. In the **Properties** dialog, you will create a Data association. Click on the pencil icon to the right of **Use Associations** to tick **Data Associations**.

14. You can find the objects `quote` and `ApprovalFlow` as input and output for the **CustomerCheck** rule.

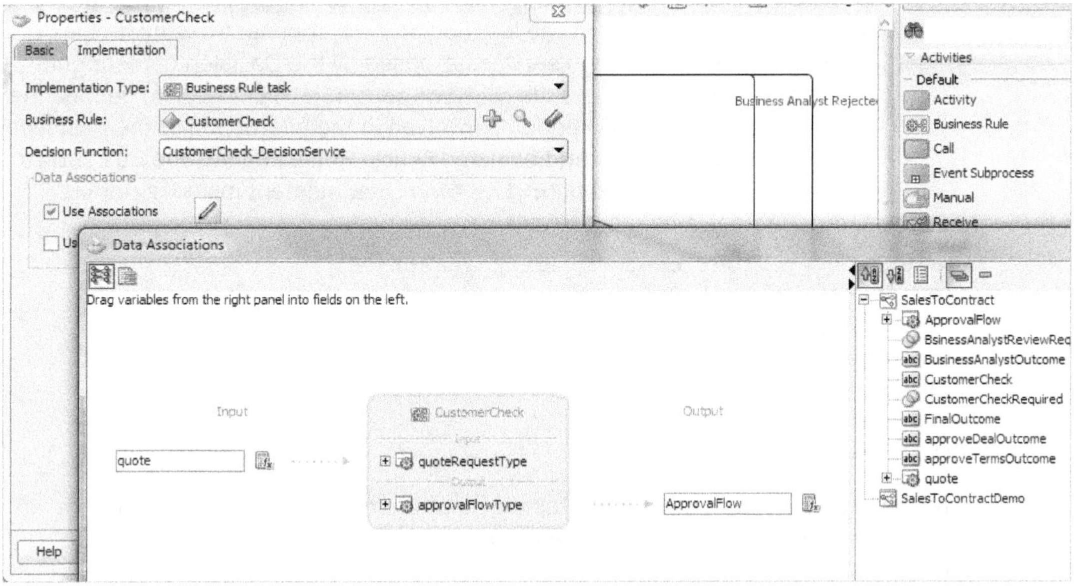

15. When finished, **Save**.
16. Go to BPM **Project navigator | Business Catalog | Rules**, and you can find a `CheckCustomer.rules` file created. This is called a rules dictionary.

> Oracle Business Rule cannot work with simple Data objects. Even if we have to use a Simple type, it needs to wrapped inside a complex element of a schema.

How it works...

Rulesets are accessed via:

- Rulesets that are defined as a service are accessed via API or Web services.
- Alternatively, the rules dictionary can be a component in the BPMN composite application and the rulesets accessed directly by the BPMN process.

When you create a dictionary, and if you go to the Application navigator, you can find that the following Decision component defining files are created:

- **Decision Service Metadata file** (`.decs`): The business rule metadata file provides information about the location of the component business rules dictionary and the Decision services exposed by the Decision component. The business rule metadata file (`business_rule_name.decs`) defines the contract between the components involved in the interaction of the business rule with the design time and backend Oracle Rules Engine. The `business_rule_name.decs` file rule `EngineProvider` element includes details about the rules dictionary to use:

```
<ruleEngineProvider name="OracleRulesSDK"
provider="Oracle_11.0.0.0.0">
<repository type="SCA-Archive">
<path>SalesToContractDemo/oracle/rules/salestocontractdemo/
CheckCustomer.rules</path>
</repository>
</ruleEngineProvider>
```

A repository-type SCA archive indicates that that the rules dictionary is located in the service component architecture archive. The path is relative and interpreted differently by the following:

- **Design time**: Metadata service **(**MDS**)** APIs open the rules dictionary. Therefore, the full path to the dictionary is as follows:

  Oramds:`/SalesToContractComposite/oracle/rules/CheckCustomer.rules`

  Runtime (business rule service engine): The business rule service engine uses the Oracle Business rules SDK Rule Repository API to open the rules dictionary located in MDS. The composite name prefix, is removed from the path and the metadata manager assumes the existence of `oracle/rules/CheckCustomer.rules`, relative to the composite home directory.

  A decision service is a web service (or SOA) enabler of business rules. It is a service in the sense of a Web service, thus opening the world of business rules to service-oriented architectures (SOA).

- **SCA ComponentType Files** (`.component`): An SCA `business_rule_name.component` type file is included with each Decision component. This file lists the services exposed by the business rules service component.

- **Composite.xml files**: They also have entries for decision components. An entry in `composite.xml` is created for a Decision component. The business rules service engine uses the information from this implementation type to process requests for the Service Engine. From an SCA perspective, a Decision component is a new implementation type.

```
<component name="CheckCustomer">
<implementation.decisionsrc="CheckCustomer.decs"/>
</component>
```

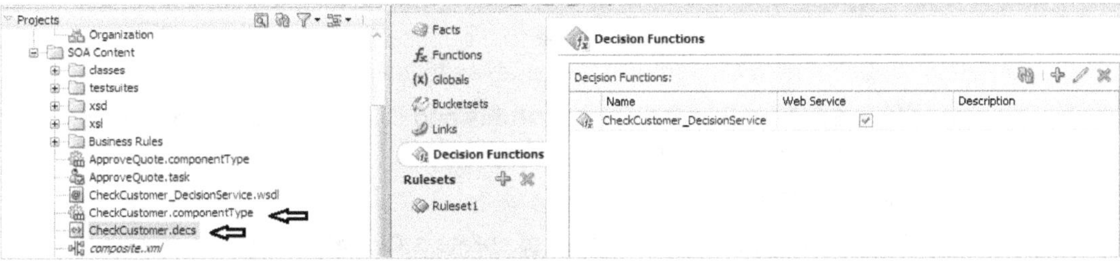

Defining Globals and Bucketsets

This rule has a `QuoteRequest` as an input fact. This rule will check for the condition of `Customer Type` and `Item Quality`, and based on these conditions, chain of management approval, level of management approval, and discount offered will be decided.

For all the cases in the `CheckCustomer` rule, your condition will keep a check on the Customer Type. For example in first case, if the `Input quote` customer type is `New` and `Quality` is in the range of `0` to `10` then `EffectiveDiscount` will have a 10% increment and others values will be set as follows:

```
If Quote.CustomerType == New and Quote.Quantity Is Between 0-10
Then
    Set ApprovalFlow.CustomerType  = True
    Set ApprovalFlow.newEffectiveDiscount = Quote.EffectiveDiscount+10
    Set ApprovalFlow..Number of Level for approval = 0
    Set ApprovalFlow.Tier1ApprovalNeeded = False
    Set ApprovalFlow.Tier2ApprovalNeeded = False
```

You can have conditions which that are evaluated to give a fixed value (`New` as Customer Type) and/or a range of values. For a fixed value, you can define Globals, and for ranges you will define Bucketsets.

As you will keep evaluating the conditions to a fixed value, you will create a for `Customer Type` of the type `Global` with value `New`. And, as your rule will evaluate to range values too, you will create a Bucketset to be used in rule.

How to do it...

In this section, we will define **Globals**, as follows:

1. Fill in the following values in the **Globals** dialog:

Global Name	Type	Value	Final
`CustomerType`	String	New	Checked

2. Oracle Business Rules a Global is similar to a public static variable in Java. You will create a Global to hold Customer Type value, as follows:
    - Go to **BPM Project Navigator | Rules** and click **CheckCustomer.rules**. This will open **rule designer2**.
    - Click on **Globals** in Rule Designer3.
    - Click on the green plus icon (**+**) to create a **Global4**.
    - Enter details as described in the preceding table. In the **Value** field, click the Expression Builder icon to enter an expression and enter the value, `New`. Checking the option **Final** means the Global is Non-modifiable.

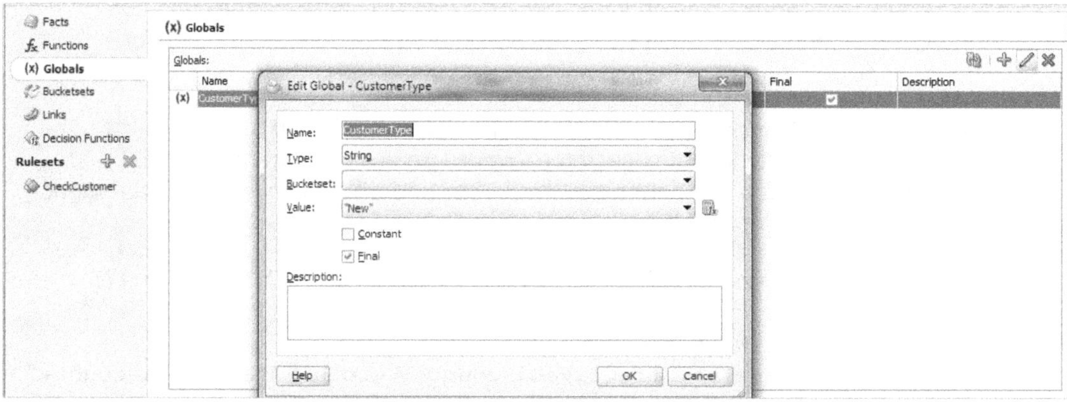

    - When done, click **OK**.
3. When you have finished this, click **Save**.
4. When you select **Final**, this specifies that you can use the Globals in a test in a rule (a non-final Global cannot be used in a test in a rule). When you select **Final**, this specifies that the global is initialized one time at runtime and cannot be changed.

Next, we define Bucketsets, as follows:

Bucketsets are created to define a list of values or a list of value ranges to limit the acceptable set of values for a fact or a property of a fact in Oracle Business rules. Bucketsets can be defined as Global Bucketsets and local Bucketsets. Global allows reuse, where a Bucketset is named and stored in the data model, and Local is specified when you define a Decision Table and only applies to one condition expression.

1. Go to the Rule designer for `CheckCustomer.rules` and select the **Bucketsets** navigation tab.
2. Click the green plus (**+**) icon to create Bucketsets and select **List of ranges**:

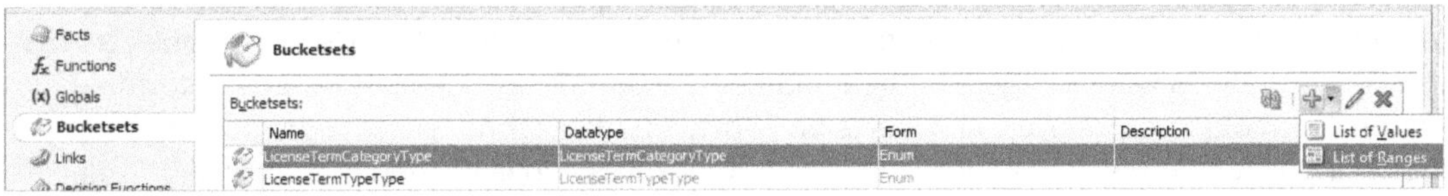

3. This will open the **Edit Bucketset** dialog.
4. Enter `QuantityBucket` as the Bucketset **Name** and `double` as the **Data Type**.
5. Click the "Add Bucket" icon repeatedly (three times) to add the number of buckets you need in the Bucketset, as shown in the following screenshot:

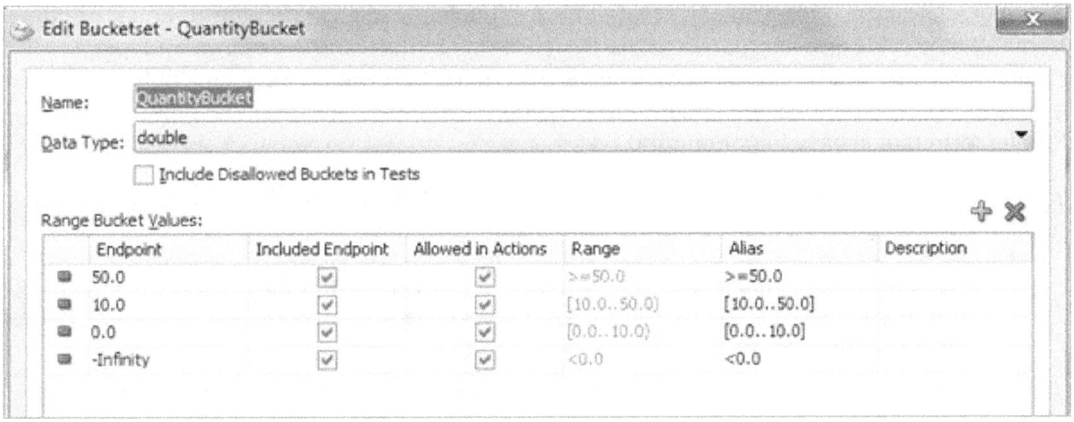

6. You will add three buckets:
    - Between 0 and 10
    - Between 10 and 50
    - Greater than 50

And by default, you will get a negative Infinity (**-Infinity**) bucket, which is less than 0. In the **Included Endpoint** field, check the checkbox to include the bucket endpoint. In the **Allowed in Actions** field, select the checkbox as appropriate, to include the bucket in the Bucketset allowable values.

7. Click **OK**.
8. When you have finished these steps, **Save**.

How it works...

When you add a bucket to a **List of Ranges** Bucketset, the value is calculated based on the currently selected bucket value and the next highest bucket value. When you change the endpoint value, the value is automatically sorted in the Bucketset. In a Decision Table, a Bucketset defines value ranges, in the condition section. The Bucketset ranges determine, for each condition expression in a Decision Table, whether it has two or more possibilities. Using a Bucketset, each possibility in a condition expression is divided into groups or ranges where a cell specifies one Bucket of values from the Bucketset (or possibly multiple Buckets of values per cell).

Defining the Rule: Decision Table

There are two ways you can define rules—either by using IF/THEN or by using Decision Tables. By using a Decision Table, you can create and use business rules in an easy-to-understand format that provides an alternative to the IF/THEN rule format, and it displays multiple related rules in a single spreadsheet-style view. In Rules Designer, a Decision Table presents a collection of related business rules with condition rows, rules, and actions, presented in a tabular form that is easy to understand.

You will use Decision Table for Check Customer rules and use if-then-else for DiscountCheck rules. For the Check Customer rule, you have following scenario :

- First case, if the input `Quote.customer type` is `New` and `Quantity` is in the range of `0` to `10` , then `Effective Discount` will have a 10% increment and other values will be set as follows:

  If `Quote.CustomerType` == `New` and `Quote.Quantity` is between 0-10, then

  ```
  Set ApprovalFlow.CustomerType  = True
  Set ApprovalFlow.newEffectiveDiscount = Quote.
  EffectiveDiscount+10
  Set ApprovalFlow..Number of Level for approval = 0
  Set ApprovalFlow.Tier1ApprovalNeeded = False
  Set ApprovalFlow.Tier2ApprovalNeeded = False
  ```

- Second case, if the input, `Quote.customer type` is `New` and `Quote.Quantity` is in the range of `10` to `50` , then `Effective Discount` will have a 10% increment and other values will be set as follows:

```
Set ApprovalFlow.CustomerType  = True
Set ApprovalFlow.newEffectiveDiscount = Quote.
EffectiveDiscount+10
Set ApprovalFlow..Number of Level for approval = 1
Set ApprovalFlow.Tier1ApprovalNeeded = False
Set ApprovalFlow.Tier2ApprovalNeeded = False
```

- Third case, if the input, `Quote.customer type` is `New` and `Quantity` is greater than `50`, `Effective Discount` will have a 15% increment and other values will be set as follows:

  If `Quote.CustomerType` == `New` and `Quote.Quantity` is between > 50, then

```
Set ApprovalFlow.CustomerType  = True
Set ApprovalFlow
.newEffectiveDiscount = Quote.EffectiveDiscount+15
Set ApprovalFlow..Number of Level for approval = 2
Set ApprovalFlow.Tier1ApprovalNeeded = False
Set ApprovalFlow.Tier2ApprovalNeeded = True
```

How to do it...

In this section, you will define the Decision Table.

I. Define Condition

1. Go to the Rule designer for `CheckCustomer.rules` and select **Rulesets | Ruleset1**.
2. Click on **Create Decision Table**, to create a Decision Table for this ruleset.

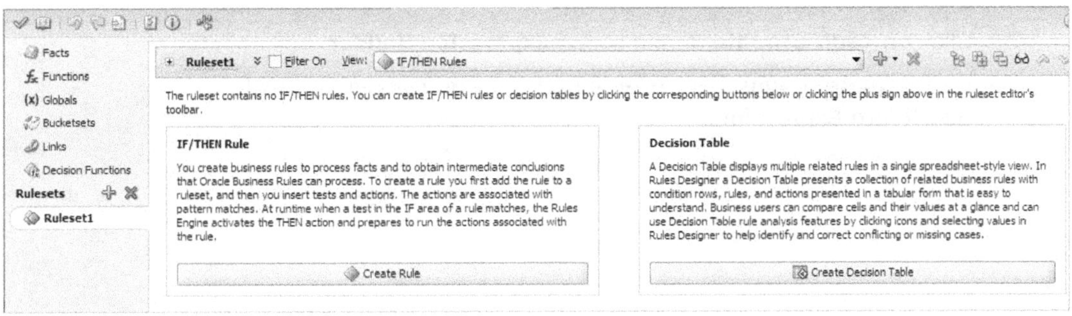

3. Give the name **CheckCustomer** to the ruleset and enter **NewCustomerQuantityCheckmatrix** as name of the Decision Table:

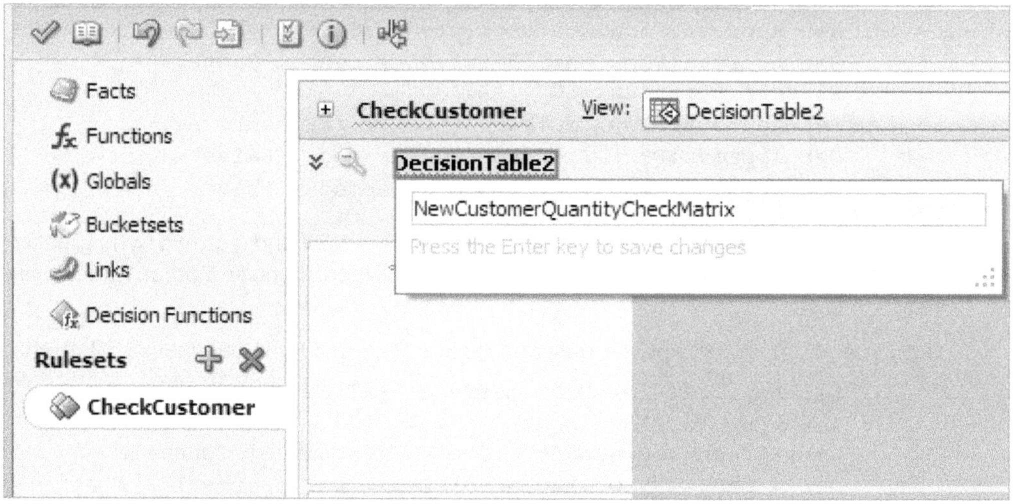

4. Click the green plus(**+**) icon and select **Condition** to create a condition:

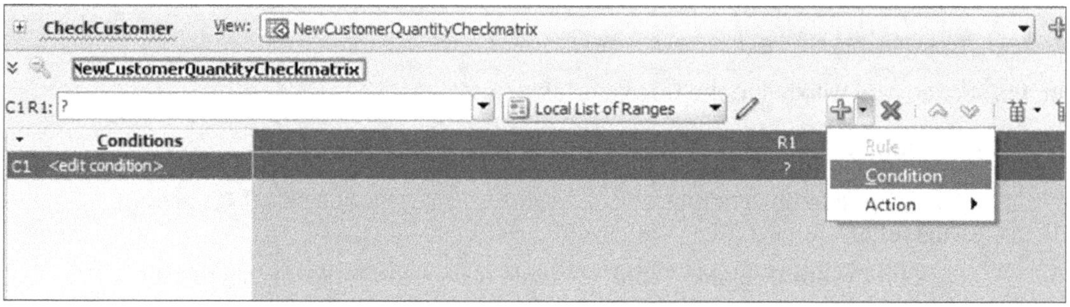

5. Click on **<edit condition>** and select **Expression Builder**.
6. Select **QuoteRequestType | Summary | customertype** and click **Insert Into Expression**.

7. Equate the expression with the **CustomerType** global which holds the value `New`.

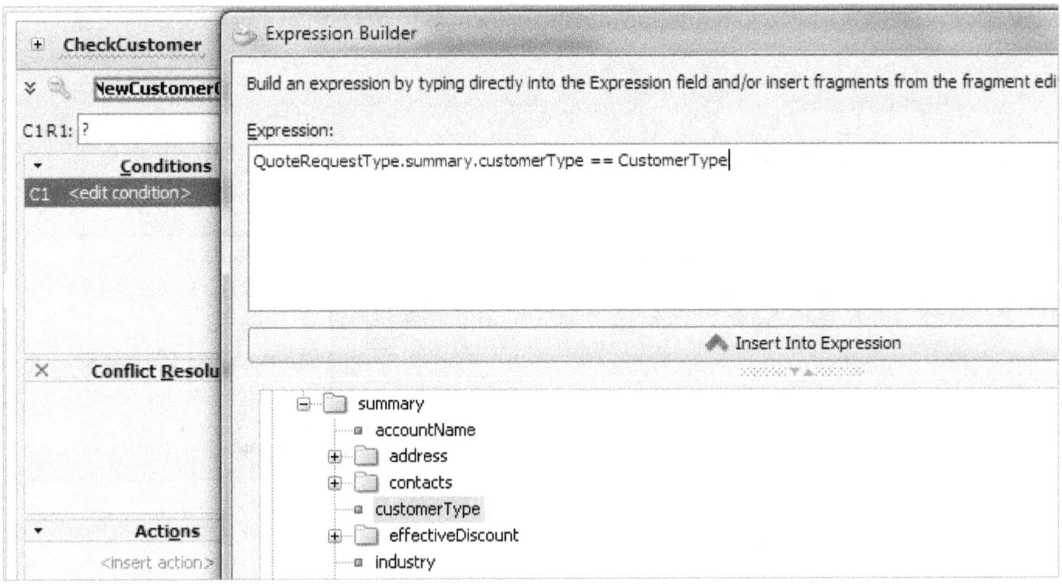

8. Click **OK**.
9. Click on the green plus (**+**) icon to add another condition to evaluate for quantity.
10. Click **Edit Condition**.
11. In the **Value Option**, select **ProductItemType | quantity**.

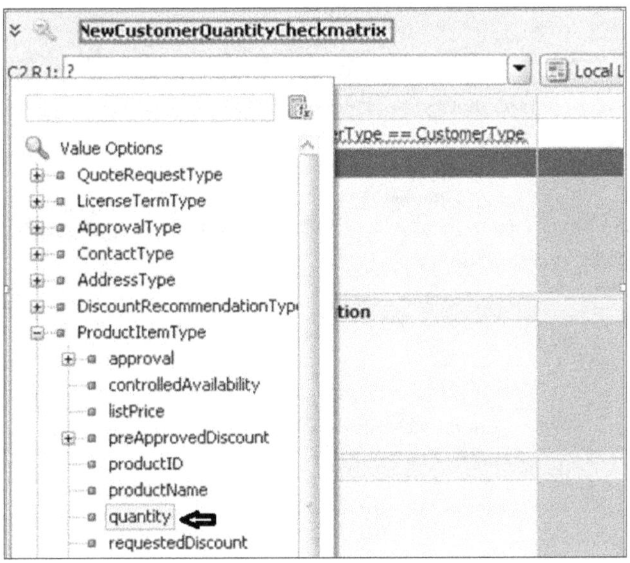

12. ProductitemType.quantityUnder this option, click on the **Local List of Ranges** pull-down menu, and select the Bucketset that you have created, **QuantityBucket**. The Conditions row requires a Bucketset from which to draw the values for each cell.

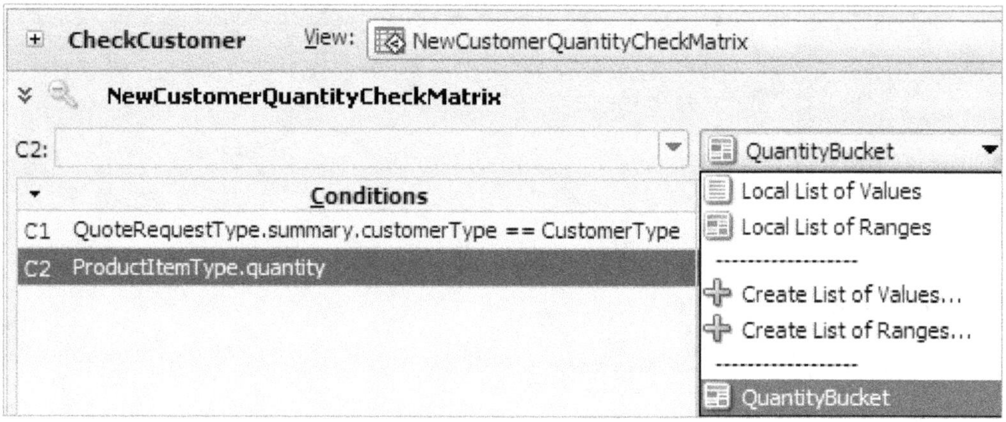

13. When finished, **Save**.

II. Define Rules

1. Click the green plus (**+**) icon and select **Rule**, to create a condition.
2. Click on the condition cell in the **R1** Rule column for the Customer Type row and you can find a pop-up with the Boolean values.
3. Check **True** so that the rule is executed if **CustomerType** = **New** is true, and actions associated in the column of this rule will also get executed.

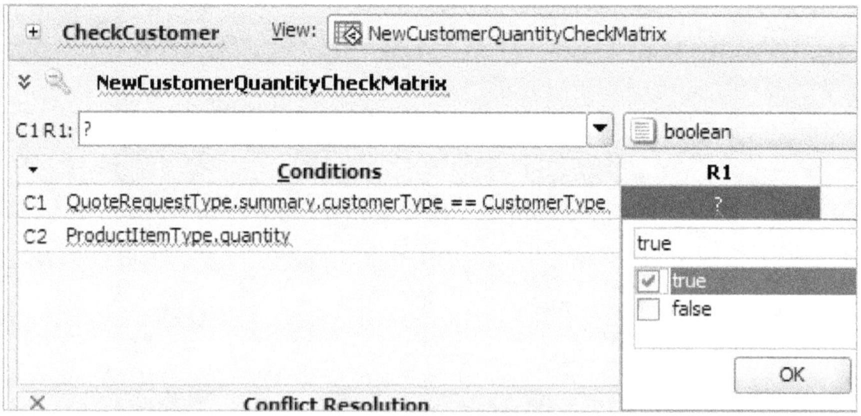

4. Similarly, click on the empty tab in the **R1** column for the Quantity row.
5. Check the range 0-10. This means if along with **CustomerType** = **New** is **True** and the quantity falls in this range, the R1 rule will get activated, and actions specified in the condition tab for this R1 rule column will get executed.

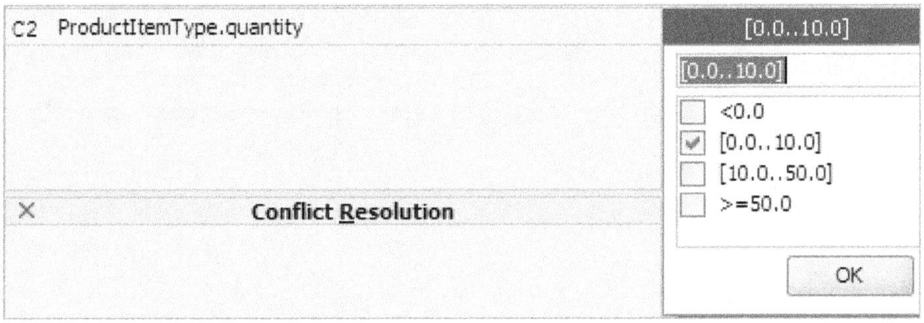

6. Repeat the preceding steps to create a Decision Rules table, as follows:

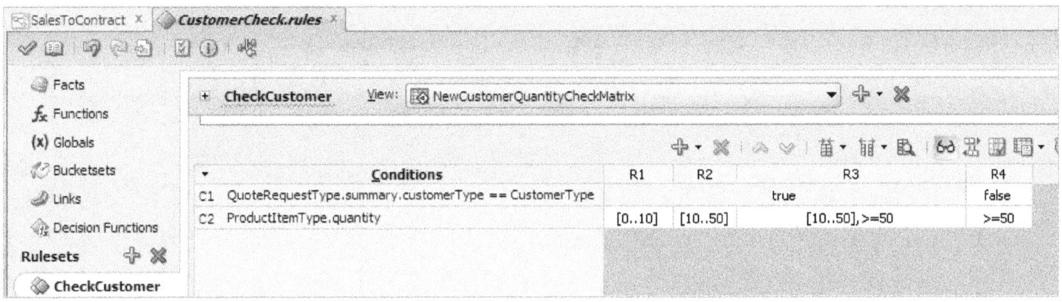

7. When finished, **Save**.

III. Add Actions

1. Click the green plus (**+**) icon and select **Action | Assert new**, to create actions.
2. Click on **Edit Actions**, and this will open **Action Editor**.

3. Chose **ApprovalFlowType**, and in **Properties**, check the properties you need. Let's take all of them.

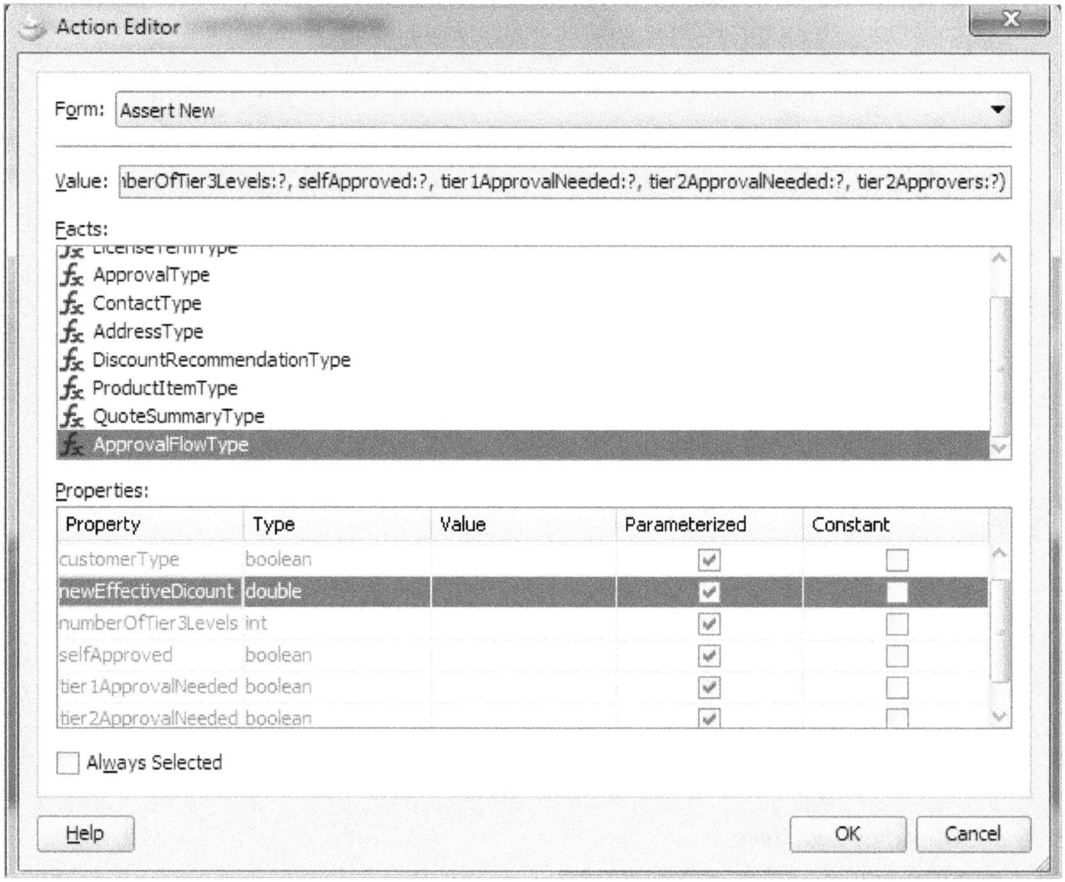

4. Enter a value in each action cell, as shown in the following screenshot:

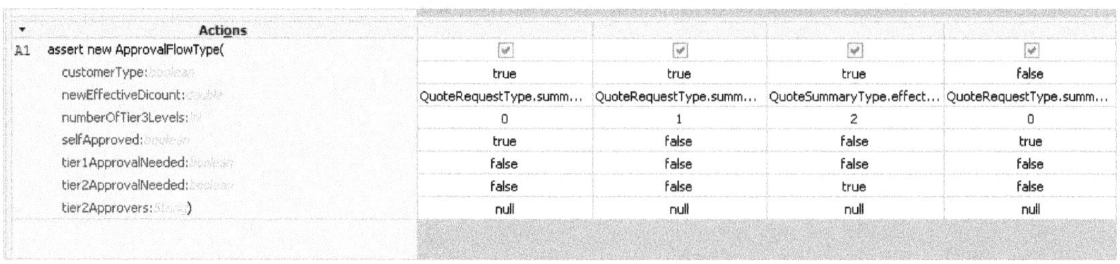

5. The values for the **Actions** cell **newEffectiveDiscount** are as follows:
   - **R1**: **QuoteRequestType.summary.effectiveDiscount+10**
   - **R2**: **QuoteRequestType.summary.effectiveDiscount+10**
   - **R3**: **QuoteRequestType.summary.effectiveDiscount+15**
   - **R4**: **QuoteRequestType.summary.effectiveDiscount+10**
6. When you have finished this, **Save**.
7. The final Rule designer with **Rules**, **Conditions** cell, and **Actions** cell entries, along with the pop-up conflicts, looks like the following screenshot:

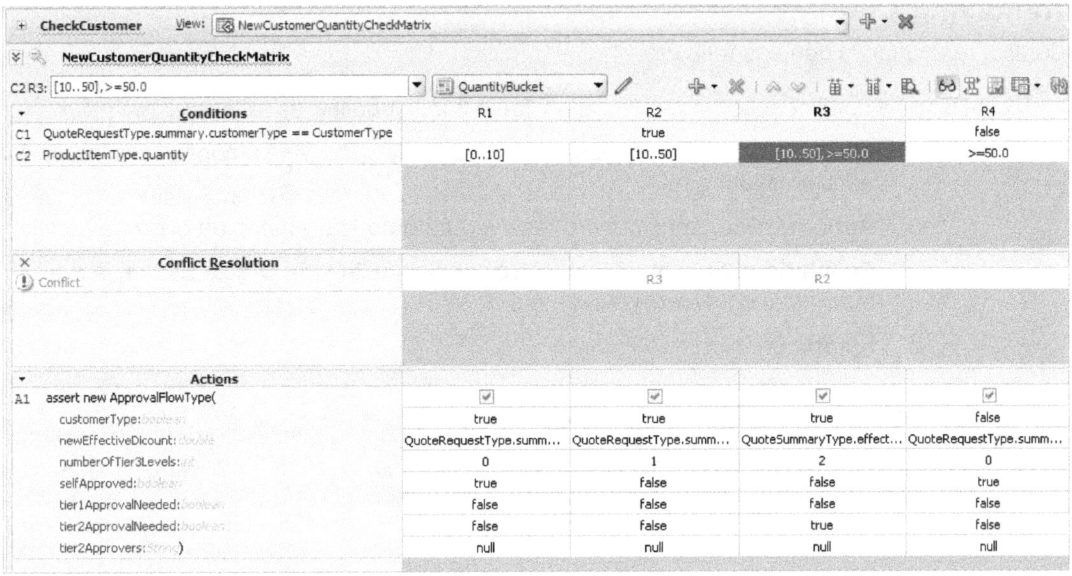

How it works...

At runtime, when facts match the **Conditions** cells, the Rules Engine prepares to run the actions associated with the rule.

Each condition row has a condition expression, and for each rule, a Condition cell. A condition expression is an expression that you build in Rules designer. The condition expression is often a fact property or a function result, but it can be any expression that has a type that can be associated with a Bucketset. Test expressions are often used. These expressions are associated with the built-in Bucketset.

Actions are associated with rules in a Decision Table. In an action, you can call a function, assert a new fact, retract a fact, or modify a fact. In the **Actions** area, the cells corresponding to an individual action for a rule are called **Action** cells. When you add multiple actions, the actions that you add in the **Actions** area are ordered; actions appearing in the higher rows run before actions in the following rows.

There's more...

Sometimes there may be conflicts in the rules in the Decision Table. Two rules conflict when they overlap and they have different actions. Two rules overlap when at least one of their condition cells has a bucket in common.

Rules designer finds conflicts and you can see the conflicts in the **Conflict Resolution** row in the Decision Table, when you click **Show Conflicts**. You can define conflict policy to handle and even resolve such conflicts.

Resolving Conflict

Conflict resolution is done as follows:

1. Define a conflict policy in the Decision Table conflict policy, as follows:
   - **Manual**: Conflicts are resolved by manually specifying a conflict resolution for each conflicting rule.
   - **Auto-override**: Conflicts are resolved automatically using an override conflict
   - **Resolution**: When possible, solve conflicts using the Oracle Business rules' automatic conflict resolution policies
   - **ignore**: Conflicts are ignored

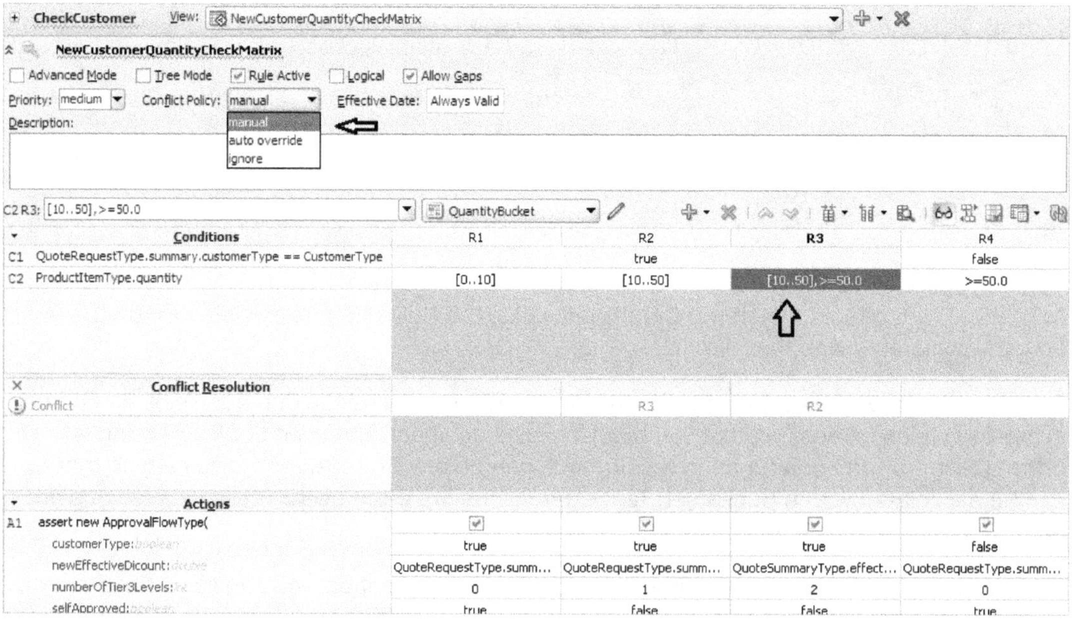

You can find that a couple of conflicts are listed in the **Conflict** section in the Rule designer.

2. Click **R3** and select one of the conflict resolution methods.
3. However, you will not follow any resolution, but will follow the strategy of **Change the Decision Table to remove an overlap**.

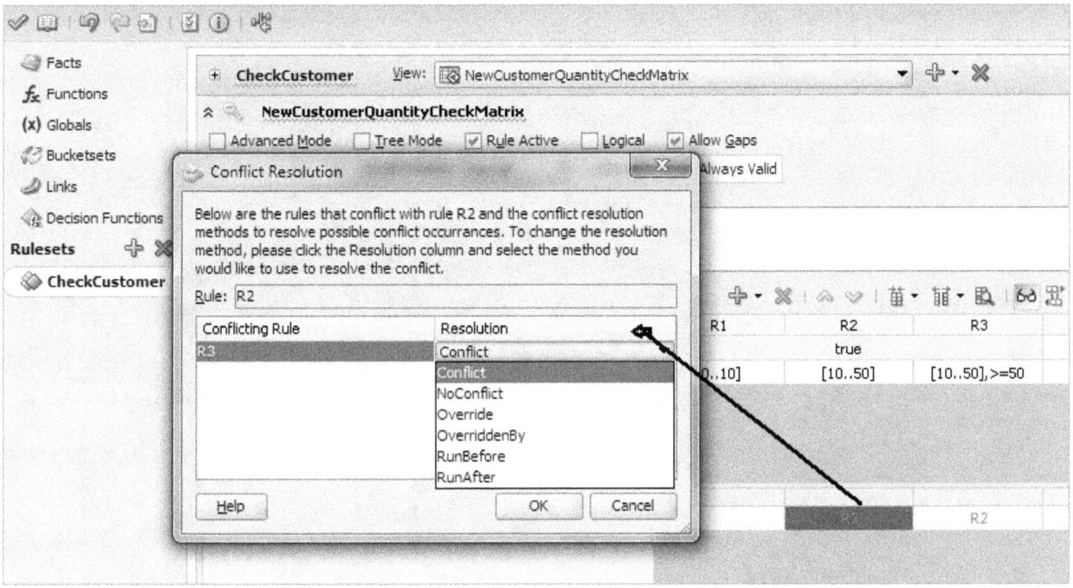

4. Click **Cancel** in the **Conflict Resolution** dialog and change the Decision Table to remove overlap.
5. Click the **R3** condition cell, uncheck the **[10..50]** range, and keep **>=50** checked.

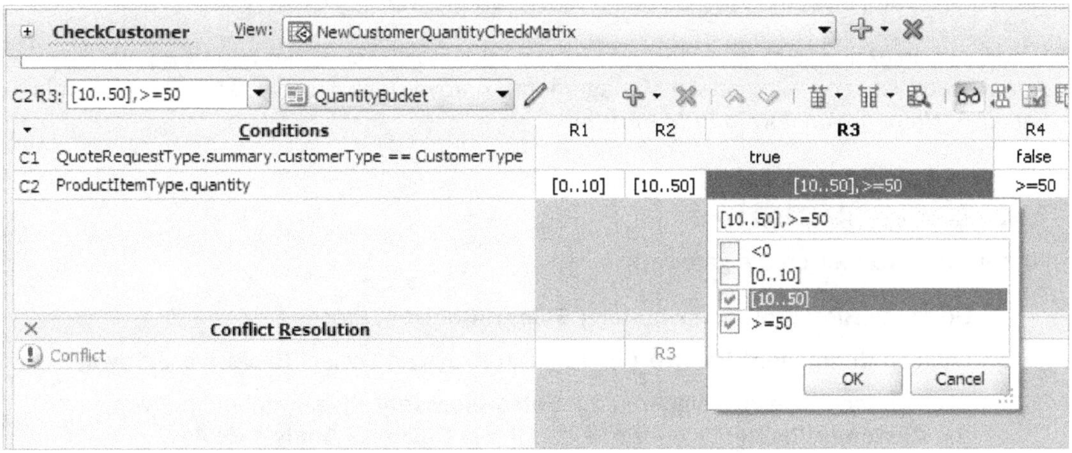

The Rule designer is created without conflict and with **Conditions** cell and **Actions** cell values.

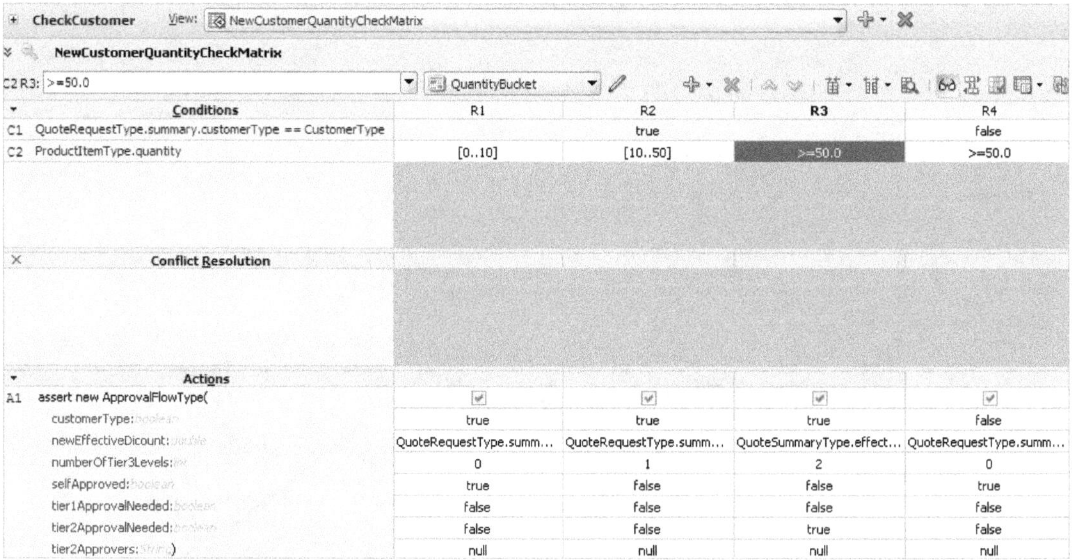

6. When finished, **Save**.

Adding gateways and Human Tasks

If `Customer Type` = `New`, then management approval is required, and the process token will pick the new path; else, the process token moves ahead with the existing path.

You will add an exclusive gateway for the process token to switch either to a new path or a non-new path. And you will model a Management Approval Task which you will implement in *Chapter 5, Human Workflow in BPM Process*.

How to do it...

In this section, you will create gateways:

1. Go to the **BPM project navigator | SalesToContract** process.
2. Click on **Component Palette | BPM | Gateways** and select **Exclusive Gateway**.
3. Click on the Process designer in the **SalesRepresentative** swimlane between the **CustomerCheck** business rule and the **Is Business Analyst Review Required?** gateway.

4. In the **Properties** dialog under the option **Enter Name** enter the value `CheckCustomerType`.
5. Click **OK**.
6. Make the sequence flow from the **CustomerCheck** rule to the **CheckCustomerType** gateway, and from there to the **Is Business Analyst Review required?** gateway.

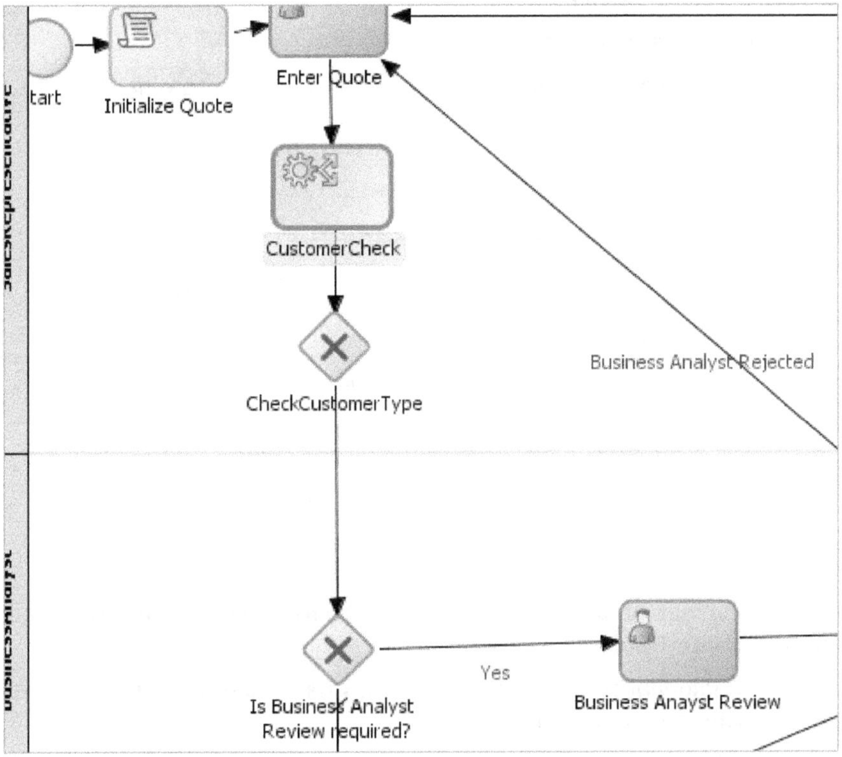

7. **Save**.
8. Click on **Activities** in the component palette and click **User Task**.
9. You know that if the Customer Type is **New**, then Process Token moves to a new Human Task that handles management approval.
10. Click on the `salesrepresentative` swimlane in front of check customer rule.
11. In the User Task properties, enter `ManagementApproval` as the name and click **OK**.
12. You will implement this Human task in *Chapter 5, Human Workflow in BPM Process*. However, for the time being, make a note of the following:
    - The outcome of this task will be **Approve** or **Reject**
    - The outcome of the **ManagementApproval** task goes to the Process Data object `'CustomerCheckOutcome'`

13. Click **Component Palette | BPM | Gateway** and select **Exclusive Gateway**.
14. In the **Properties** dialog, enter **CustomerCheckOutcome** as the name of this gateway.
15. Create a sequence flow from **CustomerCheck** rule to **ManagementApproval**.
16. In the **Properties** tab for sequence flow, enter the name **New** and **Condition | Simple Exp** as

    ApprovalFlow.customerType== true.
17. Remember this: **ApprovalFlow.customerType** values are coming from the **CustomerCheck** rule.

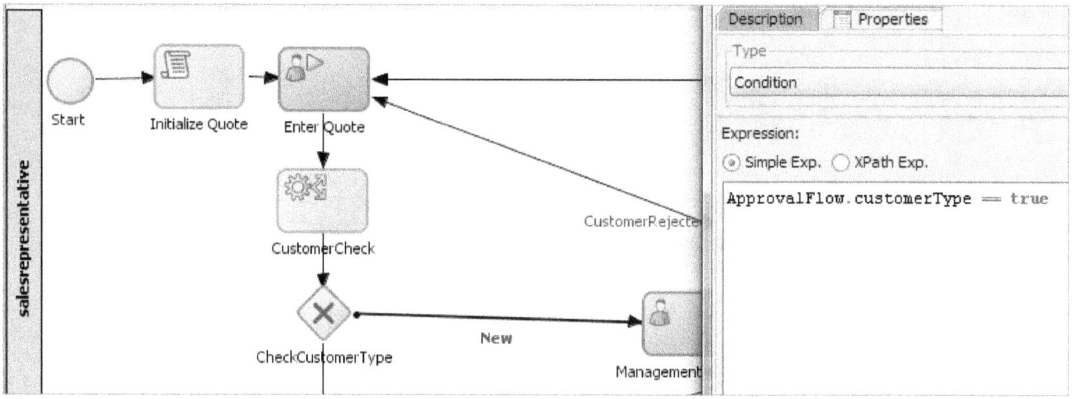

18. Make an unconditional sequence flow from the **Management Approval** task to the **CheckCustomerOutcome** gateway.
19. Create a conditional sequence flow from the **CheckCustomerOutcome** gateway to the **Enter Quote** task with details such as:
    - In the **Description** and **Properties** tabs, give the name `CustomerRejected`
    - In the **Properties** tab, select **Type** = **Condition** and choose **Simple Exp** and enter the following expression:

      ```
      CustomerCheck == "REJECT"
      ```

20. Create an unconditional sequence flow from the **CheckCustomerOutcome** gateway to the **Is business Analyst Review Required?** gateway. Your flow will resemble the following screenshot:

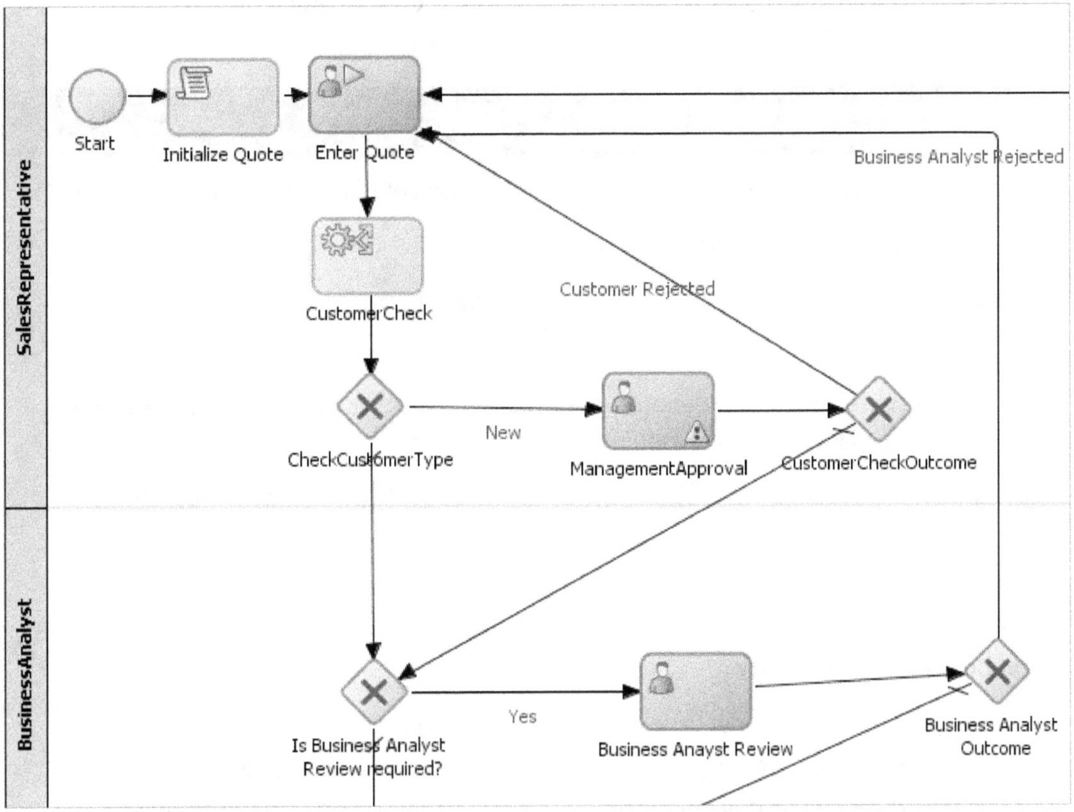

21. When you have finished this, **Save**.

> For the sake of testing, I have implemented the user task ManagementApproval and created a UI project for it. However, you will perform the implementation steps for it in the next chapter.(*Chapter 5, Human Workflow in BPM Process*).

How it works...

An exclusive gateway used for conditional switch will define the flow of process. Gateways define what path the process token will take. Exclusive gateways have outgoing sequence flows.

Defining the Rule: IF/THEN

You will now create another rule using the second method of defining rules named IF/THEN.

Using this rule you can check the following:

> *If* `EffectiveDiscount>Threashold value` *and* `CustomerType = Premium` *Then* `BusinessAnalystReview` *is not required*
>
> *If* `EffectiveDiscount>Threashold value` *and* `CustomerType != Premium` *Then* `BusinessAnalystReview` *is required*

The condition is an expression that can evaluate to true or false. The action sets the result data.

How to do it...

I. Creating a rules dictionary

1. Start Oracle JDeveloper, select **Default Role**, and click **OK**.
2. Go to **Application Navigator | Project** and click on the process **SalesToContract**.
3. Go to **Component Palette | BPM** and click on **Business Rule** from **Activities**.
4. Click in the **BusinessAnalyst** swimlane, above the **Is Business Analyst Review Required?** gateway.
5. You will find the BusinessRuleTask **Properties** dialog.
6. Enter the **Business Rule Task** name as `DiscountCheck`.
7. Click on the **Implementation** tab and click the green plus (**+**) icon to add a Business rule.
8. You will find that a **Create Business Rule** dialog opens up.
9. Go to the **General** tab of the dialog and enter a rule name `DiscountCheck`.
10. In the Input and Output section click on the green plus (**+**) icon to add input and output Data objects.

11. Click **Input Data Object**, browse for **Quote**, click **Output Data Object**, and browse for the `ApprovalFlow` object as the input and output of the Business rule.
12. Click **OK**.
13. In the **Properties** dialog, you will create a Data association. Click on the pencil icon to the right of **Use Associations** to check Data association.
14. You can find the `quote` and `ApprovalFlow` objects as input and output for the **DiscountCheck** rule, respectively.
15. When finished, **Save**.
16. Go to **BPM Project navigator | Business Catalog | Rules** and you will find a `DiscountCheck.rules` file has been created. This is the rules dictionary.
17. Create unconditional sequence flows as follows:
    - Sequence flow from the **CheckCustomerType** gateway to **DiscountCheck**
    - Sequence flow from **DiscountCheck** to the **Is Business Analyst Review Required?** gateway
    - Sequence flow **from CustomerCheckOutcome** to **DiscountCheck**
18. The process will resemble the following screenshot:

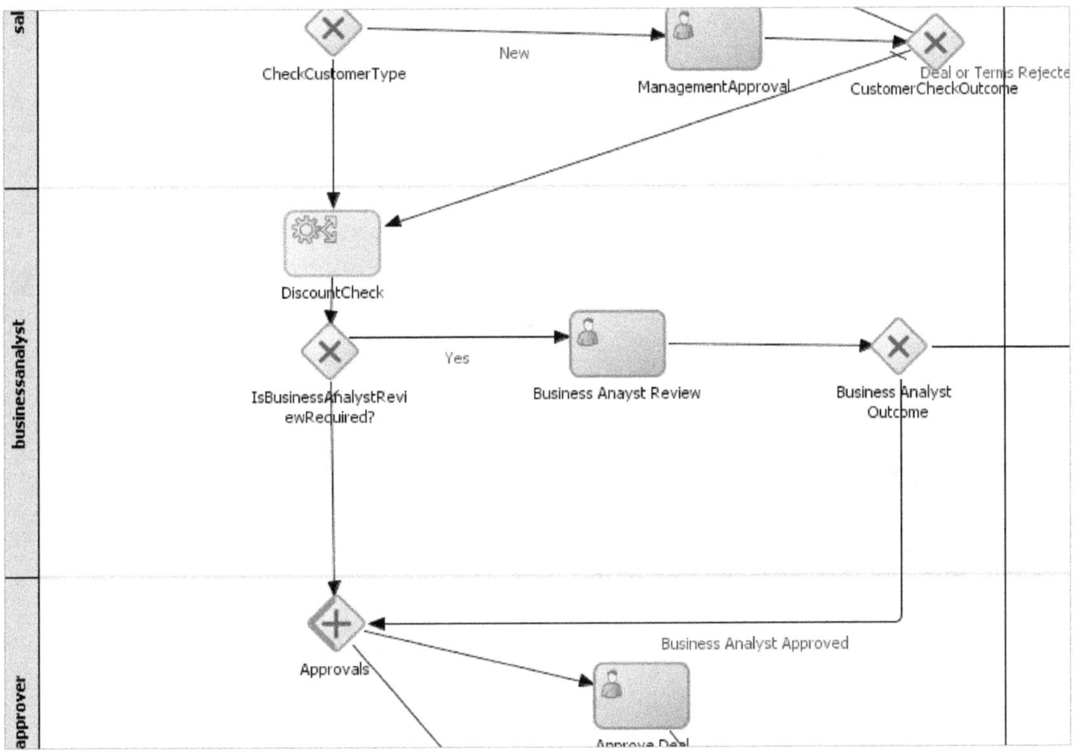

II. Defining Globals

In Oracle Business rules, a Global is similar to a public static variable in Java. You will create a **Global** to hold Customer Type values, as follows:

Global Name	Type	Value	Final
`Discountvar`	Double	30	Checked

1. Go to **BPM Project Navigator | Rules** and click **DiscountCheck.rules**. This will open the Rule designer.
2. Click on **Globals** in the Rule designer.
3. Click on the green plus(**+**) icon to create a Global.
4. Enter details as described in the preceding table.
5. In the **Value** field, click the **Expression Builder** icon to enter an expression, enter a value, **30**, and check **Final** and **Constant**. Checking **Final** means the global is non-modifiable.

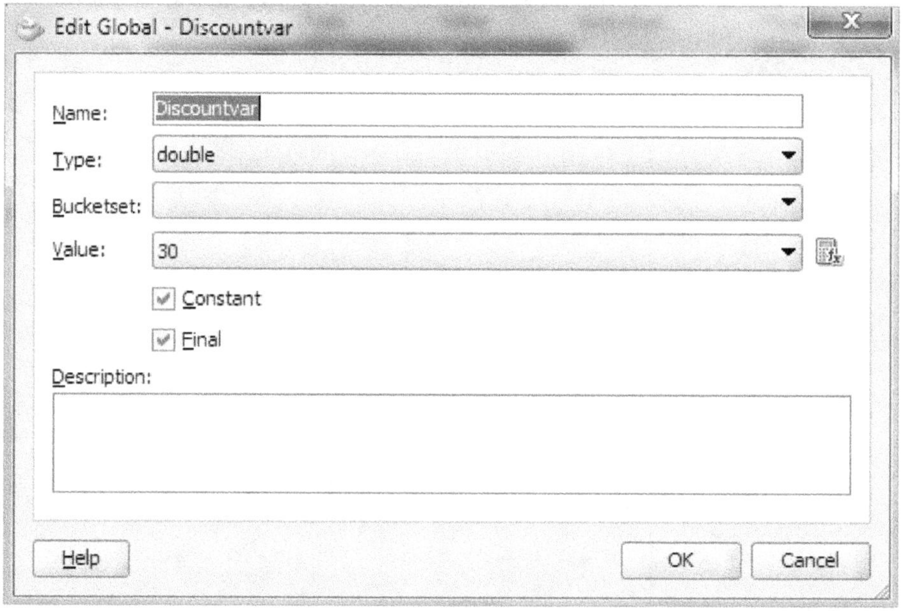

6. When you have finished this, **Save**.

III. Defining Rules

1. Go to the Rule designer for **DiscountCheck.rules** and select **Rulesets | Ruleset1**.
2. Click on **Create Rule**, to create an **IF/THEN** rule for this ruleset.

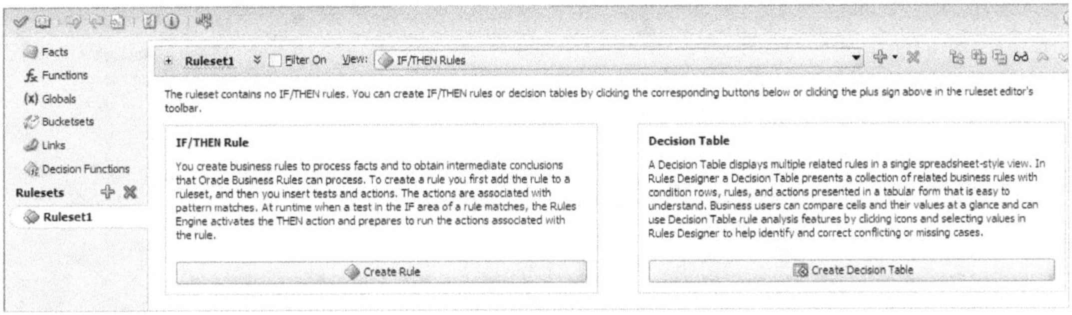

3. Name the ruleset as `DiscountCheckRuleSet`, and enter `CheckDiscount` as name of the **IF/THEN** rule.
4. Click on the green plus (**+**) icon to create another **IF/THEN** rule for this ruleset, and name it `CheckDiscountNP`.
5. In the **If** section for the **CheckDiscount** rule, click **<insert text>** and enter an IF condition, as follows:

```
QuoteRequestType.summary.effectiveDiscount>= Discountvar and
  QuoteRequestType.summary.customerType == "Premium"
```

6. In the **Then** section, click **<edit properties>**. It will open **Properties** for ApprovalFlowType; enter values for `businessPractiseReviewNeeded = false` and check `Constant` value:

    ```
    asset new ApprovalFlowType(<editproperties>businessPractiseReview
      Needed:false)
    ```

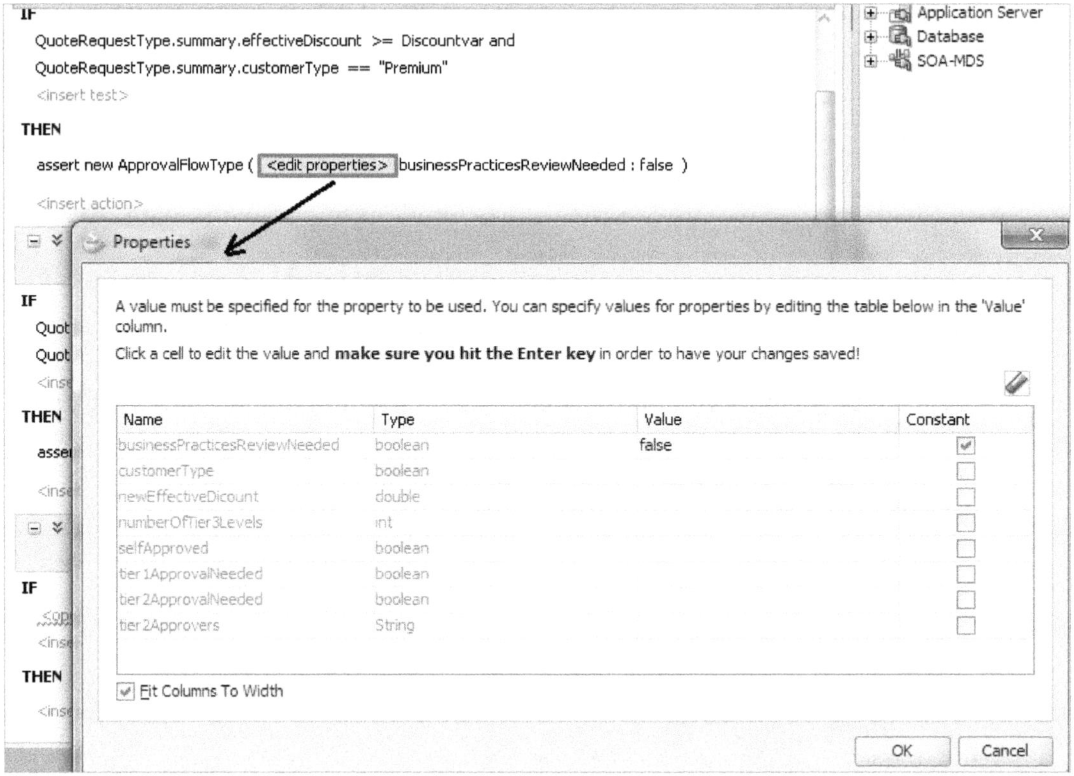

7. In the **IF** section for the **CheckDiscountNP** rule, click **<insert text>** and enter an IF condition, as follows:

    ```
    QuoteRequestType.summary.effectiveDiscount>= Discountvar and
      QuoteRequestType.summary.customerType != "Premium"
    ```

8. In the **Then** section, click **<edit properties>**. It will open **Properties** for **ApprovalFlowType**. Enter values for **businessPractiseReviewNeeded** = **true** and check **Constant** value.

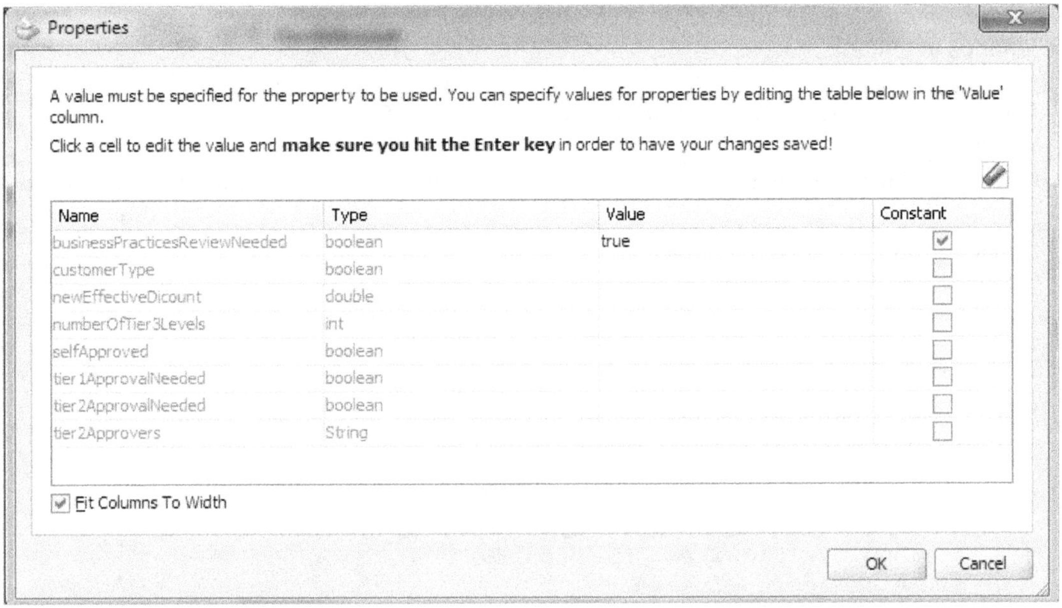

How it works...

When the process token reaches **DiscountCheck**, the If-Then-Else ruleset gets evaluated. If the effective discount is greater than 30% and the customer is a Premium customer, then a business analyst review is not required. The token moves to the Approvals Gateway.

If the effective discount is greater than 30% and customer is not a Premium customer, then a business analyst review is required. The token moves to the task **Business Analyst Review**.

Testing the rules

You will deploy the process following the steps you followed in *Chapter 3, Process Deployment and Testing*, to deploy the process. You will be using following test case scenarios to test the process:

Test # 1 Values	`Customer Type = New, Quantity = 100, Effective Discount = 40`			
Rule	**Values (Action)**	**Expected**	**Output**	**Expectance Meet**
Check Customer	`ApprovalFlowType.customerType`	true		
	`ApprovalFlowType.newEffectiveDiscount`	QuoteSummaryType.effectiveDiscount+15, that is, `55`		
	`ApprovalFlowType.NoOfTier3Levels`	2		
	`ApprovalFlowType.SelfApproved`	false		
	`ApprovalFlowType.tier1Approvalneeded`	false		
	`ApprovalFlowType.tier2Approvalneeded`	true		
Discount Check	`businessAnalystRequired`	true		
Test # 2 Values	`Customer Type = Premium, Quantity = 100, Effective Discount = 40`			
Check Customer	`ApprovalFlowType.customerType`	false		
	`ApprovalFlowType.newEffectiveDiscount`	40		
	`ApprovalFlowType.NoOfTier3Levels`	0		
	`ApprovalFlowType.SelfApproved`	True		
	`ApprovalFlowType.tier1Approvalneeded`	False		
	`ApprovalFlowType.tier2Approvalneeded`	False		
Discount Check	`businessAnalystRequired`	False		

How to do it...

1. Go to the Oracle BPM Workspace and log in as the user sales representative, to initiate the quote.

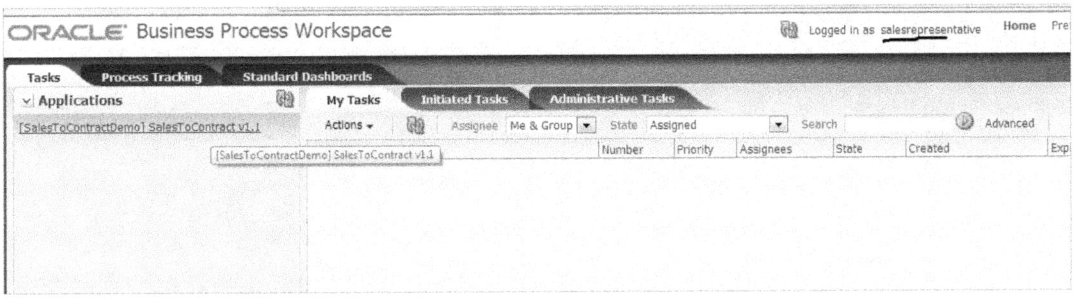

2. Enter Quote information with Test values included since **Customer Type** = **New**, **Effective Discount** = **40** and **Quantity** = **100**.

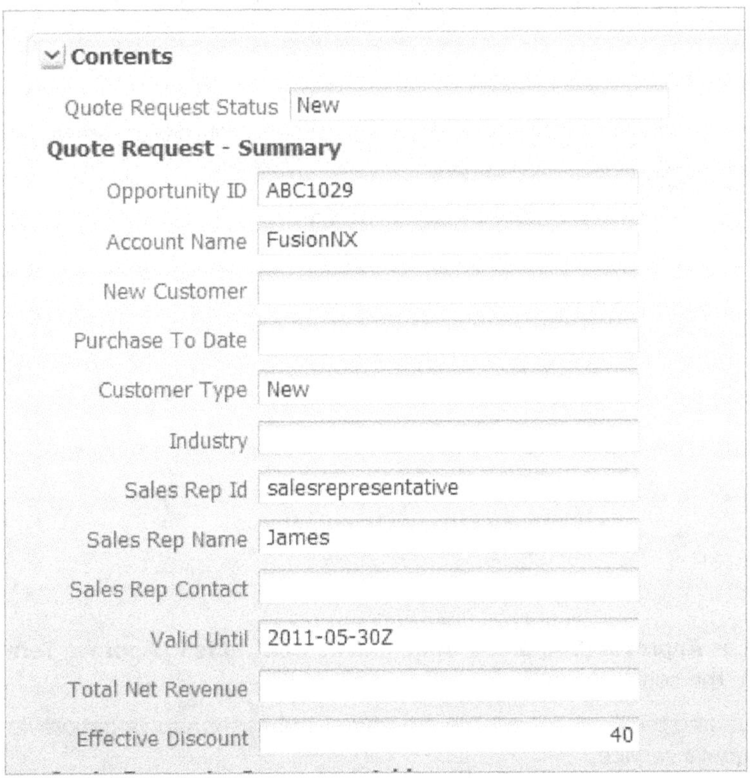

3. The quote moves ahead for managerial approval and the user/group assignment for **Management Approval** approves it.

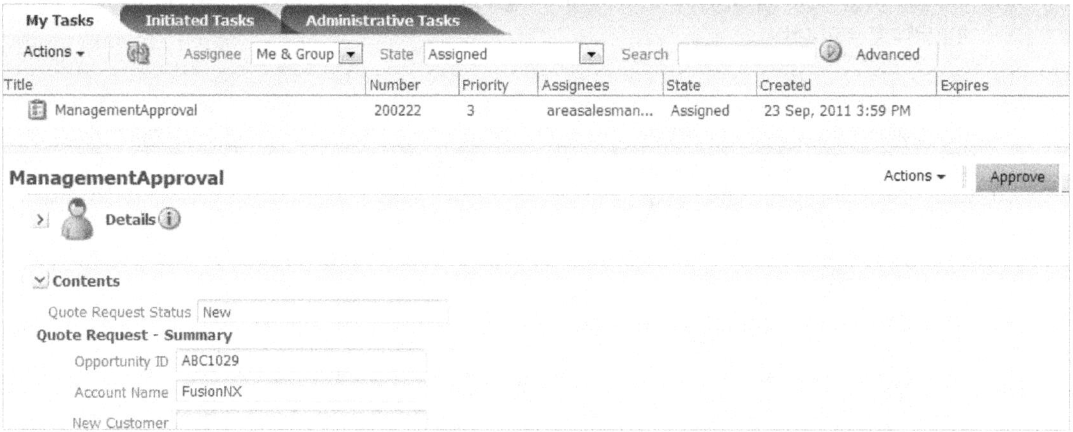

4. You can now log in as **BusinessAnalyst** and can check the quote details and approve it too.

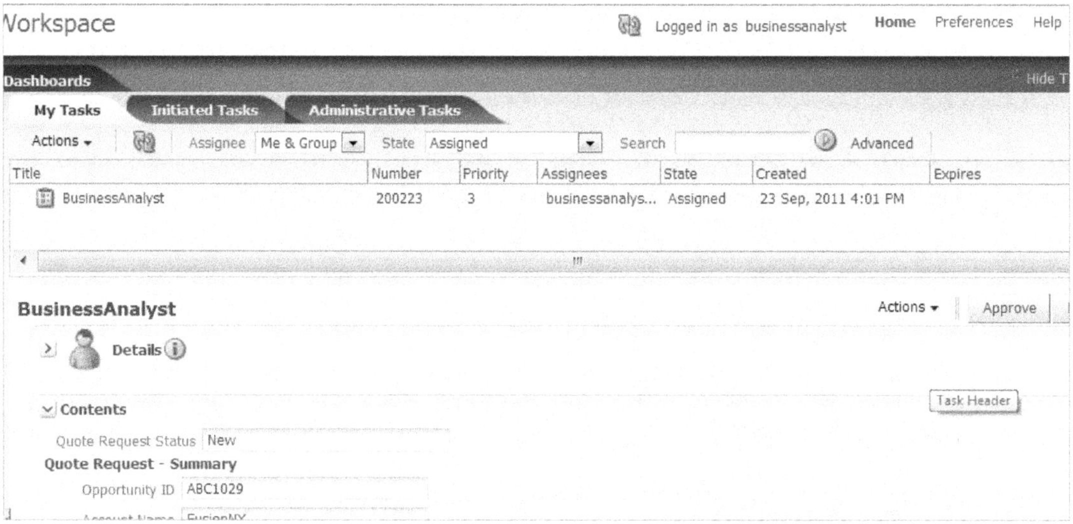

5. Log in as **Approver** to **Approve Deal**, and as **Contracts** to **Approve Terms**, and finalize the contract too.
6. You can find the `quote.xml` file created at the destination location via the **save quote** service.
7. Log in to the EM Console at `http://<hostname>:<port>/em/`.
8. Go to **SOA-Infra | default** and click on the project name **SalesToContractDemo**.

9. Click on the instance created and click on the process name in the **Trace** section, as shown in the following screenshot:

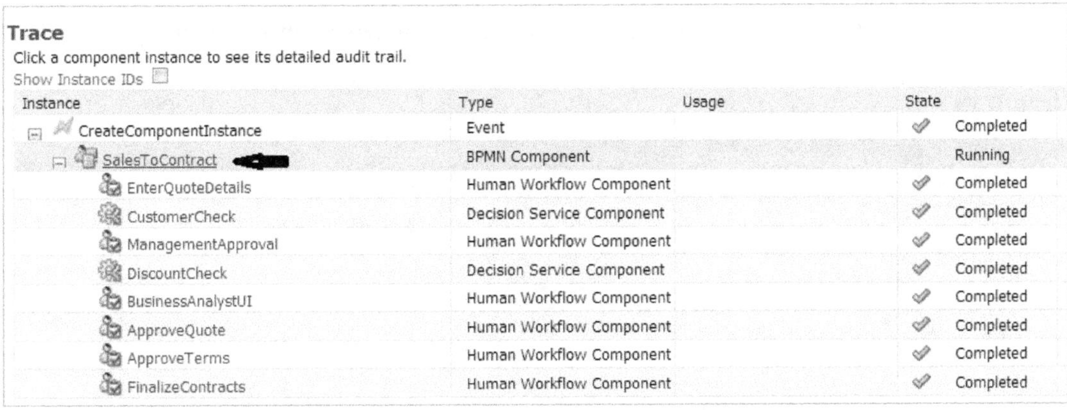

10. You are now in the **Audit Trail** section. Expand **Customer Check Rule** and click on the link **Instance Left the activity**, to show the data that was associated with this rule when the process token left this Business Rule.

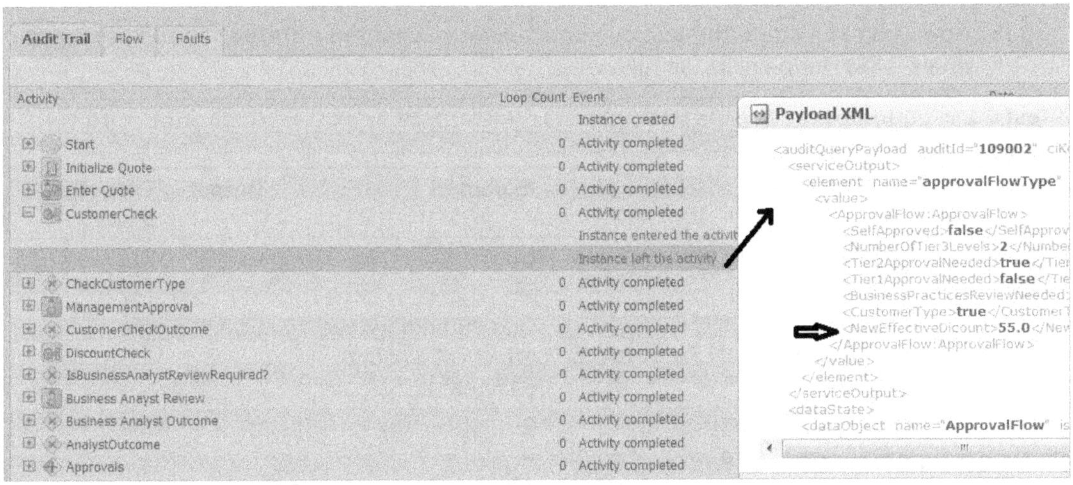

11. In the **Payload** section, check on the values and match it with the values in test scenarios.

12. Similarly, click on **Discount Check** and confirm for **BusinessPractiseReviewRequired** = **True**. As the Business Analyst Review is performed for the process, you can confirm it as **true**.

13. Similarly, run a new instance of the process, and this time, enter new `Quote` values as per **test case # 2**, with **Customer Type** = **Premium**, **Effective Discount** = **40** and **quantity** = **100**.
14. In the **Audit Trail** tab you can find that the values at **Discount Check** are as expected.

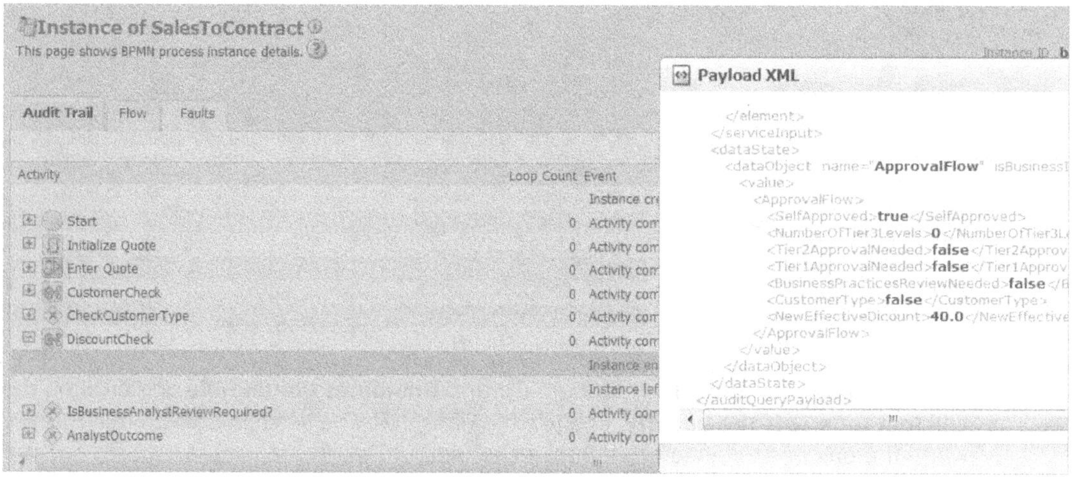

15. Now, you can update the test document where **Expected** = **Output** and **Expectance meet** = **Yes**, for all rows, as follows:

Test # 1 Values	`Customer Type = New, Quantity = 100, Effective Discount = 40`			
Rule	**Values (Action)**	**Expected**	**Output**	**Expectance Meet**
Check Customer	`ApprovalFlowType. customerType`	true	true	Yes
	`ApprovalFlowType. newEffectiveDiscount`	QuoteSummaryType. effectiveDiscount +15;that is, 55	55	Yes
	`ApprovalFlowType. NoOfTier3Levels`	2	2	Yes
	`ApprovalFlowType. SelfApproved`	false	false	Yes
	`ApprovalFlowType. tier1Approvalneeded`	false	false	Yes
	`ApprovalFlowType. tier2Approvalneeded`	true	true	Yes
Discount Check	`businessAnalystRequired`	true	true	Yes

Test # 2 Values	Customer Type = Premium, Quantity = 100, Effective Discount = 40			
Check Customer	ApprovalFlowType.customerType	false	false	Yes
	ApprovalFlowType.newEffectiveDiscount	40	40	Yes
	ApprovalFlowType.NoOfTier3Levels	0	0	Yes
	ApprovalFlowType.SelfApproved	true	true	Yes
	ApprovalFlowType.tier1Approvalneeded	false	false	Yes
	ApprovalFlowType.tier2Approvalneeded	false	false	Yes
Discount Check	businessAnalystRequired	false	false	Yes

How it works...

First, a Rule session that consists of rules, facts, and an agenda, is created. An `assert` or `retract` rule adds or removes fact instances from working memory.

After this, the following actions take place:

- Conditions for rules are evaluated
- Matching rules are added to the agenda (Activated)
- Rules that no longer match are removed from the agenda
- Rules Engine runs and executes actions (fires), for activated rules

So, for the first case, the `Check Customer` rule is executed and process token ahead for management approval and business analyst review will be required. However, for the second test case, no management approval was required and no business analyst review was required, as the conditions for the rules were set so for those two cases.

You can go ahead and run other cases, too. They would be something like `Enter Quote` with `Customer Type` as `Gold`, `Quantity` as `100` and `Effective Discount` as `40` and check for the process.

5
Human Workflow in BPM Process

Having learnt about human workflow, you are now aware of how to create user interfaces for those tasks. You have tested flows and witnessed the usage of human interaction. This chapter will focus on the advanced concepts of human workflow. In this chapter, you will look at advanced Human Task concepts like routing, defining sequential and parallel stages, skipping rules, run time AdHoc task assignments, approval groups, RL functions usage, task assignments and routing, participant types - single, serial, parallel, and FYI , participant assignments, outcome-based completion of routing flow, static, dynamic, and rule-based task assignment, task deadlines like escalation policy, and much more.

This chapter will focus on the implementation tasks, such as:

- Creating Human Task Service Components
- Creating task definition and the task payload
- Defining Assignments—stage and single participant
- Defining Assignments—sequential stage and serial participant
- Defining Assignments—management chain participant
- Defining Assignments—parallel participant type
- Testing the process

Introduction

Human Workflow is required for human interactions in processes such as approvals, assignments, routing of tasks, and so on. It is also required for performing certain activities to go forward with the process. Deadlines, notifications, and escalations can be achieved through Human Tasks, which ensure the timely performance of tasks. Human tasks even presents the tasks to end users through a variety of mechanisms such as work list applications. Reports, reassignments, and load balancing empower business owners to manage the performance of tasks.

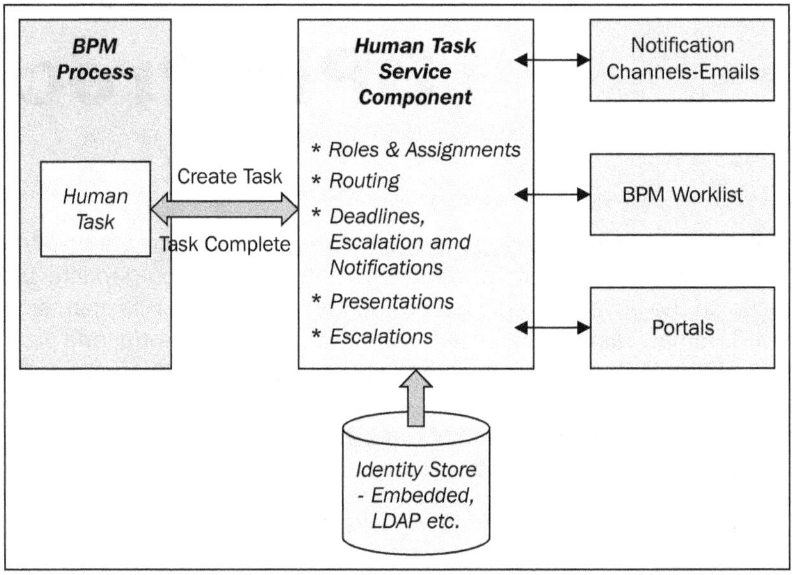

A BPM process invokes a Human Task. It creates a task in the **Human Task Service Component**. The BPM process will wait for the task to complete. The process will also watch out for any call-backs from the task and react to them. There is metadata associated with the task that is required by the Human Task Service Component to manage the lifecycle of the task, which includes information such as who performs the task, who are the stakeholders, task information, task actions, and so on.

The Human Task Service Component will use an Identity Directory such as an LDAP or an Embedded Realm to determine roles and privileges.

Human Task Service Component presents tasks to users via BPM Worklist applications, work list portlets in the form of enterprise portals, or as notifications via e-mail, phone, SMS, and other channels. Users can even perform actions on tasks from the e-mail client without connecting to Oracle BPM Worklist applications.

Starting with the release 11g that you are working on, all the Human Task metadata is stored and managed in the **Metadata Service** (**MDS**) repository. The workflow service itself consists of many services that handle various aspects of human interaction with a business process:

- **Task Service**: This has operations that can update a task, complete a task, escalate and reassign a task, and so on. A Task Service is used by Oracle BPM Worklist to retrieve tasks assigned to users. A Task Service itself consists of many services such as:
    - Task Routing Service to route, escalate, and reassign the tasks
    - Task Query Service to query a service
    - Task Metadata Service to expose operations to retrieve metadata information related to a task.
- **Identity Service**: This is a thin Web Service layer on top of WLS 11g Security infrastructure or any customer user repository to enable authentication and authorization of users.
- **Notification Service**: This is used to deliver notifications through channels such as e-mail, IM, SMS, and so on.
- **User Metadata Service**: This is used to manage metadata related to workflow users such as preferences, vacations, delegation rules, and so on.
- **Runtime Config Service**: This service supports management of task payload-mapped attribute-mappings and also provides methods for managing metadata used in the task service runtime environment.
- **Evidence Service**: This service supports storage and non-repudiation of digitally-signed workflow tasks.

During runtime, the business logic and processing rules of the Human Task Service Component are executed by the human workflow service engine. The Human Workflow Service Component has its own service engine container for performing these tasks. All Human Task service components, regardless of the SOA composite application of which they are a part of, are executed in this single Human Task service engine.

Creating Human Task Service Components

You created Human Task Service Components while you were creating Human Tasks for User tasks in your BPM process SalesToContract. However, here you will revise the method you have adopted and change how Service Components are formed and associated with the BPM process.

How to do it...

You can create Human Task Service Components in either the SOA Composite editor or in BPM Designer as follows:

I. Creating a Human Service Component in SOA Composite Editor:

1. Start Oracle JDeveloper in the default role (to enable all technologies) and go to the project `SalesToContractDemo`.
2. Click on `composite.xml` to open the Composite Editor.
3. Go to **Component Palette |SOA | Service Component** and drag-and-drop Human Task Service Components in the Composite designer, where required.
4. This will open the Human Task dialog. Give a **Name** to the Human Task. This will be created as a task file in the project.

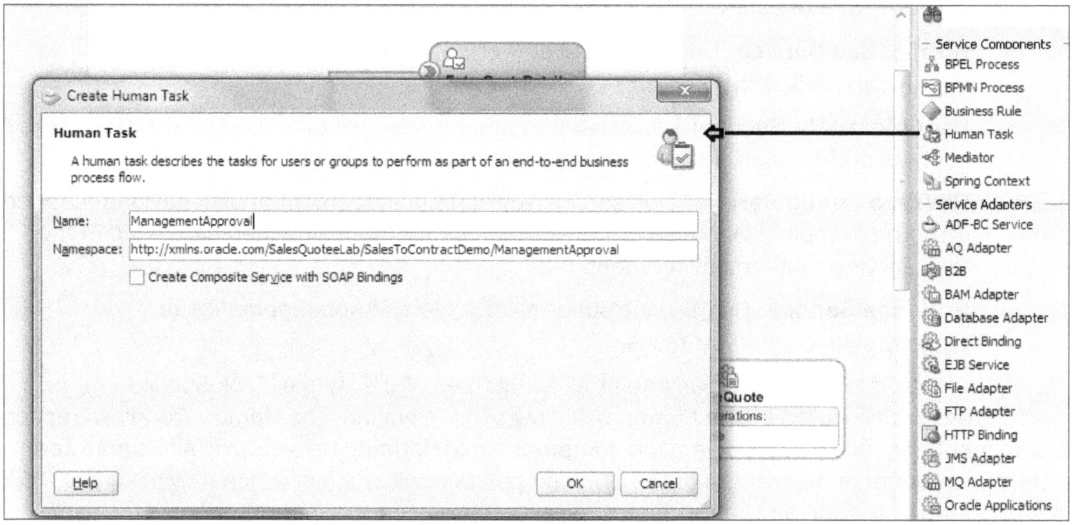

5. Don't check the **Create Composite Service with SOAP Bindings** as you want this Human Task Service Component to be associated later with the BPM process.

6. This will create a Human Task, **ManagementApproval**, which you can associate with the BPM process later.

> Clicking the **Create Composite Service with SOAP Bindings** checkbox will create a standalone component in the composite editor and a Human Task Service Component that is automatically wired to a **Simple Object Access Protocol** (**SOAP**) web service. This may be required in case we need to expose Human Task services as web services that are to be invoked by clients like OSB and so on.

7. When you have finished, click **Save**.

II. Creating a Human Service Component in BPM Process Designer:

The following method is the one you have followed while creating a Human Task in a BPM process.

1. Click on **Activities** in the component palette and click **User task**.
2. Click on the **salesrepresentative** swimlane to the right of the Check customer rule.
3. In the User Task properties, enter your name as **ManagementApproval** and click **OK**.
4. You will implement this task in the following section of this chapter.

> Remember in *Chapter 4, Business Rules in the BPM Process*, in the *Adding Gateway and Human Task* section, you have the Model Management Approval Task in a BPM process.

5. Right-click on the User task Management Approval and go to the Implementation tab.

6. Click on the green plus (**+**) icon to create a Human Task and enter details, as shown in the following screenshot:

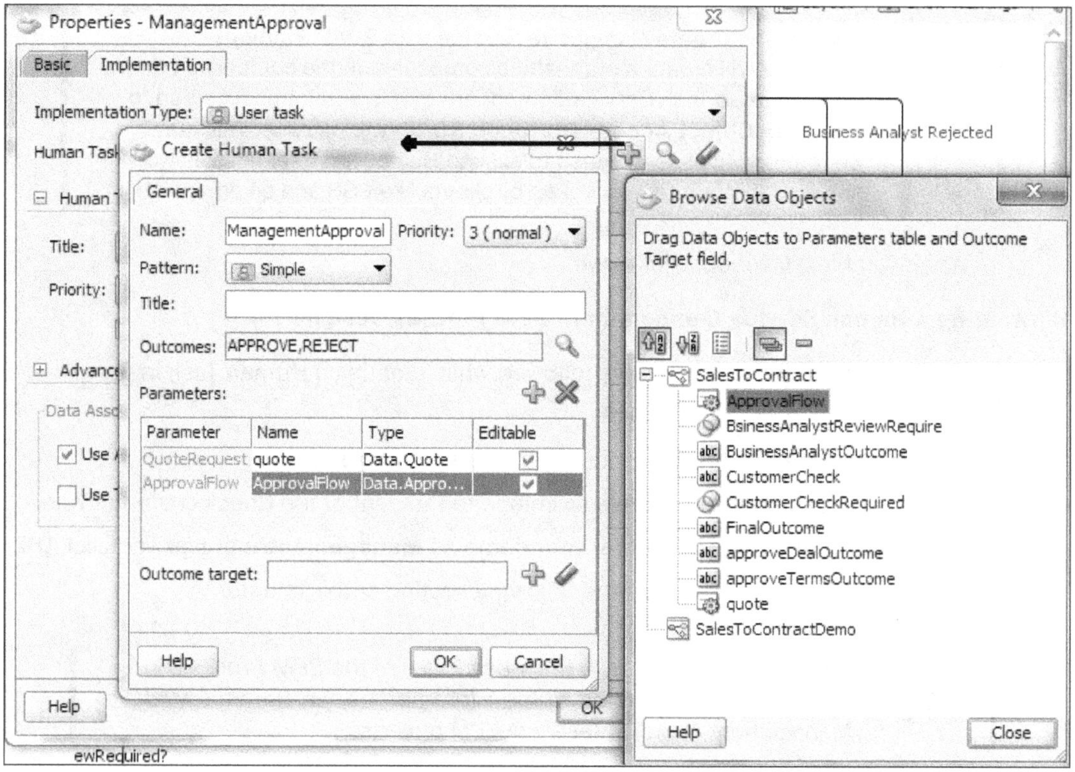

7. Click on the green plus (**+**) icon next to **Parameters** to add **Input Parameters** to the Human Task.
8. From **Browse Data Objects**, choose **ApprovalFlow** and Data objects **quote** as Input parameters.
9. This will create a ManagementApproval task which you can verify from **BPM Navigator | SalesToContractDemo | Business Catalog | Human Tasks**.
10. When you have finished, click **Save**.

How it works...

When a Human Task is created, the Human Task settings specified in the Human Task editor are saved to a metadata task configuration file in the **Metadata Service** (**MDS**) repository with a `.task` extension. This file appears in **Application Navigator | SOAProjectName | SOA Content** or **BPM Navigator | SalesToContractDemo | BusinessCatalog | HumanTasks**. You can re-edit the settings in this file by double-clicking `.task` in either of those places.

Clicking on the `.task` file will open the Human Task editor that has many sections, which are described as follows:

- **General** section: This is used to define task details such as the title, task outcomes, the owner, and other attributes.
- **Data** section: This defines the structure (message elements) of the task payload (the data in the task).
- **Assignment** section: This will enable you to assign participants to the task and create a policy for routing the task through the workflow.
- **Presentation** section: This enables you to specify Multilingual settings while the **Deadlines** section enables you to specify the expiration duration of a task, custom escalation Java classes, and due dates.
- **Notification** section: This section will enable you to create and send notifications when a user is assigned a task or informed that the status of the task has changed.
- **Access** section: This section will enable you to specify access rules for the task content and task actions, workflow signature policies, and assignment restrictions.
- **Events** section: This section enables you to specify call-back classes and task and routing assignments. Worklist events leverage the inbuilt EDN engine to publish status changes for a task example on completion, and so on.

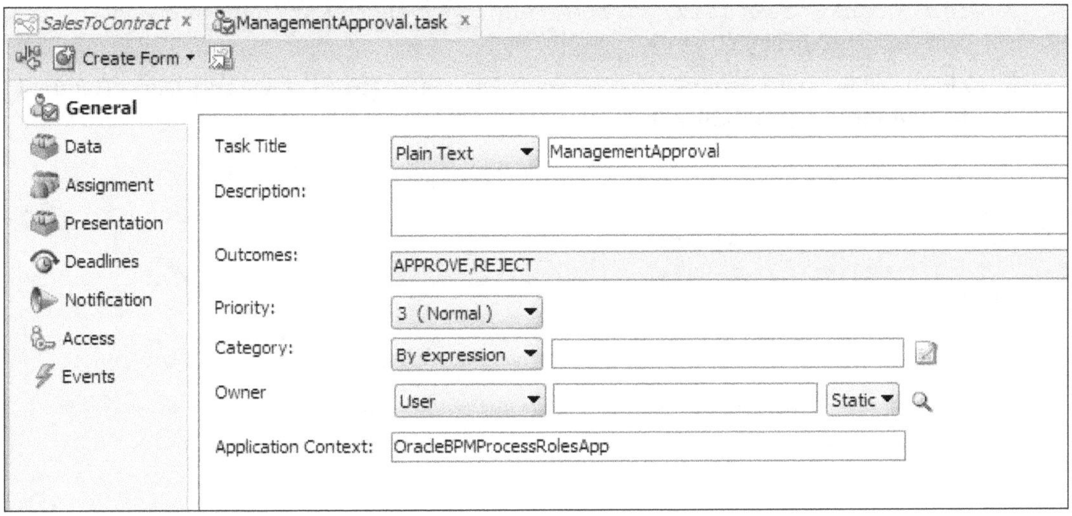

Creating task definition and the task payload

The **General** section helps you to define task definition. In this section, you can specify details such as the task title, description, task outcomes, task category, task priority, and task owner.

How to do it...

Here you will learn to create a task definition.

I. Define Task Title and Description:

1. Go to the BPM Navigator, **SalesToContractDemo | Business Catalog | Human tasks**, and click on the `ManagementApproval.task` file.
2. This will open the Human Task editor.
3. Go to the **General** section.
4. In the **Task Title**, select **Text** and **XPath** to enter a combination of **Text** and **XPath** expressions (dynamic expressions) from the input schema. Expand Schema and get the **Opportunity ID** and **Enter Text** as follows: `Management Approval for: /task:task/task:payload/ns0:QuoteRequest/ns0:Summary/ns0:OpportunityID`.
5. XPath will get auto generated when you click on the **Task | payload | QuoteRequest | Summary | OpportunityID**.

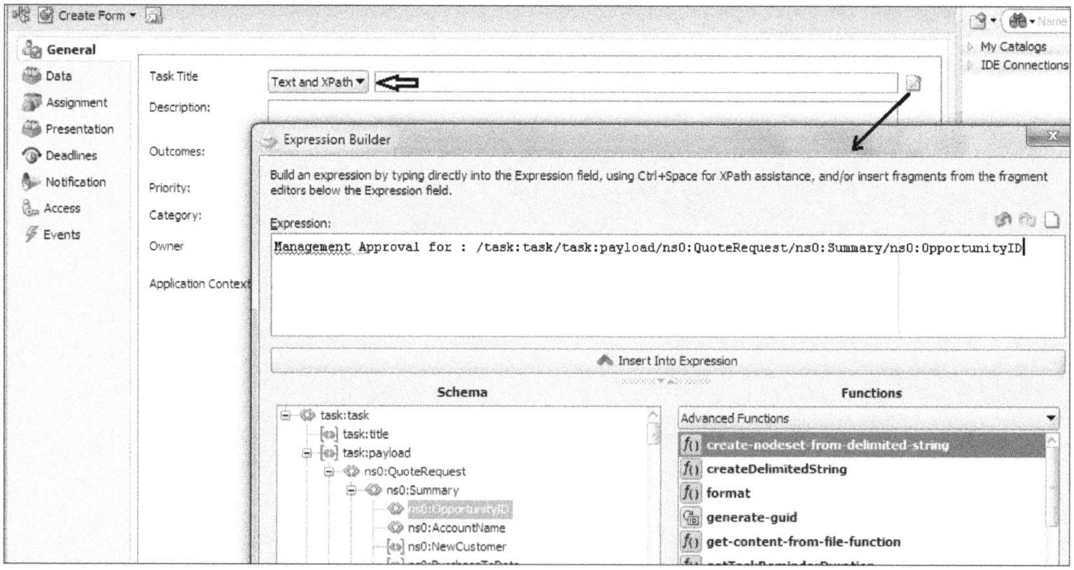

6. Click **OK** in the **Expression Builder**.
7. Enter `Management Approval for Quotation` as **Description of the Task** in the Task definition.
8. When you have finished, click **Save**.

II. Define Task outcome, priority, and category:

Task outcomes capture the possible outcomes of a task. For a Management Approval task, a manager or a group of managers will either **ACCEPT** or **REJECT** the task.

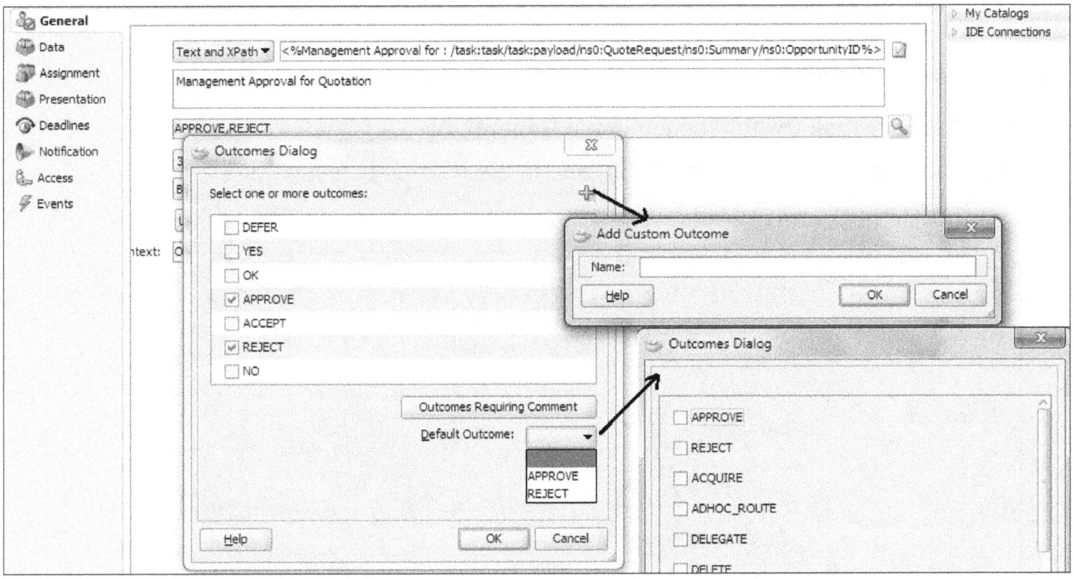

1. Click on the search icon to the right of the outcome. This will open **Outcomes Dialog**.
2. Select **APPROVE** and **REJECT** from the outcome's list.
3. Click **OK**.
4. You can even create custom outcomes by clicking on the green plus (**+**) icon in the outcome dialog. Also you can select which outcomes will have comments. Click to select an outcome to which an assignee adds comments in the Oracle BPM Worklist at runtime. The assignee must add the comments and perform the action without saving the task at runtime.

5. Click on the **Priority Drop Down** and select a **Priority**. If management approval is of normal priority, let's choose **3** as **Normal** from the priority list. **1** is considered as the highest priority.
6. Leave the **Categories** file blank as you will not categorize the Management Approval Task.
7. However, you can categorize tasks either by **Entering a Static Value** or using an expression builder to provide a dynamic value. The category displays in Oracle BPM Worklist. You can filter tasks based on category and create views on categories in Oracle BPM Worklist.
8. When you have finished, click **Save**.

III. Defining Task Owners:

1. Go to the **Task Owner** section in the **General** tab.
2. From the drop-down, select **User**, and in the method selection drop-down, select **Static**:

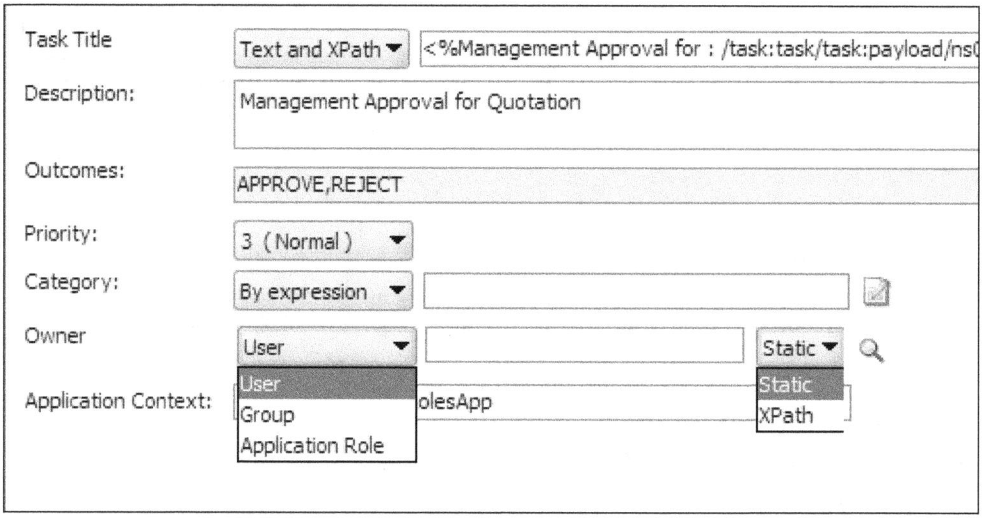

3. Click the Search icon to **Open the Identity Lookup** and choose `salesrepresentative` from the user list.

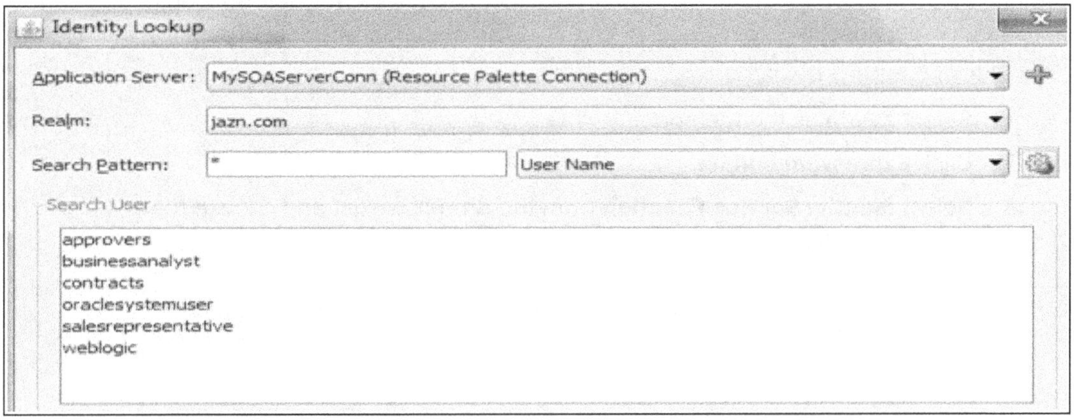

4. Here, the task owner is selected by browsing the embedded user directory.
5. Click **OK**.
6. When you have finished, click **Save**.

How it works...

The title, entered into Title in Task Definition, provides a visual identifier for the task. This task title displays in Oracle BPM Worklist.

Oracle BPM Worklist displays the outcomes you specify here as the possible task actions to perform during runtime. If you have categorized tasks, then you can filter tasks based on category and create views on categories in Oracle BPM Worklist.

There's more...

In this section, you will see how to create task owners dynamically and create a task payload.

Choosing a Task Owner dynamically

You can select the `Dynamic` method, which will open the Expression builder. If the task payload has Owner information, then you can select it in the Expression Builder. Or you can use identity functions like `getmanager()` to get the manager of the user entered into the function, as shown in the following screenshot:

1. Select **XPath** as the method.
2. Click **Expression builder**.
3. Select **Identity Service Function** from the drop-down list and choose the desired function.

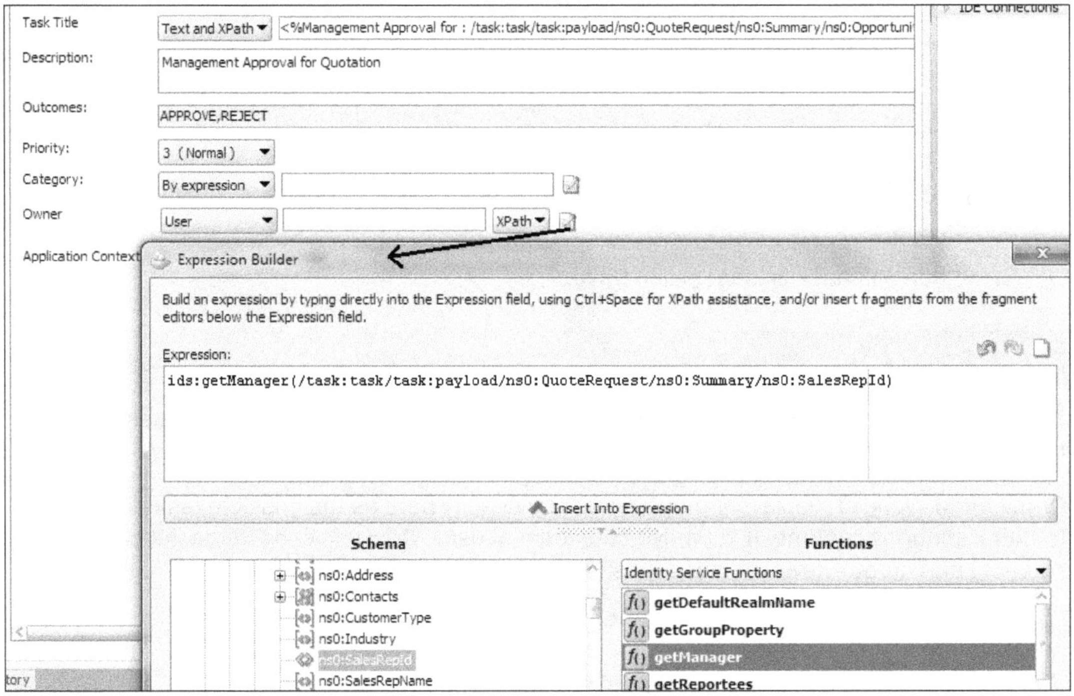

Creating a task payload

You will not be using the data section of the task payload definition for the Management Approval Human Task as you have already assigned data as input parameters to this Human Task.

However, one can use the **Data** section to specify the payload of the task defined in the schema (XSD). You create parameters to represent the elements in the XSD file by carrying out the following steps. This makes the payload data available to the workflow task.

1. Go to **Data Section** in the **Task Definition** editor.
2. Click on the green plus (+) to add a task parameter. This will open the **Add task Parameter** dialog.
3. Select variable and choose the **Element** radio and click **Browse** to choose an **Element Type** from the **Project Schema**.

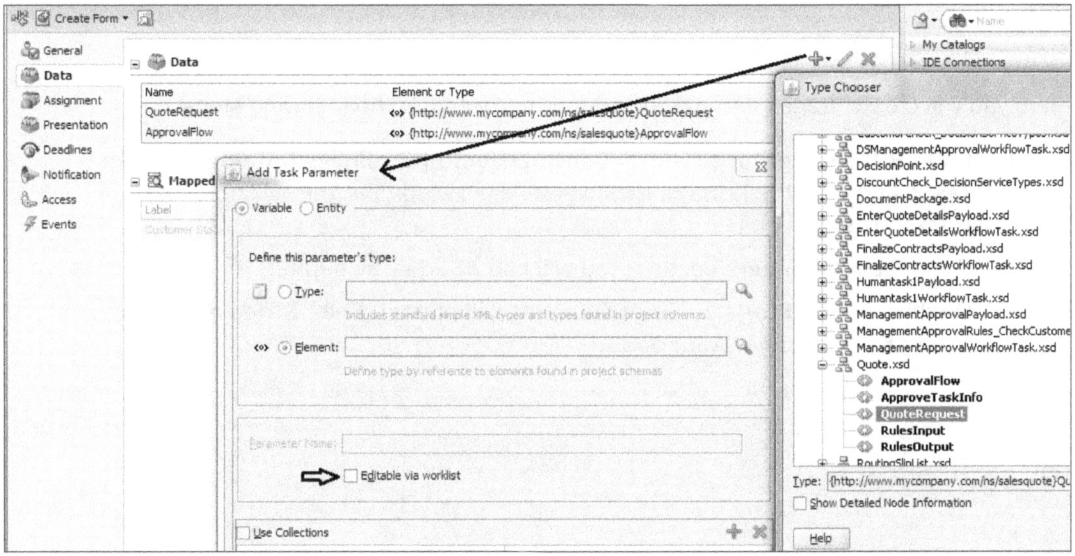

4. Select the checkbox **Editable Via Worklist** to enable users to edit this part of the task payload in Oracle BPM Worklist.
5. Click **OK** twice and then **Save**.

Defining assignments—stage and single participant

You have defined the Management Approval task and you need to define the participant type for the task. Means you will build a list of users, groups, and application roles to act upon the task (Management Approval). Simple or complex Routing Policies can be created by mixing and matching participant types. Stage organizes the blocks of participant types and participant types are grouped in a block under a stage. You can have one or more stages in sequence or in parallel. Within each stage, you can have one or more participant type blocks in sequence or in parallel.

For configuring the participant, there is an editor and the sequence in which assignees are added indicates the execution sequence. You can create parallel and sequential stages and participant types are created in these blocks.

Here you will learn how single participant type is created for management approval tasks. When the process token reaches management approval, you will build a chain of approval processes, and in this section, you will focus on creating a non-repeating stage, single name, and expression value-based participant type and you will specify a time limit for acting on a task, inviting additional participants to a task, bypassing a task participant, and implementing an escalation policy.

How to do it...

Here you will create stages and participants by carrying out the following steps:

1. Go to **BPM Navigator | SalesToContractDemo | Business Catalog| Human Tasks** and click the `ManagementApproval.task` file. This will open the **Human Task** editor.
2. Go to the **Assignment** section. You will find `stage1` as default.
3. Double-click on **Stage 1**. The **Edit** dialog will appear. Enter **Stage Name** as `TerritoryManagerApproval`.

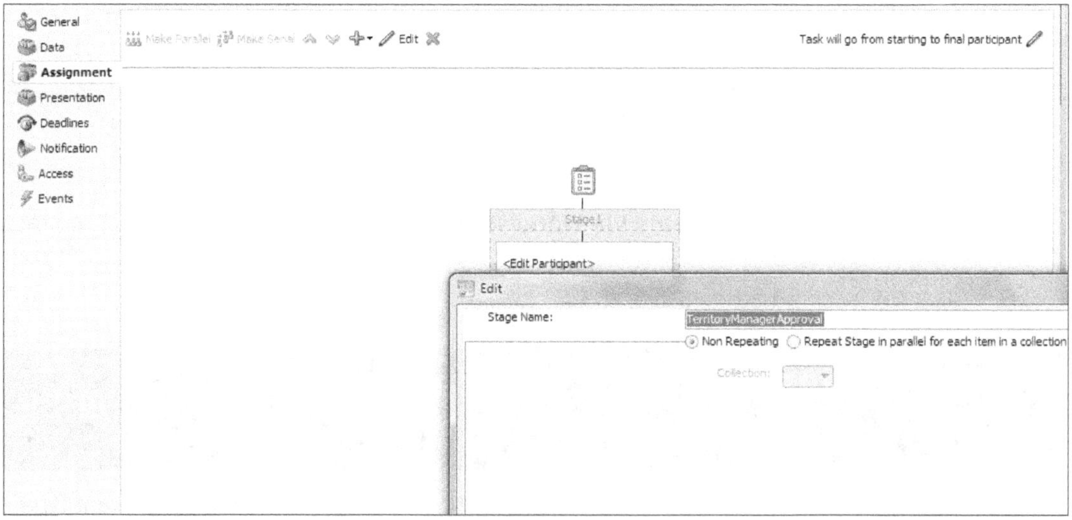

4. Choose **Non Repeating** as it specifies that there is only one stage in parallel for each element in a collection. Repeat the stage in parallel for each item in a collection - specify that the stage is to repeat in parallel for each element in a collection.
5. Click on the **Participant Type** block. It will open the **Edit Participant Type** dialog.

6. Select **Type** = **Single**. This is the `Assignment Type`. In this type of assignment list, only one user is required to act on the task. You can provide either a single user or a list of users, groups, or application roles for this pattern.
7. Enter the label for the task as **TerritoryManagerApproval**.
8. Choose **Build a list of participants using** = **Name and Expression.**
9. Check **Value Based as the method to specify the Participant Type attributes.**
10. You can create several types of lists for the single user participant (and also for the parallel, serial, and FYI user participants). Value-based name and expression lists enable you to statically or dynamically select users, groups, or application roles as task assignees.
11. Click on the green plus (**+**) icon, and from the **Identification Type** column of the **Participant Names** table, select **Add User** from the list.
12. However, you can even use expressions and dynamically select values using the expression builder. Also, you can manually enter a value by clicking the field in the **value** column.
13. Select **Data Type by name** as you will search for the username in Embedded LDAP.
14. Click on the **Browse** button as directed by the **3** in the following screenshot, and the **Identity Lookup** dialog will appear.

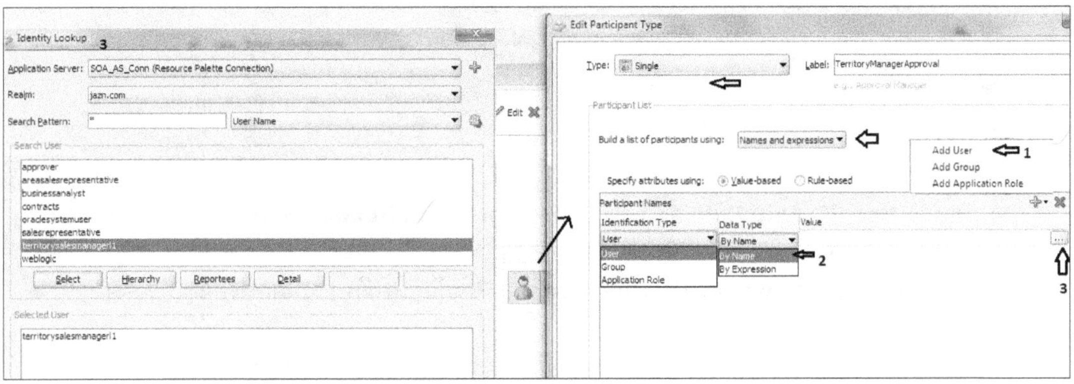

15. Select the **ApplicationServer** name and select **Realm** as **jazn.com** and while keeping the Search Pattern as ***(all)** for **User Name**, click the **Identity Lookup** button.
16. Choose the user **territorymanagerl1** as **Territory Manager Level 1**.
17. Click **OK**.
18. Scroll down on the same dialog and expand the **Advance** button.
19. You can specify the amount of time a user, group, or application role receives to act on a task. If the user, group, or role does not act in the time specified, the global escalation and renewal policies that you set in the Deadlines section (known as the routing slip level) of the Human Task editor are applied.

20. Check **Limit Allocated Duration to:** and give the time limit of one day to the Territory Manager to approve the quote.
21. If he/she doesn't approve in this time frame, the global escalation and renewal policies that you set in the Deadlines section will be applied.
22. Check **Allow this participant to invite other participants.**
23. You want to set the routing so that at runtime Territory Manager Level 1 should invite Territory Manager Level 2 before routing it to next assignee. This is also known as ad hoc routing. If this option is selected, Adhoc Route is added to the Actions list in Oracle BPM Worklist at runtime.

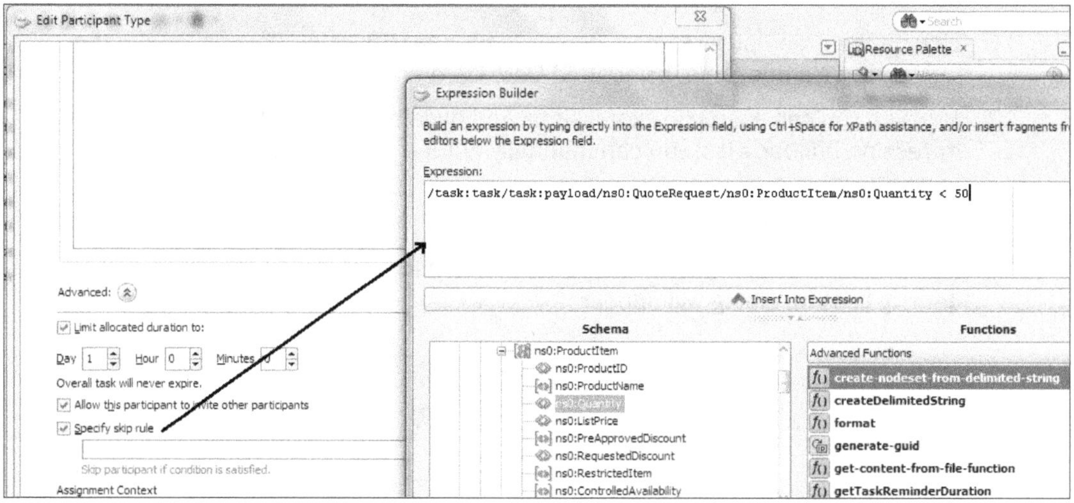

24. Check **Specify Skip Rule** and click the **Expression Builder** ahead of it, as you also want to bypass this task participant if `Product Quantity` is less than `50`.
25. Expand **Task Payload** as **QuoteRequest | ProductItem | Quantity** and enter the following:

    ```
    /task:task/task:payload/ns0:QuoteRequest/ns0:ProductItem/
    ns0:Quantity < 50
    ```

    Hence, if the incoming payload has a quantity of less than `50`, then this Task participant will be skipped.
26. Click **OK** twice to reach the Human Task editor.
27. When you have finished, click **Save**.

How it works...

When the Process Token reaches this stage and if the **Incoming Quantity** is less than fifty, the participant will be skipped. He/she may invite the Level 2 Manager too. However, if he/she fails to act on the task in one day, then the Escalation Policy will be applied.

Defining assignments—sequential stage and serial participant

Now, the assignment section has one stage with a single participant type for which a list is formed using the value-based name and expression list method.

Now you will create a Sequence of Stage, where if the Incoming Payload has an Effective Discount of or greater than 40 percent, then you will route this task to a **SalesManagerGroup**. And if approved by this group, the Process Token moves ahead and goes to the third stage which you will create for Management Chain Approval.

However, if the Effective Discount is less than 40 percent, you can assign the task to `territorymanagerl2` (Territory Manager Level 2).

How to do it...

1. You will learn to create sequential stages and add serial participants.
2. Go to **BPM Navigator | SalesToContractDemo | Business Catalog | Human Tasks** and click the **ManagementApproval.task** file. This will open the **Human Task** editor.
3. Go to the **Assignment** section. You will find the stage **TerritoryManagerApproval**.
4. Click on the stage **TerritoryManagerApproval** and click on the green plus (**+**) icon, as shown, and select **Sequential Stage** to create a second stage in sequence with the **TerritoryManagerApproval** stage.

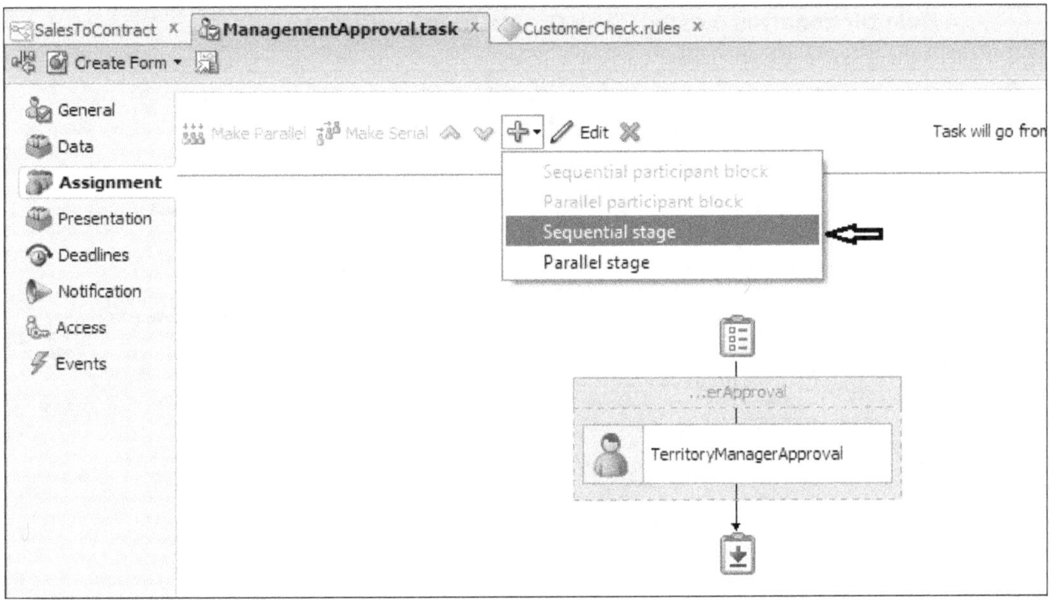

5. Double-click on the newly created stage, name it as **SalesGroupApproval**, and select **Non-Repeating** radio.
6. Click **OK**.
7. Click the **Edit** participant and it would open the **Add Participant Type** dialog.
8. Select **Type** = **Single** and **Enter Label** as **SalesGroupApproval**.
9. Use a rule-based name and expression to build the participant list.
10. Enter name of the ruleset: `SalesGroupApprovalRuleSet`. This will create a ruleset, if one is not already present.

11. Click **OK**.
12. A **Rule Dictionary** is created. Click **Create Rule** to create a rule.

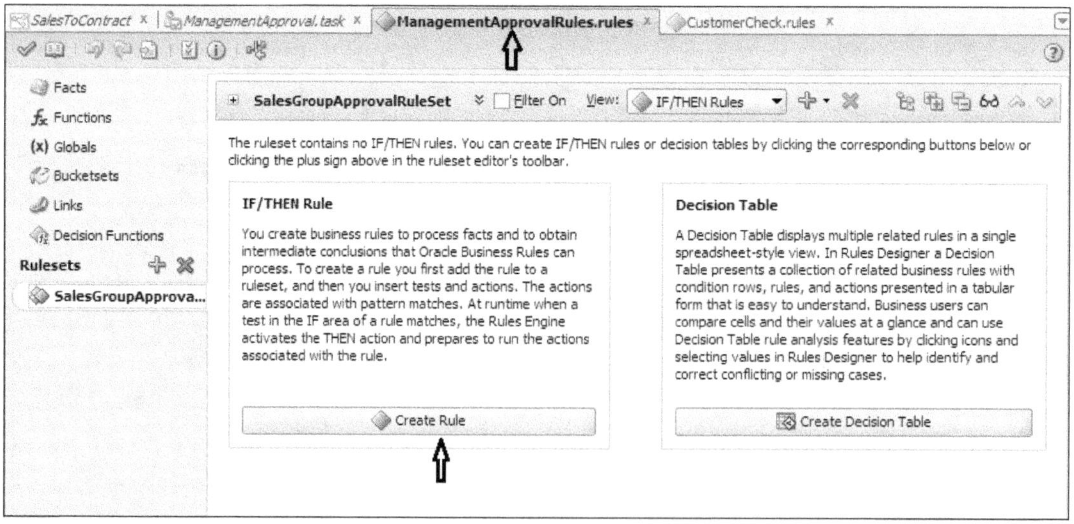

13. In the **Rule Editor**, enter the name of the rule as **SalesGroupApprovalRule**.
14. Enter the condition in the If clause, so that this condition get's executed, when Effective Discount is greater than 40 percent, as follows:

    ```
    Task.payload.quoteRequest.summary.effectiveDiscount> 40
    ```

15. In **<Insert Action>**, choose **Call**. You need to create a user list. There are a lot of Seeded functions available to create the user list.
16. You will find a pop-up list of functions. Choose the **CreateResourceList** function.
17. As you want to assign the task to a group, you will give **SalesGroup** as **Groups** into the **Function Argument**. Enter other details, as shown in the following screenshot.

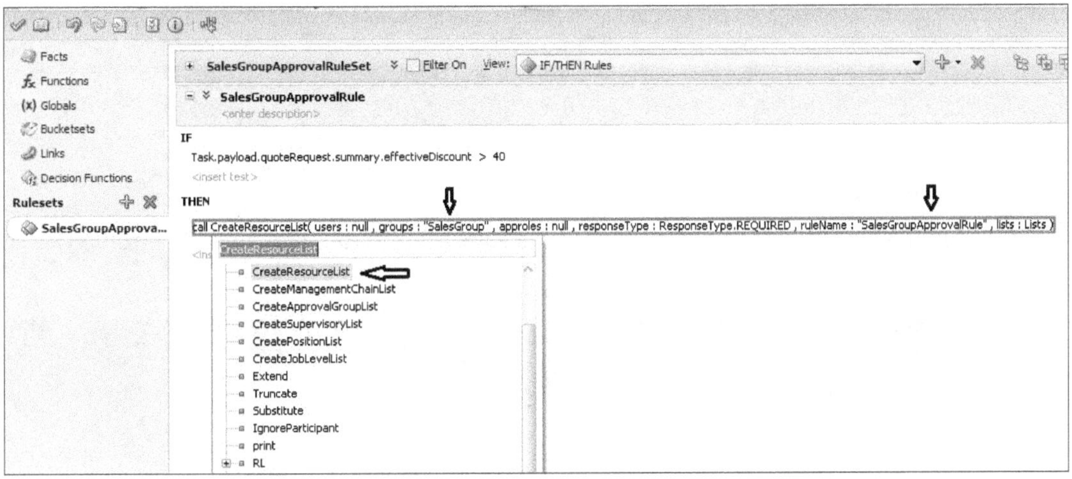

18. Click **Save**.

> You can check how to create **SalesGroup** in the the following section. Also, you cannot have app role and users' values together. So in case you have to use a value for the app role, the value for users has to be null and vice versa.

19. Click on the green plus (+) icon, as shown, to create an Else rule in the same ruleset, when Effective Discount is less than 40 percent.
20. Name the Rule as **SalesGroupApprovalRuleElse**

21. Task Action will route the task to `territorymanager12` by Creating a participant list by entering users, as shown in the following screenshot:

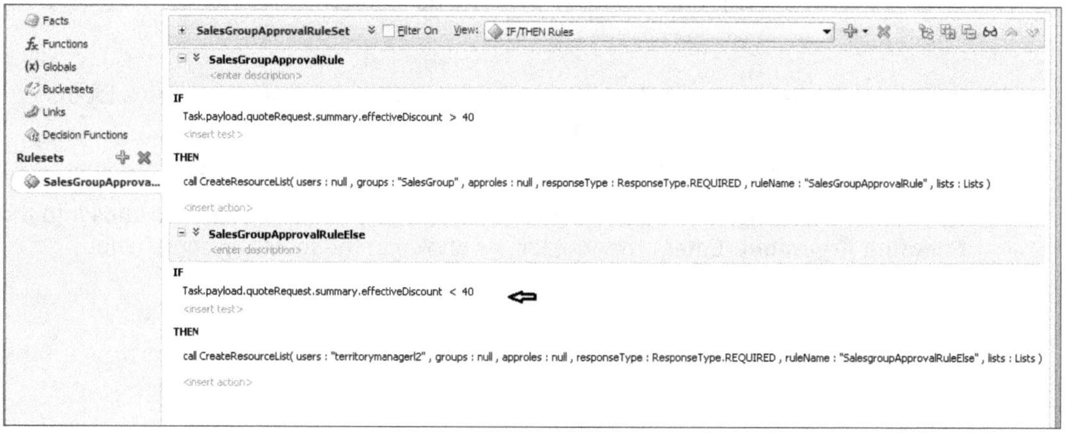

22. When finished, **Save**.
23. If an Else section is not developed in the rule, then it would result in an error in Oracle BPM Workspace as follows:

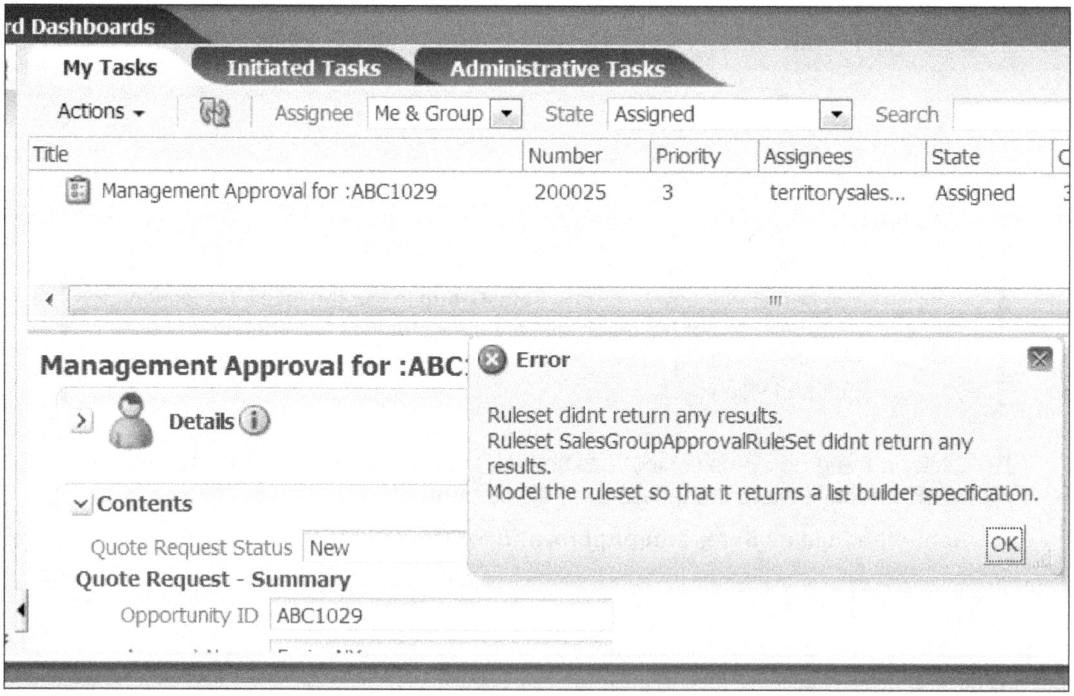

How it works...

When you name a ruleset in the edit participant type and click ok, a decision Service Component is created along with a rule dictionary.

This will create a rule dictionary, if one is not already created, and pre-seed several rule functions and facts for easy specifications of the participant list. In the rule dictionary, the following rule functions are seeded to create participant lists:

- Create Resource List
- Create Management Chain List

At runtime when process token, reaches the second stage, post Territory Manager Approval and when the condition of Effective Discount is greater than 40 percent is met, a call action gets executed. This will call the `CreateResourceList` function, which will create the list with the users of the `SalesGroup` as entered as argument in the function above. And if the Effective Discount is less than 40 percent (`< 40`), then the task action will route the task to `territorymanager12` by creating a participant list by entering users in the create resource list function.

There's more...

You will learn to create an approval group in this section.

Creating an Approval Group

1. Log in to the Oracle BPM Workspace application as a WebLogic user.
2. Click on the **Administration** link on the top of the page.
3. Click **Approval Groups** in the **Task** administration.

4. Click on the green plus (**+**) icon ahead of **Groups** and select **Create Static**.

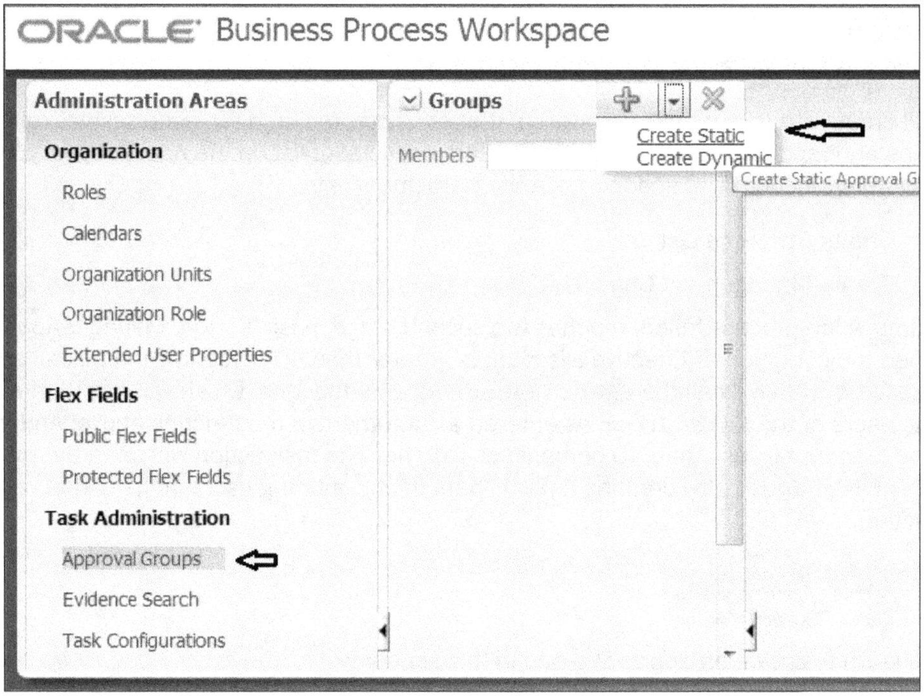

5. In the **Details** section, enter the name of the Group as SalesGroup and click on the green plus (**+**) icon to add members to the Group.
6. Search/browse for the **Members**. This will open the **Identity Browser**.
7. Select **zonalmanager** from the list. At the moment, let's have only one user belonging to this group.

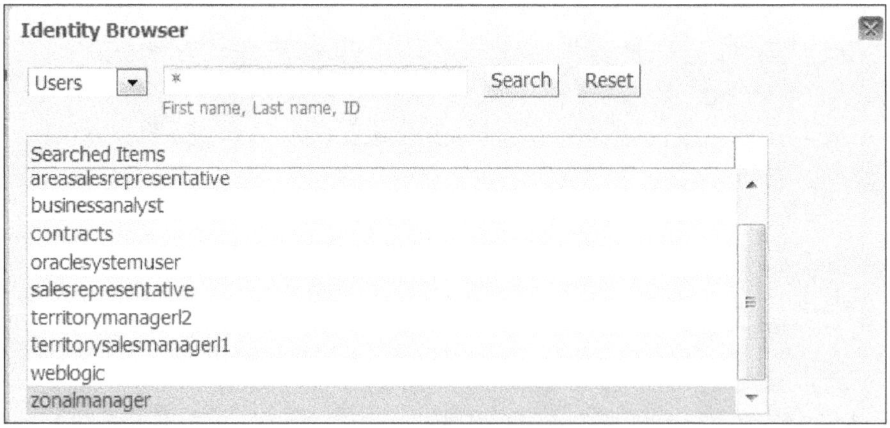

8. Click **OK**.
9. Click **OK** on the **Add to Group** box too.
10. Click on the **Apply** button and now **zonalmanager** is a member of **SalesGroup**.

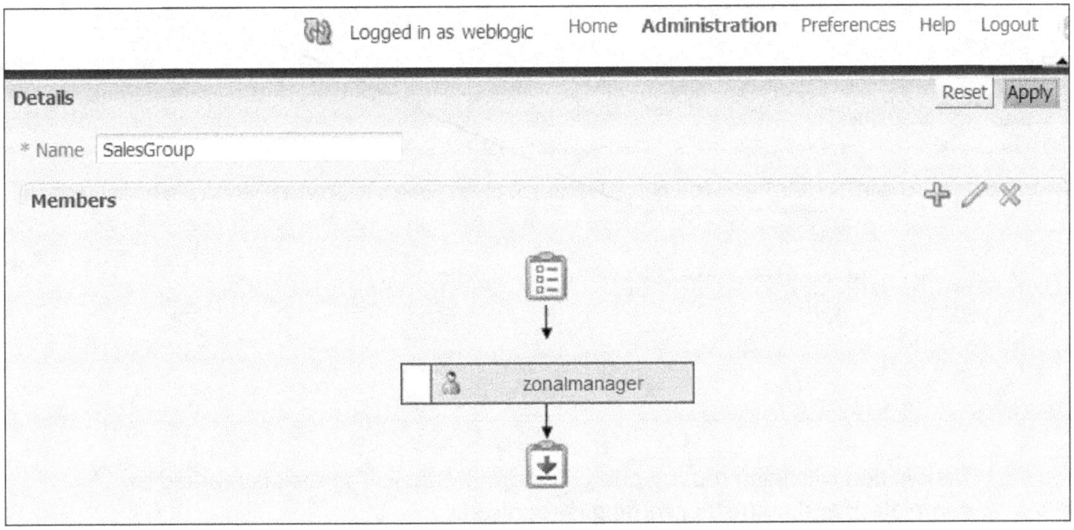

Calling RL Functions to act on the task

To instruct the task service on how to route the task, rules can specify one of many task actions. This is done by updating the `TaskAction` fact asserted into the rule session. However, rules should not directly update the `TaskAction` fact. Instead, rules should call one of the action RL functions, passing the `TaskAction` fact as a parameter. These functions handle the actual updates to the fact.

In the section, you have created a ruleset with two rules: one to handle the case when Effective Discount is greater than 40 percent and the other to handle the case when Effective Discount is less than 40 percent.

In the second rule, `SalesGroupApprovalRuleElse`, you can even use an RL function to call a `TaskAction` to complete the task.

The **COMPLETE** action finishes routing and completes the task. The task is marked as completed and no further routing is required.

1. Go to the rule designer at the rule **SalesGroupApprovalRuleElse**.

2. Enter the rule when **effectiveDiscount < 40**, as shown in the following screenshot:

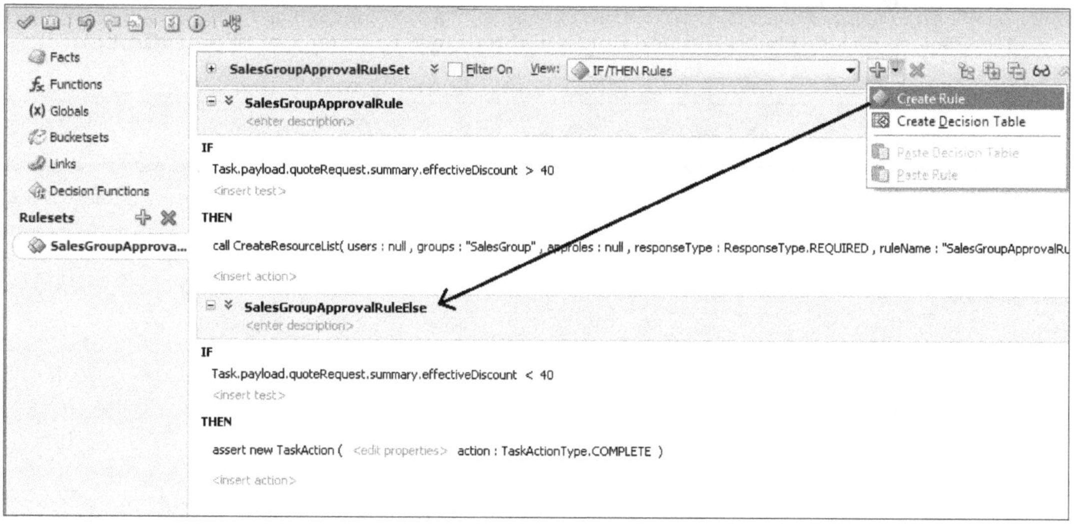

3. Task Action will finish routing and complete the task. The task is marked as completed, and no further routing is required.
4. When you have finished, **Save**.

Defining assignments—management chain participant

Management chains are typically used for serial approvals through multiple users in a management chain hierarchy. Therefore, this list is most likely to be useful with the serial participant type. This is typically the case if you want all users in the hierarchy to act upon the task. Management chains can also be used with the single participant type. In this case, however, all users in the hierarchy get the task assigned at the same time. As soon as one user acts on the task, it is withdrawn from the other users.

You will create a management hierarchy, which will get a level of elevation from the **Customer Check Rules'** Decision Table.

Remember the Decision Table has Actions in which a value is assigned to a number of **Tier3Level**, which means at what level you need to assign this task too. You will use this value to decide on the level. The maximum level defined is **2**.

The task is assigned to Sales Representative's manager AreaSalesmanager. The other people in the hierarchy who will get notified based on the **numberofTier3Level** value are **regionalmanager** and **countrymanager**.

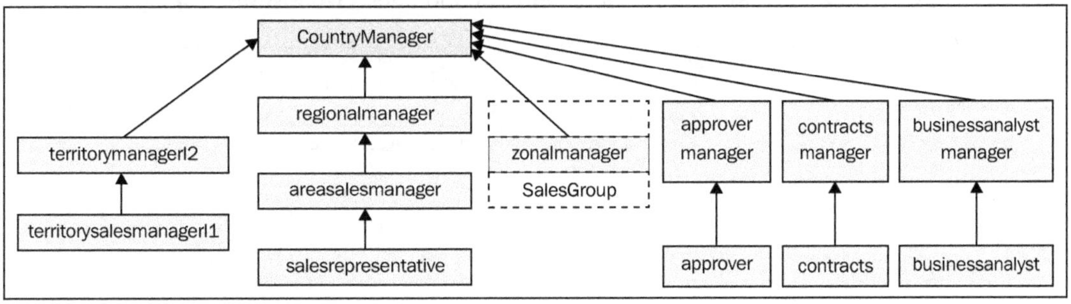

How to do it...

Let's learn to define management chain participants with the following steps:

1. Go to **BPM Navigator | SalesToContractDemo | business catalog | Human Tasks** and click the **ManagementApproval.task** file. This will open the **Human Task** editor.
2. Go to the **Assignment** section and you will find two stages created: **TerritoryManagerApproval** and **SalesGroupApproval**, as shown in the following screenshot:

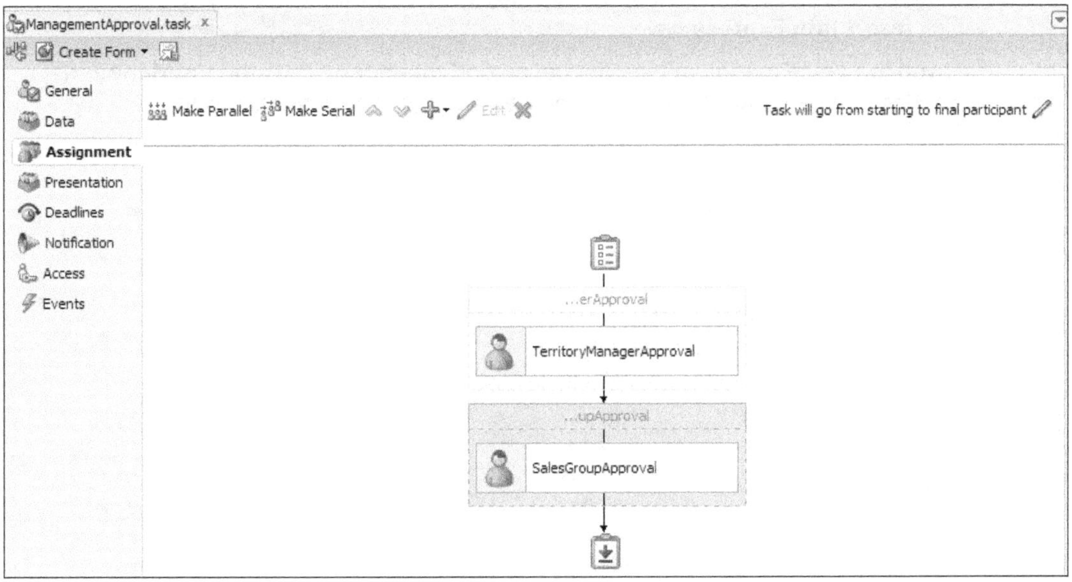

3. Click on the **SalesGroupApproval** stage, click the green plus (**+**) icon, and select **Sequential Stage** to create a **Sequential Stage** after the **SalesGroupApproval** stage.
4. Click on the default stage name **Stage 1**. In the **Edit** dialog, enter the name of the stage as **SalesManagementChainApproval** and check **Non-Repeating**.

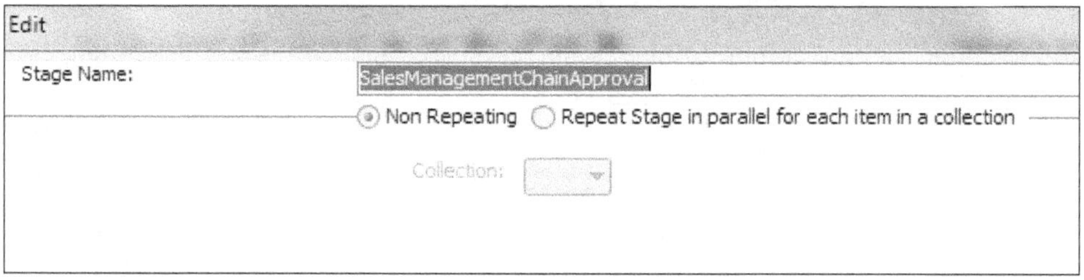

5. Click on the **Edit Participant Box**, and in the **Participant Type** dialog, select participant type as **Serial** and **Label** - **SalesManagementChainApproval**.
6. Build a list of participants using the management chain.
7. Specify the **Participant Type** attributes as **Value-based**.
8. In the **Starting Participant**, click on the green plus (**+**) icon and select **Add User** as **Identification Type**.
9. In the **Data Type**, choose **By Expression**.
10. Click on the **Browse** button to use the **Expression Builder**.
11. In the functions section, select the **Identity Service** function `getManager()` and click **Insert into Expression**.
12. As you are going to build a user list based on Embedded LDAP, the **getManager()** function accepts **SalesRepID**, and the name of the realm is **jazn.com**.

13. Expand the payload in the **Schema** section as **QuoteRequest | Summary | SalesRepId** and click **Insert into Expression**.

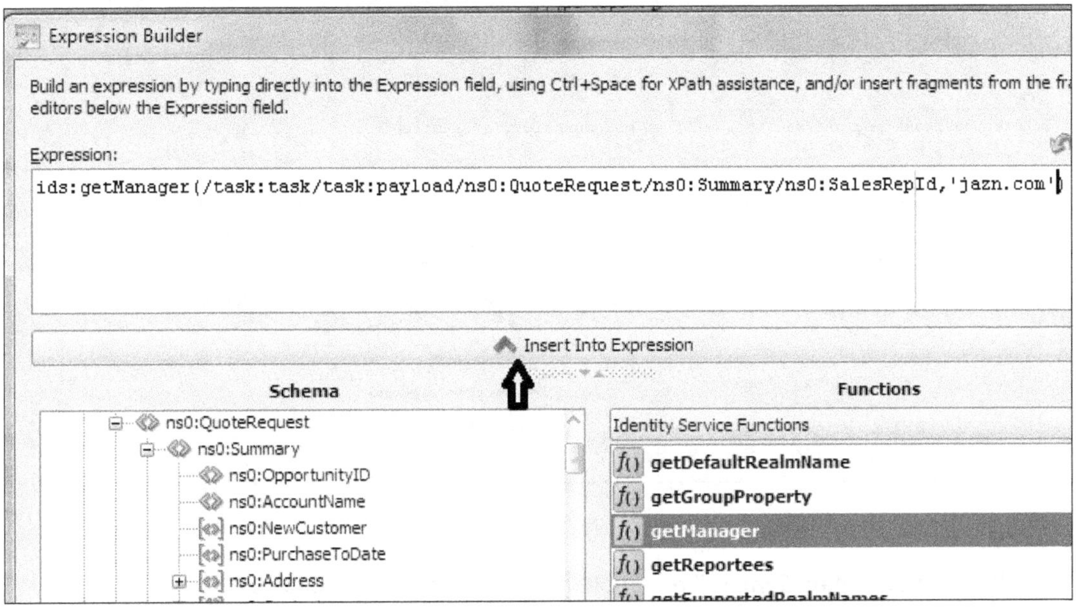

14. Click **OK**. The list will be dynamically built and level to which it would be elevated will be decided at runtime based on the Number Of Levels entered into the Participant Type dialog.
15. Select XPath from the drop-down list and click on the **Expression Builder**.
16. Expand **Payload** in the **Schema** to **Payload | ApprovalFlow | NumberOfTier3Levels**.

17. The value is populated into this field at runtime by the **Customer Check Rule** execution.

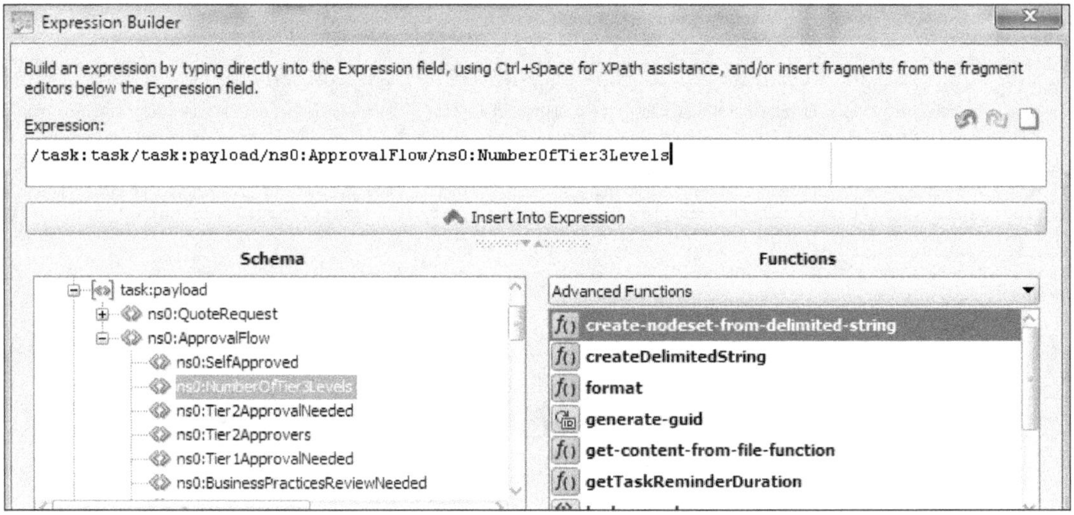

18. Click **OK**.
19. The **Participant Type** will resemble following screenshot. Click **OK**.

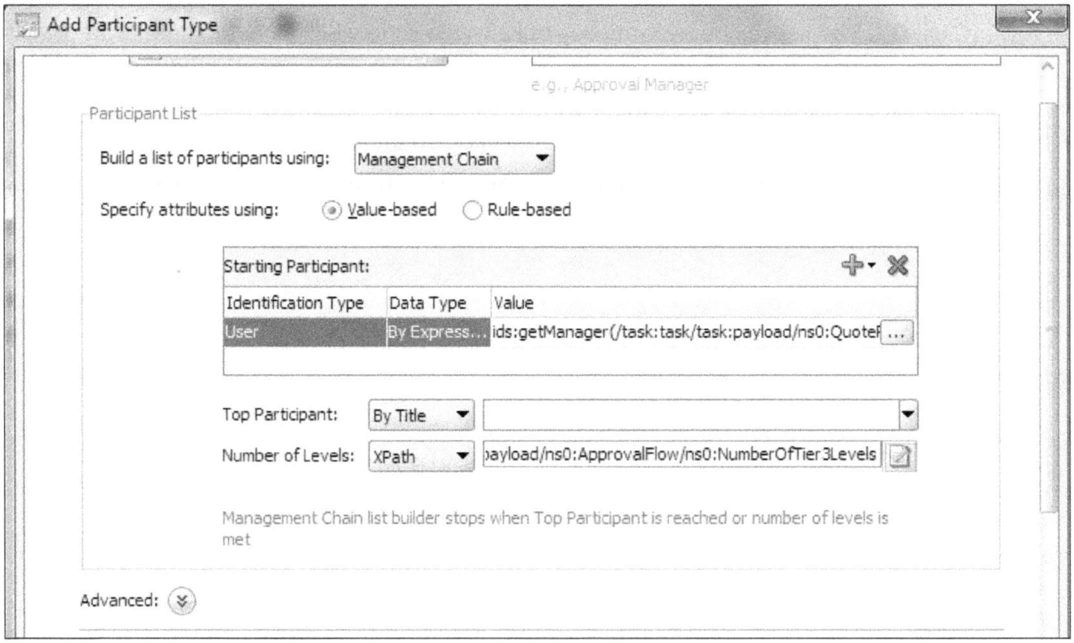

20. When finished, **Save**.

How it works...

Remember you have created a `CustomerCheck.rules` file. At runtime, when facts match condition cells (**Customer Type** = **New** and **Quantity** as entered, if it falls in the given range), the Rules Engine prepares to run the actions associated with the rule. This action will enter value into the **numberOfTier3Levels**. For example, if rule **R3** executes, action will enter value `2` into **numberOfTier3Levels**. And the task will be assigned to SalesRepID's manager **areasalesmanager** and on his/her approval, it will move ahead to **regionalmanager**.

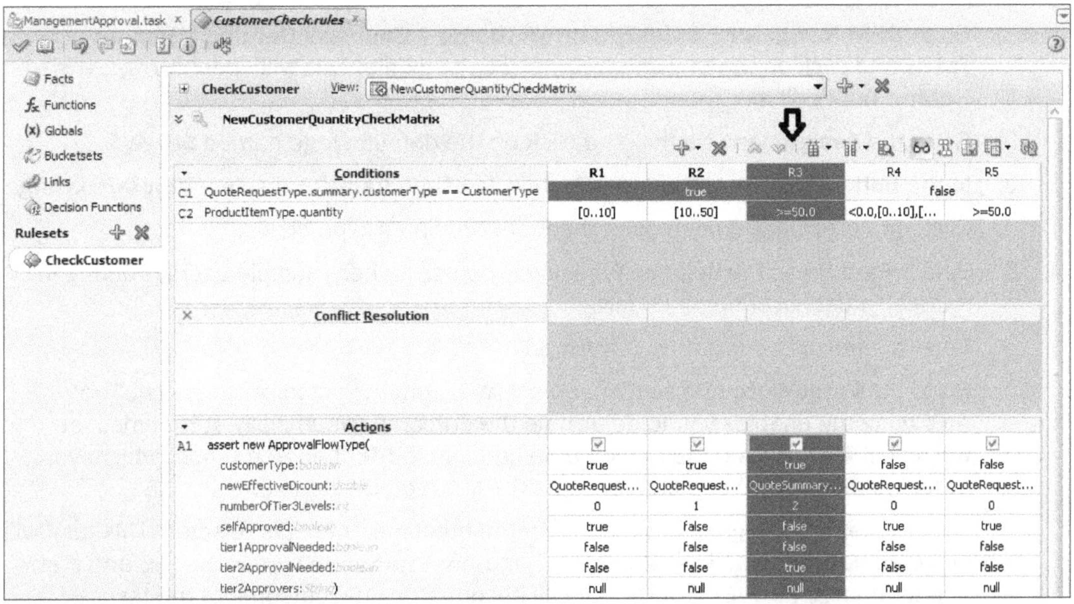

Defining Assignments—parallel participant type

When the Process Token reaches the Business Analyst Review, the `businessanalyst` user will either APPROVE or REJECT and the task outcome is assigned to the `BusinessAnalystOutcome` Process data object. You will develop a parallel scenario when multiple users, working in parallel, must act simultaneously on the Task that is assigned in parallel to the `businessanalyst` user and it's manager `businessanalyst` manager.

You will specify a voted-upon outcome that overrides the default outcome selected in the Default Outcome list. This outcome takes effect if the required percentage is reached. Outcomes are evaluated in the order listed in the table.

You specify the voting percentage that is needed for the outcome to take effect, such as a 50 percent vote.

This task will be voted between `businessanalyst` and `businessanalystmanager`, and if any one of them APPROVE/REJECT it, it will become the final outcome of the task.

How to do it...

Here you will learn to create parallel participant types as follows:

1. Go to **BPM Navigator | SalesToContractDemo | Business Catalog | Human Tasks** and click on the `BusinessAnalyst.task` file. This will open the **Human Task** editor.
2. Go to the **Assignment** section and click on the default stage named **Stage 1**.
3. In the **Edit** dialog, enter **BusinessReview** as **Stage name** and select **Non-Repeating**.
4. Click on Participant Type to open the Edit Participant Type dialog.
5. Select **Parallel** as **Participant Type**. It will be used when multiple users, working in parallel, must act simultaneously.
6. Enter a label: `BusinessReviewVoted`.
7. Go to the **Voted Outcome** section. Select **ANY** from the voted outcome list. The **ANY** outcome enables you to determine the outcome dynamically at runtime. You will select **ANY** and set the outcome percentage to **50**; then at runtime, whichever outcome reaches 50 percent becomes the final voted outcome.

   If 50 percent of assignees vote to reject the outcome, then it is rejected. This task will be voted between `businessanalyst` and `businessanalystmanager` and if any one of them APPROVE/REJECT it, it will become the final outcome of the task.
8. In the **Outcome Type** column, select **By Percentage** as a method for determining the outcome of the final task.
9. In the **value** column, specify a **50** % percentage value that determines when the outcome of this task takes effect.
10. In the **Default Outcome** list, select **REJECT** as the default outcome for this task to take effect if the consensus percentage value is not satisfied. This happens if there is a tie, or if all participants do not respond before the task expires.
11. Check **Immediately trigger voted outcome** for when the minimum percentage is met. If selected, the outcome of the task can be computed early with the outcomes of the completed subtasks, enabling the pending subtasks to be withdrawn. This means if any of the users, `businessanalyst` or `businessanalystmanager`, act on the task and APPROVE the task, the other user doesn't have to act on the task since the consensus percentage value has been satisfied. However, wait until all votes are in before triggering an outcome if selected, as the workflow waits for all responses before an outcome is initiated.

12. Check **Share attachments and Comments** to share comments and attachments with all group collaborators or workflow participants for a task. This information will be displayed in the footer region of Oracle BPM Worklist.
13. Build the list of participants using **Name and Expressions**. To specify the participant type attributes, select **Value-based**.
14. Click on the green plus (**+**) icon and select the **Identification Type**: **Add user** to add the users `businessanalyst` and `businessanalystmanager` to build the list of users.
15. Select Data Type **By Name** and click the **Browse** button to invoke the **Identity Lookup**.
16. Add the users **businessanalyst** and **businessanalystmanager**, as shown in the following screenshot:

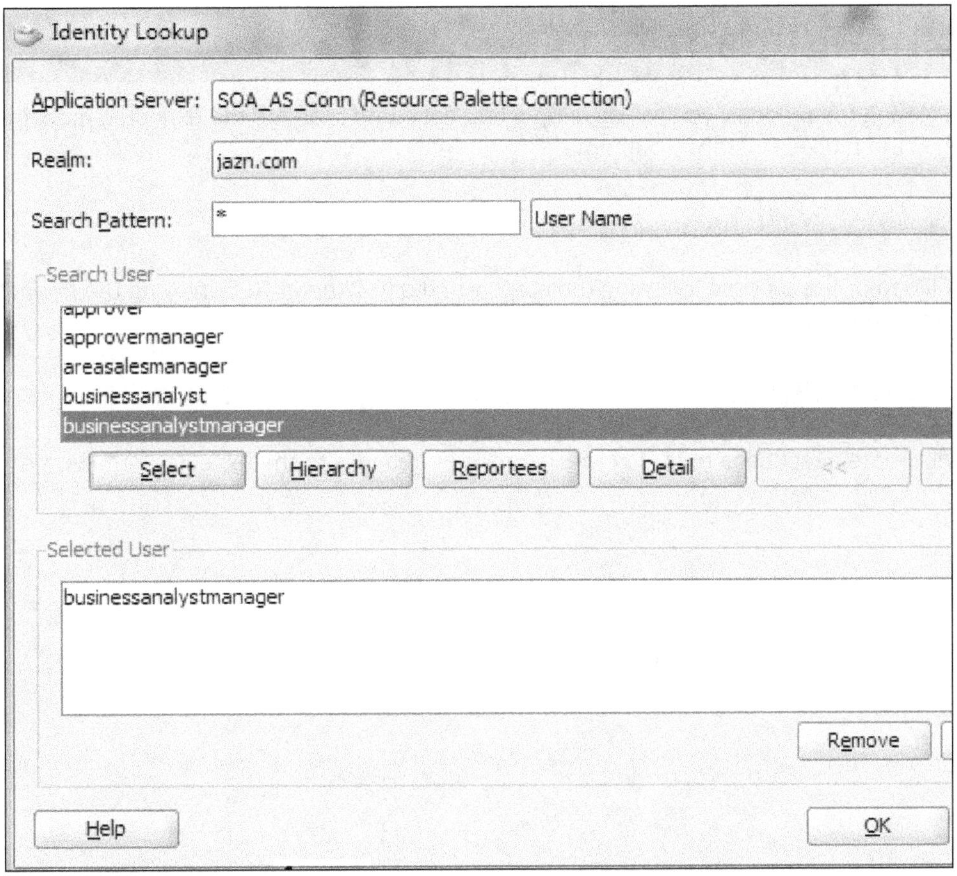

17. Click **OK** in the **Identity** dialog.
18. Click **OK** in the **Edit Participant Type** dialog as well.
19. When you have finished, **Save**.

How it works...

When the Process Token reaches the stage BusinessReview, the participant type attributes will build the participant list and a voted outcome will be expected by `businessanalyst` and `businessanalystmanager`. When a task is picked and an action is performed on the task, it will be matched with the `Percentage Set` in the `Outcome Percentage`. As there are two users, anyone's outcome will result in the 50 percent requirement, and that outcome will be considered as `Task Outcome`.

Testing the process

While testing the process, you will develop a test case and match if the expected outcome matches the process instance outcome.

Getting ready

You will deploy the process following the steps you did in *Chapter 3, Deploying the Project*, to deploy this project.

How to do it...

You will create a test case to match the instance outcome with the expected results.

Test Case # 1 Values	`Customer Type = New, Quantity = 100, Effective Discount = 30`		
Human Task Stage	**Expected**	**Output**	**Expectance Met**
Territory-Manager-Approval	In the stage TerritoryManagerApproval, the `territorysalesmanager11` user will receive the task. Once approved, it will move to next stage. You can check the title and use AdHoc Routing as set in the Participant Attributes shown below.	Task Assigned to territorysales-managerl1 user.	YES
SalesGroup-Approval	The task will move to the stage SalesGroupApproval and execute the rule—`SalesGroupApprovalRule` since `Effective Discount >40` and the task will get assigned to SalesGroup. *The discount increases from 30 percent to 45 due to the* `CustomerCheck` *rule execution.* *Log in as* `zonalmanager` *and approve the task.*	Task assigned to zonalmanager user as it is member of SalesGroup	YES
Sales-Management ChainApproval	*The task gets assigned to* `areasalesmanager` *and on approval to users* `regionalmanager` *and* `CountryManager`	On each user's APPROVE in the management chain, Task keeps elevating in the Chain	YES
Business-Review	*The task on parallel gets assigned to the users* `businessanalyst` *and* `businessanalystmanager` *and if any one of them* `APPROVE/REJECT`*, it becomes the voted outcome of the task. You can log in as* `businessanalystmanager` *and* `APPROVE` *the task.*	Log in as *businessanalyst manager* and `APPROVE` the task.	YES

- When the task is assigned to `territorysalesmanager11`, you can note that the tile is reflected as per the XPath given in task definition, as shown by Pointer **1**.
- Pointer **2** shows that the AdHoc Route is enabled and this participant can route this task to any other participant.
- Pointer **3** shows the **Created and Expires** date as set for the participant. If the participant doesn't act within a day, the task is assigned to another user, as per the Escalation policy.

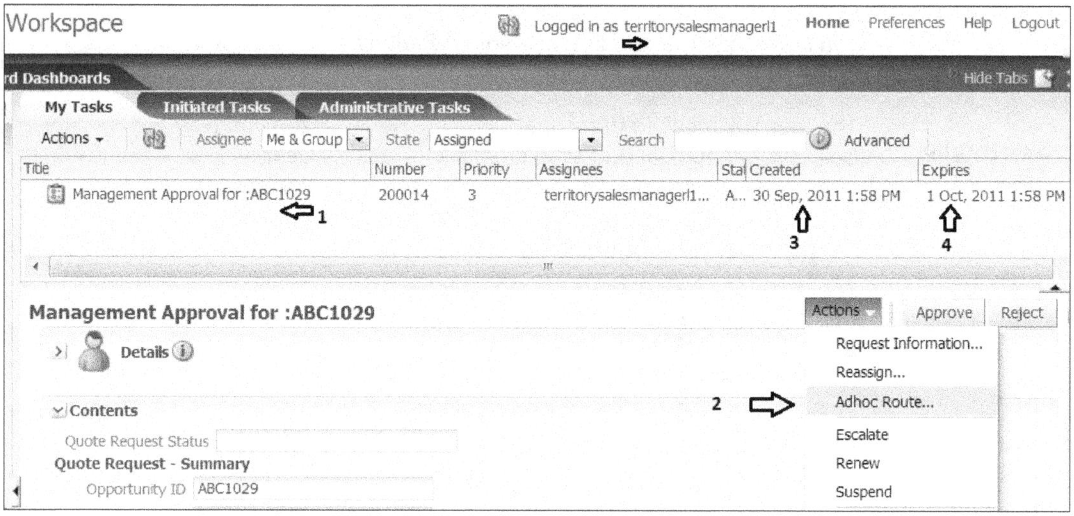

Click on Adhoc Route and you can route this task to another user too, as follows:

1. Select **Approve** from the **Task Result**. This will route the task to **territorymanagerl2** only when this user approves it.

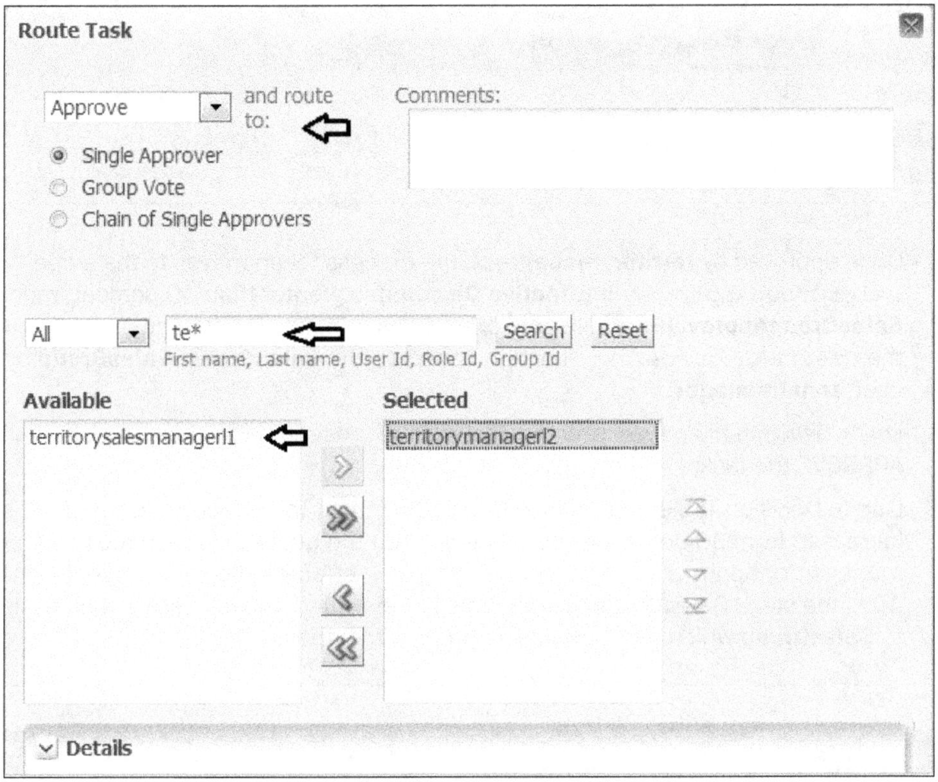

2. Log in with the **territorymanagerl2** user and you can find the task assigned to this user.

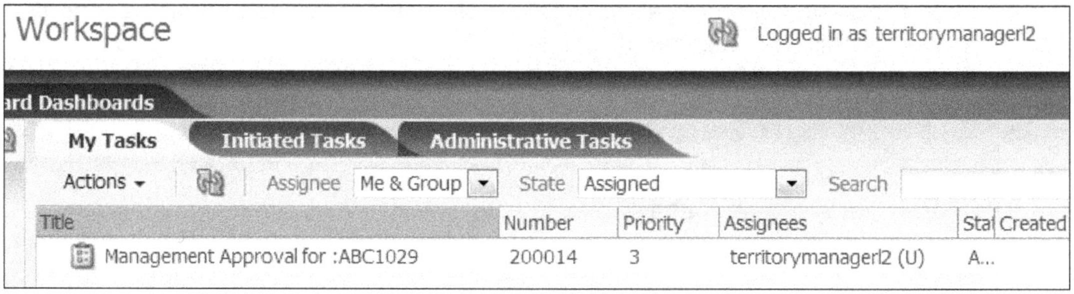

3. Once approved by **territorymanagerl2**, the process token moves to the stage `salesGroupApproval`. If **Effective Discount** is greater than 40 percent, then the **SalesGroupApprovalRule** rule gets executed and builds the Participant List using the `CreateResourceList` function based on the **SalesGroup**. **SalesGroup** has one user, **zonalmanager**.
4. Log in as `zonalmanager` and the Task will be present in its Inbox. You can APPROVE the task.

   Due to Decision Table execution in Check Customer, the effective discount will be increased from 30 percent to 45 percent. Then the quote will reach the territory manager for approval and once approved ,since effective discount is greater than 40%, the stage **SalesGroupApproval** will get executed and the task will be assigned to **SalesGroup** which has **zonalmanager** as a member.

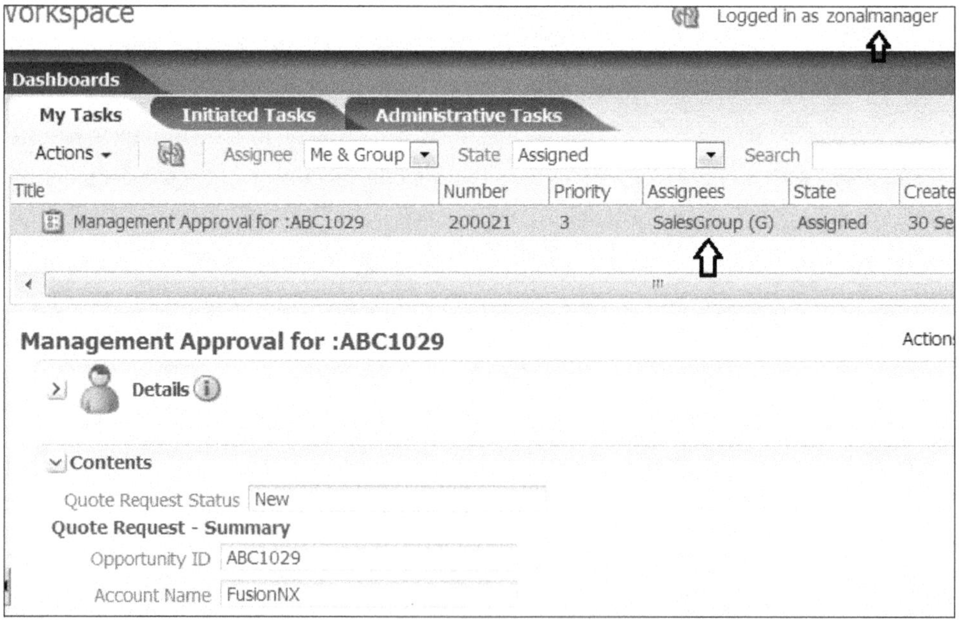

5. The task now moves to the stage **SalesManagementChainApproval**, which builds a **Management Chain of Participants** where the level is decided based on the **numberOfTier3Levels** element values. These values get populated at runtime by the `CustomerCheck` rule.

6. As `Customer Type` = `New` and `Quantity` is greater than `100`, `Rule 3` in the `Customer Check` rule gets executed and the payload with the element values will be as shown in the following screenshot:

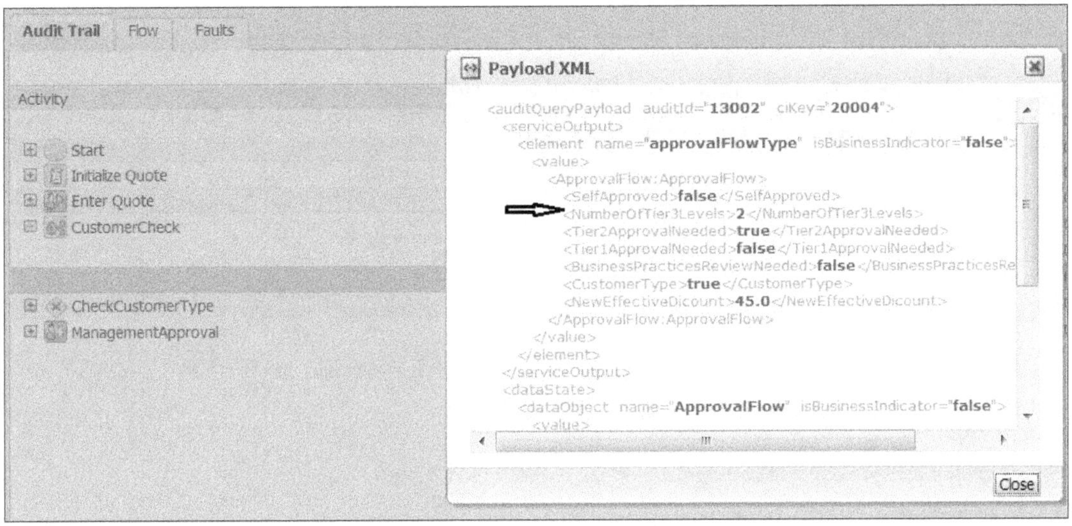

7. Log in as `areasalesmanager` and `approve` the quote. You can log in as `regionalsalesmanager` and after approval from the `CountryManager`, approve it.

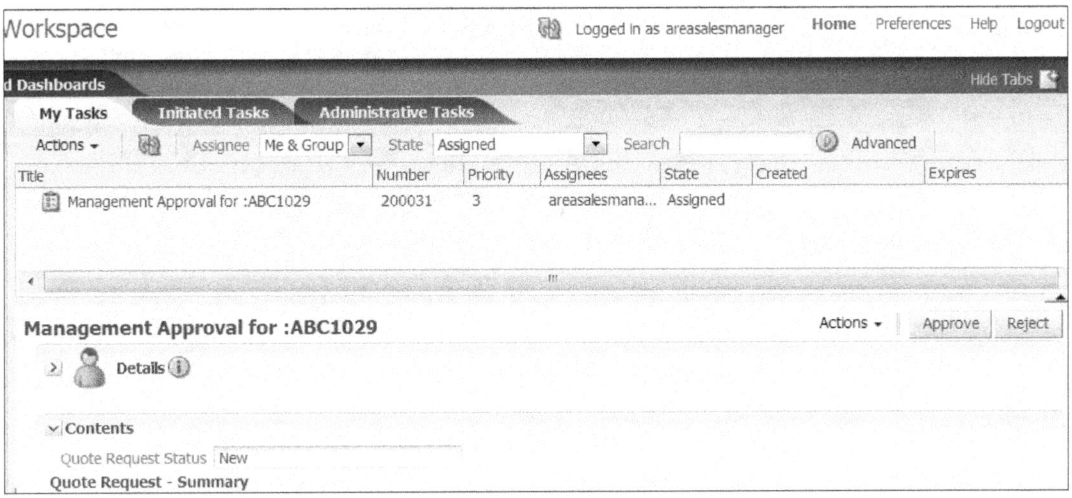

8. The Process Token now assigns the task to both users: `businessanalyst` and `businessanalystmanager`. As it's a voting with a 50 percent vote win scenario, whichever outcome reaches 50 percent becomes the final voted outcome. If 50 percent of the assignees vote to reject the outcome, then it is rejected. This task will be voted between `businessanalyst` and `businessanalystmanager`, and if any one of them approves/rejects it, it will become the final outcome of the task.

9. Log in as the user `businessanalyst` and verify the presence of the task in its Inbox. Log out of it without any action.

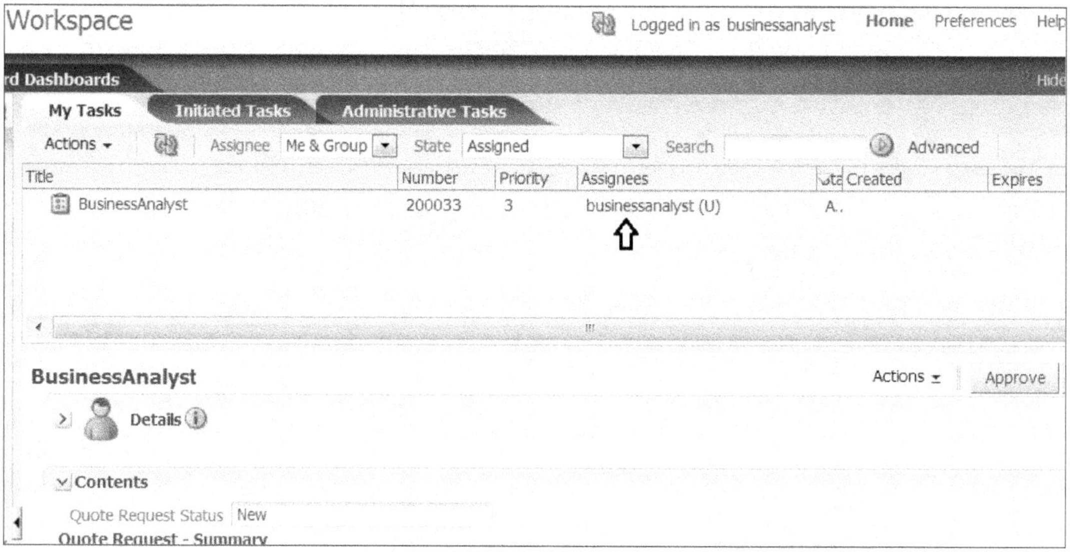

10. Log in as `businessanalystmanager` and approve the task.

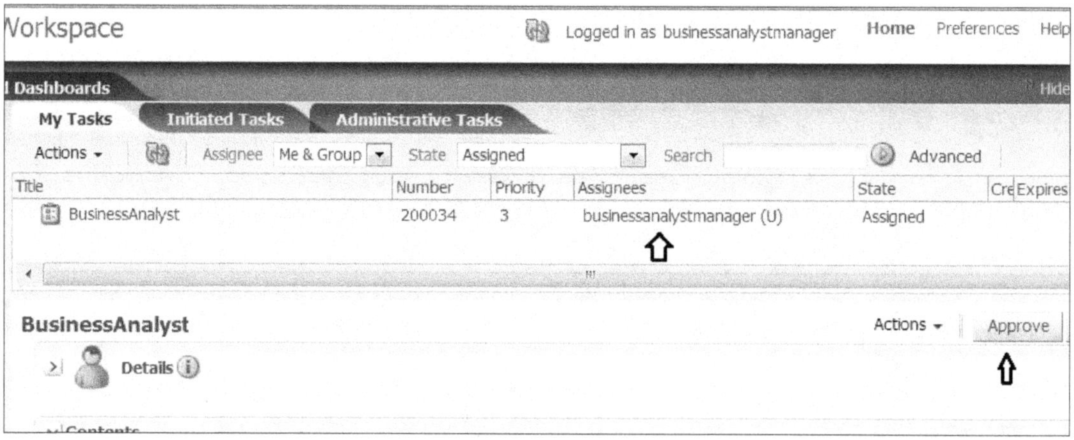

11. Log in to the EM Console. Click on **Process Instance** and on tracing you will find that the process has moved ahead to **ApproveQuote** and **ApproveTerms**.

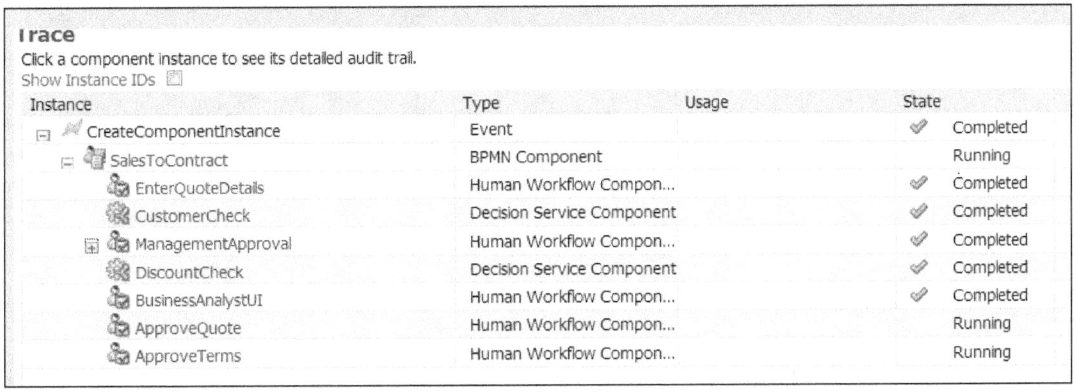

There's more...

You can execute `Test# 2`, as shown in the following table, with `Discount < 20%` and `Quantity` as `45`. This test will demonstrate the Skipping Rule that you have set in the stage `TerritoryManagerApproval` for the user `territorysalesmanagerl1` and the ruleset `SalesGroupApprovalRuleElse` when `Discount` is less than `40`.

Test # 2 values	`Customer Type = New, Quantity = 45, Effective Discount = 20`		
Human Task stage	**Values expected**	**Output**	**Expect-ance met**
TerritoryManager-Approval **SalesGroup-Approval**	In the stage `TerritoryManagerApproval`, the user `territorysalesmanagerl1` should not receive the task as the Participant Type's `Advance Attributes Skip` rule enforces the Process Token to skip the assignment of the task to this participant when `Quantity` is less than `50` The task will move to the stage SalesGroupApproval and will execute the rule—SalesGroupApprovalRuleElse as Effective Discount < 40 and the task will get assigned to `territorymanagerl2`	Task Skipped from the territorysales-managerl1 user. Task assigned to the territorymanagerl2 user.	YES

6

Process Simulation

This chapter will help you analyze the performance of your process before your process goes live in a production environment. With analysis results, you can change the parameters of your process so that the total cost and time of running a process for a business can be reduced. You will use simulation after implementation, since you should not consider simulation as a process design tool, but instead as a tool for optimizing a processes performance before it goes live. In this chapter, you will cover the following topics:

- Defining simulation models
- Defining simulation definition
- Running a simulation
- Analyzing simulation results
- Re-engineering the BPM Process to improve performance

Introduction

Simulation is an important function in Business Process Management, as it answers some of the important questions specific to process usage, such as the following:

- How much the process will cost the business
- Predicting Business Process behavior
- Checking if the process output meets the process objectives
- Identifying bottlenecks, if any
- Effect of changes on an existing process design

Simulation can be performed before implementation, but here we will be using simulation after implementation. You can perform simulation anytime—before or after implementation, however it should always be before you go live with your process. Readers can perform simulation before implementation with the methods given in this chapter. However, while reading through this section, they will understand why simulation is used for analysis after implementation.

Process Modeling focuses on getting the process right before implementation. Many use simulation before implementation because they think that direct experimentation with the business process would be disruptive or costly.

Simulation as a process design exercise makes more sense when the costs of implementation are relatively high as compared to the costs of simulation analysis. However, at present, the cost of simulation has come down significantly when used for analysis after implementation.

You are not at all delaying the benefits of implementation by positioning simulation for use after implementation. Implementation before simulation is helpful for many reasons, such as the following:

- Implementation actually provides the data required for parameterized simulation models virtually for free
- High quality of data is easy available
- Accurate data is guaranteed
- The potential for process discovery and the skills required to create meaningful simulation models are reduced, as the simulation model construction process is partially automated as a consequence of Process Implementation.
- Direct data usage increases the predictive ability of simulation models

At whatever phase you use simulation, the question is why you need it. This is because, as an Analyst post-modeling, or as a Developer post-implementation, you want to optimize the process before it goes live, so that you can reduce the cost a process brings to the business, and so that **Service Level Agreements** (**SLA**) are met. Oracle BPM Simulation addresses structural improvements most common in process redesign. It should provide useful cost and quality metrics, in addition to time-based metrics. It actively assists the user with setting model parameters to match known aggregated metrics of the as-is process.

Simulation does not execute each individual task within a process. That is, the code within an activity is not executed, forms are not displayed to the user, variables are not assigned values, external resources are not updated, and so on. However, you can mimic the behavior of an activity by configuring different attributes within a simulation model. These attributes include duration, resources, costs, queue information, and probability of sequence flows.

Process simulation models specify parameters such as the following:

- The rate at which new instances will be created
- The estimated execution times for each of the activities
- What percentage of the time a gateway will take one branch or another and so on

So, you can use the tool to create different 'what-if' scenarios based on different combinations of resource allocation and activity behavior. You can even run simulations from multiple processes simultaneously, to identify resource contention across multiple processes. Once you run the simulations, you can examine the results too.

The process of defining simulation for a BPM process comprises of defining the simulation model, defining simulation definitions, and running the simulation.

Although simulation can be used right after the modeling phase, you as a Business Analyst can analyze the process and its performance and define the operational cost to business. You will carry out the similar task as a Developer, post implementation. However, you are carrying out this step much before your process goes live in production. You have assumed that modeling, implementation, and deployment done up to this point are all carried into development instances.

Defining simulation models

The simulation model you are going to create would be a 'what-if' sort of experiment of the process that you will perform before it goes live into production. With the outcome of simulation results, you can analyze the different bottlenecks and can perform certain measures to reduce process cost to the business.

With a process simulation model, you can configure process settings. You will first create a table specifying what the process settings for different activities of the SalesToContract process would be.

Duration defines the time an activity takes to complete. It defines the distribution type, say constant, uniform, exponential, normal, and real. You will use normal distribution, which uses Gauss Bell distribution. This determines how long an activity takes to complete. You have to enter mean period and standard deviation when prompted.

Cost specifies the cost of processing the activity. For User tasks, it also specifies the cost of the resources assigned to the User task. Cost could be fixed base cost or fixed base cost with resource cost added into it. This is calculated based on the defined cost per hour and the time it takes for the resource to execute that task. Generally, this is enabled for User task.

Resources specify the number of participants assigned to a particular role. You can define this parameter in the simulation model or at a global project level in the project simulation definition.

Queue defines the simulated behavior of how process instances are queued for a given activity. It defines the Queue Size, which is the number of instances that can wait for an activity simultaneously, and Queue Info, which enables you to configure the simulated behavior of how the process instances are picked from the queue—FICO, LIFO, by priority, or randomly.

Sequence flows determine the probability percentage of instances routed through the different outgoing sequence flows. Move the slider to specify the probability of occurrence of each outgoing sequence flow.

How to do it...

In this section, you will define a simulation model:

1. Go to **JDeveloper | BPM Project Navigator** and expand the **SalesToContractDemo** project.
2. Click on **Processes | SalesToContract**.
3. Go to the **Simulations** node and expand it.
4. You will find two stores to store **Simulation Models** and its definition.
5. Select the **Simulation Model** folder, right-click it, and select **New Process Simulation Model**.
6. In the **Create Process Simulation** dialog, enter `SalesToContractSM` as **Model name**.

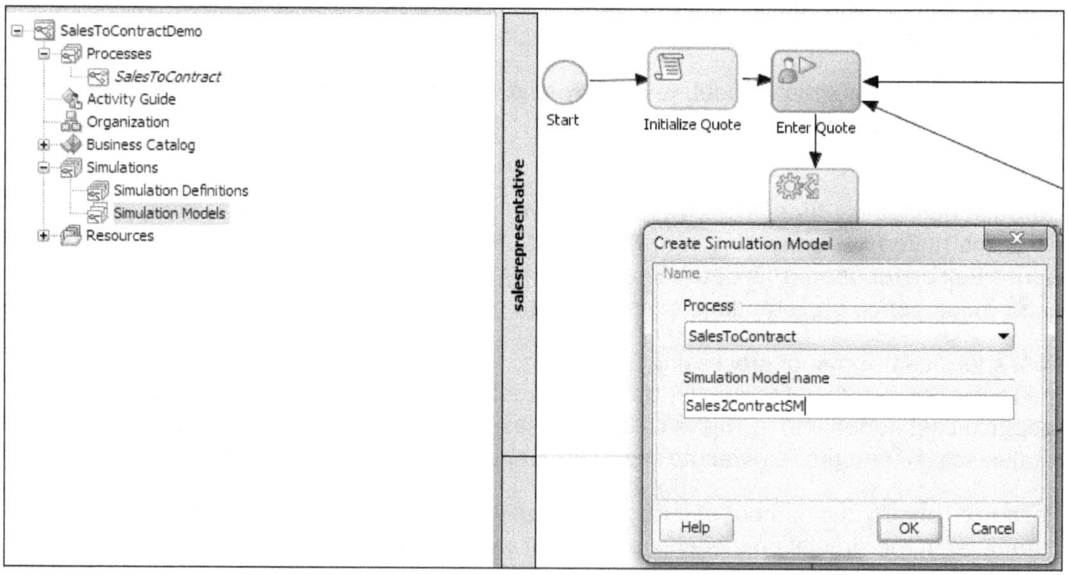

7. Click **OK**.
8. This will open the **Sales2ContractSM** simulation model.
9. Enter number of process instances to be created as `100`, as you assume that 100 Quote requests will get generated on every working day.
10. In the simulation model, go to **Start Activity** and select **Constant** as the **Distribution Type**.
11. You are doing this to configure the frequency of process instances created.
12. Enter `5` minutes as the frequency of process instance creation.

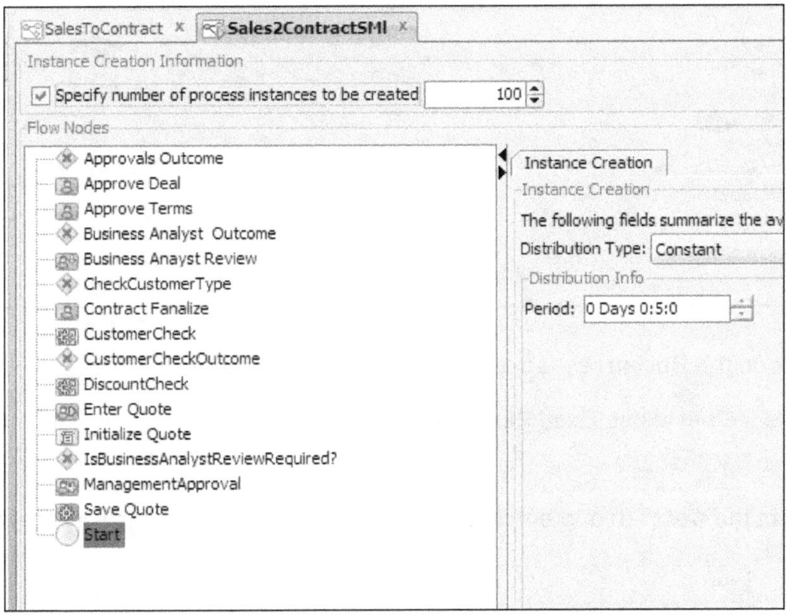

13. Click **Enter Quote** in the **Flow Nodes** list in the simulation model, and in the **Duration** tab, enter values as follows:
    - **Distribution Type: Normal**
    - **Mean: 30** minutes

- **Standard Deviation: 3** seconds

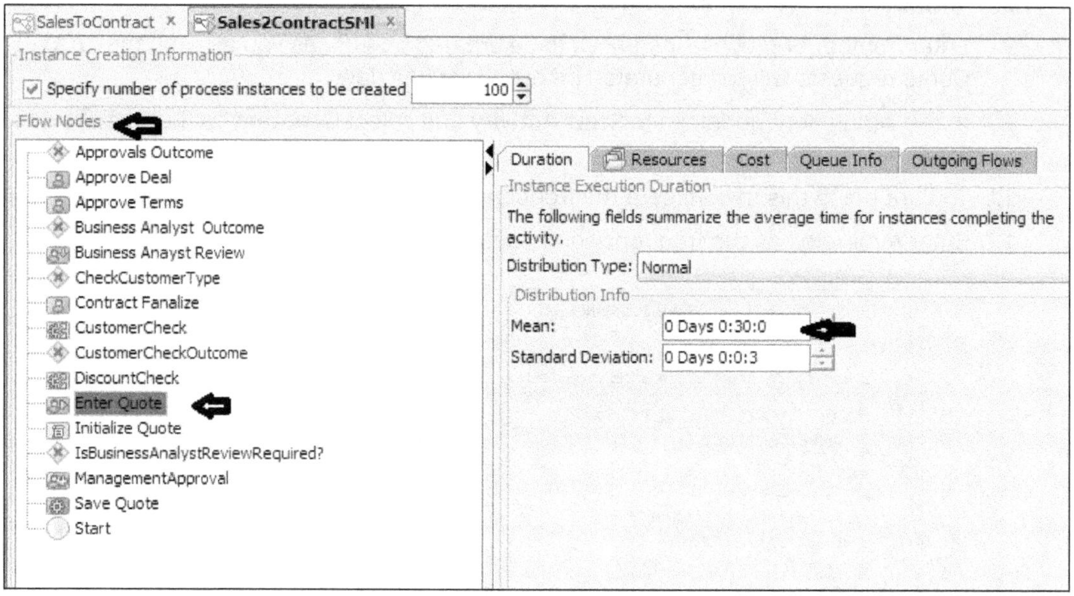

14. Click on the **Resources** tab and enter the following values:
    - Check: Use Fixed Resources
    - Value: 1
15. Select the **Cost** tab and enter values, as shown in the following screenshot:

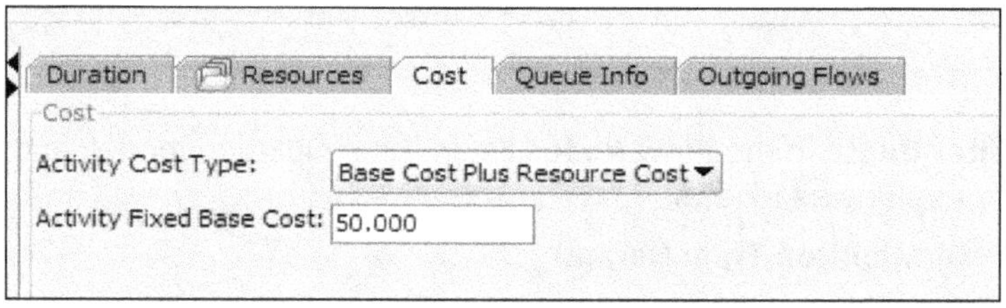

16. Click on the **Queue Info** tab and enter **2** as **Warning Size**.

17. Click the **IsBusinessAnalystReviewRequired?** activity, and in the **Outgoing Flows** tab, set values as shown in the following screenshot:

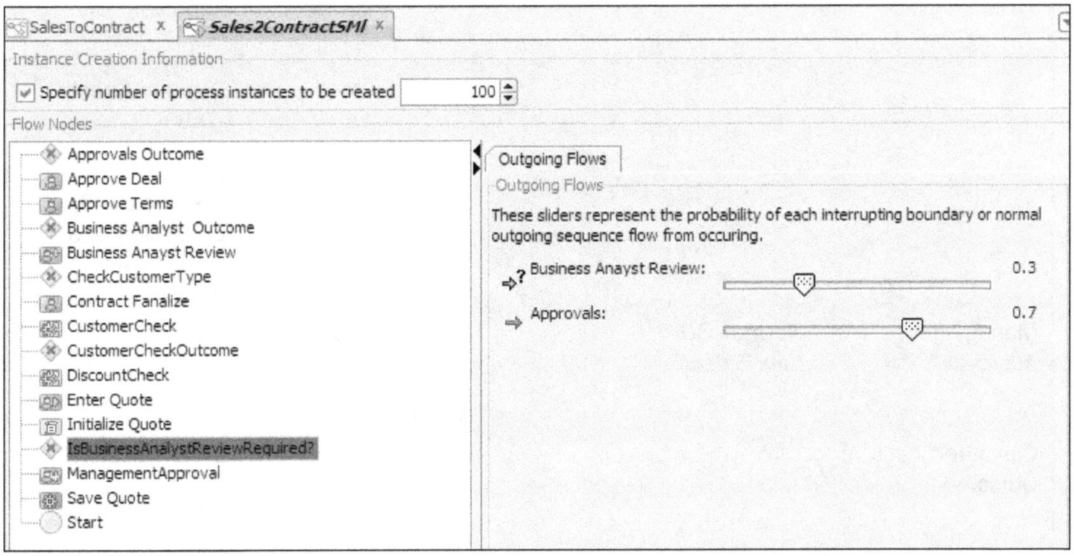

18. You will assume that 30 percent (**.3** probability) of cases go for **Business Analyst Review** and 70 percent of the cases move ahead for **Approvals.**
19. You can similarly use the following table to enter values for other activities as well.
20. You will use the following table to enter values for activity parameters such as Duration, Resource, Cost, Queue, and Flow.

Activity	Duration	Resources	Cost	Queue	Flow
Initialize Quote	Normal-10 sec, 3 sec	-	Fixed - $0	1	-
Enter Quote	Normal-30 min, 3 sec	5	Fixed + Resource - $50	2	-
CustomerCheck	Normal- 3 sec, 3 sec	-	Fixed - $0	1	-

Activity	Duration	Resources	Cost	Queue	Flow
CheckCustomer Type					Management Approval Flow - 0.2 DiscountCheck - 0.8 (You can assume that the probability of a 'New' Customer is 0.2.)
Management Approval	Normal- 30 min, 3 sec	6	Fixed + Resource - $300	1	-
CustomerCheck Outcome					Enter Quote - 0.2 DiscountCheck - 0.8 (Assuming only 20 percent of the cases go back for Reviews.)
DiscountCheck	Normal- 3 sec, 3 sec	-	Fixed - $0	1	-
IsBusinessAnalyst ReviewRequired					Business AnalystReview - 0.3 Approvers - 0.7 (Assuming 30 percent of the cases need Business Analyst Review)
BusinessAnalyst Review	Normal- 30 min, 3 sec	2	Fixed + Resource - $100		-

Activity	Duration	Resources	Cost	Queue	Flow
BusinessAnalyst Outcome					EnterQuote - 0.3 Approvals - 0.7 (Assuming only 30 percent get rejected.)
ApproveDeal	Normal- 10 min, 3 sec	1	Fixed + Resource - $50		
ApproveTerms	Normal- 10 min, 3 sec	1	Fixed + Resource - $50	-	-
ApproversOutcome	-	-	-	-	EnterQuote - 0.3 Finalize Contract - .7 (Assuming 70 percent of the quotes move for finalization.)
Contract Finalize	Normal- 20 min, 3 sec	1	Fixed + Resource - $100		
Save Quote	Normal- 5 min, 3 sec	1	Fixed + Resource - $50		

You have assumed that this is the Cost meant for 1 day for the process.

21. When you have finished, click **Save**.
22. Close the **Simulation Model** tab.

How it works...

Simulation models allow you to simulate the behavior of an individual process. Here, you have defined the activities parameters. They enable you to define how a process behaves as part of a simulation definition. You can define multiple simulation models for each process, creating different simulations based on different combinations of resource allocation and activity behavior.

Defining simulation definition

Oracle BPM projects may consist of many processes, and each project simulation can consist of one or more processes and their corresponding simulations. You need to create a **simulation definition**, as this is what actually determines which processes and process simulation models should be used and how resources should be configured for the simulation.

In simulation definition, you can also customize many parameters that influence the performance of your project, such as Starting Time and Duration of simulation.

Also, you can associate which process simulation models you want to include in the project simulation and can include the participant resources.

How to do it...

You will define a simulation definition to determine which simulation models should be used as follows:

1. Go to **JDeveloper | BPM Project Navigator** and expand the **SalesToContractDemo** project.
2. Click on **Processes | SalesToContract**.
3. Go to the **Simulation** node, expand it, and select **Simulation Definitions**.
4. Right-click **Simulation Definitions** and select **New Simulation**.

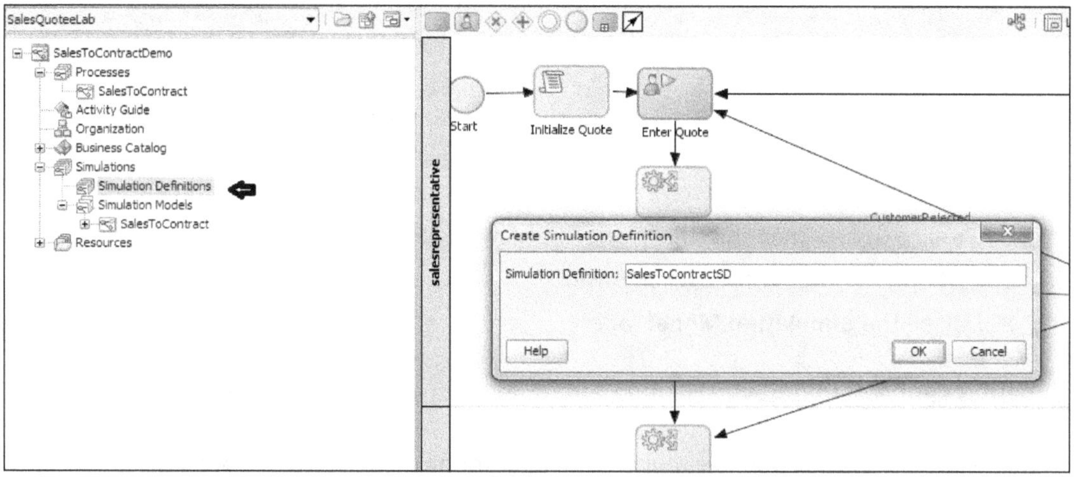

5. Enter `SalesToContractSD` as the **Simulation Definitions** name in the **Create Simulation Definition** dialog.
6. Click **OK**. A **Simulation Definitions** editor will open up.

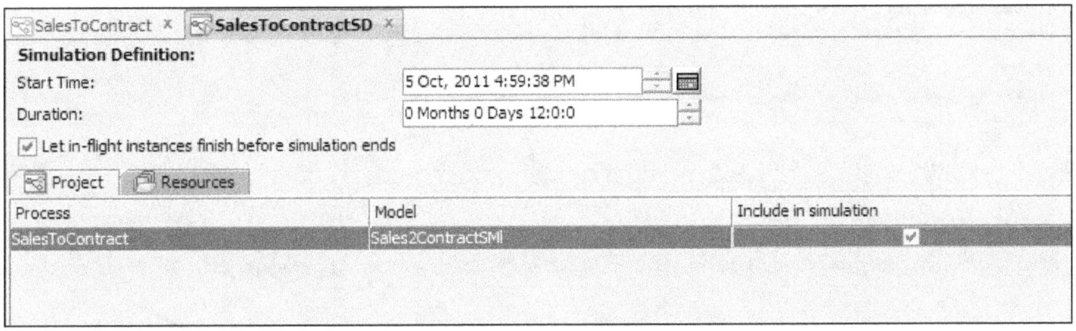

7. Let the **Start Time** be as it is. This time is used only for logging. It is not used for scheduling purposes.
8. Enter **12** hours as the period the simulation runs for.
9. Tick the option **Let in-flight instances finish before simulation ends**. This means simulation ends only when the specified number of instances complete. If unselected, simulation stops after the simulation duration is completed. At that point, all incomplete instances are shown in either "in-process" or "queue" status.
10. Click the **Project** tab, and tick **Include in Simulation**. This specifies that the process must be included in the simulation. Here, you can find all the processes that belong to the listed project. As there is one process for this project, it will be listed.
11. Go to the **Resource** tab and click on the green plus (**+**) icon to add the resources to use within the simulation.
12. Enter the name of the **Resource**, say `salesrepresentative`. Enter `$50` as **Cost**, for the cost of resource per hour. Set their **Availability** and **Efficiency** as **100%**. Click the green plus (**+**) icon, to set the participants for the roles you already have included in this project. Set capacity to **5**.

13. Click on the **Roles** cell and then the "browse" button to select a role, and assign it to a row, for example, assign the **contracts** role to the fourth row, and so on.

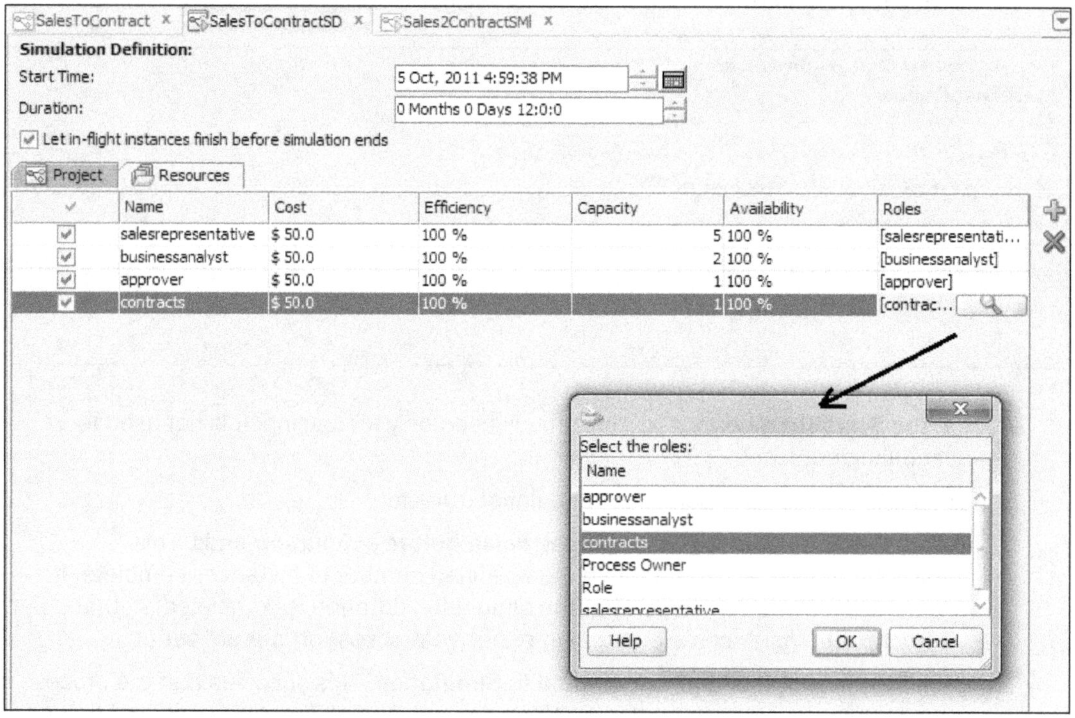

14. Fill the table, as shown in the preceding screenshot.
15. When you have finished, click on **Save**.

Running a simulation

Now that you have created a simulation model and a definition for it for the SalesToContract process, let's run this simulation, and later you will analyze the results of the simulation.

How to do it...

1. Click on **View** | **Simulations** to open the **Simulations** section in JDeveloper.

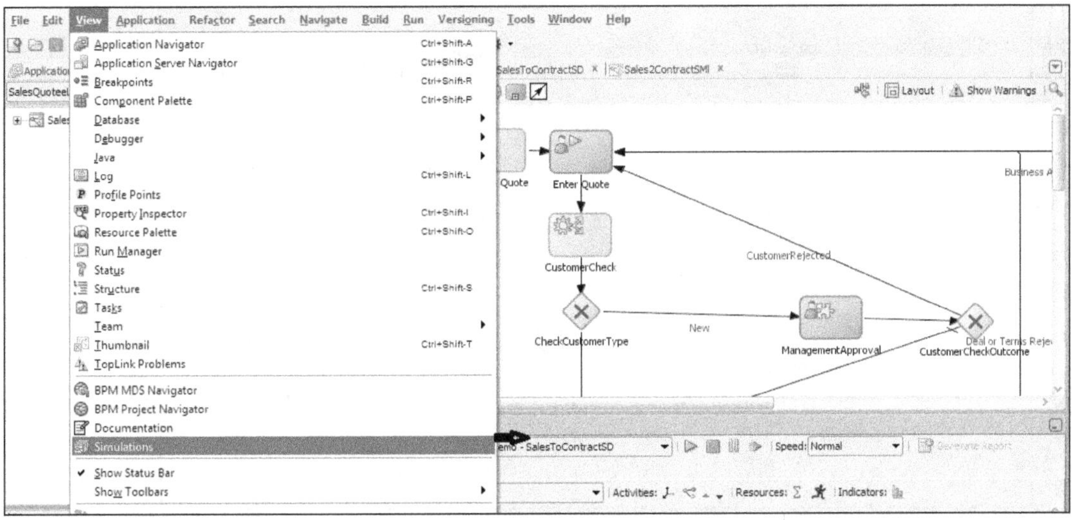

2. This will open a **Simulations** window as shown in the preceding screenshot. Select the simulation definition you have created and want to run. In this case, you will select **SalesToContractSD**.
3. Click on the **Run** button in the **Simulation** window to run the simulation.

4. When you run the simulation, you will find that it starts in an interactive mode and you can find **Process Progress** in the **Animation** section. You can place the mouse over a column in the **Animated Chart**, which will indicate the value of the activity.

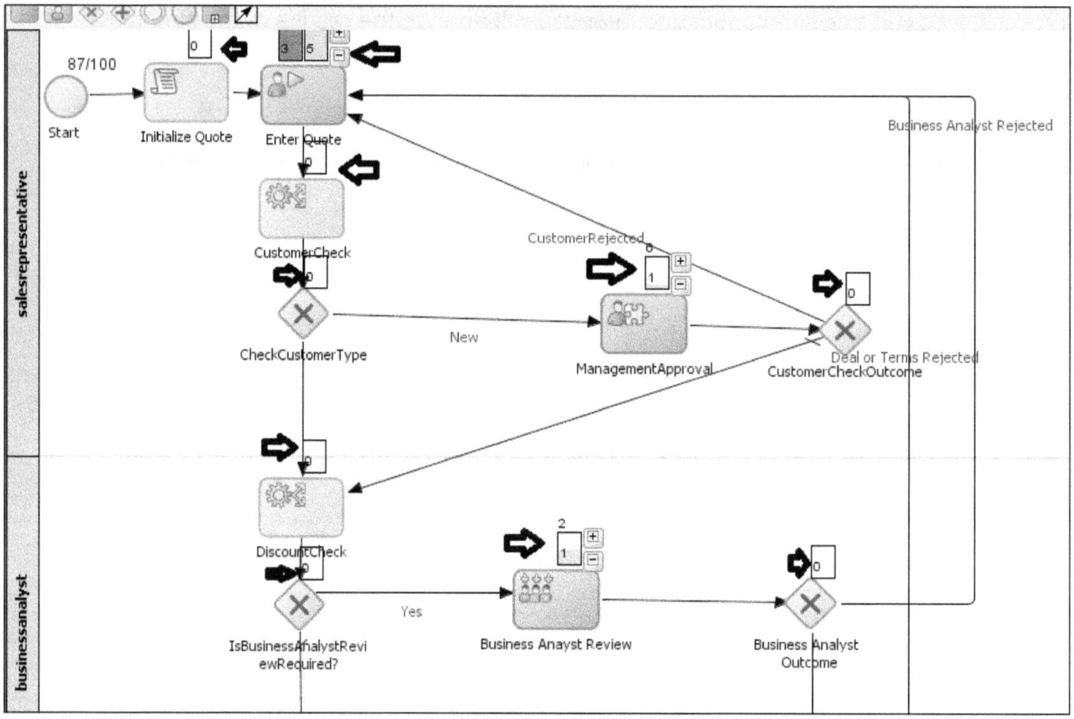

5. At any time, you can stop the simulation run. Click on the **Stop** button in the **Simulations** window to stop the simulation.

How it works...

When you run the simulation, the animation of the simulation appears in the project editor, and the results appear according to your specifications in the **Simulations** page. You can stop the simulation at any time without waiting for the entire simulation to complete and can analyze the results.

You will find that a **Simulations** view is created in the simulation area as shown in the following screenshot:

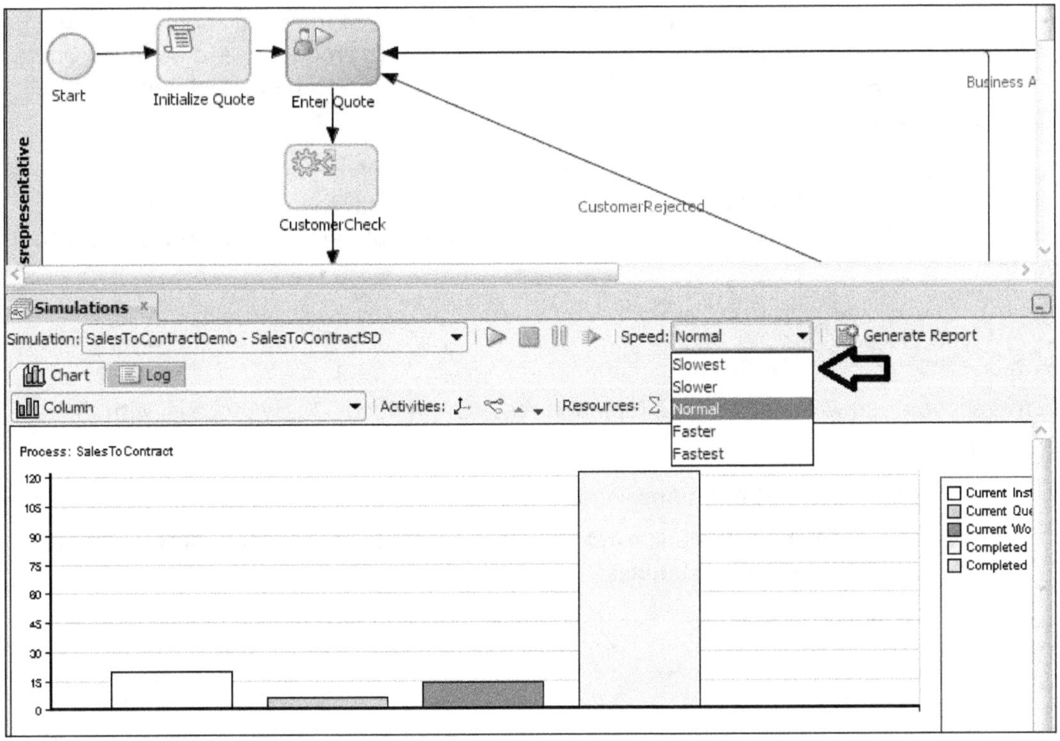

There's more...

You can set the speed of the simulation run by following the ensuing section.

Selecting the running speed

You can select the speed at which to run the simulation from the **Speed** list. At normal speed, instances are created at a rate of one per second.

1. Click on the **Speed** drop-down list, as shown in the preceding screenshot.
2. Select a **Speed**, in this case **Normal**, to create instances at a rate of one per second.

Analyzing simulation results

You will analyze the simulation results. Based on the analysis of the simulation results, the as-is Sales Quote process model is used as a starting point to produce the to-be Sales Quote process model. Simulation of the to-be Sales Quote process model helps to determine the benefits of the changes.

You can display results in either charts or as an log file, too. With charts, you can select the type of chart, such as **Bar**, **Column**, **Table**, and so on, to display the results. You have the choice to select which activities you want to analyze and what parameters you want to focus on, too.

How to do it...

In this section, you will analyze the simulation result to produce a to-be process, with the following steps:

1. Double-click the **Simulations** window to bring it to full view mode.
2. Next, you can chose the unit's indicator, as shown, and select **Only Current Queue Size** and **Completed Instances**:

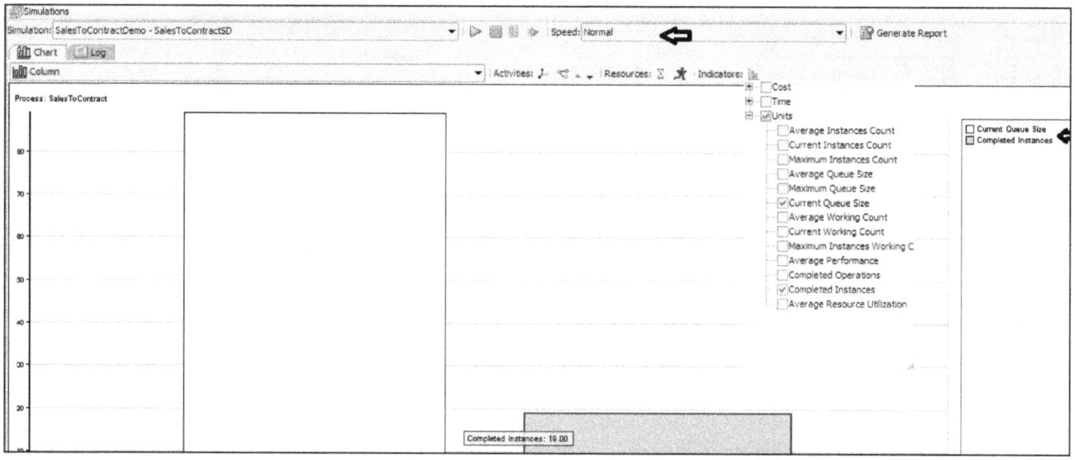

3. You will find that **Current Queue Size** is greater than **Completed Instance Size**. This indicates that **Queue Size** is more.
4. Now, you can analyze the time required for processing the process.

5. Click on **Indicators**, choose **Time**, and select **Average Waiting Time** and **Average process time**.

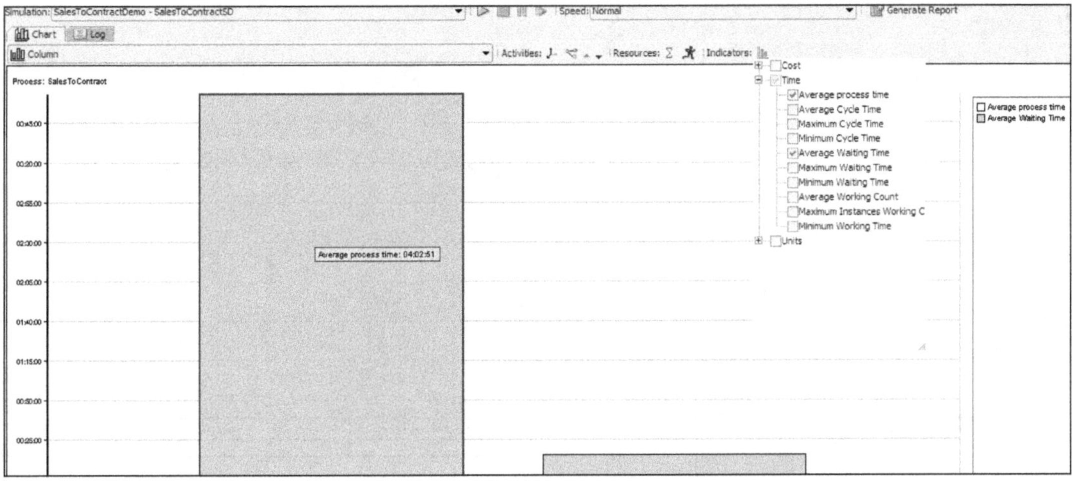

6. It shows that **Average process time** is more than four hours and waiting time is also high.
7. Click on **Activities** and select the activities **Enter Quote**, **Approve Deal**, **Approve Terms**, **Finalize Contract**, and **Business Analyst Review**, for which you want to analyze the processing time, as shown in the following screenshot:

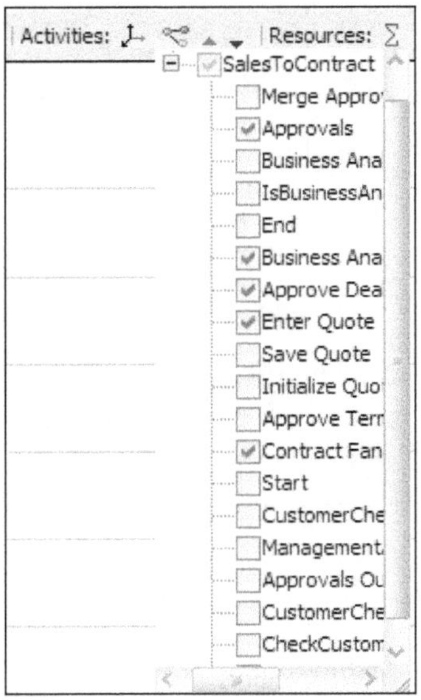

8. You will find that **Average process time** for all major activities is quite high, and even the waiting time is high.

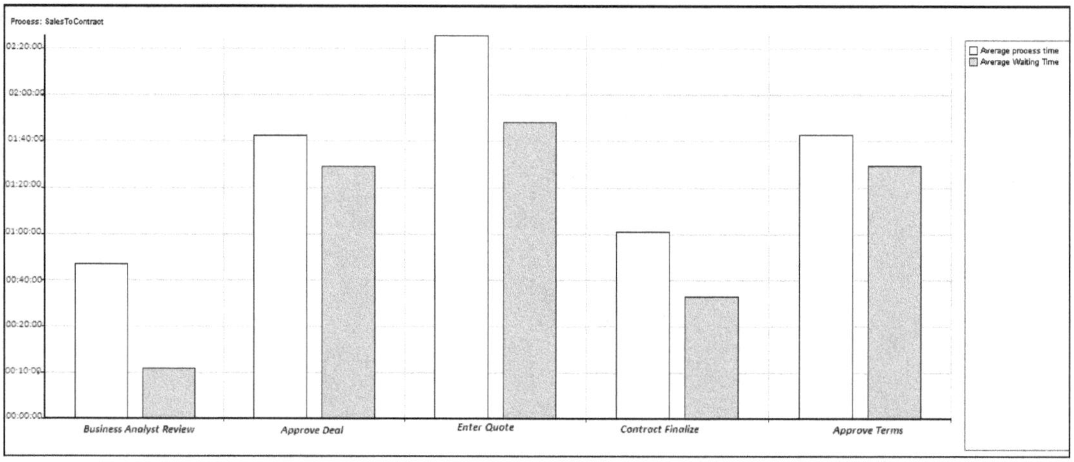

9. Go to **Indicators** and tick **Total Cost**.
10. You will find that the total cost comes to **$17250**, which is the cost to run this process for a day.

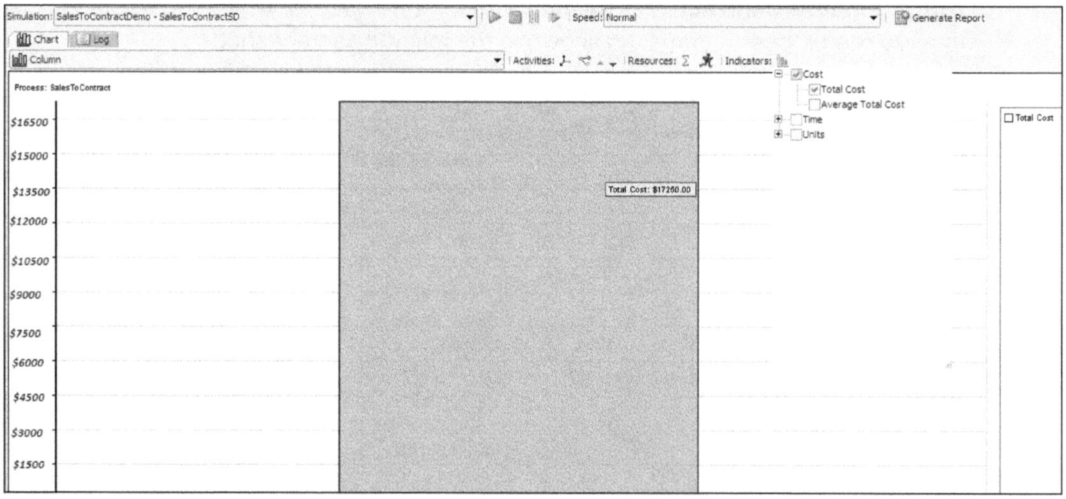

How it works...

1. Simulation will calculate results based on the indicators you choose. You can summarize the **Analysis**, as follows:

Process	Units	Time	Cost
SalesToContract	Current Queue Size = 89	Average Processing Time- 4 hrs 30 min	$17250

There's more...

In this section, you will learn to create a **Simulation Report**.

Creating Simulation Reports

1. In the Simulation window, click on the **Generate Documentation** button, which will generate reports for this simulation run. The **Simulation Report** dialog opens.
2. In the **Directory Location** field, enter a directory to store the report or click the button next to it to browse the file system and select a directory.
3. In the **Activities** tab, select the option **Summary**
4. In the tree below it, select the activities to include in the report. You can specify which activities to include, such as the ones you have selected for analyzing the results—**Enter Quote**, **Approve Deal**, **Approve terms**, **Business Analyst Review**, and **Finalize Contracts**.

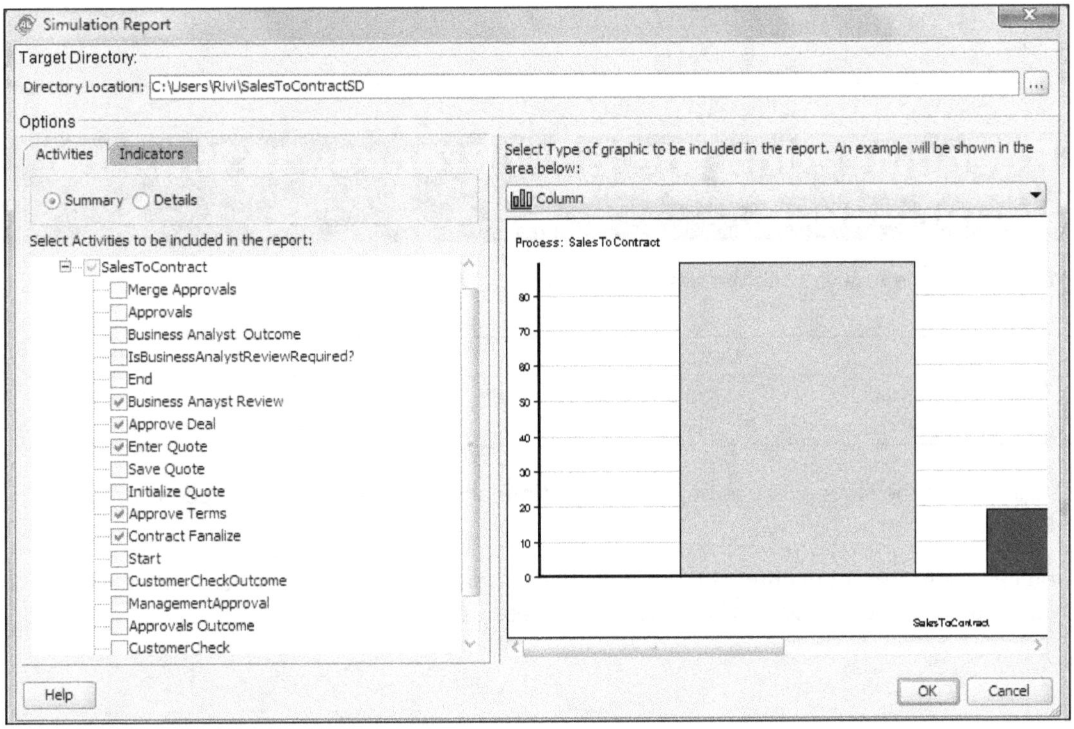

5. Select **Column** as the chart type.
6. Click **OK**.

   You will find that a directory is created using the name and location you have provided and that it contains an HTML file, as shown in the following screenshot. This graphically shows the simulation result and has a link to CSV files that have simulation data and simulation resource data.

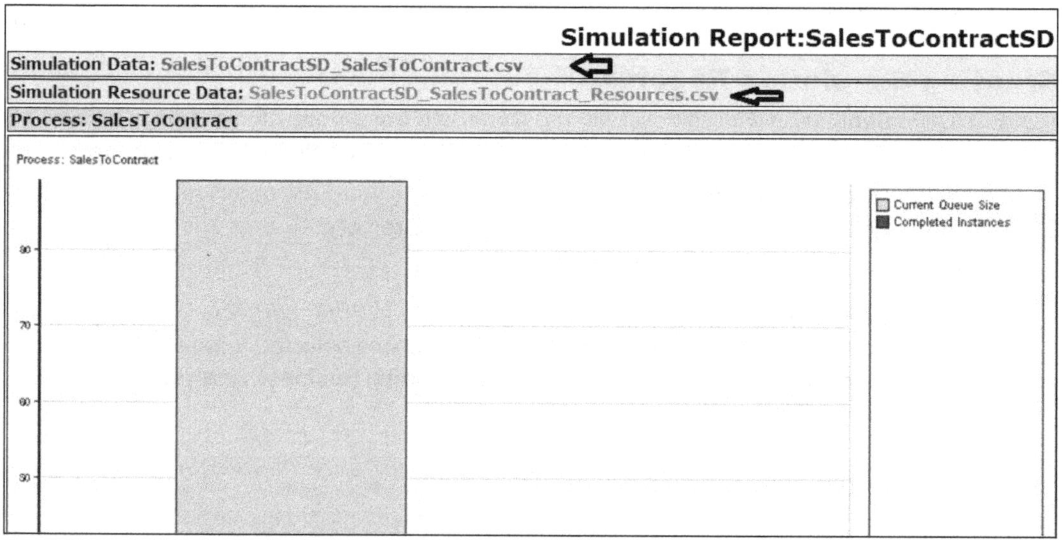

Reengineering the BPM Process to improve performance

You will find the Analysis results are as follows:

Process	Units	Time	Cost
SalesToContract	Current Queue Size = 89	Average Processing Time - 4 hrs 30 min	$17250

It shows that the Queue Size is huge and that time and cost taken for the process are also very high.

You can perform a lot of change to improve the performance of your process and hence can reduce the operational cost of running this process to the business.

How to do it...

You can reengineer the process to increase process performance with the following steps:

1. Go to the **Simulation Definitions** dialog for the process and click the **Resources** tab.
2. Increase the capacity of **businessanalyst** from **2** to **5**, **contracts** to **5**, and **approver** to **5**, as they are the most problematic areas.

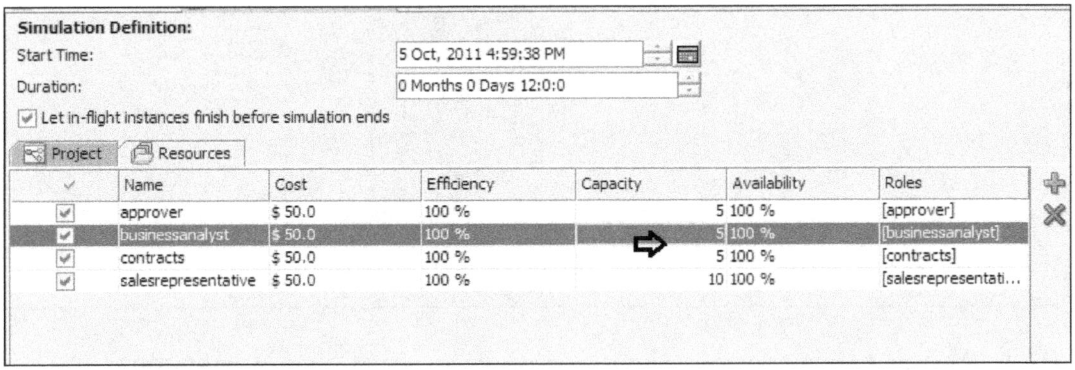

3. Click **Save**.
4. Click **Run** in the **Simulation** window to rerun the simulation.
5. Click on the **Time | Average Processing Time** checkbox. You will find that **Average Processing Time** has reduced to **45** minutes.

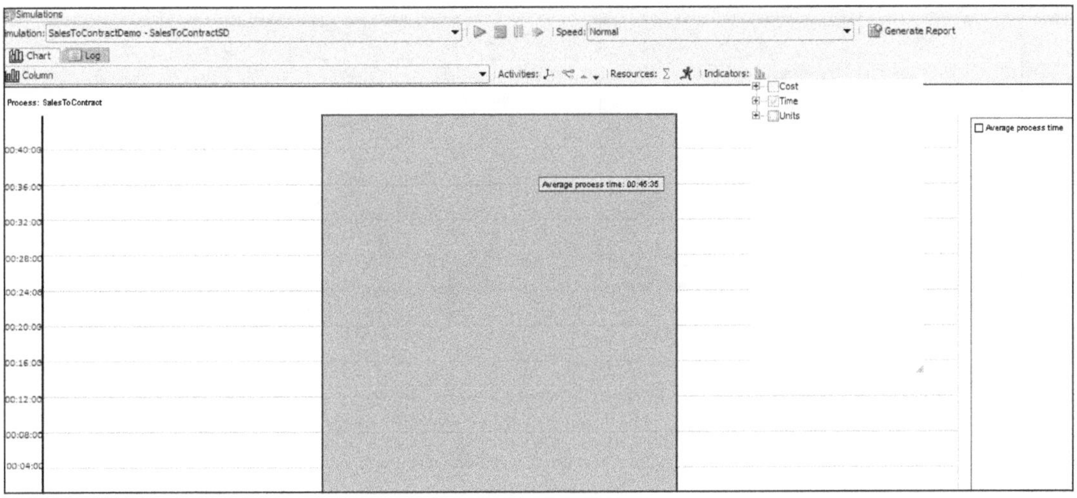

6. Click **Units | Average Queue Size | Completed Instances** and you will see that the number of completed instances is greater than before.

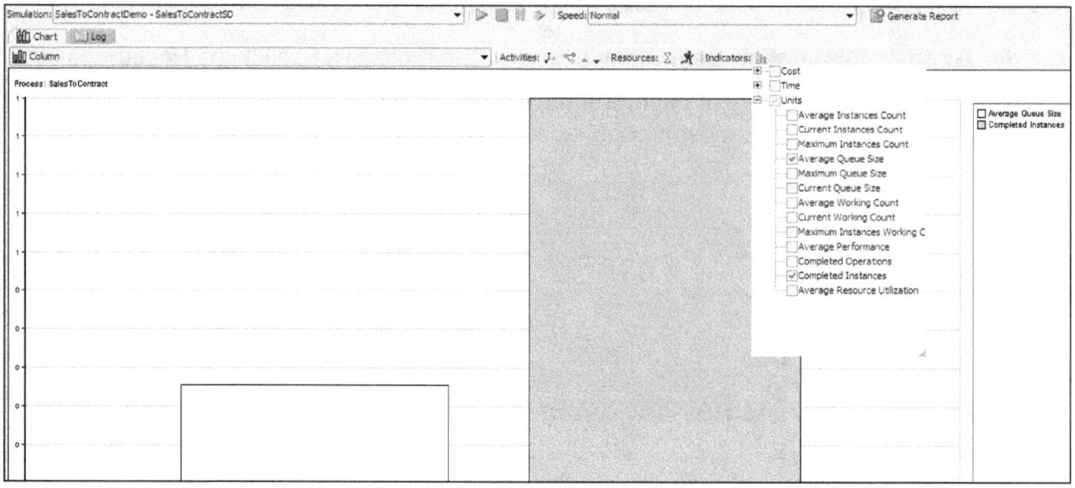

7. Click on **Cost**, and you will find a dramatic decrease (in the cost) to **$3000**.

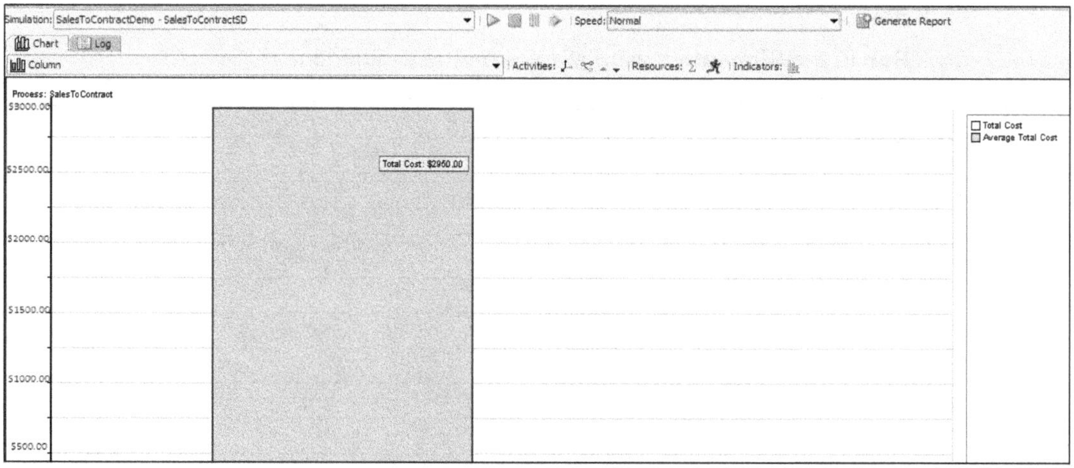

7
Developing UI using Oracle ADF

So far, you have learnt to model, implement, and simulate the Oracle BPMN process. During implementation, you have infused Business Rules and have created a Human Task. While creating Human Tasks, you have created user interfaces for the participant/users to interact with your Human Task and to act on them. You have adopted an auto-generation mechanism to generate a user interface for Human Task. You have witnessed the use of human interaction in an earlier chapter (*Chapter 5, Human Workflow in BPM Process*). Human interaction provides user interfaces to the people to interact with Human Tasks. Oracle BPM 11g sits on top of SOA and leverages the Oracle Application Development Framework (ADF). **Oracle ADF** is a powerful framework that includes rich user interface capabilities. In this chapter, you will learn ways to create UI pages for interacting with Human Tasks.

In this chapter, we will cover the following topics:

- Creating ADF Task Forms
- Creating a task display form
- Creating task display forms—using individual Drop handlers
- Implementing routers
- Creating a Task Form sequence flow
- Creating a Task Form with ADF business components
- Creating a task display form using Wizard

Introduction

Oracle ADF sits on top of a standard Java platform—Java EE—and takes advantage of it. Its an end-to-end application development framework and is built on top of model-view-controller architecture.

You have created ADF forms using the auto-generate facility provided for Oracle Human Tasks. This is because Oracle ADF is preintegrated with Oracle BPM 11g for the generation and development of Task Forms. These Task Forms are the user interface used by process participants to start a process or work on a task. One can even go beyond using auto-generation mechanisms and can use the Oracle ADF capabilities and framework to build Oracle BPM 11g Task Forms and applications.

You had created BPM Task Forms earlier. BPM Task Forms are user interfaces that an end user uses to initiate processes and to perform activities in the process. You will find that a BPM Task Form is a form for viewing and editing data. It empowers end users with the power to take actions such as approve, reject, and so on, on the work items. Oracle ADF is pre-integrated with Oracle BPM 11g for the generation and development of Task Forms. There are different ways to generate these Task Forms:

- **Auto generate**: You can use this mechanism to generate Task Forms. When you use this option, you are presented with a ready-to-deploy Task Form.
- **Wizard Driven**: This is an option from the `.task` file. However, it offers more options such as temple and multi-row-column layout.
- **Task flow based on Human Tasks**: In this case, you only get task flow and task data, however the UI page must be created using ADF designer's drag-and-drop form creation capabilities leveraging Human Task data control.

  Whatever option you choose, you will get a task data control and a bounded task flow. With the first two options, you get a complete page corresponding to the activity `view` in the task flow. In the last option, a page is not generated, however the Human Task **drop handler** can be used to create a complete page.
- **Data Control**: Whatever option you use to generate an ADF UI page, an artifact that is always generated is Human Task data control. It follows the naming convention `<user Interface Project name>.<Task Name>`. It has a child node named `Tasks`, which contains some elements that are important to understand, such as:
  - Payload
  - Task Attributes
  - System Attributes
  - Human Task Drop Handler

When you drag-and-drop task elements on the canvas, there are Human Task-specific drop handlers available, which offer the option of creating task headers, task actions, comments, and so on.

In this chapter, you will learn to create a task display form using Auto generate, Wizard driven, and Task flow based on Human Tasks. You will uncover how to create a bounded task flow, how to work with drop handlers, and how to create a task display form using individual drop handlers. You will also witness how to declaratively route control to activities. You will create Task Form sequences (that is, multiple Task Forms in task flow) and learn to use ADF-BC component and Web Service data control while learning about Entity Objects and View Objects.

Creating ADF Task Forms

You have created Human Tasks for users/participants to interact with your process and perform activities/actions on those tasks by logging in to the Oracle BPM workspace.

Each task that you create has two parts. One is the metadata and other one is the Task Form, which is used to display the contents of the task in the user's Worklist when he/she logs in to Oracle BPM Worklist applications. When a user logs in to Worklist applications and drills down into a task, the task display form renders the details of the task.

For Human Tasks, you create a task display form, which is a Java Server Page XML (`.jspx`) file that you create in the Oracle JDeveloper designer where you created the SOA composite containing the task. There are many ways to create a task display form for Human Tasks—Auto Generate, Wizard Driven and Task flow based on Human tasks. Whatever mechanism you adopt, you must have a previously created Human Task (`.task` file) as part of an SOA composite, before you can create task flow.

In this section, you will create a Task Form for the Enter Quote Details Human Task. Earlier, you created it using Auto Generate and Wizard driven mechanisms; here, you will create it using task flow.

> Delete the earlier UI project for the `Enter Quote Details` Human Task. Open JDeveloper, right-click on the **EnterQuoteUI** project and select **Delete Project**. Choose **Remove project from applications** and click **OK**.

How it works...

In this section, you will learn to create Task Forms.

I. Create task display forms based on Human Tasks

1. Open JDeveloper in the default role.
2. Open the application containing the **SalesToContractDemo** project.
3. Create a new project by clicking **New Project**.

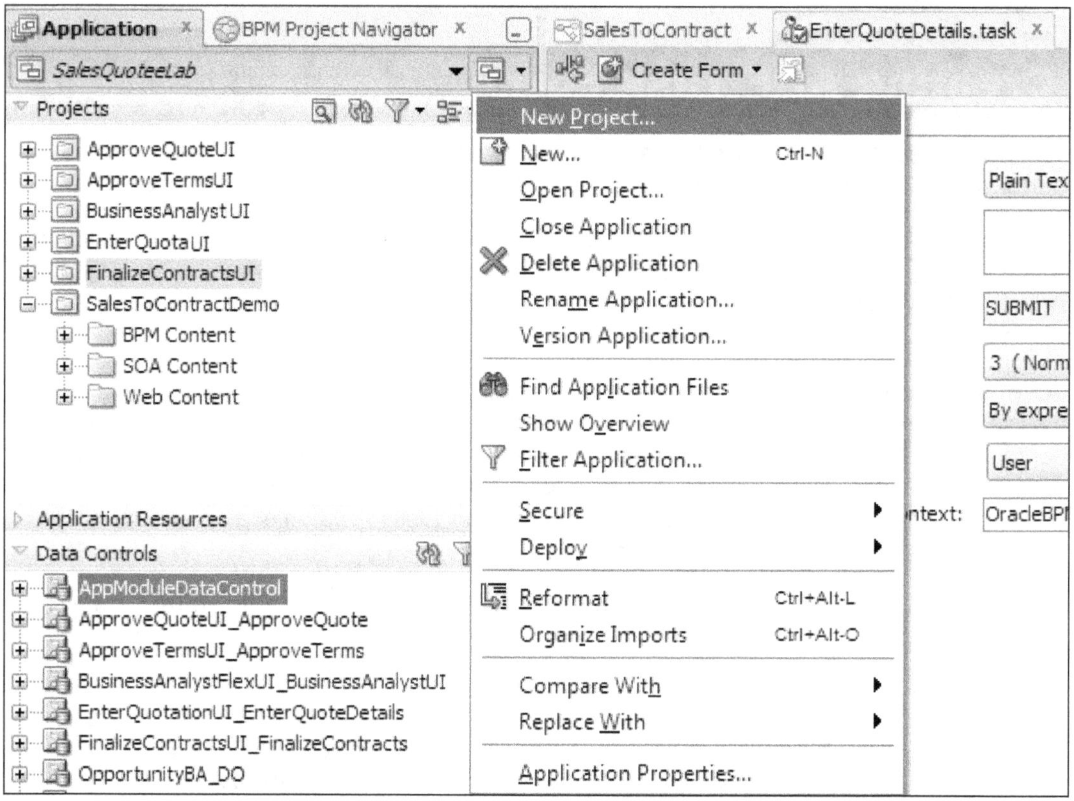

4. Go to **All technologies | General | Projects** and select **Generic Project**.
5. Click **OK**.

6. Enter `EnterQuoteDetailsUI` as the name of the project and click **Finish**.
7. You will find that a project is created in the application navigator in the same application in which the **SalesToContractDemo** project is located.
8. When you have completed the preceding steps, click **Save**.
9. Right-click on the new, empty project, **EnterQuoteDetailsUI**, and select **New**.
10. In the **New Gallery** dialog, go to **All Technologies | Web tier | JSF** and select **ADF Task Flow Based on Human Task**, within **Items**.
11. Click **OK**.

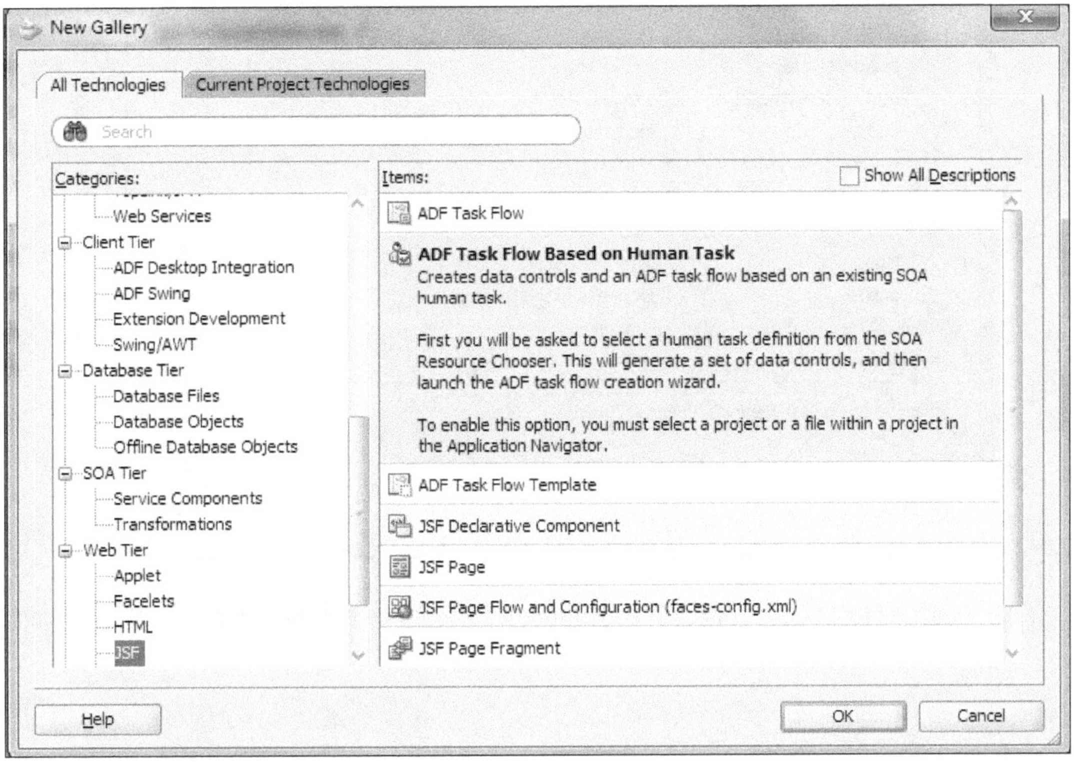

12. In the **SOA Resource Browser** dialog, find the `EnterQuoteDetails.task` file. This is the task metadata where you have defined the Enter Quote Human Task.

13. Click **OK**.

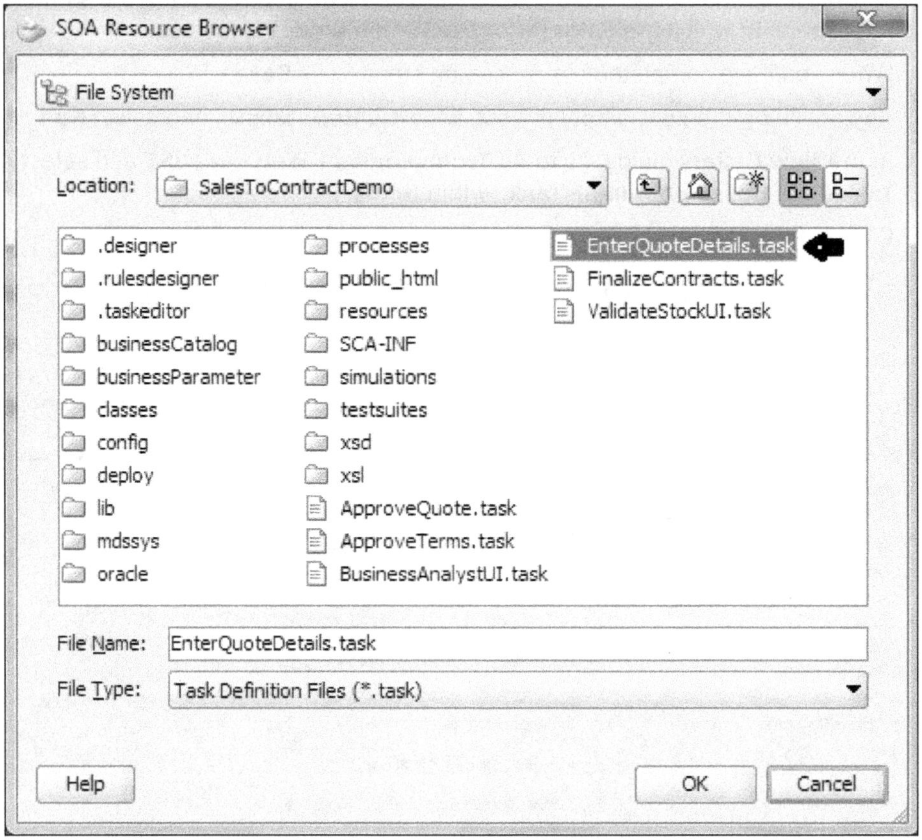

14. Place a check next to **Create as Bounded Task Flow**, in the **Create Task Flow** dialog.

15. The **Task Flow** dialog provides a modular approach for defining control flow in an application.

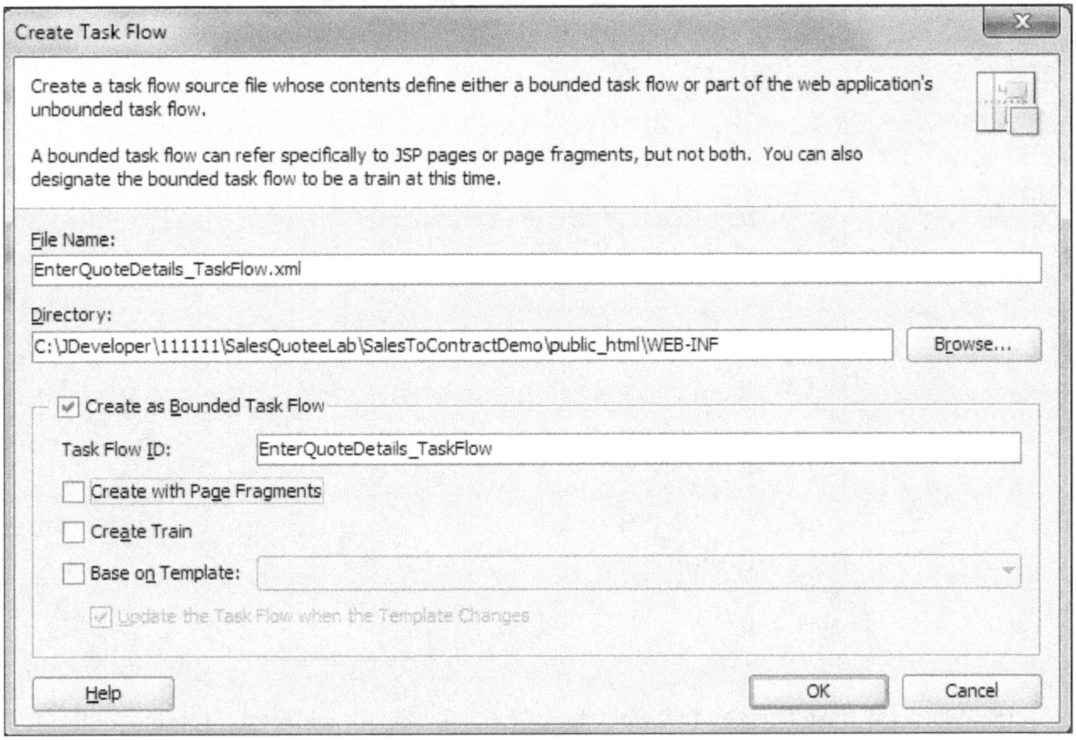

16. Let the other entries remain default and click **OK**.

> Bounded task flow is a specialized form of task flow that has a single entry point and zero or more exit points. It contains its own set of private control flow rules, activities, and managed beans. An ADF bounded task flow allows reuse, parameters, transaction management, and reentry.

17. You can find the **taskdetails1_jspx** icon in the designer.

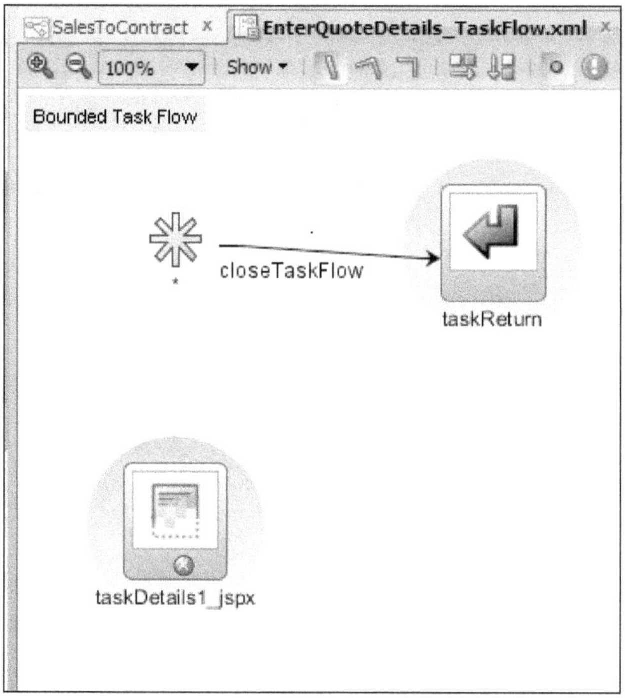

18. When you have finished following the preceding steps, click **Save**.

How it works...

You have created this task flow based on a Human Task. You can find drop handlers, parameters, and operations in the **Data Controls** section. They wire the task flow application with the workflow services. Navigate to **Data Controls** in JDeveloper and verify that Human Tasks are aware of data controls that wire the task flow application with the workflow services.

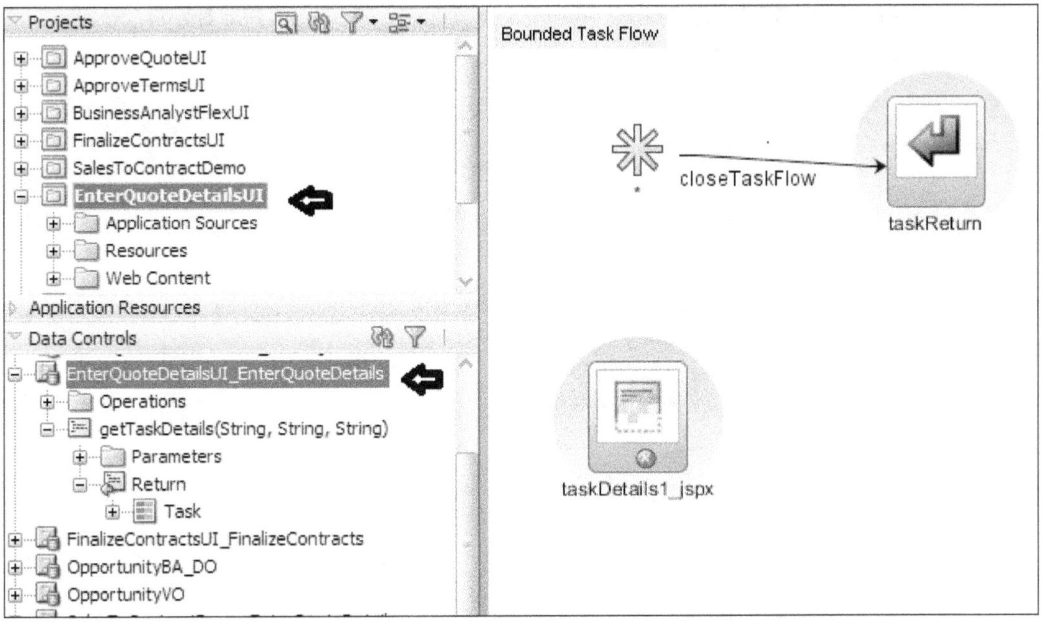

Creating a task display form

Along with parameters and operations, data control also offers handlers. You can create interface regions to display the contents of the task. Human Task drop handlers can auto-generate a task with or without payload, and other task components, such as header, action, history, comments, and attachments. You will create a task display form using the complete task with a payload drop handler, in this section.

You will implement a router mechanism in the later sections. The router will switch between different pages based on the input payload data (which you will cover later in the section *Implementing Routers*, in this chapter).

In this recipe, you will create a task display form, which will have many sections. Later, you will create a task display form without product sections.

If Account Name is not FusionNX: Then the task display form will have all the sections.

Else: It will not have the product section.

How to do it...

In this section, you will learn to a create task display form, as follows:

1. In JDeveloper, go to **EnterQuoteDetailsUI project | Web Content | Page Flows** and click **EnterQuoteDetails_TaskFlow.xml**.

2. In the **Create JSF Page** dialog, enter `SalesQuote.jspx` as **File Name**, accept default values, and click **OK**.

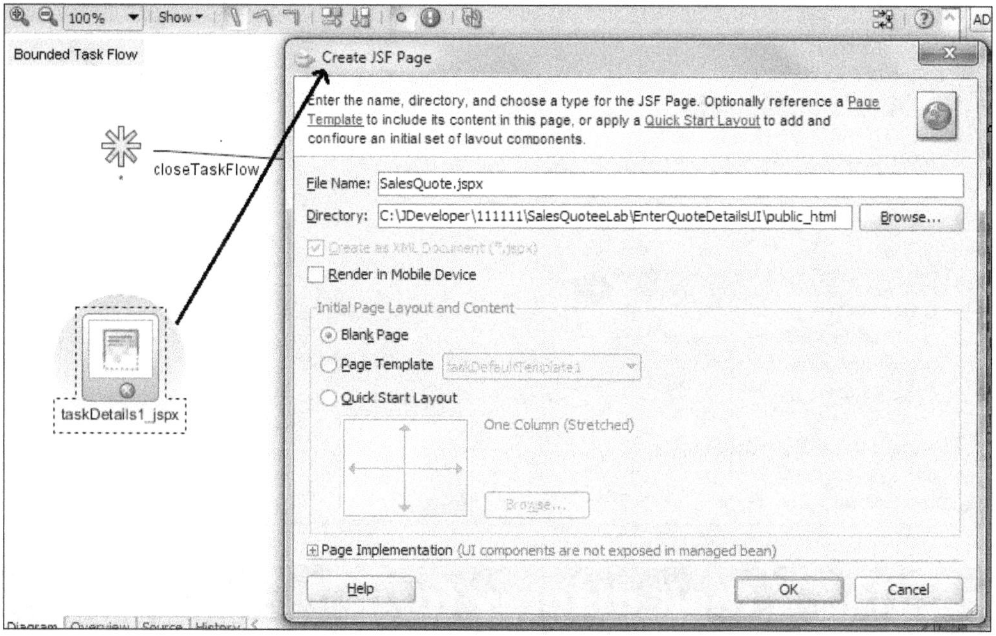

3. In the **Data Controls** section, expand **EnterQuoteDetailsUI_EnterQuoteDetails | gettaskDetails | Return**.
4. Select the task icon, and drag-and-drop it into **SalesQuote.jspx**.
5. Click **Human Task** and select **Complete task with Payload**.

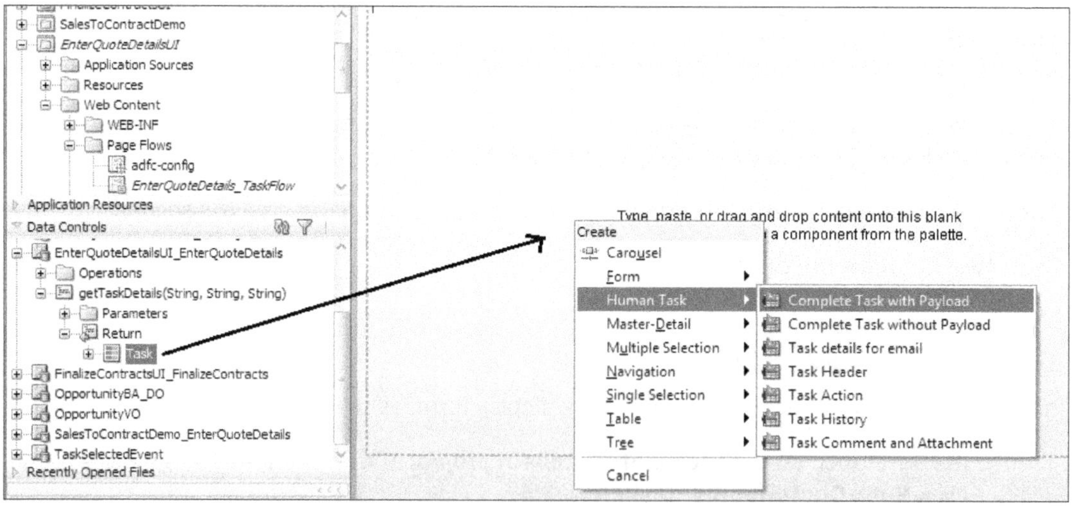

6. In the **Edit Action Binding** dialog, accept defaults and click **OK**.
7. Action binding is used by UI command components such as hyperlinks or buttons to invoke built-in or custom operations on data collections or data control, without writing code.

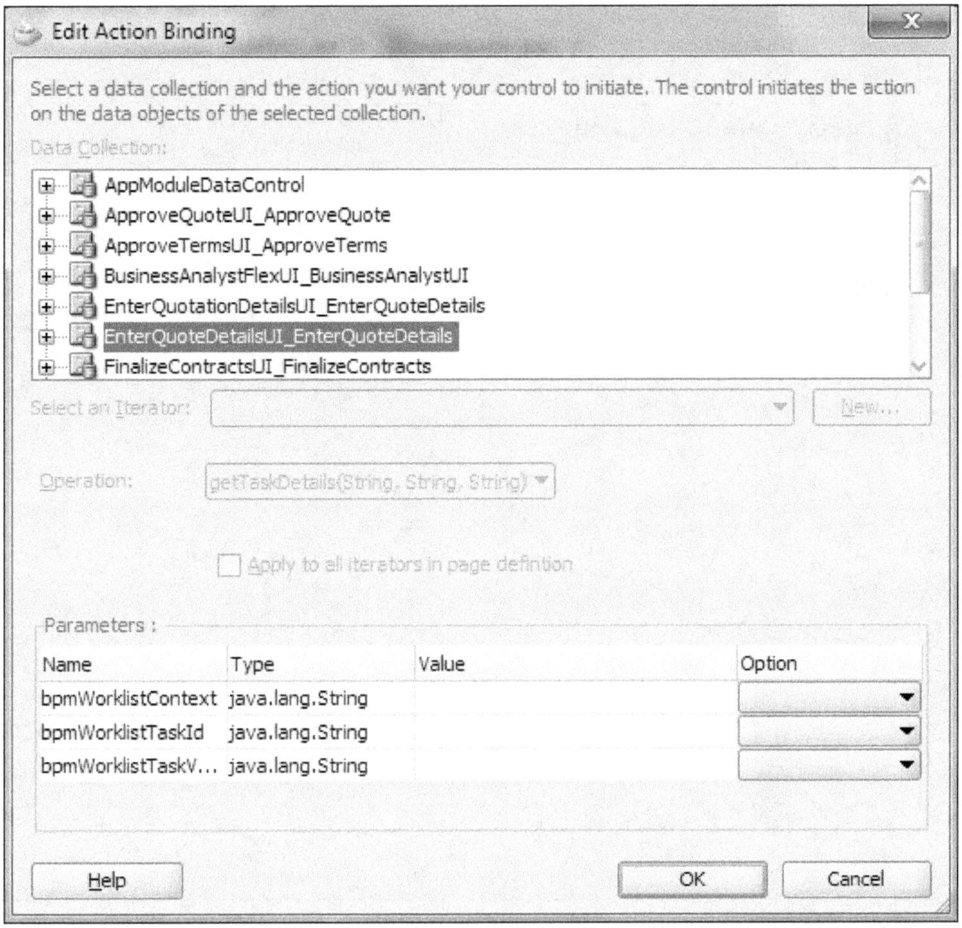

8. In the next dialog (for data binding), select the data collection, as shown in the following screenshot, and click **OK**.

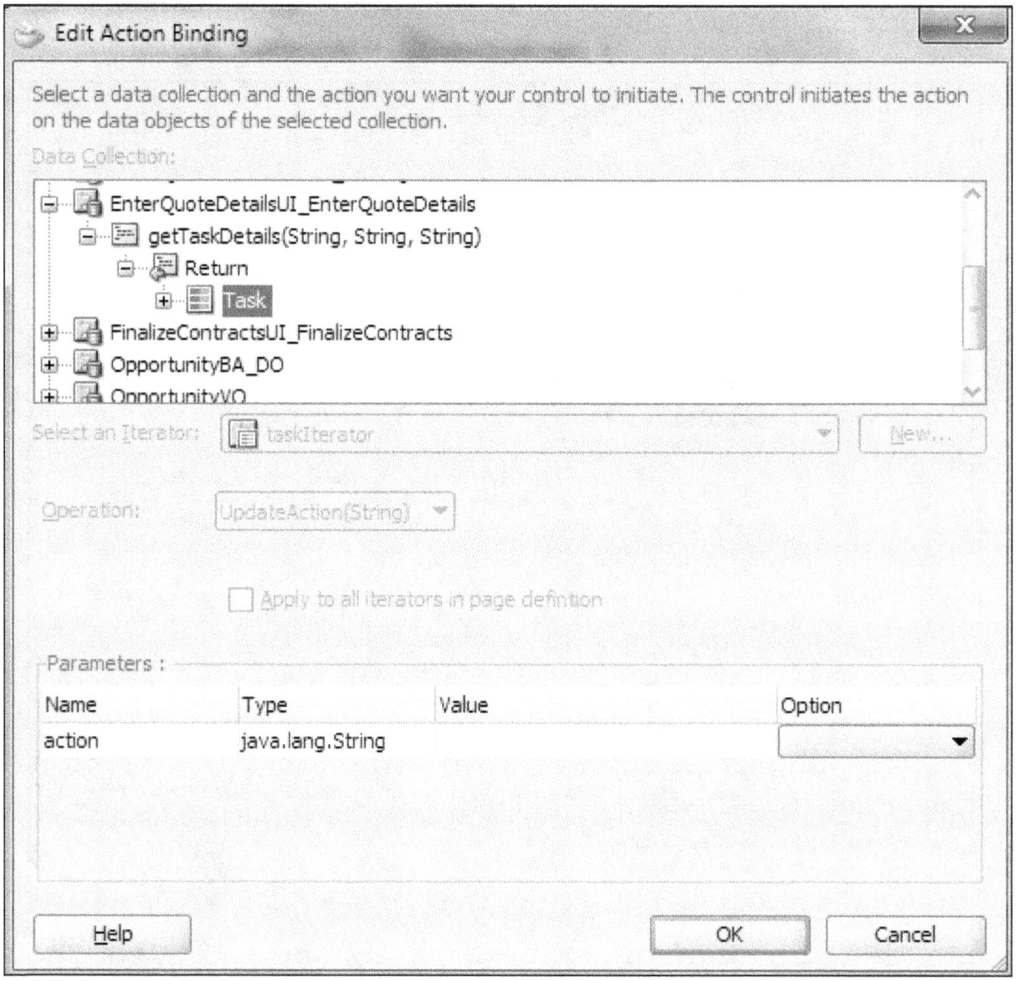

9. You will find the task display form, as follows:

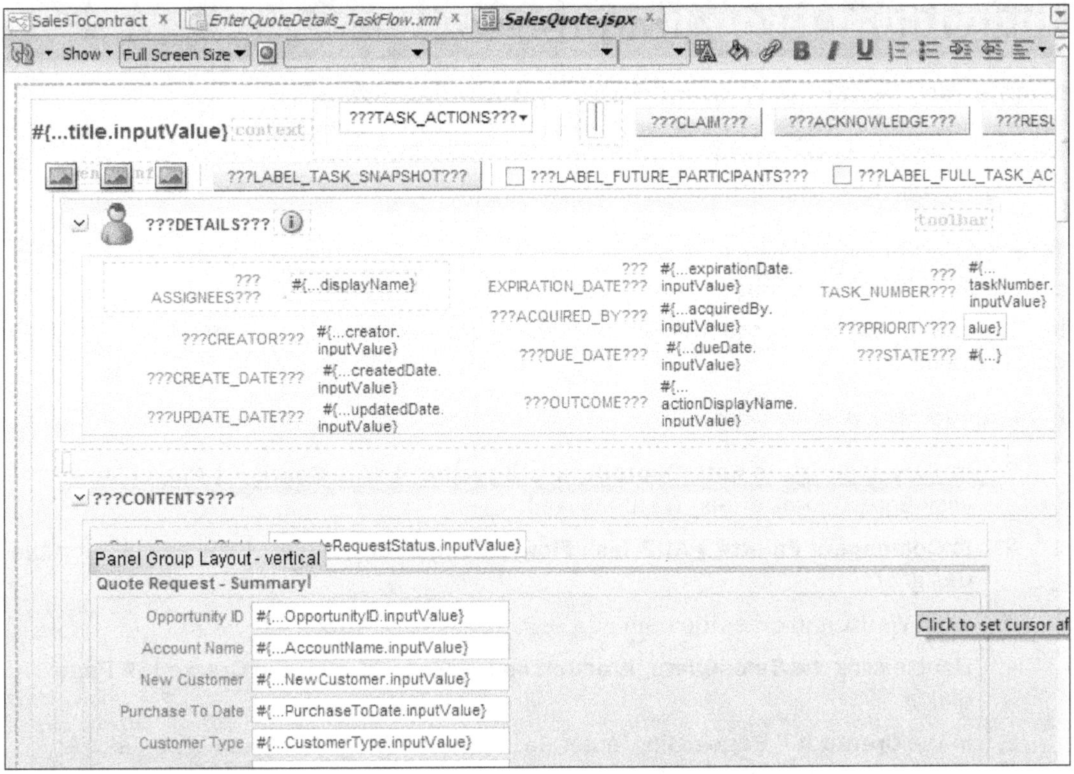

10. When you have completed the preceding steps, click **Save**.

How it works...

You have designed the `SalesQuote.jspx` file. This is the task display form (using the complete task with payload drop handler) and is available at `jDev_Oracle_Home/mywork/ApplicationName/ProjectName/public_html`.

This task display form is ready to be deployed; you can deploy the project and test it.

What you did is similar to what the Auto-generate task UI wizard does for you. However, you now have some understanding of what happens in the background.

Creating a task display form—using individual Drop handlers

In this section, you will create a task display form in the same task flow `EnterQuoteDetails_TaskFlow.xml`, in which you have created a task flow in an earlier section. As you will be trying to implement routers, as discussed before, you will create a task display form without product details.

How to do it...

In this section, you will discover how a task display form is created using individual drop handlers.

I. Creating a task display form

1. In JDeveloper, go to **EnterQuoteDetailsUI project | Web Content | Page Flows** and click **EnterQuoteDetails_TaskFlow.xml**.
2. In **Component Palette | ADF Task Flow | Components**, select **View** and click on the designer.
3. Click **View1** and enter the name `SalesQuote_ProductLess` for it.
4. Double-click the **SalesQuote_ProductLess** view; it will open the **Create JSF Page** dialog.
5. In the **Create JSF Page** dialog, enter `SalesQuote_ProductLess.jspx` as the filename, accept defaults, and click **OK**.
6. In the **Data Controls** section, expand **EnterQuoteDetailsUI_EnterQuoteDetails | getTaskDetails | Return** and select the **Task** icon.
7. Drag-and-drop the **Task** icon onto **SalesQuote_ProductLess.jspx**.

8. Click **Human Task** and select **Task Header**, as shown in the following screenshot:

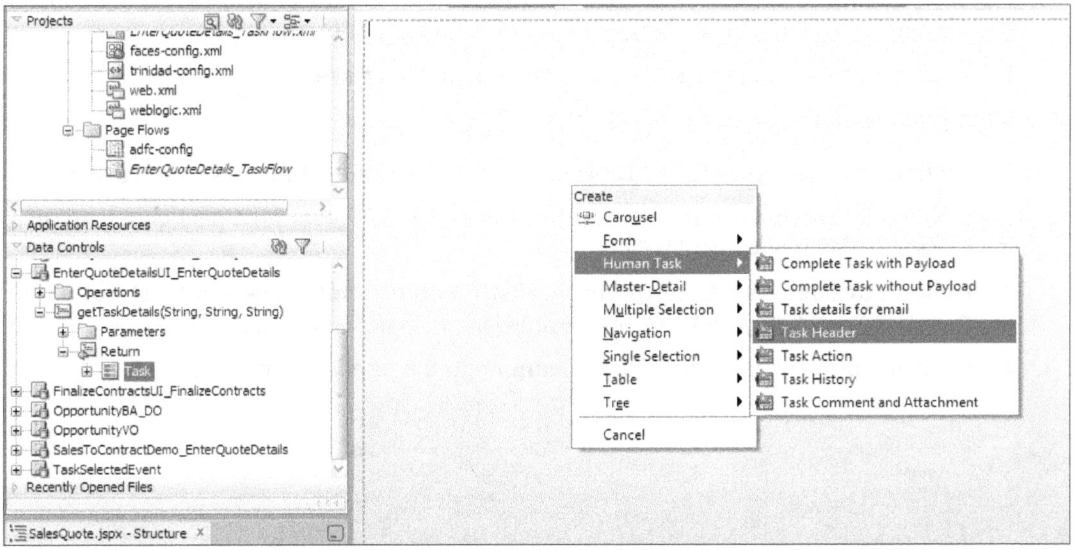

9. This will create **Task Action** buttons and the **Task Header** task.

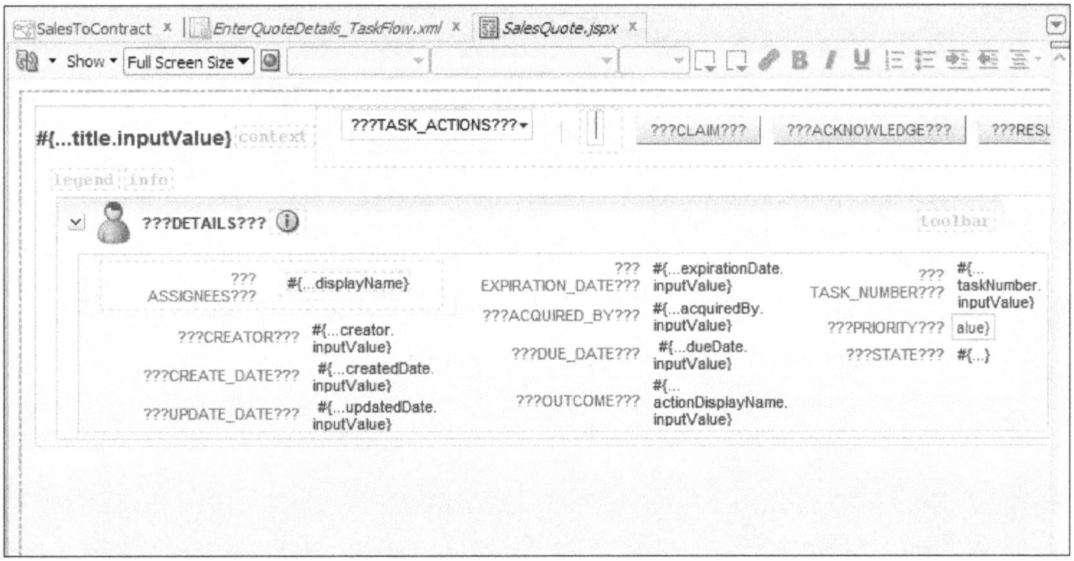

10. Again, drag-and-drop the **Task** icon into **SalesQuote_ProductLess.jspx**.
11. Click **Human Task** and select **Task History**. This will create a **Task History** section. You can repeat the same for task comments and attachments.
12. When you have completed the preceding steps, click **Save**.

II. Adding payload to the task display form

1. Go to **Component Palette | ADF faces | Layout** and select **Panel Group Layout**.
2. Drag **Panel Group Layout** between the header and the rest of the sections (**HISTORY**, **COMMENTS**, and **ATTACHMENT**).
3. Go to **Data Controls | EnterQuoteDetailsUI_EnterQuoteDetails | getTaskDetails | Return | Task | Payload | Quote_Request** and select **Summary**.
4. Drag-and-drop the data collection **Summary** to the panel layout area, as shown in the following screenshot:

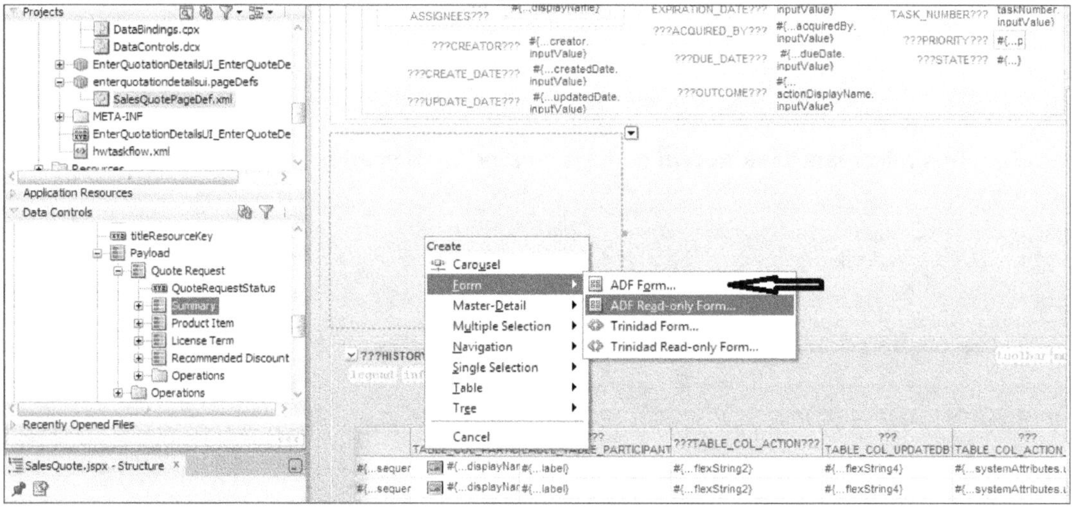

5. From the context menu, select **Form | ADF Forms**.

6. Accept the defaults in the **Edit** dialog and click **OK**. This will create the payload region, as shown in the following screenshot:

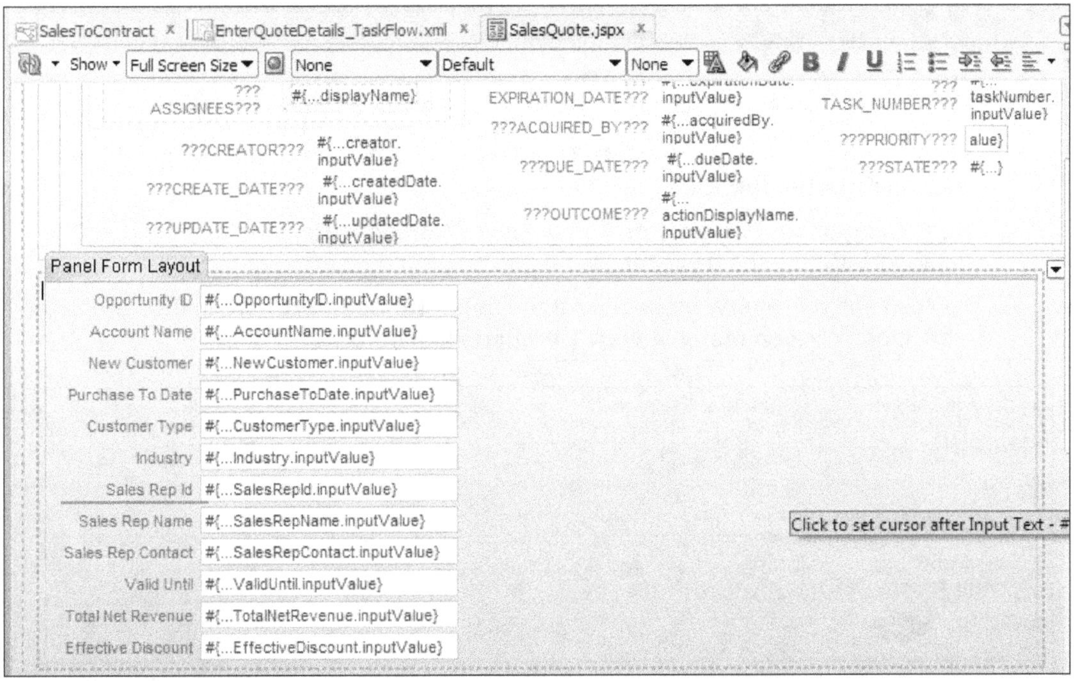

How it works...

You have designed the `SalesQuote.jspx` file. This is the task display form (using the complete task with payload drop handler), and is available at `jDev_Oracle_Home/mywork/ApplicationName/ProjectName/public_html`.

The payload drop handler allows you to display chosen elements selectively in the task UI.

Implementing routers

Router activities are used to declaratively route control to activities, based on logic specified in an EL expression. They are used to branch to multiple control flows leading from it, to different activities.

Each router case contains the elements Expression and Outcome. They are used to choose the activity to which control is next routed:

- **Expression**: This is an EL expression evaluating to either true or false. The first expression that evaluates to true is used to determine the corresponding outcome.

- **Outcome**: This is a value returned by the router activity if the EL expression evaluates to true.

How to do it...

In this section, you will cover how to implement declarative route control, as follows:

1. In JDeveloper, go to **EnterQuoteDetailsUI project | Web Content | Page Flows** and click on **EnterQuoteDetails_TaskFlow.xml**.
2. Go to **Component Palette | ADF Task Flow | Components** and drag-and-drop the activity **Router** on the designer. Name it `RouteEnterQuote`.
3. You can find a **Property Inspector** for the router **RouteEnterQuote** in the lower-right side. If not, click on **Menu** at **View | Property Inspector**.

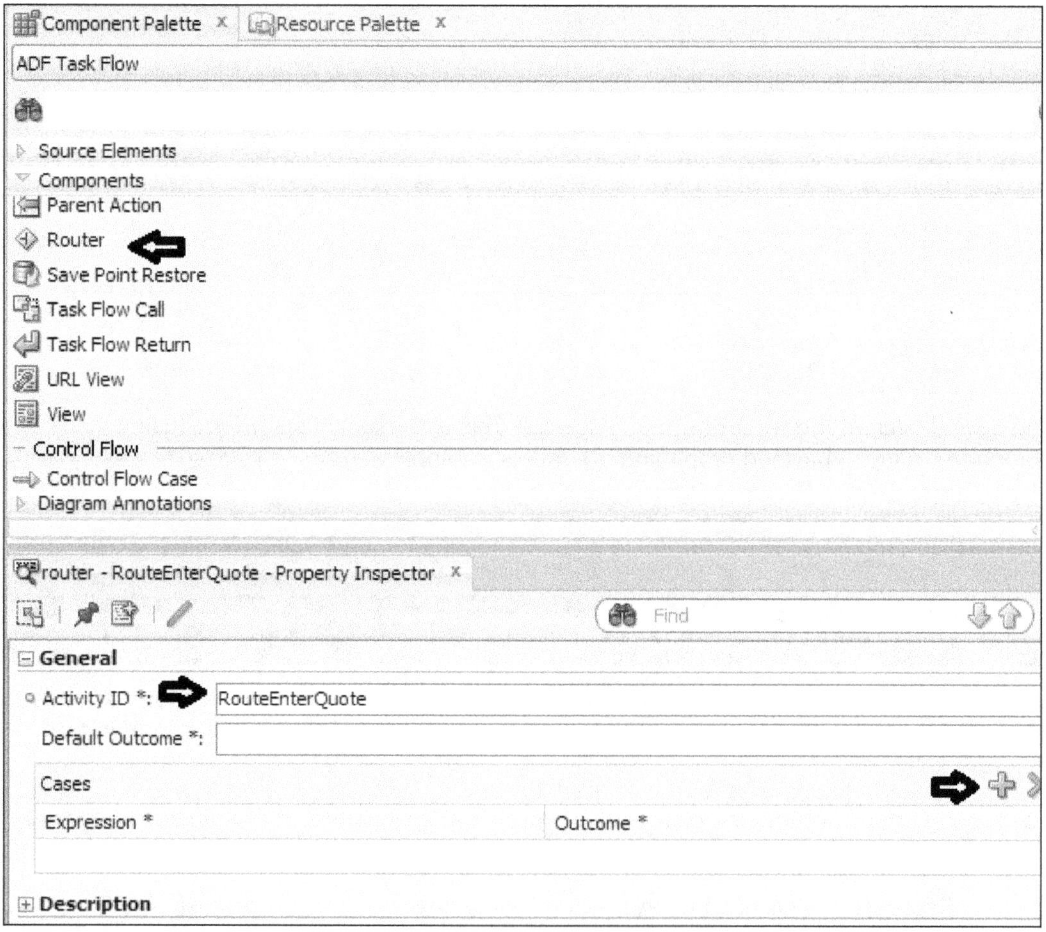

4. Go to **Component Palette | ADF faces | Components** and click on **Control Flow Cases**.
5. Create a flow case from the **RouteEnterQuote** router to the **SalesQuote_ProductLess** view and name it `WithoutProduct`.
6. Create a flow case from the **RouteEnterQuote** router to the **SalesQuote** view and name it `WithProduct`.
7. Click on the **RouteEnterQuote** router in the designer and go to **Properties**.
8. Click on the green plus (**+**) icon to the right of the cases.
9. Choose **Expression Builder** from the the drop-down menu.
10. In **Expression Builder**, expand **Data** | **EnterQuoteDetailsUI_SalesQuotePageDef** and select **AccountName**.
11. Enter the following expression:

```
#{data.enterquotedetailsui_SalesQuotePageDef.AccountName ==
"FusionNX"}
```

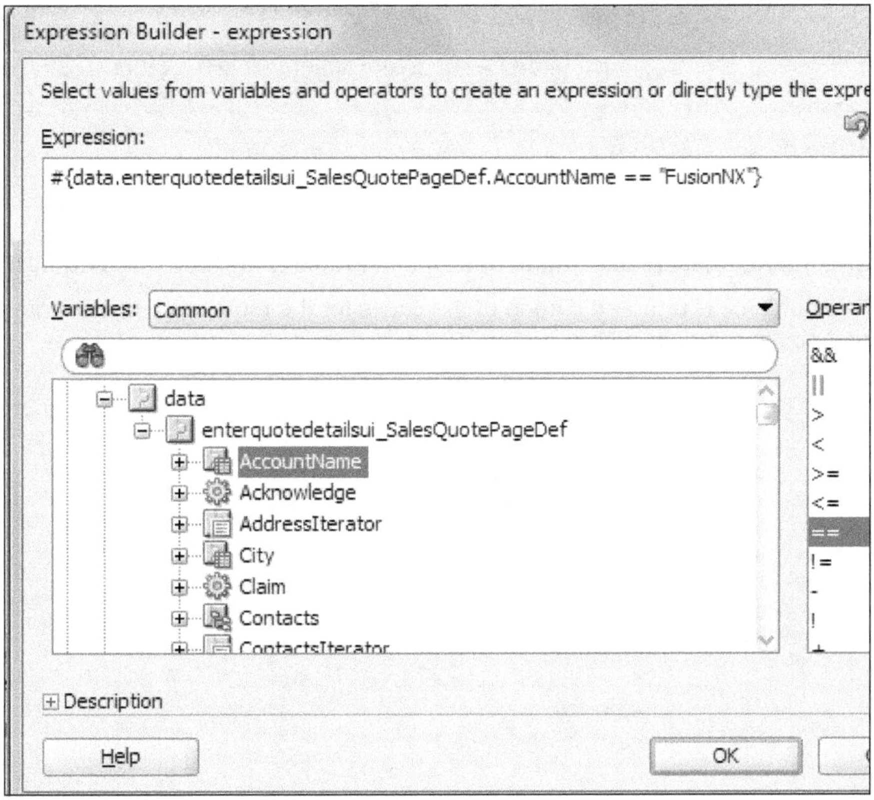

12. Click **OK**.

13. In the **Outcome** drop-down menu, select **WithoutProduct** as the outcome.
14. Similarly, add another expression:

    `{data.enterquotedetailsui_SalesQuotePageDef.AccountName!=`
    `"FusionNX"}`

    Then, select the outcome **WithProduct**.

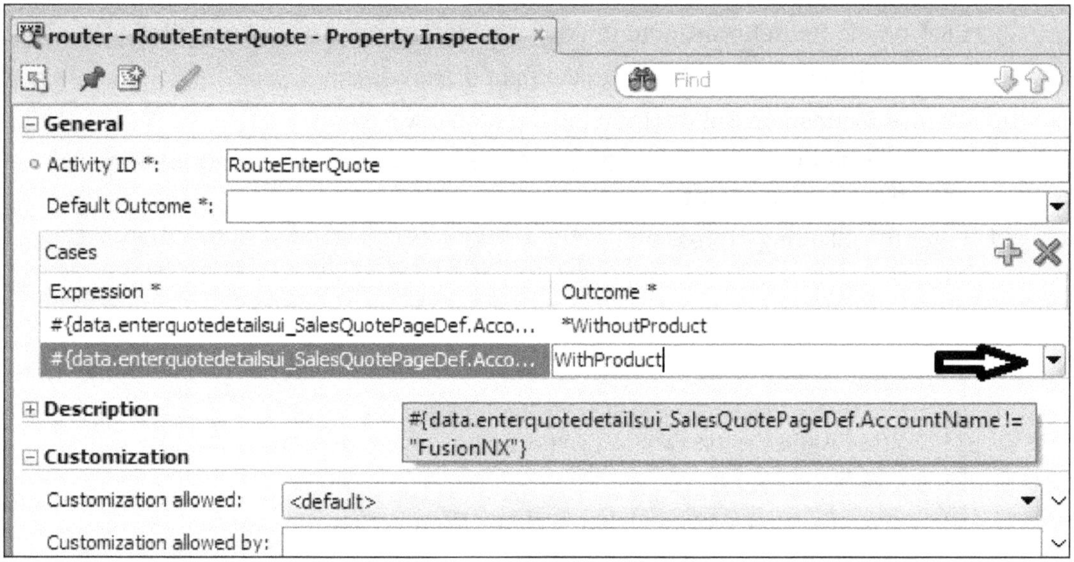

15. Click **Router** and set the default outcome in **Property Inspector** as **WithoutProduct**.
16. This outcome is returned if none of the cases for the router activity evaluate to true, or if no cases are specified.

17. Right-click the router **RouteEnterQuote**, click **Mark Activity**, and select **Default Activity**. This will ensure that the router is called.

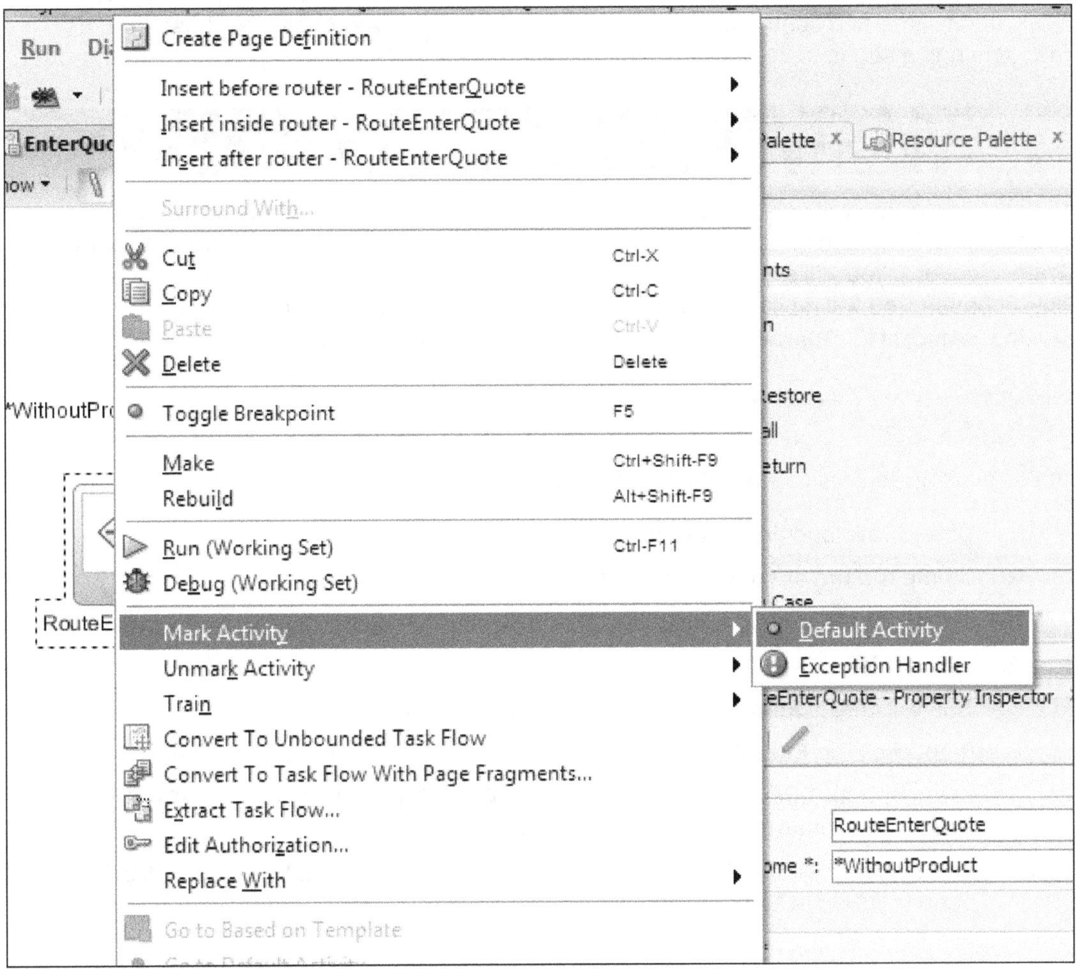

How it works...

When the router expression evaluates to true, control passes to the activity that the the control flow case points to, based on the outcome specified in the properties, for that expression. If none of the cases for the router activity evaluate to true, or if no cases are specified, the outcome specified in the router default outcome field (if any) is used.

Hence, when the quote payload (initialized by a Script Task) or the Quote Message arrives to the **SalesToContract** process (in case the **SalesToContract** process is exposed as a service or accepts messages), with value of account name as FusionNX, the first expression gets evaluated to true and control passes to the **SalesQuote_ProductLess** view, based on the outcome being set as `WithoutProduct`, in **Properties**.

Creating Task Form sequence flow

In this section, you will create multiple Task Forms in a task flow. These Task Forms will be in sequence. You have already witnessed creation of task flow. There, you have a **Create Train** checkbox. You will select this option to create a task flow that allows a sequential flow of pages. You will do it for **EnterQuoteUI**, however you can repeat the same for **BusinessAnalystUI**, **Approve Terms/Deal**, and **Finalize Contracts**, too.

How to do it...

In this section, you will create a Task Form sequence flow:

1. Open JDeveloper in the default role.
2. Delete the pre-existing **EnterQuoteUI** project.
3. Create a new project by selecting **New | Generic Project**, and name it **EnterQuoteUI**.
4. Click **Finish**.
5. This will create **Empty Project** in the application navigator.
6. Right-click the **EnterQuoteUI** project and select **New**. This will open the new gallery.
7. Select the **All Technologies** tab and go to **Web Tier | JSF**, select the **ADF Task flow Based on Human Task** item and click **OK**.
8. In the **SOA Resource** browser, select **EnterQuoteDetails.task** and click **OK**. This will open the **Create Task Flow** dialog.

9. In the **Create Task Flow** dialog, select **Create as Bounded Task Flow** and check **Create Train**.

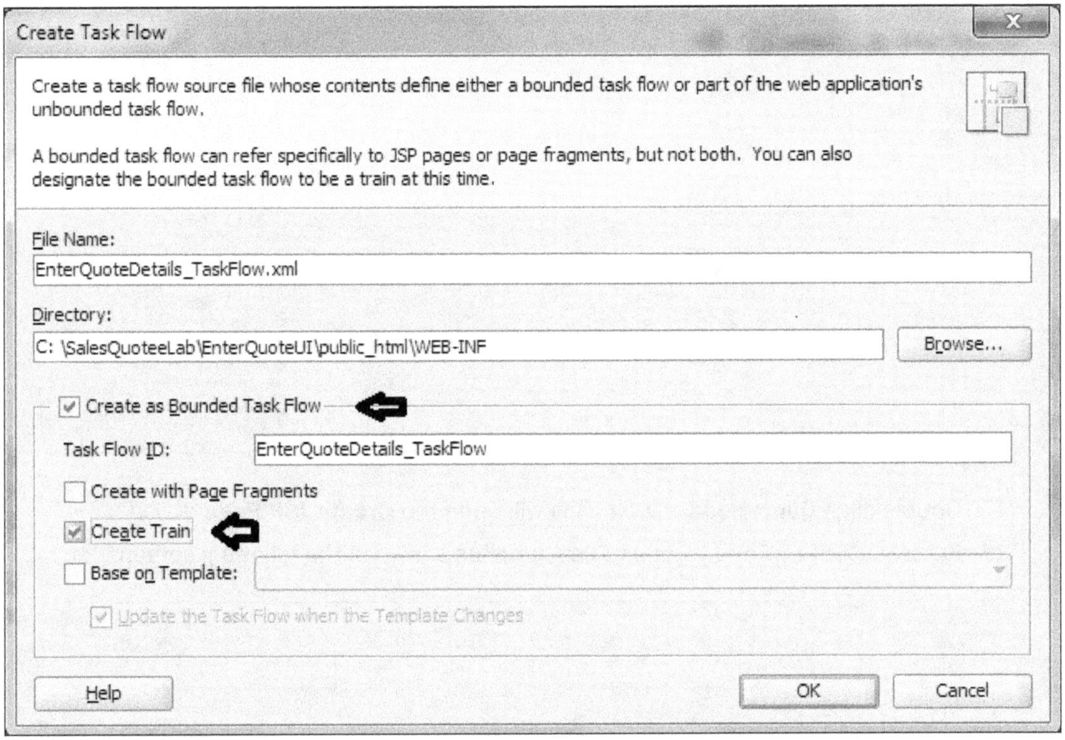

10. Click **OK**.
11. This will open `EnterQuoteDetails_TaskFlow.xml`.
12. Rename `taskDetails1_jspx.jspx` as `QuoteHeader.jspx`.
13. Go to **Component Palette | ADF Task Flow | Components** and drag-and-drop **View** into the designer.
14. Name the **QuoteLines** activity as **View**.
15. Go to **Component Palette | ADF Task Flow | Components** and click **Control Flow Case**.

16. Create a flow from **QuoteHeader** to **QuoteLines** and then to **QuoteLines** and **taskReturn**, as shown in the following screenshot:

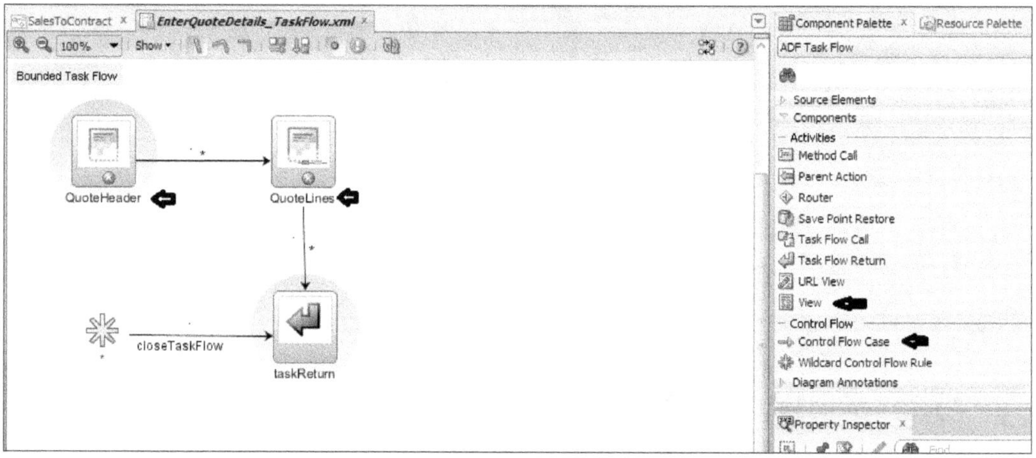

17. Double-click **QuoteHeader** view. This will open the **Create JSF Page** dialog.
18. Enter `QuoteHeader.jspx` as **File Name**, as shown in the following screenshot:

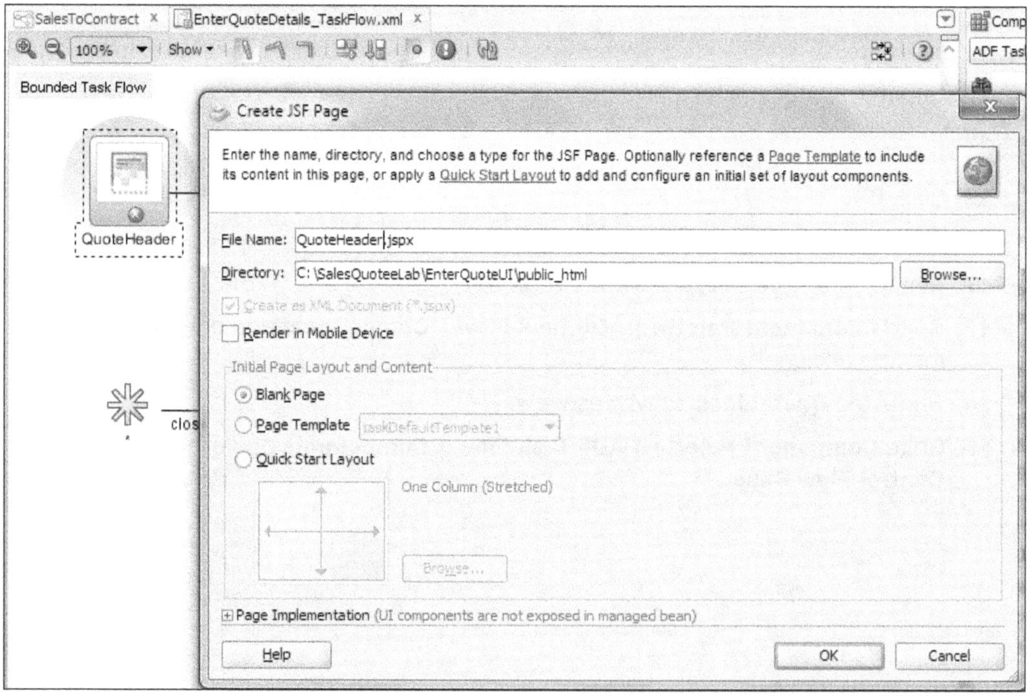

19. Let the details be default, and click **OK**. This will open the `QuoteHeader.jspx` file.

20. Go to **Data Control | EnterQuoteUI_EnterQuoteDetails | getTaskDetails | Return** and drag-and-drop **Task** into the designer.
21. Click **Human Task** and select **Task Header**, to create a task header for the page.

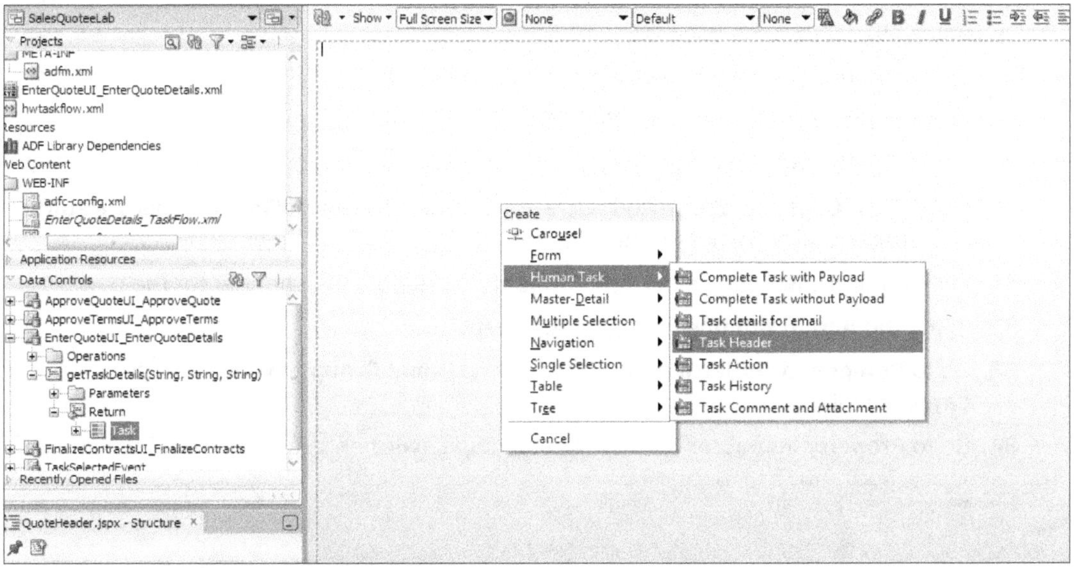

22. In the **Edit Action Binding** dialog, click **OK** twice.
23. Go to **Component Palette | ADF faces | Layout** and drag-and-drop **Panel Group Layout**.

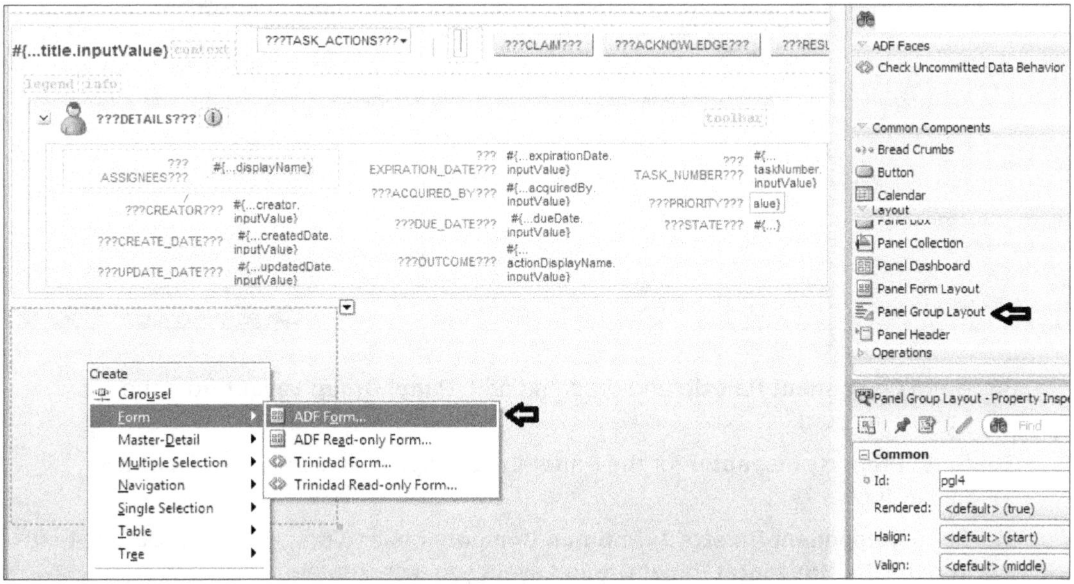

24. Go to **Data Control | EnterQuoteUI_EnterQuoteDetails | getTaskDetails | Return | Payload** and drag-and-drop **Summary** into **Panel Group Layout**, which you have just created.
25. Click **Form** and select **ADF Form**.
26. In the filled **Edit** form, click **OK**.
27. When you have completed the preceding steps, **Save**.
28. Go to **EnterQuoteDetails_TaskFlow.xml** and double-click **QuoteLines**.
29. In the **Create JSF Page** dialog, click **OK**. This will open the `QuoteLines.jspx` file.
30. Go to **Data Control | EnterQuoteUI_EnterQuoteDetails | getTaskDetails | Return** and drag-and-drop **Task** into the designer.
31. Click **Human Task** and select **Task Header**, to create a task header for the page.
32. In the the **Action Binding** dialogs, click **OK** twice.
33. Go to **Component Palette** and drag-and-drop **Panel Group Layout** from the **Layout** menu.
34. Go to **Property Inspector** for the **Panel Group Layout** and select **Vertical** as **Layout**.

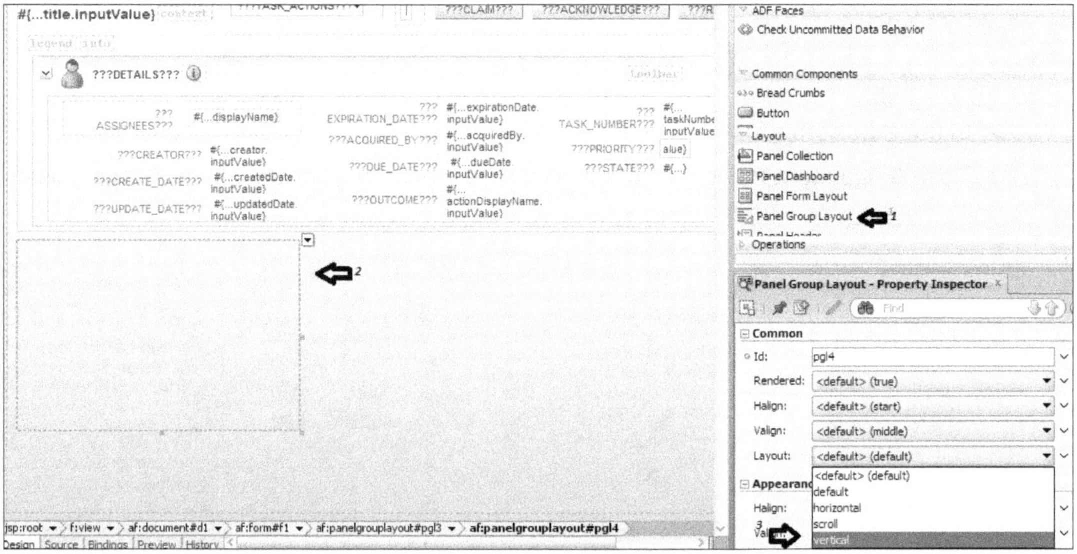

35. Go to **Component Palette** and drag-and-drop **Panel Group Layout** from the **Layout** section.
36. Go to **Property Inspector** for the **Panel Group Layout** and select **Horizontal** as **Layout**.
37. Go to **Component Palette | Common Components** and drag-and-drop **Output Text** into the the **Horizontal Panel Group Layout** you just created.

38. In the **Property Inspector** of this text box, enter `Quote Summary` as **Value**.

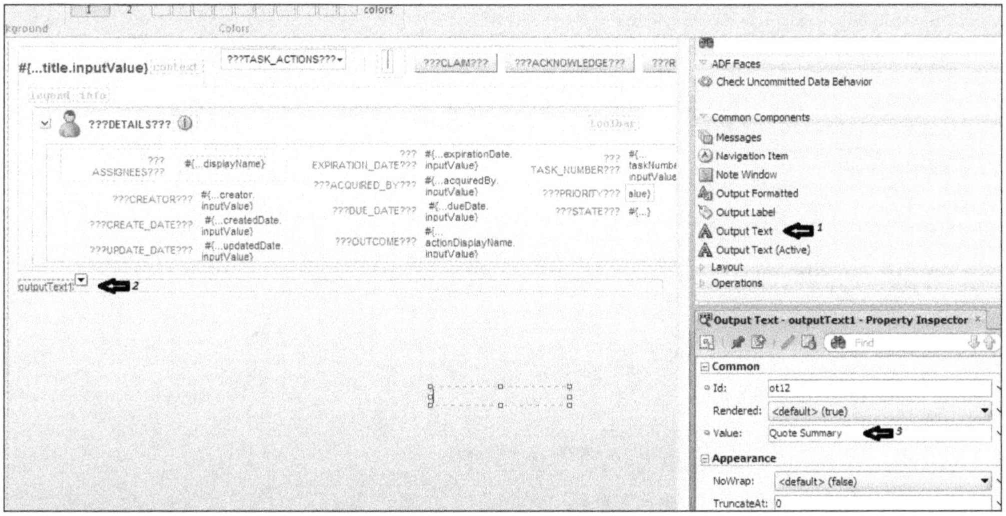

39. Select the **Horizontal Panel**, click the drop-down and select **Insert inside**. Choose **Button** from the list.

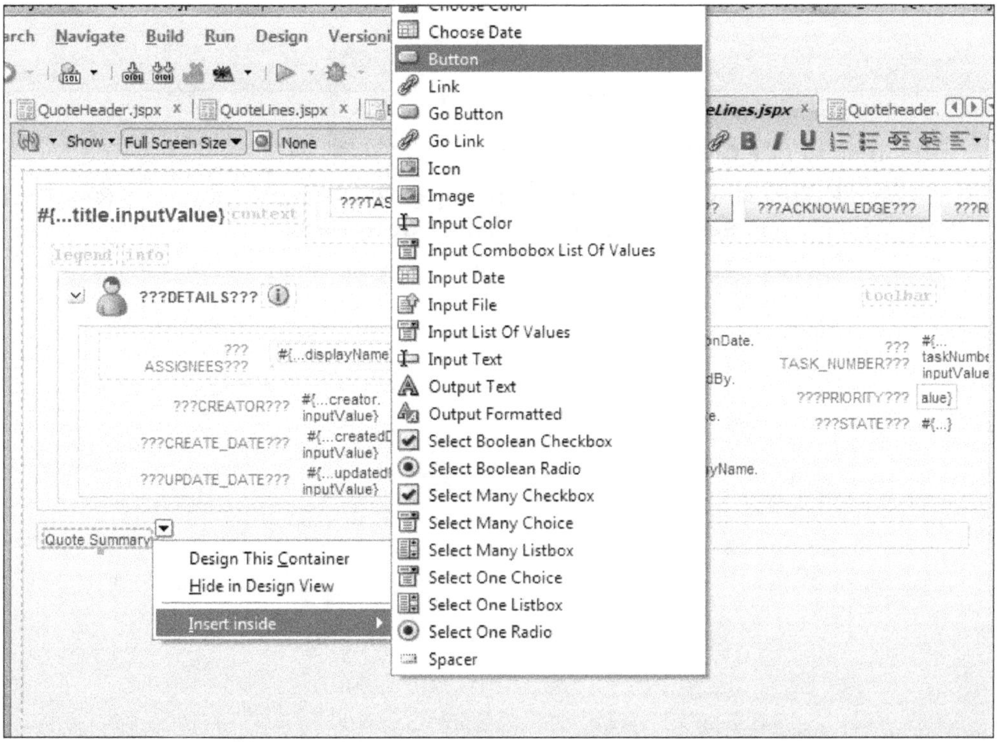

40. Click on the **Button** action icon, and select **Bind to ADF Control**.

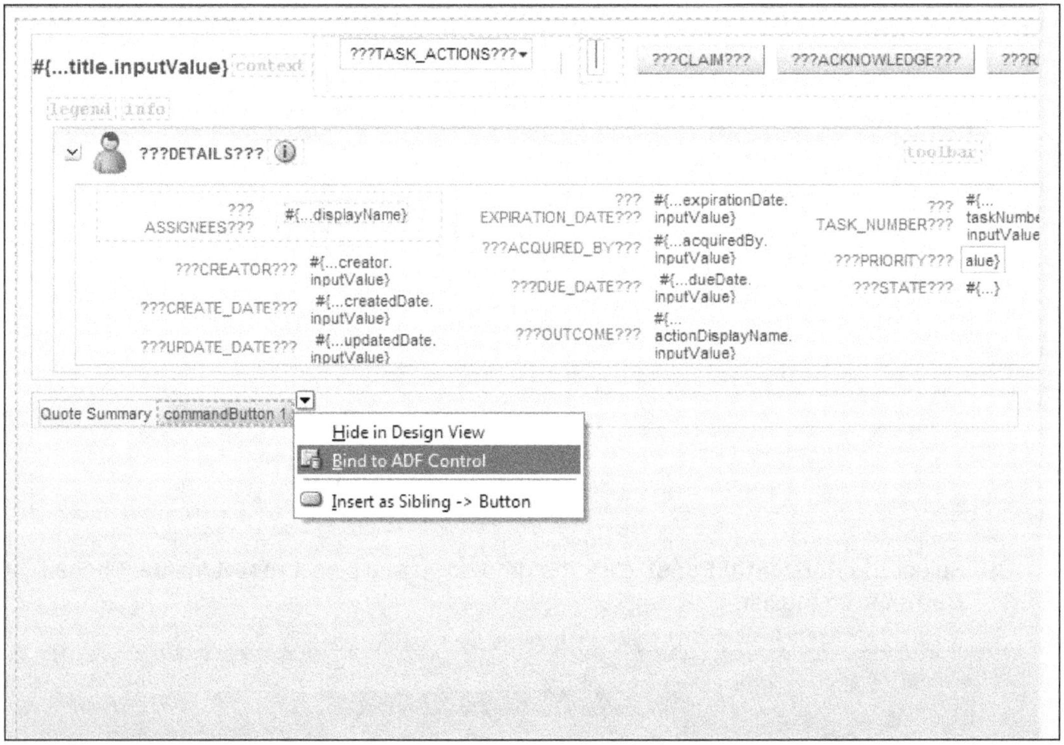

The **Bind to ADF Control** dialog will open.

41. Expand **EnterQuoteUI_EnterQuoteDetails | getTaskDetails | Return | Task | Payload | Quote Request | Product Items | Operations**.

42. Select **Create** under **Operations** as the bind to ADF Control setting for this button in the **Bind to ADF Control** editing dialog,and click OK.

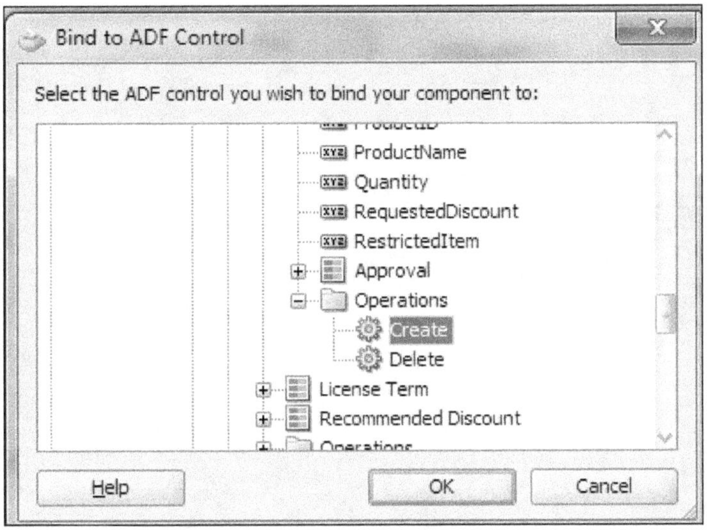

43. Select the horizontal panel, click the drop-down, and select **Insert Inside**. Choose **Button** from the list.
44. Click on the button, click the button action icon, and select **Bind to ADF Control**.

    A **Bind to ADF Control** dialog will open.
45. Expand **EnterQuoteUI_EnterQuoteDetails | getTaskDetails | Return | Task | Payload | Quote Request | Product Items | Operations**.
46. Select the **Create** operation under **Bind to ADF Control**, for this button and click **OK**.
47. In the **Edit Bind Action** dialog, click **OK**.
48. Go to **Data Control** and expand **EnterQuoteUI_EnterQuoteDetails | getTaskDetails | Return | Task | Payload | Quote Request**.

49. Drag-and-drop **Product Item** in the vertical panel.
50. Click **Table** and select **ADF Table**.

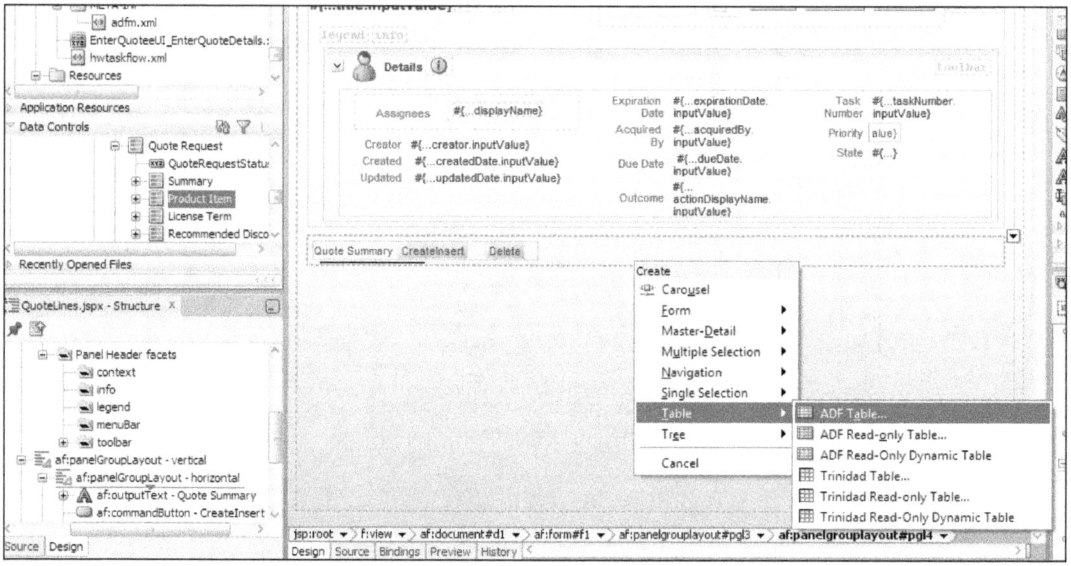

51. In the **Edit Table Column** dialog, accept defaults and click **OK**.
52. When you have completed the preceding steps, click **Save**.
53. You created **Task Actions**, attachment, and comments, as you have done before.

How it works...

You can verify the JSPX page in the project navigator and from its physical location, too.

1. You can verify that `QuoteHeader.jspx` and `QuoteLines.jspx` are created. The flow can be verified from the task flow XML file.

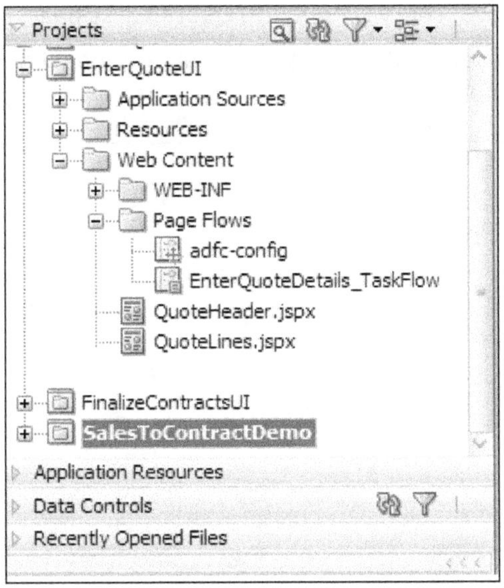

2. You can find these files in the `/Public_HTML` folder in the project directory.

Deploying and testing

You can now deploy the project and can test it, and verify payload from the EM Console, as follows:

1. Log in to Oracle BPM Workspace as user **salesrepresentative**.
2. Click on the process name in the **Applications** list.
3. Enter quote details for the **Quote Header** page, as follows:

4. Click **Actions | Save**. This will open the **Quote Lines** page.
5. Click the **CreateInsert** button and you can enter product details, as shown in the following screenshot:

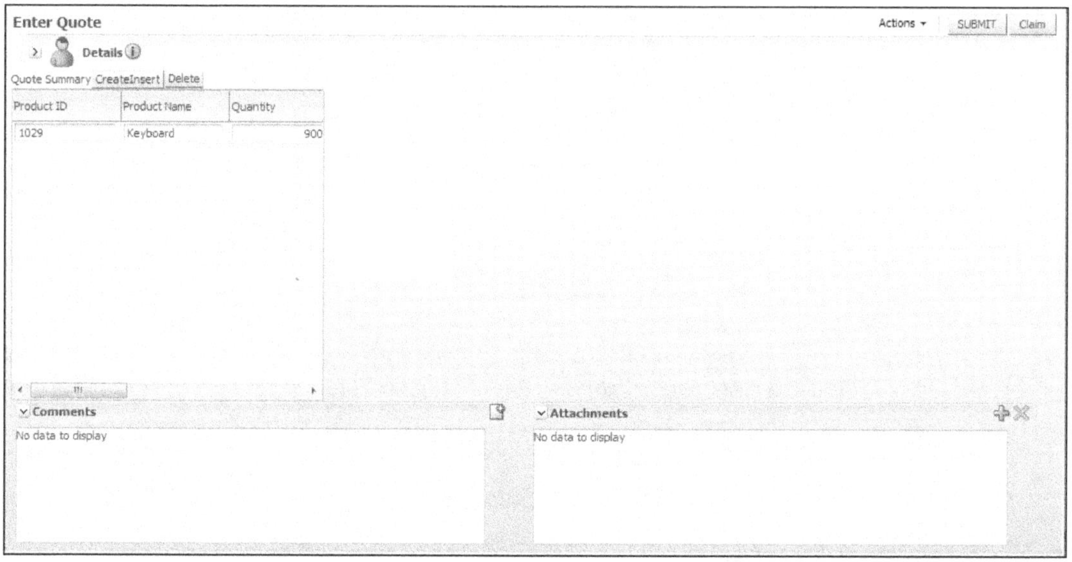

Once this has been done, you can click the **Submit** button.

6. Log in to the Oracle EM Console and click **Running Instance** for the **SalesToContractDemo** project.
7. You can verify the product details you have entered from the Payload of the activities.

Creating a Task form with ADF Business Components

ADF-BC is the data model layer for ADF. It has the following prime components:

- **Entity Objects**: They represent a row in the data source, and you can modify their attributes. They encapsulate business logic as well, to validate your data. Entity objects are defined by specifying a table as they represents its rows, and rows are identified based on row key.

- **View objects**: They encapsulate the SQL queries. You can create a read-only view object when updates to data are not necessary. You can create entity-based View objects, static View objects, and programmatically populated View objects, too. Custom View objects can also be created. It's the View objects that collaborate with Entity Objects.
- **View Links**: They are used to represent the master-detail relationship between two View objects.
- **Application Module**: It is a smart data service that contains the data model of master-detail-related queries that your client interface needs to work with. It's a transactional component used by UI to work with application data. It can contain procedures and functions (referred to as service methods) that are encapsulated within the service implementation.

Getting ready

ADF Business Components, known as **ADF-BC**, are used for creating complex Task Forms, and one can use ADF-BC View objects as facts in Oracle Business Rules. For ADF, the main data source, which is also called the data model, is based on ADF-BC.

Oracle JDeveloper provides a very easy way to bind components from the Business Services layer to your controller and view layers using an innovative binding layer approach. The data control palette provides a view into the Business Services layer. Developers can simply drag-and-drop Data objects and bind them to their user interface implementation.

The functionality of the process SalesToContract says that the `salesrepresentative` user will enter the quote, and based on **Discount Check**, the task will be guided to the `businessanalyst` user. You have created the Task UI earlier, using the Auto-generate mechanism, however here, you will also add some information about `Opportunity`, to the user interface presented to the `businessanalyst` user.

How to do it...

In this section, you will develop expertise in creating ADF-BC components and creating Task Forms based on ADF-BC components.

I. Create a table and a procedure based on it

1. You will create a table named `ValidateOpportunity`. This table will contain `OpportunityID`, which is a part of the quote payload. When one queries the table based on `OpportunityID`, details about `OpportunityID` data are fetched. You will create a procedure that inputs `OpportunityID` and results in `OpportunityType` and `OpportunityRevision`.

2. Create a table named `ValidateOpportunity` in the `DEV_SOAINFRA` schema, or in any schema that you have configured for your DB connection, as follows:

```
create table ValidateOpportunity (OpportunityID
varchar2(20),OpportunityType varchar2(10),OpportunityRevision
varchar2(1));
```

3. Insert some demo data, as follows:

```
insert into ValidateOpportunity values('ABC1029','New','Y');
insert into ValidateOpportunity values('ABC1030','Old','Y');
```

4. Create the procedure, as follows:

```
CREATE OR REPLACE PRODECURE CHECKOPPORTUNITY (
OPPID IN VARCHAR2,
OPPTYPE OUT VARCHAR2,
OPPREV OUT VARCHAR2) AS
BEGIN
SELECT OPPORTUNITYTYPE, OPPORTUNITYREVISION INTO OPPTYPE, OPPREV
FROM VALIDATEOPPORTUNITY
WHERE OPPORTUNITYID = OPPID;
END;
```

5. You can use JDeveloper to create a table and procedure, or you can use any other tool such as TOAD or SQL*PLUS to achive the desired goal.

II. Create a Synchronous Service based on the procedure CHECKOPPORTUNITY

1. Assuming you have basic knowledge about creating a BPEL service, we will not go into the details of service creation.
2. Open JDeveloper in the default mode.
3. Create a synchronous BPEL service that accepts `OpportunityID` and returns `OpportunityType` and `OpportunityRevision`.
4. You can use the Oracle DB adapter in the BPEL process.
5. Let the name of the service be `OpportunityCheckingService`.
6. Deploy it to the WebLogic server on which you have SOA installed.

III. Create an ADF-BC View object, based on web service

1. Go to JDeveloper and click the application containing the **SalesToContractDemo** project.
2. Right-click the **BusinessAnalystUI** project, and click on **Properties**.
3. In the **Properties** dialog, select **Libraries** and **Class path**.
4. Add the library **BC4J Service Runtime**.
5. Click **OK**.
6. As your goal is to provide input to the UI form from the service, you will need to follow the ensuing steps:
    - In the application navigator, right-click the **BusinessAnalystUI** project and select **New**
    - In the **New Gallery** dialog, go to **All Technologies | Business Tier | Data Controls** and select **Web Service Data Control**

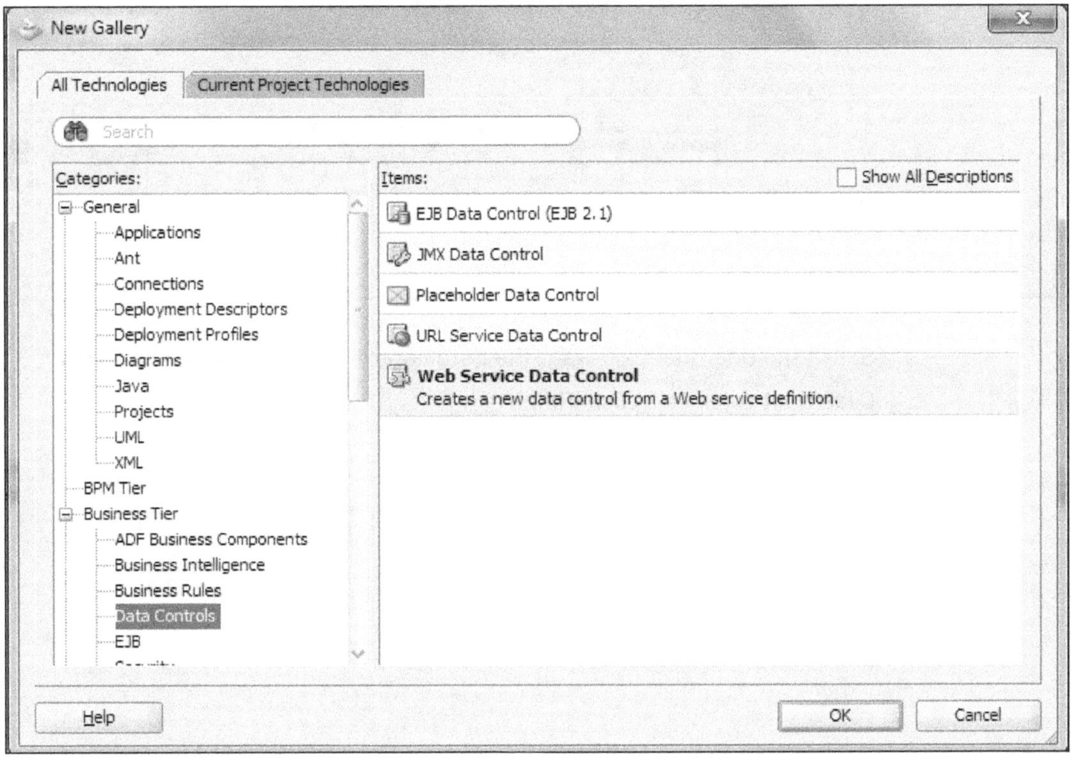

This will open the Create Web Service data control wizard.

- Enter `OpportunityVO` as **Data Source Name**, and `OpportunityCheckingService WSDL` as the BPEL service in **URL**, and click **Services**
- The service section will list the **Service: OpportunityCheckingService**. Select it and click **Next**

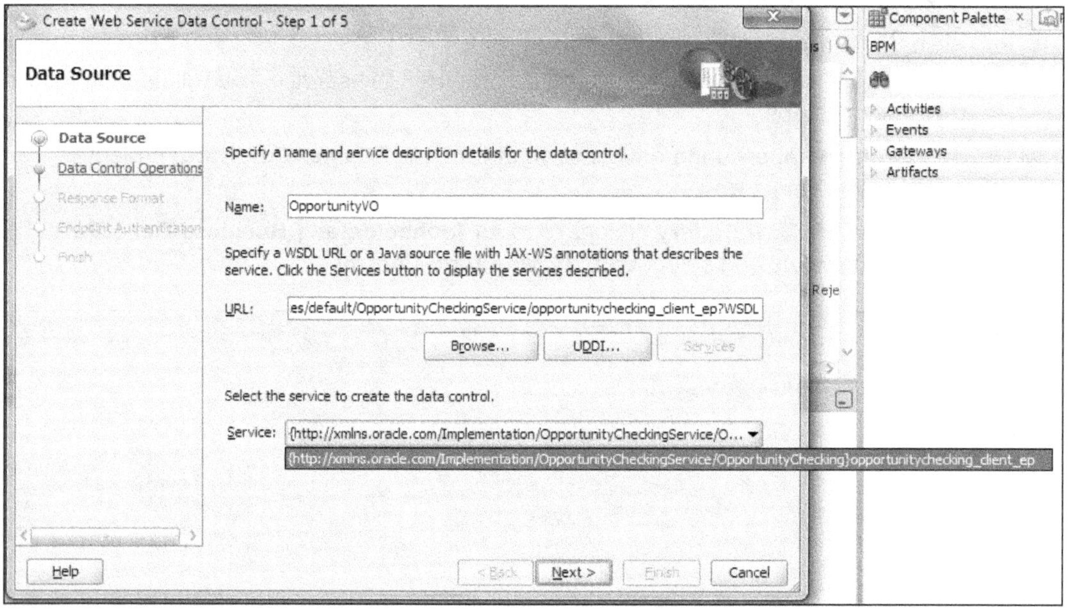

- Select the operation you want the data control to support and click **Next**
- Click **Next** twice and click **Finish**

7. To verify data control creation, go to **Data Controls | OpportunityVO**.

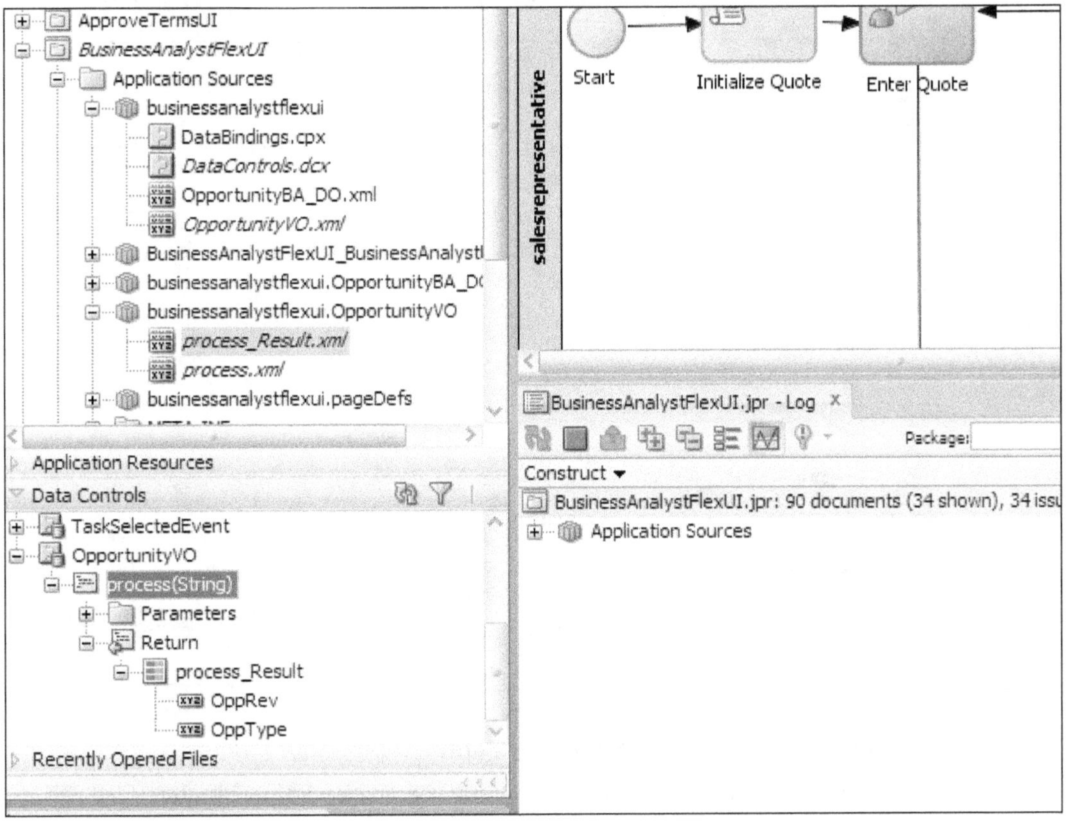

This confirms that you can include this data control in your UI ADF forms.

8. Go to **BusinessAnalystUI project | Web Content** and click on the `taskDetails1.jspx` page.
9. Select the **CONTENTS** showDetailHeader.
10. From the menu, select **Design this Container**.

11. From **Data Controls | OpportunityVo | Process | Return**, drag-and-drop **process_result** into the contents container, as shown in the following screenshot:

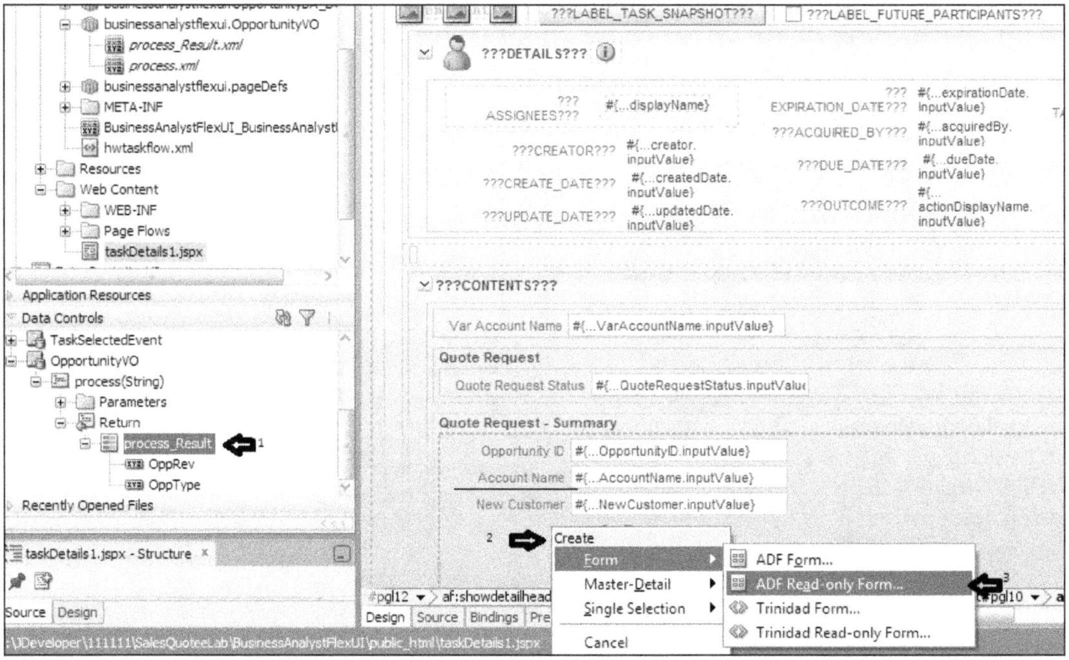

12. Click on **Form** and select **ADF Read-Only Form**.

13. This will open the **Edit Form Fields** dialog and will display **Value Binding**. Click **OK**.

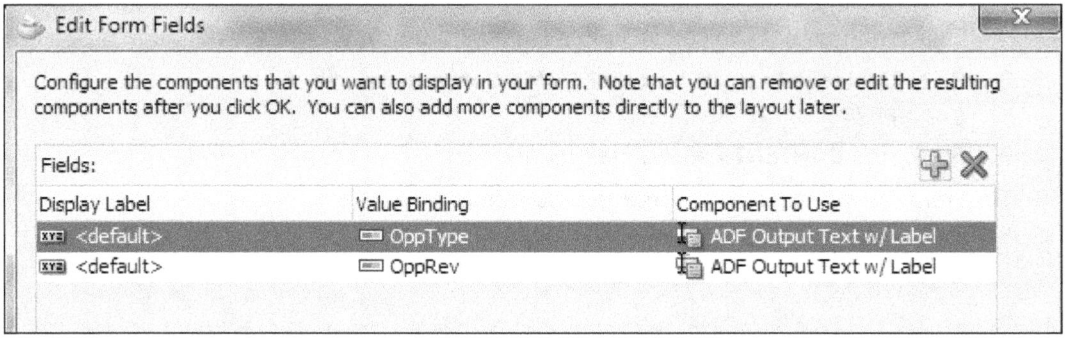

14. In the **Parameters** section, in the **Value** field, select **Show El Expression Builder**.

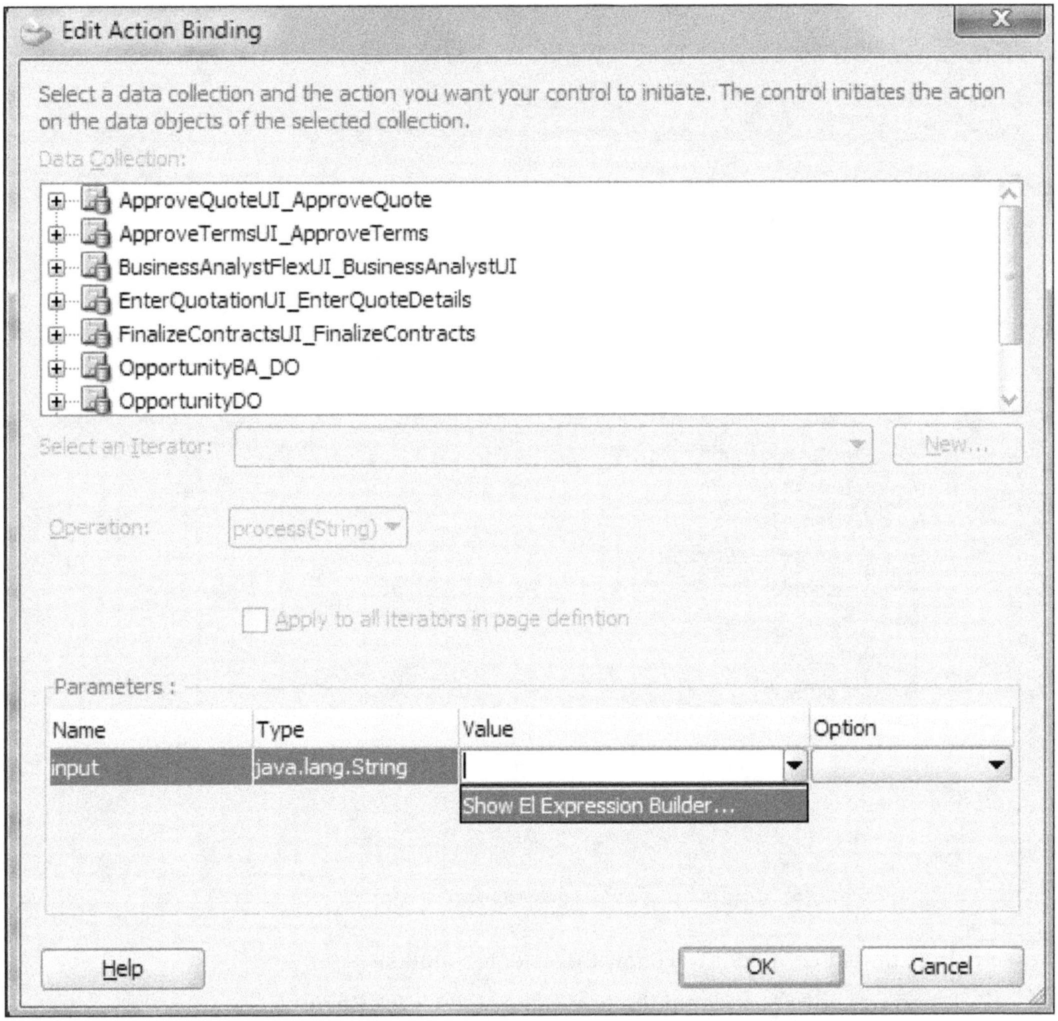

15. The **Variables** dialog is displayed.

16. Expand **ADF Bindings**, select **OpportunityID**, and click **OK**.

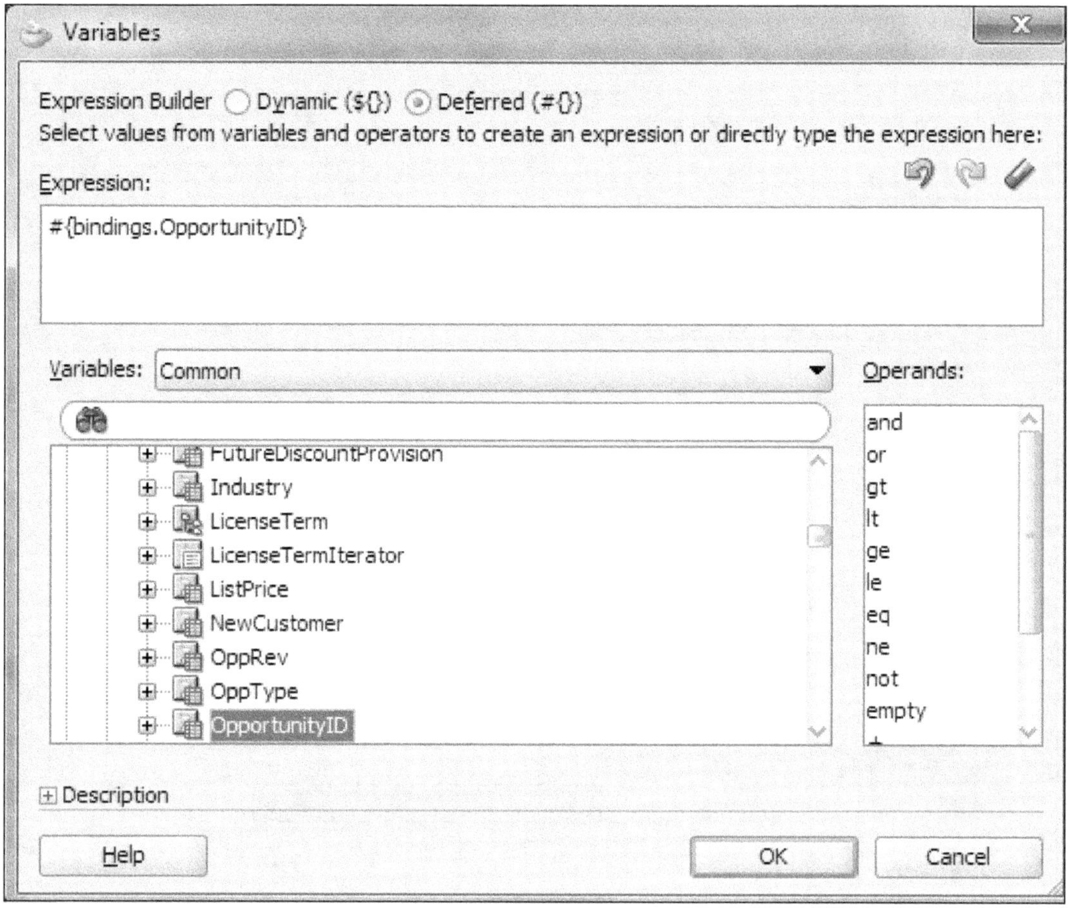

The content container will show the selected inputs.

17. When you have completed the preceding steps, click **Save**.

How it works...

Deploy the project and go to the Oracle BPM workspace as the `salesrepresentative` user and enter the value for**Enter Quote**. The quote will move to BusinessAnalyst user. Log in as the `businessanalyst` user in Oracle BPM workspace. You will find that **OppType** and **OppRev** are selected based on the **Opportunity ID** entered. In this case, the **Opportunity ID** enteredis **ABC1029**. Verify it with the data you have inserted into the preceding table. You will find an instance created for **OpportunityCheckingService** in the EM console, too.

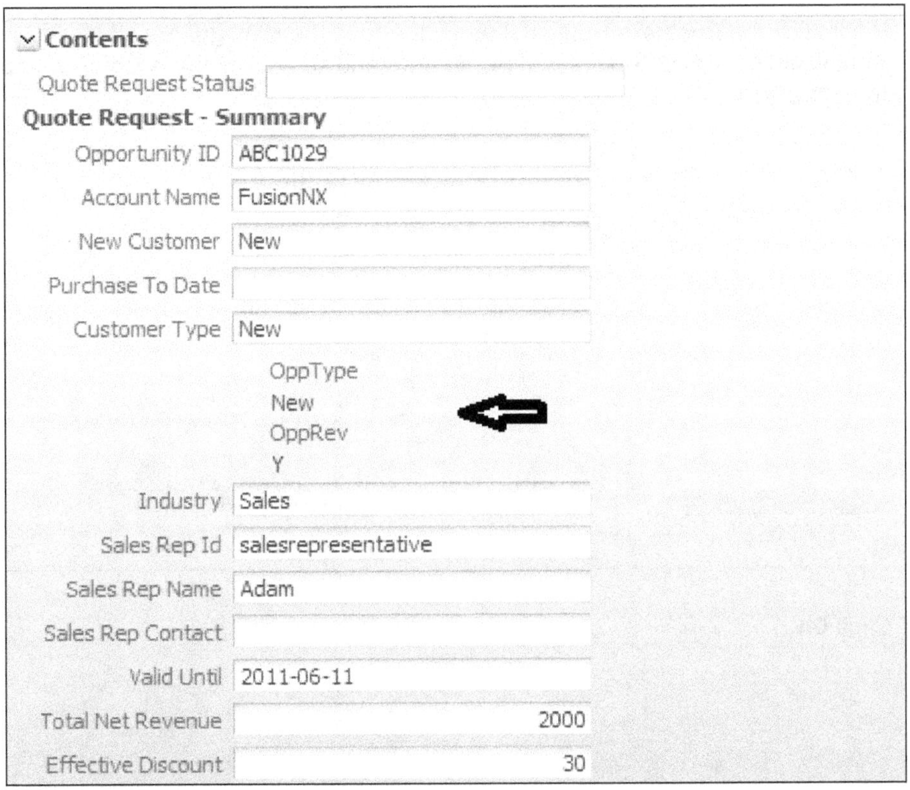

This is useful when, say `businessanalyst` user needs more information about the opportunities available, to help him/her make a decision about either approving or rejecting the quote.

There's more...

Let's learn to create entity and View objects in the following section.

Creating Entity and View objects

You have created data control based on the web service. You can even create ADF-BC Entity objects and corresponding View objects, based on tables, and can use them via ADF Data Controls in the Task Form.

1. Right-click the **BusinessAnalystUI** project, and in the **New gallery** dialog, go to **Business Tier | ADF Business Components** and select **Business Components from Tables**.

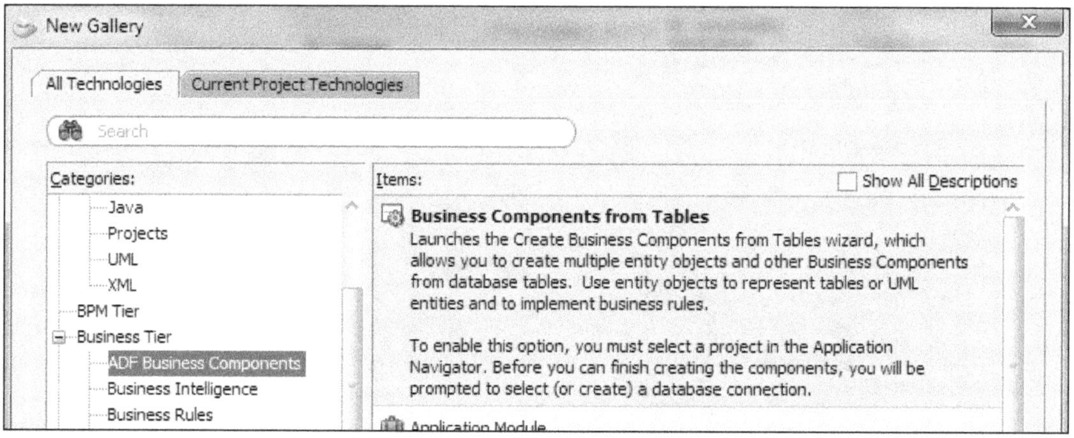

2. Click **OK**.

3. Specify the data connection information for the `Business Components.jpx` file and click **OK**.

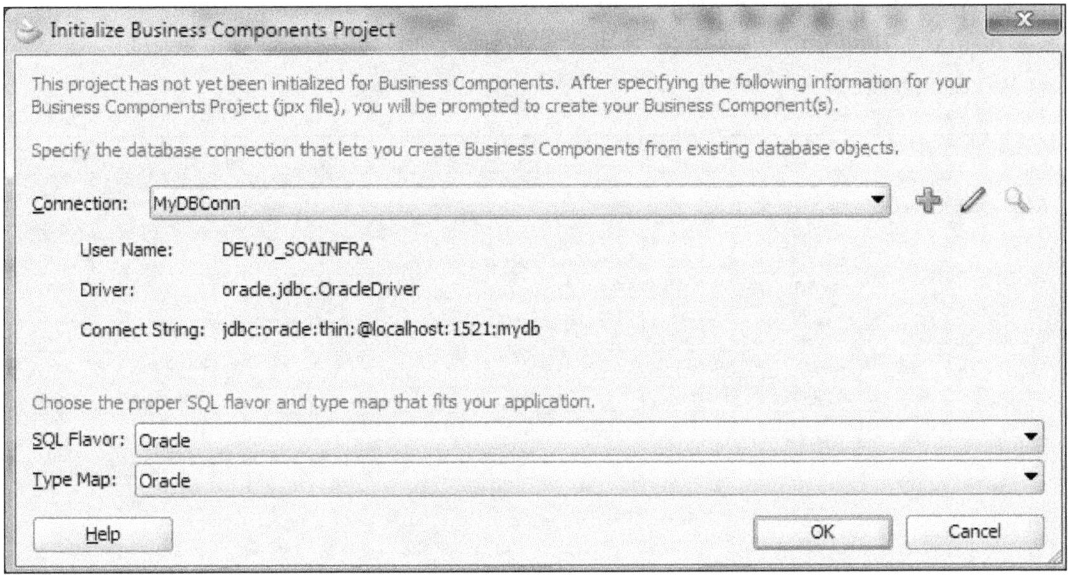

4. Enter the **Package** name, select the **Schema**, and click **Query** after entering a search string for the table.

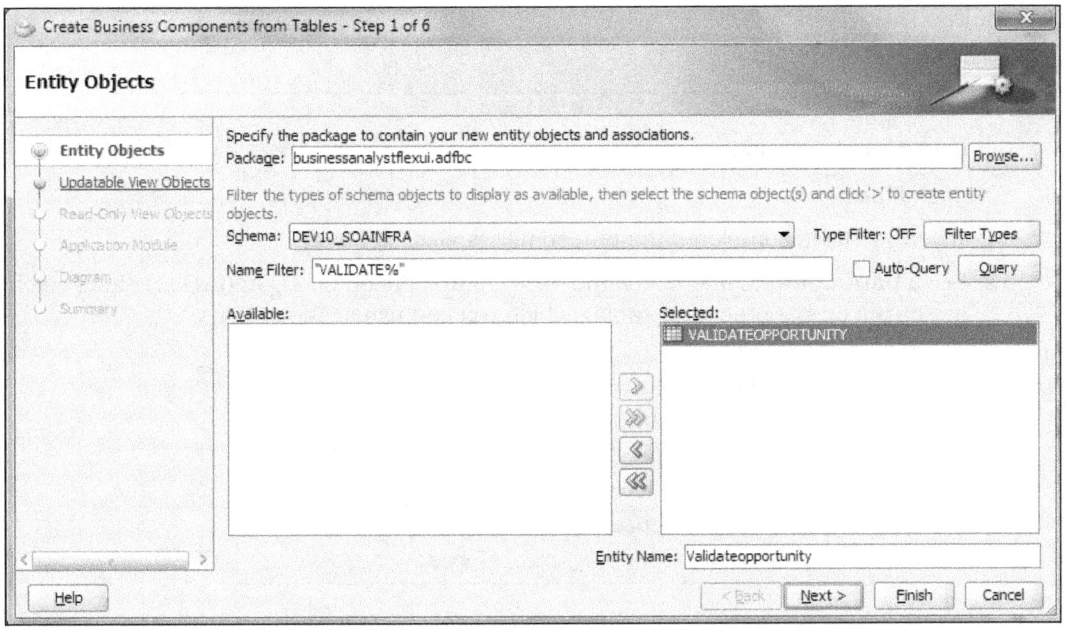

5. You will find the **VALIDATEOPPORTUNITY** table in the available column. Select it and click **Next**.
6. Click **Next**, without selecting anything.
7. In the **Read-Only View Objects** dialog, query again for the table and select it.
8. Click **Next**.

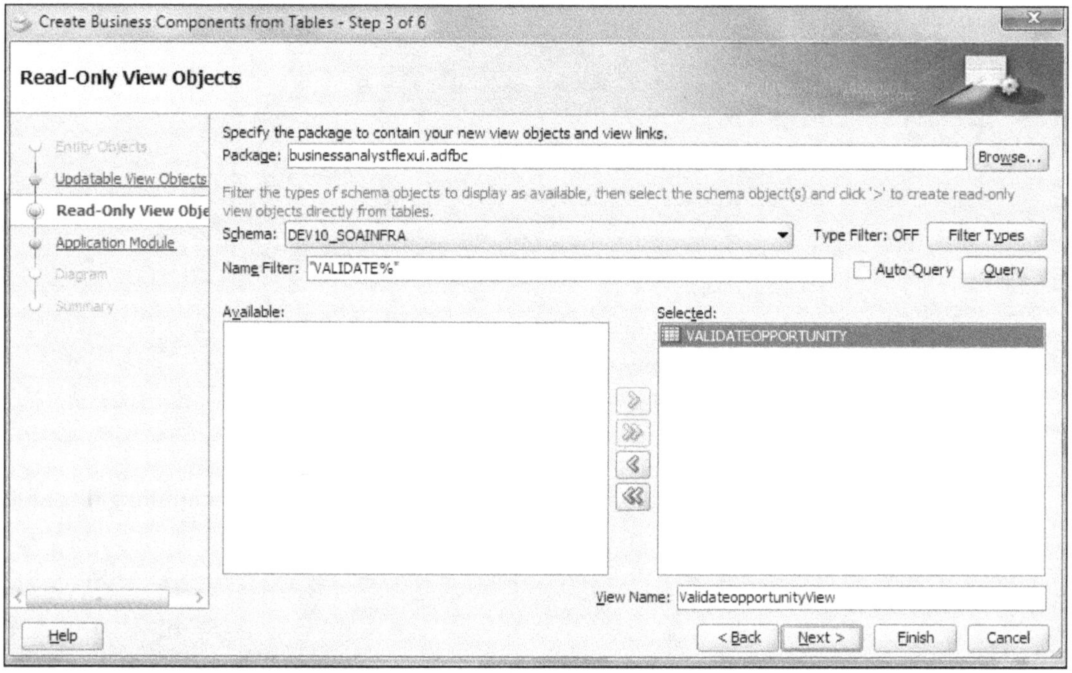

9. Click **Next** twice more.
10. Click **Finish**.
11. When you have completed the preceding steps, click **Save**.
12. Go to **Data Controls** and check the data control, based on EO and VO created (which are based on the preceding table), which you can use in Task Forms.

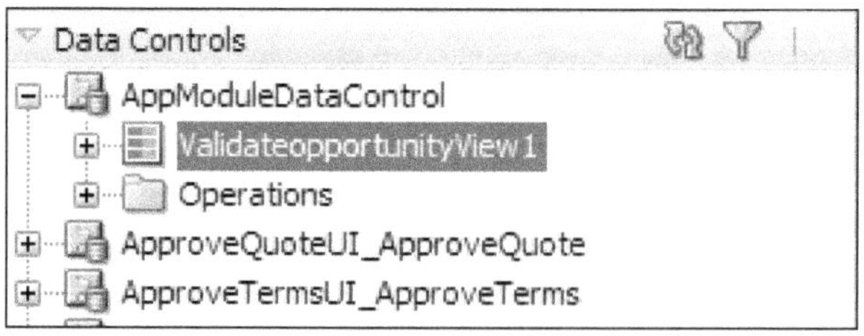

Creating a task display form—using a wizard

There are many ways to create a task display form for a Human Task, and one of them is using wizards. **Wizard Driven** is also an option in the `.task` file. However, there are more options available, such as temple and multi-row-column layout, which you will learn in this section.

In this section, you will create a task display form for the Business Analyst Human Task.

How to do it...

Let's create a task display form using wizards, as follows:

1. Open JDeveloper in the default role.
2. Go to the **BPM Project Navigator** tab.
3. Expand **Business Catalog | Human Tasks** and click **Approve Quote**.
4. Click **Create Form**.
5. From the drop-down menu, select **Launch Task Form Wizard...**.

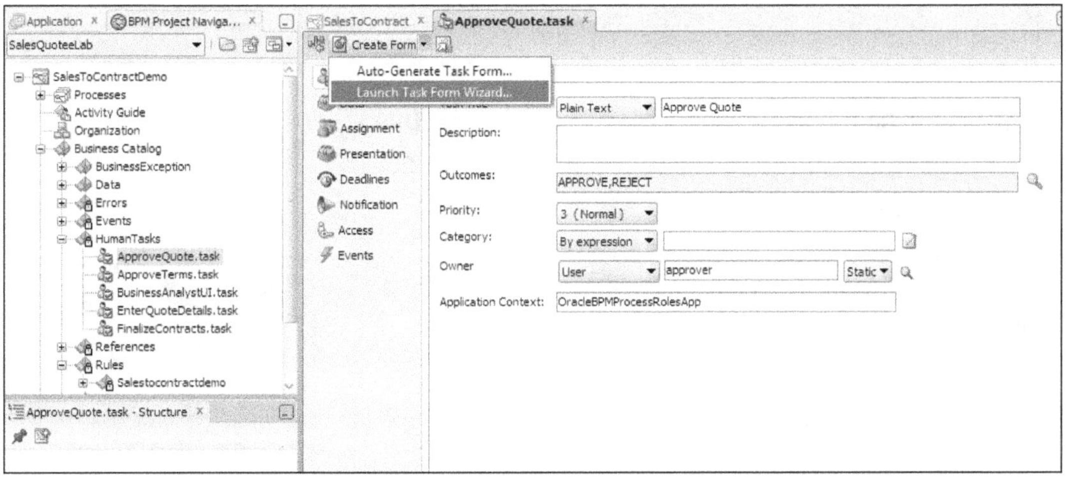

6. Enter the name of the project. Let's keep the older **ApproveQuoteUI** project as it is and create a new project named **ApproveQuoteDetailsUI**.
7. Click **OK.** This will open the wizard.
8. In the **Name** dialog, enter `ApproveQuoteDetailsUI` as the form name and click **Next**.

9. In the **Header Page** section, let the number of columns be **2**, and select all the available header contents in the same order.

   You can select the desired one and can even change the order from here.

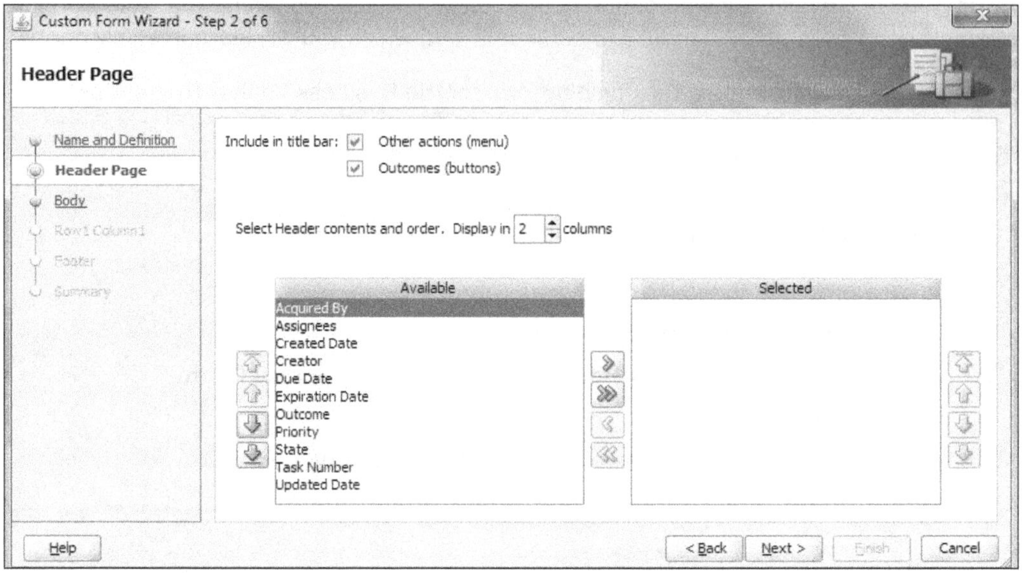

10. In the **Body** page, enter `Quote Lines` as **Panel title**.
11. Select number of columns as **3** and add rows as **2**.
12. Click **Next**.

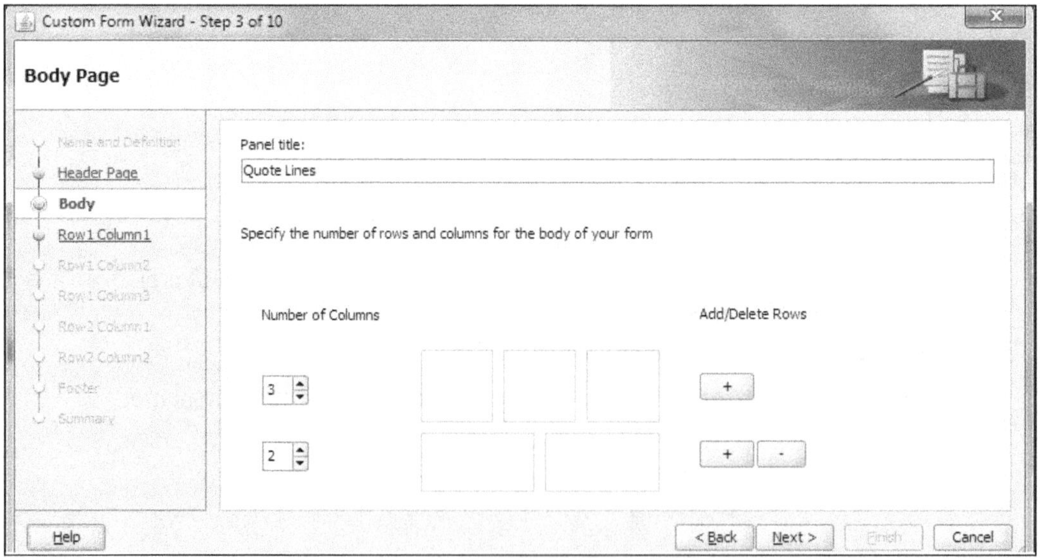

13. For the **Row 1 Column 1** dialog, select **QuoteRequestStatus** and **Summary** from the payload.

    You will find that a position indicator also is displayed at the top.

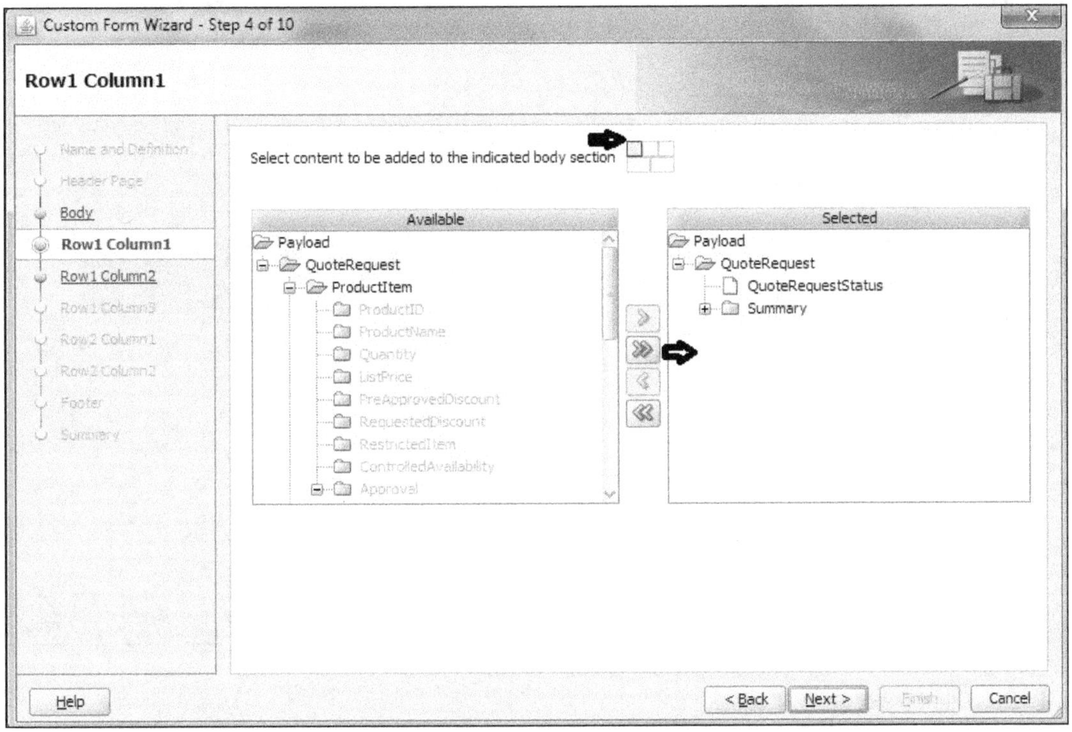

14. Click **Next.**
15. For **Row 1 Column 2**, you can select **Address** from **Payload | Summary** and click **Next.**
16. For **Row 1 Column 3**, you can select **Contact** from **Payload | Summary** and click **Next.**
17. For **Row 2 Column 1**, select **Product Items** and click **Next.**
18. For **Row 2 Column 2**, select **License Terms** and click **Next.**

19. Enter `Quote Attachments` as the title for **Footer** and select all the available fields.

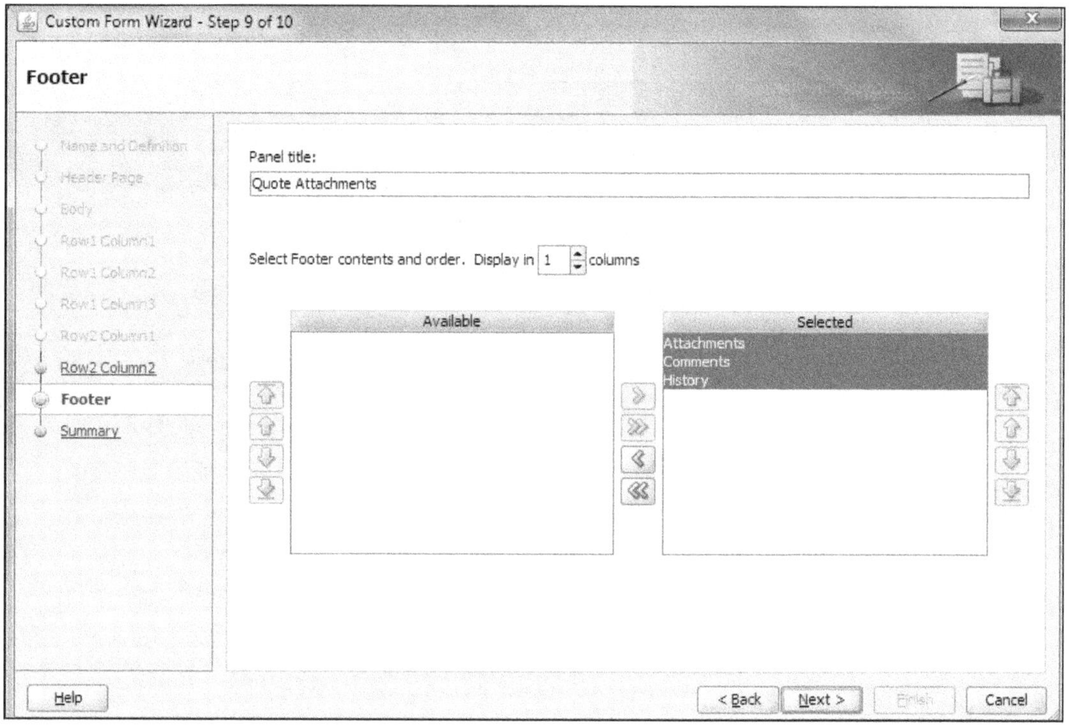

20. Click **Next**.
21. The last page summarizes your selection. Click **Finish**, if you are happy with the content.
22. Click **OK** on the **Edit Table Column** dialog.

How it works...

You will find that a new project called **ApproveQuoteDetailsUI** is created. You can verify the Task Form from `/public_html/ApproveQuoteDetailsUI.jspx`.

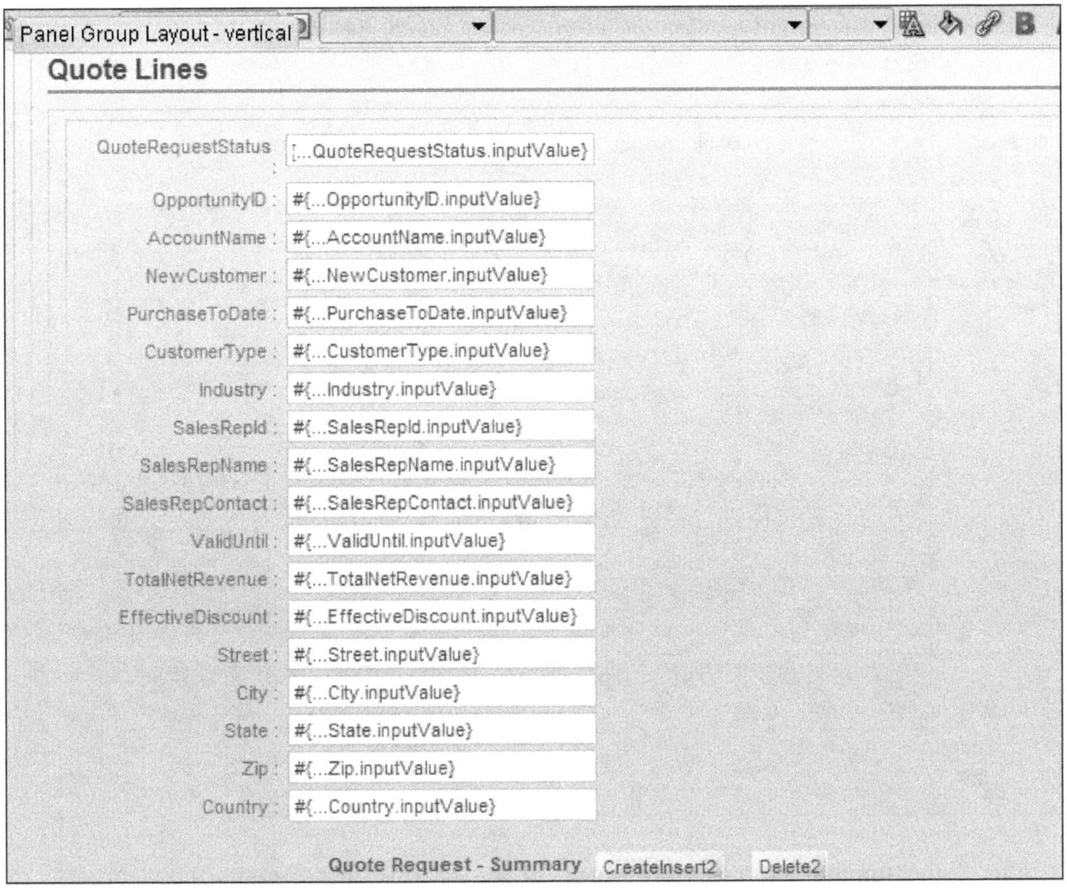

You can now deploy and test the Project.

There's more...

You have just created an **ApproveQuoteDetailsUI** project, using wizards. You can deploy this UI project as a single EAR file. As you already have a ApproveQuoteDetailsUI project EAR file in the same root, you must undo deployment for that, first.

Deploying an individual project

Let us explore how to deploy an ADF UI project:

1. Create a **Deployment Profile** by clicking on **Menu | Application | Application properties**.
2. Select **Deployments** and enter a Deployment Profile **Name**, say `ApproveQuoteDetailsUI`.

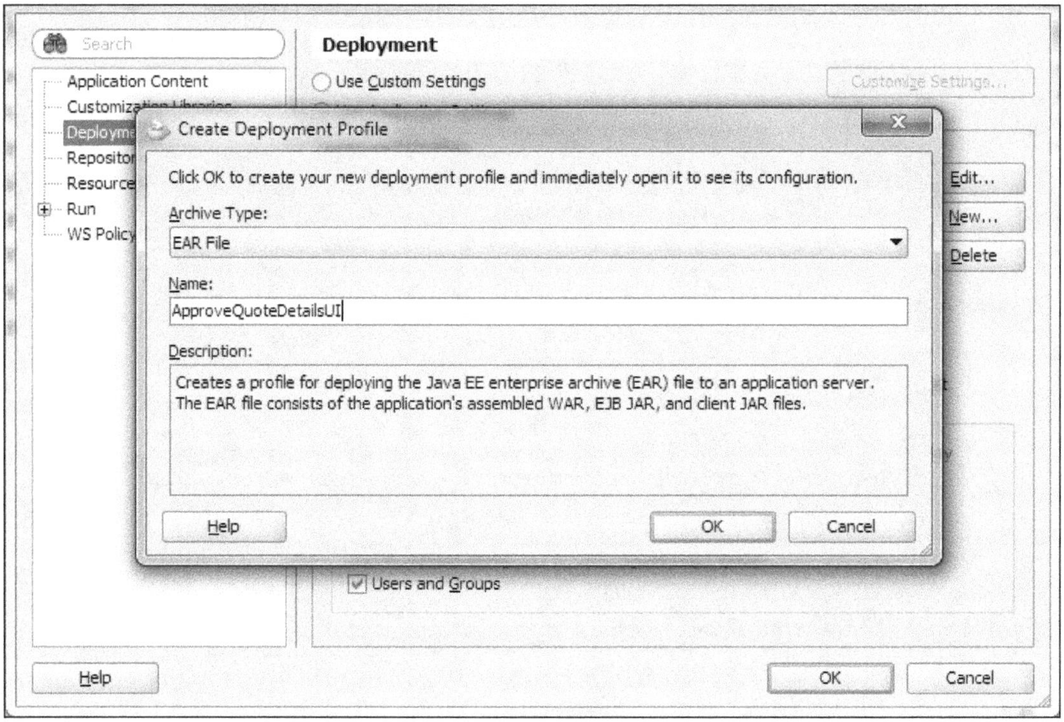

3. Select **Application Assembly** and check the **ApproveQuoteDetailsUI** project, as shown in the preceding screenshot, and click **OK**.
4. Now you can deploy it from **Menu | Application | Deploy** and select the **Deployment Profile**.

8
Exception Management

This chapter will help you learn how to handle system exceptions and business exceptions in Oracle BPM 11g. Exceptions can occur in tasks or in the subprocess. You will explore how exceptions are thrown and how exceptions are caught, for a task and for a subprocess. In addition, you will infuse exception handling for task and subprocesses using either the `boundary catch` event or an event subprocess.

We will cover the following topics to gain expertise in exception management:

- Handling business exceptions in a task
- Handling business exceptions in a subprocess
- Handling a system exception-Fault Management Framework
- Handling the timeout exception-Timer event
- Faulting the process

Introduction

Errors can happen in a process. They might be caused either due to system failure or maybe a business issue. When an error occurs due to system failure, software failure, hardware failure, and so on—broadly speaking due to infrastructure failure, they are termed as system errors. Infrastructure issues such as 'database not available', 'server not up and running', and so on, cause system errors.

Any errors due to problems in process behavior (say that a process was designed in such a way that if inventory doesn't have the stock availability, then the quotation cannot be processed normally and this would lead to a process exception) are called **business exceptions**, as they are caused due to interference of problems in your regular process flow.

System exceptions are used to handle system errors and business exceptions are used to handle process errors.

In this chapter, you will explore the following scenarios:

- Stock unavailability leads to a business exception that is handled by a subprocess. You will use the `catch error boundary` event to handle this business exception.
- You will invoke a service in which unavailability will lead to a system exception. You will use the following mechanism to handle the following system exceptions:
  - You will use fault-policy framework to handle system exceptions
  - You will use the subprocess `Error handled by Event Sub process Boundary` event
  - The `Catch Timer` event will handle timeout exceptions
- Handling business exceptions in a task

You have a service, `StockValidator_EBS`, a BPEL web service that checks for the availability of stock (items) based on **PRODUCTID**. And as a response, if the item is not available in the inventory, it shows a Business Error **SOPFault**.

You can create a **StockValidator_EBS** BPEL web service, based on a PLSQL procedure, which checks for item availability in the **MTL_SYSTEM_ITEMS** table and returns `SOPFault` if the item is not available.

You will implement a service task in your BPM process to invoke this **StockValidator_EBS** service.

If Stock is available: Then the process token follows the normal path
Else, if Stock is not available: Then the service task throws an error

You will use the **Boundary Catch Event** to handle the exception, in this case. Boundary error catch events enable you to resume the main process flow after handling the exception.

How to do it...

In this section, you will learn to handle business exceptions, as follows:

1. Go to **JDeveloper | Application Navigator | SalesToContractDemo Project** and click on the **SalesToContract** process.
2. Go to **Component palette | BPM | Activities** and click the activity `SubProcess`.
3. Click anywhere in the **salesrepresentative** swimlane to create a subprocess in it.
4. This will open the **Subprocess | Properties** dialog. Enter the name `Stockvalidation_ExceptionHandler` for the subprocess and click **OK**.

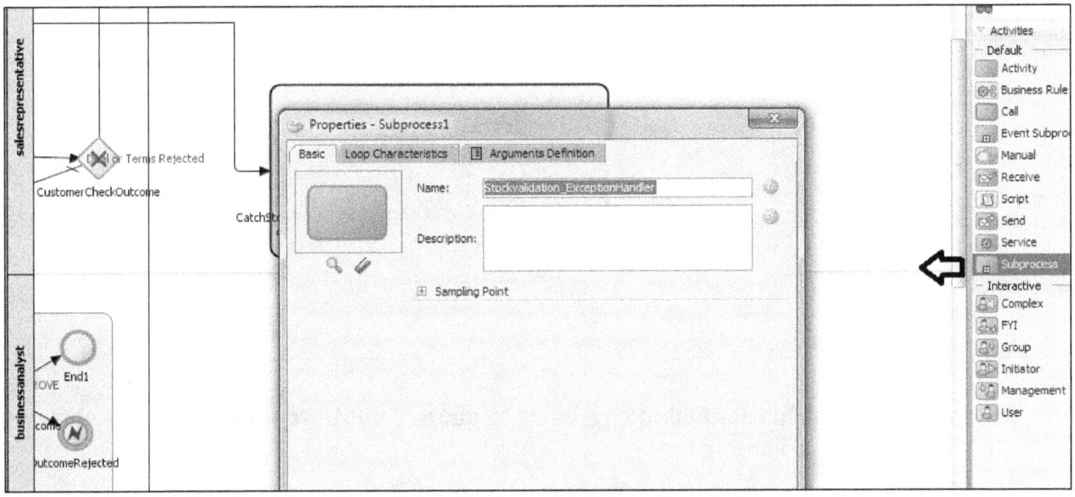

5. For the **Start** and **End** activities in the subprocess, click on them and enter `StartStockvalidationException` and `EndStockvalidationException` as **Name** for the **Start** and **End** activities, respectively. Keep their **Implementation type** as **None**.
6. Go to **Component Palette | BPM | Activities** and click on the **Script** activity.
7. Click on the subprocess between the **Start** and **End** activities. This will create a **Script Task** in the subprocess.

8. In the **Script** task properties, enter `AssignStockStatus` as the name, and in the **Implementation** tab, check **Data Associations** and drop **quote** as variable.

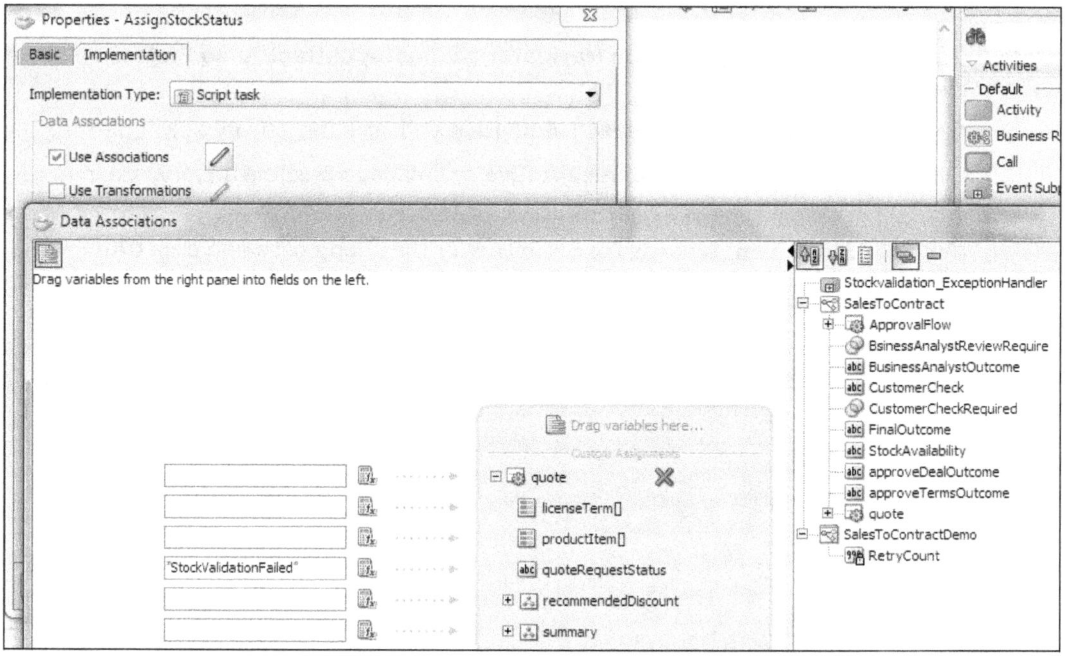

9. Assign **StockvalidationFailed** as a value to **quote | quoteRequestStatus**, as shown in the preceding screenshot.
10. Click **OK** twice to return to **SubProcess**.
11. Click on **Component Palette | BPM | Interactive user task**.
12. Click between **AssignStockStatus** script and **EndStockValidationException**.
13. This will open User task properties. In the **Basic** tab, enter **Name** of the User task as **StockValidation**.
14. In the **Implementation** tab, create a Human Task `StockValidationNotification` and assign the object **quote** as input, as shown in the following screenshot:

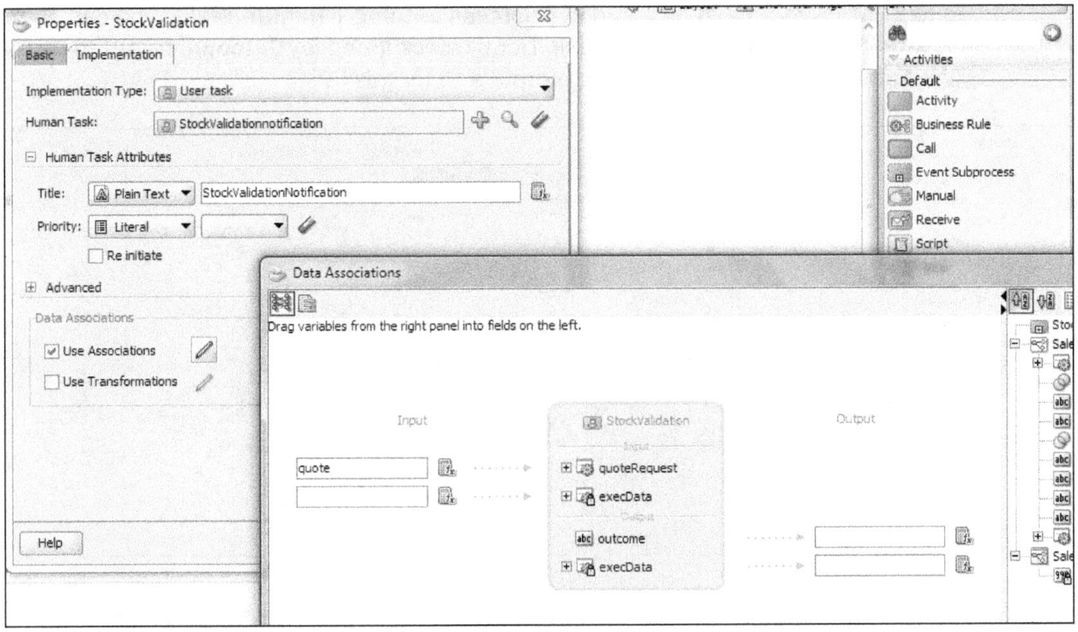

15. Click **OK** twice and you are back to the subprocess.

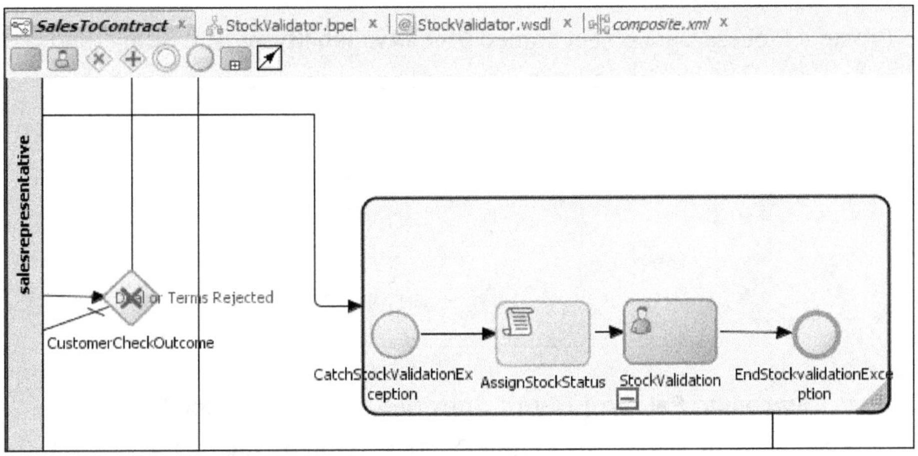

16. Go to **BPM Project navigator** and in **Business catalog | Human Tasks**, you can find the **StockValidationNotification** task. Double-click it and let **Outcome** be set to **OK**; click **Auto-Generate task form** to generate a UI for this task.

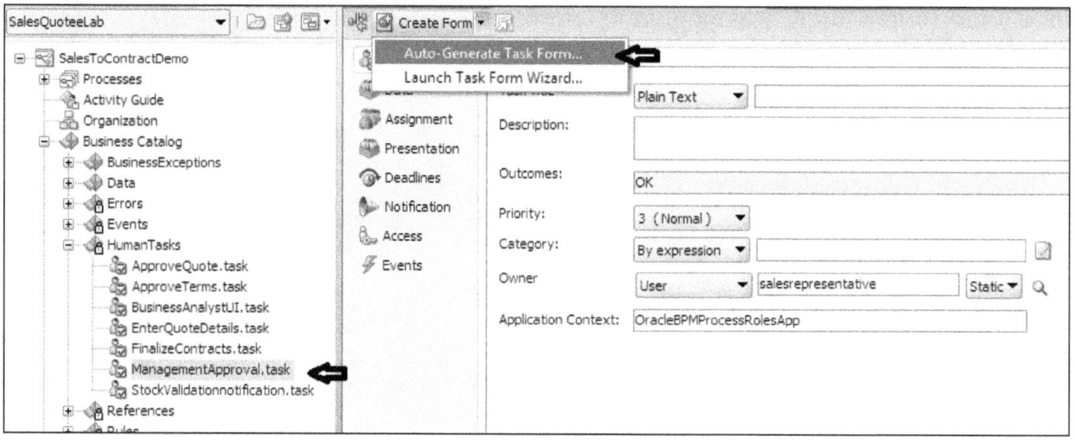

17. In the **Create Project** dialog, enter `StockvalidatorUI` as the **Project Name** and click **OK**.
18. Once the UI is created, you can validate it from **Application Navigator | SalesToContractDemo** project.
19. Create a Process Data object named **StockAvailability**, of type **String**, and click **OK**.

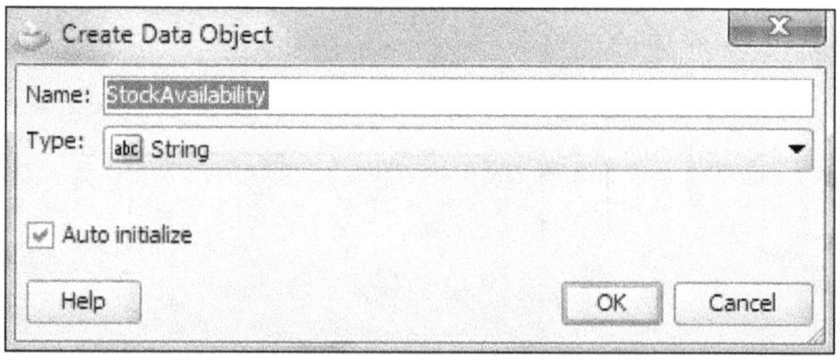

20. Go to **Component Palette | BPM | Activities** and click **Service Task**.
21. Click on the designer, between **Enter Quote** and **Check Customer**. This will open the service task **Properties**.

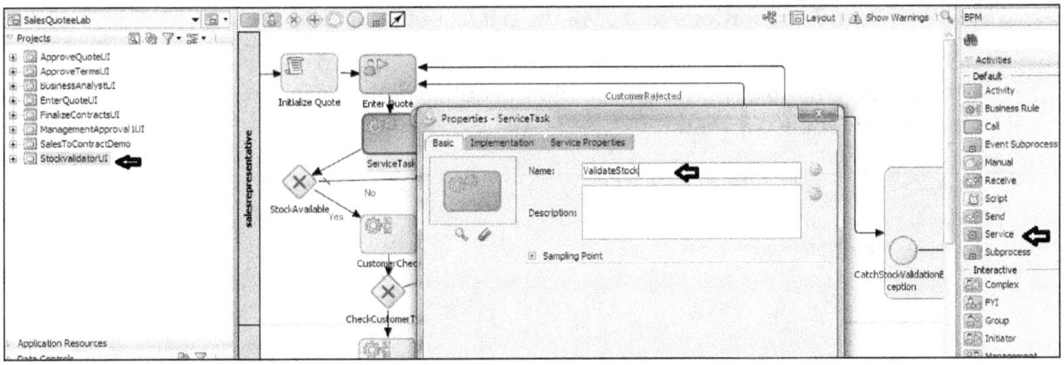

22. Enter `ValidateStock` for the service task **Name**, and click on the **Implementation** tab.
23. In **Service Task**, on the **Implementation** tab, choose **Service Call**
24. Click on the "browse" button to the right of **Name** to select the service **Stockvalidator_EBS** and click **OK** on the **Type** dialog. The operation **process** will pop-up automatically.

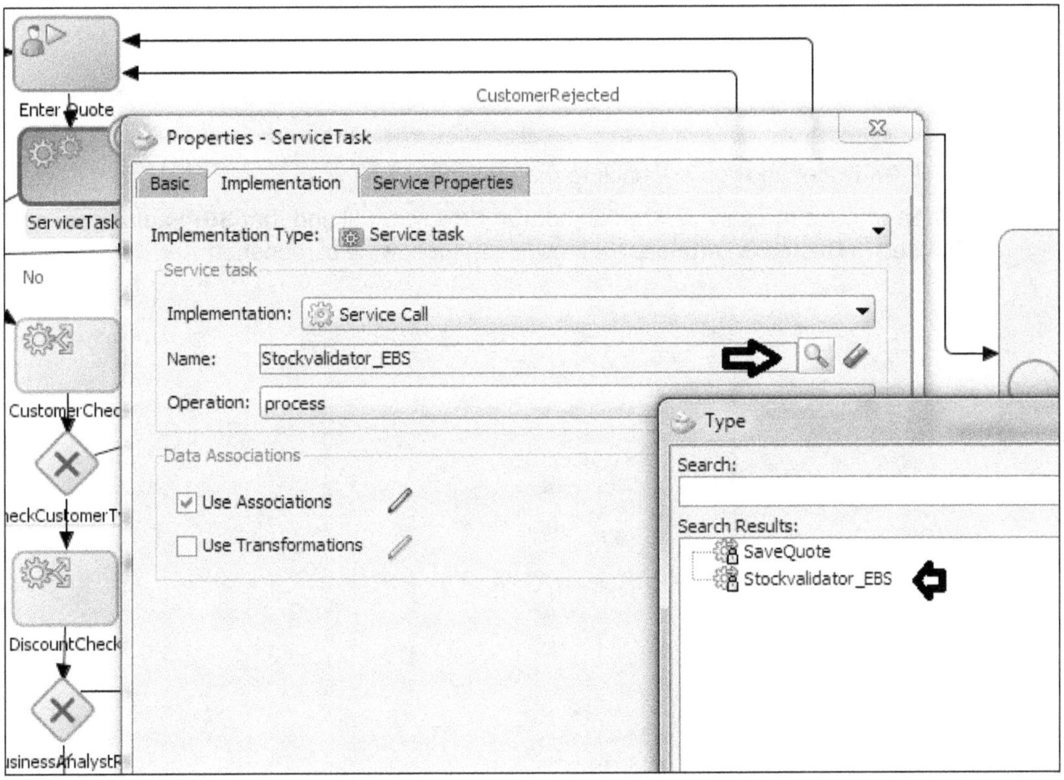

25. Check **Data Associations** and click the pencil button to edit.
26. Drag-and-drop **quote** from the Data objects as an input to service task, and the **StockAvailability** Data object into the output, which gets populated by **processResponse | result**.

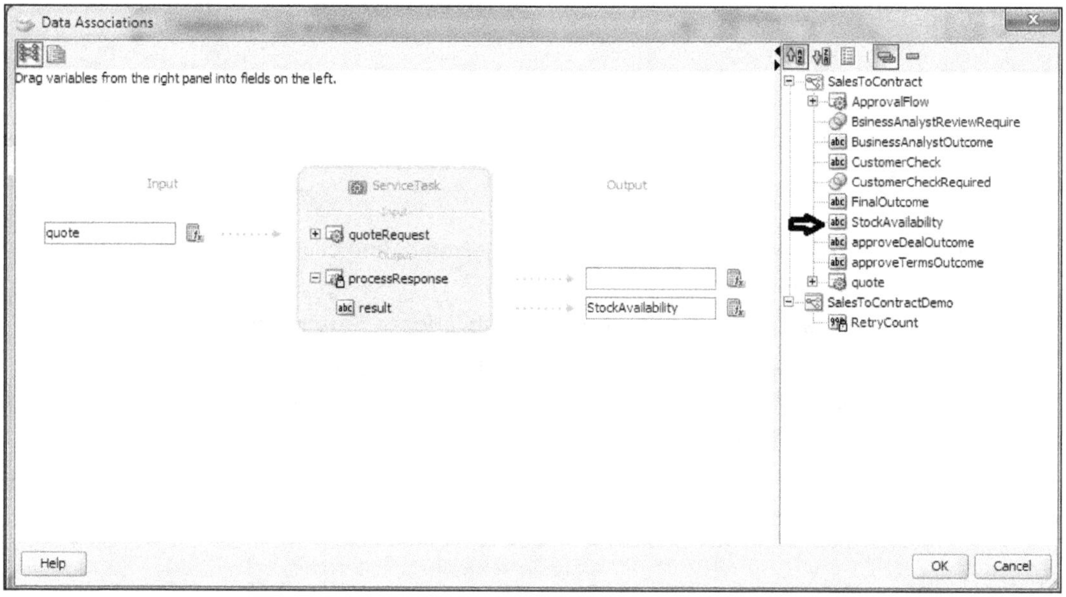

27. Click **OK** twice, and you are back to the designer.
28. When you use the service **Stockvalidator_EBS**, you will find that **SOPFault** errors get infused in **Business Catalog**, as shown in the following screenshot:

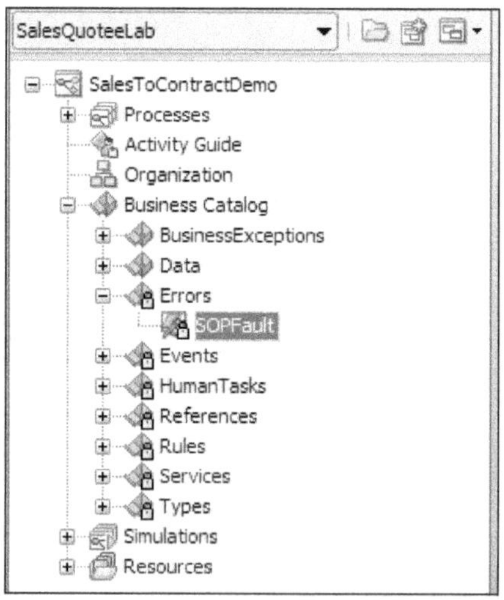

29. Go to **Component Palette | BPM | Gateways** and click **Exclusive Gateway**.
30. Click between the **ValidateStock** service task and **Customer Check** rule. This will open the **Properties** dialog. Enter `StockAvailable` as the gateway name.
31. Create a sequence unconditional flow from **ValidateStock** to **StockAvailable**.

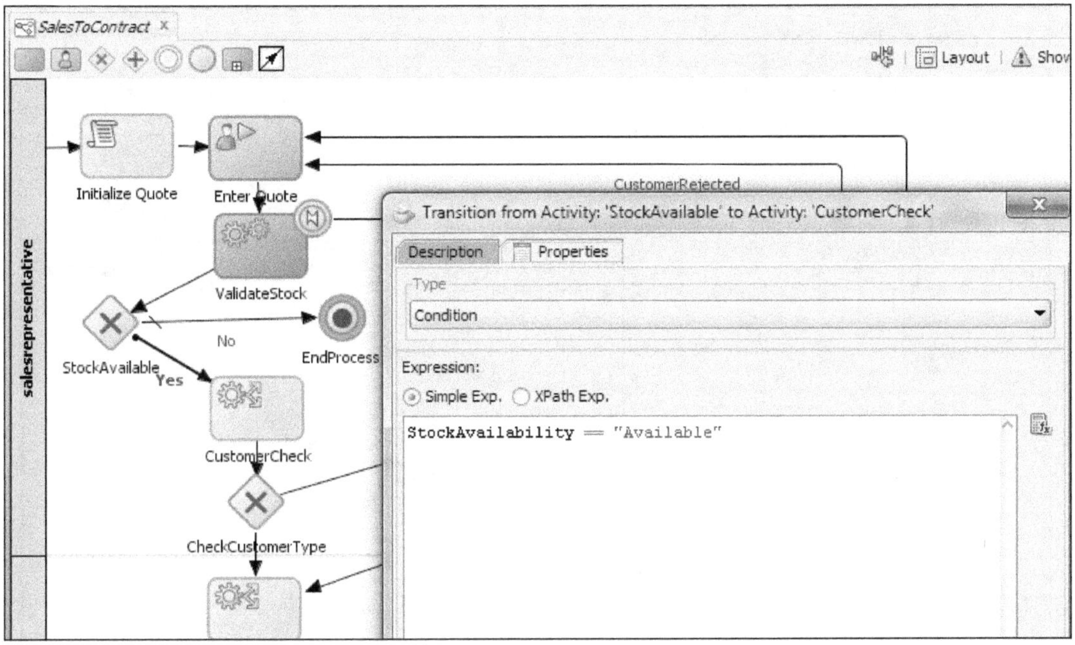

32. Go to **Component Palette | BPM | Events**, click **Terminate End Event**, and name it `EndProcess`.
33. Click to the right of the **StockAvailable** gateway and create an unconditional flow from **StockAvailable** to the **EndProcess** End event.
34. Create an unconditional flow from the **StockAvailable** gateway to **CustomerCheck** rule task and name it `Yes`.
35. Create a conditional flow from the **StockAvailable** gateway to the **EndProcess** activity. Choose **Simple Expression** and enter the expression, as follows, and then click **OK**:

```
StockAvailability == "UnAvailable"
```

36. Go to **Component Palette | BPM | Events**, click on the **Error Catch** event, and drag it on to the **ValidateStock** service task. This will open the **Properties** dialog.

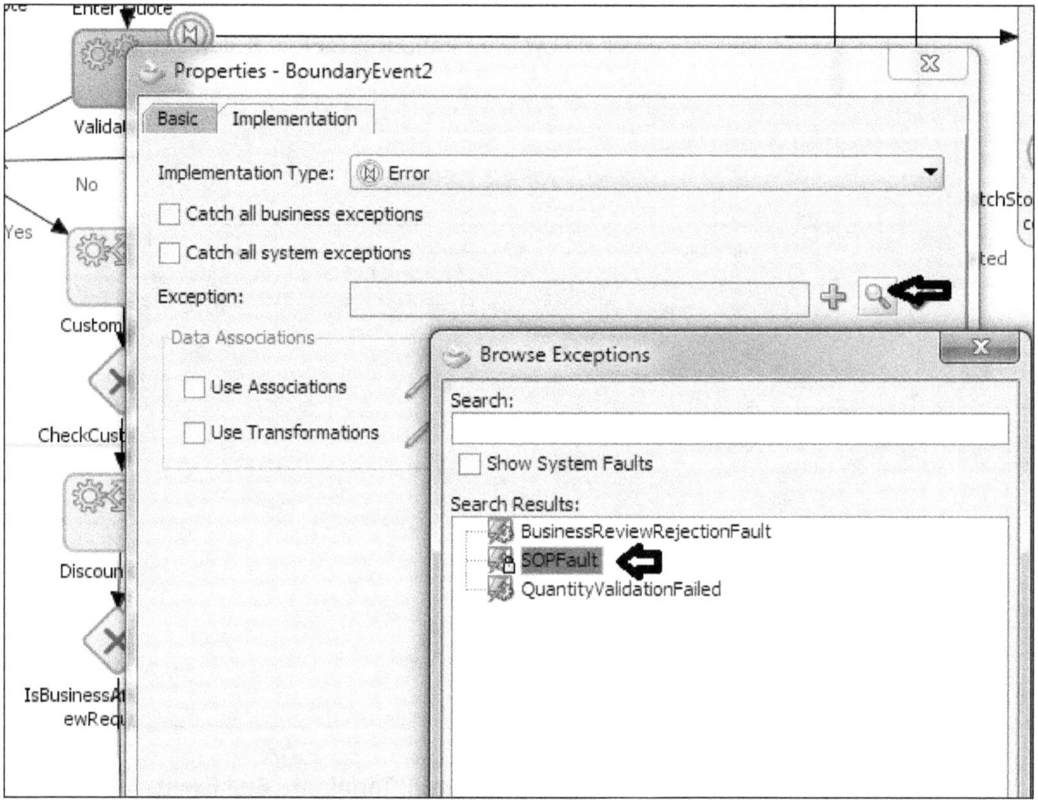

37. Let the implementation type be **Error** and click the "browse" button to the right of **Exception**, to browse for the errors. Select **SOPFault** from the list, as shown in the preceding screenshot, and then click **OK**.

38. Add **Default sequence** from **ValidateStock** to the **Stockvalidation_ExceptionHandler** option.

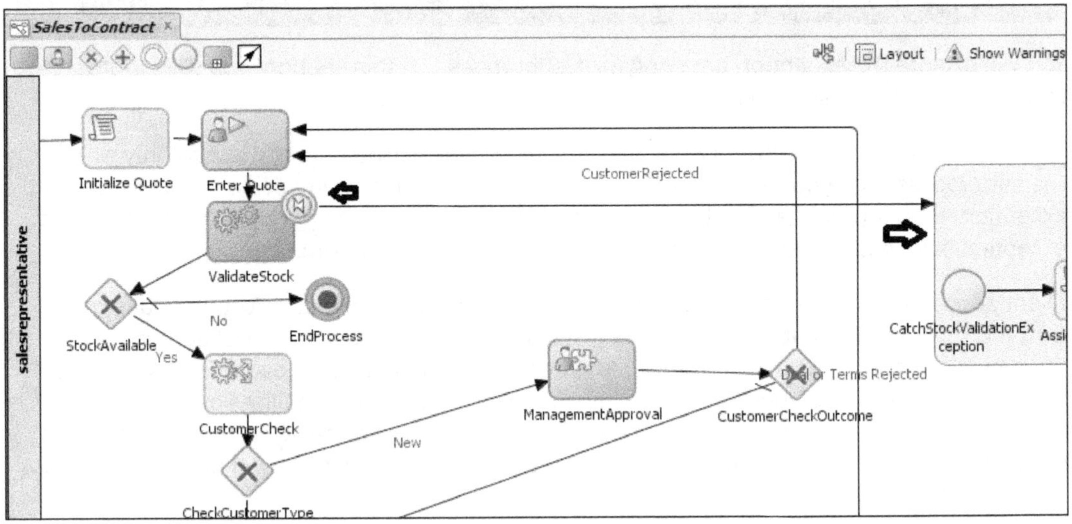

39. When you have finished the preceding steps, click **Save**.

How it works...

BPMN service engine runs the task **ValidateStock**, which calls **StockValidator_EBS**. **StockValidator_EBS** will raise an error if the stock is not available. The task fails with a SOAP error, which will be converted by BPMN service engine into an exception.

When an error occurs while running the task **ValidateStock**, which has a boundary error catch event attached, BPMN Service Engine will follow the flow defined by the boundary error catch event. The exception handling flow, defined by the boundary error catch event, can rejoin the main process flow if stock is available, or end the process.

Handling Business Exception in a subprocess

You will explore the exception handling for a subprocess, in this section. You will create a subprocess and that subprocess will end with an Error event.

When the process ends with an Error event, it's handled by the parent process only when the subprocess has a boundary catch event attached to it. If the process cannot handle the exception, then it propagates it to its parent process. If there is no parent process, then the exception is logged to the Enterprise Manager fault recovery system.

Event subprocesses enable you to define a cleaner process with less effort, because the **Catch** Error event is located within the event subprocess. To reuse an exception handling flow using boundary catch events, you must define a boundary catch event for each of the tasks and then connect those boundary events to the exception handling flow. If the exception handled in the event subprocess occurs while running any of the tasks in the process, then the BPMN Service Engine continues running the exception handling flow defined in the event subprocess.

How to do it...

You will first create a **Sub Process**, and then use an **Error End Event** to **Throw** a business error, and finally, you will create **Event Sub Process** to catch the business exception.

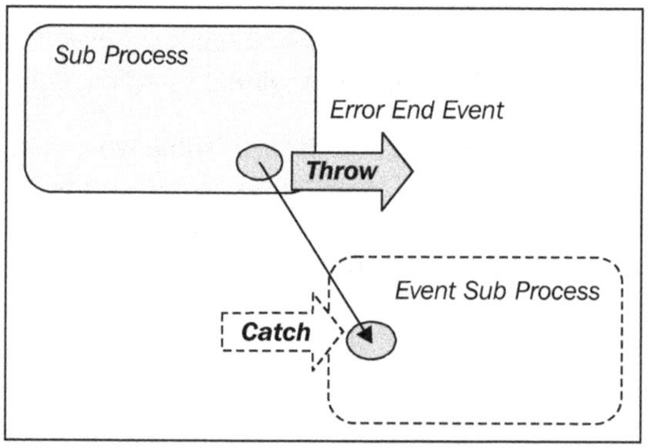

You have a **Business Analyst** User task to perform business reviews. Let's recreate the same task in a subprocess, and if the Business Analyst task has the outcome REJECT, then the subprocess throws an error. This error would be caught in **Event Sub Process**.

I. Create Business Exception

1. Go to **BPM Project Navigator | SalesToContractDemo Project | Business Catalog** and right-click **Business Catalog**.
2. Click **New | Business Exception**.

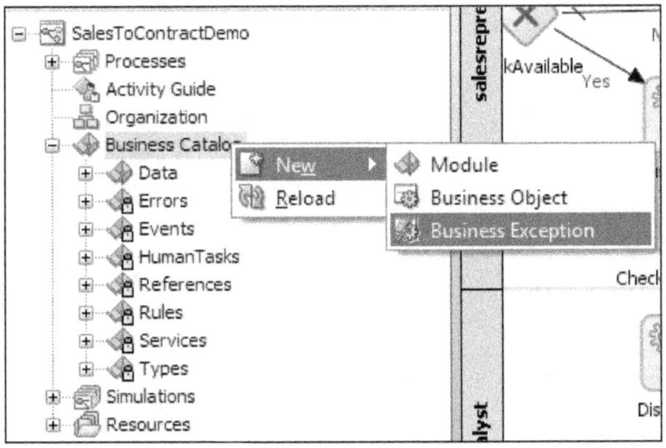

3. In the **Create Business Exception** dialog, click on the **Browse Modules** button.
4. Click on the "create module" (**+**) icon to create a module.
5. Enter `BusinessException` as the name for a new module.

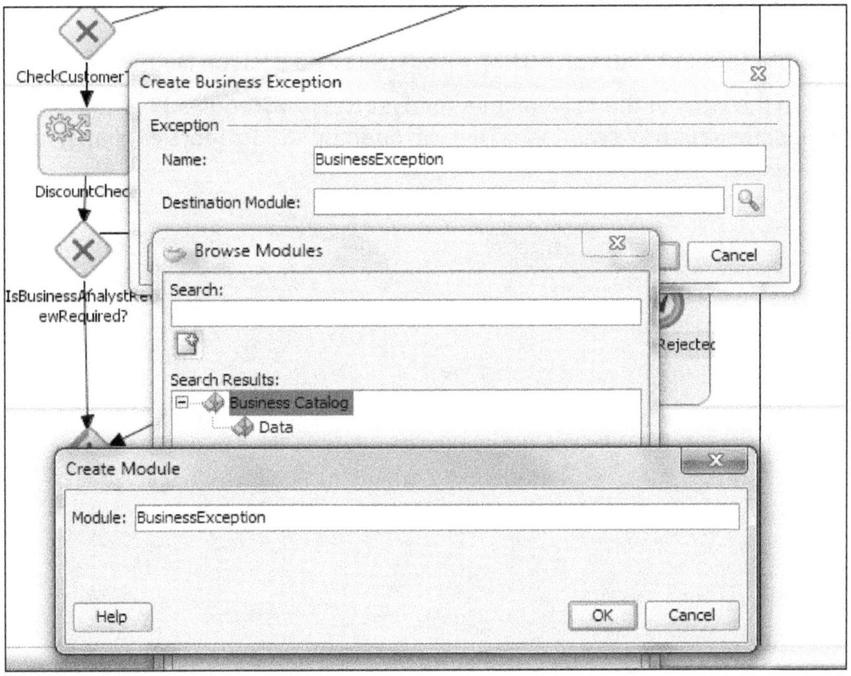

6. Click **OK** twice to go back to the **Create Business Exception** dialog.
7. Enter `BusinessReviewRejectionFault` as the name for the **Exception** and click **OK**.

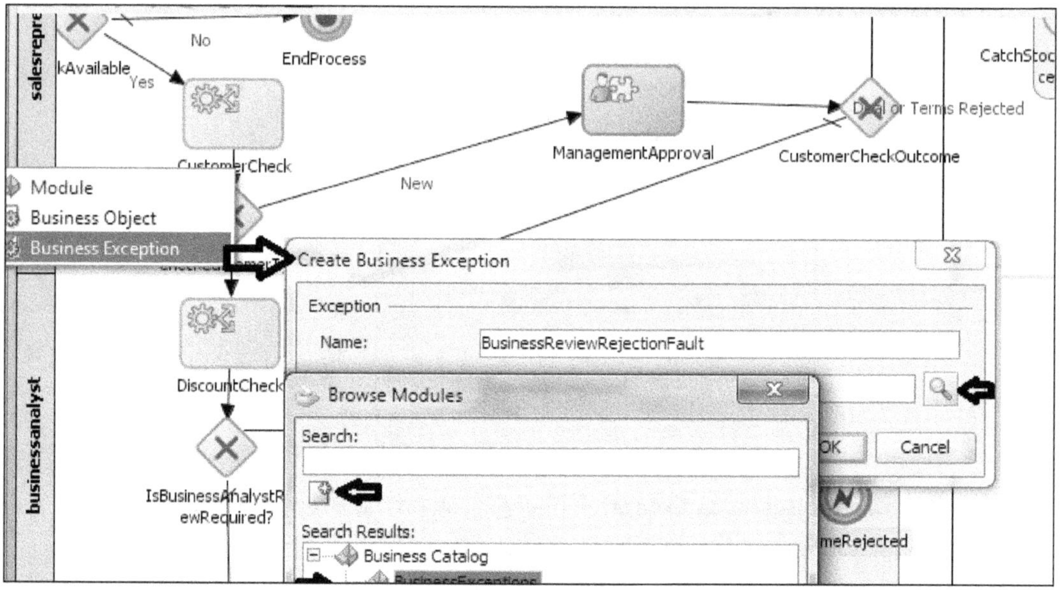

II. Create Subprocess

1. Go to **Component Palette | BPM | Activities** and click on **Subprocess**.
2. Click to the right of the **Is Business Analyst Review Required?** gateway, in the **businessanalyst** swimlane. This will open up the **Properties** dialog for the subprocess.

3. Enter name of the subprocess as `BusinessAnalystReviewSubprocess`, in the **Basic** tab.

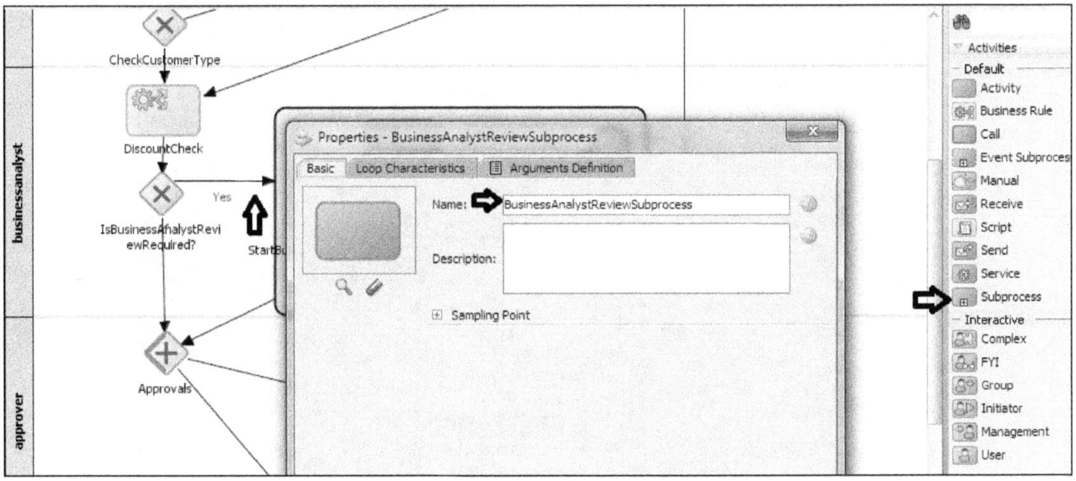

4. Name the **Start** and **End** activities in the subprocess `StartBusinessAnalystReview` and `EndBusinessAnalystReview`, respectively.
5. Click on **User task** in **Component Palette | BPM | Interactive Activities**.
6. Click between the **Start** and **End** activities in the subprocess.
7. In the **Properties** dialog, enter `BusinessAnalystReview` as the name for the task.
8. In the **Implementation** tab of the **Properties** dialog, browse **Human Task**, select the **BusinessAnalystUI** task and click **OK**.

9. Enter the title **BusinessAnalystReview**, as shown in the following screenshot:

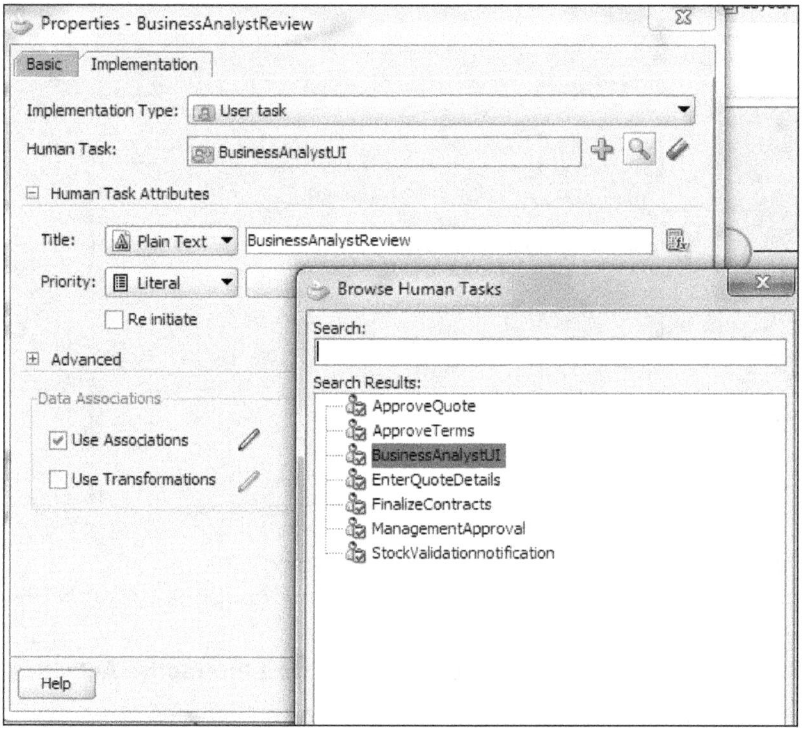

10. Place a checkmark next to the options for **Data Associations**, drag **quote** into the **Input** and **Output** sections, and drag the **BusinessAnalystOutcome** Data object into the **Output** section of the task outcome.

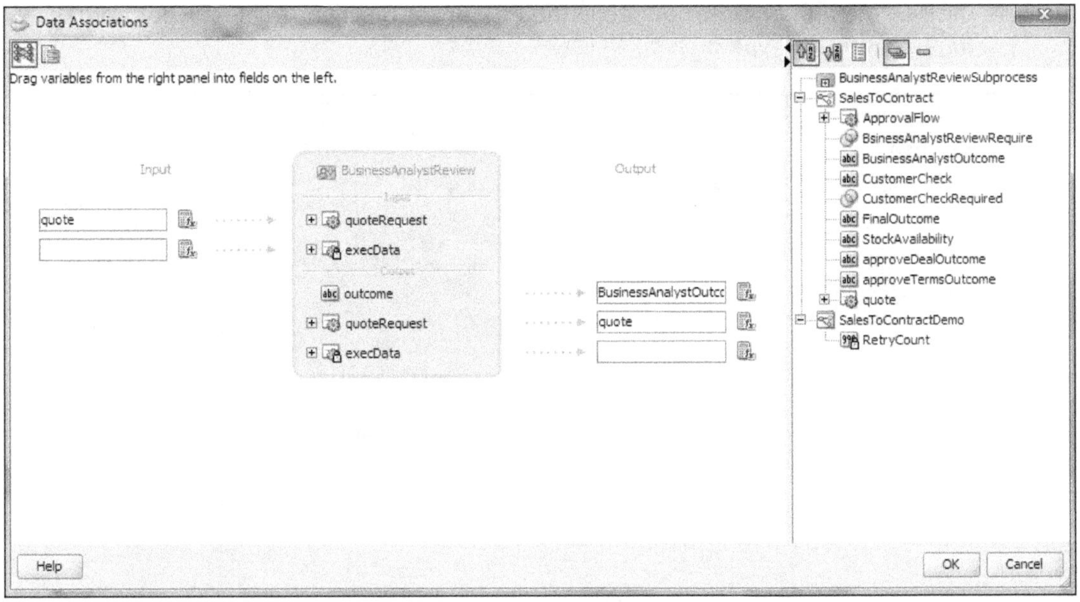

11. Click **OK** twice, to reach the subprocess.
12. Go to **Component Palette | BPM | Gateways** and click on **Exclusive Gateway**.
13. Click to the right of the **BusinessAnalystReview** User task and enter the name **BusinessAnalystOutcome** in the **Basic** tab of the **Properties** dialog of the gateway.
14. Go to **Component Palette | BPM | Events** and click **Error End Event**.
15. Click to the right of the **BusinessAnalystOutcome** gateway and this will open the **Properties** dialog for **Error End Event**.
16. Enter `OutcomeRejected` as the name for **Error End Event**, in the **Basic** tab.

17. Click on the **Implementation** tab in the **Properties** dialog and select **Error** from the **Implementation Type** drop-down list.

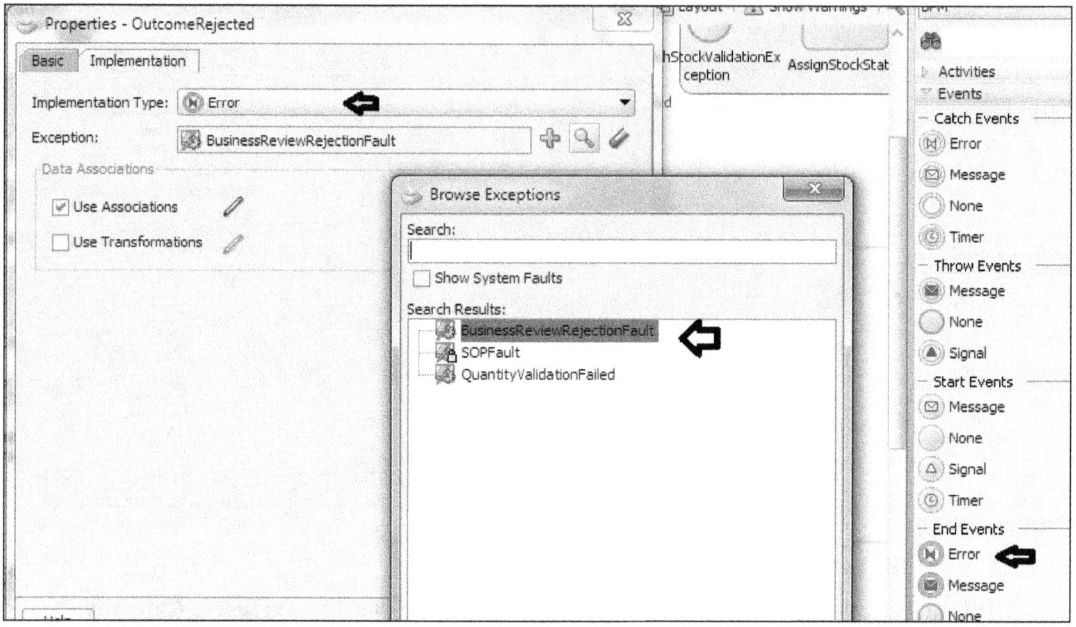

18. Click the "browse" button to browse for **Exceptions** and select the **BusinessReviewRejectFault** exception, which you have created in this section. Click **OK** twice.

III. Create sequence flows

1. Create an unconditional sequence flow from the **StartBusinessAnalystReview** activity to the **BusinessAnalystReview** task, and then to the **BusinessAnalystOutcome** gateway.
2. Create a conditional flow from the **BusinessAnalystOutcome** gateway to the **EndBusinessAnalystReview** activity.
3. In the **Properties** dialog for the conditional sequence flow in the **Description** tab, enter **APPROVE** as the name, and in the **Properties** tab, select **Condition** as the **Type**. Enter a simple expression(**Simple Exp**) based on the **BusinessAnalystReview** outcome Data object, as follows:

```
BusinessAnalystOutcome == "APPROVE".
```

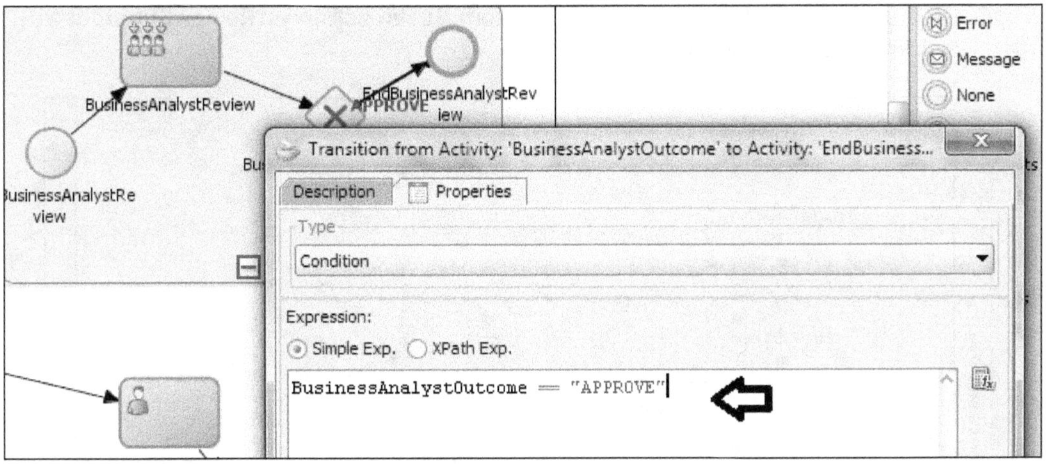

4. Click **OK**.
5. Create a unconditional sequence flow from the **BusinessAnalystOutcome** gateway to the Error End Event, **Outcome Rejected** and click **OK**.
6. The subprocess will look like the following screenshot:

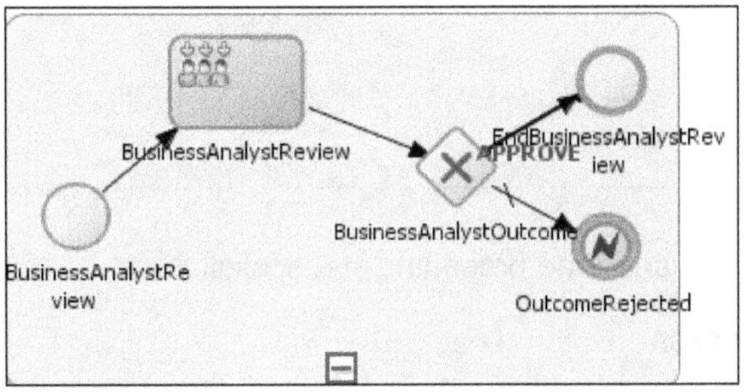

7. Create a conditional sequence flow from the gateway **Is Business Analyst Review Required?** to the subprocess **BusinessAnalystReviewSubprocess**.
8. Name this flow as **Yes** and enter a simple expression condition, as follows:

```
ApprovalFlow.businessPracticesReviewNeeded == true
```

9. Remember, you did the same when the **BusinessAnalystReview** task was a simple task. You are now doing it for the subprocess.

10. Create an unconditional sequence flow from **BusinessAnalystReviewSubprocess | SubProcess** to the **Approvals** gateway.

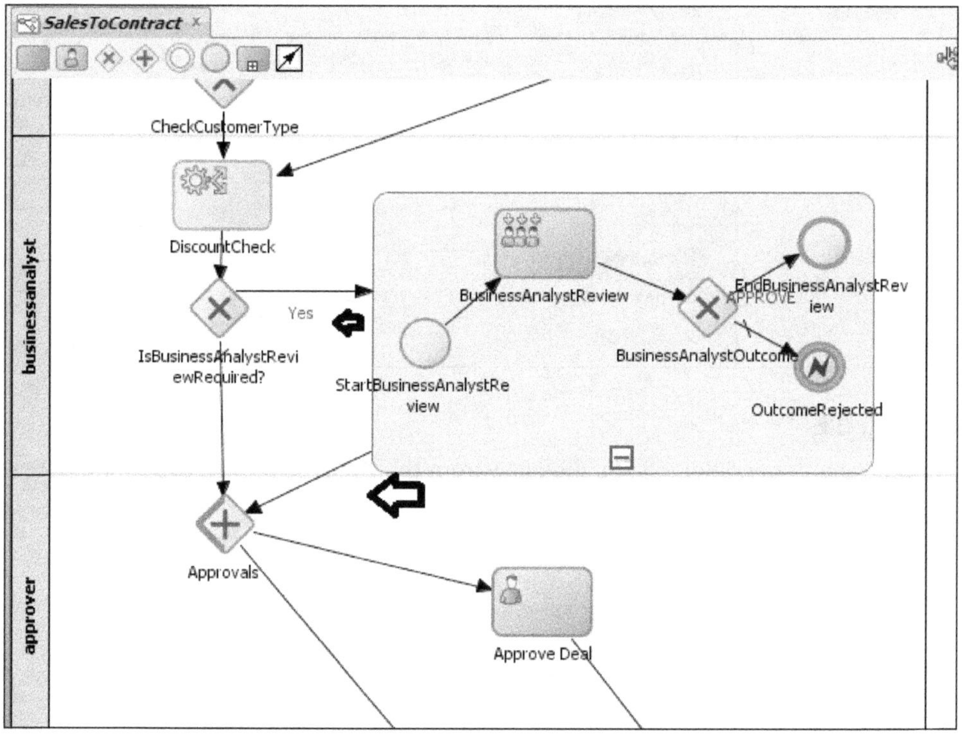

11. When you have finished the preceding steps, click Save.

IV. Create an Event Process

1. In the designer, right-click just below the **contracts** swimlane to create a new swimlane.
2. Select **Add Role** and in **Role Properties** and click the **New** button. Enter `Admin` as the role name and click **OK** twice.

3. You can find an **Admin** swimlane created just below the **contracts** swimlane.

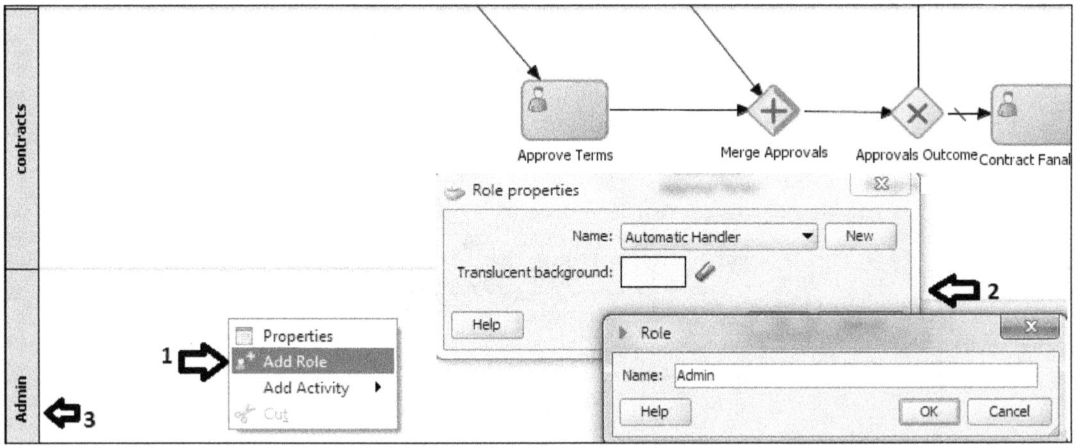

4. Go to **Component Palette | BPM | Activities** and click on **Event Subprocess**.
5. Now click anywhere in the **Admin** swimlane. This will create an Event subprocess.
6. Right-click the start of the **Event Sub Process** and select **Properties**.
7. In the **Basic** tab, enter the **Start Event** name as **CatchBusinessFault**, and in the **Implementation** tab, select **Error** from the **Implementation Type** drop-down menu.

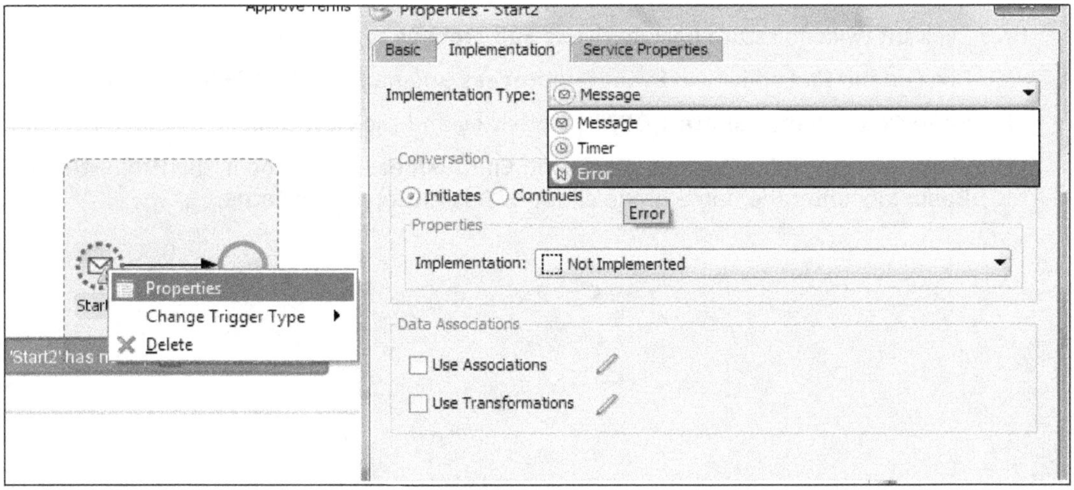

8. Click the "browse" button, as shown in the following screenshot, to browse for **Exceptions** and select **BusinessReviewRejectionFault**.

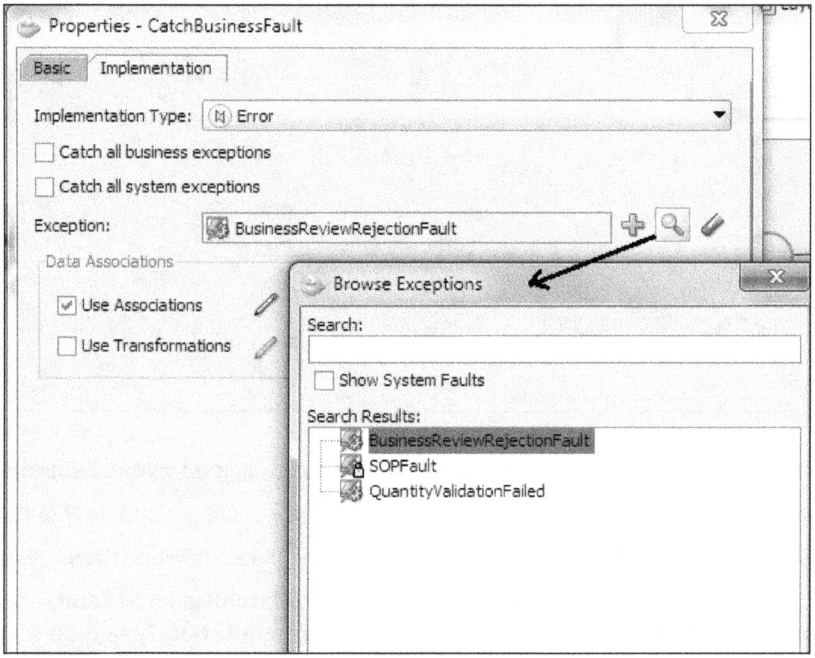

9. Click **OK** twice to return back to **Event Sub process**.
10. Click on the **End** activity in **Event Subprocess** and name it **EndBusinessFault**.
11. Go to **Component Palette | BPM | Activities** and click **Scripts**.
12. Click between **CatchBusinessFault** and **EndBusinessFault**, and in the **Properties | Basic** tab, enter the name of the script as **AssignRejectionStatus**.

13. Click **Data Association**, and in the **Edit** panel, drag the Data object **quote** and assign **Rejected** to **quoteRequestStatus**.

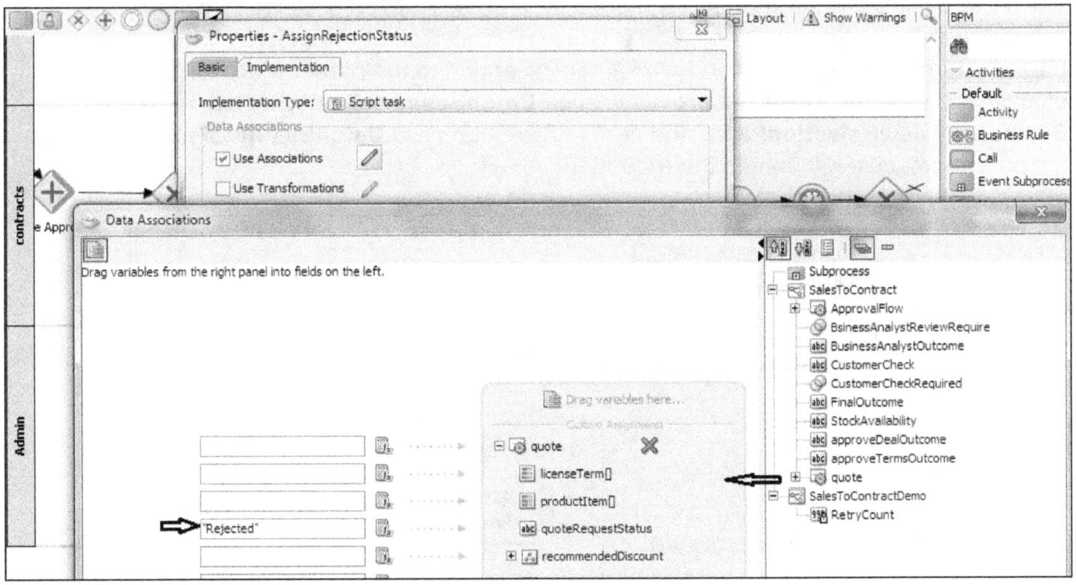

14. Click **OK** twice, to get back to **Event Subprocess**.
15. Create a sequence flow from **CatchBusinessFault | AssignRejectionStatus | EndBusinessFault**.
16. When you have finished, click **Save**.

How it works...

When the Business Analyst rejects the quote, the process token reaches **Error End Event**. It will then throw the exception **BusinessReviewRejectionFault**. BPMN Service Engine interrupts the process and throws the exception to the parent process. The parent process will have the **Event Subprocess** called **CatchBusinessFault** defined. It can catch **BusinessReviewRejectionFault**, and hence the subprocess **CatchBusinessFault**, defined in the parent process, will handle the exception.

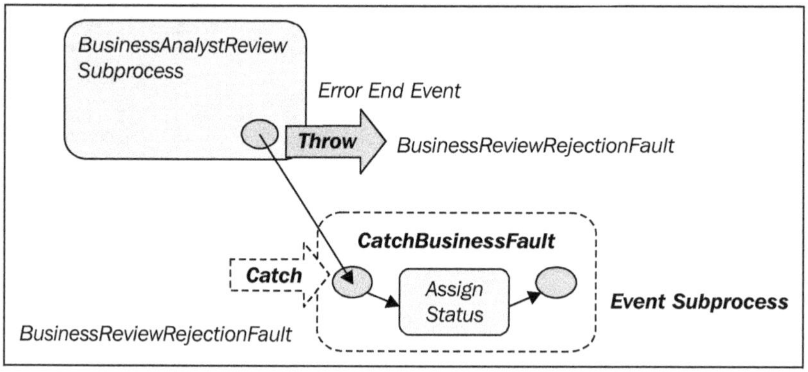

There's more...

You have used the **Event Subprocess** activity to catch a specific error—**BusinessReviewRejectionFault**. However, you can even implement this event subprocess to handle all system or business exceptions.

Implementing Catch All

1. Go to **Implementation** properties at the beginning of Event subprocess.
2. Select **Error** as the **Implementation Type**.

3. Tick **Catch all business exceptions**; or tick **Catch all system exceptions**, if you want to handle all business or system exceptions, rather than a specific exception.

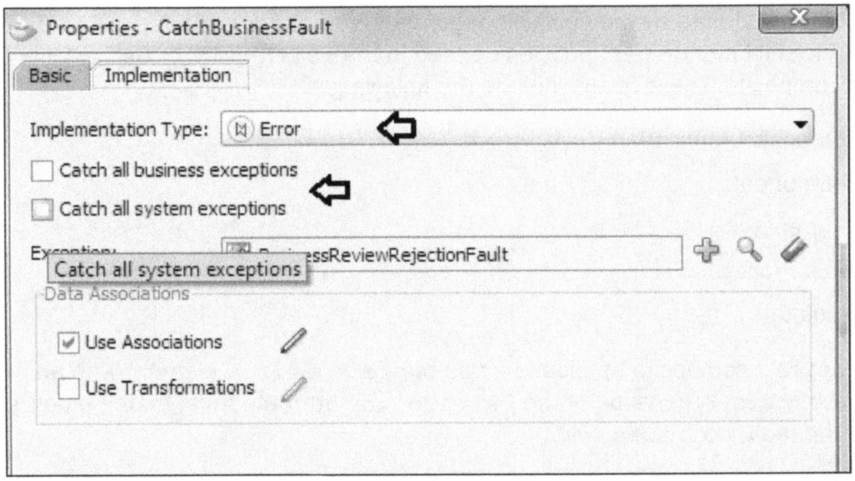

Handling a system exception—Fault Management Framework

The purpose of the **Fault Management Framework** is to provide error handling that is external to SOA and does not impact the SOA/BPEL design or runtime. The framework is implemented using policies defined in XML.

These policies are reusable across composites/components and can catch both runtime and business faults. Once a fault is caught, the policy defines actions that can be used for the SOA instance, such as retry, human intervention, replay scope, rethrow fault, abort, and custom Java actions.

These policies can be bound to composites and/or components. When the policies have been defined and bound to composites and/or components, the framework will intercept the fault before the standard fault handler comes into play.

You will create two XML policy files required to set up the Fault Management Framework in SOA, the first of which is `fault-policies.xml`. This file contains one or more Fault Policy definitions, fault definitions (which can also include conditions), and actions. The second policy file that is required by the Fault Management Framework is `fault-bindings.xml`. This policy file will bind (or map) policies defined in the `fault-policies.xml` file to levels within the composite. These levels include the following:

- Composite Application
- Component
- Reference
- BPEL Process
- Mediator

When binding to a composite application, use the `<composite>` element with an attribute called `faultPolicy`. The value of the `faultPolicy` attribute must match a policy ID defined in the fault, `policies.xml`.

When binding to a reference, use the `<reference>` element with an attribute called `faultPolicy`. The value of the `faultPolicy` attribute must match a policy ID defined in the fault, `policies.xml`.

When binding to a component, use the `<component>` element with an attribute called `faultPolicy`. The value of the `faultPolicy` attribute must match a policy ID defined in the `fault-policies.xml`. You will also need to specify a `<name>` element containing the name of the process.

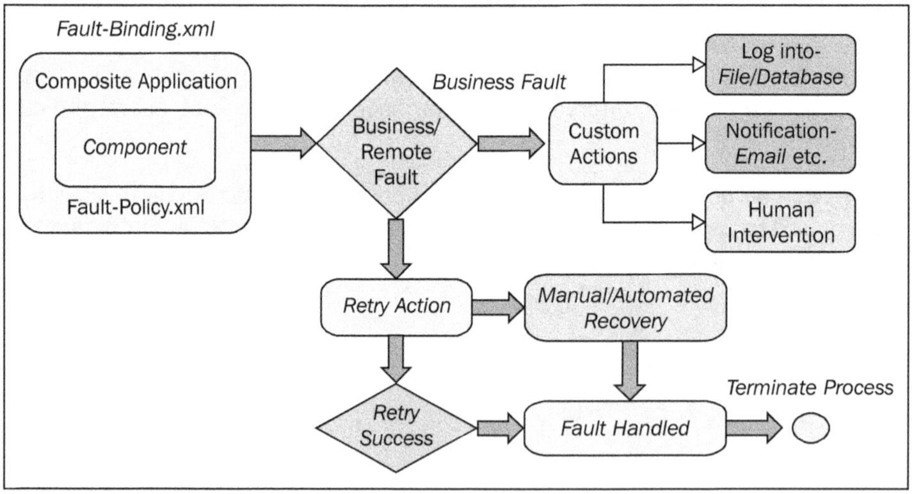

How to do it...

You have created a service task **ValidateStock** in the **salesrepresentative** swimlane. This task invokes the `Stockvalidator_EBS` service. If `Stockvalidator_EBS` throws a binding or remote fault, you will use the fault-policy framework to catch the exception.

1. Create a `fault-policy.xml` file. For the sample scenario, you will keep this file as simple as possible and would create it only for system faults—binding and remote faults.

```
<?xml version="1.0" encoding="windows-1252" ?>
<faultPolicies xmlns="http://schemas.oracle.com/bpel/faultpolicy">
 <faultPolicy version="2.0.1" id="SystemFaults"
              xmlns:env="http://schemas.xmlsoap.org/soap/
envelope/"
              xmlns:xs="http://www.w3.org/2001/XMLSchema"
              xmlns="http://schemas.oracle.com/bpel/faultpolicy"
              xmlns:xsi="http://www.w3.org/2001/XMLSchema-
instance">
  <Conditions>
   <faultName xmlns:bpelx="http://schemas.oracle.com/bpel/
extension"
              name="bpelx:remoteFault">
    <condition>
     <action ref="ora-retry"/>
    </condition>
   </faultName>
   <faultName xmlns:bpelx="http://schemas.oracle.com/bpel/
extension"
              name="bpelx:bindingFault">
    <condition>
     <action ref="ora-terminate"/>
    </condition>
   </faultName>
   <!-- Business faults -->
  </Conditions>
  <Actions>
<Action id="ora-retry">
    <retry>
     <retryCount>3</retryCount>
     <retryInterval>2</retryInterval>
     <exponentialBackoff/>
     <retryFailureAction ref=" ora-human-intervention "/>
     <retrySuccessAction ref=" ora-terminate"/>
    </retry>
```

```
      </Action>
      <Action id="ora-rethrow-fault">
        <rethrowFault/>
      </Action>
      <Action id="ora-human-intervention">
        <humanIntervention/>
      </Action>
      <Action id="ora-terminate">
        <abort/>
      </Action>
      <Action id="ora-java">
        <!-- this is user provided class-->
      </Action>
    </Actions>
    <Properties></Properties>
  </faultPolicy>
</faultPolicies>
```

2. Create a `fault-binding.xml` file, as follows:

```
<?xml version="1.0" encoding="windows-1252" ?>
<faultPolicyBindings version="2.0.1"
                     xmlns="http://schemas.oracle.com/bpel/
faultpolicy"
                     xmlns:xsi="http://www.w3.org/2001/XMLSchema-
instance">
  <composite faultPolicy="SystemFaults"/>
  <!-- Below listed component names use polic SystemFaults -->
  <component faultPolicy="SystemFaults">
    <name>Stockvalidator_EBS</name>
  </component>
</faultPolicyBindings>
```

   You can find that the component `Stockvalidator_EBS` is bound with `fault-policy.xml`, as the value of the `faultPolicy` attribute matches the policy ID defined in the `fault-policies.xml` file.

3. Add two properties in `composite.xml`, to let the composite use them.
4. The `fault-policy` files are loaded at start-up, so when any changes are made to them, a server restart is required. The location for the Fault Policy files can be in the same directory as `composite.xml` or in a location identified by a property in `composite.xml`:

```
<property name="oracle.composite.faultPolicyFile">fault-olicies.
xml></property>
<property name="oracle.composite.faultBindingFile">faultbindings.
xml></property>
```

How it works...

When the process token reaches the `ValidateStock` service task and invokes the `StockValidator_EBS` service, if the service throws a binding/remote fault, it gets propagated as no boundary catch events are defined. For this component, Fault Policies are defined and hence the Fault Policy framework will handle the exception. As per your definition, in `fault-policy.xml`, on infusion of binding or remote fault, you would just terminate the process. Hence, in an error scenario this process will get terminated.

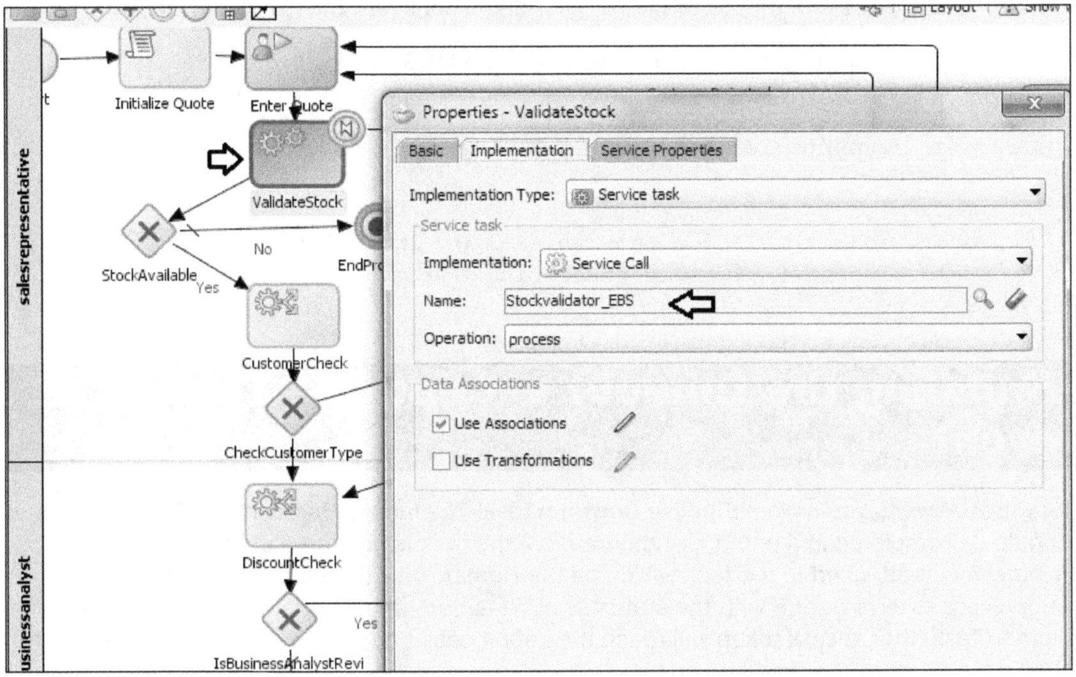

> Once a fault is caught, the policy defines actions that can be used for the SOA instance, such as retry, human intervention, replay scope, throw fault again abort, and custom Java actions.
>
> At present, `fault-policies.xml` can catch and act on both system and business faults for the BPEL and Mediator components. However, they cannot manage business faults in a BPMN process. They have to be handled within the process.

There's more...

You can use MDS location for Fault Policy files. In this way, the same files can be used across different composite projects.

Use MDS location for Fault Policy files

We can use different names and locations for the Fault Policies and fault binding files, by setting the properties `oracle.composite.faultPolicyFile` and `oracle.composite.faultBindingFile`, in the `composite.xml` file, to configure these custom files.

For example, we can refer to these files even from the MDS.

```
<property name="oracle.composite.faultPolicyFile">
oramds://apps/faultfiles/fault-policies.xml
</property>

<property name="oracle.composite.faultBindingFile">
  oramds://apps/faultfiles/fault-bindings.xml
</property>
```

Handling the timeout exception—Timer event

As you are aware, you have a **Finalize Contract** task. The idea is that contract finalization should be completed in a one-hour time frame. If the task is not completed in one hour, a Timer event attached to the task will catch the Human Task timeout. You will develop a subprocess to save `quote` with the status `SLAVoilated`, and when timeout happens on the Human Task, the process token will reach the subprocess and save `quote` to a location with the status `"SLAVoilated"`.

How to do it...

I. Create a Catch subprocess

1. Go to **Component Palette | BPM | Activities** and click on **Sub Process**.
2. Click just below the **Finalize Human** task in the **Contracts** swimlane.
3. This will open the **Properties** dialog. In the **Properties** | **Basic** tab, enter the name of the subprocess as `CatchSLA`. Keep the default settings for the other tabs.

4. Name the **Start** and **End** events of the subprocess as **CatchSLAError** and **EndSLAError** respectively.
5. Let the **Implementation type** for both **CatchSLAError** and **EndSLAError** be **None**.
6. Go to **Component Palette | BPM | Activities** and click on **Service Task**.
7. Click between the **CatchSLAError** and **EndSLAError** activities in the subprocess. This will open the **Properties** dialog.
8. In **Properties**, enter name of the service task as `"SaveSLAVoilatedQuote"`.
9. In the **Implementation** tab, select **Service Call** from the **Implementation** drop-down.
10. Click on the "browse" button to the right of the of **Name** field and select **SaveQuote** from the list.
11. Place a check next to **Data Associations** and click the pencil button to edit.
12. In the **Data Associations** editor, drag **quote** from the Data object list into the input section and enter `"SLAViolated"` as **quoteRequestStatus**.

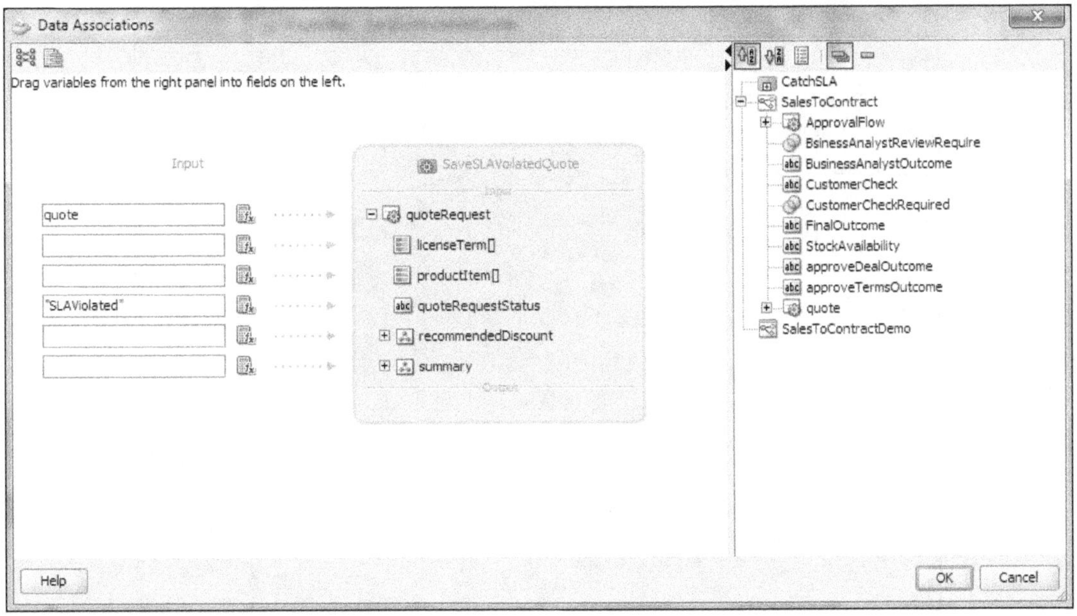

13. Click **OK**.
14. When you have finished, click **Save**.

II. Create a Timer event

1. Go to **Component Palette | BPM | Events** and click on **Timer Catch Events**.
2. This will open the **Properties** dialog.
3. Enter `ThrowSLAVoilation` as the name for the **Timer Catch Event**.
4. In the **Implementation** tab, select **Implementation Type** as **Timer** and tick **Interrupting Event**.
5. In the interrupting **Boundary Timer Event**, process execution does not continue on the normal sequence flow and executes the exception flow path.
6. Specify a time period in the **Time Cycle**. Let's set it to `1` minute for the time being, to facilitate testing. However, it should be `1` hour for this scenario.

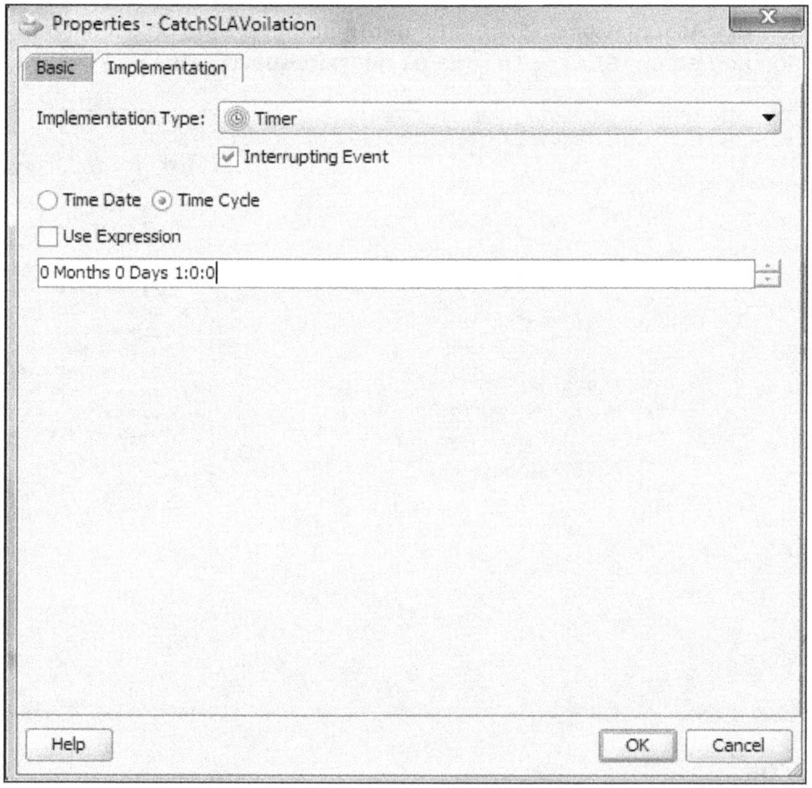

7. Click **OK**.
8. Create a default sequence flow from the Timer Event `CatchSLAVoilation` to `CatchSLA` subprocess.
9. When you have finished, click **Save**.

How it works...

The process token reached the **Finalize Contract** Human Task and the task is assigned to the Contracts user to finalize it. A timer implies that if the task is not completed in one hour, the **Catch Timer** event will execute and the process token will follow the sequence path defined for the **Timer Catch** event and will reach the `CatchSLA` subprocess. This subprocess will save the quote with the `SLAVoilated` request status.

There's more...

You have invoked the `SaveQuote` service twice. Let's build a Catch All for the system exception if it occurs while invoking `SaveQuote`.

Catch all system exceptions

1. Go to **Component Palette | BPM | Activities** and click on **Event Subprocess**.
2. Enter `CatchSystemExceptions` as the name of the **Event Subprocess** activity.
3. Rename the **Start** activity in **Event Subprocess** as `CatchAllSystemExceptions`.

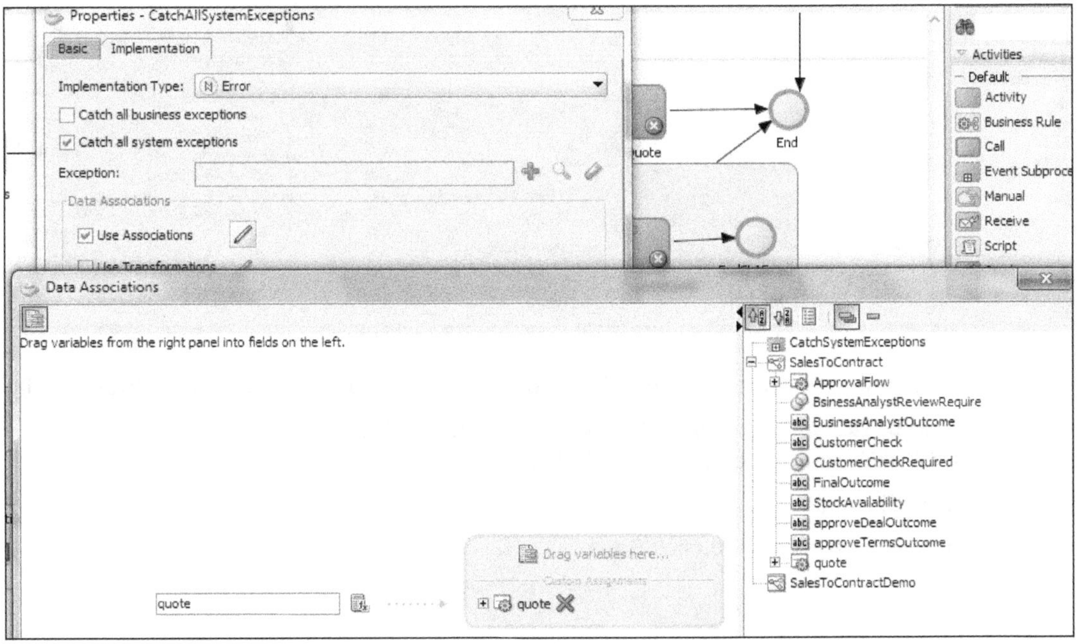

4. In the **Implementation** tab, select **Implementation Type** as **Error** and tick **Catch all system exceptions**.

5. Tick **Use Data Associations** and click the pencil button to edit.
6. In the **Data Associations** editor, drag the Data object **quote** into variables and assign **quote** Data object to it, as shown in the preceding screenshot.
7. Click **OK** twice, to reach the designer.
8. Go to **Component Palette | BPM | Activities** and click on **Script Task**.
9. Click between the **Start** and **End** activity in **Event Subprocess**. This will open the Script Task **Properties** dialog.
10. Enter `SystemException` as the name of the Script Task.

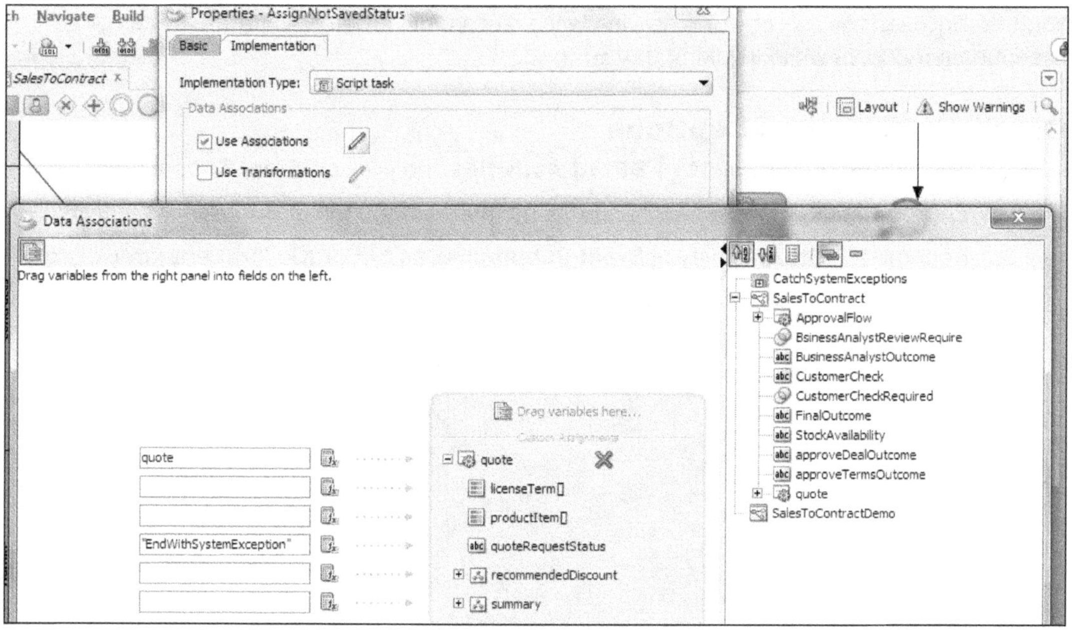

11. In the **Implementation** tab, tick **Data Associations** and click the pencil button to edit.
12. In the **Data Associations** editor, drag **quote** as input and assign **EndWithSystemException** to **quoteRequestStatus**.
13. Click **OK** twice.
14. When you have finished,click **Save**.

Faulting the process

Deploy the process, following the deployment methods in *Chapter 3, Process Deployment and Testing*.

Now that you have implemented exception handling for the business and system exception points, it's time to test whether they are working.

- When process token reaches the task `ValidateStock`, which calls `StockValidator_EBS`, `StockValidator_EBS` will raise a `SOPFault` business exception, if stock is not available.
- When process token reaches the `ValidateStock` service task and invokes the `StockValidator_EBS` service, if the service throws binding/remote fault, it gets propagated as no boundary catch events are defined. For this component, Fault Policies are defined, and hence the **Fault Policy framework** will handle the exception. You have defined in `fault-policy.xml` that, on infusion of binding or remote fault, you will just terminate the process. Thus, on error, this process will get terminated.
- When the Business Analyst rejects the quote, the process token will reach `Error End Event` and throw `BusinessReviewRejectionFault`. BPMN Service Engine interrupts the process and throws the exception to the parent process. The parent process has the event subprocess `CatchBusinessFault` defined, which can catch `BusinessReviewRejectionFault`, and hence the subprocess `CatchBusinessFault` will handle the exception.
- The process token reaches the Finalize Contract Human Task, and the task is assigned to Contracts user to finalize it. A timer checks if the task is not completed in one hour, and if so, the `Catch Timer` event will execute and the process token will follow via the sequence path defined for `Timer Catch` event and will reach the `CatchSLA` subprocess. This subprocess will save the quote with the `SLAVoilated` request status.

How to do it...

In this section, you will learn to test business exceptions.

I. **Test the SOPFault Business Exception**

1. Go to Oracle BPM Workspace and log in as the user `salesrepresentative`.
2. Initiate the process and enter quote information.

3. Enter a **PRODUCTID** value that you are aware is unavailable.

   For instance, let's enter `1030` as **PRODUCTID**, for which **AVAILABILITY** is **N**.

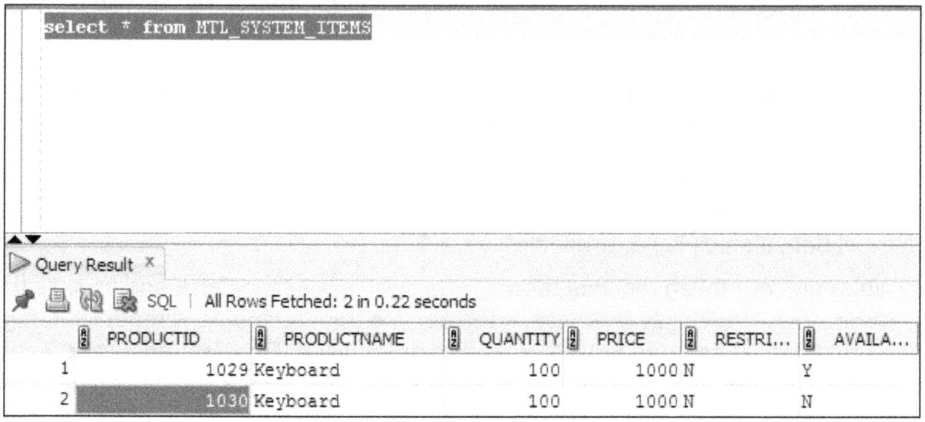

4. `StockValidator_EBS` will raise a SOPFault business exception. Boundary Catch Event will handle the exception, in this case. And the process token reaches `Stockvalidation_ExceptionHandler`.
5. Log in to the Oracle EM console and click on the instance created.
6. Go to the flow; you can trace the process token movement with the green lines.

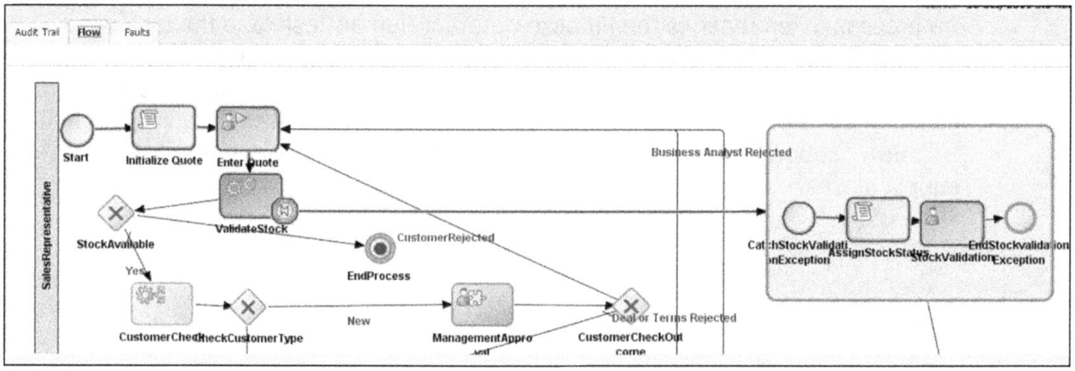

7. You will find that the **StockValidationNotification** task is assigned to the user **salesrepresentative**, as defined in the subprocess.

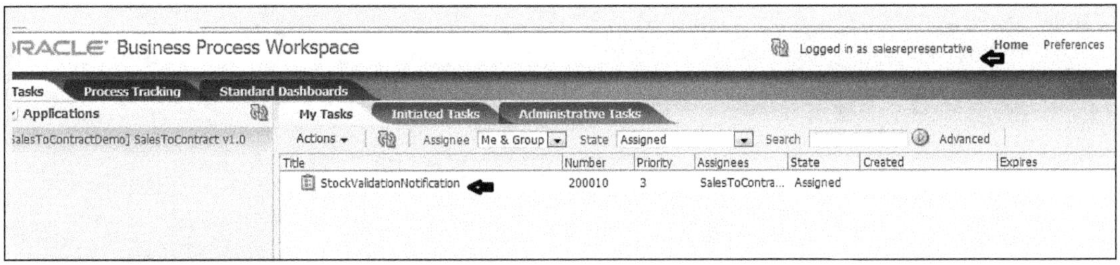

II. Handle system exceptions with the Fault Policy framework

1. Go to the Oracle EM console and shut down the `StockValidator_EBS` service.
2. Go to Oracle BPM workspace, log in as `salesrepresentative`, and initiate the `SalesToContract` process. Enter quote data.
3. The service task `ValidateStock` will invoke the `StockValidator_EBS` service. As this service is down, it will raise fault, and as no boundary catch event is defined, it gets propagated. For this component, Fault Policies are defined and hence Fault Policy framework will handle the exception.
4. You have said that, in `fault-policy.xml`, on infusion of a binding or remote fault, you would just terminate the process. Hence, on an error, this process will get terminated.
5. Log in to Oracle EM Console and verify the same in **Traces**.

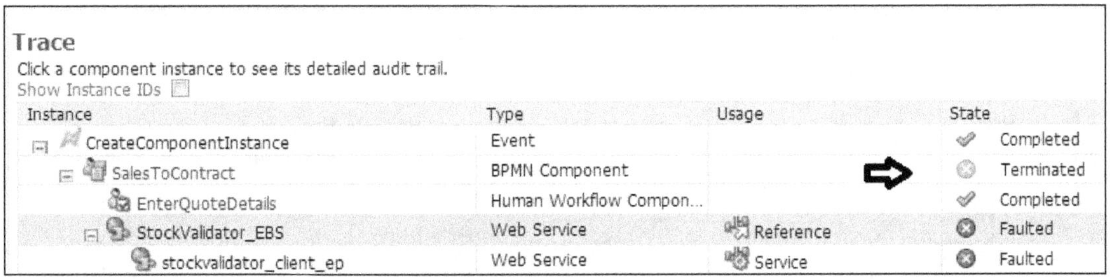

III. Handle a business exception in a subprocess

1. Go to Oracle BPM workspace, log in as `salesrepresentative`, and initiate the **SalesToContract** process. Enter quote data.
2. Log in as the user `BusinessAnalyst` and reject the quote.

3. Log in to the Oracle EM console, and verify that there is a **BusinessReviewRejectFault** exception.

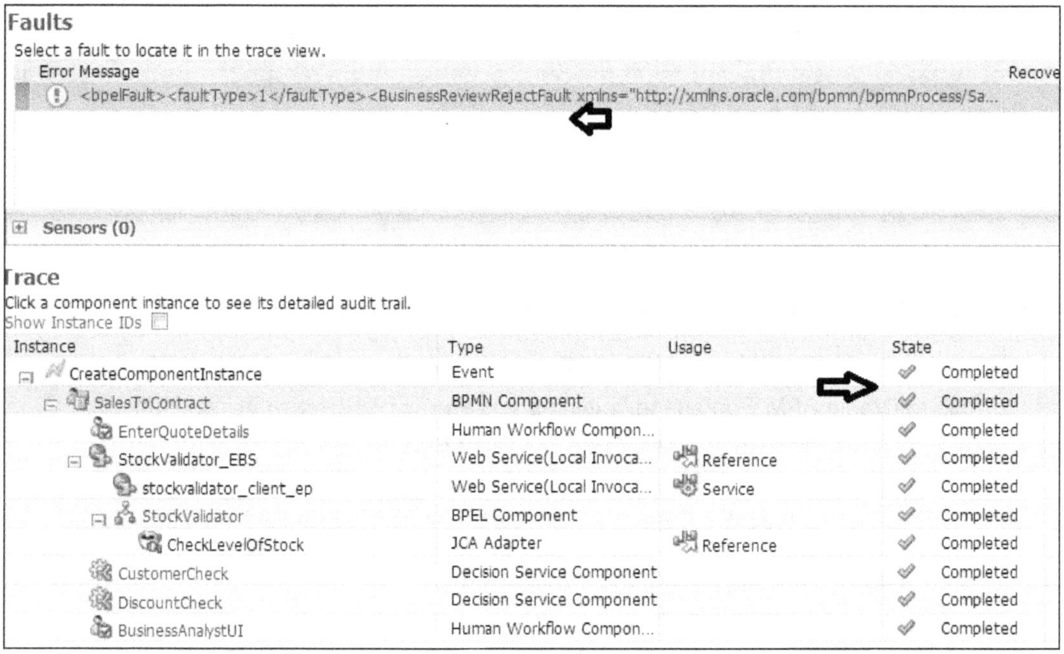

4. The parent process has the event subprocess **CatchBusinessFault** defined to catch **BusinessReviewRejectionFault**.

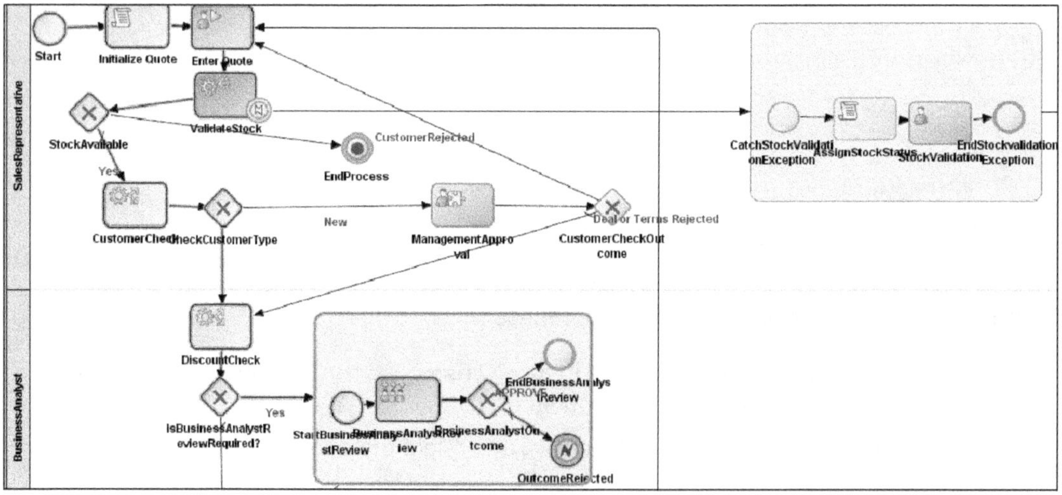

IV. Handle Timeout exception

1. Log in to Oracle BPM workspace as the user `salesrepresentative` and enter quote data with a **PRODUCTID** value that is available. In this case it can be `1029`.
2. Log in as the user `BusinessAnalyst` and approve the quote.
3. Log in as the users `Approver` and `Contracts` to perform the **Approve Terms** and **Contracts** tasks respectively.
4. Now, you will find that the **Finalize Contracts** task is assigned to user `Contracts`.
5. Do not perform any action for one hour. The `Catch Timer` event will execute and the process token will follow the sequence path and reach the `CatchSLA` subprocess.

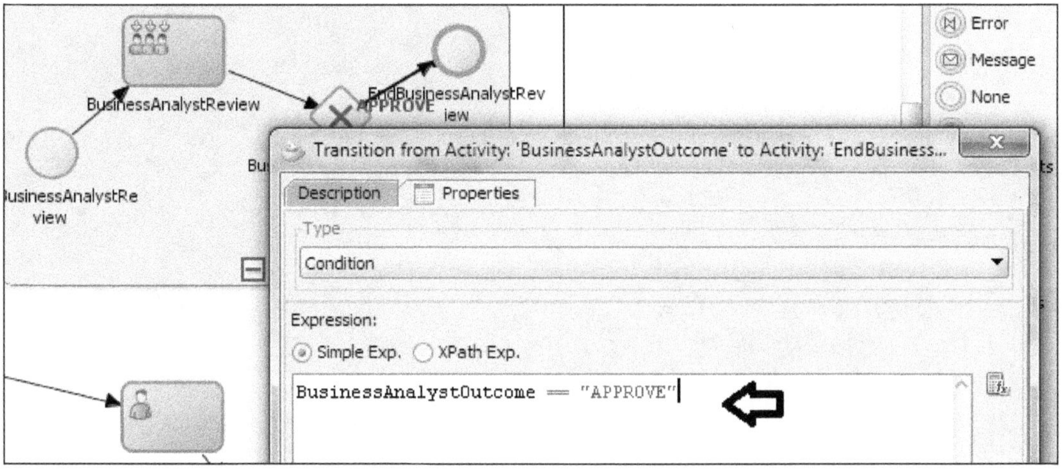

6. The `CatchSLA` subprocess will save the quote with the `SLAVoilated` request status.

9
BPM and SOA in Concert

This chapter explores how Oracle SOA and Oracle BPM, in tandem, can help in enabling the success of enterprise-wide BPM. Together, they provide an enterprise computing - an end-to-end enterprise BPM offering.

In this chapter, you will explore the common integration approach in Oracle BPM. You will uncover how the BPM process invokes other processes and services, and how BPM processes get invoked. You will explore JMS queue-based auto invocation of BPM processes, how to expose the BPM process as a reusable service, how a BPM process can invoke other processes, and synchronous and asynchronous operations for services.

In this chapter, you will learn the following topics:

- Invoking an asynchronous service using message events
- Invoking a synchronous service using service task
- Calling a BPM process
- Initiating BPM from JMS
- Exposing the BPMN process as a service

Introduction

BPM provides higher-level abstraction for defining businesses processes as well as other important capabilities of monitoring and managing those processes. Services provide the functions that support those processes.

SOA provides the ability for services to be combined together and to support and create an agile, flexible, and dynamic enterprise. Still, some interconnectivity and cohesiveness can be evolved if BPM and SOA are put together.

SOA will support the creation of reusable and reliable services for appropriate orchestration. These services are agile and reusable. An agile application is a loosely coupled set of services, it is easily modified to address changing business needs, and it is scalable by design. But without BPM your services will not have the ability of continuous improvement and optimizing themselves.

On the other hand, if BPM is employed without SOA in a business enterprise, application can be built in an organization, but that business organization will not be able to extend. BPM does not require SOA, as it can work alone, but SOA simplifies BPM implementation in a business organization. SOA provides a layer of control and governance for IT underneath BPM.

A common integration approach is Oracle BPM consuming OSB services, BPEL service, or any web services. Oracle BPM consuming synchronous and asynchronous operations of web service, BPEL services will be explored in this chapter. Just like any other web service, Oracle BPM can consume the proxy services that are exposed from Oracle Service Bus by providing the `WSDL` file to Oracle BPM process and having a web service object generated in your process's component catalog.

Similarly, there are cases when you need to expose Oracle BPM services to be consumed by BPEL, Mediator, and more specifically, by Oracle Service Bus. There are many ways by which Oracle BPM processes can be exposed as services, such as exposing Oracle BPM process as service or using JMS. Exposing a process as a web service is a built-in capability of Oracle BPM. Web services, such as BPEL/Mediator Service or OSB, can post messages on JMS queues, and Oracle BPM can subscribe to listen to those queues. A message on the queue will result in instance creation based on the incoming message.

Invoking asynchronous service using message events

Your BPM process can invoke other processes and services in many ways. It could be messages, send or receive tasks, signals, calls, service tasks, and so on. Generally, it's the operations used to communicate with other process or service. It could be synchronous or asynchronous.

You have the SaveQuote service, which you have used up until this point, to save quote information to a file location. It's an asynchronous service that you have created. You will learn to use the message throw event to invoke this service and a message catch event to receive a call-back of the asynchronous service.

How to do it...

In this section, you will learn to invoke an asynchronous service using message events:

1. Navigate to **JDeveloper** | **SalesToContractDemo** and click on the **SalesToContract** process.
2. You will locate the point where you need to perform an asynchronous service invocation and call-back. In the **contracts** swimlane, just after the **Contract Finalize** service task, you will use the indicated first point for service invocation and second point for service call-back:

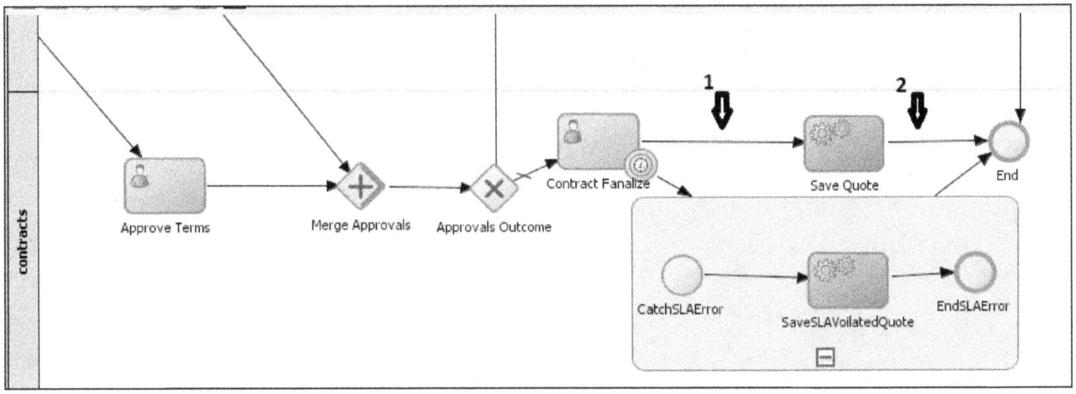

3. Go to **Component Palette** | **BPM** | **Events** and click on **Throw Message Event**.
4. Drag-and-drop it to point **1** between the **Contract Finalize** and **Save Quote** tasks. This will open the **Properties** dialog.
5. Enter the name of the message event as `Invoke_SaveQuote`, in the **Basic** tab.
6. In the **Implementation** tab, let the **Implementation Type** be `Message` and select **Initiates** for **Conversation**
7. In the **Properties** dialog, select **Service Call**.
8. Click on the "browse" button next to **Name**, to browse for an asynchronous service.

9. From the **Type** dialog, select the **SaveQuote** asynchronous service and click on **OK**.

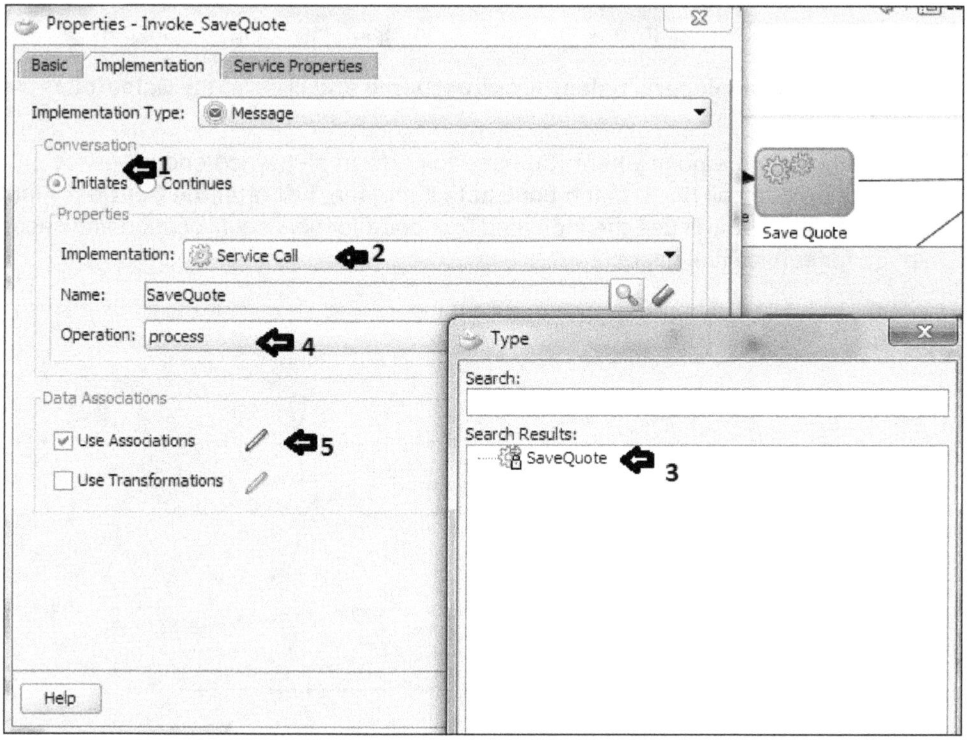

10. Select the operation to invoke from the service.
11. Click on **Data Association** and assign `quote object` as input argument to the service.
12. Click on **OK**.
13. When you have finished this, click on **Save**.
14. Go to **Component Palette** | **BPM** | **Events** and click on **Catch Message Event**.
15. Drag-and-drop it to point **2**, between **Invoke_SaveQuote Event** and **End Activity**. This will open the **Properties** dialog.
16. Enter `Callback_SaveQuote` as the name, in the **Basic** tab.
17. In the **Implementation** tab, let the **Implementation Type** be `Message` and select **Continues** for **Conversation**.
18. You will find that **Initiator Node** appears.

19. You have to select an activity that invokes the asynchronous service. You can select **Invoke_SaveQuote**.
20. You will find that the **Name** field and **Operations** will auto-populate.

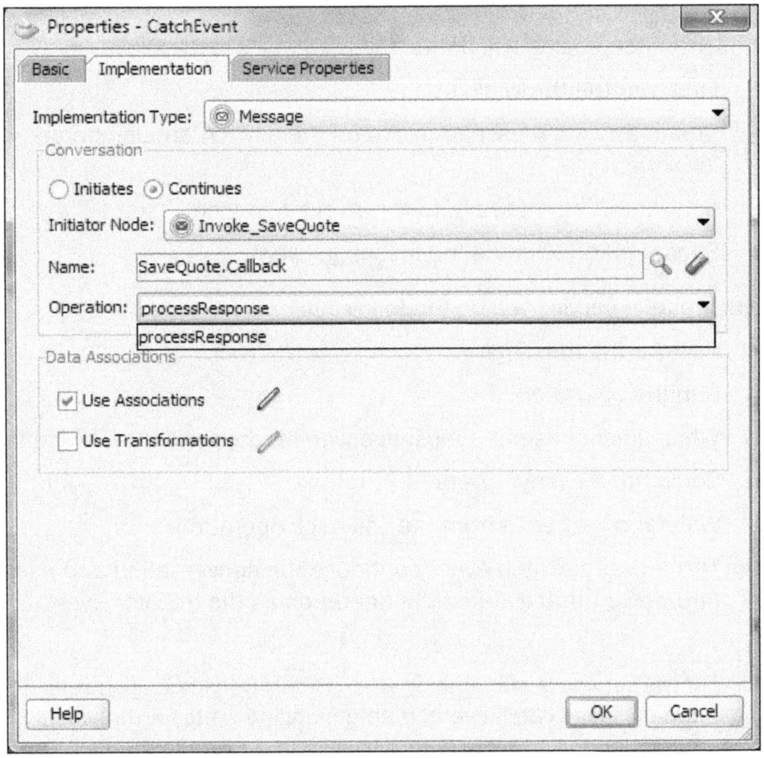

21. When you have finished this, click on **Save**.
22. You can find a slightly renovated process design, as follows:

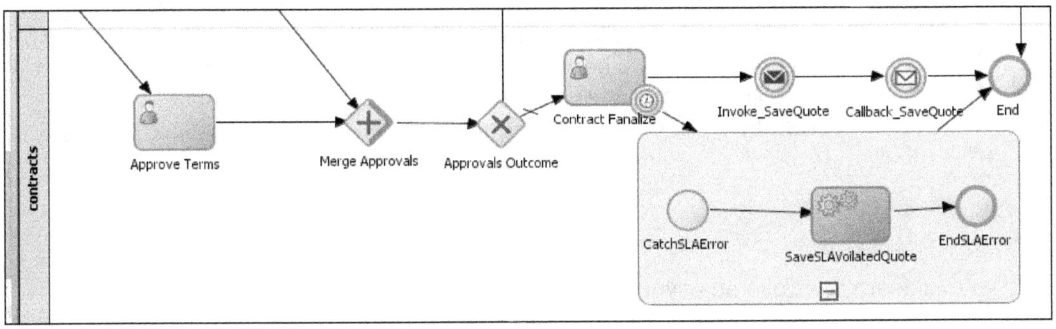

How it works...

Invocation is carried out by the throw message event, which is configured to initiate a conversation. The BPMN service engine performs the invocation and callback.

- The BPMN service engine will do the following:
    - First, run the throw event
    - Create an XML message based on the asynchronous operation that it's invoking
    - Send this XML message to the invoked service
    - Send a token to catch the message event
- An asynchronous service will do the following:
    - Receive the message
    - Run the operation
    - When finished, send a message with response to the service that invoked it
    - Catch the message event
    - Wait for a response from the call-back operation
    - This message catch event continues the conversation and uses the message throw event that invoked the operation as the initiator event.

> If the service is still running when BPMN Service Engine runs the message catch event, then the engine waits for the service operation to complete before passing the token to the next flow object in the process. Oracle BPM Suite supports automatic correlation through WS-Addressing headers. If you need a message-based correlation, the approach is to delegate the correlation tasks to a BPEL process. However, with Oracle BPM Suite 11g FP, out of the box support for message-based correlation is provided in addition to automatic correlation. Correlation keys can be based on one or more correlation properties to form a unique key to locate the process instance. Just as you set data association, you can use the wizard to define correlation keys.

There's more...

Here you will learn to invoke an asynchronous BPMN process:

Invoking an asynchronous BPMN Process

An asynchronous BPM process can be invoked using the message throw event. The invoked BPM process response can be obtained by invoking the service call-back operation using a message catch event:

1. Find a point in the BPM process where you need to invoke another BPM process.
2. Drag-and-drop message throw event from the **Component Palette** to that point.
3. In the **Properties** of Throw Message Event, set **Conversation** to **Initiates**.
4. Select **Process Call** as **Implementation**.
5. Click on the "browse" button to browse for the process and select an asynchronous BPM process.
6. Select the node from the node list.
7. Use data association to assign parameters to invoke the BPM process.

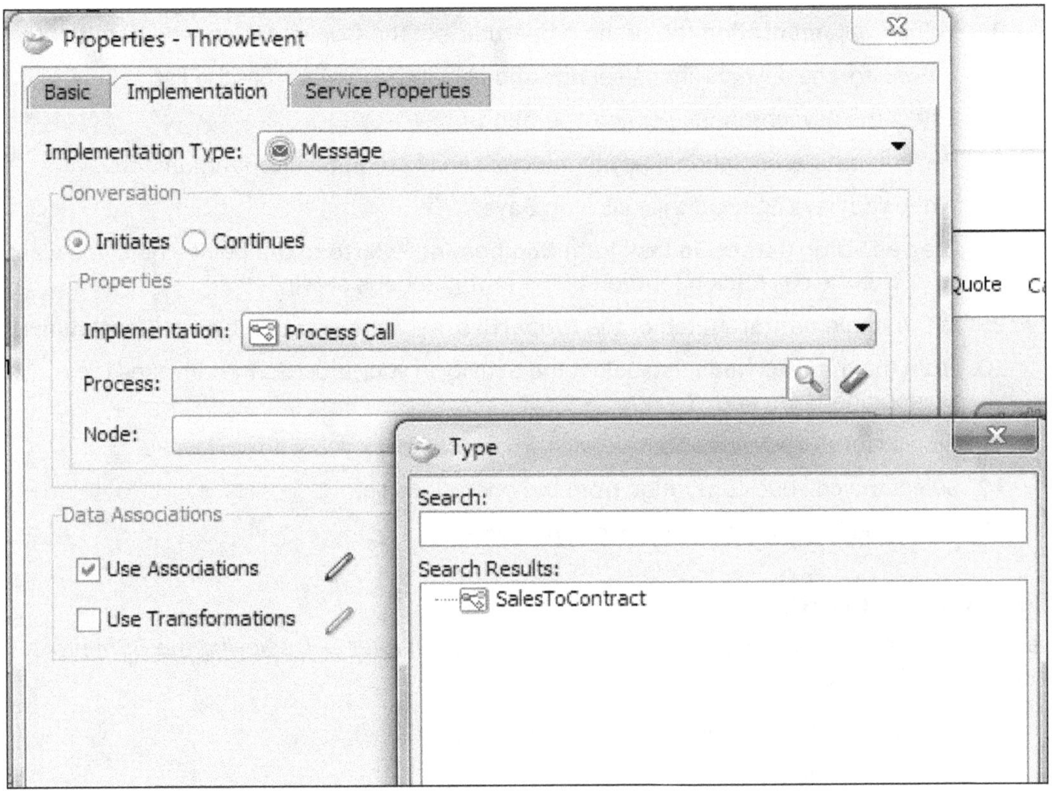

8. Drag-and-drop the catch message event to the point where you want to invoke call-back operation of the asynchronous BPM process.
9. In the **Implementation** tab of properties of the message catch event, select **Continues** as the **Conversation** type.
10 .In the **Initiator Node**, select the activity that invoked the asynchronous BPM process.
11. In the **Node list**, select **Invoke** as the callback operation.
12. When you have finished this, click on **Save**.

Send and receive task to invoke asynchronous service operations

You can use send and receive tasks too for invoking asynchronous services and BPMN processes.

1. Select the process on which you want to invoke an asynchronous service operation.
2. Drag-and-drop a **Send** task from the component palette.
3. In the **Implementation** tab of the properties, set the **Conversation** type to **Initiates**.
4. Browse for the asynchronous service and select the server from the list.
5. Select the asynchronous service operation.
6. Perform data association if asynchronous service requires input arguments.
7. When you have finished this, click on **Save**.
8. Drag-and-drop a **Receive** task from **Component Palette** to the point where you want to invoke the call-back operation of the asynchronous service.
9. In the **Implementation** tab of the **Properties**, set **Conversation** type to **Continuous**.
10. From the **Initiator Node** list, select the activity in your process that invokes the asynchronous service.
11. Browse for the asynchronous service whose call-back you want to invoke.
12. Select the call-back operation from the operations list.
13. When you have finished this, click on **Save**.

Deploying and testing

Deploy the process, as shown in the following steps, in *Chapter 3, Deploying the BPM project*. You can test the process up to this stage:

- Log in to BPM workspace as sales representative user.
- Enter Quote details.

- Advance the process till **Contract Finalize**.
- Finalize the contract.
- Log in to Oracle EM Console.
- You can find a completed instance created for the SalesToContract process.
- Click on the instance and go to trace.
- Click on the name of the process **SalesToContract**.
- Click on the **Flow** tab.
- You will find that the process token followed the desired path of Throw and Catch Message Events. You can find a `quote.xml` file created at the specified location, too:

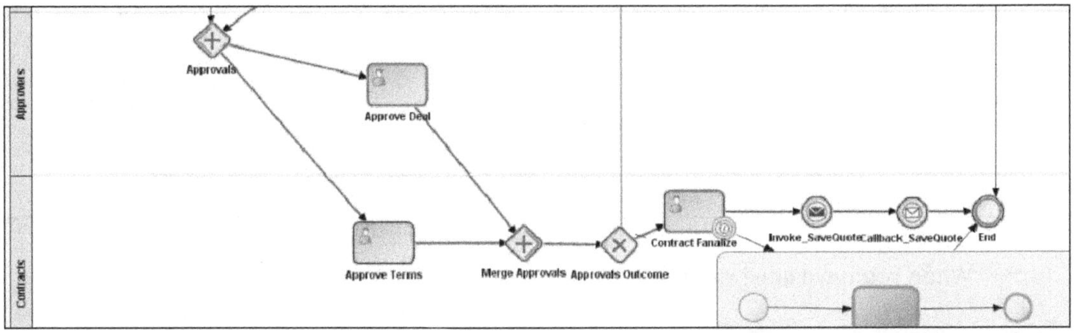

Invoking synchronous service using service task

You have being using service task for invoking synchronous operations in services. You have invoked the synchronous service **StockValidator_EBS**, to validate stock in *Chapter 8, Exception Management*. However, in this section, you will learn how synchronous service invocation works.

How to do it...

Here, you will learn to invoke a synchronous service using a service task:

1. Add a service task to the point where you want to invoke a synchronous operation on a service.
2. In the **Implementation** tab of the properties of the service task, browse for the service.

3. Select the **StockValidator_EBS** service from the list.
4. Select the synchronous operation from the list.
5. Check data association and assign the **quote** object as **Input** and the **StockAvailability** object as **Output**, to the **ValidateStock** service task, which invokes the **StockValidator_EBS** service.

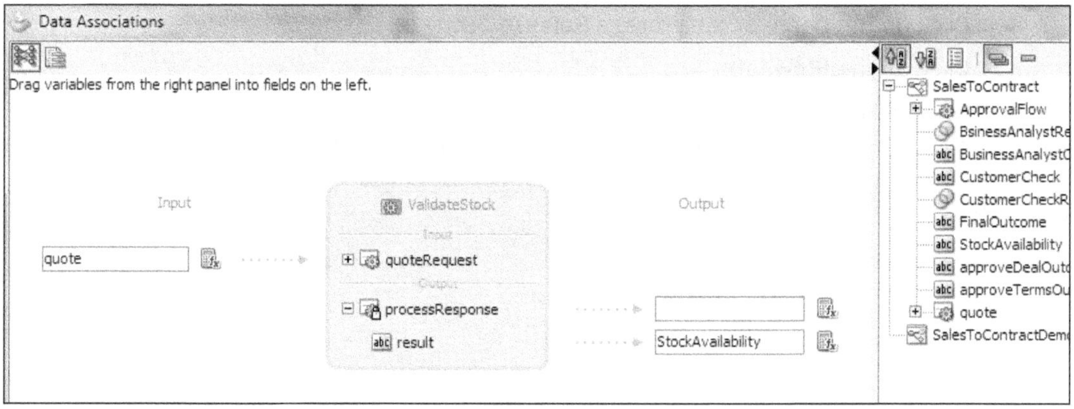

6. When you have finished this, click on **Save**.

How it works...

BPMN Service Engine runs a service task and waits for the service to respond before continuing with the process flow. When the service finishes running, it sends a response to the service task. If the service operation returns output data, then this data is mapped to the data objects in the project using the service task data association.

There's more...

In the way you have implemented the invocation of a synchronous operation on a service, you can also invoke a BPM synchronous operation using service task.

Invoking a synchronous BPM process operation

A synchronous BPM process operation can be invoked using a service task, as follows:

1. Select a point in the BPM process where you need to invoke another BPM process.
2. Drag-and-drop the service task from **Component Palette** to that point.
3. In the properties of the service task, set **Implementation** to **Process Call**.
4. Click on the "browse" button to browse for the process and select a snchronous BPM process.
5. Select the Node from the Node list.
6. Use data association to assign parameters to the invoked BPM process.
7. When you have finished this, click on **Save**.

In case of a synchronous BPMN process invocation, BPMN Service Engine waits for the response. When the synchronous BPMN process completes, it sends a response, and if the response has returned the data, it gets mapped to the data objects assigned to output of the service task.

Calling a BPM process

You will create a reusable BPM process and will call it from your `SalesToContract` process. Let's create a `Quotation Saving` process, which performs the task of saving quotes through the SaveQuote service that we have been using. You have created the CatchSLA subprocess to handle SLA errors when the timer gets expired for the **Finalize** task. You will call this new BPMN process in the CatchSLA subprocess, to perform quote saving.

You will create a child process that will be a reusable process and can be invoked from many processes. Reusable processes can be started only by invoking from a call activity.

> Reusable processes are not part of the SOA composite and hence you cannot access reusable processes from other SOA components.

How to do it...

In this section, you will learn to call a BPMN process from another BPMN process:

1. Create a BPMN reusable process.
2. Open JDeveloper in default mode and go to the **SalesToContractDemo** project in the application navigator.
3. Navigate to **Processes**, right-click on **Process**, and select **New**.
4. From **Gallery**, select **BPM Tier** as the categories and select **Processes** as the **Items**.
5. Click on **OK**.
6. In the **Create BPM** project dialog, enter `QuotationSavingProcess` as **Name** for the new BPM process, select **Reusable Process** as **Type**, and click on **Next**:

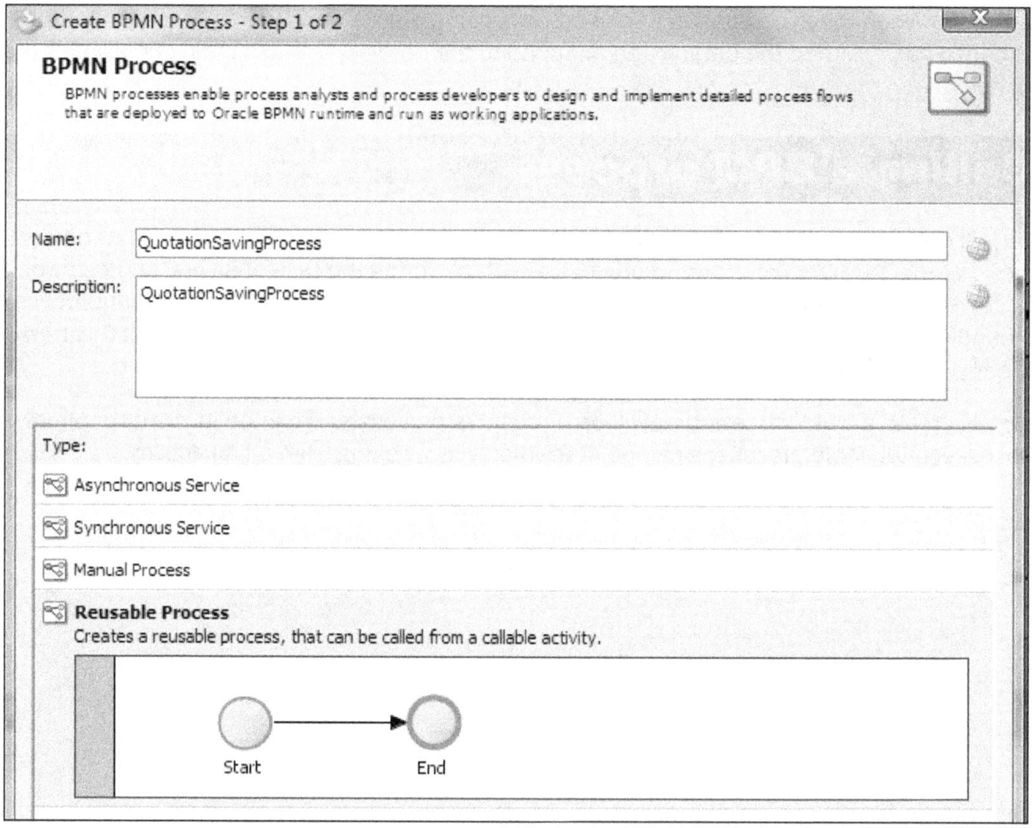

7. For **Arguments Definition**, supply `IN` as the **Name**, set **Type** to `Component`, and choose **Quote** from the **Component** list:

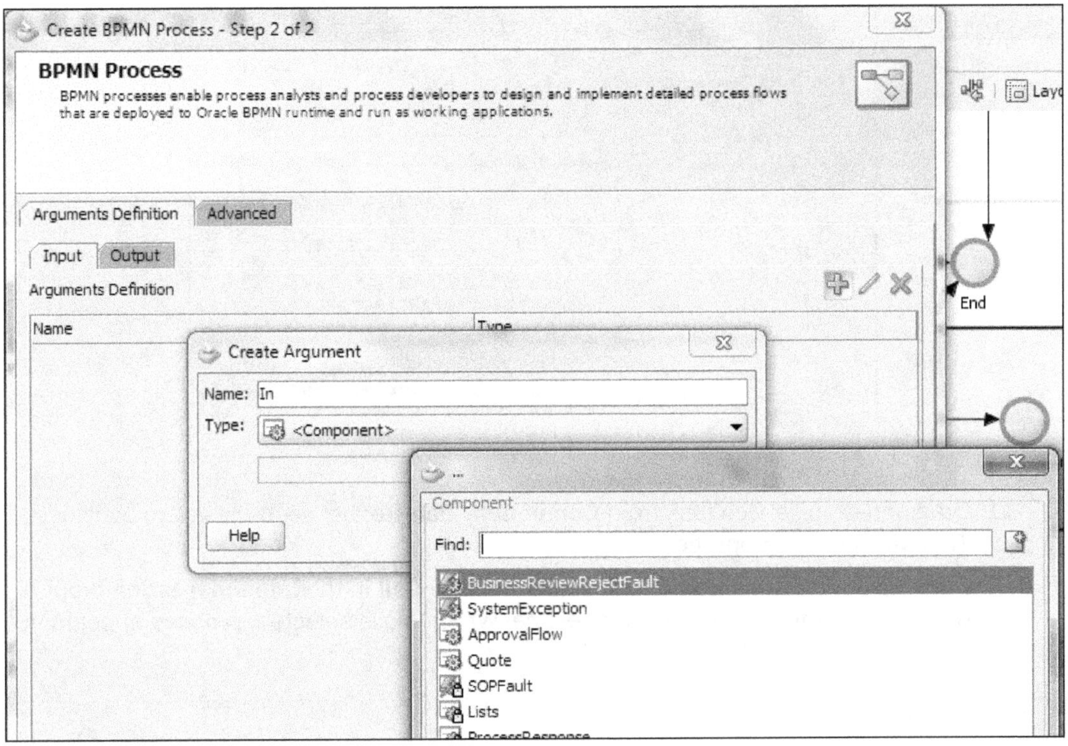

8. Click on **OK** twice.
9. You will find a new process with a **Start** and **End** activity, as shown in the following screenshot:

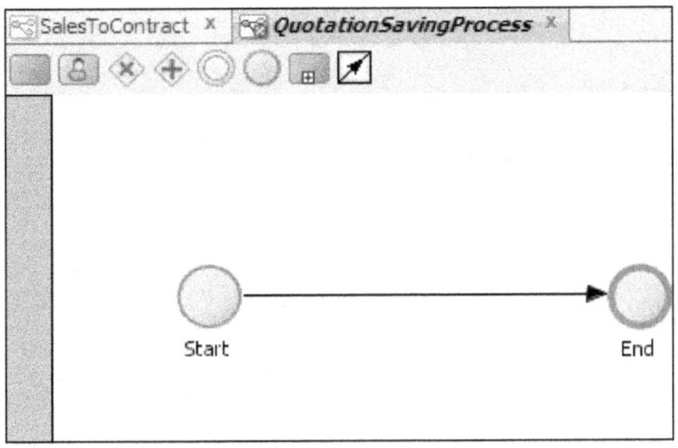

10. Create a data object `quote` of component type **Quote**:

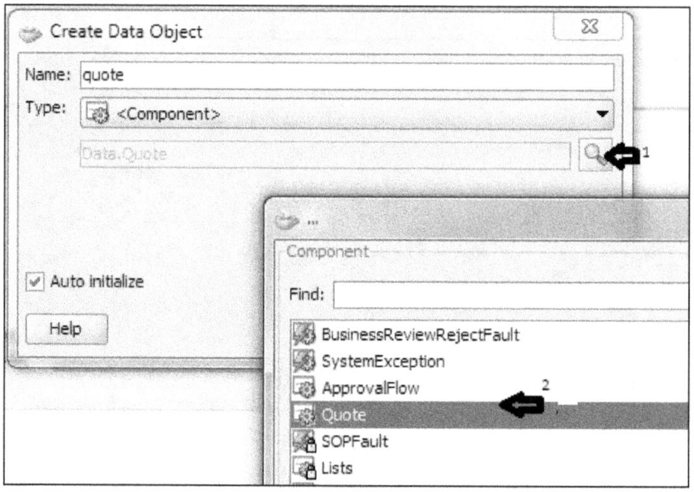

11. Drag-and-drop service task from **Component Palette**, between these two activities. This will open its properties.

12. Enter `SaveQuote` as **Name**, and select **Service Call** in the **Implementation** drop-down. Browse for the **SaveQuote** service. When this is selected, **process** appears in the **Operation** field automatically:

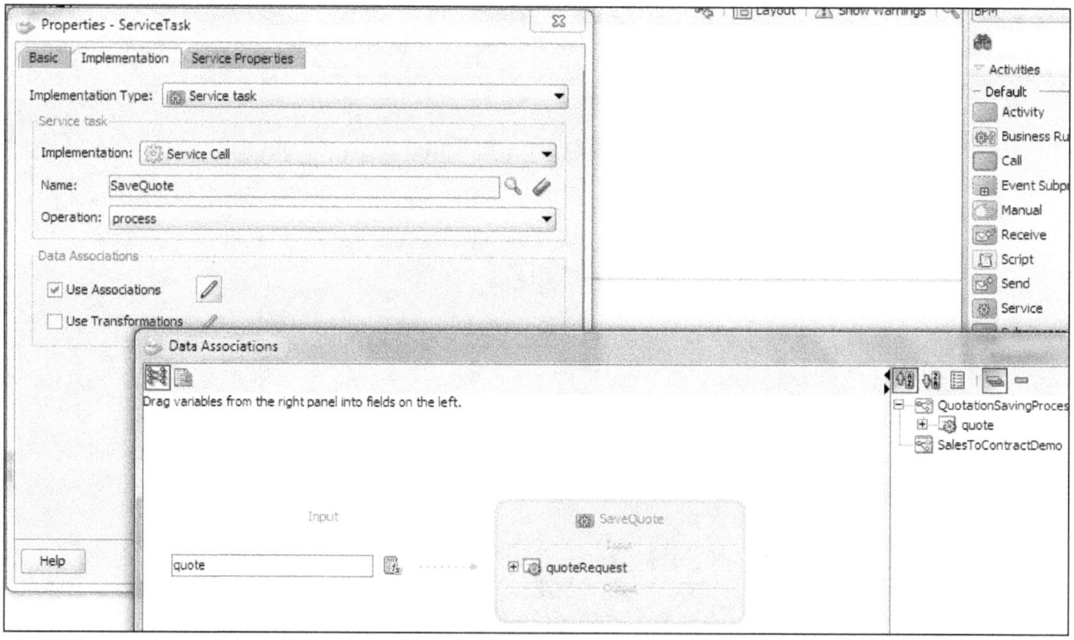

13. Drag-and-drop the **quote** object as **Input** to the **SaveQuote** service.
14. Click on **OK**.
15. When you have finished this, click on **Save**.

> The **Start** event of a reusable process must always be of type none. The **End** event can be an error or a message event.

16. Call **Process**.
17. Go to the designer area of the **SalesToContract** process.
18. Go to the contracts swimlane and expand the CatchSLA subprocess.
19. Delete the **SaveSLAVoilatedQuote** service task.
20. Drag-and-drop **CallActivity** from the BPM **Component Palette**.
21. In the **Properties** for **CallActivity**, enter `SaveSLAVoilatedQuote` as the name.
22. In the **Implementation** tab, select the process **QuotationSavingProcess** and check the data association:

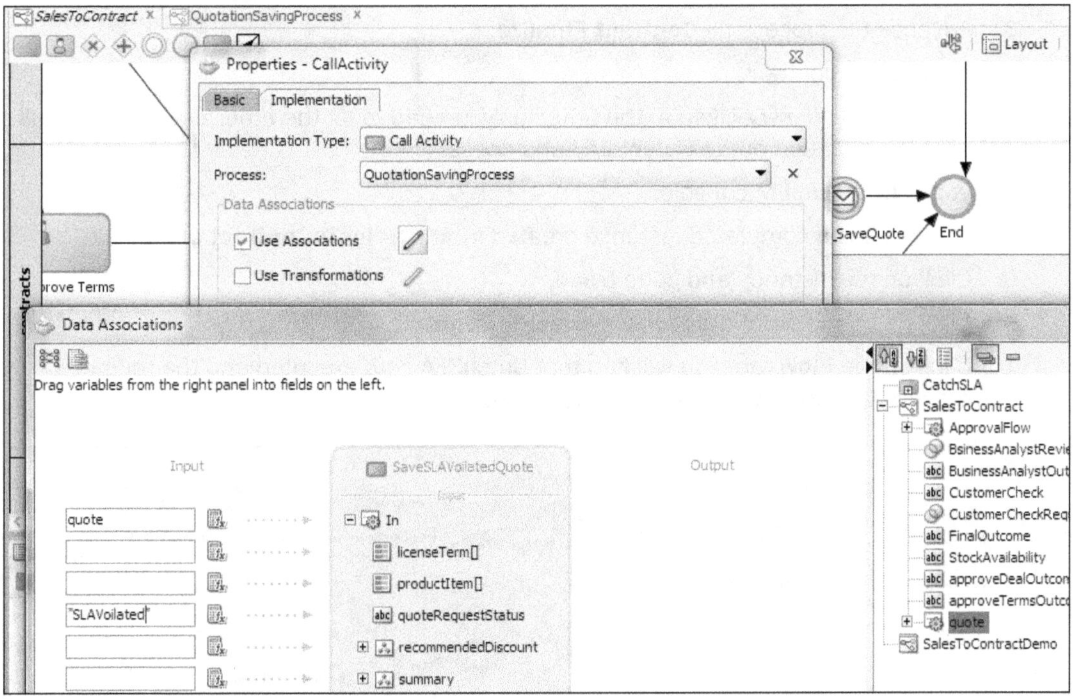

23. Drag-and-drop the **quote** object as **Input** to the BPM process.
24. Enter `"SLAVoilated"` for **quoteRequestStatus**.
25. When you have finished, click on **Save**.

How it works...

When the token reaches the CatchSLA subprocess, **QuotationSavingProcess** becomes a child process of the invoking **SalesToContract** process. The parent process passes the process token to the child process as no new tokens are created. Token on completion from child process reaches back to the parent invoking process.

There's more...

You can deploy and test the process till this point. Follow the *Deploying the BPM Project* section in *Chapter 3, Process Deployment and Testing* for deployments:

1. Log in to BPM workspace as **salesrepresentative** user.
2. Enter Quote details.
3. Advance the process till **Contract Finalize**.
4. Finalize the contract.
5. Wait for the time specified in the timer, as you need to let the timer expire, which will lead to invocation of the CatchSLA subprocess.
6. Log in to Oracle EM console.
7. You can find a completed instance created for the **SalesToContract** process.
8. Click on the instance and go to **trace**.
9. Click on the name of the process, **SalesToContract**.
10. Click on the **Flow** tab. You will find that CatchSLA gets executed and the reusable process **QuotationSavingProcess** is invoked, too:

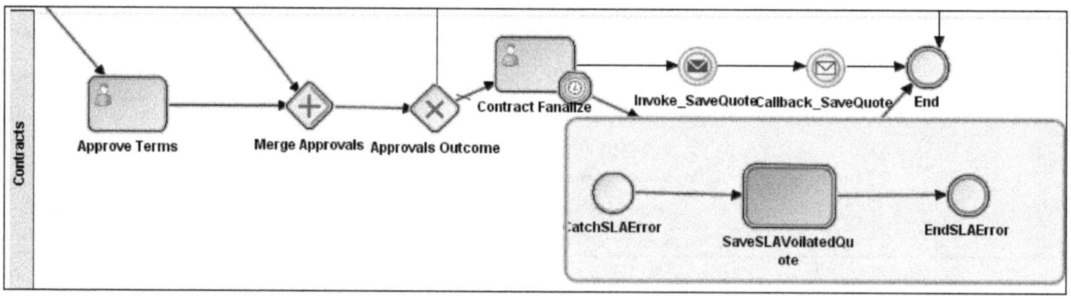

11. In the audit trail, you can verify the payload modified by the `QuotationSavingProcess` reusable process:

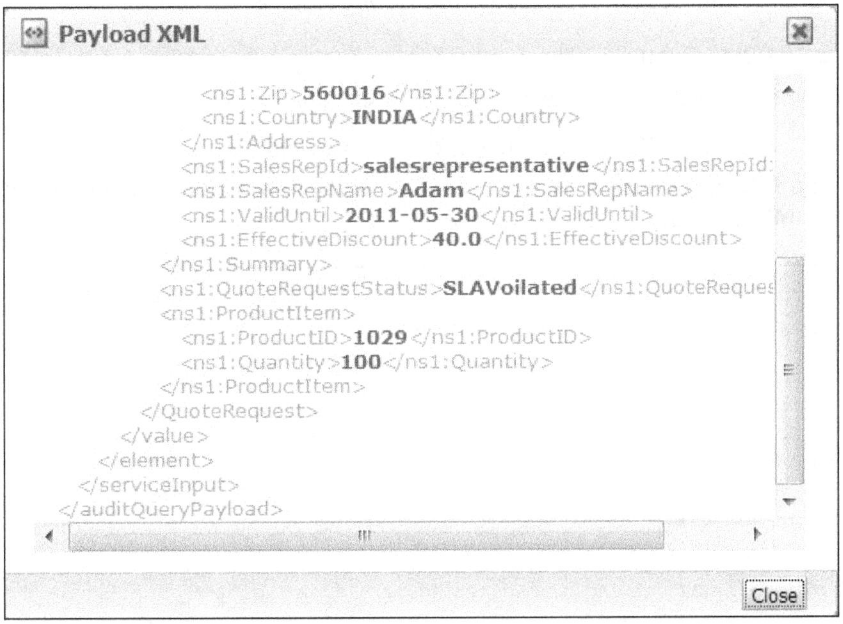

Initiating BPM from JMS

Up to now, for all the phases of the BPM development lifecycle, you have used Human Tasks to initiate the BPM **SalesToContract** process. However, in real-time scenarios, this is rare case. Initiation of the BPM process takes place through either exposing the BPM process as a web service, through BPM reading a JMS, or through BPM PAPI APIs. Other mechanisms may include processes instantiated with e-mails/file/batch (that is, from enterprise information systems) and scheduled mechanisms, such as using timers. In this section, you will explore how to initiate a BPM process through JMS queue.

The **SalesToContract** process is a part of the supplier process. **Supplier_ABCS** will be created, which will produce the **QuoteRequest** message on a JMS queue. Your **SalesToContract** process will consume those messages by subscribing to the same JMS queue. This will eventually lead to initiation of the **SalesToContract** BPM process.

You will create a JMS queue and a **Supplier_ABCS** BPEL service to produce **QuoteRequest**, and finally, you will modify your **SalesToContract** BPM process to subscribe to this queue.

How to do it...

In this section, you will learn how to initiate the BPMN process using JMS:

1. Create a JMS Queue.
2. Log in to Oracle EM console as weblogic user.
3. In the domain structure, expand **Services** | **Messaging** and click on **JMS Modules**.
4. In the **JMS Modules** list, on the right-hand side of the domain structure, click on **SOAJMSModule**:

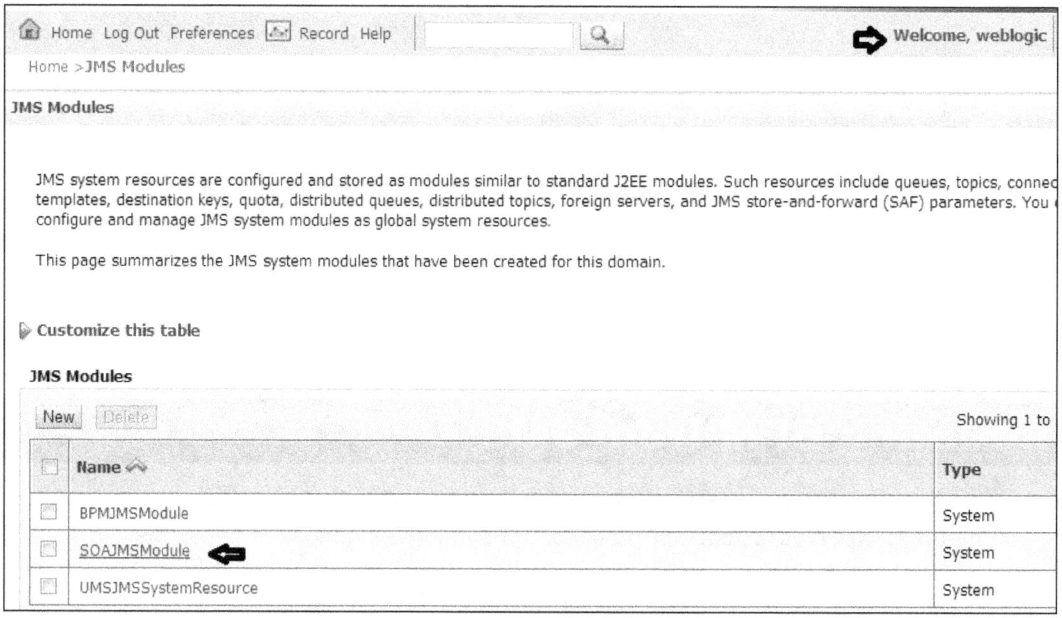

5. You will create a JMS Queue. These queues are configured and stored as modules.
6. This will open the **SOAJMSModule** settings page. Click on the **New** button, in the **Summary of Resources** section, as shown in the following screenshot, to create a new queue resource:

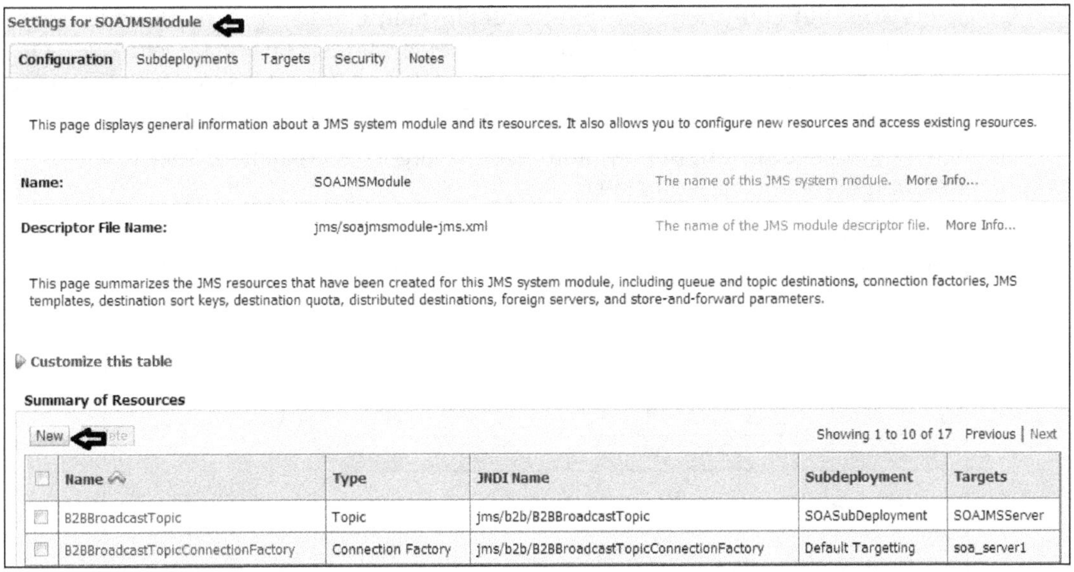

7. On the **Create a New JMS System Resource** page, place a check next to **Queue** and click on the **Next** button, as you are going to create a queue resource.
8. Enter `QuoteReqQueue` as queue **Name** and `eis/jms/QuoteReqQueue` as **JNDI Name**. Let the **Template** be **None**, as set by default, and click on **Next**:

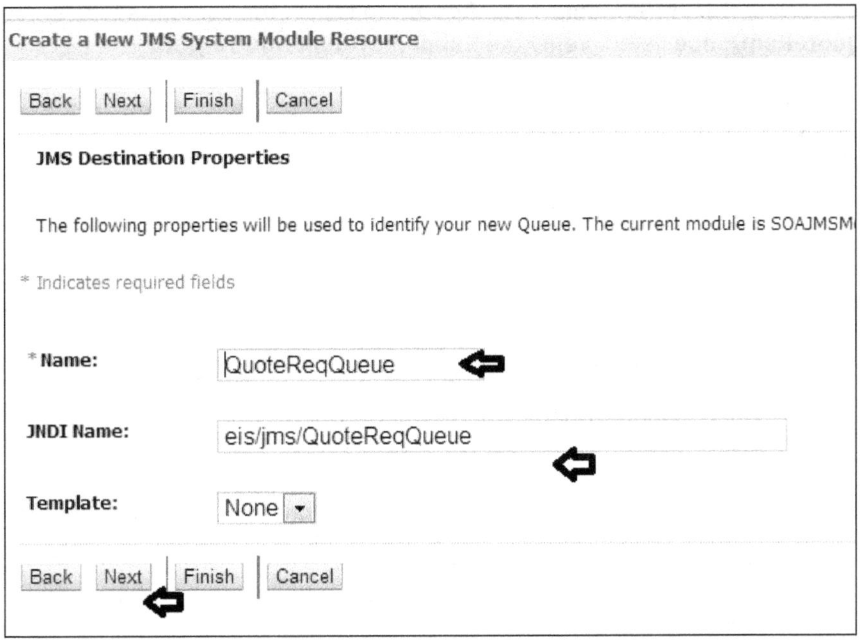

9. Select **SOASubDeployment** from the **Subdeployments** drop-down. You have to target this queue to a server instance. By using subdeployments, you can target a queue to SOA Server Instance. The server already has a subdeployment created with the name `SOASubDeployment`. However, you can create a new subdeployment, too.
10. When you select **SOASubDeployment**, a list of targets is presented. Select **SOAJMSServer** and click on **Finish**:

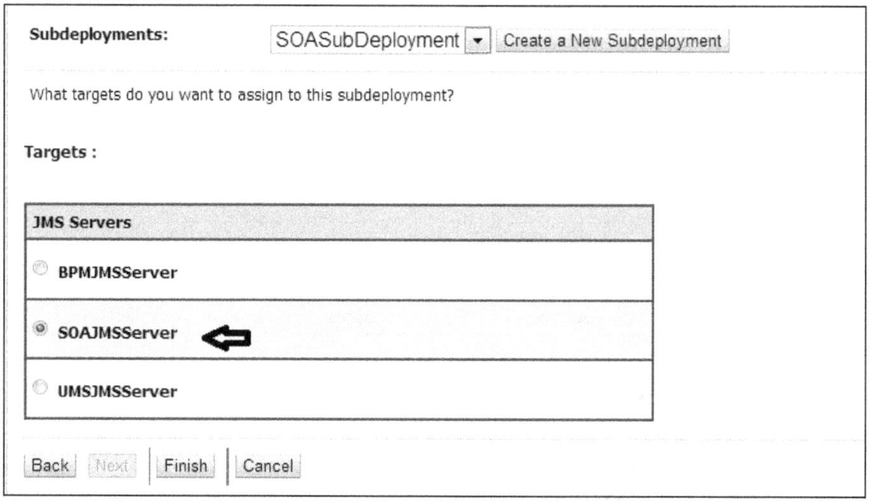

11. Go back to **SOAJMSModule | Configuration** tab. In the list of resources, you will find **QuoteReqQueue** listed. Verify the **Subdeployment** and **Targets**:

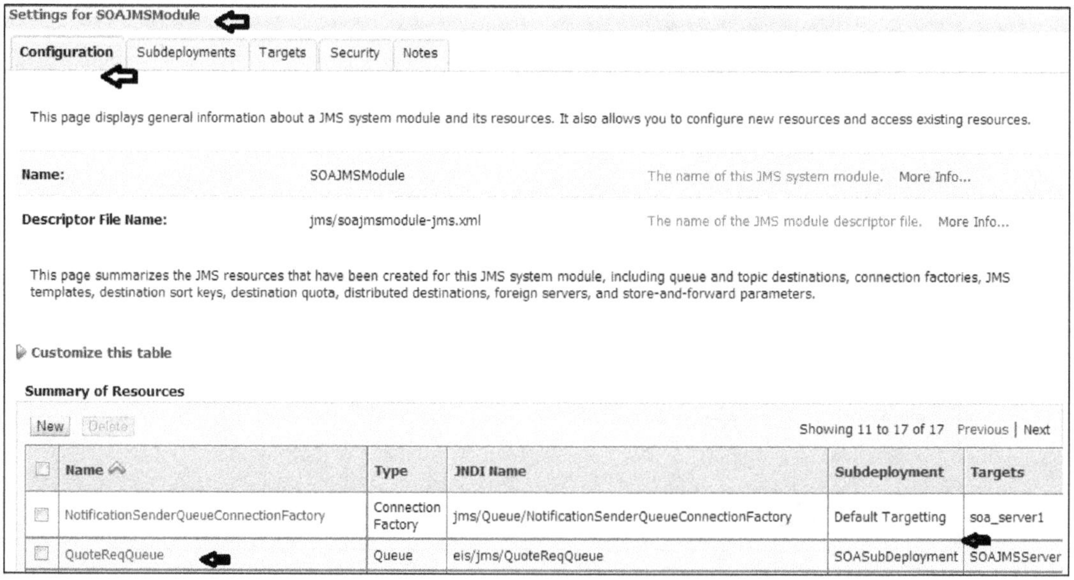

12. Create **Supplier_ABCS** BPEL service Message Producer Service.
13. Open JDeveloper in default mode.
14. Create a new project. Select projects from the categories, select the **SOA** project from the items list, as shown in the following screenshot, and click on **OK**.
15. In the **Create SOA Project** dialog, enter `Supplier_ABCS` as the **Project Name**, make sure **SOA** is selected, and click on **Finish**:

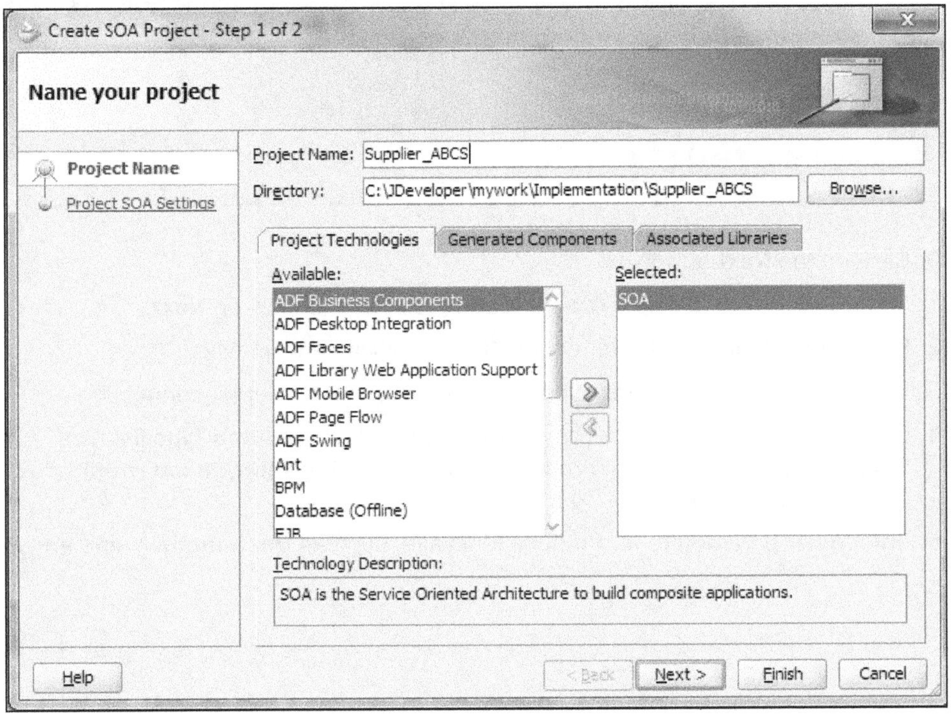

16. This will open a blank `composite.xml` designer.
17. Import `Quote.xsd` into the project.

18. Go to **Component Palette** | **SOA** | **Service Adapters** and drag-and-drop JMS Adapter into the reference swimlane. This will open the **JMS Adapter Configuration Wizard**.
19. On the wizard, supply `QuoteRequest` as **Service Name** for the JMS adapter service:

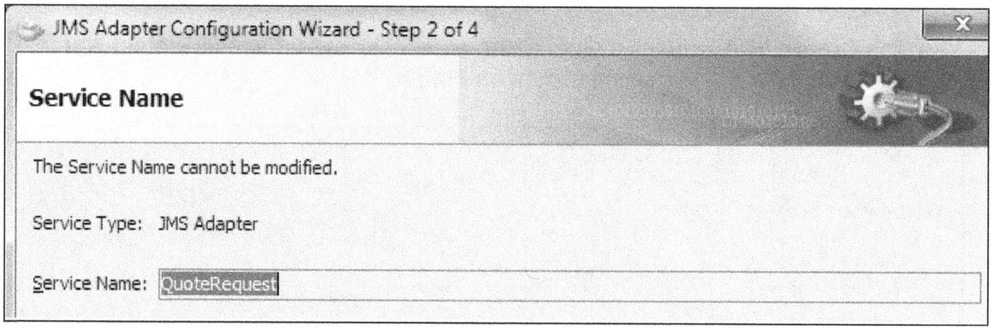

20. Click on the **Next** button.
21. In the JMS Provider, select **Oracle Weblogic JMS** and click on **Next**.
22. Select the application server connection and click on **Next** twice.
23. By now, you must be aware of having a SOA application server connection.
24. Select Produce Message as the operation from the **Operation Type** list. The **Supplier_ABCS** service will produce messages to **QuoteReqQueue**—a JMS queue. Click on **Next**.
25. Enter other parameters for Produce Message, such as **Destination Name** and **JNDI**.

26. On the **Produce Operation Parameters** dialog, click on the "browse" button next to **Destination Name** and select **QuoteReqQueue** from the list of resources .You can find **QuoteReqQueue** in the **SOAJMSModule** resource list:

27. You are aware that the **JNDI Name** for JMS connection is `eis/wls/Queue` by default. You will use the same one. Once you are done, click on **Next**.

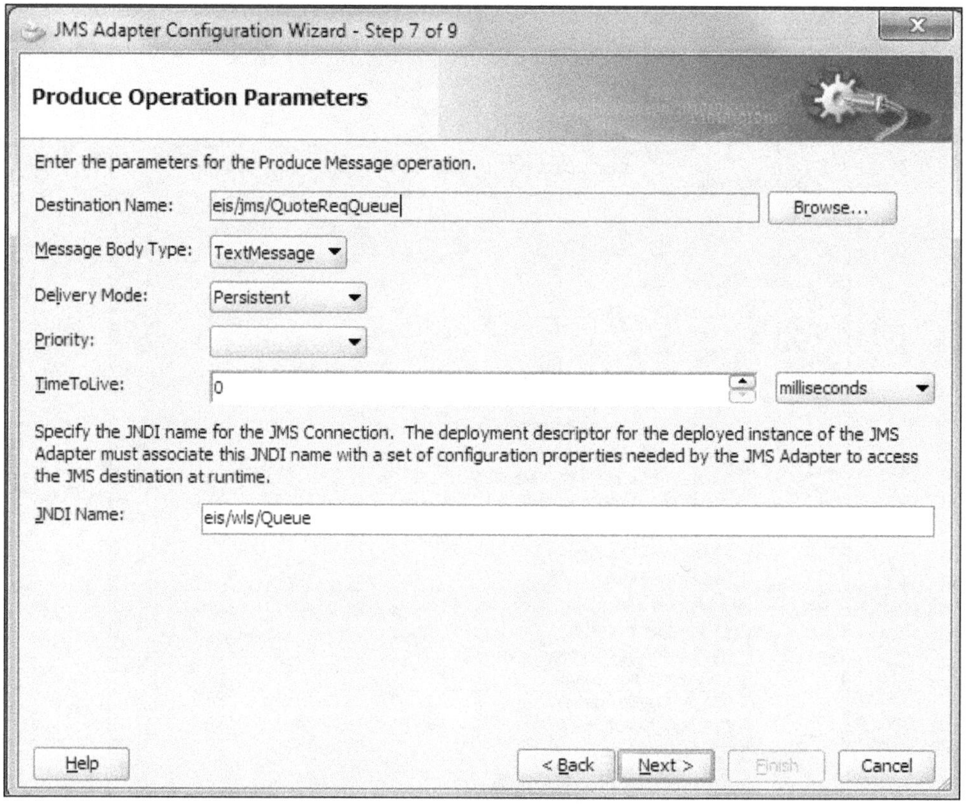

28. Click on the "browse" button next to the message URL, and as you have imported `Quote.xsd` into the project, you can browse the schema in the project. Select the **QuoteRequest** element from the schema. Click on **OK** in the **Type Chooser** dialog, and **Next** in the JMS Wizard dialog.

29. The schema you have chosen here will define the message payload for the JMS destination.

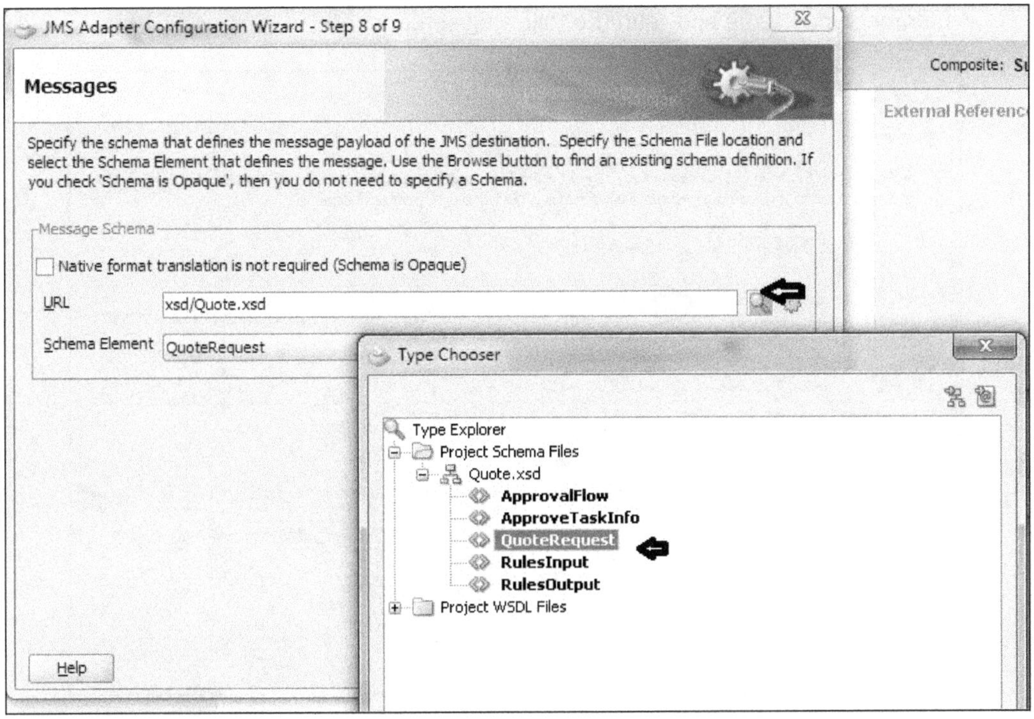

30 Click on **Finish** in the last dialog.

31. You will find that a JMS Adapter is created on the reference swimlane in the composite designer.

32. Go to **Component Palette** | **SOA** | **Service Component**. Drag-and-drop **BPEL** from the component list into composite designer's component middle swimlane. This will open the **Create BPEL Process** dialog.

33. Choose **BPEL 1.1 Specification**. Enter `Supplier_ABCS` as the name of the BPEL service, and expose it as a service. Let the service be an asynchronous service. Browse for the input schema type and select **QuoteRequest** from the Schema Element type list, as shown in the following screenshot:

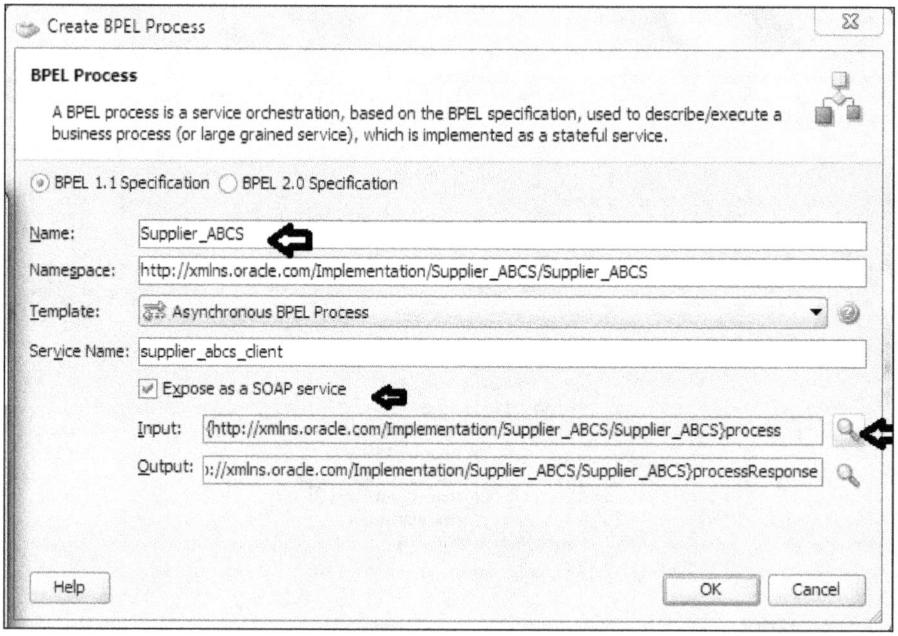

34. Create a wire between the **Supplier_ABCS** and **JMS Adapter** services in the composite designer.
35. Double-click on the BPEL Service **Supplier_ABCS**. This will open the `Supplier_ABCS.bpel` designer.
36. Go to **Component Palette** | **BPEL 1.1** | **BPEL Constructs** | **Webservice**, drag-and-drop **Invoke** between **ReceiveInput** and **Call-Back Client**, and rename it to `Invoke_QuoteRequest`.
37. Create a **Partner Link** with the **QuoteRequest** JMS service. **Produce Message** will auto-appear as an operation.

38. Click on the green plus (+) icon, to create an input variable and click on **OK**:

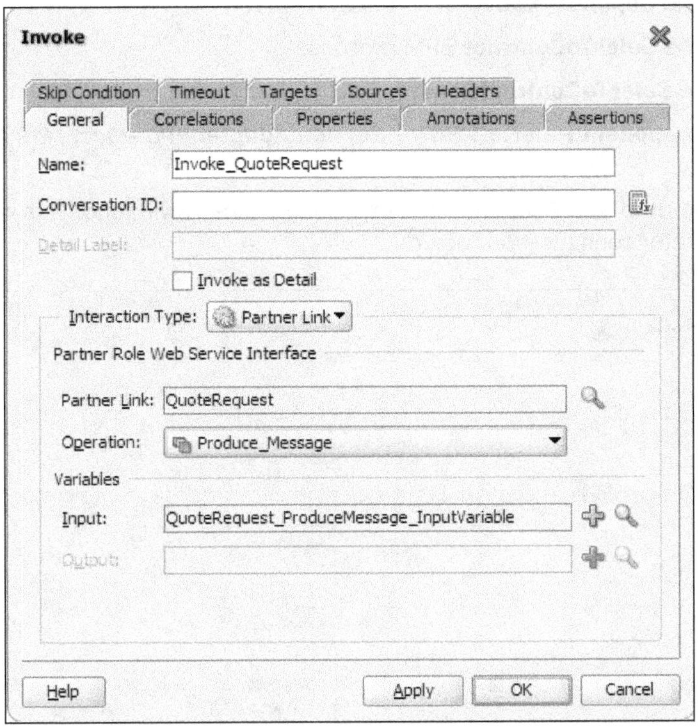

39. Go to **Component Palette** | **BPEL 1.1** | **SOA Extensions** and drag-and-drop the **Transform** activity between receive input and invoke `QuoteRequest`.
40. Rename it to `Transform_Input_QuoteRequest` and create a transformation between input variable and `QuoteRequest_ProduceMessage_Inputvariable`.
41. Name transformation file `Transformation_Input_QuoteRequest.xsl` and create the transformation between source and target:

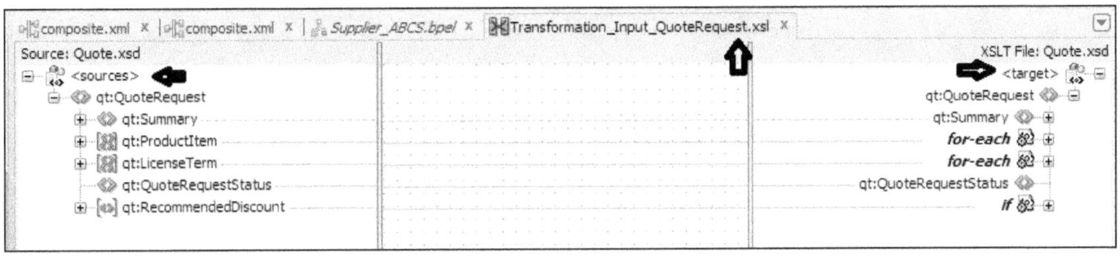

42. When you have finished this, click on **Save**.
43. Deploy the **Supplier_ABCS** service to SOA server.
44. Modify the **SalesToContract** BPM process.
45. Go to the **SalesToContractDemo** project in JDeveloper and click on **composite.xml**.
46. Go to **Component Palette** | **SOA** | **Service Adapter** and select **JMS Adapter** from the list.
47. Drag-and-drop JMS Adapter to the exposed services swimlane. This will open the JMS adapter configuration wizard:

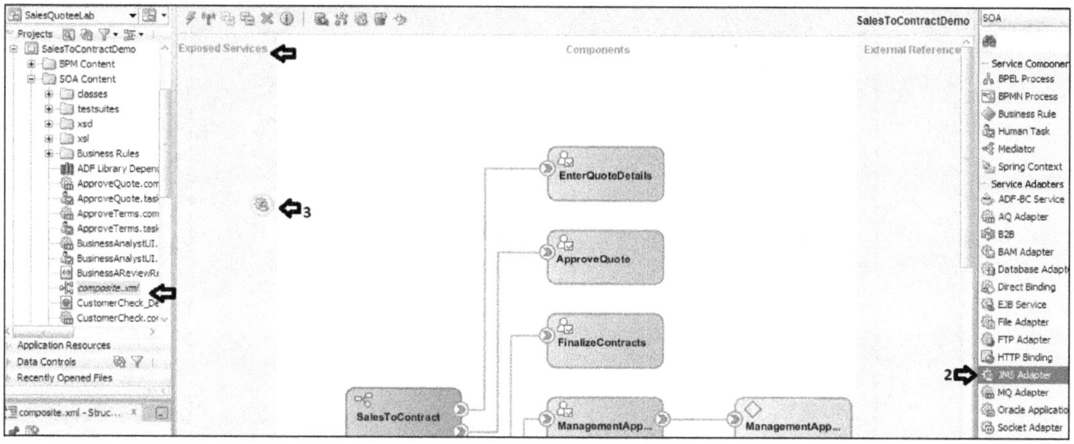

48. Enter name of the JMS Adapter service as `ReadQuoteRequest` and click on **Next**.
49. Select **Oracle Weblogic JMS** from the JMS provider list and click on **Next**.
50. Select **Application Server** from the drop-down list and click on **Next** twice.
51. Select **Consume Message** from the **operation type** list.

52. In the **Consume Operation Parameters**, click on the "browse" button next to **Destination Name** and select **QuoteReqQueue** from the resource list. This was you are configuring the Adapter Service to be a consumer:

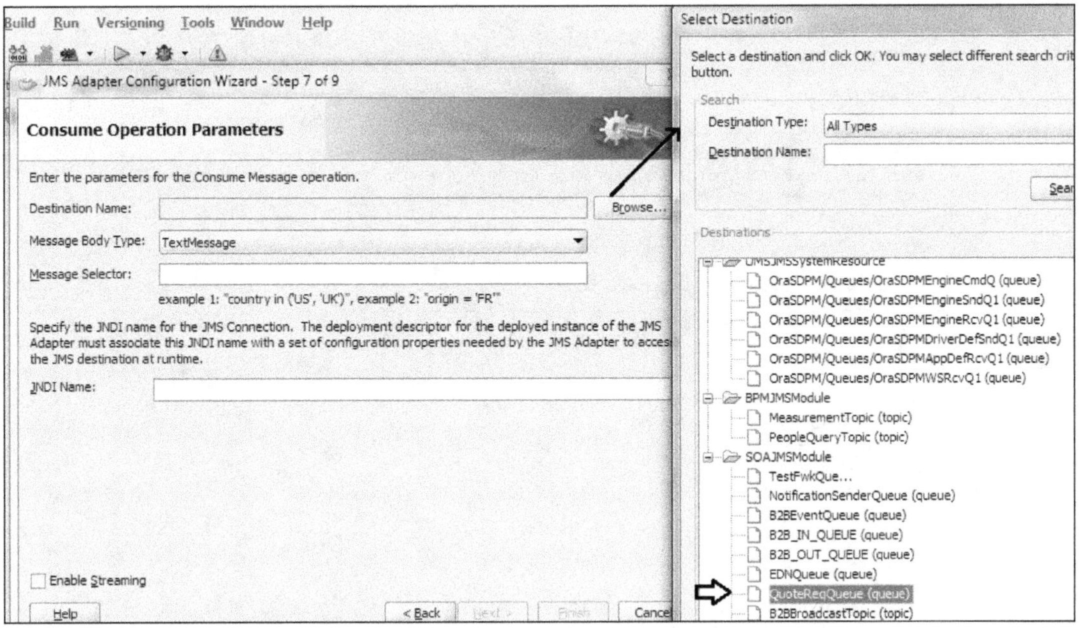

53. Let **JNDI Name** be `eis/wls/Queue`, which you have used for the produce operation also.
54. Click on **Next**.

55. In the **Messages** dialog, click on the **Browse** button to choose the message type for the JMS payload. Select **Quote** | **QuoteRequest** from **Quote.xsd** in the project schema:

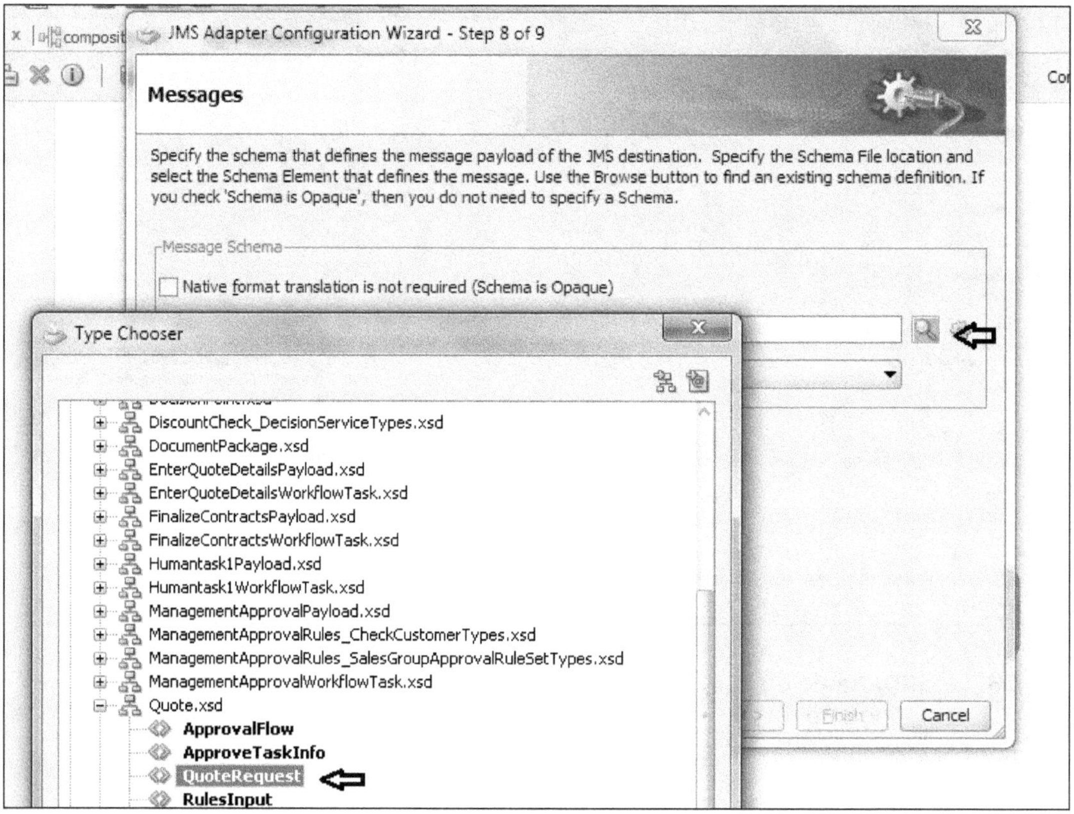

56. Click on **OK**.
57. Click on **Next**, on the **Messages** dialog.

58. Click on **Finish**.
59. When you have finished this, click on **Save**.
60. This will create a service in the exposed service swimlane.
61. Click on the **SalesToContract** process in the project.
62. Right-click on **Start** | **Change Trigger Type** | **Message**:

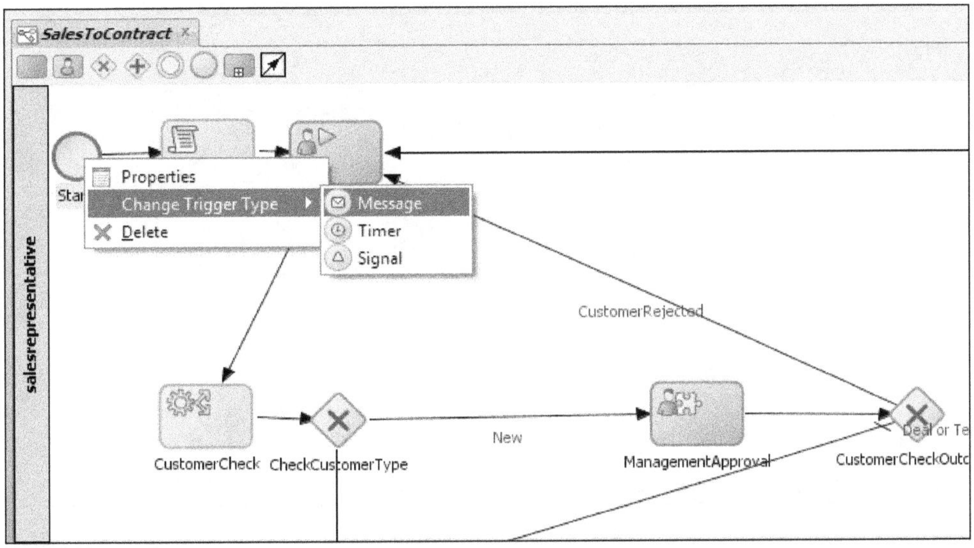

63. In **Properties**, go to the **Implementation** tab and select **Interface from Catalog** from the **Implementation** drop-down.

64. Click on the "browse" button next to **Name** and select the JMS service **ReadQuoteRequest** created as consumer from the list:

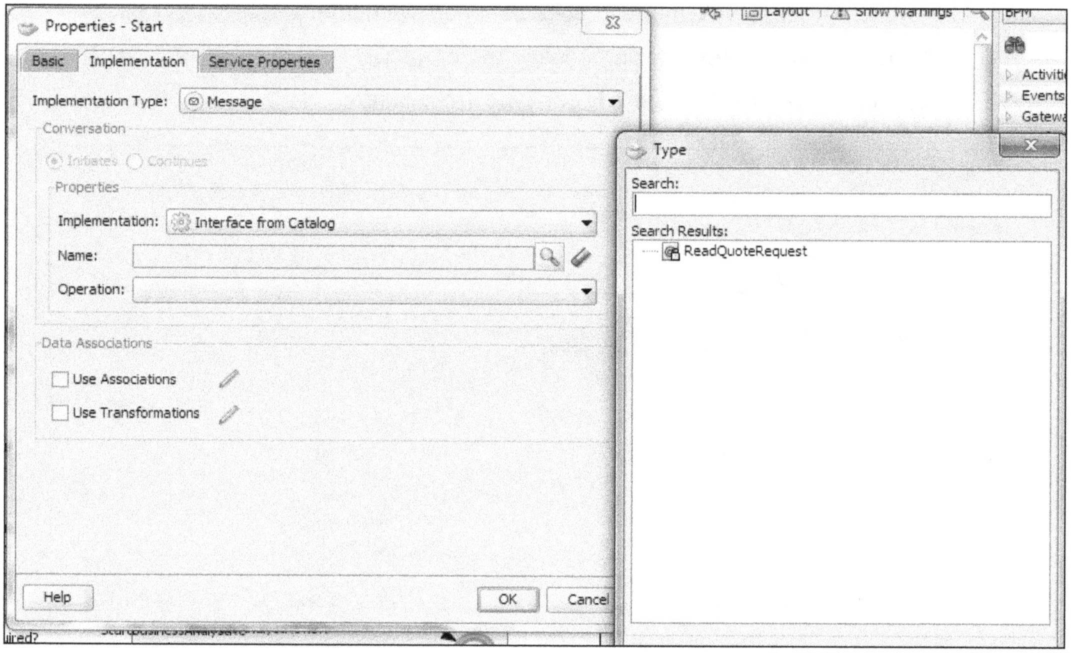

65. Click on **OK** and an operation consume message will automatically pop up.
66. Check the data association and click on the pencil button next to it.
67. In the **Data Associations** editor, drag-and-drop **quote** from the data object list into the **Output** section:

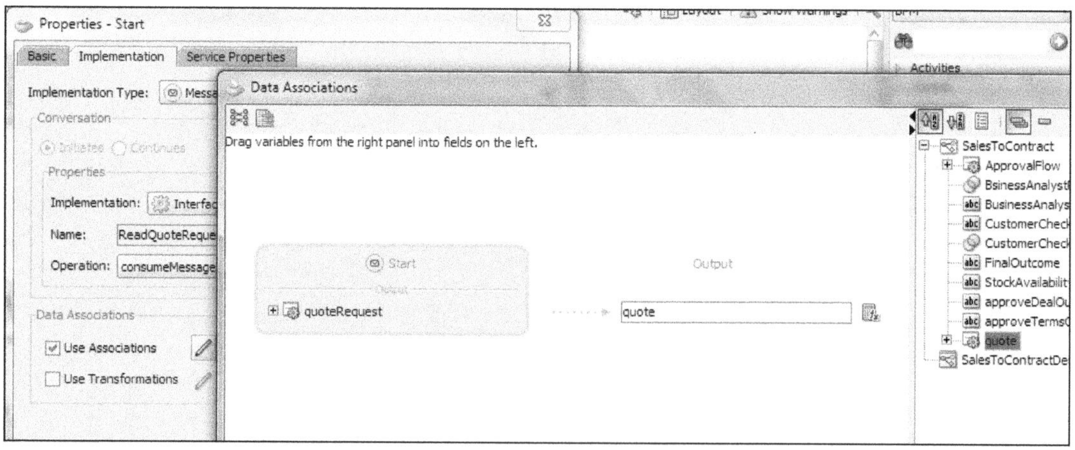

68. Click on **OK**.
69. Check the **Use Transformation** checkbox and click on the pencil edit button ahead of it.
70. In the **Create Transformation** dialog, click on the green plus (**+**) icon to select the source. Select **QuoteRequest** as the source and **quote** as the target.

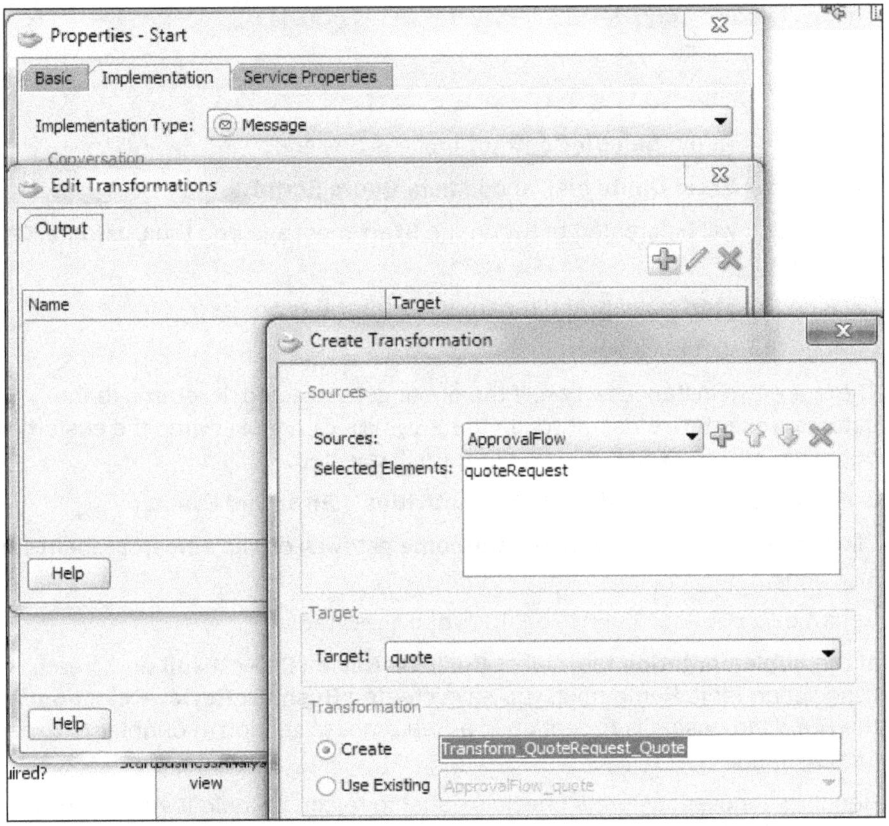

71. Select the **Create** radio button, enter `Transform_QuoteRequest_Quote` as the transformation name, and click on **OK** twice.
72. Click on the **OK** button on the **Properties** dialog, too.

73. Create the transformations, as shown in the following screenshot and click on **Save All**:

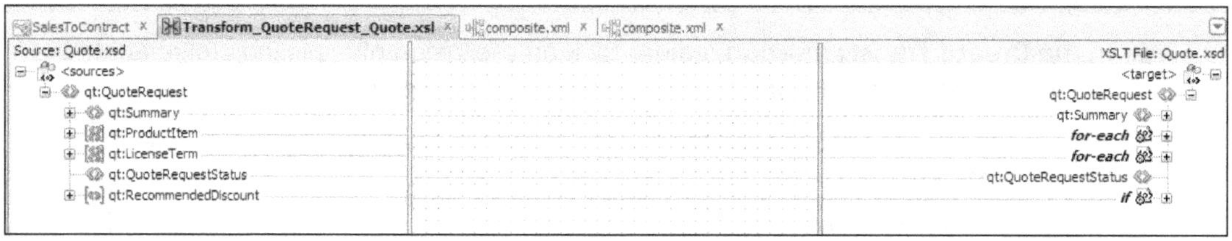

74. You are now at the **SalesToContract** process designer.
75. Remove the **Enter Quote** task and initiate **Quote Script**.
76. An auto link will be created between the **Start** message and the **CustomerCheck** decision rule.
77. Click on the **Start** activity and rename it to `QuoteRequest`.
78. Change the sequence flows.
79. There are two instances when, if the quote gets rejected, it returns to the **salesrepresentative** user through the `EnterQuote` task—when the customer check outcome fails and when the deal or term is rejected.
80. Go to **Component Palette | BPM | Activities | Error End Event.**
81. Click on **Next** to **CustomerCheckOutcome** gateway on the **salesrepresentative** swimlane.
82. Rename `Error End Event` to `EndCustomerCheck`.
83. In the **Implementation** tab, select **BusinessReviewRejectFault** and create a data association for it. Remember, you have created **BusinessReviewRejectionFault** in the *Handling Business Exception in a Sub process* section in *Chapter 8, Exception Management*.
84. Hence, whenever customer check is equal to reject, it would lead to a business fault and would be handled by the **Event** subprocess, which you have created in *Chapter 8*, to handle **BusinessReviewRejectFault**:

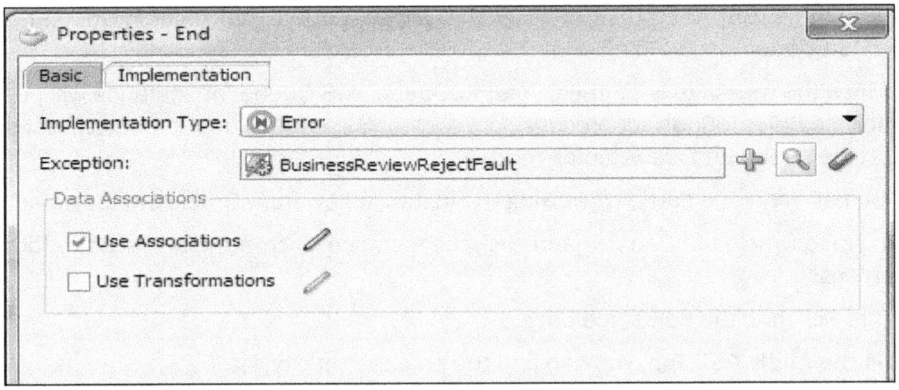

85. Create a conditional sequence flow from **CustomerCheckOutcome** to **EndCustomerCheck** and name it **CustomerRejected** with a simple condition, as follows:

    ```
    CustomerCheck == "REJECT"
    ```

86. Go to **Component Palette** | **BPM** | **Activities** and click on **Error End Event**.
87. Click on in the **Contracts** swimlane, just above the **Approval Outcome** gateway
88. Rename `Error End Event` to `EndDealORTerms`.
89. In the **Implementation** tab, select **BusinessReviewRejectFault** and create a data association for it. Remember, you created **BusinessReviwRejectionFault** in *Chapter 8*.
90. Hence, whenever a deal or term is equal to reject, it would lead to a business fault and would be handled by the Event subprocess, which you have created in *Chapter 8*, to handle **BusinessReviewRejectFault**.
91. Point Deal or Terms Rejected sequence flow to EndDealORTerms End Event.
92. When you have finished this, click on **Save**.
93. Deploy and test.
94. Deploy the project. Refer to the *Deploying the BPM project* section in *Chapter 3, Process Deployment and Testing* if required.

95. Run the `Supplier_ABCS` service. This will post quote message on QuoteReqQueue JMS Queue
96. Once the message is on the QuoteReqQueue JMS Queue, an instance will be created for the SalesToContract process, too, as your SalesToContract process is subscribed to the queue and it's listening to it.
97. You can verify the same by viewing the instance flow from Oracle EM console
98. Log in to Oracle EM Console and click the instance ID created for the SalesToContract process
99. This will open the flow trace page.
100. In the **Audit Trail** Tab, you can find the process activity list.
101. You can verify that an instance has been created for the Start activity, and quote payload can be verified by clicking on the activity details, too:

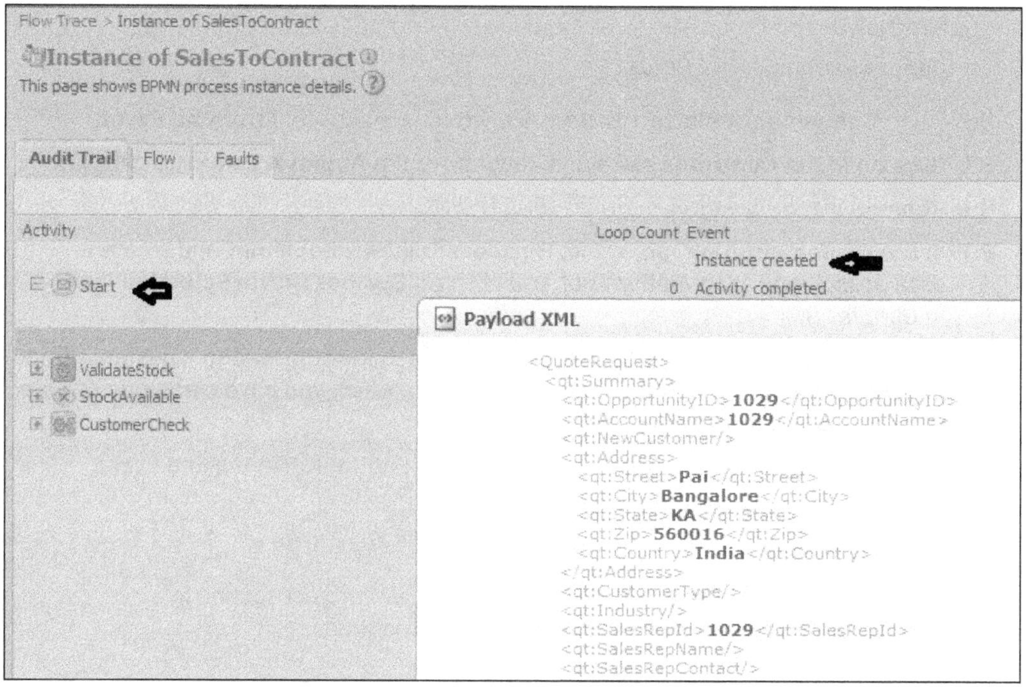

How it works...

Web services, such as BPEL/Mediator Service or OSB, can post messages on JMS Queues, and Oracle BPM can subscribe and listen to those queues. A message on the queue will result in instance creation, based on the incoming message.

When **Supplier_ABCS** puts a Quote Message on **QuoteReqQueue**, **SalesToContract** process is listening to the same queue and hence an instance gets created. You can carry forward the process movement the way you did every time. Log in as a Business Analyst user and approve/reject the queue.

Exposing BPMN process as a service

A common integration requirement is to expose the BPMN process as a service. There are cases when you need to expose Oracle BPM services to be consumed by BPEL, Mediator, and more specifically, by Oracle Service Bus. Exposing process as a webservice is a built-in capability of Oracle BPM. Process instance creation or process notification can be exposed as a service.

In a real world scenario, it would not be practical to have tasks initiated from within the BPM Workspace using the **User Task Initiator** component as you were doing till now. So you would use the `SalesToContract` BPM process as a web service.

All the BPMN processes that define a process interface appear in the SOA Composite.
To connect to a BPMN process using a custom web service client you need the following information:

- Web Service Location: `http://host:port/soa-infra/services/partition/compositDNe!revision/process.service`
- WSDL Location: `http://host:port/soa-infra/services/partition/composite!revision/process.service?WSDL`

How to do it...

In this section, you will learn to expose the BPMN process as a service :

1. Go to **JDeveloper** | **Project** | **Composite.xml**.
2. Delete the **ReadQuoteRequest** service you have created to listen to the JMS queue:

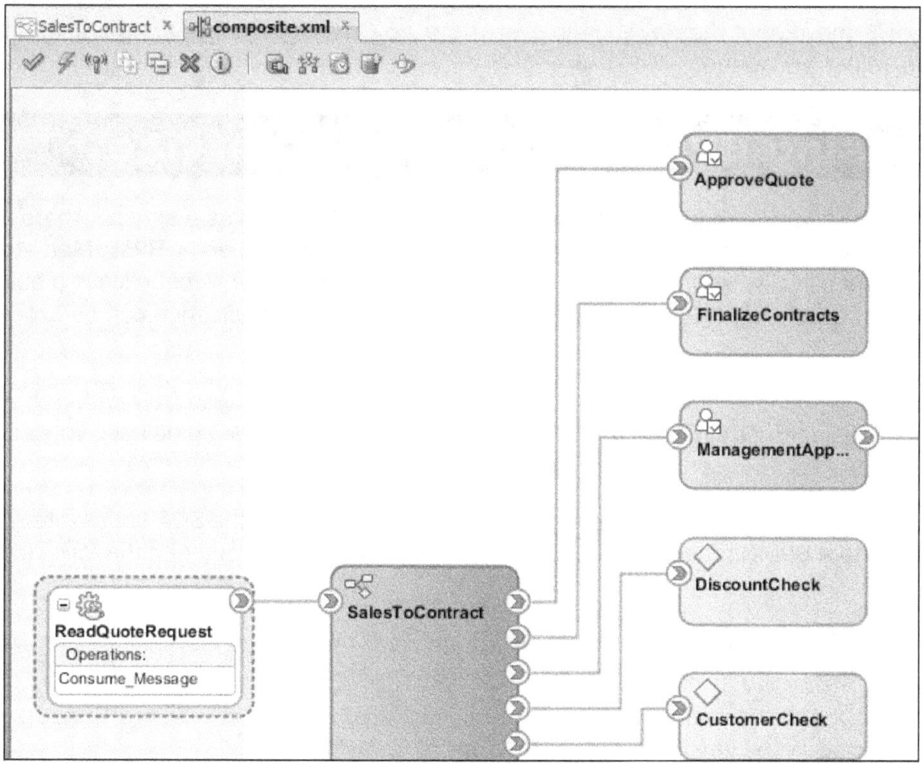

3. Right-click on the **Start** activity and select properties.
4. Select **Define Interface** from the drop down,as **Implementation**, in the **Properties** area.
5. Click the green plus (**+**) icon to add arguments.
6. In the **Create Argument** dialog, enter name as **'QuoteInput'** for the input argument and select type as **Component**.
7. Click on the "browse" button to browse for the components and select **Quote** from the list.

8. Click on **Ok** twice to reach back to Properties of the Message Activity.

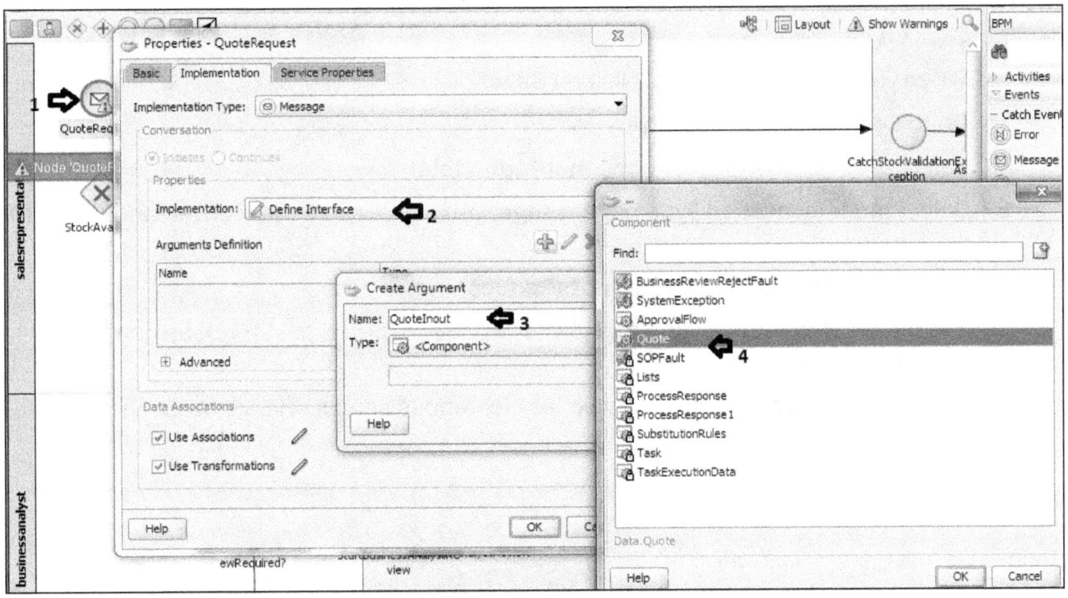

9. Expand the **Advance** section, check the **Asynchronous** operation, and enter `requestoperation` as operation name.

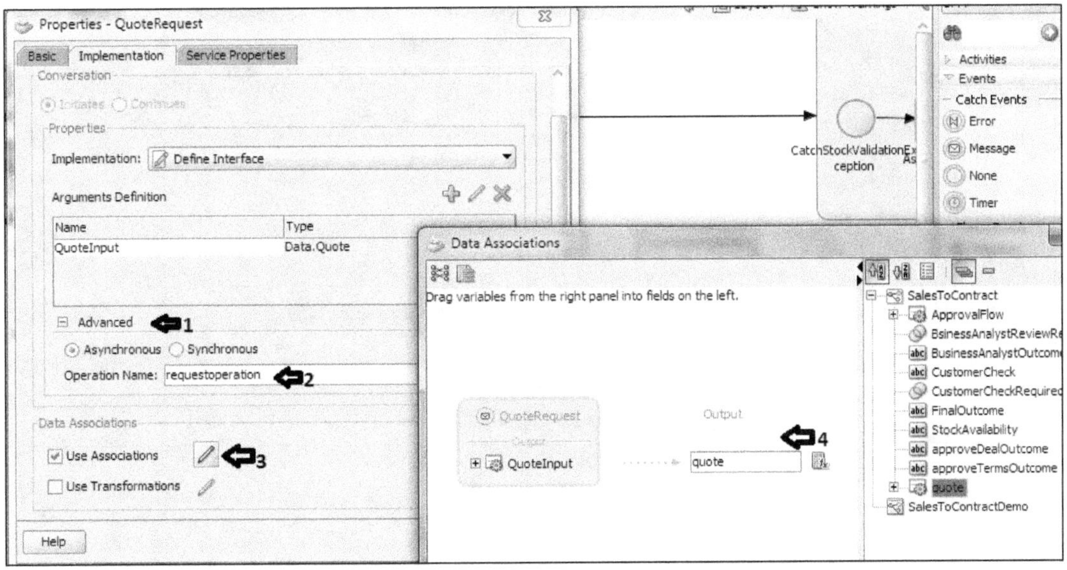

10. Check data association, click on edit pencil button to edit the data association.
11. Drag-and-drop **quote** from objects into the Output QuoteRequest message.
12. Click on **ok** twice.
13. When you have finished this, click on **Save**.
14. Go to **End** activity and right-click on it.
15. Select properties and go to **Implementation** tab.
16. Select **Implementation Type** as **Message**, you will observe that conversation will be continuous.
17. Select **Initiator Node** which is **QuoteRequest** in this case.
18. Expand the **Advance** section and give `operationQuoteCallback` as name of the call-back operation.
19. You BPMN process is now a service, asynchronous service. Hence, would have a call-back operation too:

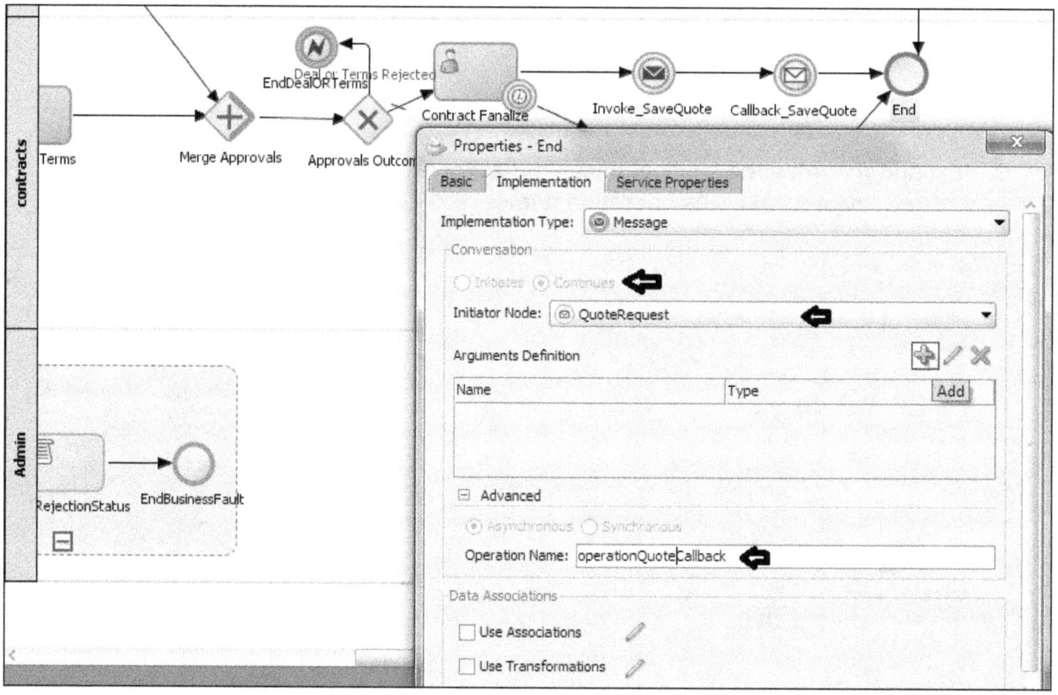

20. Create a data association if you want this BPMN Asynchronous process to return data.
21. Let's assign quote objects as output.
22. When finished, click on **Save**.

How it works...

When you create a BPMN process with a message **Start** event and a message **End** event, it becomes a service provider. This service can be invoked from a web service, web service client, BPEL Service, OSB Service, or from the service task of another BPMN process

The BPMN process that you have converted into a service is an asynchronous service, because the operation type of its message **Start** event is asynchronous. However, if the operation type of its message **Start** event is synchronous, then the BPMN process is a synchronous service.

There's more...

You can test the process at this stage to check if the BPMN process can be invoked by BPEL, OSB, or other services.

You can either use a web service client to test it or you can create a BPEL process and invoke this service. You can even go to Oracle EM console to fetch the endpoint URL of the service and can use the default to test the service.

To connect to a BPMN process using a custom web service client, you need the following information:

- Web Service Location: `http://host:port/soa-infra/services/partition/compositeDN!revision/process.service`
- WSDL Location: `http://host:port/soa-infra/services/partition/composite!revision/process.service?WSDL`

Invoking BPMN process asynchronous Service

1. Log in to Oracle EM Console as WebLogic user
2. Click on the **Service Endpoint and WSDL** button and copy the **Endpoint URI** of the service:

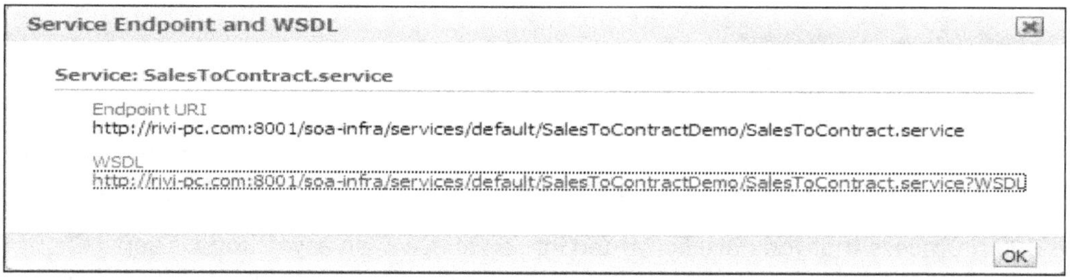

3. Visit the Endpoint URL in a browser.
4. You will find an HTML **Test** page, which you can even use as XML source to enter Quote data.
5. You can verify **requestoperation**, which you provided when implementing the `Start` message event:

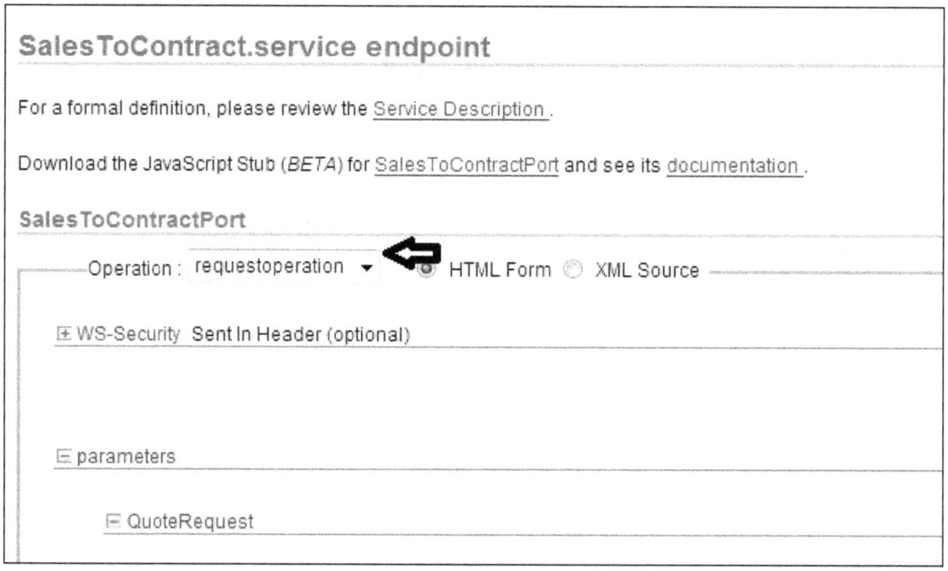

6. Enter Quote data and click on **Invoke**, at the end of this HTML page.
7. You can find an instance being created in a running state.
8. Click on the instance and go to the **Audit Trail** page.
9. Click on the **Audit Trail** tab and verify instance creation and input payload.

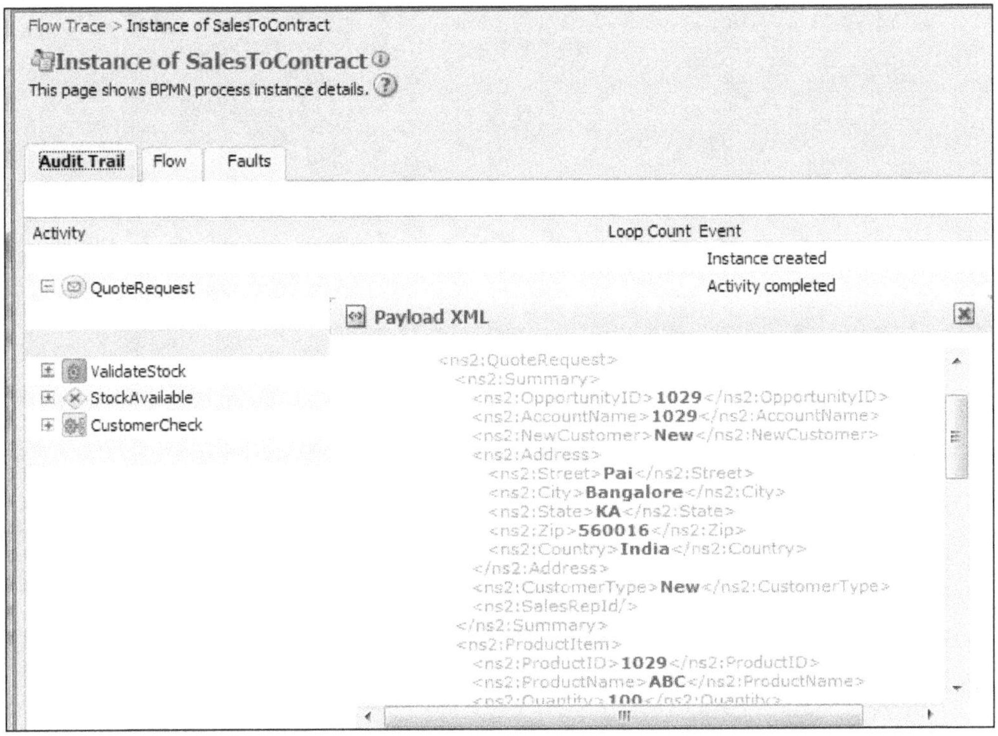

10. Now you have WSDL, which can be used to invoke this BPMN asynchronous service.

10

End User Interaction

So far, you have learnt how to model, implement, and simulate the Oracle BPMN process. Using Enterprise architect, you have created a BPM Roadmap, and with the process analyst you have modeled the flow, which the developer has implemented and deployed. Post deployment, it's the end users who will interact with the process by participating in it. In this chapter, you will focus on end-user interaction in the running process. While learning about end-user interaction, you will also experience the power of Social BPM.

In this chapter, you will interact with BPM Workspace and learn to work with tasks, process tracking, and dashboards. The latter half of this chapter will discuss building a Social Collaborating Team Space using WebCenter spaces. By the end of this chapter, you will have learnt how to create a social collaborating space, announcements, discussions, blogs, and polls. You will cover the following topics:

- Interacting through BPM Workspace
- Working on Process Instance
- Interacting through Process Spaces

Introduction

End users are participants who perform interactive activities. Oracle BPM flow will automatically route these tasks to a participant based on his/her role and they have to log in (either to Oracle BPM Workspace or Process Spaces) and perform their activity. You have already witnessed how a participant with a *salesrepresentative* role will enter the Quote. And then, if required, a participant with a *businessanalyst* role will review the process and will perform the activity on the task, which is to either accept or reject the Quote.

End user interaction with a running process is performed by logging in to either Oracle BPM Workspace or Process Spaces. With Business Process Workspace, you as an end user can perform tasks, track process instances, and monitor performance, workload, and business indicators. **Process Space** is a workspace build on top of Oracle WebCenter Spaces. Process workspace enables a more effective and a more productive BPM.

In this chapter, you will first learn to work on Oracle BPM workspace and will later explore Process Spaces. Different categories of users/participants can interact with the running process using Workspace.

To enable collaboration within the context of process and process instance, Oracle Process Spaces, which is based on Oracle WebCenter group spaces, offers different types of collaboration communities. These communities offer to share and collaborate the following, within the context of business process with the process team:

- **Process space**: This is meant for task collaboration and is used to view details for all running processes
- **Instance space**: This is meant for instance collaboration and is used to view details of all running instances and can share through discussions, documents, wikis, and blogs
- **Modeling space**: This is meant to collaborate on the design of the model. Participants involved in design can share and collaborate on the designed model

This ensures that right set of people are involved, from process design and modeling to end users, who can participate, collaborate, and share.

Interacting through BPM Workspace

Oracle BPM workspace is a web interface for end-user participation/interaction. You can perform a number of activities using Workspace. However, in this section, you will learn about working on Tasks.

How it works...

In this section, you will master interaction through BPM workspaces:

I. Working with Task Details:

1. Log in to the Oracle BPM workspace, at `http://localhost:8001/bpm/workspace`.
2. The Task is already initialised by a *salesrepresentative* user. Enter with *businessanalyst* credentials.

3. Click on **Actions**, and you can act on this assigned task from here too, in addition to the **Tasks** page you have been using till now:

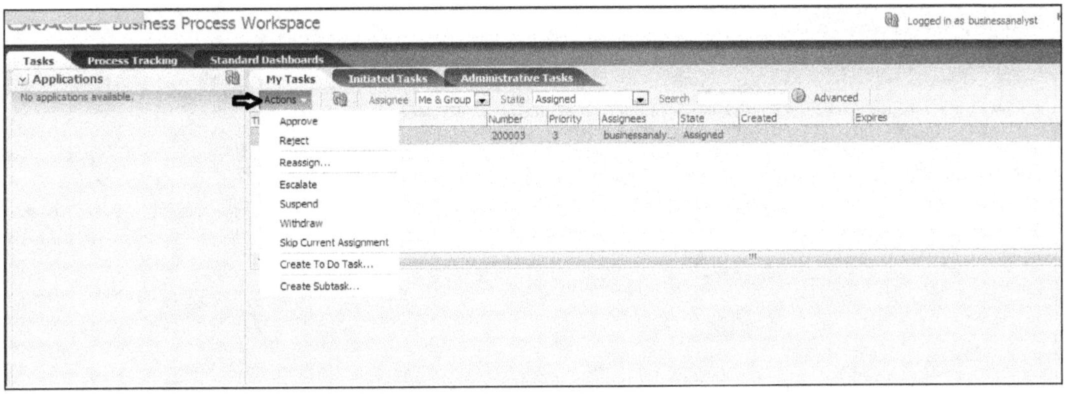

4. You can even **Reassign**, **Escalate**, **Suspend**, or **Withdraw** it.

II. Customizing Task pages:

You can customize the **Tasks** pages; for example, you can add views, select/add new columns, and display a part of task, too:

1. Add a new column. Visit the *Flexfields* section in the next chapter to add a new column to the task.
2. *Flexfields* will store the custom attribute values coming from task Payload and would make the new column available to the custom view. For mapped attributes to get populated, administrators create mapped attribute mappings by specifying a label for the mapped attribute to be populated and map the payload attribute that contains the data to the label.
3. You will find an `AccountName` column with `FusionNX` as the value:

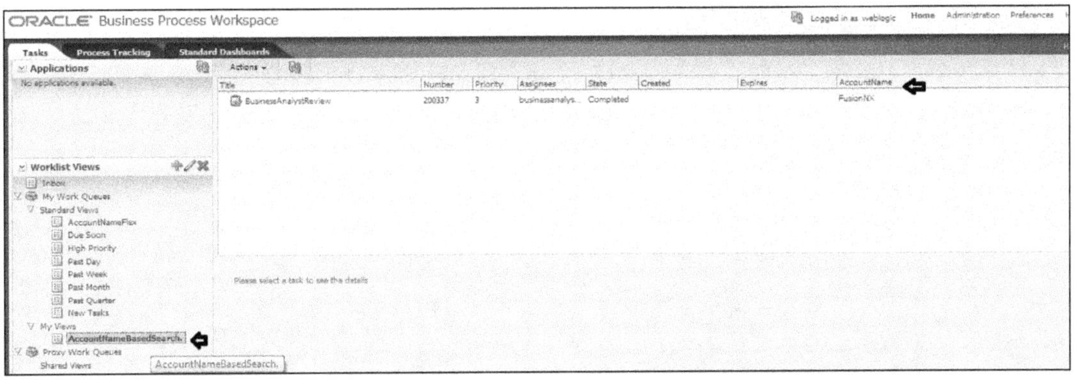

4. Click on the **Advanced** tab, as shown in the following screenshot, and a search Box Pop-Up.

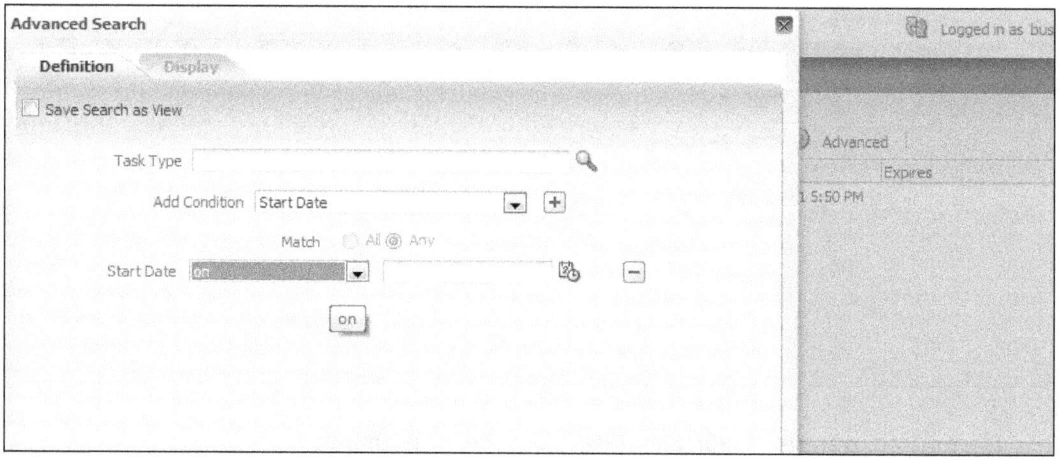

5. You can click on the "browse" button next to **Task Type** and add conditions to base the search on
6. You can check the **Save** box, to save this search too.

III. Create Custom Worklist view:

1. Select **Inbox** and click on the green plus (**+**) icon in **Worklist Views**, as shown in the following screenshot.
2. A **Create User View** page gets displayed:

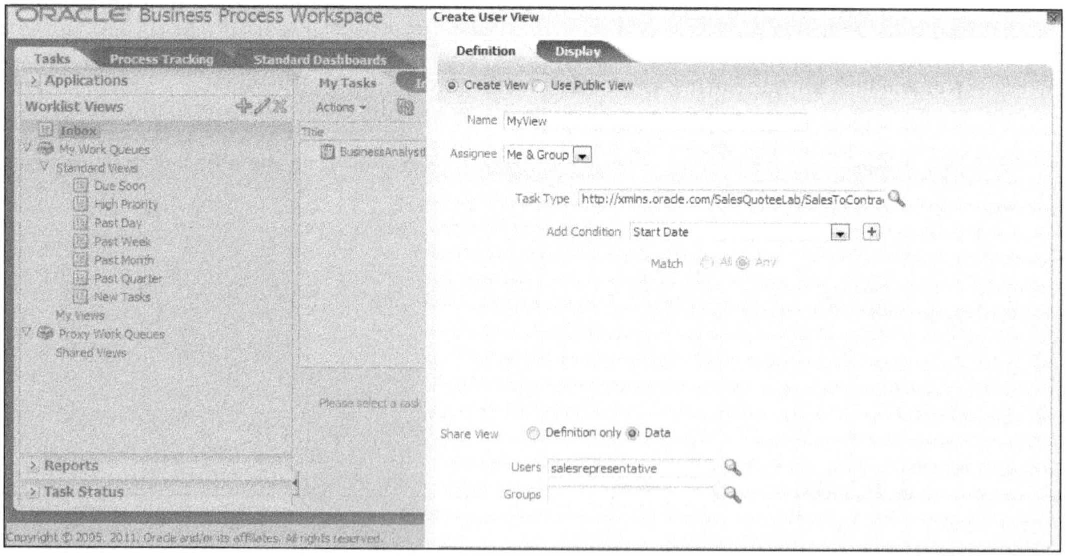

3. Enter `MyView` as **Name** and let it be a new View.
4. Select **Me & Group** as **Assigne** and BusinessAnalystUI as **Task Type**.
5. Enter `salesrepresentative` as the users which can share data and your view.
6. You will find that a new View, with the name **My View**, is created and that your tasks are present in it, too:

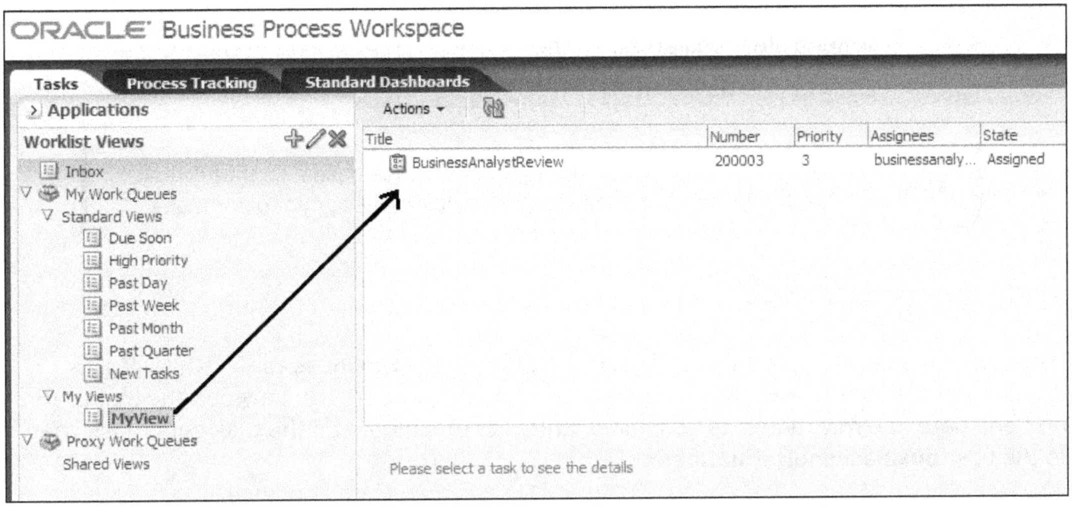

7. Log in to BPM Workspace as the user **salesrepresentative**, and you will find **MyView** with data shared in it:

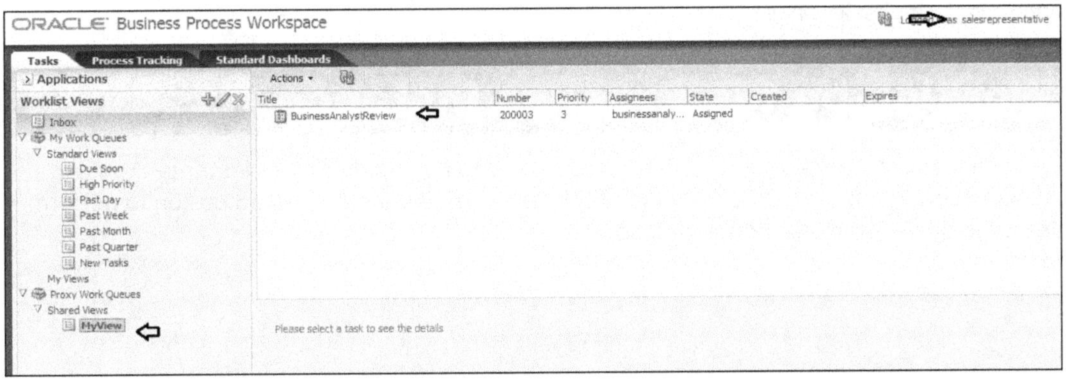

IV. Creating Rules:

1. Rules act on tasks. They can be designed to either act on a specific Task.

2. You will learn to create a Rule in section, *BPM Admin—Setting Rules* in the next chapter. Here let's enable a Vacation Rule.

    - Click on the Preferences in BPM Workspace while logged in as *salesrepresentative* user
    - Click on **Rules**.
    - Check Enable Vacation Period.
    - Enter a start and an end date.
    - Click on the **Save** button.

> You can inbuilt reassignment policy on such cases, so that if Task Assignment falls in vacation period, it gets assigned to someone.

How it works...

When the rule meets its filter conditions, it is executed. If a **BusinessAnalystUI** task gets assigned to the **businessanalyst** user and this task assignment falls between the start date and end date, the rule meets its conditions and gets executed, and the task gets reassigned to the user **businessanalystmanager**.

Flexfields will store the custom attribute values coming from task payload and would make it available to the custom view. For a mapped attribute to get populated, administrators create mapped attribute mappings by specifying a label for the mapped attribute to be populated and map the payload attribute that contains the data to the label. You get those labels as columns in the **Tasks** page.

Working on the Process Instance

From the **Process Tracking** tab in Workspace you can initiate a process instance. You can also add comments and attachments to that instance. Use the **Advanced** button to perform searches based on roles, status, and so on.

How to do it...

In this section, you will cover how to check the graphical audit trail of a process instance:

1. Click on the Process Instance, as shown in the following screenshot.
2. Expand the **Audit Trail** section, on **Details** page.
3. Click on **Graphical**, to view the graphical details of the Process Instance:

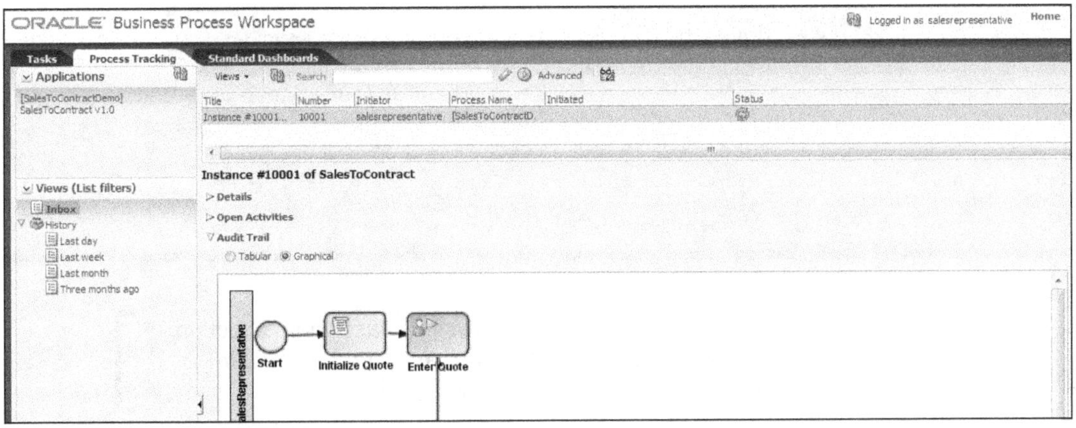

There's more...

In this section, you will unleash the features of BPM Workspace Standard Dashboard.

Working with Standard Dashboard

Standard Dashboards are graphical data based on process cube schema. They display the metrics gathered during the execution of a process. With these dashboards, you can analyze the workload and performance of the participant. You can even analyze the number of process instances waiting for completion and the average time taken per process.

1. Click on the **Standard Dashboard** tab within BPM Workspace.
2. Click on the **Show** drop-down list and select any dashboard, for example, **Performance per participant**.

3. Click on the left panel to view details that will display average time taken per participant:

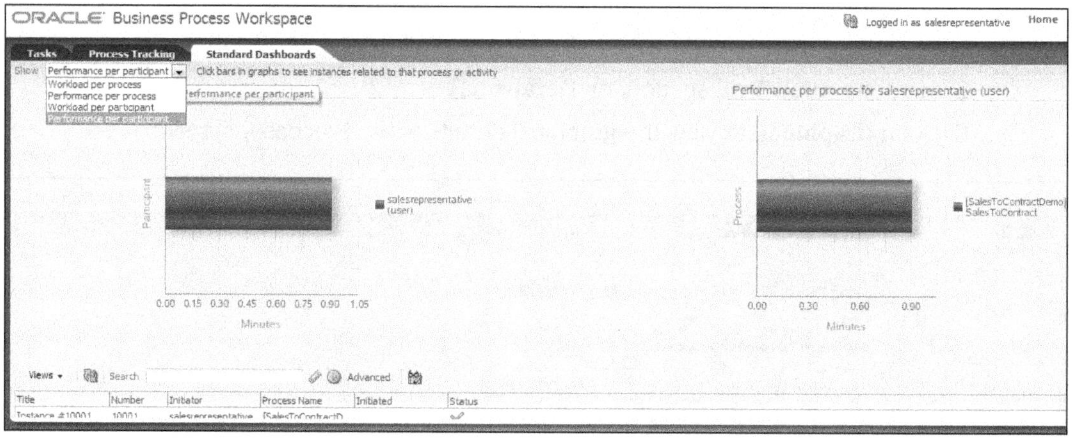

> Check the *Deploy and create custom dashboards* section, in *Chapter 11, Manage, Monitor, and Administer BPM Process* to create custom dashboards.

Interacting through Process Spaces

If you need a team-based site along with your enterprise portals, or if you wish to connect with people, collaborate content and business objects, the answer is the ready-to-use application Oracle WebCenter Spaces. With WebCenter Spaces you can customize the look and feel of your pages, create pages, add content, publish and edit content stored in Oracle **Universal Content Management** (**UCM**), manage tasks, projects, people, and their content, and much more. WebCenter Spaces has Process Spaces built on top of it.

> Process Spaces = Process Workspace + WebCenter.

Process Spaces provides Process Workspace, Process Modelling Spaces, and Process Instance Spaces:

- **Process Workspace**: This has a **Process Tracking** page to provide process-related information. You have witnessed all these features in Oracle BPM Workspace. It's quite similar to that. You can act on a task, filter a task, add documents to a task, participate in discussions, and view recent activities in a process space.

- **Process Modelling Spaces**: With this, you can collaborate on process definitions. It contains a process catalog, which displays processes represented as squares.
- **Process Instance Spaces**: This allows you to collaborate on a process instance. Here you can view all the instance details of the process, such as audit trail information, details of the instance, open activities, comments and attachments, calendars, and other stuff, such as initiate, filter, or cancel a instance from process workspaces.

In this section, you will create a team site where members can collaborate. FusionNX team with Sales Interest needs to exchange information in the form of ideas, opinions, and so on. To help groups to stay connected, you will use templates that cater your needs. These templates are provided by Oracle WebCenter Spaces. You will build a team site to explore WebCenter Spaces' social networking capabilities.

How to do it...

In this section, you will master the art of interacting with process spaces.

I. Create a Space:

1. Log in to Oracle WebCenter Spaces, at `http://localhost:8888/webcenter`.
2. Click on **Spaces**, on the banner and click on **Create Space**. This will open a **Create a Space** dialog.
3. Enter `FusionNXConnect` as the name and a key to enable people to find this space. Let it be `FusionNXConnect`:

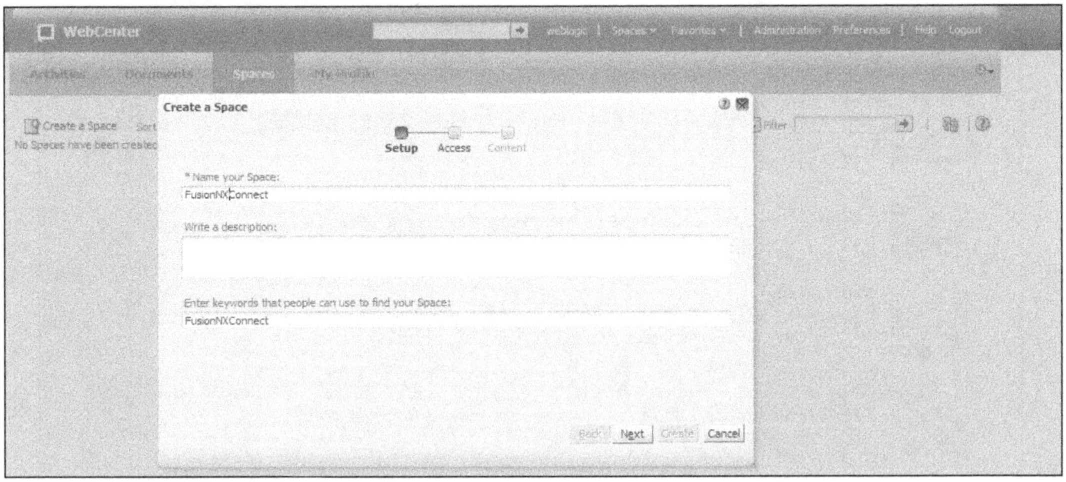

4. Click on **Next**.
5. On the **Access** dialog, enter a URL for the Space. Complete it by entering `FusionNXConnect`.

6. Your direct URL to access the FusionNXConnect team site will be `http://localhost:8888/webcenter/spaces/FusionNXConnect`:

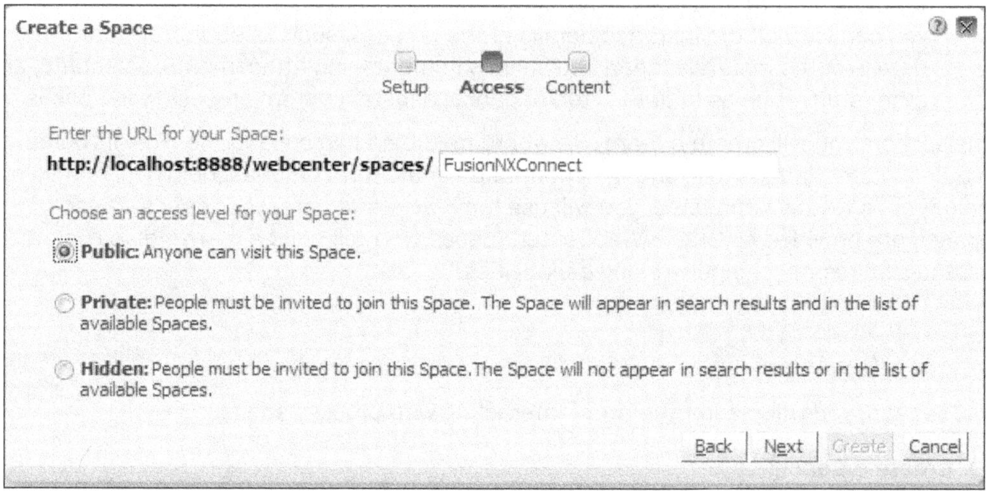

7. Let the access level be **Public**.
8. In the list of the templates, choose **Team Site**, as this template has services such as announcements, discussions, events, and so on, for a team to collaborate.

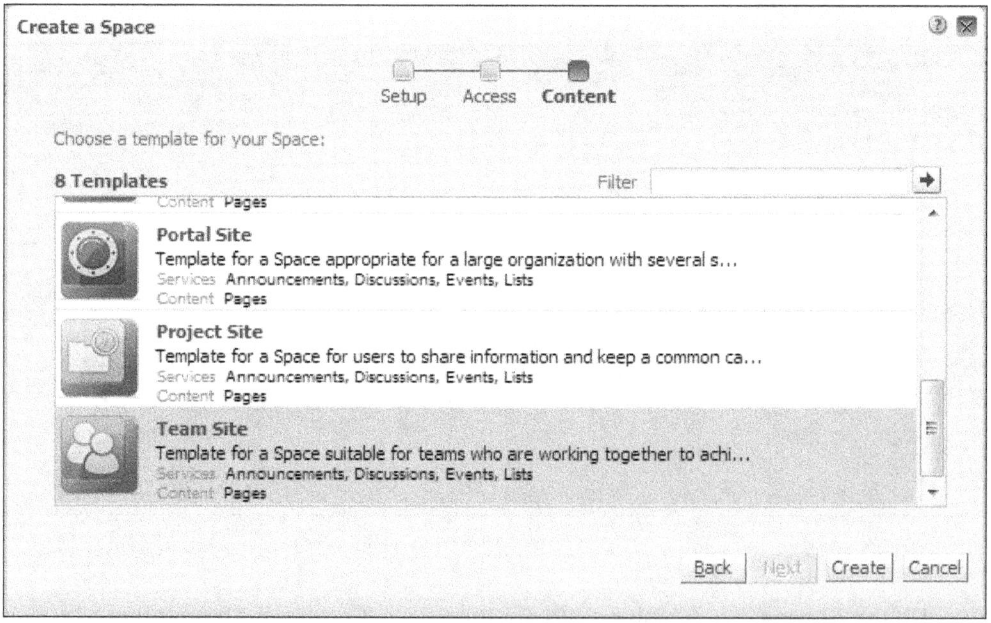

9. Click on **Create**, and a team site is created.

II. Add members:

1. You are in the **FusionNXConnect** Space. Click on **Members** in the left-hand navigation. This will open **FusionNXConnect - Settings** page
2. Click on the **Members** tab
3. Click on **Add People** to add members.
4. Search for the `salesrepresentative` user, and once it appears in the list of names, select **Participant** as a role and click on the **Add** button.
5. Repeat step 4 for the `businessanalyst` user, too:

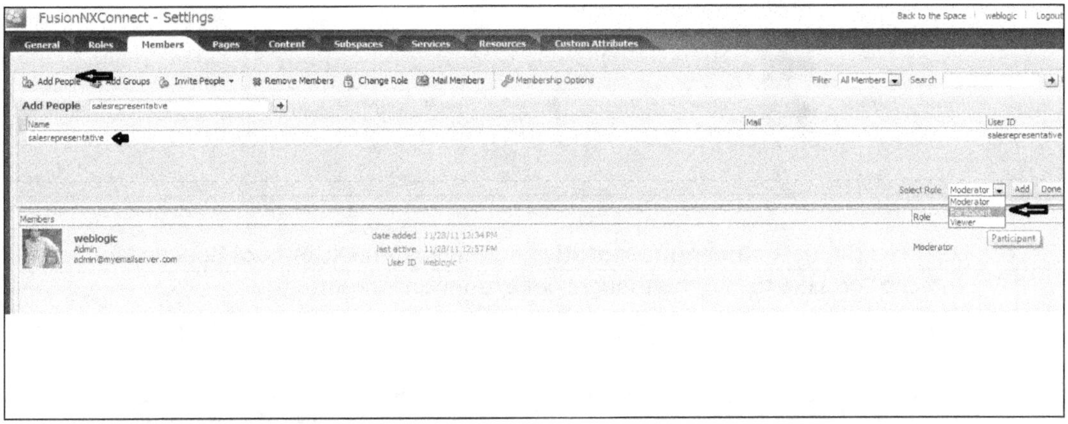

6. Click on **Back to the Space** on the top-right of the banner, and you are back to the FusionNXConnect Space team site.

III. Create announcements to share thoughts and ideas:

1. You must be aware that announcements must be used to share your thoughts and ideas on various social networking sites, such as Facebook, Orkut, LinkedIn, and so on. BPM WebCenter Spaces lets you do the same.
2. You are at the **FusionNXConnect Spaces** home page. Write something to share with your members.
3. Say `Hi Everyone, Welcome to FusionNX Connect..!!.`

4. Click on the **Publish** button, as shown in the following screenshot.
5. The message gets displayed in the banner:

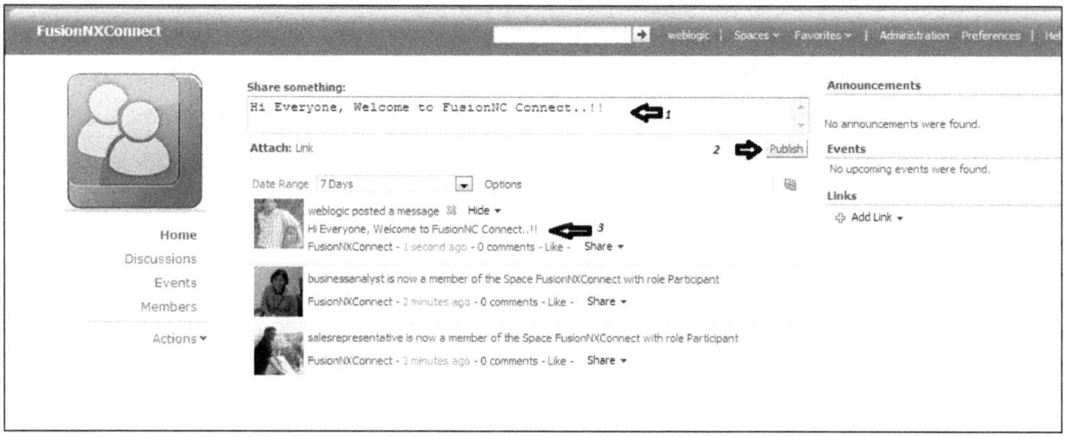

6. Log in as the user **salesrepresentative**, to the **FusionNXConnect** Spaces team site, and click on **Like** to like the thought/idea/announcement.
7. You can also comment on the shared content, as shown in the following screenshot:

IV. Create an announcement:

1. Log back in to **FusionNXConnect** Spaces as the user **weblogic**.
2. Click on **Action** | **Manage** and select **Announcements**. You will find that there are no announcements in the banner now:

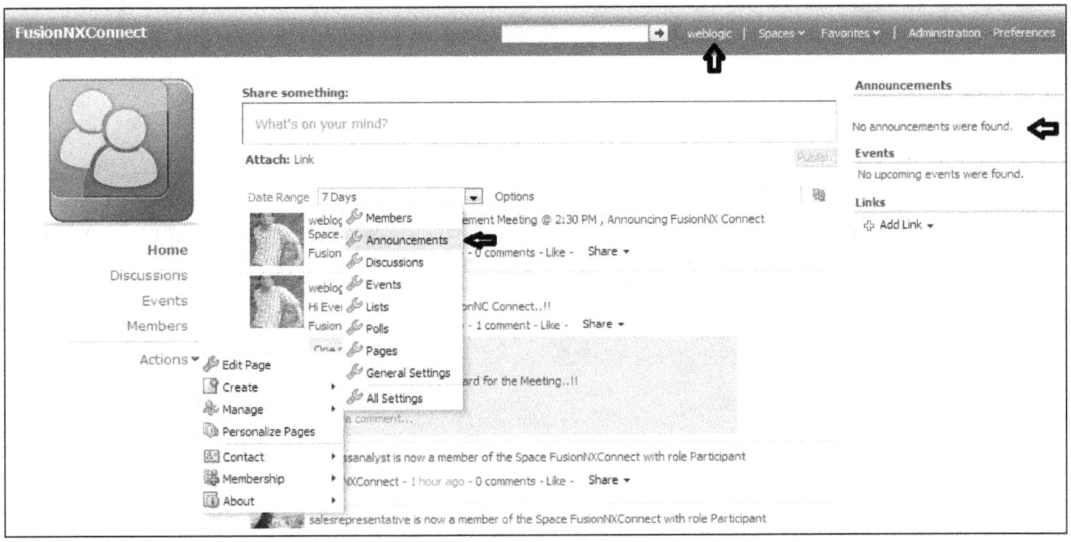

3. In the **Create Announcement** dialog, enter the subject and an announcement, as shown in the following screenshot.
4. You can fix a time when you want this announcement to be active and can even fix an expiry date for the announcement:

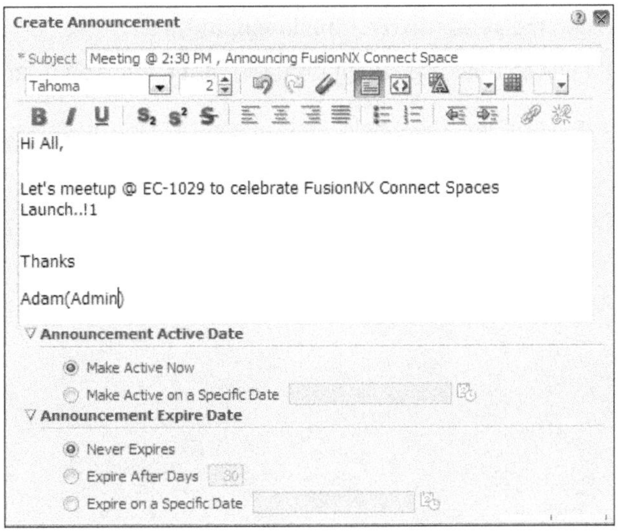

5. Click on **OK** in the dialog
6. Now, you can verify the announcement that appears on the FusionNXConnect banner.

> Basically, you can use events to schedule a meeting, and **Announcement** to perform an announcement, such as the starting of a team site or an outing, and so on.

V. Create Discussion:

1. Log in as the user **weblogic** to the **FusionNXConnect** team site.
2. Click on **Discussions**.
3. Click on **Create Topic** and enter topic details, as shown in the following screenshot. Click on the **Create** button to create the discussion:

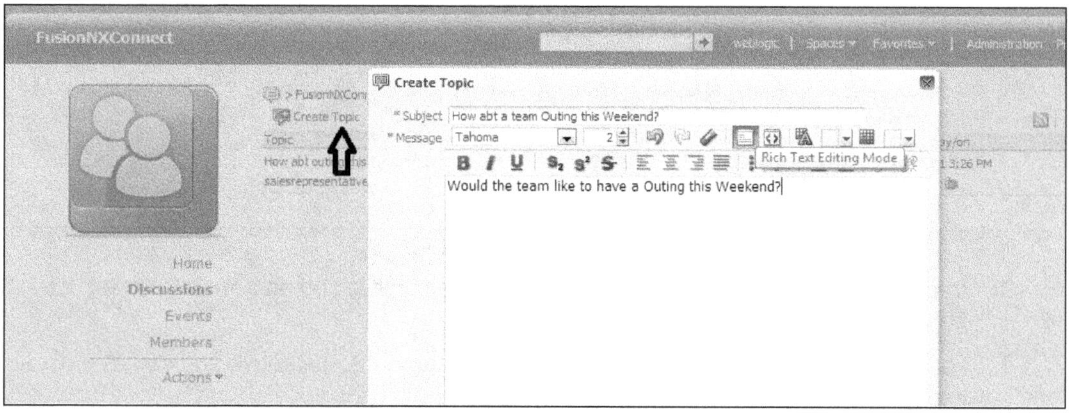

4. Log out and then log in as the user **businessanalyst**.
5. You can find a link to this discussion on the banner. Click on it, and a dialog appears.

6. You can click on **Reply Topic** to respond on this discussion:

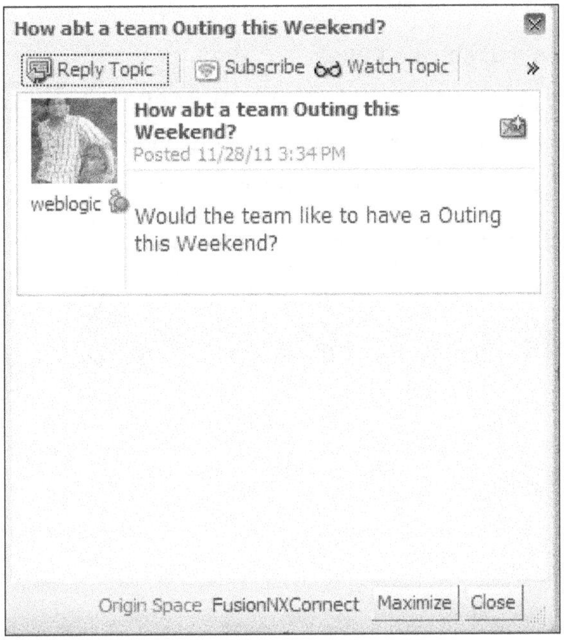

How it works...

Here, you have explored social networking features in WebCenter Spaces. With WebCenter Spaces, you can even build a portal site.

There's more...

If you have UCM configured, a **Document** tab also appears in the same template. Also, you can create a wiki, blog, and so on.

Creating a blog

To create a blog, follow the ensuing steps:

1. Click on **Blogs** in the panel.
2. Select the **Team Blog** page.
3. Click on **New Post**, to create a new blog.
4. Enter title and text, and click on the **Create** button.
5. You will find that a new blog is created.

Creating a poll

To create a poll, follow the ensuing steps:

1. Click on **Actions** and choose **Polls**.
2. Give a name to poll such as `Is Social BPM an Excellent Idea?`
3. Use green icon on the right, to create a poll question in the **Design** tab.
4. You can schedule the poll and perform settings for it.

Poll is an excellent mechanism to infuse polling in the space:

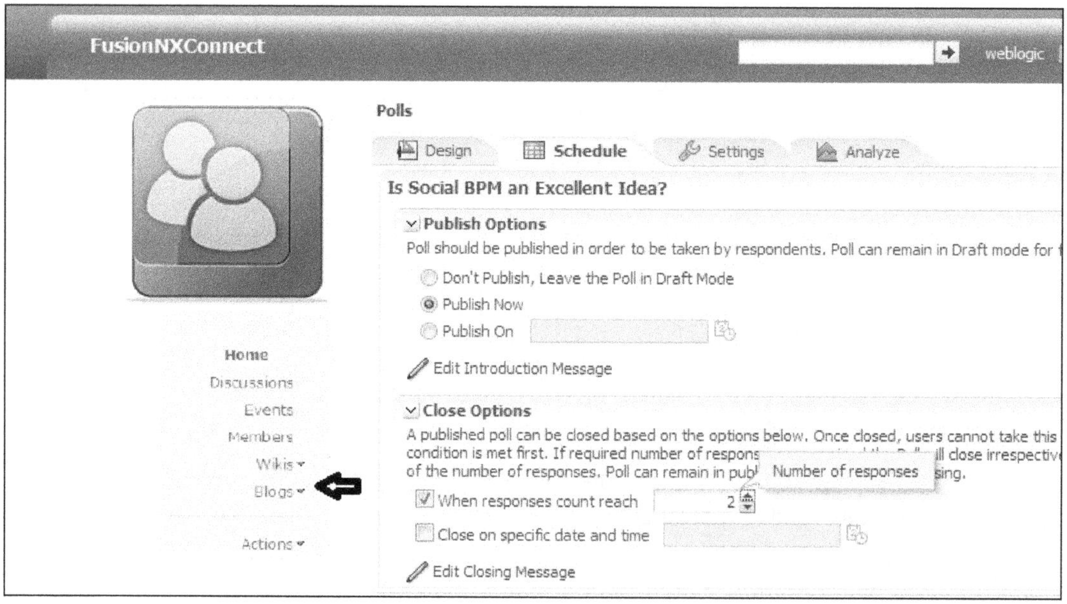

Adding log and settings

1. On the **FusionNXConnect** page, click on **Actions** | **General Settings**.
2. In the **Display** setting, browse for the icon and logo.

3. You can apply a new skin and can even set a language for this page:

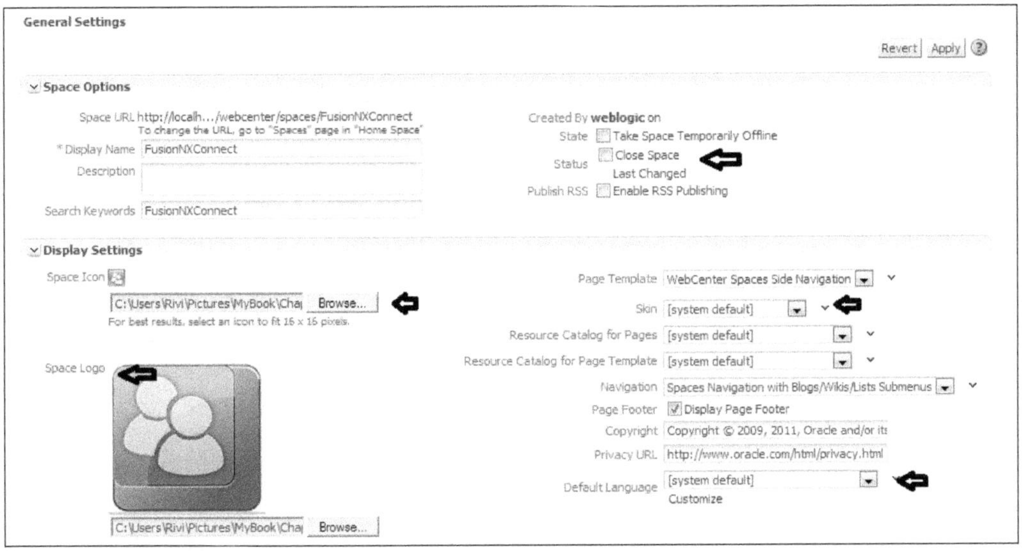

4. Click on **Apply**, when you are finished with the changes.
5. The final team site with social collaboration, will look like the following screenshot:

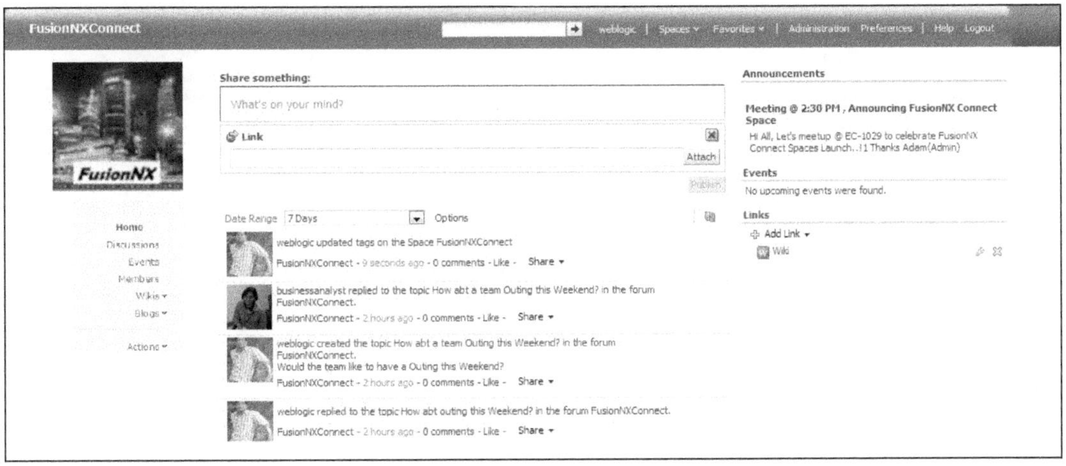

11

Manage, Monitor and Administer BPM Process

You have modeled the process, implemented it, performed a simulation, and deployed and tested the process. Process owners will want to monitor the running process to see how it is performing. They need to have an insight into the working of the process in order to track process performance, access process design, process design refinements, and correlate process performance with related business activities and KPIs. BPM and SOA administrators manage the deployed application and they ensure that it is running properly and also resolve any issues that occur.

In this chapter, you will first look at process analytics, monitoring, and then administration. You will configure process analytics by specifying the business indicators to the processes in your project, and assign values to them, identify sampling points for capturing business indicators, configure the project to use BPM Cubes or Oracle BAM or both, and then use BPM workspace or BAM architect to configure custom dashboards.

As a BPM administrator you will manage BPM roles, Organization Units, and approval groups, and perform a few other BPM-process-specific administrative tasks. As a SOA administrator you will configure and monitor the whole SOA suite system along with its deployments. Their main tool is Enterprise Manager.

We will first look at SOA Admin tasks and then switch to BPMN Admin tasks.

In this chapter we will look at the following:

- Creating a custom dashboard in the BPM workspace
    - Create business indicators
    - Data assignment to business indicators
    - Create measurement marks
    - Add counters
    - Deploy and create custom dashboards
- Configuring BAM Architect to create custom dashboards
    - Create a Data object folder in Oracle BAM Architect
    - Enable BAM in a BPMN project
    - Create BAM data objects
    - Create BAM custom dashboards
    - View custom dashboards
- SOA Admin—Configuring SOA infrastructure properties
- SOA Admin—Monitoring SOA infrastructure
- SOA Admin—Administering BPMN applicationdeployment
- SOA Admin—Fault recovery for BPMN processes
- SOA Admin—Configuring notification settings
- BPM Admin—Integrating Oracle BPM with Oracle Business Activity Monitoring
- BPM Admin—Managing roles, Organization Units, and groups
- BPM Admin—Setting rules
- BPM Admin—Using flex fields/mapped attributes
- BPM Admin—Monitoring BPM processes.

Introduction

Business Process Analytics enables you to monitor the performance of your deployed processes. It measures the key performance indicators in your project and stores them in a database. Process analysts can view the metrics stored in the Process Analytics databases using workspace dashboards or Oracle BAM, depending on the database you select to store the information.

Process developers can define process specific metrics using business indicators. **Business indicators** are a special type of project Data object that the BPMN service engine stores in the Process Analytics databases when it runs the BPMN processes.

BPM Suite 11g has an audit service that continuously audits process metrics and user defined business indicators. This audit information is pushed to process STAR schema or BAM Data objects. You can then create customized dashboards ontop of the process STAR schema or the information can be consumed by external business intelligence tools such as OBIEE and others.

Oracle BPEL has sensors and it can be monitored on BAM dashboards; AIA has audit logging mechanisms which you have to invoke, to get the information logged. In BPM you have BAM Data Objects as well as BPM Process Cubes.

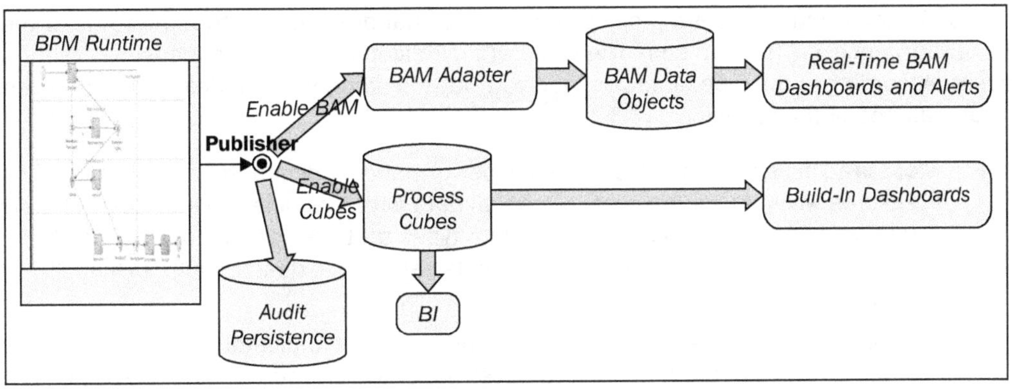

The following list describes the typical tasks you perform when you use Process Analytics in a BPM project:

- Adding business indicators to the processes in your project and assigning values to them
- Identifying sampling points for capturing business indicators
- Configuring the project to use BPM cubes or Oracle BAM, or both
- Deploying your project
- Using BPM workspace or BAM architect to configure custom dashboards

I. Adding business indicators to the processes in your project and assign values to them

Process Analyst will define the key performance indicators and process metrics you want to monitor while developing your process. There are standard predefined metrics for activities and processes, including active instance count and average time to completion, broken out by process, activity, and participant. Supported predefined measures are the number of active instances, average time to complete an activity, average time to complete a process, and so on. The supported predefined dimensions are process, activity, and participants.

You can also define custom measures according to your needs. To define custom measures, you use business indicators. The different types of business indicators enable you to measure specific values, keep track of categories, or count the times an instance completes one or more activities. Oracle BPM provides you with a set of predefined cubes you can use to store the Process Analytics data. Cubes are a structure used to organize a database, so that it enables you to analyze data in real time and view it from multiple perspectives. You can also choose to store these data to Oracle BAM or use both systems simultaneously.

You can use business indicators to store the value of an indicator you want to measure in your process, or to store a category you want to use to group the values you measured in your process. Business indicators are project Data objects that are used to store the value of the KPIs of your process. They can store the value of an indicator you want to measure in your process. According to the type of information you want to store, you can define your business indicator as one of the following:

- **Measure** This stores the value of a key performance indicator that you can measure. Measures will help you capture numerical data which signifies a value that will help you in analytics. Measures only allow data types that are continuous. You must use them with measurement marks such as sales total, deal amount, discount percentage, and so on.
- **Dimension** This stores the value of a key performance indicator that you can use to group the values of the measure business indicators in your process. It specifies how the data needs to be picked. Dimensions store the value of a KPI that you can use to group the values of the measure business indicators in your process. If you use a continuous data value to define a dimension, then you must add at least one range. The Process Analytics database only stores the range value if the data value is a continuous one such as region, order type, deal range, or industry type.
- **Counters** These are the type of measures used to keep track of the number of times an instance completes a certain activity. You must use them with counter marks.

II. Identifying sampling points for capturing business indicators

At runtime, when the BPMN Service Engine runs the activity in the process, it stores data about the process in the BPM Cubes and Oracle BAM Data Objects. This data comes from the sampling points defined in the project.

Add measurement marks or counter marks in the processes where you want to track the value of the business indicators and configure sampling points generation for the project or process.

Sampling points are broadly divided into two types:

1. Built-in sampling point—configured at project, process, and activity level:
   - Generate sampling for all user tasks
   - Generate sampling for start/end of process
   - Generate sampling for start/end of activity

2. User defined sampling point:
    - **Measurement marks** store the following data in the Process Analytics databases:
        - The value of the process default measures
        - The value of the measure business indicators associated to that measurement mark
        - The value of the dimensions defined in the process
    - **Single measurement** sample business indicators at a specific point in the process
    - **Counter mark** is used to track the number of times the instance runs the particular activity interval (start and end)

This will measure a business indicator in a section of your process. Always use these measurement marks to monitor critical sections of your process.

III. Configuring the project to use BPM Cubes or Oracle BAM, or both

Oracle BPM provides a set of predefined cubes you can use to monitor the activity of your processes. These predefined process cubes are enabled by default. If cubes are enabled when the BPMN Service Engine runs the processes in your project, then it populates the cubes. You can then view the data stored in these cubes using the dashboards provided by the BPM workspace application.

The BPMN Service Engine populates the predefined cubes each time it runs an activity or completes a process. The engine uses the sampling points configuration you defined, to populate the cubes. If you configure a process to not generate sampling points, then the BPMN Service Engine does not store this information in the predefined cubes.

You can use Oracle BAM to monitor the activity of the process in your project, leveraging the capabilities of Oracle BAM while using Oracle BPM. When you run a process that has Oracle BAM enabled, the BPMN service engine populates the Oracle BAM database with information about the business indicators measured in that process. The BPMN Service Engine generates this information based on the sampling points preference you defined in your project.

IV. Deploying the project

Refer to the section *Deploying the project* mentioned in *Chapter 3, Process Deployment and Testing*, to learn more about the deployment mechanism.

V. Use BPM workspace or BAM Architect to configure custom dashboards

After publishing, the application business analysts can use the default dashboards BPM workspace provided or create custom dashboards to view the metrics the BPMN service engine gathered while running BPMN processes.

End users can create custom (user defined) dashboards by defining graphs in the BPM workspace and assembling those graphs to define a dashboard.

You can even use BAM Architect to create a BAM dashboard, with the BPM business indicators defined in your process. You can enable BAM Architect to create BAM dashboards with the following steps:

Create Data object folder in Oracle BAM Architect.

Enable BAM in BPMN project.

Create BAM data objects.

Create BAM custom dashboards.

View custom dashboards.

There are two types of administrators in Oracle BPM:

- SOA Administrators: They configure and monitor the whole SOA Suite system along with its deployments

  Tool: Enterprise Manager

- BPM Administrators: They manage BPM roles, Organization Units, Approval Groups, and perform other BPM process-specific administrative tasks

  Tools: They use Business Process Composer, Business Process Workspace, and Oracle Enterprise Manager

SOA Administration includes configuring SOA Infrastructure properties, monitoring SOA Infrastructure, deploying SOA Composite applications, monitoring SOA Composite application, fault recovery for BPMN Processes, and notification settings.

BPMN Administrator activities includes configuring BPMN Process Service Engine properties, integrating Oracle BPM with Oracle Business Activity Monitoring, monitoring BPMN process service components and engines, managing the Oracle BPMN service components and engines, and flex fields.

Creating a custom dashboard in BPM workspace

You will analyze the quantity ordered to understand its distribution across regions and the price range.

In this scenario, you add a counter to count the number of times the quote needs to be revised.

You will use Script Activity to assign data to the business indicators.

Open the version of the project youcreated in *Chapter 8, Exception Management*. For the sake of simplicity, remove the validation section and **CustomerCheck** rules. Remove the **Exception** section and the process should look as follows:

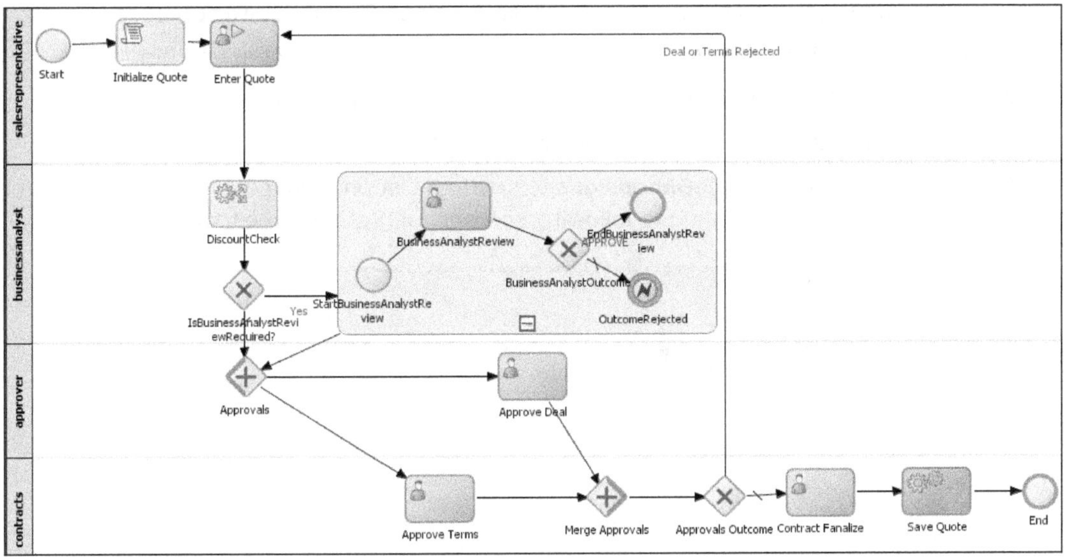

The process will now allow the **salesrepresentative** user to **Enter Quote**, and then the discounts will be checked.

If the discount is greater than 30 percent and customer type is *Premium*, then Business Practice Review is not required. The process token will move ahead for **Approve deal** and **Approve Terms**. Once approve deal and approve terms are approved, the contract waits to be finalized. Once it is finalized, a quote is saved to a file location.

Measurement marks are used to measure a business indicator of type **Measure** at a certain point in the process or in a section of the process. You can use one measurement mark to measure multiple business indicators.

When storing the value of a measure business indicator, the BPMN Service Engine also stores the value of the dimensions you defined in your process. Later on, when you build the dashboards to monitor your process, you can use these dimensions to group the values into different categories. For example, in the Sales Quote process you might want to view the total quantity ordered by region. Measurement marks are of single measurement type, interval start type, and interval stop type.

How to do it...

I. Create business indicator

1. Open JDeveloper in **default** role.
2. Go to **Application Navigator** | **Project**, and click on **SalesToContract** process.
3. Go to **View** | **Structure** to open the structure window, if it's not open after step 2.
4. In the **Structure Windows**, right click on **Business Indicators**.
5. Click **New** | **Dimension** to open the create dimension dialog.
6. Enter name **PriceRangeDimensions** to create a List price range dimension and enter range values as shown in the following screenshot. Set the **Type** to **Int**:

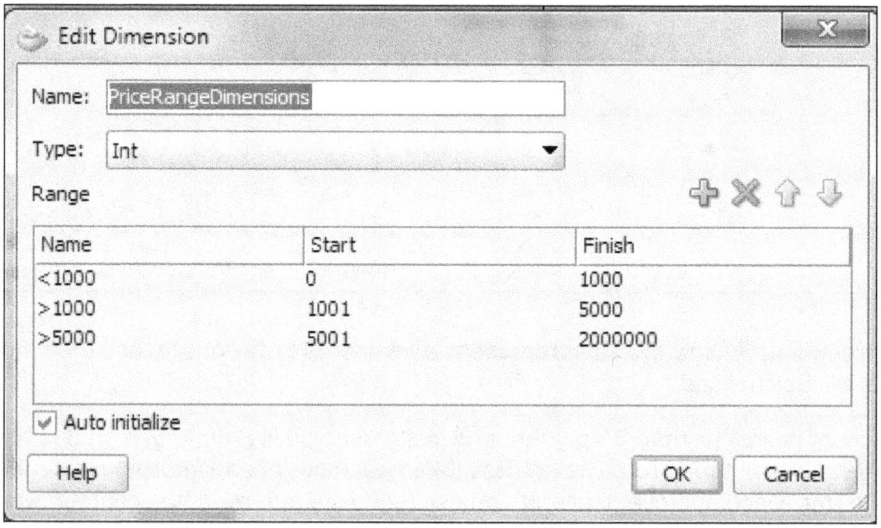

7. Click on **OK**.
8. Click on **New** | **Dimension**, to open the **Create Dimension** dialog. We will create another dimension for **Region**.

9. Enter **Name** as **Region** and **Type** as **String**.

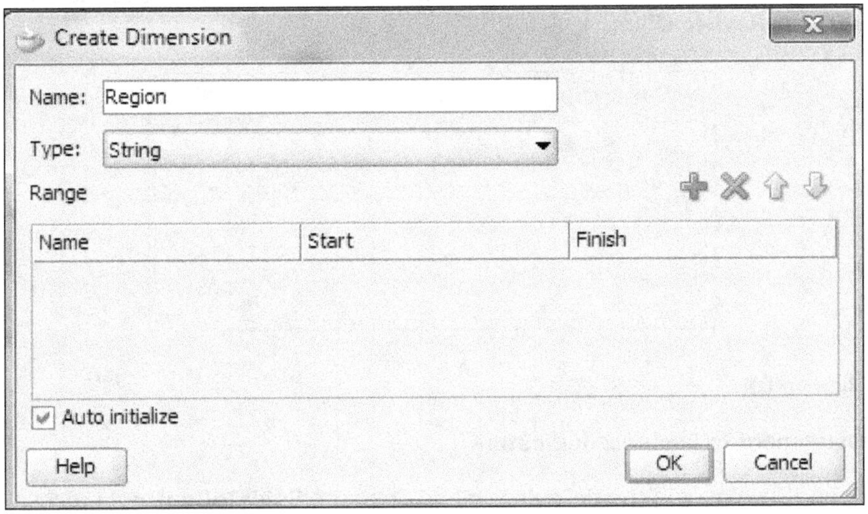

10. Click on **OK**.
11. In the structure window, click on **Business Indicator** | **New** | **Measures**.

    You will create a measure business indicator for quantity.

12. In the **Create Measure** dialog, enter **Name** as **Quantity** and set **Type** as **Int**.

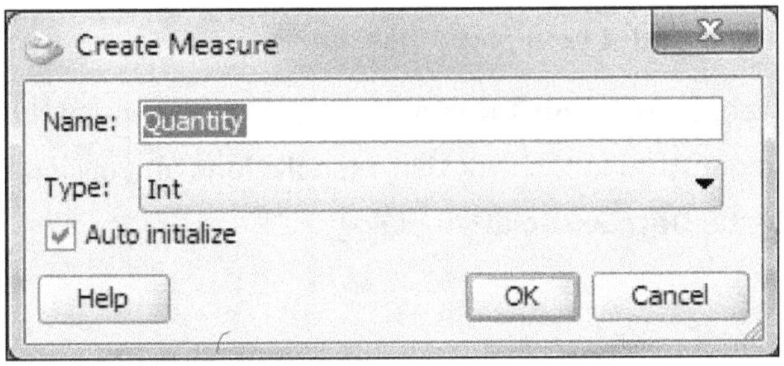

13. Click on **OK**.

14. In the structure window, click on **Business Indicator** | **New** | **Counter** . Add a counter business indicator for counting the number of times the quote is revised. Enter **Name** as **QuoteRevisionNum**.

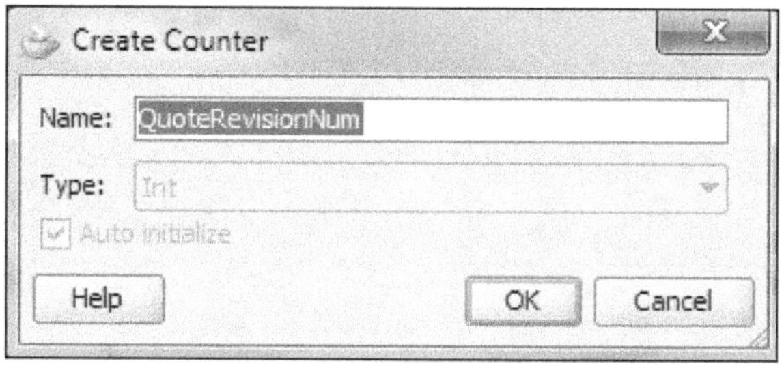

15. Click on **OK**.

II. Data assignment to business indicators

1. Open JDeveloper in the **default** role and open the **SalesToContract** process in the canvas.
2. Go to **Component palette** | **BPM** | **Activities** and click on **Script Activity**.

   You will use a script activity to assign data to the business indicators from the quote Data object.

3. Click on the **Sequence Flow** between **Enter quote human task** and **Discount check rule** in the **salesrepresentative** swimlane.

   This will open the **Script task** properties dialog.

4. In the **Basic** tab, enter**AssignToBizIndicators** as the name of the script task.
5. In the **Implementation** tab, check **Use associations** and click on the edit pencil sign.

   This will open the **Data association** dialog.

6. Drag-and-drop **Quantity**, **Region**, and **PriceRangeDimensions** into the variable section in the **Data association** dialog.

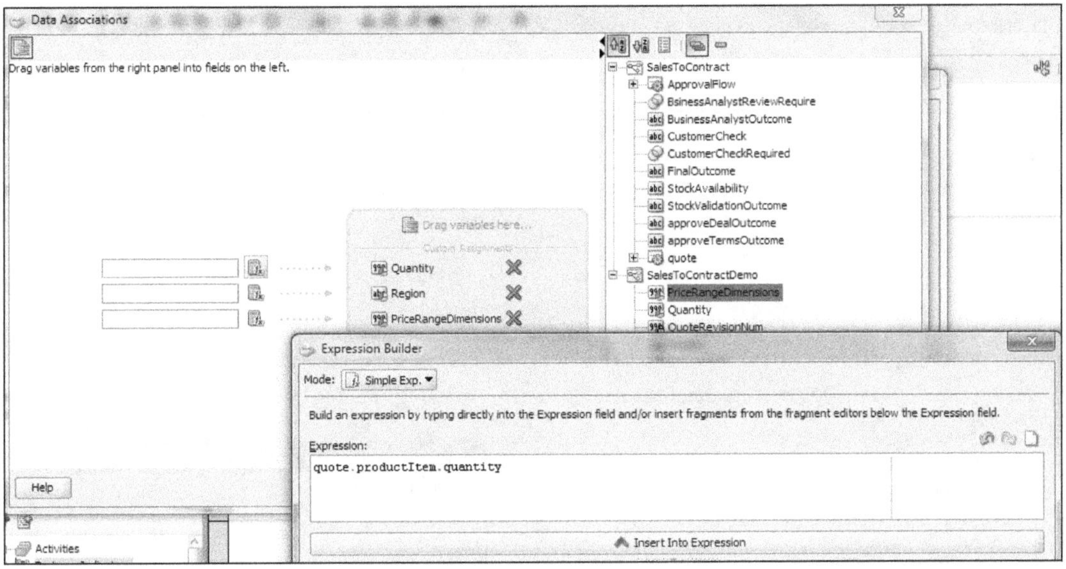

7. To set the **Quantity**, **Region**, and **PriceRangeDimensions** values, click on **Expression Builder**, on the right of input box. This will open the **Expression Builder**.

8. For the **Quantity** input box's **Expression Builder**, expand **quote** | **productItem** | **quantity** and click on the **Insert into expression** button.

9. For the region input box's expression builder, Expand **quote** | **summary** | **address** | **country** and click on **OK**.

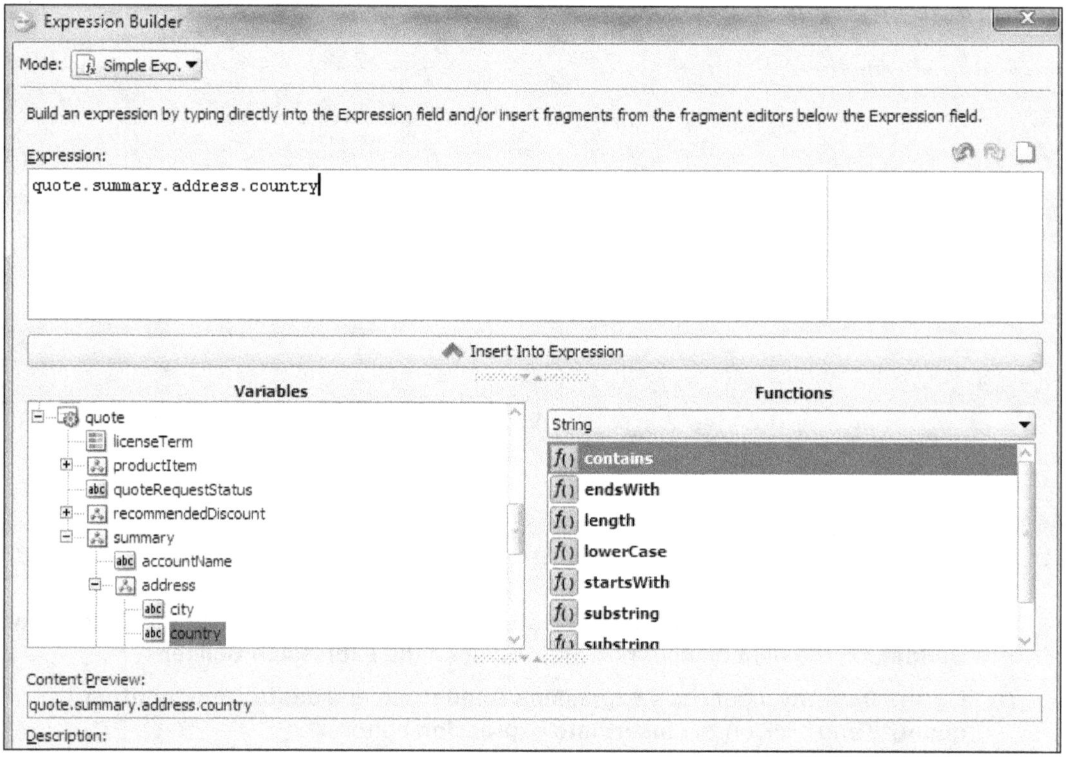

10. For the **PriceRangeDimensions** input box's **Expression Builder**, expand **quote** | **Product Item** | **list price** and click on **OK**.
11. Click **OK** twice and, when you have finished the preceding steps, click on **Save**.

III. Creating measurement marks

You have to measure quantity values coming out of the enter quote details activity. To do that you need to create a measurement mark.

1. Open the BPMN process.
2. Go to **Component Palette** | **BPM** | **Artifacts** and click on **measurement**.
3. Click between **AssignToBizIndicators** script task and **DiscountCheck** rules.

   This will open **Measurement Mark Properties**.
4. Set the **Measurement Type** as **Single Measurement**. As you have already defined business indicators in your process, you must add single measurement marks in the process where you want those business indicators.

5. Enter **Name** as **EnterQuoteMeasure**.
6. From the available business indicators, select **Quantity[Measure]**.

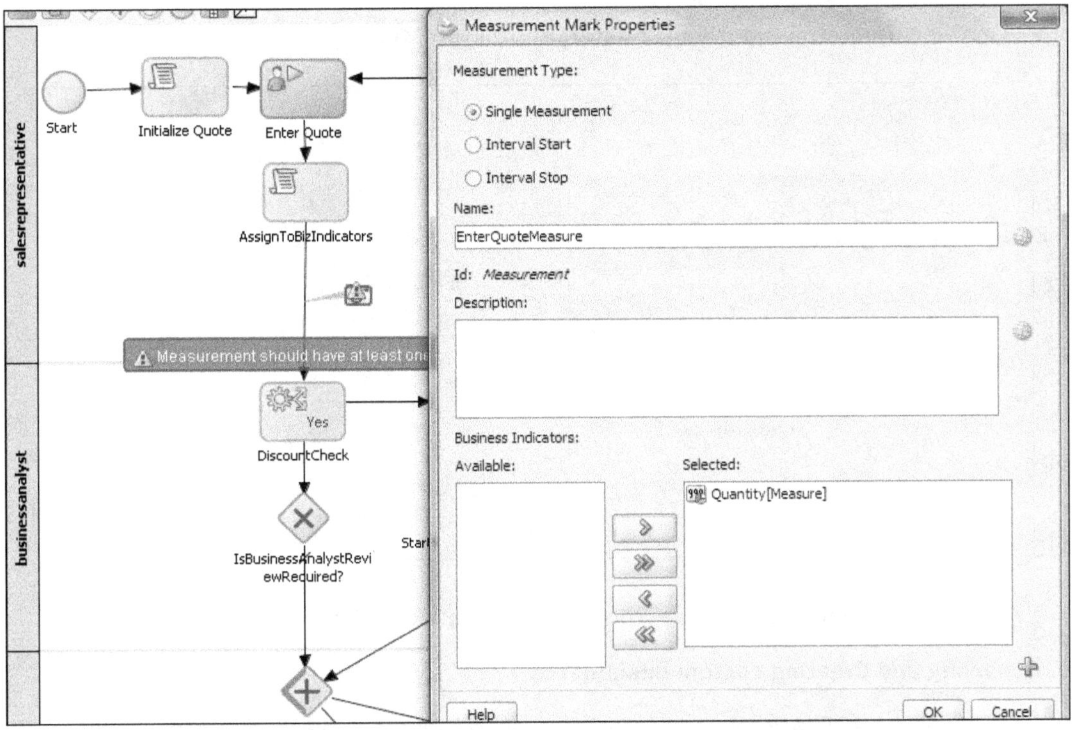

7. Click on **OK**.

> Single measurement marks indicate the BPMN Service Engine to store the value of the measured business indicators associated to that measurement mark. The BPMN Service Engine also stores the values of the default process measures and the dimension business indicators at this point in the process.

IV. Adding counters

Counter marks are used to update the value of the counter business indicators defined for your process. Counter marks are used for auditing, identifying performance issues, and so on. When a token arrives at an activity that has a counter mark defined, the BPM Service Engine updates the value of its associated counters in the Process Analytics databases. Each time the BPM Service Engine updates a counter business indicator, it adds one unit to the current value. Here, you will track how many times a quote has to be revised due to rejections.

1. Open the process **SalesToContract**.
2. Right-click on the **Enter Quote** details task and select **Add Counter Mark**. This will open a properties dialog.
3. Select **QuoteRevisionNum[Counter]** and click on **OK**.

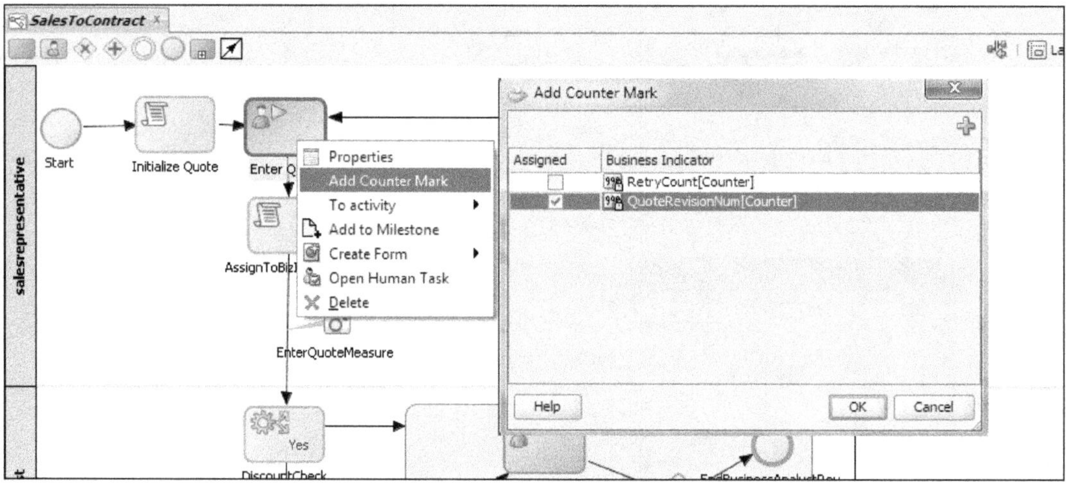

4. When you have finished the preceding steps, click on **Save**.

V. Deploying and Creating custom dashboards

1. As all the ADF task forms are already available on the server, just deploy the SOA project.
2. Log in to Oracle BPM workspace as a **BusinessAnalyst** user.
3. Click on the new page icon in the top-right corner.
4. Give the name of the panel as **SalesQuoteCustomPage** and click on the **Add Panel** button.

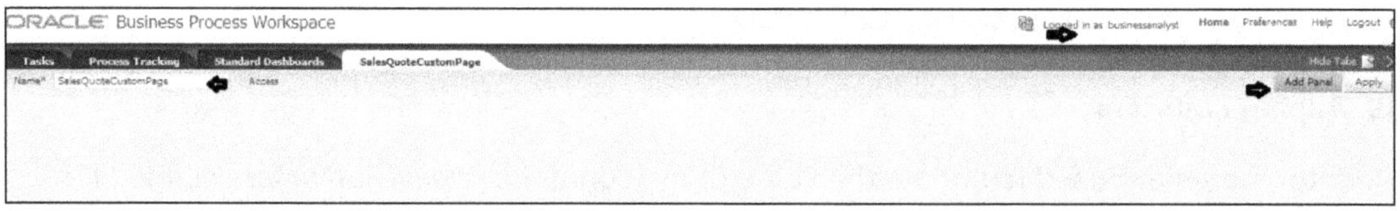

5. In **Add Panel**, select **Dashboard (Charts)** and click on **OK**.

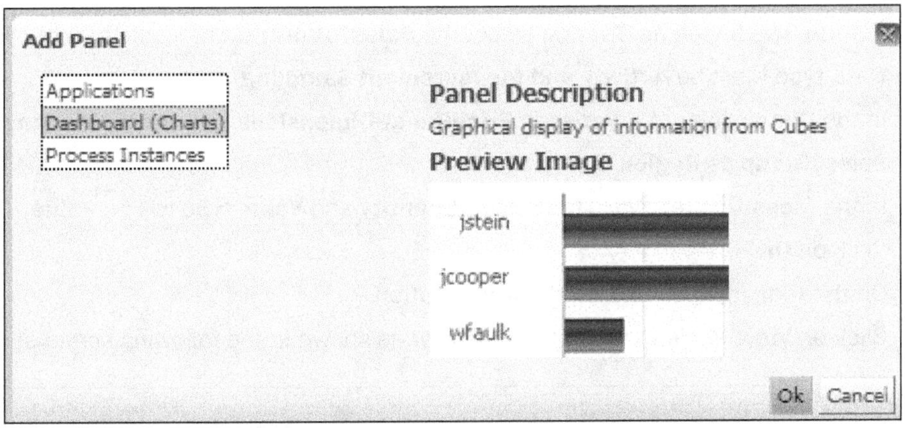

6. Name the panel **QuantityRegionPrice** and click the magnifying glass ahead of **Data Source**.

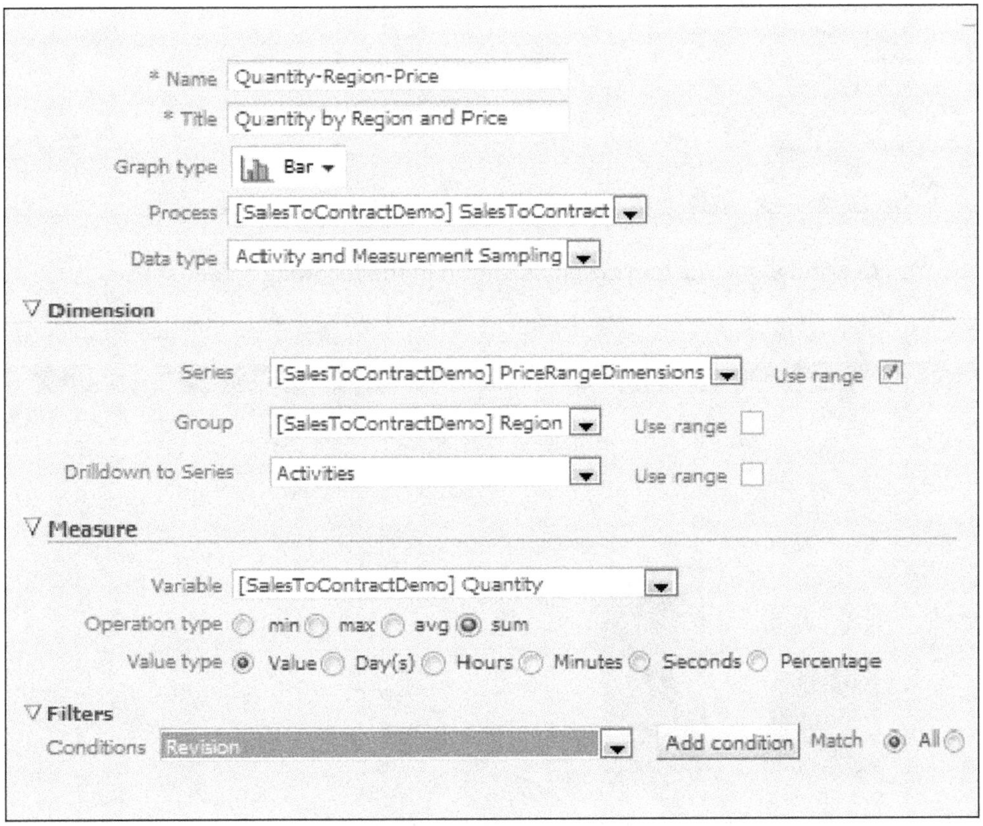

7. Enter **Quantity-Region-Price** for **Name** and provide a **Title** as shown in the previous screenshot.
8. Set the **Graph type** as **Bar** and select the **SalesToContract** process from the list.
9. **Data type** must be **Activity and Measurement Sampling**.
10. In the **Dimension** area, **Series** is **PriceRangeDimensions** and check **Use range**.
11. Select **Group** as **Region**.
12. In the **Measure** area, **Variable** will be **Quantity** and **Value type** will be **Value**.
13. Click on **OK**.
14. On the widget page, click on the **Apply** button.
15. Click on **View Mode** in the top-right corner as shown in the following screenshot:

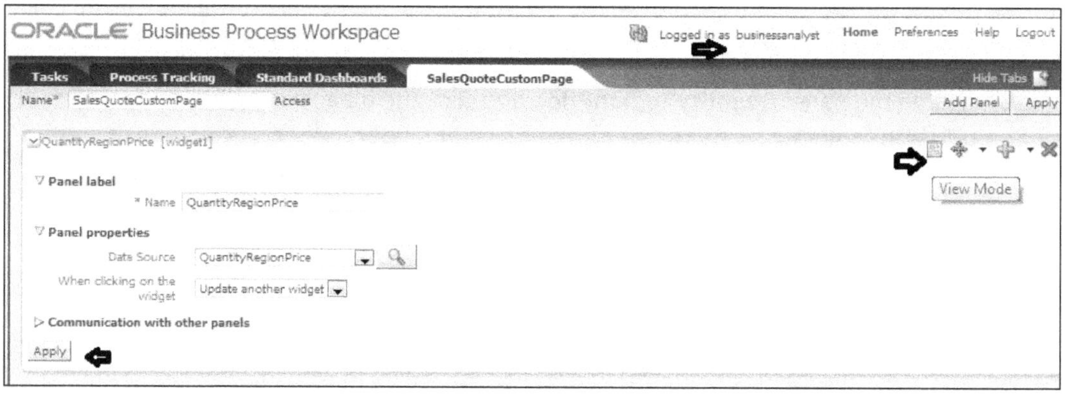

16. You can find a new custom graph as shown in the following screenshot:

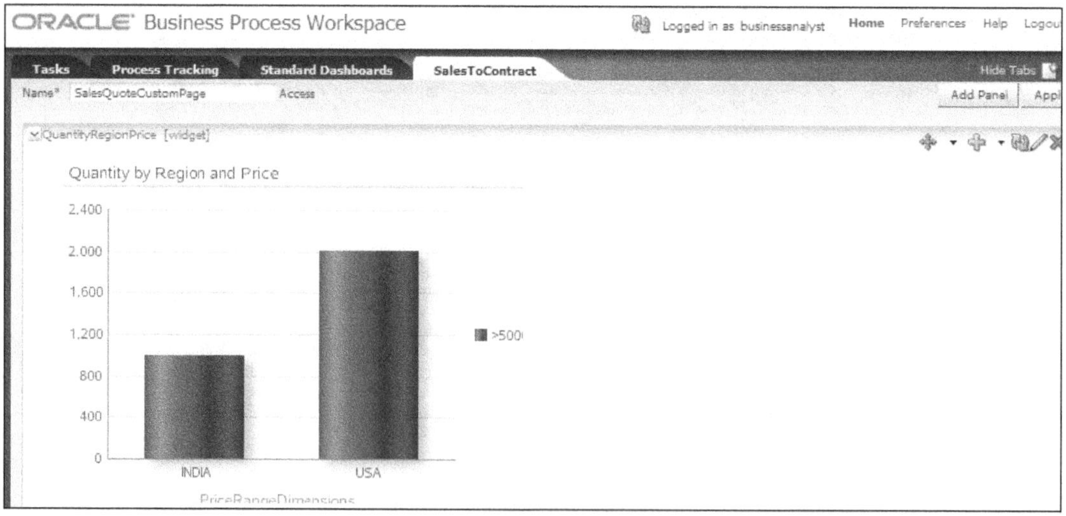

[While entering the quote details, you have entered quantity for India region as 1000 and Quantity for USA region as 2000. However, price was less than 5000 in both the cases.]

How it works...

When the process token reaches measurement marks, it will measure the business indicators of type Measure in the process. While storing these values, the BPMN Service Engine will also store the value of the dimensions you defined in your process.

In the last section, you will build a custom dashboard using BPM workspace, which will be used to monitor your process. There you will use dimensions to group the values into different categories.

The BPMN Service Engine populates the predefined cubes each time it runs an activity or completes a process. The engine uses the sampling points configuration you defined to populate the cubes. If you configure a process not to generate sampling points, then the BPMN Service Engine does not store this information in the predefined cubes.

There's more...

In this section, you will learn how to configure BPM process cubes.

Configuring BPM process cubes generation in a project

If you use BPM process cubes to monitor the performance of your project, then you must enable the generation of the process cubes at developing time. When you deploy your application, Oracle BPM uses this configuration to enable BPM process cubes.

Use the following steps to enable BPM process cubes in a project:

1. Go to BPM project navigator and right-click on the project.
2. Select **Project Preferences**.
3. In the **Category** tree, select **Process Analytics Summary**.
4. In the **Process Analytics Summary** section, click on the **Data Targets** tab.
5. Select **Enable Cubes** to enable cubes generation.
6. Click on **OK**.

[By default, cubes are enabled. Hence, you were able to view data in the custom workspace dashboards you have created.]

Configuring BAM Architect to create custom dashboards

After publishing the application, business analysts can use the default dashboards the BPM workspace provided or create custom dashboards to view the metrics the BPMN Service Engine gathered while running the BPMN processes.

End users can create custom (user-defined) dashboards by defining graphs in the BPM workspace and assembling those graphs to define a dashboard.

However, you can also use BAM Architect to create a BAM dashboard with the BPM business indicators that you created. You need a BAM Data object for the business indicators you defined in your process.

In this section, you will learn to do the following:

- Create a Data object folder in Oracle BAM Architect
- Enable BAM in BPMN project
- Create BAM data objects
- Create BAM custom dashboards
- View custom dashboards

In order to integrate Oracle BPM and Oracle BAM you have to perform a couple of one-time setup tasks such as configuring the BAM adapter in the Oracle EM console and enabling BPMN engine to send events to BAM by configuring BPMN Service Engine's MBean properties. You will learn these tasks in the administration section; however, here it's assumed that the setup task and event enabling are both performed by administrators.

How to do it...

I. Creating data object folders in Oracle BAM Architect

When the process token reaches measurement marks, process specific analytic events are raised. With user defined configurations, these events are passed to Oracle BAM. In Oracle BAM, you need Oracle BAM Data objects to capture those events. And these Data objects are defined in a folder in BAM Architect. This folder path is what you will provide when you set data target preferences for your project **SalesToContractDemo**.

1. Log in to Oracle BAM at `http://localhost:9001/OracleBAM` (use 9001 if the BAM server is a managed server; else use 7001 if you have single Admin Server configuration).
2. Log in as the WebLogic user.

3. Click on the **Architect** button, as you need to create Data object managing folders.

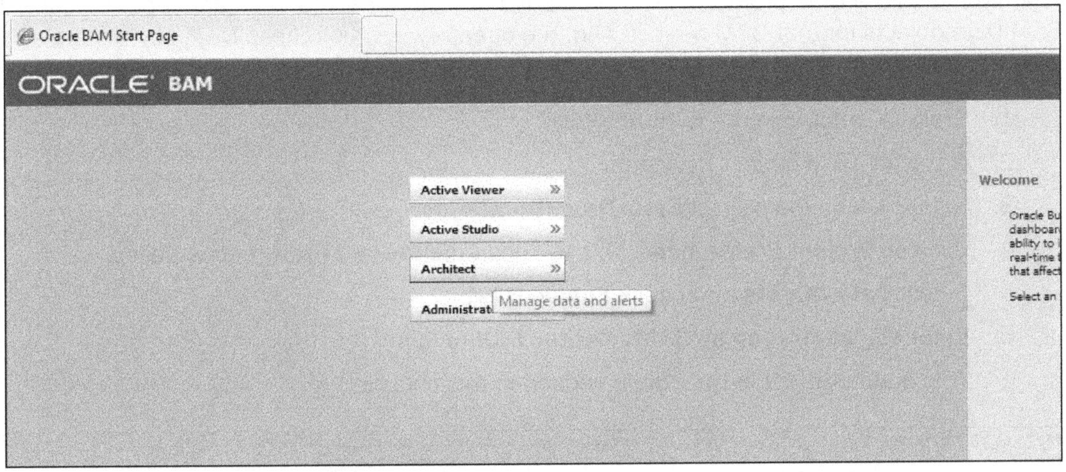

4. On the BAM Architect page, select Data objects from the drop-down list.
5. Click on **Data Objects** and click on the **Create subfolder** on the right-hand side window.
6. Name the folder as **SalesToContractSamples** and click on **Create folder**.
7. Similarly, create a **ProcessDataObjects** folder inside the **SalesToContractSamples** folder.

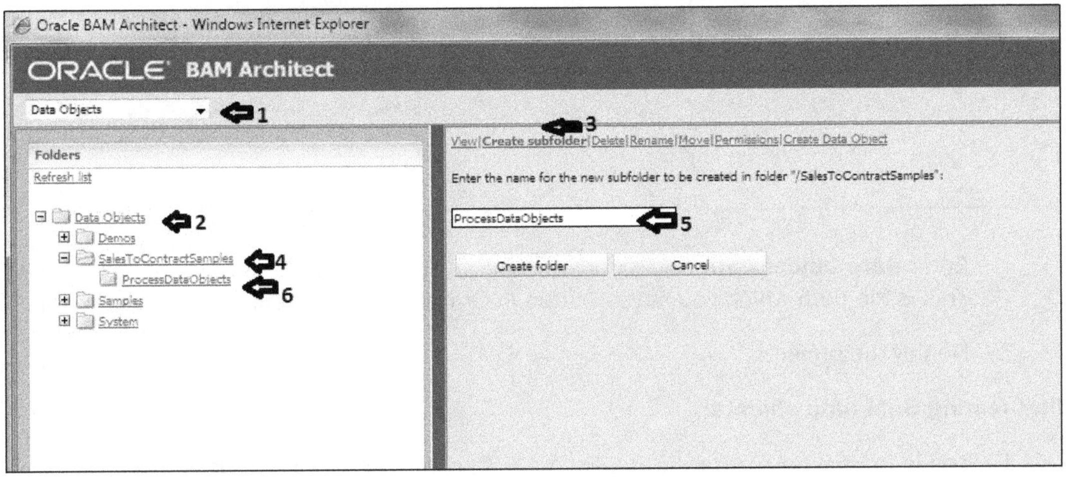

8. Note down the folder path, which is `/SalesToContractSamples/ProcessDataObjects`.
9. Close the BPM Architect window.

II. Enabling BAM in BPMN projects

When you deploy a BPM project, Oracle BAM automatically creates the custom and predefined BAM Data objects for that BPM project. And, the directory in which these Data objects are created is defined in the project preference that you will set as follows:

1. Start JDeveloper in the **default** role.
2. Go to the BPM project navigator.
3. Right-click on the project **SalesToContractDemo**.
4. Click on **Project Preferences**. This will open the **Project Preferences** dialog.
5. Select **Data Targets** and check **Enable BAM**.
6. Enter **eis/bam/soap** as **BAM Adapter JNDI** name.

   This adapter is set in the admin section of this chapter.

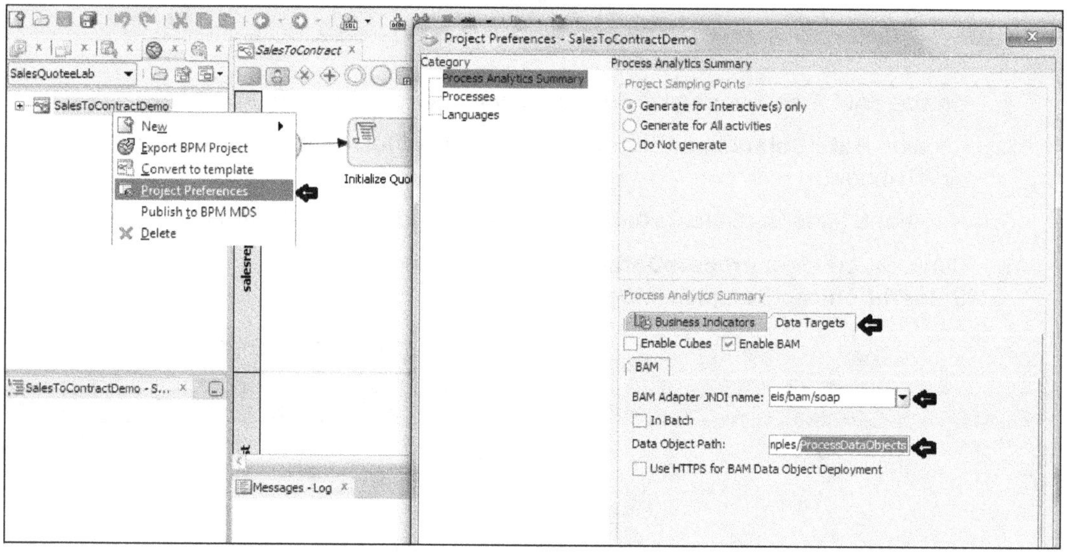

   Enter **Data Object Path** as `/SalesToContractSamples/ProcessDataObjects`. This is the path which you have created in Oracle BAM Architect in previous section.

7. Deploy the project.

III. Creating BAM data objects

1. Log in to `http://localhost:9001/OracleBAM` as WebLogic user.
2. Select **BAM Architect**.

3. Expand **Data Objects** | **SalesToContractSamples** | **ProcessDataObjects**.

   You can find a Data object created as `BI_default_<Composite Project Name>_<ProcessName>` in the same way you can find **BI_default_SalesToContractDemo_SalesToContract** Data object you created.

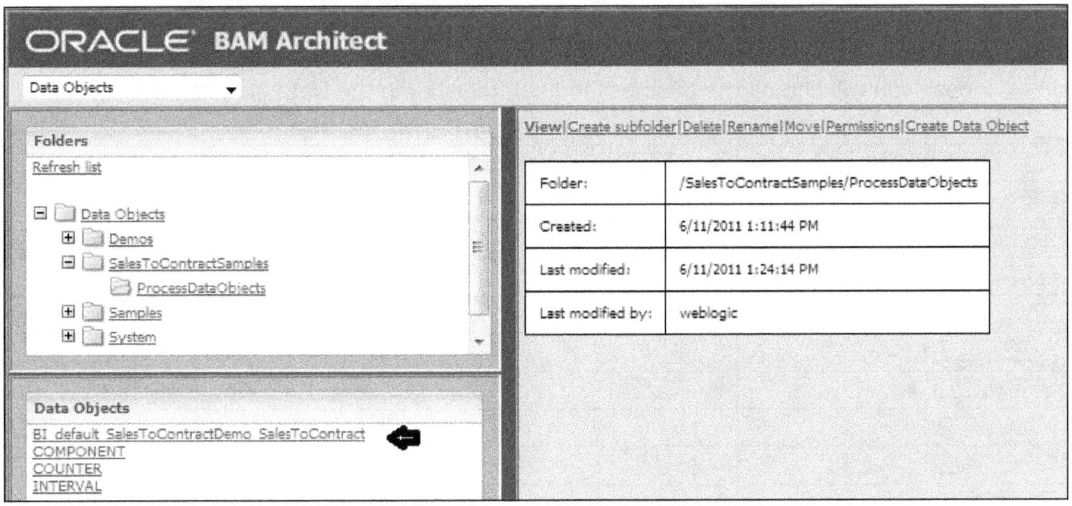

4. Double-click on the **BI_default_SalesToContractDemo_SalesToContract** Data object.
5. This will open the Data object editor section on the right of the Data object list as shown in the following screenshot:

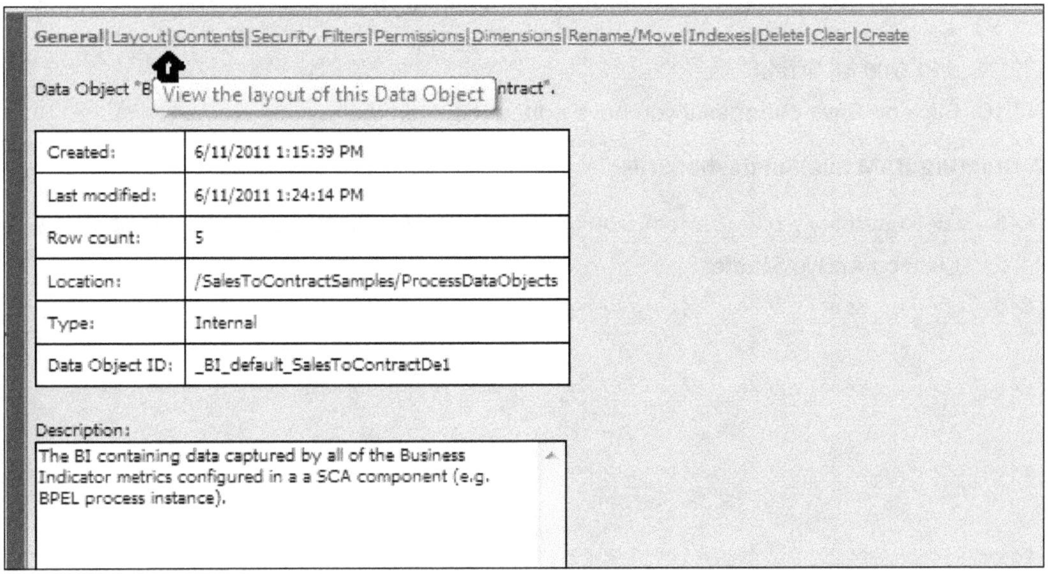

6. Click on the **Layout** tab. This will open the layout of the Data object **BI_default_SalesToContractDemo_SalesToContract**.
7. Click on the **Edit layout** button.
8. You can find that all the data object columns have been created for the business indicators.

   However, you can create a data object field by clicking on the **Add Field** tab. In this case you will find all the business indicators listed in the Data objects section.

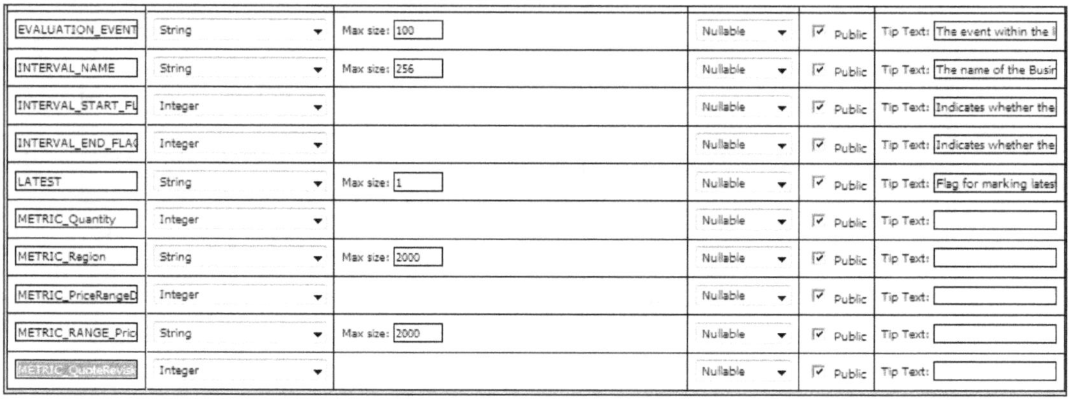

9. If you want to bring changes to their name, or add a description, you can do it. However, a Data object column must follow a naming convention; for example, a column created for a business indicator in the Data object must be `METRIC_<Business Indicator Name>` and it's type should match. Similarly, you can find that for **RANGE_PriceRangeDimensions**, there is a column created. This column followed the convention as `METRIC_RANGE_<Business Indicator Name>` and type as **String**.
10. Click on **Save changes** if you have edited the columns.

IV. Creating BAM custom dashboards

1. Go to `http://localhost:9001/OracleBAM/` and login as WebLogic user.
2. Click on **Active Studio**.

3. Click on the **Shared Reports** tab and then click on the **Create A New Report** button.

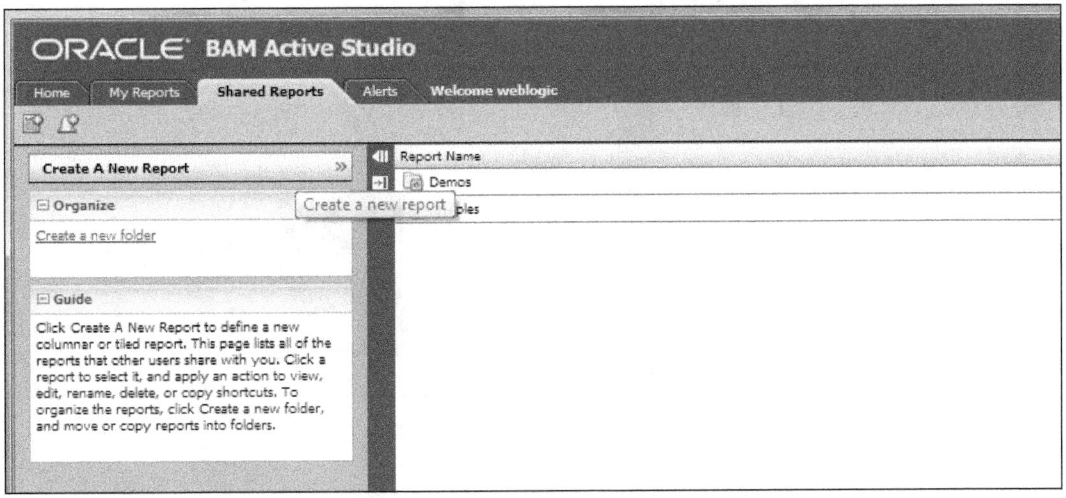

4. In the title Section, select two horizontal tile within separator report template.
5. Enter the report title as **SalesToContractCustomDashBoard**.
6. Select **3D Bar Chart**.

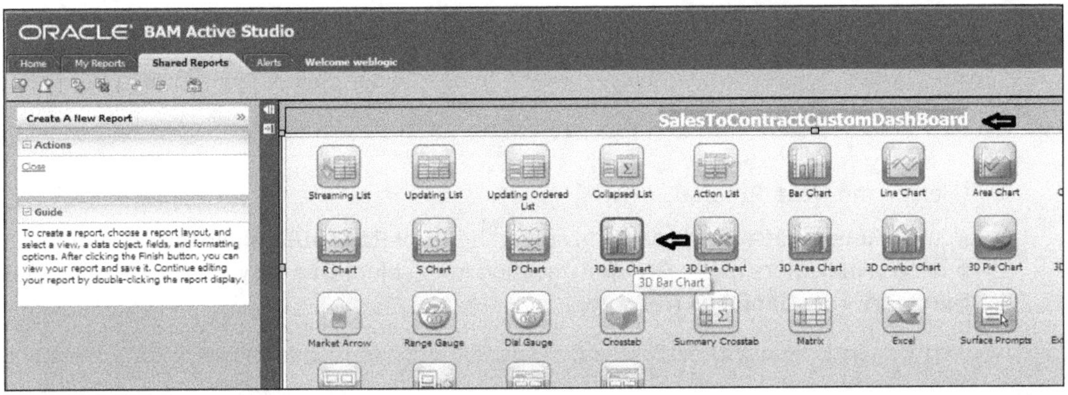

7. In the **Choose Data Object** section, go to **Data Objects** | **SalesToContractSamples** | **ProcessDataObjects** and select the **BI_default_SalesToContractDemo_SalesToContract** Data object.

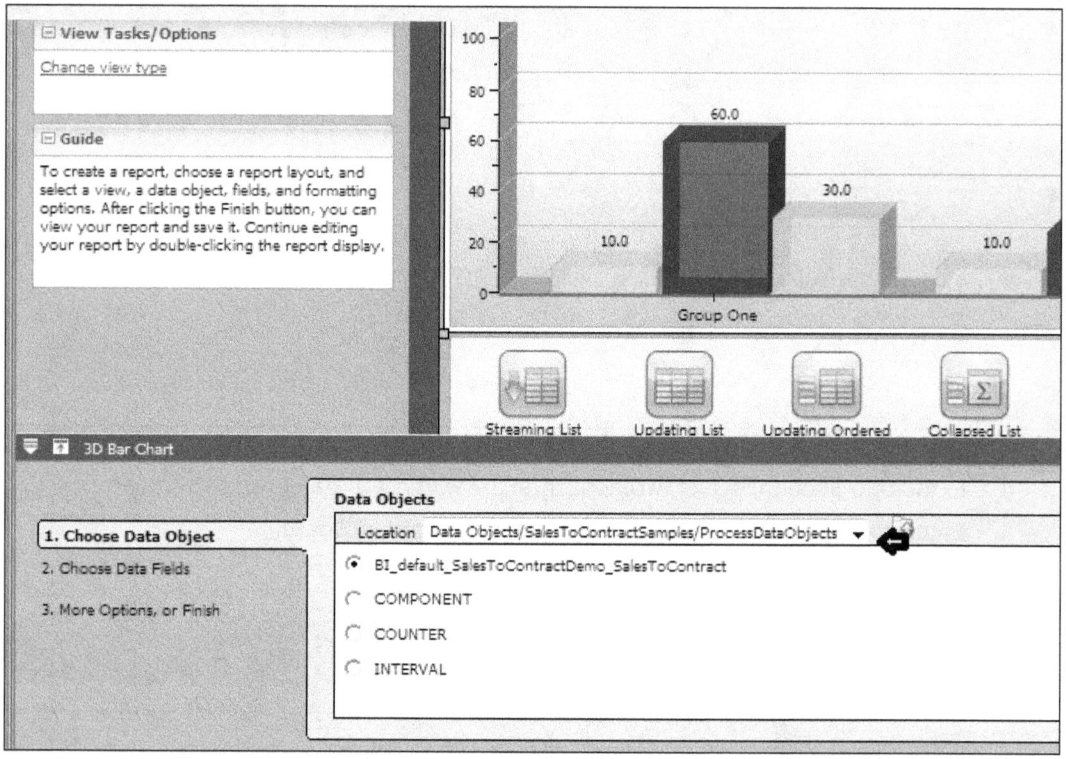

8. Click on the **Next** button.

9. In the **Choose Data Fields** section, select the **PriceRangeDimensions** and **Region** business indicators in the **Group By** section, and select **Quantity** in **Chart Values**. Set **Summary Function(s)** as **Average**.

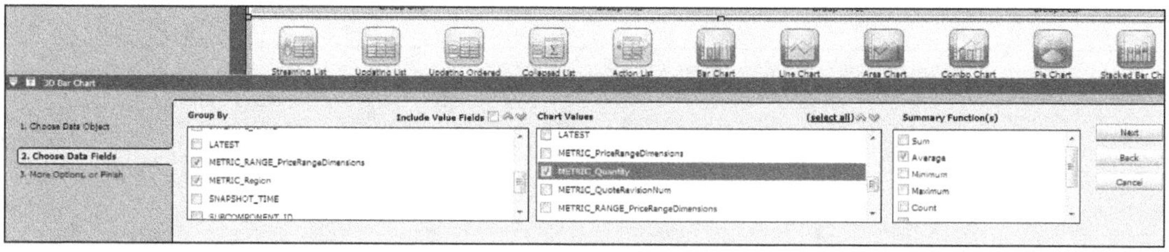

10. Click **Next**.

11. In the **More Options, or Finish** section, click on **Change View Properties**. You can also change the report properties in this section.

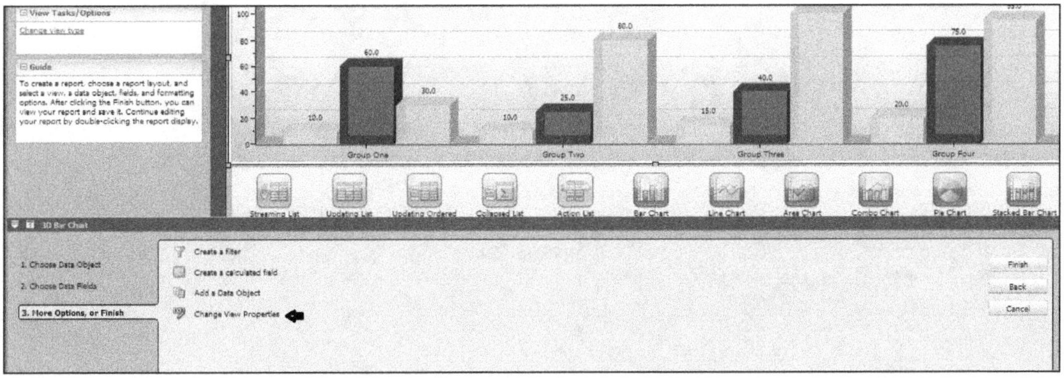

12. In the title for the report, enter **Quantity By Region and Price**.
13. Check **Vertical Axis Label** and enter the name to appear on the vertical section as **Quantity**.

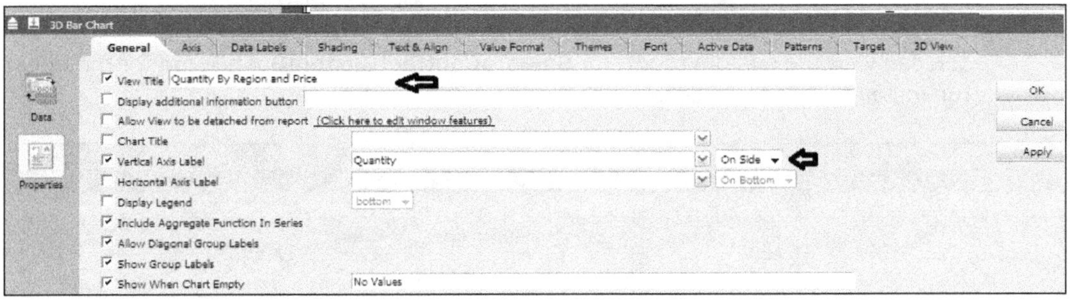

14. Click on **OK**.
15. If you are satisfied with the report attributes, click on **Apply**.
16. Click on **Save as**, to save the report at `Shared Reports/Demos/SalesToContractSamples/ProcessDataObjects`.

V. Viewing dashboards

1. Log in as the WebLogic user at `http://localhost:9001/OracleBAM`.
2. Click on **Active Viewer**.

3. Select the **SalesToContractCustomDashBoard** report and click on **OK**.

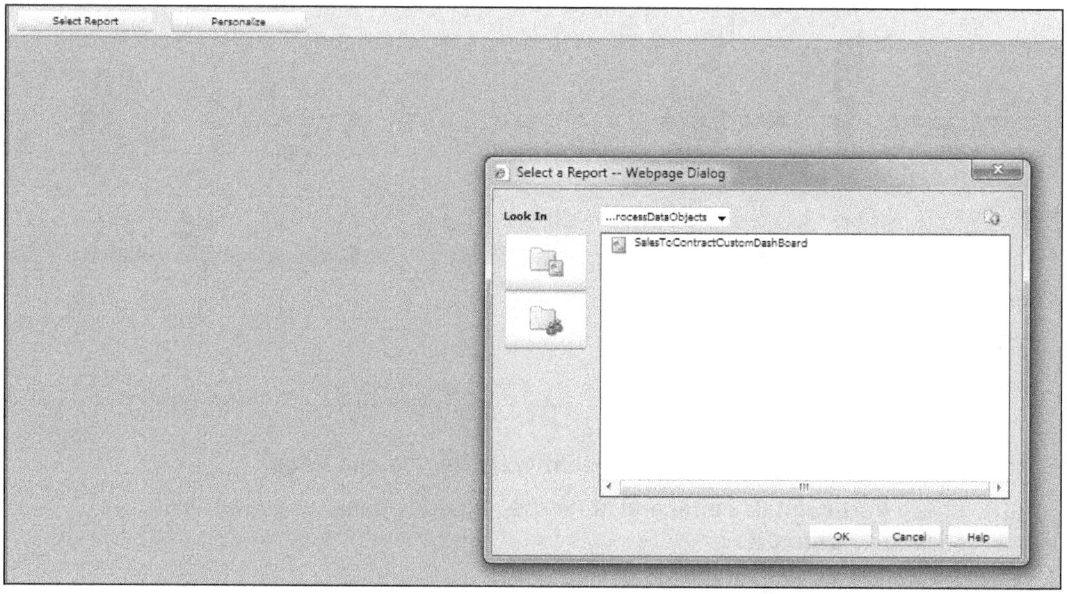

4. You can view the custom report for **SalesToContractCustomDashBoard** for the latest run instances of the process.

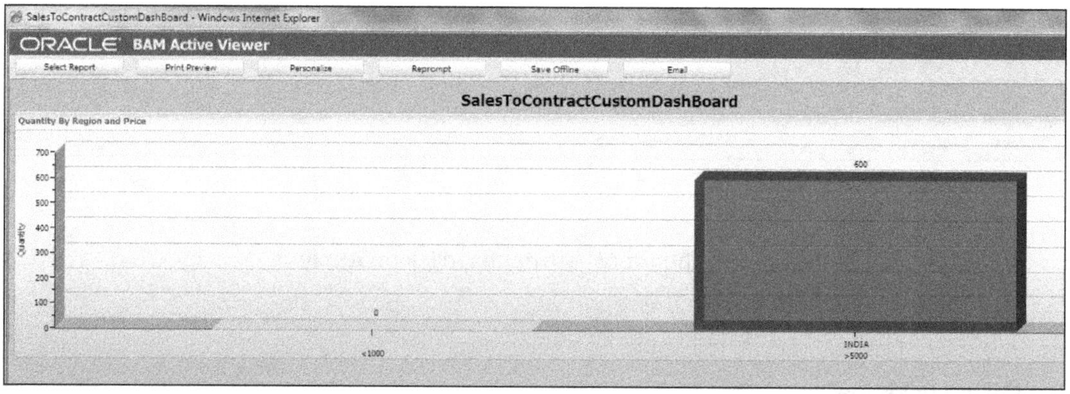

How it works...

When the process token reaches measurement marks, process specific analytic events are raised. Events are passed to Oracle BAM Data objects, defined as path. /`SalesToContractSamples/ProcessDataObjects` specified in **Project preferences**. When you deploy a BPM project, Oracle BAM automatically creates the custom and predefined BAM Data objects for that BPM project.

SOA Admin—Configuring SOA infrastructure properties

You can configure many properties for the SOA infrastructure, such as **Audit Level**, **Payload Validation**, **UDDI Registry**, **JNDI Data Source**, **Binding Properties**, and so on.

When these properties set, they impact all deployed SOA composite applications.

While you are testing the process and things are not working as expected such as process instance takes the wrong branch or the approval flow is not that which you were expecting, then you can debug the process by setting the **Audit Level** to **Development**. Setting the **Audit Level** is carried out in Enterprise Manager. First, you set **Audit Level** to **Development** mode, and then initiate a new process instance in the **Business Process** workspace to witness the effect of this change in debugging.

How to do it...

1. Go to the Enterprise Manager console | **soa-infra** | **SOA Administration** and click on **Common Properties**. This will set the **Audit Level** to the **Development** mode.

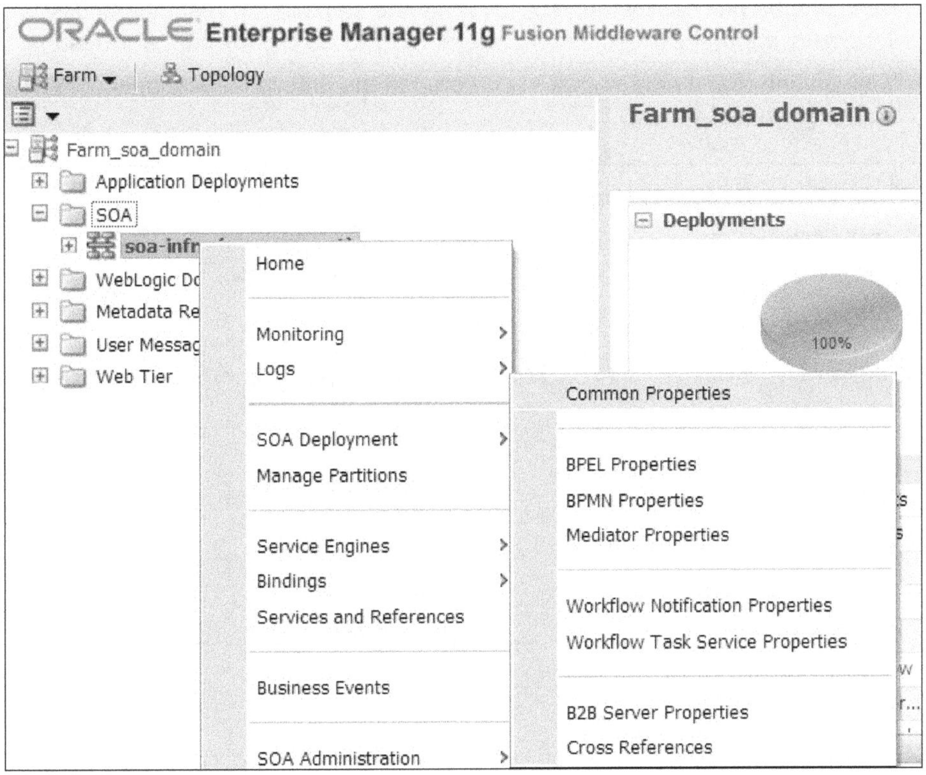

2. Also, check **Capture Composite Instance State**.

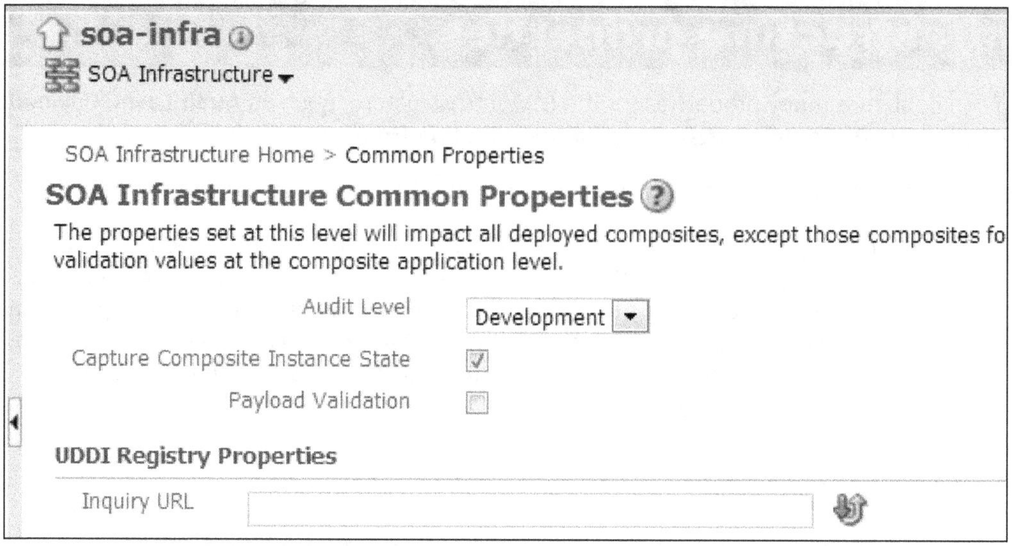

3. Log in to Oracle BPM workspace with the **salesrepresentative** credentials and reinitiate the process instance by following the steps in the *Testing process: Triggering the process* section of *Chapter 3, Process Deployment and Testing*.
4. You can find that a new instance is created in the Enterprise Manager console. Click on the given **Instance ID**.

5. In the **Trace** section, click on the process name **SalesToContract**.

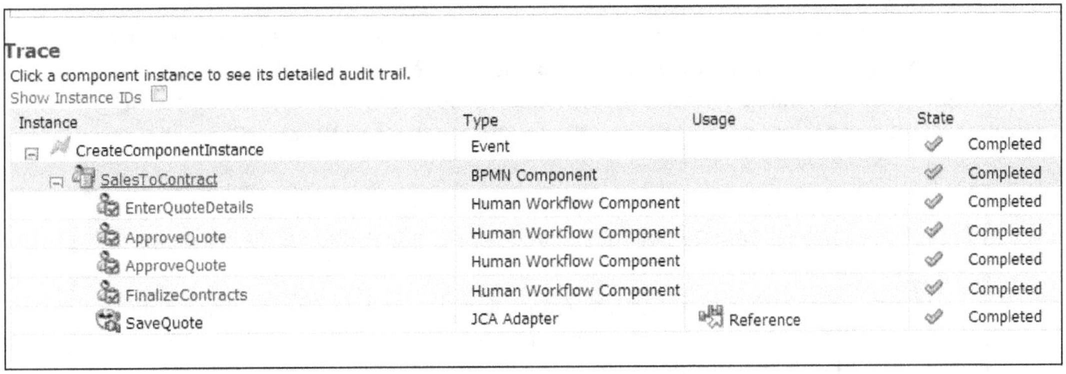

6. In the **Audit Trail** tab, you will find that the blue links are clickable and display data values at that particular point in the process.

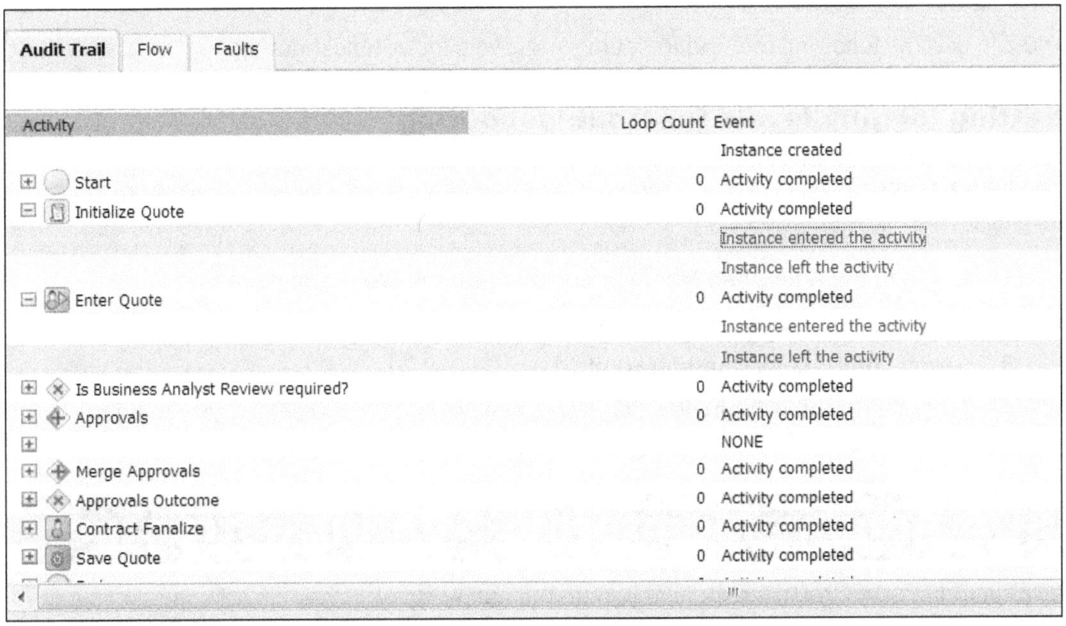

7. Click on **Instance entered the activity** for the **Enter Quote** task, and you can find the data associated with the activity.

How it works...

Development mode makes available far more of these data value links, which is why it is so useful for debugging. Setting **Audit Level** to **Development** enables both composite tracking and payload details tracking. This option provides for separate tracking of the running instances. All instances are captured as either running or not running.

> You can enable the validation of incoming and outgoing messages. Non-schema compliant payload data is intercepted and displayed as a fault.
>
> Also, the capture instance state flag should have these values only in development and testing environments, as they seriously affect the overall performance of the infrastructure.

There's more...

You can use the following method to set logging levels for troubleshooting.

Setting logging levels for troubleshooting

To make troubleshooting simple, it is recommended that you set logging levels to the **TRACE:32 FINEST** level in Oracle Enterprise Manager Fusion Middleware Control. To set logging levels for troubleshooting:

1. Log in to the Enterprise Manager console with the WebLogic user.
2. Right-click on **SOA infrastructure**.
3. Select **Logs** | **Logs Configuration**.
4. From the **Oracle Diagnostic Logging Level** list, set the parent loggers to the **TRACE: 32 FINEST** level.

SOA Admin—Monitoring SOA infrastructure

By monitoring SOA infrastructure, you can do the following:

- Monitor the BPM composite applications deployed to the SOA infrastructure
- Monitor SOA infrastructure processing requests
- Monitor the Service and Reference Binding components

How to do it...

1. Log in with the WebLogic user to `http://localhost:7001/`.
2. Expand **soa-infra** | **default** and then click on the deployed project, **SalesToContractDemo**.

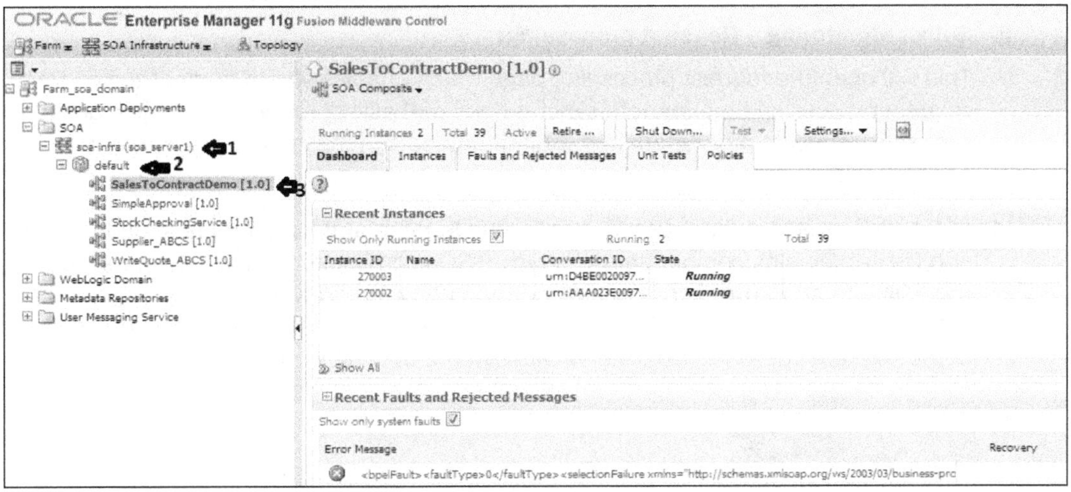

3. This will open the composite dashboard.

   You can find that recent running instances are displayed along with their details, such as **Instance ID**, status, time, and so on.

4. Uncheck **Show Only Running Instance**, if you want to list instances which are not running.
5. You can recover from faults identified as recoverable at the SOA infrastructure, SOA composite application, service engine, and service component levels.
   - In the **Error Message** column, click on an error message to display the complete information about the fault.
   - If the fault is identified as recoverable, click on the **Recover Now** link to perform fault recovery.
6. You can retire the composite by clicking on the **Retire** button on the SOA infrastructure dashboard. Retiring the composite will not allow new instances to be created; however, old instances will be completed.
7. You can shut down the composite by clicking on the **Shut Down** button on the SOA infrastructure dashboard. Shutting down the composite will not allow new instances to be created, and processing of existing instances will be stopped.

8. Click on the **Settings** button to set:
    - Composite Level Audit Levels
    - Payload Validations
    - Enable/Disable BAM Monitoring
9. To monitor processing requests, right click on **SOA-Infrastructure**.
10. Select **Monitoring** | **Request processing**.

    This will open the request processing page which enables you to monitor the average request processing time for both synchronous and asynchronous messages, active requests, requests processed, and faulted requests in the service engines and service infrastructure.
11. Right-click on **SOA-Infrastructure** and select **Service and References** to monitor the service and binding components used in all SOA composite applications deployed to the SOA infrastructure. Services provide the outside world with an entry point to the SOA composite application. References enable messages to be sent from the SOA composite application to external services in the outside world.

How it works...

The SOA infrastructure processing requests have metrics for message delivery between the service engines, service infrastructure, and binding components. You can find details about the names and types of the services, the SOA composite applications in which the services are used, the total number of messages processed, the average processing time, and the number of faults occurring in the services.

SOA Admin—Administering BPMN application deployment

You have learnt the deployment of BPM application in *Chapter 3, Process Deployment and Testing*. You can deploy a BPM application from Oracle EM console too. To deploy a BPMN application via the Enterprise Manager console, you have to first create a deployable archive in either JDeveloper or using ANT or WLST scripts. The archive can consist of a single SOA composite application revision in a JAR file or multiple composite application revisions (known as a **SOA bundle**) in a ZIP file.

How to do it...

In this section, you will learn to deploy BPM projects from the Enterprise Manager console.

1. Log in with WebLogic user to the Oracle Enterprise Manager console (`http://localhost:7001/em/`).

2. Expand **soa-infra** and click **SOA Partition** as shown in the following screenshot:

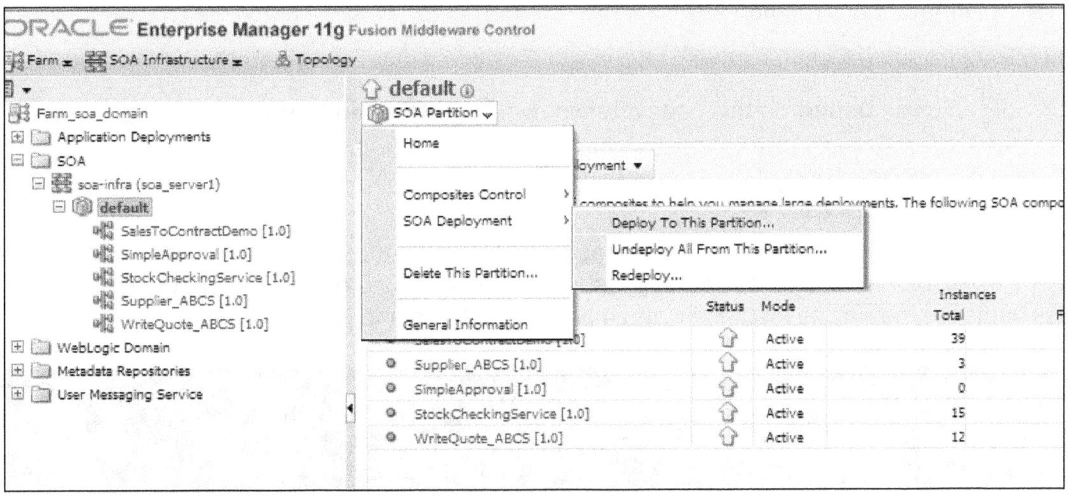

3. Select **SOA Deployment | Deploy To This Partition...**.
4. Click on the **Browse** button in the **Archive or Exploded Directory** section, to specify the archive of the SOA composite application to deploy.

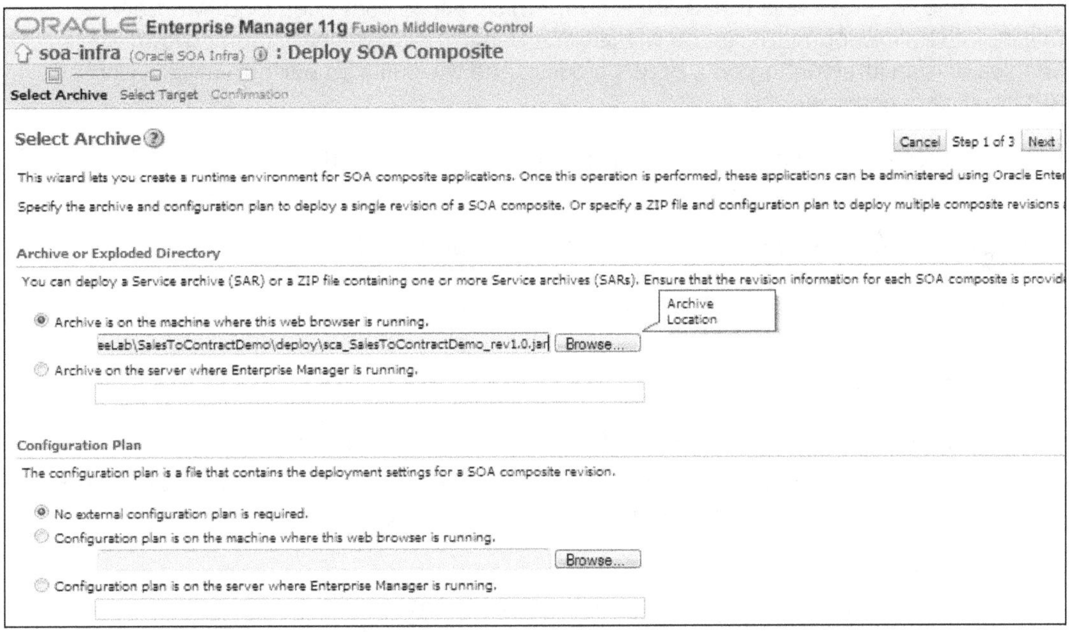

You can even attach a configuration plan to include with the archive. The configuration plan enables you to define the URL and property values to use in different environments.

5. Click on **Next**.
6. Click on **Deploy** on this page after verifying the **Revision Details**.

How it works...

Once you have deployed the composite application in SOA Infrastructure, you can perform administration tasks, such as creating instances, configuring properties, monitoring performance, managing instances, and managing policies and faults.

SOA Admin—Fault recovery for BPMN processes

You learnt how to define fault policies for a BPMN process in *Chapter 8, Exception Management*, in the *Handling a system exception—Fault Management Framework* section.

In *Chapter 8, Exception Management*, BPMN Service Engine runs the task `ValidateStock`, which calls `StockValidator_EBS`. `StockValidator_EBS` will raise an error if stock is not available. The task fails with a SOAP error, which will be converted by BPMN Service Engine into an exception. Here, you will use the framework to define a fault policy that enables human intervention on a BPMN process and you will also perform recovery on BPMN process components.

You will implement a service task in your BPM process to invoke this `StockValidator_EBS` service.

If Stock = Available Then Process Token follows the Normal path

else if Stock != Available then service task throws a Error

How to do it...

1. Open the `fault-policy.xml` file and add the following code:

```
<faultName xmlns:client="http://xmlns.oracle.com/Implementation/
StockCheckingService/StockValidator"
              name="client:SOPFault">
  <condition>
      <test>$fault.payload = "UnAvailable"</test>
    <action ref = "ora-human-intervention"/>
  </condition>
</faultName>
```

If availability is 'N', then `StockValidator_EBS` will raise a `SOPFault` and will be handled by the policy framework.

2. In `fault-policy.xml`, you have defined human intervention action. Without fault policies, BPMN instances do not generate recoverable faults (instead they are non recoverable); the ora-human-intervention action makes the fault recoverable.
3. Deploy and run an instance of the process. Enter the product as **1030**, as with this Product Code; `StockValidator_EBS` will have availability as 'N' and this service will result in `SOPFault`, which you will handle using the fault policy framework.

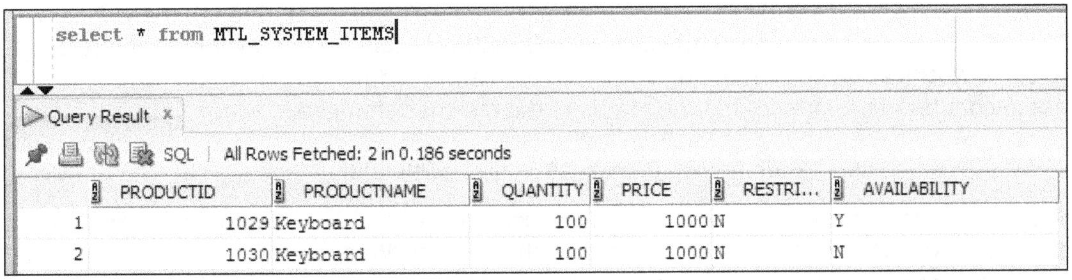

You can find that a fault instance is created.

4. Log in to the Enterprise Manager console as WebLogic user and go to **soa-infra**.
5. Click on **Faults and Rejected Messages**.
6. Select the fault that has been identified as recoverable and select it.
7. In the **Recovery** column, click on **Recover**. The **Faults** page for that BPMN process instance is displayed. You can find the fault recovery section at the bottom of the page.
8. Select **Retry** from the **Recovery Action** list.
9. From the **Variable** list, select a variable which contains the **Availability Data** and **In the Value** field, enter the correct value **Y**.
10. Click on **Set Value**, and click **Yes** when prompted to continue.
11. Click **Recover** to recover from the fault, then click **Yes** when prompted to continue.

You should see that the page will get refreshed and indicates that no faults occurred.

How it works...

You created a `StockValidator_EBS` BPEL web service ,based on a PLSQL procedure, which checks for item availability in `MTL_SYSTEM_ITEMS` table and returns `SO0050Fault` if item not available.

When this fault is raised, policy framework will handle this fault, in this case. And you can perform the fault recovery from Oracle EM console.

SOA Admin—Configure notification settings

In *Chapter 5, Human Workflow in BPM Process*, you have learnt about Human Task which has many sections. The **General** section is used to define task details such as title, task outcomes, owner, and other attributes. The **Data** section defines the structure (message elements) of the task payload (the data in the task). The **Assignment** section enables you to assign participants to the task and create a policy for routing the task through the workflow. Similarly, you have learnt about **Presentation**, **Deadlines**, **Access**, and **Events** sections too. And, the **Notification** section enables you to create and send notifications when a user is assigned a task or informed that the status of the task has changed.

Notifications can be sent via e-mail, phone, SMS, and other channels.

You can develop a scenario for which once the contract is finalized by **contracts** user, then **salesrepresentative** user must be informed with an e-mail. Whenever the contract finalizes, the **salesrepresentative** user will receive an e-mail.

For Human Task, you can perform many admin tasks such as notification settings, adding authentication provider, migrating Human Workflow stuffs between environments, and managing notification.

How to do it...

In this chapter, you will learn to configure notification settings.

I. Define a notification

1. Open JDeveloper in **default** role, go to BPM project navigator and click on the **SalesToContractDemo** project.
2. Expand the **Business catalog | Human Tasks** and click on **FinalizeContracts.task**. This will open the task editor.
3. Go to **Notification** section in the task editor.
4. In the **General** tab, set the **Task Status** as **Complete**, as you want to send a notification to **salesrepresentative** user only when this task is completed.

5. Click on the **Browse** button to open the **Identity Lookup**, select the **salesrepresentative** user and click **OK**.

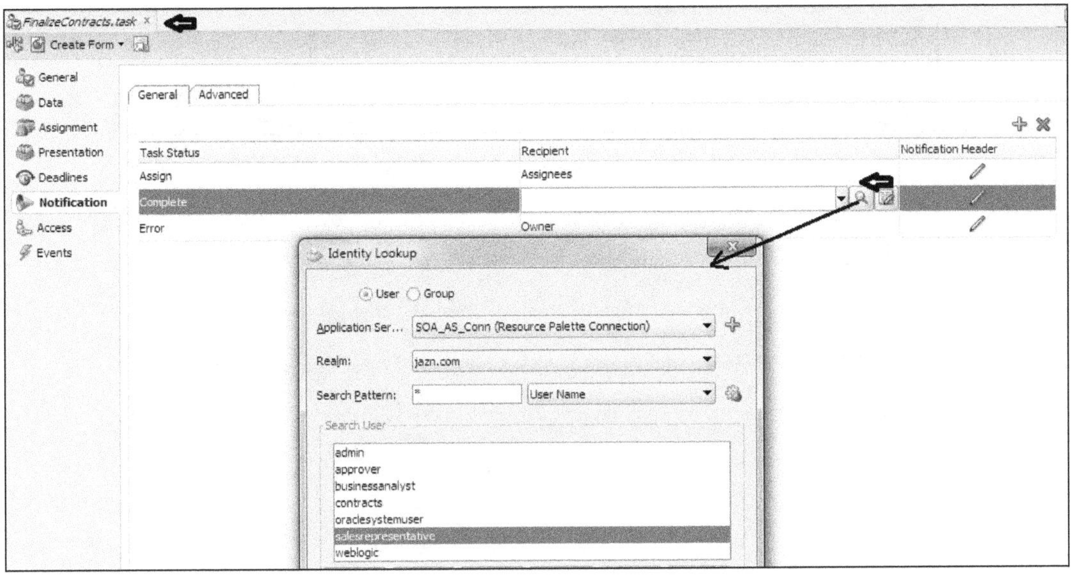

6. Click on the edit pencil button, in the **Notification Header** column to define the header that is to be sent with the notification. The header is defined using an expression and can include elements from the task definition such as payload data.
7. When you have finished the preceding steps, click **Save**.

II. Configure notification settings

1. Install an e-mail server - in this case, you can use *James Server*. It's free and available to download. My e-mail server name is **myemailserver.com**, **SMTP Port** is **35** and **Pop3** is set to run on port **210**.
2. Log in to Oracle EM console (`http://localhost:7001/em/`) as WebLogic user.

3. Expand **User Messaging Service**, right-click on **usermessagingdriver-email** and select **Email Driver Properties**.

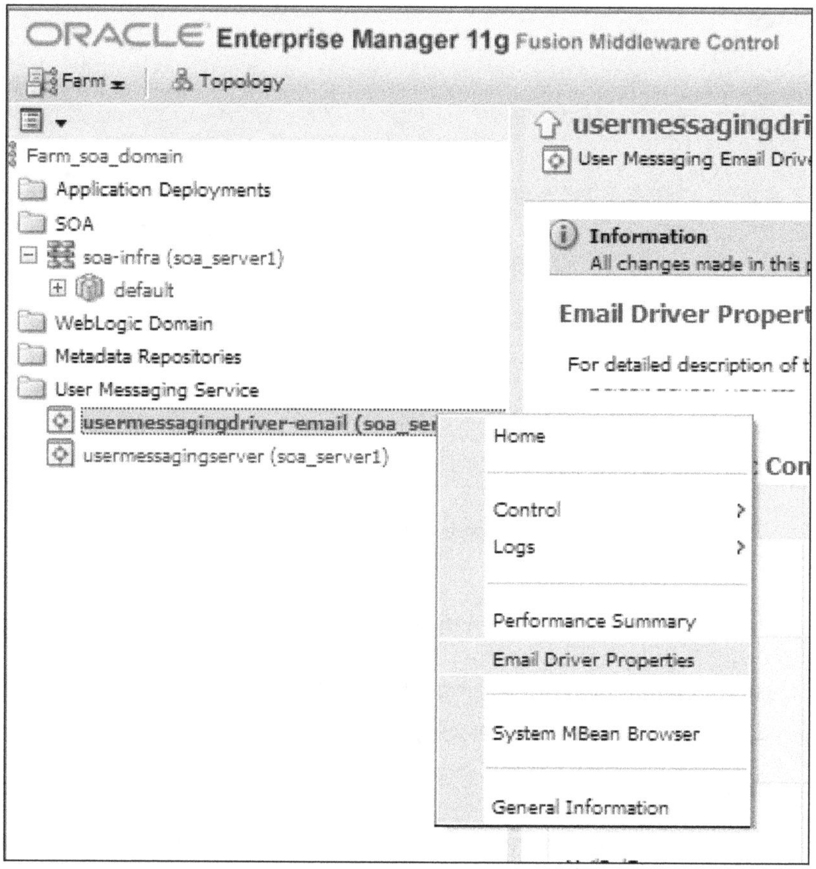

4. Set **Email Driver Properties** as the following:
   - **Default Sender address** - **admin@myemailserver.com**
   - **Mail Access Protocol** - **POP3**
   - **Receive Folder** - **INBOX**
   - **Outgoing Email Server** - **myemailserver.com**
   - **SMTP Port** - **35**
   - **Outgoing Default Sender** - **admin@myemailserver.com**
   - **Outgoing Username** - **admin**
   - **Incoming Mail Server** - **myemailserver.com**
   - **Incoming Port** - **210**

- **Incoming Mail Id** - **salesrepresentative@myemailserver.com**
- **Incoming User Id** - **salesrepresentative**
- Set **Email Password** to the one you have entered while creating accounts in James Server.

5. Click **APPLY**.
6. Deploy the project and run a test instance. You can find an e-mail in the **salesrepresentative** user account when contract is finalized.

> You can install James Server 2.3.2 as the e-mail server and can use Mozilla Thunderbird as the e-mail client.

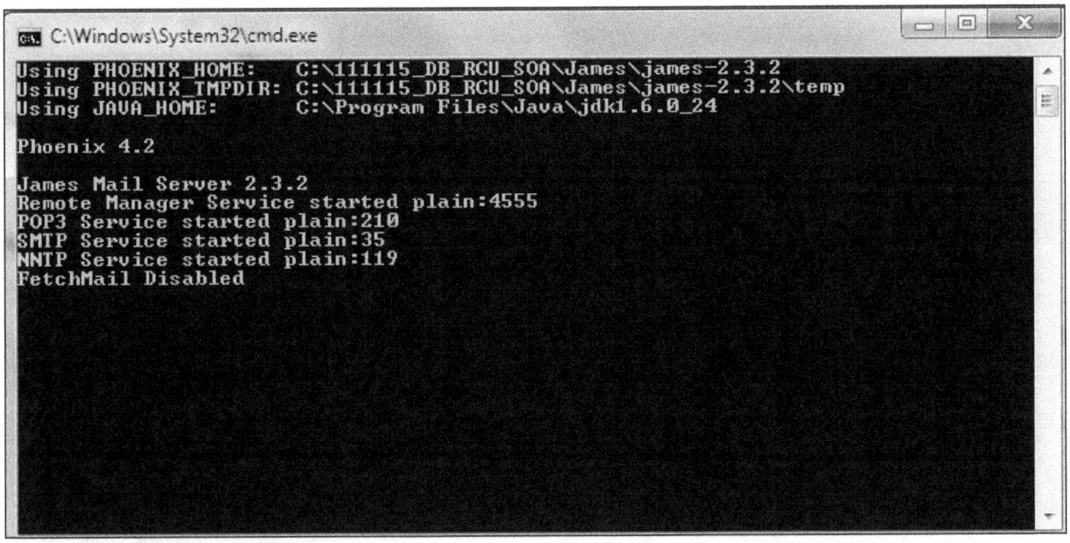

How it works...

Human Workflow Framework is basically integrated with **Oracle UMS** (**Oracle Unified Messaging Services**), to deliver notifications through a variety of channels and based on a user's personal preferences.

You have set the UMS Email driver in Oracle EM console and when Human Workflow engine runs the notification, as its integrated with UMS, it sends an e-mail to the specified user.

There's more...

In this section, you will cover how to manage notifications.

Managing notifications

You can even manage outgoing notifications and incoming e-mail notifications from Oracle EM console.

1. Go to Oracle EM console and log in as the WebLogic user.
2. Right-click on **soa-infra** | **Service Engines** and select **Human Workflow**.

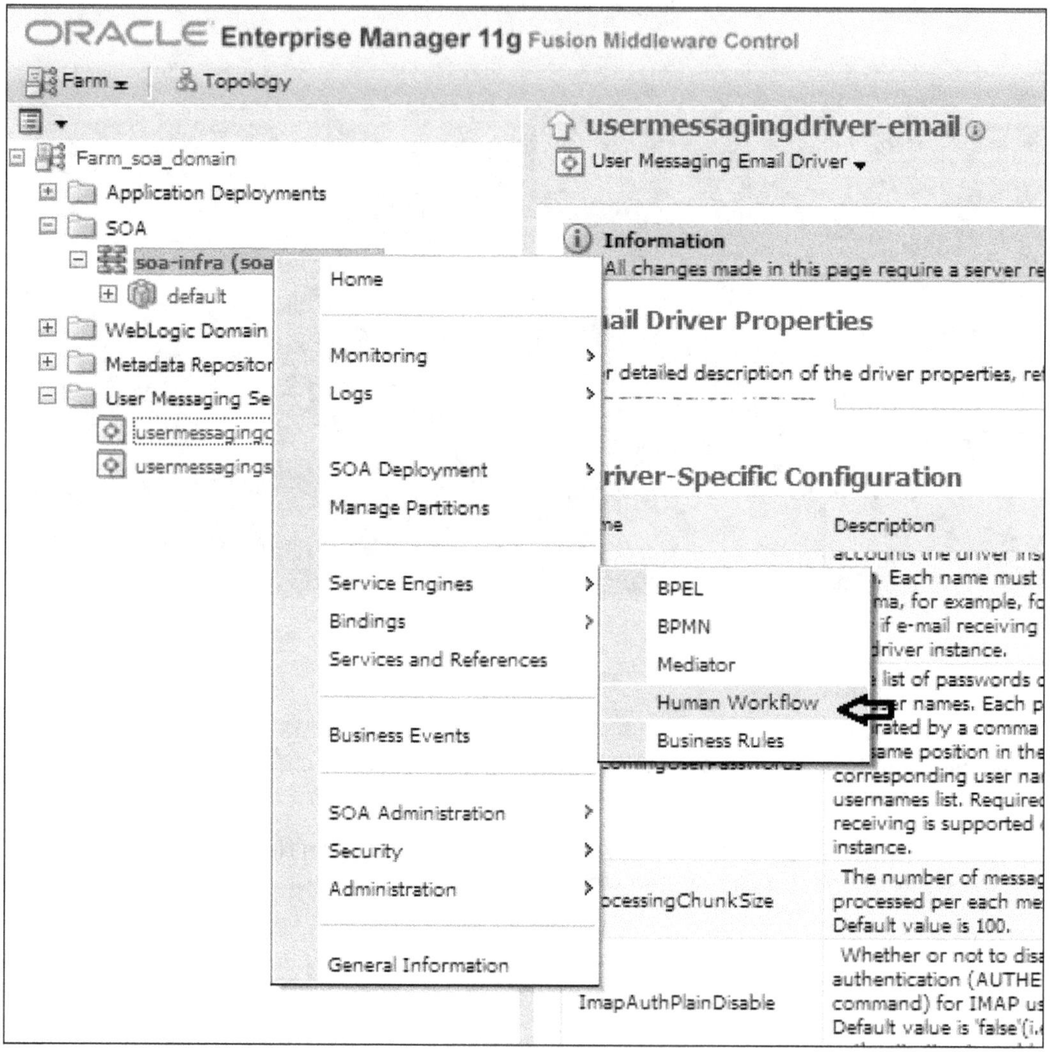

3. Click on the **Notification Management** tab.
4. In the **Outgoing Notifications** section, you can find the outgoing e-mails sent to **salesrepresentative** user's e-mail address.

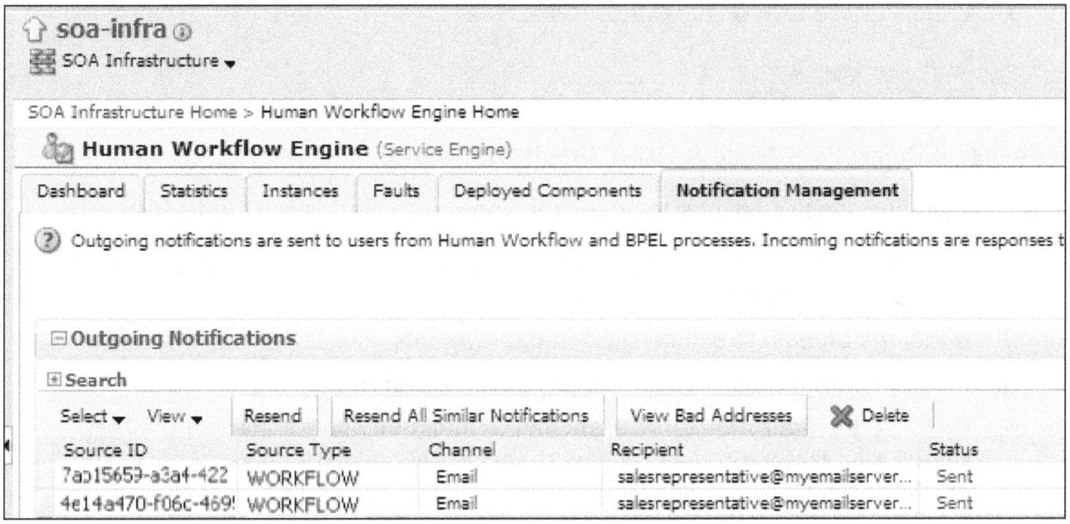

5. Similarly, you can find incoming e-mails in the **Incoming Notifications** section too.

   You can perform a number of tasks on these messages such as **Resend**, **Delete**, and so on.

BPM Admin—Integrating Oracle BPM with Oracle Business Activity Monitoring

There are two types of administrators in Oracle BPM—SOA Administrators and BPM Administrators. This section will cover BPMN Administrator activities, which includes configuring BPMN Process Service Engine properties, integrating Oracle BPM with Oracle Business Activity Monitoring, monitoring BPMN Process service components and engines, managing Oracle BPMN service components and engines, and flex fields.

You learnt to create custom dashboards in the section *Use BPM workspace or BAM Architect to configure custom dashboards*, in this chapter. You also created `data object` folders in Oracle BAM Architect, enabled BAM in BPMN project, created BAM Data objects, and finally created BAM custom dashboards.

However, there are couple of settings which we need to configure to enable integration between Oracle BPM and Oracle BAM. They are as follows:

- Configure Oracle BAM Adapter on the Oracle BPM server
- Enable Oracle BAM on the Oracle BPM server

How to do it...

I. Configure Oracle BAM Adapter on the Oracle BPM server

This configuration enables adapter to understand how to connect to the BAM server.

1. Go to the WebLogic Server Administration console (`http://localhost:7001/console`) and log in as WebLogic user.
2. Under the **Domain** structure, click on **Deployments**.
3. In the **Deployments** list, click on **Oracle BAM Adapter**.
4. Go to the **Configuration** tab | **Outbound Connection pools** and expand **SOAP Connection factory**. You can configure Oracle BAM Adapter to use either SOAP or RMI to communicate with Oracle BAM.
5. Click on the `eis/bam/SOAP JNDI` name.
6. In the **Properties** tab, enter the outbound connection pool server details as shown in the following screenshot:

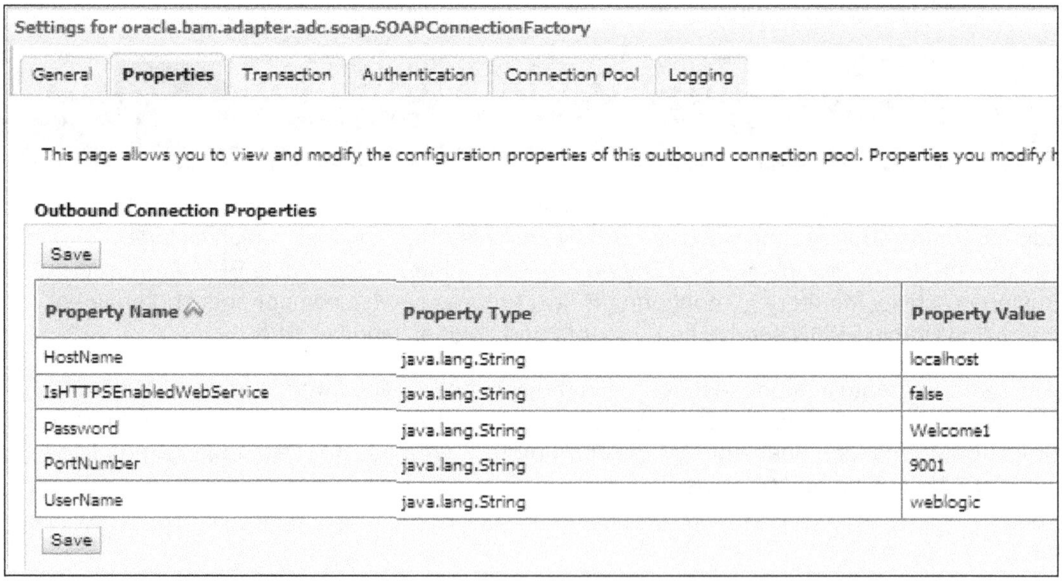

7. Click on **Save**.

   After you enter value in the **Property Value** field, press *Enter* to persist them.

8. Select the deployment plan location to complete the dialog.
9. Click on **Deployments** again, in **Domain** structure, and select **Oracle BAM Adapter**.
10. Click on **Update** and complete the dialog.
11. Click on **Finish**.

II. Enable Oracle BAM on the Oracle BPM server

By setting MBean properties, you are enabling BPM to send events to BAM.

1. Log in to Oracle EM (`http://localhost:7001/em/`) as WebLogic user.
2. Expand **Weblogic Domain**, right-click on **soa_domain** | **bam_server1** and select **System MBean Browser**.

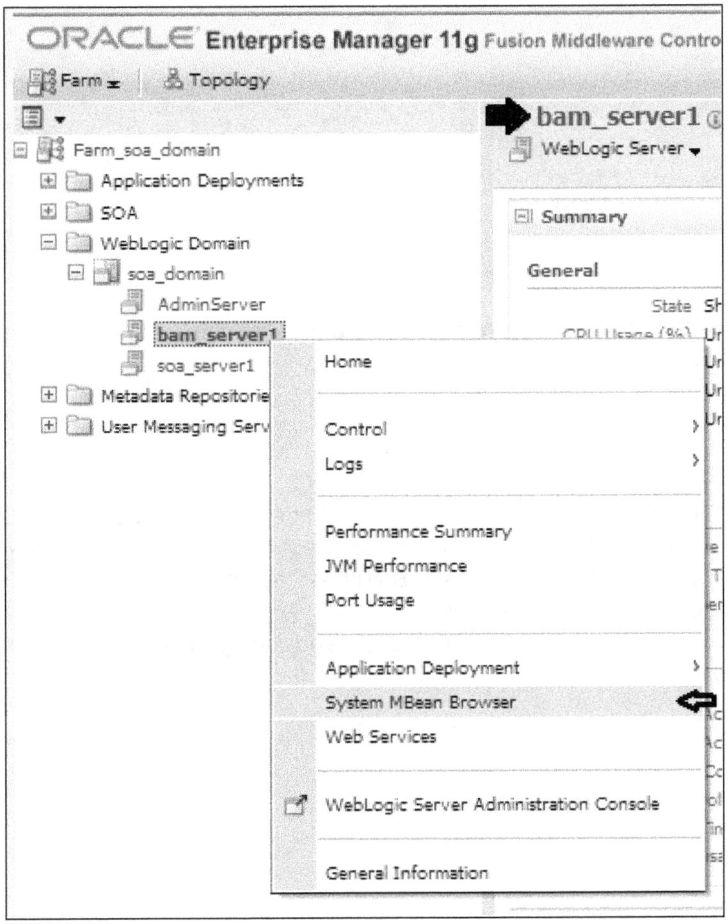

3. In **System MBean Browser**, expand **oracle.as.soainfra.config** | **BPMNConfig** and select **bpmn**. This will open the bpmn MBean's properties.

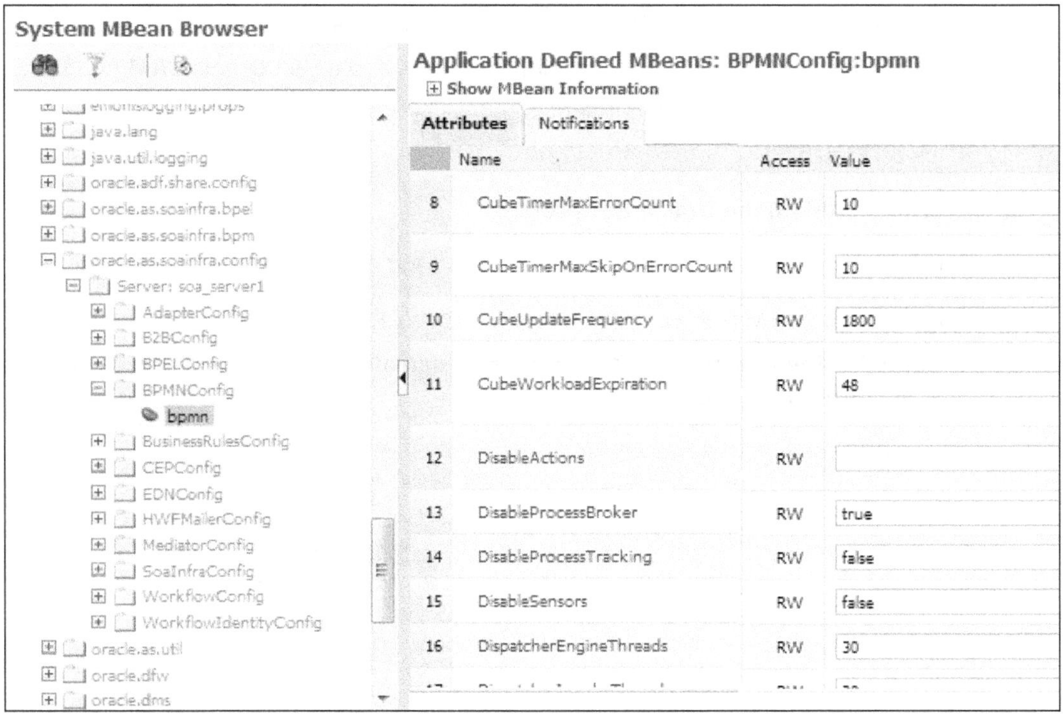

4. Scroll to **DisableActions** properties and delete its value.
5. Click on **Apply**.

How it works...

You configured BAM Adapter as it's used by the BPM server to push events to BAM. And to enable Oracle BAM on the BPM server, you have to set **DisableAction** property in BPMN MBean. When you deploy the BPM project, BAM Data objects are generated (as you have seen in earlier sections) with a name `BI_default_Project_Process`(`BI_default_SalesToContractDemo_SalesToContract`), and then you can create custom dashboards and view them.

BPM Admin—Managing roles, organization units, and groups

In *Chapter 1, Process Modeling*, you defined roles and organization units. Roles authorize the people with a set of responsibilities (task) to perform. Later, you divide the tasks based on these roles by creating swimlane in the process. And each horizontal swimlane is associated with a role.

The method you adopted in Chapter 1, *Process Modeling*, for role assignment was static. However, there could be situations where a user is on vacation or leaves the organization, and in these cases you need to have new users to be assigned to roles in a dynamic fashion. You can assign users dynamically to roles using Oracle BPM workspace.

You have a user **BusinessAnalystManager** which will be assigned a Business Analyst role, as the user **businessanalyst** will be on vacation.

How to do it...

I. Manage roles

1. Log in to Oracle BPM workspace (`http://localhost:8001/bpm/workspace/`) as WebLogic user.
2. Click on the administration link.
3. Click on **Roles**, in the **Administration Areas** panel on the left, to list all the different roles across all the deployed processes.
4. Select **SalesToContractDemo.BusinessAnalyst** role and this will list the user assigned to the role. You can find that only **businessanalyst** user is assigned to **SalesToContractDemo.BusinessAnalyst** role.
5. Click on the add icon on the lower panel, to add a user to this role.

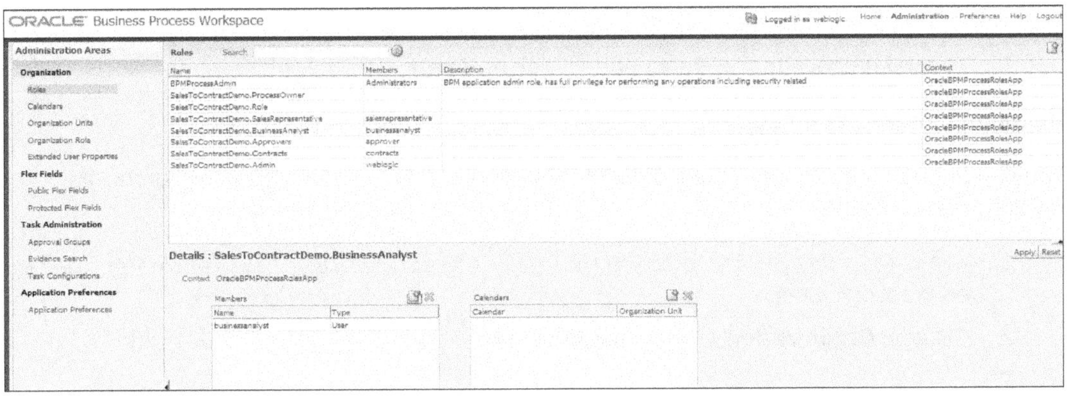

6. Select users from the drop-down list and search for users. Select **businessanalystmanager** and click **OK**.

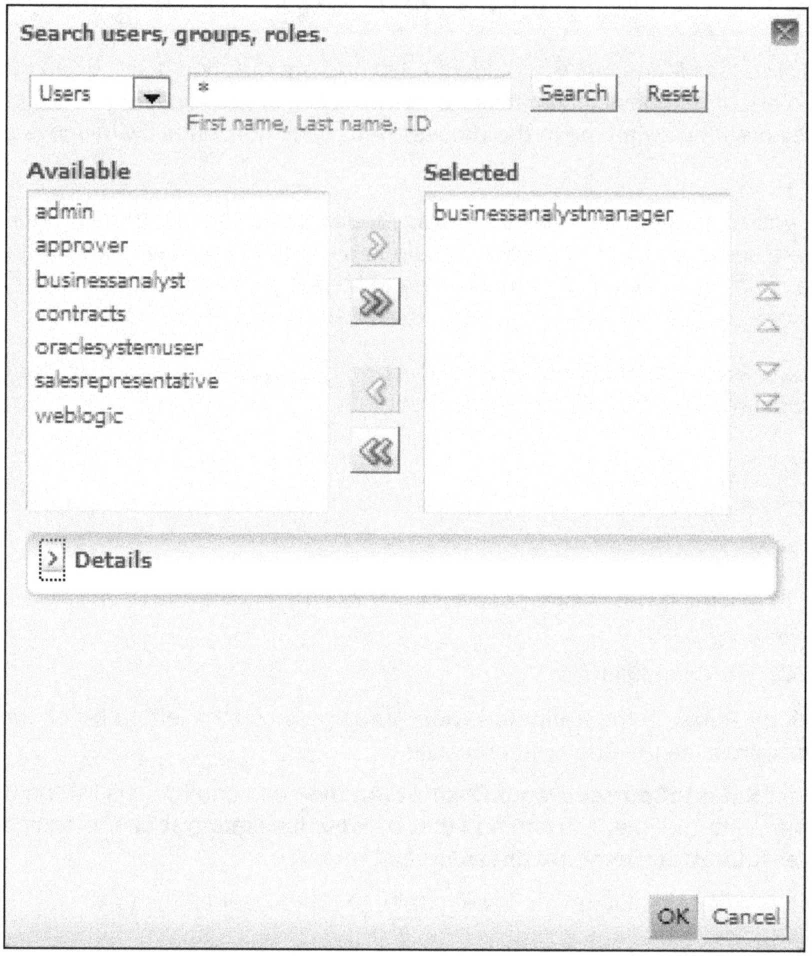

7. You will be back to the **Roles** page. Click on **Apply**.

II. Manage organization units

You can define organization units in Oracle BPM workspace and can define hierarchy of organization units too.

1. Log in to Oracle BPM workspace (`http://localhost:8001/bpm/workspace/`) as WebLogic user.
2. Click on **Organization** | **Organization Units**.

3. Click on add button and from the list, select **Root Organization Unit**.

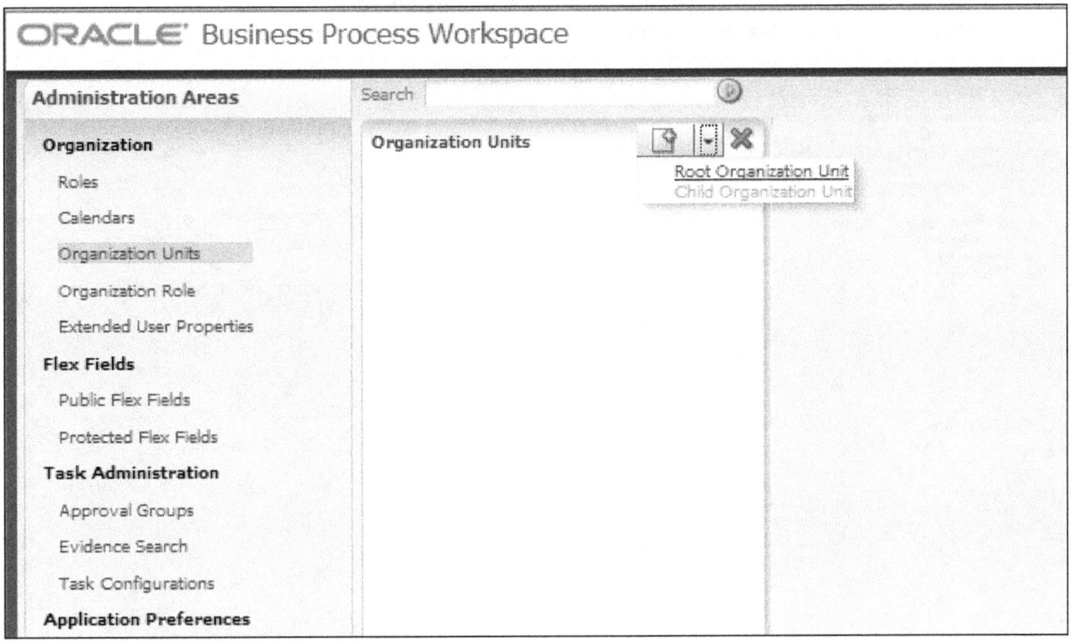

4. Enter **Name** of organization unit as **APJ Sales Unit**.
5. Click on the add button and select **Child Organization Unit** to add a child organization to **APJ Sales Unit**.

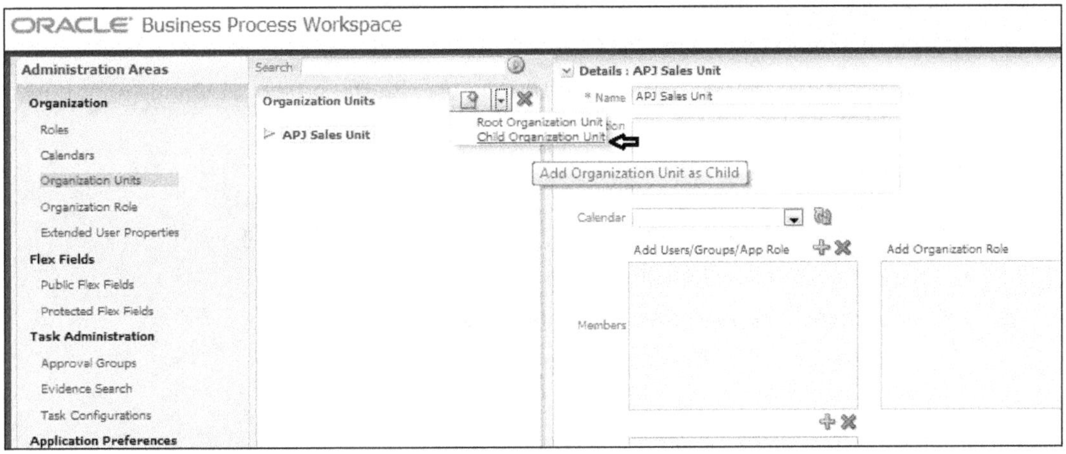

6. Enter **India Sales Unit for Name** of the Child Organization .
7. Click on **Apply**.

8. Open JDeveloper in the **default** role.
9. Go to the BPM project navigator and click on **Organization** in the **SalesToContractDemo** project, as shown in the following screenshot:

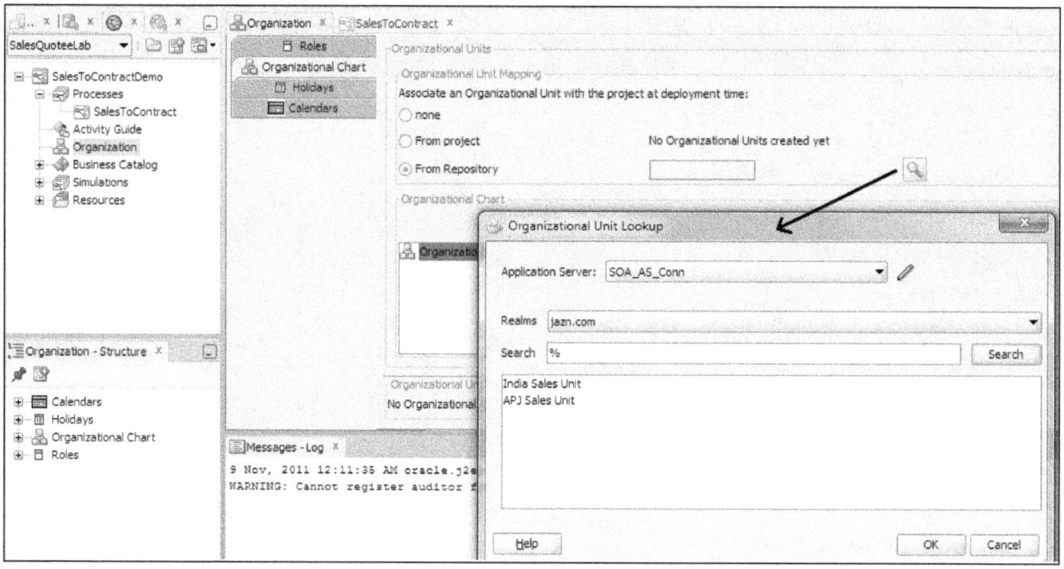

10. Check **From Repository** and click the browse button to open **Organization Unit Lookup**.
11. Select the **Application Server** and search for all.
12. You can find the Organization Units you have created.
13. Select the one required and click **OK**.

    This way you can associate an organization unit with the project at deployment time from repository.

III. Creating Approval Groups

1. Log in to the Oracle BPM workspace application as the WebLogic user.
2. Click on the administration link at the top of the page.
3. Click **Approval Groups** in **Task Administration**.

4. Click on the green plus (+) icon next to **Groups,** and select **Create Static**.

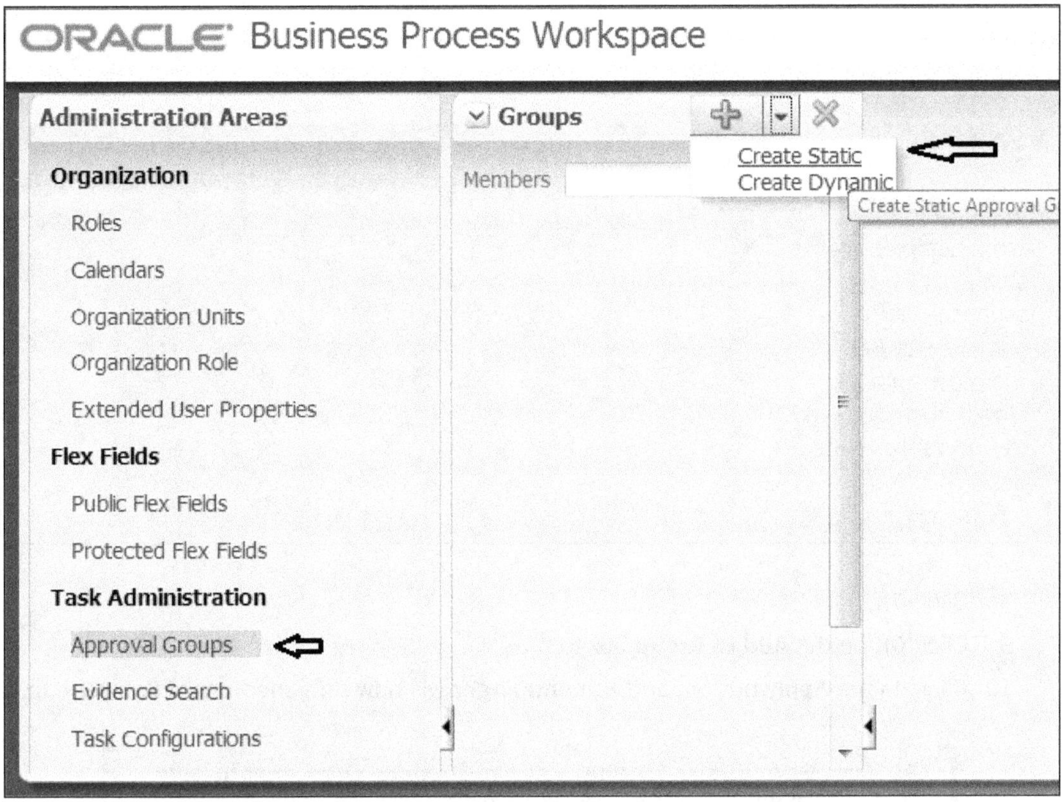

5. In the **Details** section, enter **Name** of the group as **SalesGroup** and click on the green plus (+) icon to add members to the group.
6. Search/browse for **Members**. This will open the **Identity Browser**.

7. Select **zonalmanager** from the list. Let's have only one user belonging to this group at the moment.

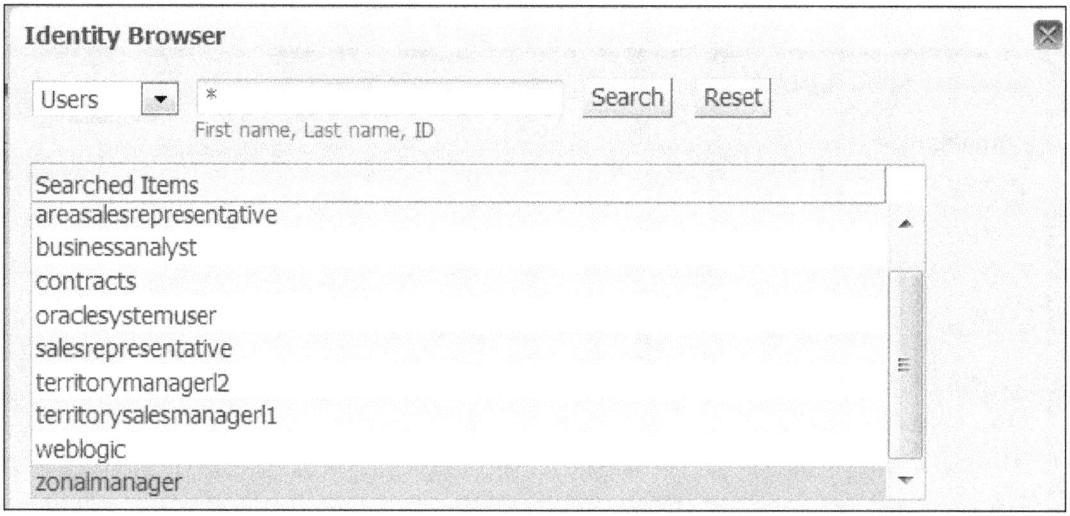

8. Click **OK**.
9. Click **OK** on the **Add to Group** box too.
10. Click on the **Apply** button, and **zonalmanager** will now be a member of **SalesGroup**.

> Go to `http://acharyavivek.wordpress.com` to learn about Dynamic Approval Group.

IV. Managing organization roles

Organization roles are logical roles that define the members of an organization unit. They are groups of users specified by using a query. For example: all **Members** of **SalesGroup** belong to a logical **Organization Role** named **SalesAgents**.

1. Go to Oracle BPM workspace and log in as the WebLogic user.
2. Click on **Organization Role** as shown in the following screenshot.
3. Click on the add icon to add an organization role.

4. Enter **Name** as **SalesAgents** and select **SalesGroup** in the **Grantees Group** list.

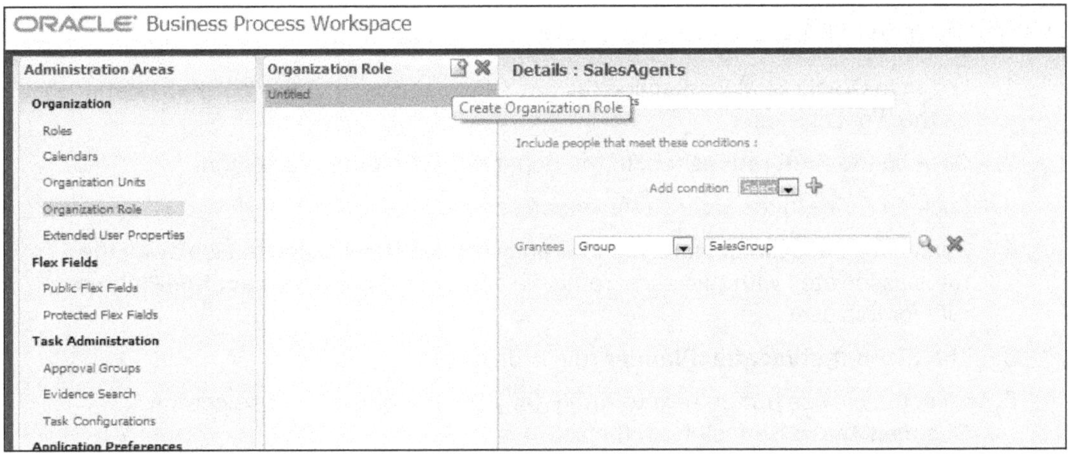

5. Click on **Apply**.

There's more...

The following section will guide you through the necessary steps to revoke a role.

Revoking a role

1. From the **Business Process Workspace** toolbar, select **Administration**. The **Administration Areas** panel appears.
2. In the **Organization** panel, select **Roles**.
3. Select a role. The **Details** panel displays the details for the selected role.
4. Choose the member in the **Members** section and click on **Revoke the role from user, group, or role**.
5. Click on **OK**.

BPM Admin—Setting rules

You have a user **businessanalystmanager** which will be assigned the Business Analyst role, as user **businessanalyst** will be on vacation. You can handle such a situation dynamically, by using rules on tasks.

If a rule meets its filter conditions, then it is executed and no other rules are evaluated.

How to do it...

In this section, you will explore how to use rules.

1. Log in to Oracle BPM workspace (`http://localhost:8001/bpm/workspace`) as the WebLogic user.
2. Click on the **Preferences** tab, in the upper-right corner of the screen.
3. Click on **Rules** in the **User Preferences** section.
4. Search for the **businessanalyst** user and click on **Show Rules** to display all the rules associated with this user. You have created a **BizAnalystVacationPlanner** rule for this user.
5. The **BizAnalystVacationPlanner** rule is displayed.
6. Click the browse button next to **Apply Only to task type(s)** and select the **BusinessAnalystUI** task from the list.

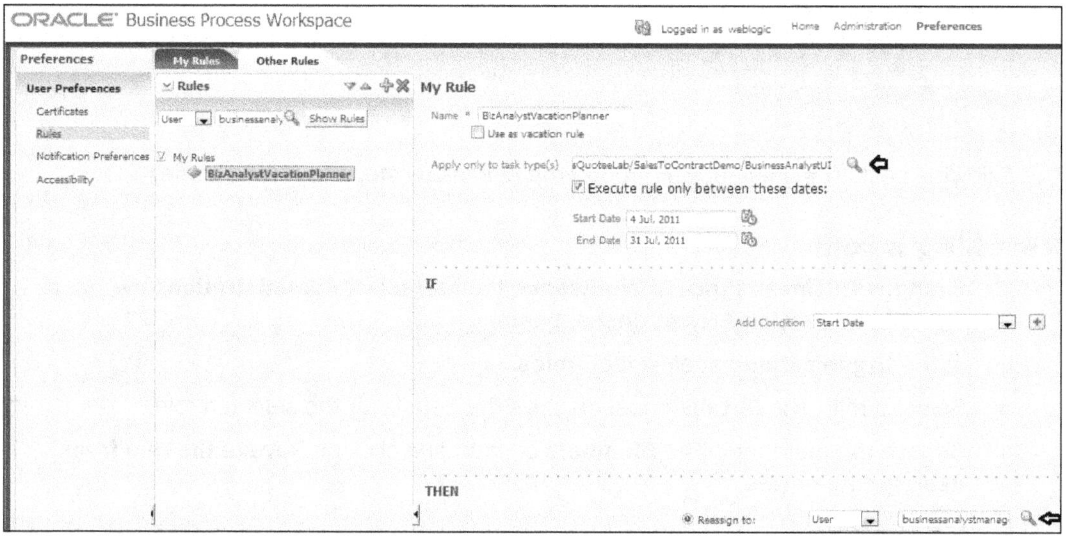

7. Check **Execute rule only between these dates**, to get rule eligibility between these dates.
8. Enter a **Start Date** and **End Date** as shown in the previous screenshot.
9. Set **IF** condition as **Start Date**.
10. Reassign the task to the **businessanalystmanager** user.
11. Click on **Save**.

How it works...

When the rule meets its filter conditions, it is executed. If a **BusinessAnalystUI** task gets assigned to the **businessanalyst** user and this task assignment falls between the **Start Date** and **End Date**, the rule meets its conditions and is executed, and the task is reassigned to the **businessanalystmanager** user.

BPM Admin—Using flex fields/mapped attributes

A user can have many tasks assigned. Let's say he wants to prioritize tasks and work on those tasks which he wants to access at that instant. You can create a custom column in the task list and the user can see these custom column values in the task list after logging into the Process workspace; they can then decide which task to access.

How will these column values be populated? These column values will be populated from the task payload itself. Say you have a **businessanalyst** user. You will create a custom attribute in a task list which displays *Account name* from the quote payload. Account name has values such as FusionNX, APJSales, USASales, and so on, and **businessanalyst** has priorities for the day and he/she just wants to work on account name FusionNX for the day.

You can achieve this by using **flex fields**. Human Workflow flex fields store and query use case specific custom attributes. These custom attributes typically come from the task payload values. Storing custom attributes in flex fields provides the following benefits:

- They can be displayed as a column in the task listing
- They can filter tasks in custom views and advanced searches
- They can be used for a keyword-based search

How to do it...

I. Adding variables

1. Log in to JDeveloper with the **default** role.
2. Go to BPM navigator | **Project** | **Business Catalog** | **Human tasks** and click on **BusinessAnalystUI.task**.
3. Click on the **Data** section to open the task editor.
4. Click on the green plus (**+**) icon to add a data variable.

5. Let the variable **Type** be **string**. Enter **Parameter Name** as **VarAccountName** and check **Editable via worklist**.

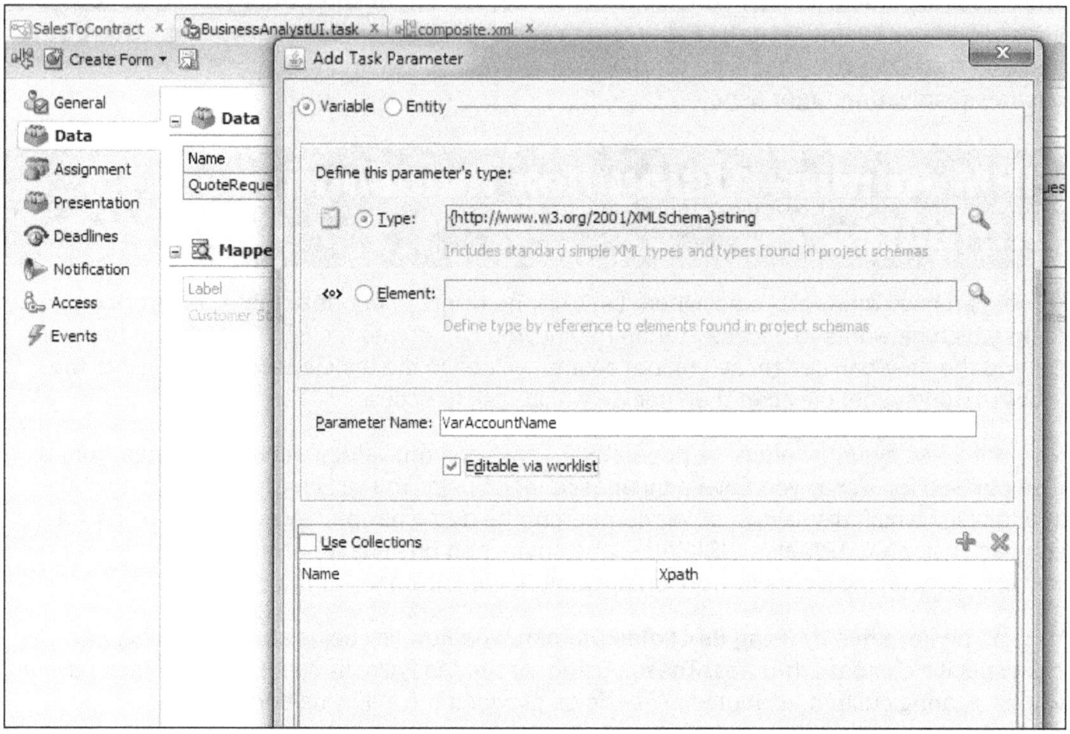

6. Click **OK**.
7. Click on the **SalesToContract** process and go to the **Business Analyst** swimlane.
8. Double-click on the **BusinessAnalystReview** Human Task.
9. Go to the **Implementation** tab and edit the Data association.

10. Enter a simple **Expression quote.summary.accountname** from the quote payload as input to the **VarAccountName** variable as shown in the following screenshot:

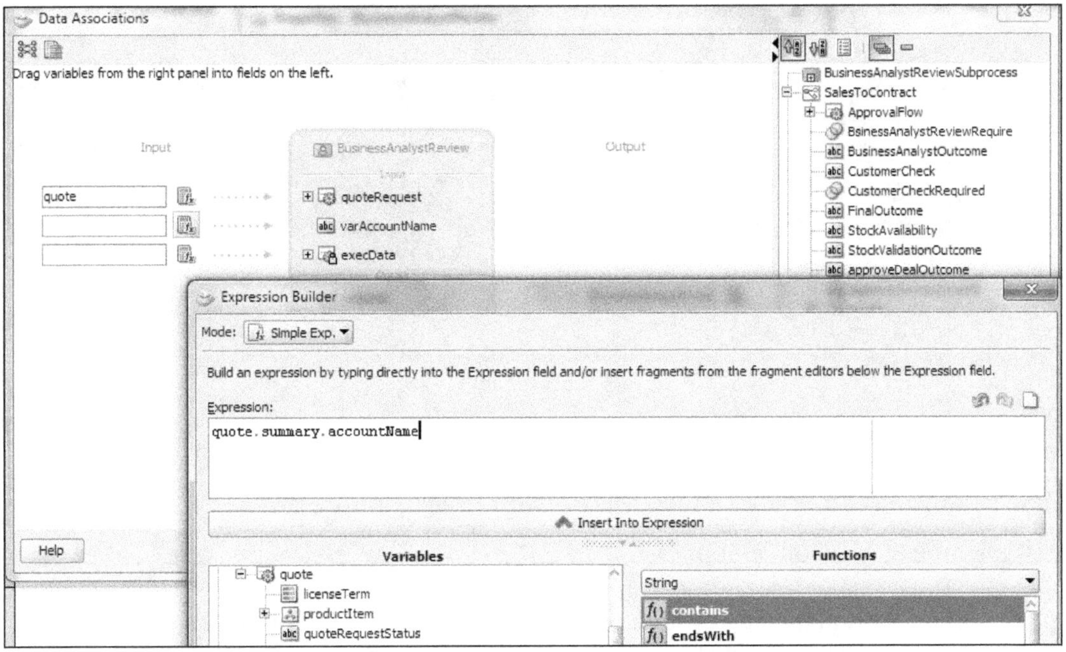

11. Click **OK** on the Data association dialog.
12. Click **OK** on the **Properties** dialog too.
13. When you have finished the preceding steps, click **Save**.
14. Deploy the project as per *Chapter 3, Process Deployment and Testing*.

II. Creating flex fields for BusinessAnalystUI tasks

1. Log in to Oracle BPM workspace as the WebLogic user.
2. Click on the **Administrator** tab and in the **Administration Area**, click **Public Flexfields.**
3. In the **Create Flexfields** section, click on the green plus (**+**) icon. This will open a label box.

4. Create a label **AccountName** as shown in the following screenshot and click on the **Create** button to create it:

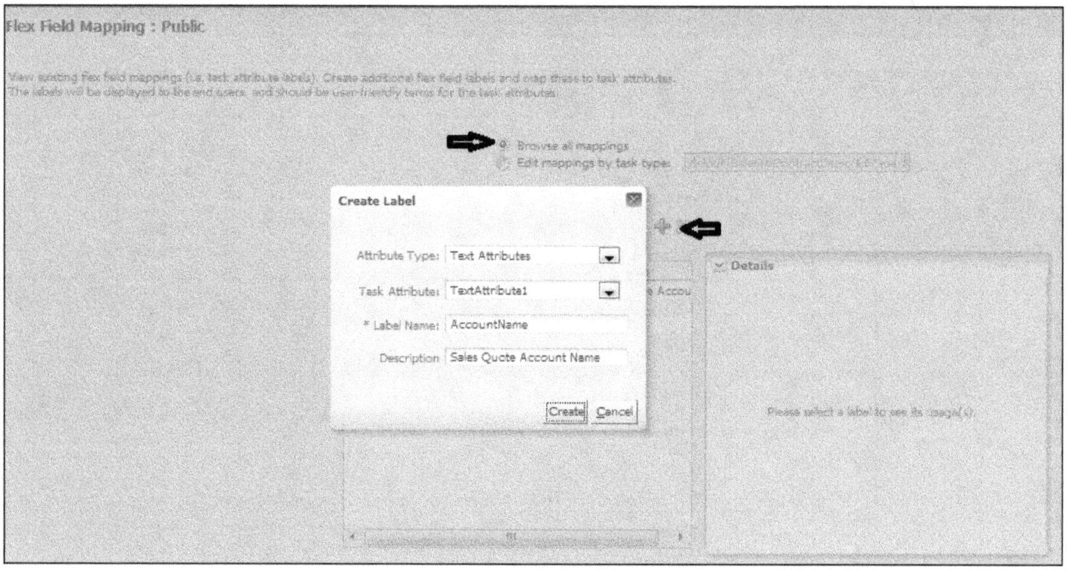

5. Check **Edit mappings by task type** and click on the browse button as shown in the following screenshot.
6. Select the **BusinessAnalystUI** task from the list.
7. You can select **VarAccountName** from the drop-down list as the **Map Payload Attributes**.
8. Select the **AccountName** label in the text box adjacent to the **Map Payload Attributes** drop-down list.

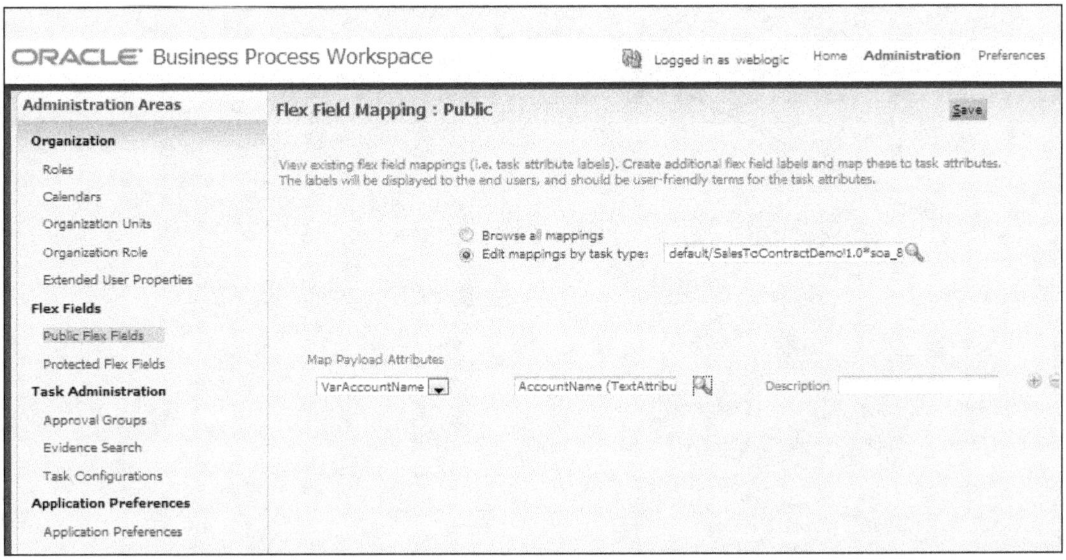

9. Click on the **Save** button in the top-right corner.
10. Click on the **Home** tab and go to **Worklist Views** section.
11. Click on **Inbox** and click on the green plus (**+**) icon to add a user view.

    This will open a **Create User View** dialog.

12. Enter **Name** as **AccountNameBasedSearch**.
13. Select the **BusinessAnalystUI** task in **Task Type** and keep the defaults for the rest.

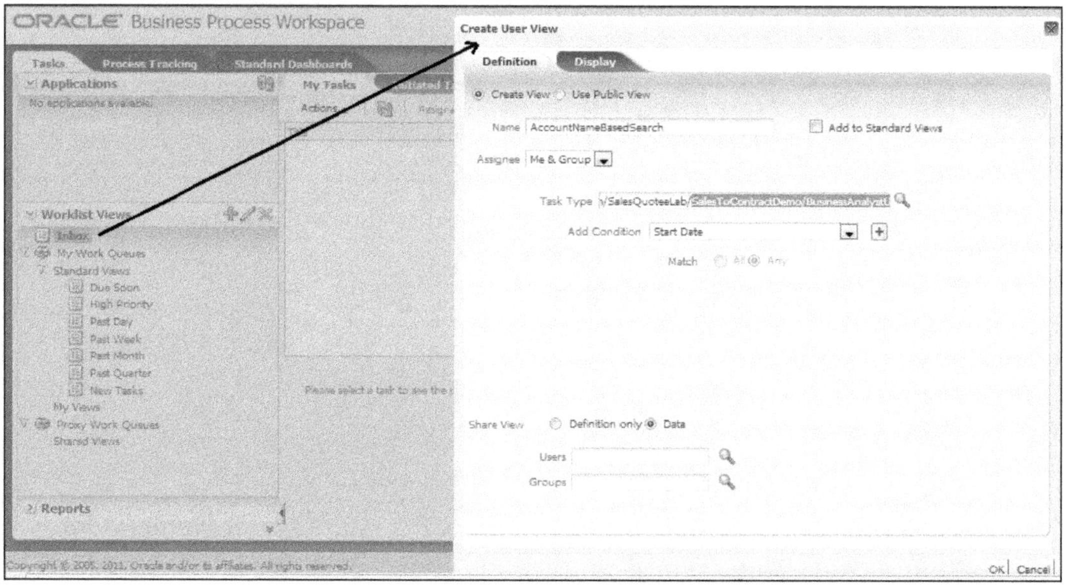

14. Click on the **Display** tab.
15. Scroll through the **Available** column list and you will find the column label **AccountName** listed there.
16. Add the column to the **Selected** section by clicking the **>** arrow.

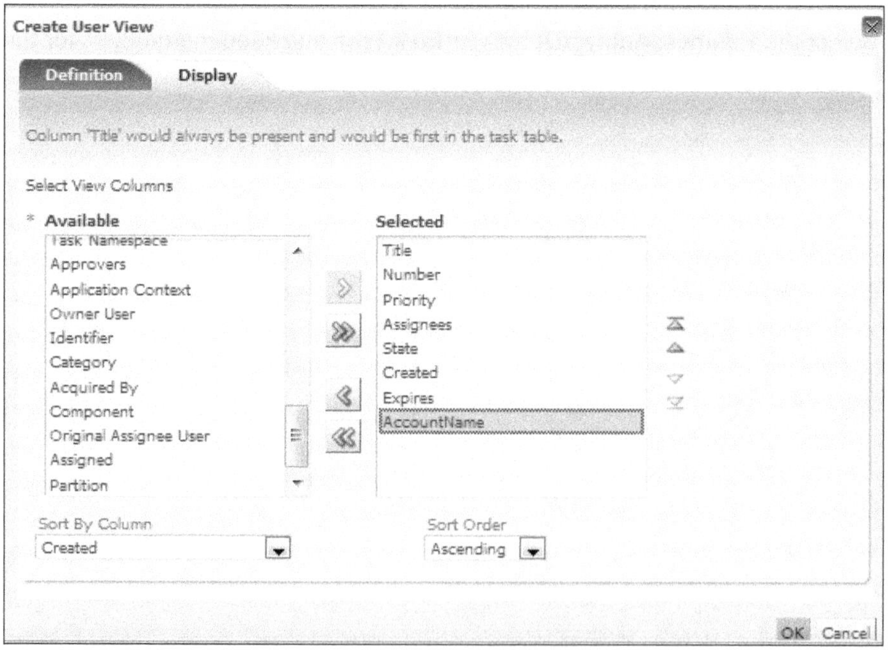

17. Click **OK**.
18. Initiate a process instance.
19. Log in again to Oracle BPM as the WebLogic user.
20. In the **Worklist Views**, you will find the custom view **AccountNameBasedSearch**.
21. You will find **AccountName** as the column and **FusionNX** as the value.

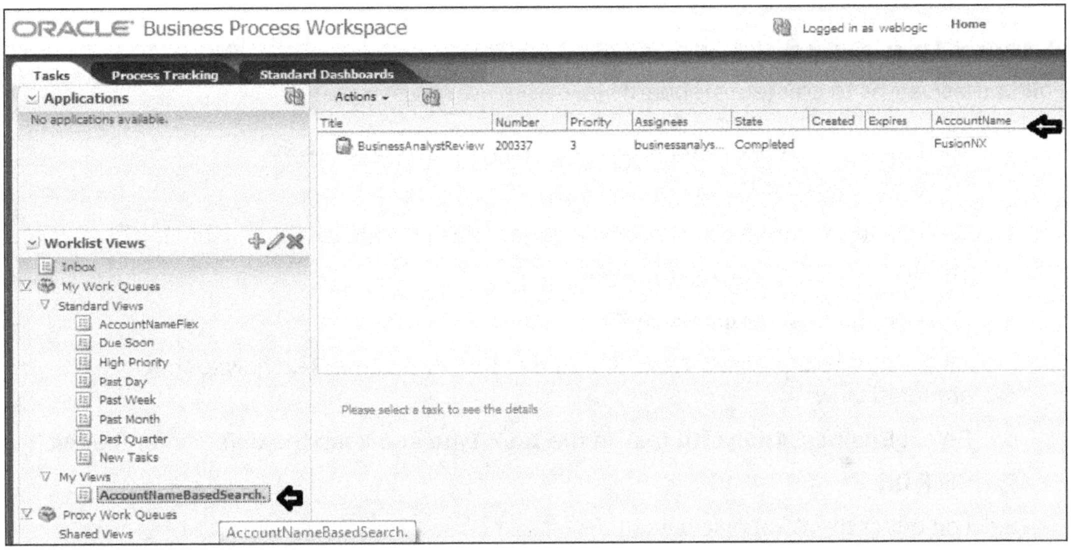

22. You can log in to Oracle EM console and verify the value from the running process instance.

How it works...

Flex fields will store the custom attribute values coming from the task payload and make them available to the custom view. For the mapped attribute to get populated, administrators create mapped attribute mappings by specifying a label for the mapped attribute to be populated and map the payload attribute, which contains the data, to the label.

After the mapping is complete and a new task is initiated, the value of the payload is transferred to the mapped attribute that has just been mapped. Tasks initiated before the mapping do not contain the value in the mapped attribute. Only top-level, simple type attributes in the payload can be transferred to a mapped attribute.

These mappings are valid for a certain task type.

You have witnessed that the Human Task editor is used only when defining the payload for a task. All other operations are performed at runtime by the administrator.

There's more...

You created this custom view **AccountNameBasedSearch** in the **Inbox** earlier. And you have selected the **BusinessAnalystUI** task in the task type and kept the defaults for the rest.

You have noticed that there is a checkbox **Add To Standard View**, which you have kept as unchecked by default. You can create a custom view in **Standard Views** too.

Adding to a standard view

Follow these steps to create a standard view:

1. Go to Oracle BPM workspace and log in as the WebLogic user.
2. Go to the **Worklist Views** section.
3. Click on **Inbox** and then click on the green plus (**+**) icon to add a user view.

   This will open a **Create User View** dialog.
4. Enter **Name** as **AccountNameFlex**.
5. Check **Add To Standard View**, to add this **AccountNameFlex** view to the standard view.
6. Select **BusinessAnalystUI** task in the **Task Type** and keep the defaults for therest.
7. Click **OK**.
8. Log out of the WebLogic user.
9. Run an instance on the process.
10. Log in as **BusinessAnalyst** user in the Oracle BPM workspace.
11. Go to **Worklist Views** and you can witness **AccountNameFlex** in **Standard View**.
12. You will find the **AccountName** column and data from payload too.

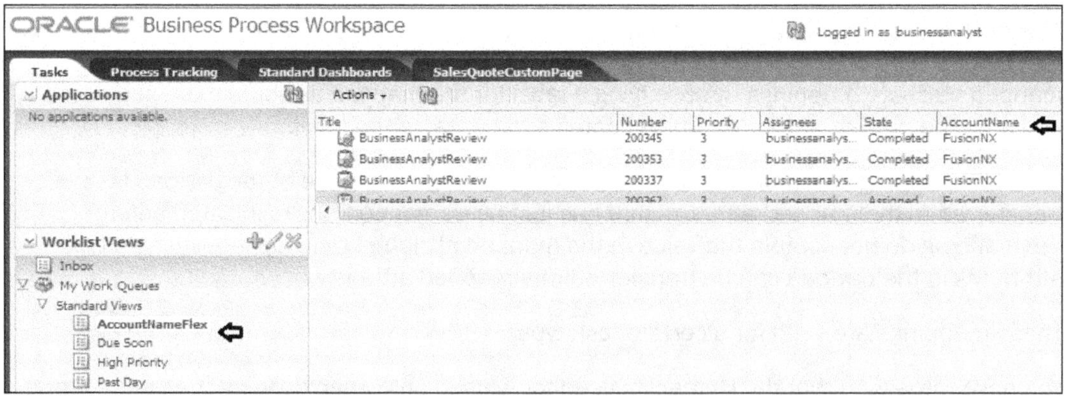

BPM Admin—Monitoring BPM processes

Oracle EM helps you track the execution of your BPM processes. A BPM project has SOA composite and other components wired. You have deployed the project and run an instance of the project. Now, you can use Oracle EM console to monitor it.

How to do it...

Learn to monitor processes using the EM console in the following section:

1. Log in to the Oracle EM console as the WebLogic admin user.
2. Go to **soa-infra** and click on the BPMN project name in the **default** domain.
3. You can find the instance created for it in the display.
4. Un-check the running instance box and you can find instances which have been completed or have different states than **Running**.

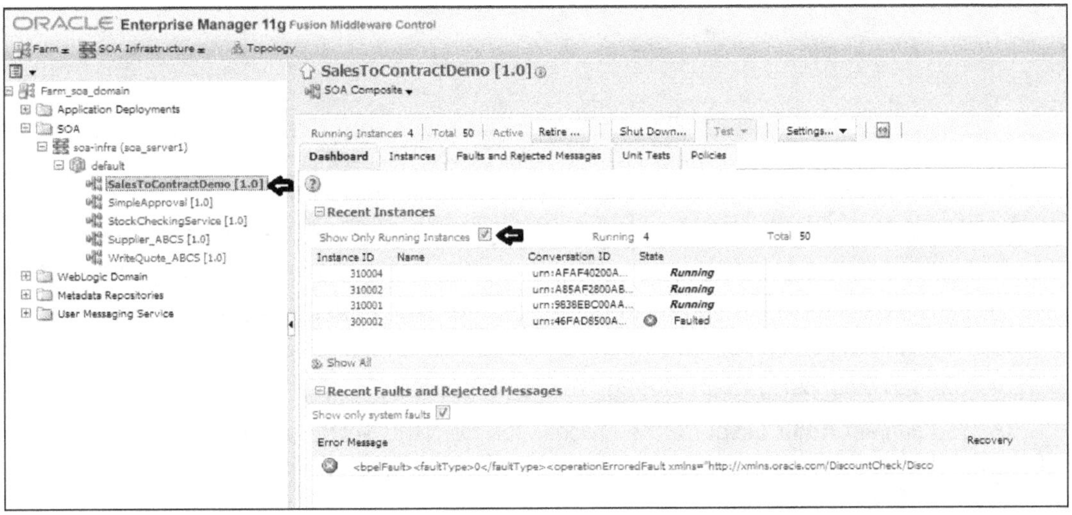

5. You can retire, shutdown, and perform different settings changes related to **Audit Level**, payload validation, and BAM monitoring from this page.
6. Click on **Instance ID**. This will open the flow trace page.
7. Click on the process name **SalesToContract**.
8. You are at the **Audit** page. In the **Audit Trail** tab, you can find all the activities being listed.
9. Expand the **BusinessAnalystReview** activity and click on **Activity Link** to drill into the input and output of the activity.

10. You can find the variable **VarAccountName** being populated with **FusionNX**, which youused as the custom column in the previous section.

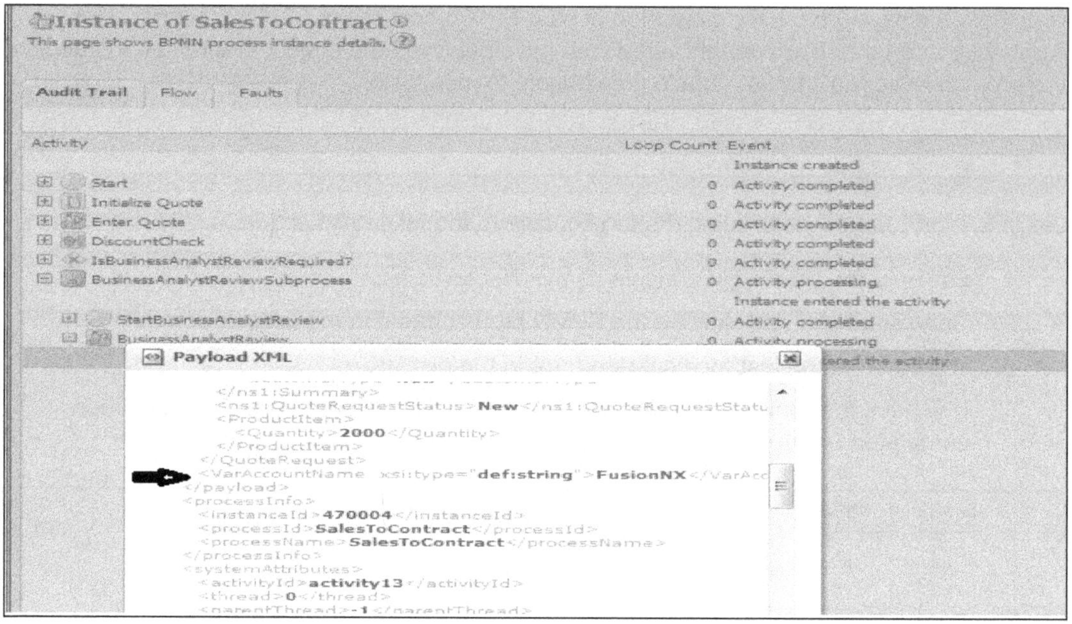

11. Similarly, you can click on the **Flow** tab to view the process flow.
12. In the main process dashboard, you can use the **Faults and Rejected Messages** tab to check on process faults and can even perform recovery of recoverable faults.
13. Policies can be attached and detached too from the **Policies** section on the main dashboard.
14. You can even perform unit testing to the processes.
15. You can set **Audit Level** for the process too from the **Settings** button.

How it works...

Monitoring BPMN processes from the Oracle EM console provides drill-down facilities to an instance. And tasks such as error recovery, setting **Audit Level** of the process, payload validation, enabling BAM, unit tests, and policy attachment and detachment can all be performed from one place.

A

Oracle BPM— Application Development Lifecycle

Business Process Management (**BPM**) is for process transparency, process intelligence, business empowerment, and business alignment. What makes the heart of an enterprise? What makes or breaks an enterprise? What's the differentiating factor? What provides operational efficiency, business visibility, and agility to an enterprise? It's the business process, and Oracle BPM is all about business process and business process management. BPM encompasses the vision, modelling, collaboration, simulation, implementation, measurement, execution, monitoring, management, and administration of business processes.

Business architecture lays the blueprint for operating and transforming the enterprise. It includes various models and defines business goals, objectives, initiatives, and metrics, and models business functions both internal and external. It also encompasses organizational models to depict roles, responsibilities, and collaborations, to define how and by whom defined functions will be provided and used. Along with all of this, business architecture defines business rules and policies to infuse governance, so that stakeholders can adhere and enforce policies. They also define steps to achieve business transformation objectives.

However, one business architecture element that is of interest for us in this book, is Business Process Models. Business Process Models defines the activities, steps, and information flows between processes, to carry out business functions.

As Oracle BPM is a part and element of Enterprise architecture. BPM needs to be designed, so that the enterprise can fully reap the rewards of Oracle BPM. While designing business processes, it's not just automating and managing processes, it more about how an enterprise adapts to a comprehensive view of business processes, where they have to take the overall Enterprise architecture into account and not just automating and managing business processes. Therefore, you can look at BPM adoption in an enterprise as an element of Enterprise architecture.

With BPM, the enterprise can achieve the goal of automation. Enterprise can now model a business process, make associations with Human Workflow and IT applications, and infuse **Business Rules Management Systems** (**BRMS**) . And, in combination with SOA and BRMS, enterprises can achieve extremes of agility. Oracle BPM offers business agility. Process impact is directly proportional to process complexity. BPM is for continuous process improvement, too.

Oracle BPM methodology is an agile strategy and an iterative approach to Business Process Management. And they are best suited in this era of ever-changing business processes, where there is a demand for continuous incremental improvement. Traditional methodologies were code-centric, rarely model-driven, always overlooked the KPI, lacked continuous improvement, and had no vision beyond the current single project. For BPM, a methodology was required that could address these inadequacies, that could bridge the gap between IT and business.

Oracle BPM methodology as a foundation for business process implementation as an enterprise element offers many benefits such as the follows:

- Business in Oracle BPM lifecycle, business leadership, and Enterprise architect, work closely, which leads to process improvements with continuous alignment with business needs.
- **Evaluation**: Evaluation of IT assets enables effective planning. Gaps in the IT landscape can be identified and assessed, and required enhancements can be specified.
- **Predictability**: With simulation and analysis of processes, Oracle BPM incorporates predictability, as results and costs can be determined in advance and with a high degree of accuracy and confidence.

- **Bridging Business and IT Gap**: Business stakeholders are involved at every step of process design and development. Information is exchanged at every engineering step. Process or business analysts always work with process architects. Business process analysts with their process, business, and modelling skills, capture and model processes, drive process optimization, recommend changes, incorporate change requests from business, direct UAT, identify rules, define KPIs, and work with process architects for technical coordination.
- **Traceability**: With process analysis, you can capture the key decisions and associated motivation artifacts to support impact analysis and enable traceability throughout the business process lifecycle.
- **Measurability**: With process analysis, you can monitor your business processes, which enables a feedback loop enabling continuous improvement.
- **Adaptability**: BPM methods and activities can be integrated with existing methods and new methods, with ease.
- **Role Definition**: Clear definition of duties.

Oracle BPM Methodology has put more control in the hands of business leadership. The following figure shows the Oracle BPM Application development lifecycle. It has many phases, such as:

- Vision
- Model
- Implementation
- Deployment
- Run-time

This application development lifecycle is equally applicable to any type of BPMN process, be it a standard process, an orchestration process, or a choreographic process. Most process modellers, and even you, after reading this book and creating a model, must be familiar with defining the flow of activities. This is called standard process or an orchestration process. In choreography processes, the focus is not on orchestrations of the work performed by these participants, but rather on the exchange of messages/information between participants.

You can refer to `http://acharyavivek.wordpress.com/`, for more information about choreography and orchestration.

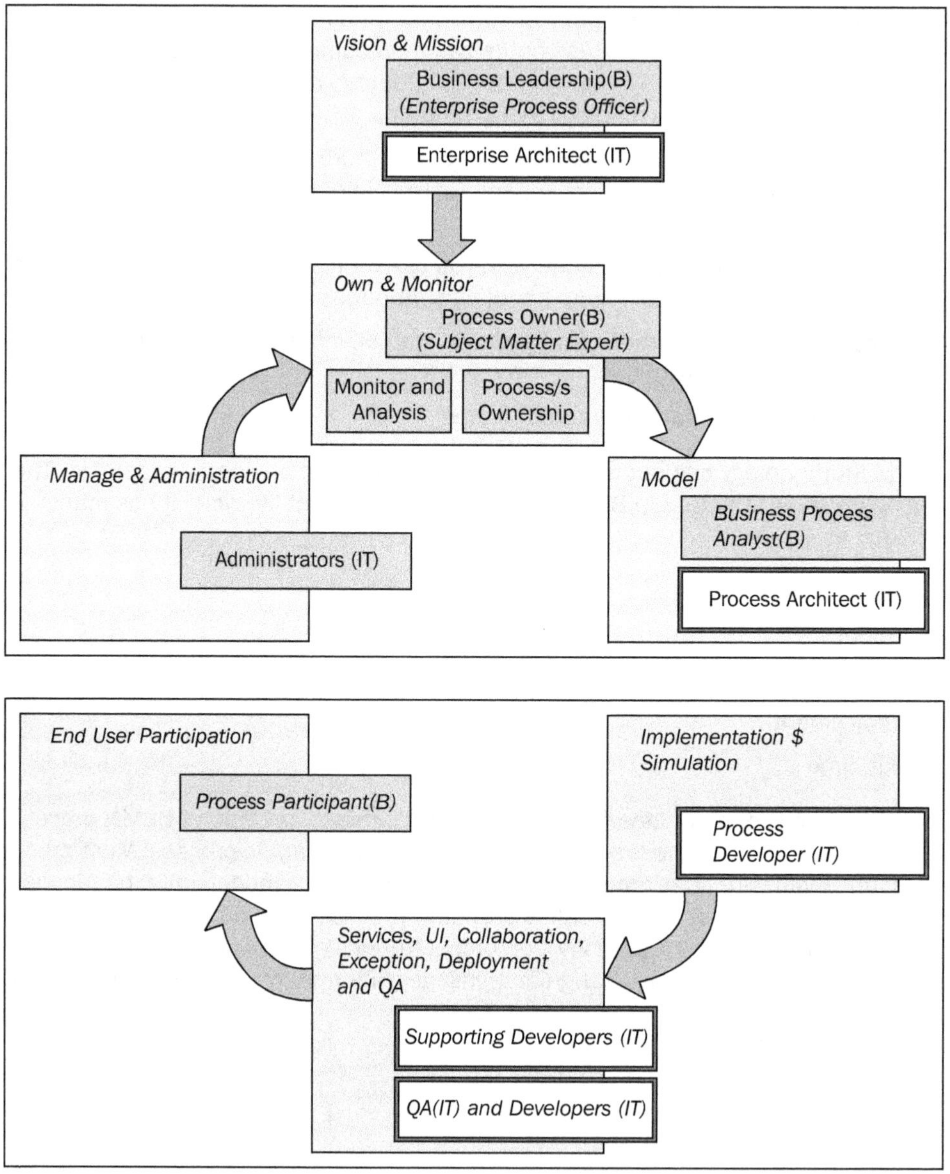

In the screenshot, **B** stands for a business role or a participant from Business and **(IT)** means a participant from IT.

Vision

Adopting BPM into an enterprise to make it business-driven is the vision laid by leadership and coordinated by enterprise-wide architects. It brings both business and process agility. As you can see in the screenshot, business leadership and enterprise architects work closely, for vision and mission, and this leads to improvements in process, with continuous alignment to business needs.

This phase lays the foundation for BPM adoption in the enterprise, with automation and continuous improvement guaranteed, and at the same time staying aligned with business needs.

You can term it as planning, strategy, analysis, and design. Planning is must for a BPM initiative to succeed. BPM planning needs to go beyond departmental level and must incorporate a comprehensive view of the entire enterprise, its goals, operations, processes, and IT systems.

Alignment with business objectives must be the strategy for BPM vision. Business leadership along with process owners will analyze processes and find other high-value processes that are amenable to automation and have a high benefit-to-risk ratio. And these high-value processes are BPM process candidates.

Enterprise architects will then analyze the technical aspects of the BPM process candidates and will create a BPM road map. This road map will describe the current state and future vision, and will also identify the gaps between the two. The road map to get from the current state to the desired state is defined as the *Mission*. The participants in this phase are business leadership and enterprise architects.

- **Business leadership** (business participant) will drive the business requirements by setting business goals, objectives, and priorities. Business leadership provides initial inputs, such as high-level vision, definition, and mission statements and funds the BPM initiative. Business leadership may include many roles, such as, executive management, line-of-business, and so on. However, let's define them as enterprise process officers responsible for developing a process-centric culture, system, and behaviours. They use BPM Analytics to determine business process changes. Business leadership is supported by enterprise architects.
- **Enterprise architects** ensure that IT strategies and standards are applied. Along with Business leadership, they identify business architecture inputs to BPM and help with determining the needs for a major business process change.

Model

During this stage, a process analyst creates process models based on real-world business processes and problems. Oracle BPM provides three distinct tools for modelling business processes. Each tool has a different role within the Oracle BPM Suite. The tool you use depends on your business requirements, the stage of the application development cycle, and your user persona.

- Oracle BPM Studio
- Oracle Business Process Composer
- Oracle Business Process Analysis Suite (BPA)

Models are simply a way for process analysts to document processes in a structured way. A **Process analyst** models the flow of a business process and documents its steps. Process analysts are assisted by process architects with their technical skills. Process analyst and process architect are the critical roles in the automation of business process. One has a greater business focus and the other has technical orientation. This bridges the business and IT gap. Business process analysts, with their process, business, and modelling skills, capture and model processes, drive process optimization, recommend changes, incorporate change requests from business, direct UAT, identify rules, define KPIs, and work with process architects for technical coordination.

Modelling participants are process analysts and process architects, described as follows:

- **Process analyst**: They are also termed as business process analysts. They are involved in process modelling and own process modelling skills. They are responsible for the following:
    - Capturing and managing graphical business process models
    - Driving process optimization
    - Recommending changes
    - Handling process change requests from the business
    - Incorporating incremental process improvements
    - Identifying and coding business rules
    - Working in user acceptance testing
    - They work closely with process architects for technical coordination.
- **Process architects**: - They coordinate with process analysts in process modelling. It's a role also identified as solution architect. However, they have modelling skills and process implementation skills, too. They are responsible for:
    - Analysis and design of technical aspects for the process
    - Defining technical integration strategies
    - Technical specification for new IT capabilities
    - Directing system and integration testing

Implementation

After process analysts model business processes, process developers are responsible for creating business applications based on these models. Using Oracle BPM studio, process developers implement reusable services and integrate other business systems. Implementation may include the following types of tasks generally performed by process developers:

- Refining process model
- Making technical configurations

They implement defined rules. They can create a user interface and can incorporate exception management. However, they have secondary developers to perform specialist technical tasks. For example, an Oracle ADF expert can create dynamic ADF pages to be used as task forms. Some other developer with exception handling expertise can perform that on the process. An integration expert can incorporate SOA into the process, and so on.

After a process developer finishes the implementation, the application is compiled and deployed like other SOA composite applications. It can be compiled and deployed using Oracle BPM Studio.

Process developers are also termed as process designers. They implement the process model to make it executable by configuring data mappings, defining data, and transforming activity input and output. They may not be knowledgeable about business processes, however they rely on process models for implementations. They have the following responsibilities:

- Rapidly create business processes using tools; tools required: BPM Studio
- Create implementation artifacts
- Populate business catalogs with rich implementation artifacts.

Deployment

This phase includes testing and deployment. Process developers or a supporting deployment team can perform process deployment.

For testing, either a developer or **Quality Analyst** (**QA**) can be involved. Testing with different phases can see different people participation. Generally, developers will perform the unit testing; system and integration testing will be performed by QAs and directed by process architects. User acceptance testing will witness involvement of process analysts and QAs. Once UAT is completed, the process is deployed to runtime.

Deployment is the process of transferring an Oracle BPM project from the development environment to the run-time environment. This can be either a testing or production run-time environment. After finishing the integration of business processes with back-end systems and reusable services, process developers create and compile a working process-based application. This application is then deployed to Oracle BPM runtime. Oracle BPM Suite contains the following typical scenarios for deploying to Oracle BPM Runtime:

- Deployment directly from Oracle BPM Studio
- Deployment directly from Business Process Composer
- Deployment using an exported SAR file
- Deployment using the WebLogic Scripting Tool (WLST or ANT)

Once the process is deployed to runtime, it's available to end users.

Runtime

After an application is deployed, the run-time environment makes the Oracle BPM application available to process participants, based on the roles assigned in the organization where the business processes were deployed. This stage is divided into the following distinct functions:

- **End-user interaction**: Process participants and process owners are responsible for interacting with the running application using the process workspace. Process analysts and owners can also monitor the process and revise Oracle Business Rules at runtime.
- **End-user participants**: Process participants are the end users or process performers in a business process who perform the human aspects of the business process task and perform interactive activities. They provide task execution details to the process analyst and are involved in acceptance testing. They should be contacted and interviewed at the time of process automation as it's a must for process designers to know what they actually do. They have many roles, such as supervisor, sales manager, sales representative, business analyst, agent, clerk, and so on.

Oracle BPM flow will automatically route these tasks to a participant, based on his/her role, and they have to log in (either to Oracle BPM Workspace or Process Spaces) and perform their activity. Everything, from end-user interaction to running the process, is performed by logging in to either Oracle BPM Workspace or Process Spaces.

Administration Business administrators are responsible for maintaining running business applications and the overall run-time infrastructure using Oracle Enterprise Manager and the Oracle WebLogic Server administration console.

Administrators or operation managers are responsible for:

- Configuring and monitoring SOA Infrastructure
- Configuring BPMN process service engine
- Integrating the server with organization directory store and allowing logical/process roles to be mapped to real organizational users or groups. Integrating Oracle BPM with external monitoring, such as Oracle Business Activity Monitoring and much more.

Process management and monitoring process owners are responsible for monitoring and maintaining running processes using process workspace. Process analysts and owners use Oracle Business Activity Monitoring to monitor the real-time performance of business processes and KPIs. The participant in this phase is the process owner.

Process owners are the subject matter experts for business processes. They own a process or processes. They are responsible for:

- Assisting Business Process Analysts (B) throughout modeling.
- Assisting Business Process Administrators (IT) throughout runtime.
- Managing process flow.
- Assigning Tasks.
- Defining Rules and Objectives.
- Analysing end-to-end Business Process Performance.
- Making process-specific decisions to resolve conflicts, such as the gap between departmental silos of business process activity, where ownership is undetermined and knowledge is sparse. Process owners resolve such issues as they are the process experts responsible for the end-to-end flow of key business processes.
- Advocating recommendations for enterprise-wide process improvements.
- They are also responsible for monitoring the business processes they own.

Oracle BPM is the leading technology for supporting business process management. Oracle BPM lifecycle supports the entire process improvement lifecycle, vision,modeling, collaboration, simulation, implementation, measurement, execution, monitoring, management, and administration of business processes. Its model-driven approach enables business and IT professionals to work together more collaboratively throughout the Oracle BPM lifecycle. It is collaboration with excellence.

B
Approval Management

With the evolution of business processes and compliance, companies are emphasising on documents and approvals. Many applications use **Approval Management Extension** (**AMX**) for approvals. With Oracle BPM AMX, you can define approval rules based on your business processes and decisions, such as whether to route documents to approvers in series or parallel and whether approvals should be based on employee supervisory hierarchy, position hierarchy, job levels, or Approval Groups. The approval tasks are defined in Oracle JDeveloper's Human Task editor and approvals are managed in BPM Worklist applications or BPM Workspace applications. You used BPM Workspace in this book and will be using the same application for AMX too.

Introduction

The following are the key elements that are involved in understanding and setting up approval routing rules:

- **Approval Request Task**: Business processes need human intervention such as you have used in the **SalesToContract** process in this book. The document **Approval Request Task** lets you send approval requests to approvers, enabling them to make decisions and thus advance the process:

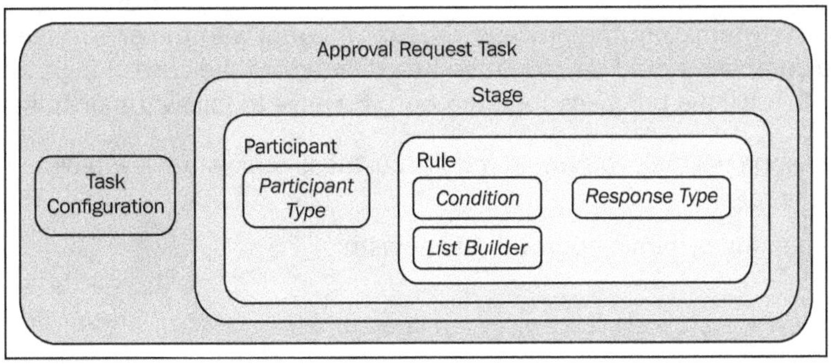

- **Task Configuration**: You need to configure event-driven and data-driven configuration for the document approval task before submitting documents for approval.
- **Stage**: Stages let you organize your approval routing rules into logical groupings, and each stage is associated with a collection. A collection contains a set of attributes at a specific purchasing document level, such as header, lines, and so on, which can be used to author routing rules.
- **Participant**: You can add or edit task participants inside stages. Participants are assigned based on routing patterns, such as single, parallel, serial, and FYI.
- **Rule**: Approval rules, within a participant, are composed of rule name, condition, list builder and its attributes, response type, and auto action. The rule name will identify the approval rule:
    - **Condition** will indicate when the approval rule will be applied. A condition is defined based on the attributes seeded in a collection. Once the condition is satisfied, **List Builder** will identify the type of users needed to approve or receive notification.
    - **List Builder**: There are many list builders supported, such as Approval Group, job level, position, supervisory, and resource. Each list builder has a set of properties that defines it. **Response Type** indicates if the participants are required to approve the task. If not, they are FYI participants.
    - **Auto action**: specifies if the list builder will automatically act on tasks. The auto action value specifies the outcome to be set, such as approve or reject.

Your business requirement is to generate approvers list dynamically. They have a basic business fulfillment to be taken care of, based on the industry type, and then as per business defined logics, a list of approvers will be generated. The business needs to incorporate the following logic to derive approvers dynamically:

```
If Industry IS 'Sales' Then
Approvers are - Salesbusinessanalyst1 and Salesbusinessanalyst2
If Industry IS 'IT' Then
Approvers are - ITbusinessanalyst1 and ITbusinessanalyst2
Else
Approvers are - businessanalyst and businessanalystmanager
```

To generate a list dynamically, the process needs to interact with the enterprise database. The enterprise database would have a procedure defined to take care of logic and to return approvers list. To fulfill the business requirement, you have to follow the ensuing steps:

- Modify approval task you would modify business analyst review task to build list using business rule
- Implementing dynamic approval mechanism

You have defined user hierarchy in the *Defining assignments—management chain participant* section in *Chapter 5, Human Workflow in BPM Process*. Ensure that following users are created in security realm in Oracle SOA or are available in your identity management solution:

- Salesbusinessanalyst1
- Salesbusinessanalyst2
- itbusinessanalyst1
- itbusinessanalyst2
- businessanalyst
- businessanalystmanager

Modifying Approval Task

The Task has a task metadata and assignment section, which has the stages defined. There can be many participants in a stage. You can set properties on the participant to determine routing (serial or parallel) for the task. There are two kinds of participants—value-based and rule-based.

You have created a rule based participant in *Chapter 5*. Rule-based participants are also called rulesets, and approval routing rules are authored inside a ruleset. It's the ruleset that you would view in the Oracle BPM Workspace and BPM Worklist applications.

How to do it...

You will modify the **BusinessAnalystReview** task so that it will be based on business rules:

1. Open JDeveloper in the default role.
2. Go to project **SalesToContact** | **BusinessAnalystReview.task** in the Project Hierarchy.
3. In the **Task** metadata, click on the **Assignments** section.
4. Double-click on the participant block.
5. Follow the ensuing details to create a list builder based on Rule.

6. Enter name of **List Ruleset** as `DynamicApprovalGroup`:

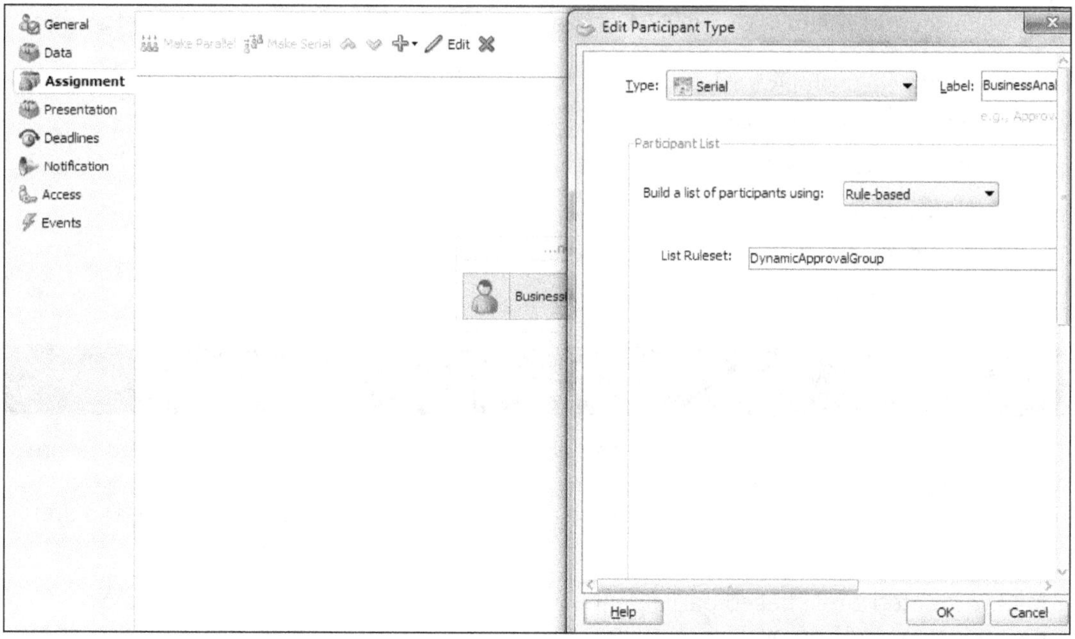

7. This will create **Decision Service** components and a Ruleset in it. The following is the **Decision Service** component:

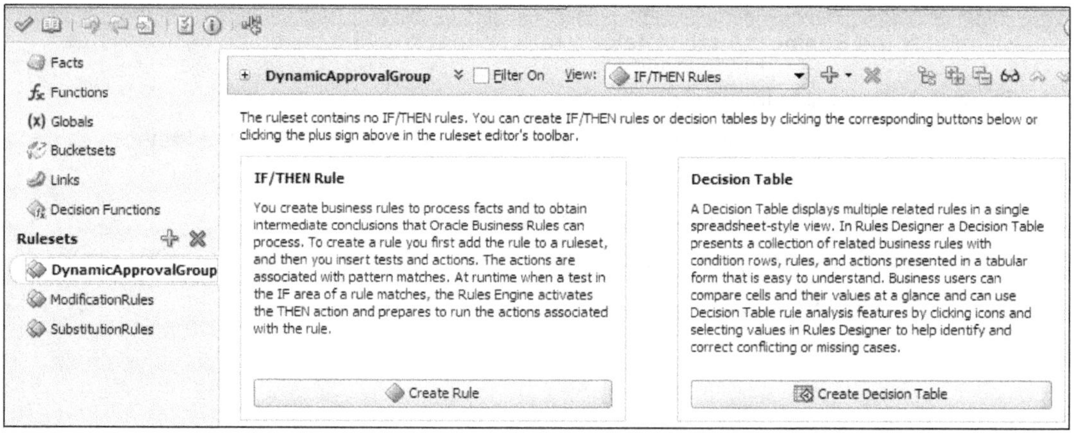

8. Click on **Create Rule**.

9. Create a Rule with name `DynamicApprovalGroupRule` and invoke the **CreateApprovalGroupList** API with the following parameters:
    - Name of the Group: `DynamicAG`: This is the name of the dynamic Approval Group, which you have created in BPM Workspace
    - `allowEnptyApprovalGroup: true`
    - `responseType :ResponseType.REQUIRED`: As it's an Approvers list and not a FYI list, we would use the ResponseType required
    - `rule Name: Enter the Rule name DynamicApprovalGroupRule`
    - `lists: Lists:`

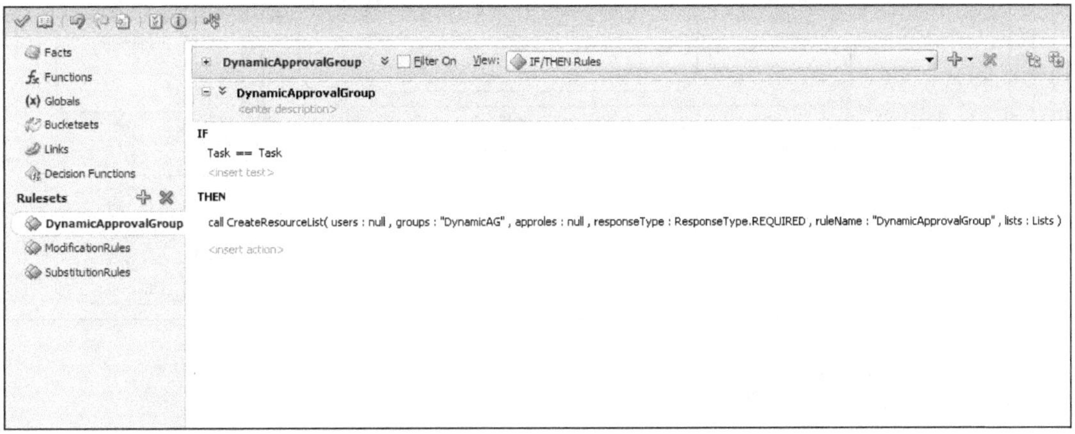

10. Deploy the process as outlined in the *Deploy BPM projects* section in *Chapter 3, Process Deployment and Testing*.

How it works...

When the process token reaches for approvals, it would be routed to the stages defined in task metadata, and inside these stages there are participants. You have defined participants as rule-based, and hence an approval rule gets executed. Rule name will identify the rule and when the condition gets satisfied, the **Rule** gets executed. **Rule** will build the participant list based on the **List Builder** Approval Group.

Approval Group will be defined in the Oracle BPM Workspace; it will invoke a Java class, which in turn calls the PL/SQL procedure to dynamically build the list of participants. These participants will be returned to the **Rule**, and tasks get assigned to them. Based on the response type, it's decided if the participant will act on the task or if it is a FYI participant:

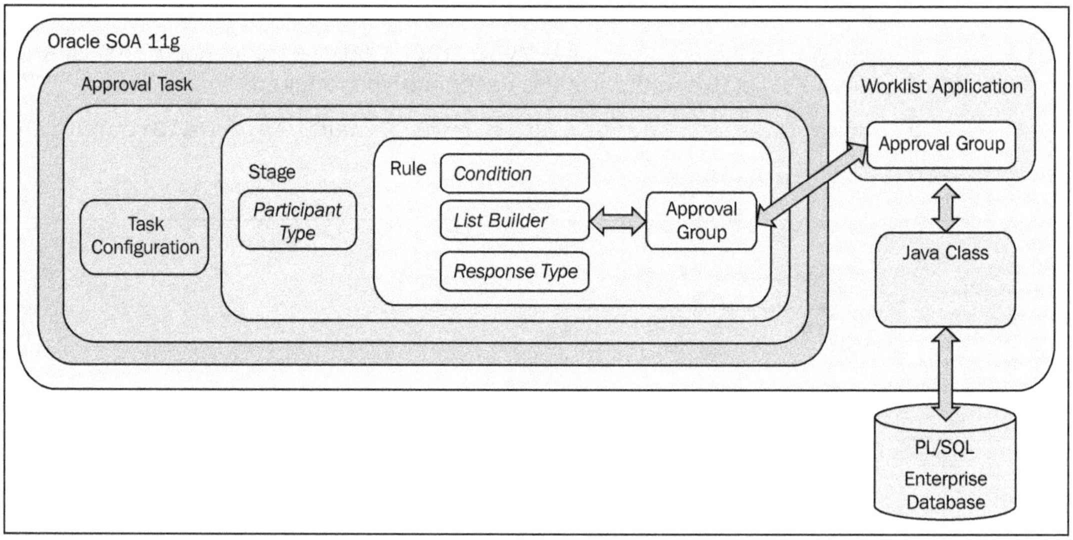

There's more...

Once you have deployed the process, you can verify task configuration from the Oracle BPM Workspace and BPM Worklist applications.

Verifying configured task

To verify configured tasks, you have to log in to Oracle BPM Workspace application with admin role. You can even change task configuration from here. Follow the ensuing steps:

1. Log in to Oracle BPM Workspace at `http://localhost:8001/bpm/workspace`.
2. Click on **Administration Areas | Task Administration | Task Configuration**. To configure the **Task** section, click on **BusinessAnalystReview(1.0)**. This is the task that you have modified to include the business rule for dynamic approval. Task is here as a part of the process being deployed, which has **BusinessAnalystReview.task**.
3. Click on the **Data Driven** tab and select the Ruleset **DynamicApprovalGroup**.

4. Expand **DynamicApprovalGroupRule**, which will get listed when you select the ruleset.

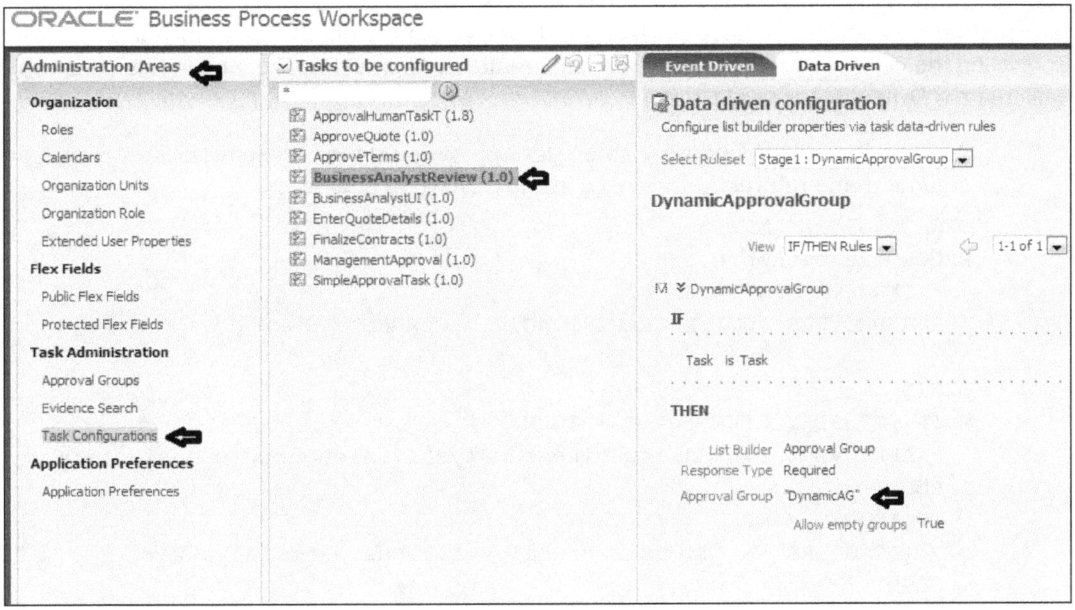

You can verify the Approval Group listed that you have entered in the business rule in JDeveloper.

Implementing dynamic approval mechanisms

To implement dynamic approval mechanism, follow the ensuing steps:

- Create a PL/SQL procedure in the DEV_SOAINFRA schema of the enterprise database. This schema comes as a part of SOA installation. However, any business-specified custom schema can be used for a similar operation.
- Create a Java class that accepts task as a parameter and invokes this PL/SQL procedure by passing argument and receiving approvers list.

How to do it...

You will create a PL/SQL procedure in the enterprise database and a Java class in JDeveloper or any other java editor. You have to place the Java class at a globally known location specifying the classpath in SOA. Then you can create an Approval Group, and in this case you will create a Dynamic Approval Group:

1. Create a PL/SQL procedure (named `GetApprovers`) that accepts `Industry` as argument and returns `Approvers` list, in SOAINFRA schema:

   ```
   CREATE OR REPLACE
   PROCEDURE GetApprovers(
       INDUSTRY IN VARCHAR2,
       APPROVERS OUT VARCHAR2 ) AUTHID CURRENT_USER
   AS
   BEGIN
     IF INDUSTRY LIKE 'SALES' THEN
       APPROVERS := 'Salesbusinessanalyst1,Salesbusinessanalyst2';
     END IF;
     IF INDUSTRY LIKE 'IT' THEN
       APPROVERS := 'ITbusinessanalyst1,ITbusinessanalyst2';
     ELSE
       APPROVERS := 'businessanalyst,businessanalystmanager';
     END IF;
   END GetApprovers;
   COMMIT;
   ```

2. Create a Java class (named `XXDynamicAG`) that accepts Task as a parameter and invokes this PL/SQL procedure `GetApprovers` by passing `Industry` as argument and receiving Approvers list.
3. Develop a custom Dynamic Approval Group class.
4. Place the class file at a globally known directory, which is the path for the SOA classpath.
5. For custom classes and JAR, Oracle offers `oracle.soa.ext_11.1.1` dir to place custom components, such as classes and JAR files. Place your custom class at `$BEAHOME/Oracle_SOA/soa/modules/oracle.soa.ext_11.1.1/classes/oracle/apps/XXDynamicAG.class`.
6. You would define an implementation class using the interface file `IDynamicApprovalGroup.java`, defined in the package `oracle.bpel.services.workflow.task`; this class contains only one public method that gets the Approval Group members, and the task object is the only input parameter:

   ```
   import java.sql.CallableStatement;
   import java.sql.Connection;
   import java.sql.DriverManager;
   ```

```
import java.sql.SQLException;

import java.util.ArrayList;
import java.util.List;

import oracle.bpel.services.workflow.IWorkflowConstants;
import oracle.bpel.services.workflow.runtimeconfig.impl.
RuntimeConfigUtil;
import oracle.bpel.services.workflow.runtimeconfig.model.
ApprovalGroupMember;
import oracle.bpel.services.workflow.task.IDynamicApprovalGroup;
import oracle.bpel.services.workflow.task.model.Task;

import org.w3c.dom.Element;
import org.w3c.dom.NodeList;

public class XXDynamicAG implements IDynamicApprovalGroup {
    public XXDynamicAG() {
        super();
    }

    public List getMembers(Task task) {

        Element payloadElem = task.getPayloadAsElement();
        String IndustryName = null;
        IndustryName = getElementValue(payloadElem, "Industry");

        String getStatus = "";
        String[] results = { };
        try {
            Class.forName("oracle.jdbc.driver.OracleDriver");
            System.out.println("========== class loaded");
            }
        catch (ClassNotFoundException ex) {
            System.out.println("========== class load error");
            ex.printStackTrace();
        }
        Connection connection = null;
        CallableStatement cstmt = null;
        try {
            connection = DriverManager.getConnection("jdbc:oracle:
thin:@localhost:1521/mydb", "DEV20_SOAINFRA", "Welcome1");
```

```
        System.out.println("========== connection=" +
        connection);
        // prepare call
        cstmt = connection.prepareCall("{call GetApprovers
        (?,?)}");

        cstmt.setString(1, IndustryName);

        //Register Output
        cstmt.registerOutParameter(2, java.sql.Types.VARCHAR);
        // Call the stored procedure
        cstmt.execute();

        System.out.println("========== procedure executed");
        //Get the output parameter array
        String Approverstr = cstmt.getString(2);
        results = Approverstr.split(",");

        System.out.println("done");
        System.out.println(getStatus);
        }
        catch (SQLException ex) {
        ex.printStackTrace();
    } finally {
        try {
            if (cstmt != null)
            // close the callable statement
            {
                cstmt.close();
                cstmt = null;
            }
            System.out.println("========== stmt closed");
            } catch (SQLException ex) {
            System.out.println("========== stmt close err");
            ex.printStackTrace();
        }
        try {
            if (connection != null)
            // close the connection
            {
                connection.close();
                connection = null;
            }
```

```
                System.out.println("========== conn closed");
            } catch (SQLException ex) {
                System.out.println("========== conn close err");
                ex.printStackTrace();
            }
        }
        List approversList;
        approversList = new ArrayList();

        for (int i = 0; i < results.length; i++) {
            ApprovalGroupMember taskAssignee =
                RuntimeConfigUtil.getFactory().
                 createApprovalGroupMember();
            taskAssignee.setMember(results[i]);
            taskAssignee.setType
              (IWorkflowConstants.IDENTITY_TYPE_USER);
            taskAssignee.setSequence(i);
            approversList.add(taskAssignee);
        }
        return approversList;
    }

    public static String getElementValue(Element payloadElem,
                                         String pElementName) {
        String value = null;
        NodeList myNodeList = payloadElem.getElementsByTagName
          (pElementName);
        Element myElement = (Element)myNodeList.item(0);
        NodeList myChildNodeList = myElement.getChildNodes();
        for (int i = 0; i < myChildNodeList.getLength(); i++) {
            value = (myChildNodeList.item(i)).getNodeValue().
             trim();
        }
        return value;
    }
}
```

7. Register the Dynamic Approval Group using the BPM workspace applications.
8. Create a Dynamic Approval Group in BPM Workspace with name `DynamicAG`, based on the Java class `XXDynamicAG`.
9. Log in to Oracle BPM workspace with **weblogic** as the **Administration** account.
10. Click on **Administration**.

11. Click on **Administration Areas | Task Administration | Approval Groups**.
12. Create a dynamic group by clicking on the **Create Dynamic** option and entering the name of the group as `DynamicApprovalGroup`:

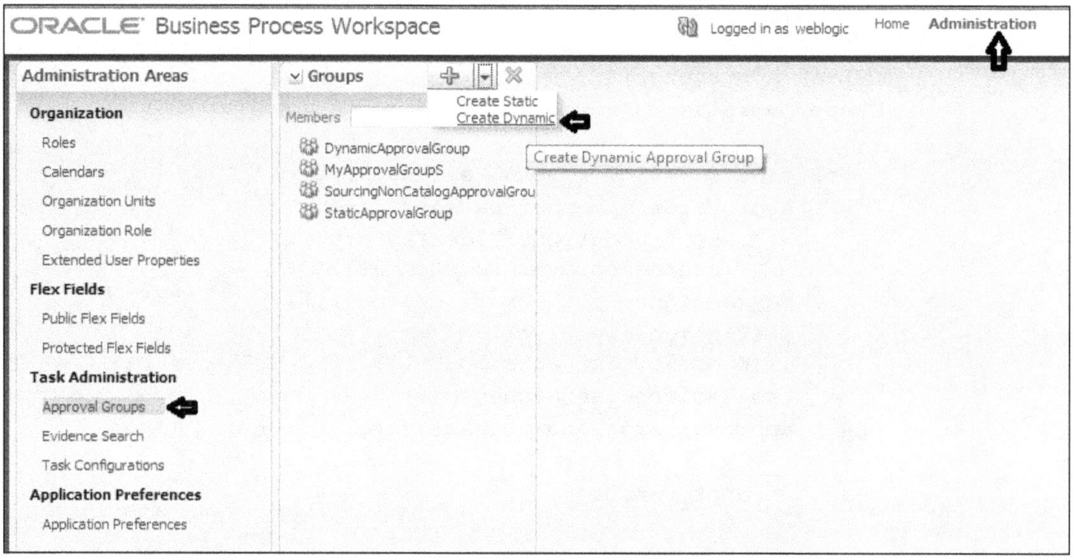

13. Click on **Apply**.

There's more...

You can now test the BPM process. Initiate the **SalesToContract** process. Enter `it` as Industry.

Testing the process

1. Go to Oracle BPM Workspace.
2. Log in as **salesrepresentative**, to initiate the quote.
3. Enter `it` as Industry and enter other quote details.
4. Submit the quote.

5. Log in as **itbusinessanalyst1**, and you can verify that the task is assigned to it:

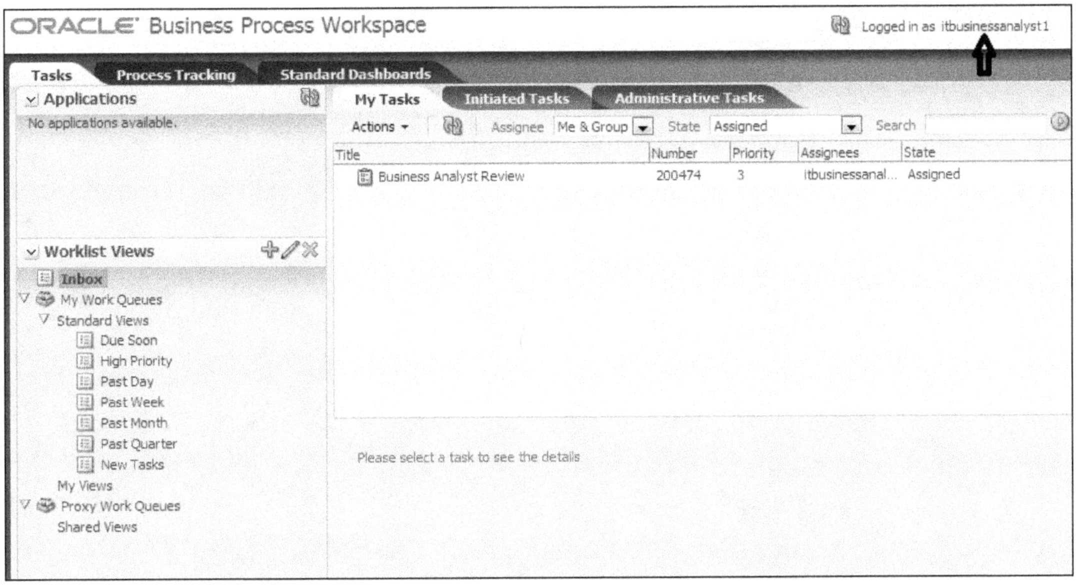

When the process token reaches the BusinessAnalystReview **Approval Task**, the list of approvers is built through a call to Dynamic Approval Group, which would invoke a Java class that, in turn, calls the PL/SQL procedure to dynamically build the list of participants. These participants will be returned to the **Rule** and the task gets assigned to them. As the Industry type entered in quote was `it`, PL/SQL would return users **itbusinessanalyst1** and **itbusinessanalyst2**, and you can verify the task assignment to these users from Oracle BPM Workspace.

> You can use Oracle BPM Worklist application to perform similar operations that you have performed using Oracle BPM Workspace applications.

Index

A

B

C

D

E

F

Q

R

T

U

V

W

Thank you for buying
Oracle BPM Suite 11g Developer's Cookbook

About Packt Publishing

Packt, pronounced 'packed', published its first book "*Mastering phpMyAdmin for Effective MySQL Management*" in April 2004 and subsequently continued to specialize in publishing highly focused books on specific technologies and solutions.

Our books and publications share the experiences of your fellow IT professionals in adapting and customizing today's systems, applications, and frameworks. Our solution-based books give you the knowledge and power to customize the software and technologies you're using to get the job done. Packt books are more specific and less general than the IT books you have seen in the past. Our unique business model allows us to bring you more focused information, giving you more of what you need to know, and less of what you don't.

Packt is a modern, yet unique publishing company, which focuses on producing quality, cutting-edge books for communities of developers, administrators, and newbies alike. For more information, please visit our website: `www.PacktPub.com`.

About Packt Enterprise

In 2010, Packt launched two new brands, Packt Enterprise and Packt Open Source, in order to continue its focus on specialization. This book is part of the Packt Enterprise brand, home to books published on enterprise software - software created by major vendors, including (but not limited to) IBM, Microsoft and Oracle, often for use in other corporations. Its titles will offer information relevant to a range of users of this software, including administrators, developers, architects, and end users.

Writing for Packt

We welcome all inquiries from people who are interested in authoring. Book proposals should be sent to `author@packtpub.com`. If your book idea is still at an early stage and you would like to discuss it first before writing a formal book proposal, contact us; one of our commissioning editors will get in touch with you.

We're not just looking for published authors; if you have strong technical skills but no writing experience, our experienced editors can help you develop a writing career, or simply get some additional reward for your expertise.

[PACKT] enterprise
professional expertise distilled
PUBLISHING

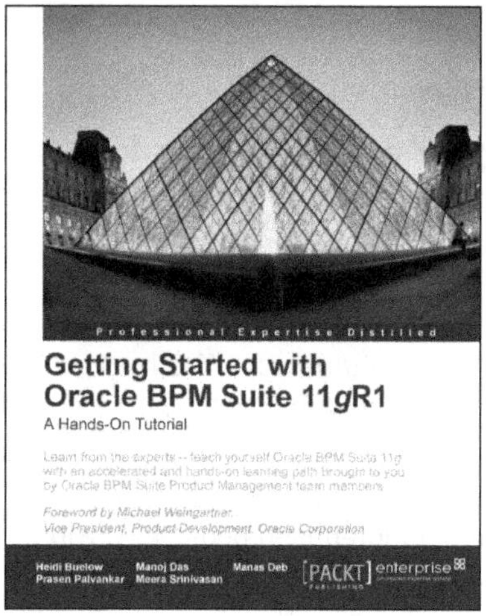

Getting Started with Oracle BPM Suite 11gR1 – A Hands-On Tutorial

ISBN: 978-1-84968-168-1 Paperback: 536 pages

Learn from the experts – teach yourself Oracle BPM Suite 11g with an accelerated and hands-on learning path brought to you by Oracle BPM Suite Product Management team members

1. Offers an accelerated learning path for the much-anticipated Oracle BPM Suite 11g release
2. Set the stage for your BPM learning experience with a discussion into the evolution of BPM, and a comprehensive overview of the Oracle BPM Suite 11g Product Architecture
3. Discover BPMN 2.0 modeling, simulation, and implementation

---

Oracle SOA Suite 11g R1 Developer's Guide

ISBN: 978-1-84968-018-9 Paperback: 720 pages

Develop Service-Oriented Architecture Solutions with the Oracle SOA Suite

1. A hands-on, best-practice guide to using and applying the Oracle SOA Suite in the delivery of real-world SOA applications
2. Detailed coverage of the Oracle Service Bus, BPEL PM, Rules, Human Workflow, Event Delivery Network, and Business Activity Monitoring
3. Master the best way to use and combine each of these different components in the implementation of a SOA solution

Please check **www.PacktPub.com** for information on our titles

Oracle ADF Enterprise Application Development —Made Simple

ISBN: 978-1-84968-188-9 Paperback: 396 pages

Successfully plan, develop, test, and deploy enterprise applications with Oracle ADF

1. Best practices for real-life enterprise application development
2. Proven project methodology to ensure success with your ADF project from an Oracle ACE Director
3. Understand the effort involved in building an ADF application from scratch, or converting an existing application

---

Oracle JDeveloper 11gR2 Cookbook

ISBN: 978-1-84968-476-7 Paperback: 406 pages

Over 85 simple but incredibly effective recipes for using Oracle JDeveloper 11gR2 to build ADF applications

1. Encounter a myriad of ADF tasks to help you enhance the practical application of JDeveloper 11gR2
2. Get to grips with deploying, debugging, testing, profiling and optimizing Fusion Web ADF Applications with JDeveloper 11gR2 in this book and e-book
3. A high level development cookbook with immediately applicable recipes for extending your practical knowledge of building ADF applications

Please check **www.PacktPub.com** for information on our titles

www.ingramcontent.com/pod-product-compliance
Lightning Source LLC
LaVergne TN
LVHW082024200926
848481LV00010B/2916